To

Sophie, Alana and Stephen
A.J.L.

Patricia, Colm, Nessa and Ben
B.M.W.

LECTURERS!
SUPPORT MATERIAL

For your support material check our website www.gillmacmillan.ie

Support material is available to lecturers only within a secure area
of this website.

To access support material for *The Macroeconomy of the Eurozone:*

1. Go to www.gillmacmillan.ie

2. Click on the 'logon' button and enter your username and
password. (If you do not already have a username and password,
you must register. To do this click the 'register' button and
complete the online registration form. Your username and
password will then be sent to you by email.)

3. Click on the link 'Support Material'.

4. Select the title *The Macroeconomy of the Eurozone*

Contents

Preface   xiii

Chapter 1: Introduction to Macroeconomics   1
1.1   Introduction   1
1.2   A Rising Standard of Living   1
1.3   Real Growth and Inflation   4
1.4   The Business Cycle   5
1.5   Unemployment   6
1.6   Inflation   8
1.7   Macroeconomic Policy   14
1.8   Summary   17
1.9   Conclusion   18

Chapter 2: Introduction to the Theory of Income Determination   19
2.1   Introduction   19
2.2   Macroeconomic Models   19
2.3   The General Theory   20
2.4   The Goods and Services Market   21
2.5   Aggregate Demand   22
2.6   Aggregate Supply   25
2.7   Equilibrium   28
2.8   Demand-side and Supply-side Shocks   29
2.9   Real GNP and Unemployment   31
2.10   Natural Real GNP and the Long-run AS Curve   34
2.11   Adjusting to Economic Shocks in the Long Run   38
2.12   Keynesian Economics   41
2.13   Classical Economics   41
2.14   Modern Macroeconomics   43
2.15   Conclusion   44
Appendix 1: The role of stocks in establishing equilibrium   44
Appendix 2: Nobel prize winners in economic science winners   45

Chapter 3: The Consumption Function and Income Determination   48
3.1   Introduction   48
3.2   Disposable Income, Consumption and Saving   48
3.3   Evidence from the Irish economy   52
3.4   The Keynesian Multiplier   53
3.5   Average Propensity to Consume and Save   59

3.6   Theories of Consumer Behaviour   61
3.7   Conclusion   66
Appendix: Deriving the multiplier formula with saving, taxation
          and import leakages   66

Chapter 4: Fiscal Policy and the Business Cycle   68
4.1   Introduction   68
4.2   Stabilisation Policy   68
4.3   The Budget   70
4.4   Assessing the Stance of Fiscal Policy   74
4.5   Problems in Implementing Stabilisation Policy   77
4.6   Taxation and the Supply-side of the Economy   82
4.7   Conclusion   85

Chapter 5: Fiscal Policy in Ireland   86
5.1   Introduction   86
5.2   Economic Programming and Planning   86
5.3   The Irish Experience with Stabilisation Policy   92
5.4   Conclusion   103

Chapter 6: Money and Banking   104
6.1   Introduction   104
6.2   What Is Money?   104
6.3   Types of Money   105
6.4   The Banking System in a Modern Economy   108
6.5   Money Creation in a Modern Economy   112
6.6   The Role of a Central Bank   114
6.7   High-powered Money and the Money Multiplier   117
6.8   Instruments of Monetary Policy   118
6.9   Conclusion   120

Chapter 7: The Price Level and the Money Supply in the Long Run   122
7.1   Introduction   122
7.2   The Quantity Theory of Money   122
7.3   Hyperinflation   125
7.4   Keynesian Perspective on the Quantity Theory   128
7.5   Evidence from the Irish Economy and the Eurozone   129
7.6   The Development of the Irish Currency   131
7.7   The Evolution of Central Banking in Ireland   135
7.8   Conclusion   139
Appendix: The structure of the Irish financial sector   139

Chapter 8: Money and Interest Rates in a Closed Economy 142
8.1 Introduction 142
8.2 Monetary Policy 142
8.3 The Demand for Money 144
8.4 Money Market Equilibrium 149
8.5 Nominal and Real Interest Rates 150
8.6 Aggregate Demand and Interest Rates 152
8.7 Monetary Policy in a Closed Economy 153
8.8 Monetary Policy and the Keynesian, Classical Debate 156
8.9 Crowding-out 158
8.10 Conclusion 160
Appendix: Net present value 160

Chapter 9: The Foreign Exchange Market and Exchange Rates 163
9.1 Introduction 163
9.2 The Balance of Payments 163
9.3 The Foreign Exchange Market 168
9.4 The Rise and Fall of the Irish Foreign Exchange Market 169
9.5 The Exchange Rate of the Irish Pound and the Euro 171
9.6 Exchange Rate Determination 173
9.7 The J Curve 175
9.8 Shifts in Supply and Demand 177
9.9 Factors Influencing Exchange Rates in the Medium-term 177
9.10 Speculation 179
9.11 The Trade-weighted Exchange Rate Index 181
9.12 Conclusion 182

Chapter 10: Inflation and Interest Rates in Open Economies 184
10.1 Introduction 184
10.2 Purchasing Power Parity 184
10.3 The PPP Exchange Rate 186
10.4 PPP and the Real Exchange Rate 189
10.5 An Alternative Measure of Competitiveness 192
10.6 PPP: Graphical Representation 194
10.7 Relative PPP 195
10.8 PPP under Flexible Exchange Rates 198
10.9 PPP under Fixed Exchange Rates 198
10.10 Uncovered Interest Rate Parity (UIP) 200
10.11 The Irish UK Experience with UIP 203
10.12 The Euro and UIP 205
10.13 Excess Returns and the Peso Problem 205

10.14 The Open Economy Monetary Model   206
10.15 Conclusion   209

Chapter 11: Fixed Exchange Rate Systems: Theory and History   210
11.1   Introduction   210
11.2   How a Fixed Exchange Rate System Works   210
11.3   The Monetary Adjustment Mechanism   212
11.4   Sterilisation   214
11.5   Why Fixed Exchange Rate Systems Do Not Endure   215
11.6   The Gold Standard   217
11.7   The Bretton Woods System, 1945–71   220
11.8   The European Snake, 1972–74   222
11.9   Which Exchange Rate Regime Is Best?   223
11.10 Conclusion   225
Appendix: The monetary approach to the balance of payments (MAB)   225

Chapter 12: The European Monetary System: Precursor to the Euro   227
12.1   Introduction   227
12.2   The European Monetary System, 1979–98   227
12.3   Inflation Convergence in the EMS   230
12.4   History of EMS   227
12.5   The Currency Crisis of 1992–93   233
12.6   The Responses to the 1992–93 Crisis   237
12.7   Conclusion   238
Appendix: Chronology of main events relating to the EMS   239

Chapter 13: Irish Exchange Rate Policy from the Sterling Link to EMU   241
13.1   Introduction   241
13.2   The Sterling Link, 1922–79   241
13.3   The Rationale for Joining the EMS   243
13.4   Policy Credibility and the Speed of Adjustment   244
13.5   The Experience in the EMS   245
13.6   Why Ireland Did Not Initially Benefit from the ERM   248
13.7   The Irish Pound and the Crisis of 1992–93   251
13.8   Was There an Alternative to Devaluation?   255
13.9   Irish Exchange Rate Policy after the 1992–93 Crisis   258
13.10 Conclusion   259

Chapter 14: European Monetary Union   260
14.1   Introduction   260
14.2   The Run-up to Economic and Monetary Union   260

14.3   The Political Benefits of EMU to Ireland   264
14.4   The Economic Benefits of EMU to Ireland   265
14.5   The Economic Costs of EMU to Ireland   269
14.6   Factors Constraining Adjustment within the Eurozone   270
14.7   Adjusting to Economic Shocks within the Eurozone   273
14.8   Conclusion   277
Appendix 1: Chronology of the EU and EMU   278
Appendix 2: The Maastricht convergence criteria and their application   280

Chapter 15: The European Central Bank and Economic Policy in EMU   **282**
15.1   Introduction   282
15.2   The Design of the ECB   282
15.3   What Is 'Price Stability'?   284
15.4   Central Bank Independence   286
15.5   Monetary Policy in the EMU   290
15.6   Conclusion   296

Chapter 16: Interest Rate, Exchange Rate and Fiscal Policy in the Eurozone **297**
16.1   Introduction   297
16.2   Controlling the Money Supply   297
16.3   The ECB's Interest Rate Policy   298
16.4   Other Factors Influencing Interest Rates in the Eurozone   304
16.5   The Euro as a Global Currency   308
16.6   Exchange Rate Policy in the Eurozone   310
16.7   Who Decides Exchange Rate Policy?   312
16.8   Fiscal Policy in EMU   314
16.9   The Implications of the Stability Pact for Economic Policy   318
16.10 Conclusion   319
Appendix: The dynamics of debt accumulation   320

Chapter 17: The IS-LM Model   **323**
17.1   Introduction   323
17.2   Equilibrium in the Goods Market: the IS Curve   323
17.3   Equilibrium in the Money Market: the LM Curve   326
17.4   Equilibrium in the Goods and Money Markets   328
17.5   Government Spending and Private Investment: Crowding-out   332
17.6   The Relative Effectiveness of Fiscal and Monetary Policy in the
       IS-LM Model   333
17.7   The Fiscal-Monetary Policy Mix   335
17.8   Conclusion   336

Chapter 18: The Mundell-Fleming Model   **338**

18.1   Introduction   338

18.2   Internal and External Balance   338

18.3   Introduction to the Mundell-Fleming Model   342

18.4   Applying the Model under Fixed Exchange Rates   343

18.5   The Model under Floating Exchange Rates   346

18.6   Economic Policy, Output and the Trade Account   349

18.7   Conclusion   353

Chapter 19: Hedging against Exchange Rate and Interest Rate Risk   **354**

19.1   Introduction   354

19.2   Internal Hedging Techniques   354

19.3   External Hedging Techniques: the Forward Market   356

19.4   Interest Rate Parity Theory   359

19.5   The Unbiased Predictor Hypothesis (UPH)   361

19.6   Forward Market Efficiency   364

19.7   Interest Rate Risk   367

19.8   Anticipating Interest Rate Movements   367

19.9   Hedging Against Interest Rate Risk   368

19.10   Futures Contracts   370

19.11   Comparing Forward and Futures Contracts   374

19.12   Conclusion   374

Chapter 20: The Labour Market   **376**

20.1   Introduction   376

20.2   The Aggregate Production Function   376

20.3   The Labour Market   377

20.4   The General Model   382

20.5   The Keynesian Model   384

20.6   Deflationary Demand-side Shock   387

20.7   Deflationary Supply-side Shock   390

20.8   Monetarism   392

20.9   The Neoclassical Model   395

20.10   Conclusion   398

Chapter 21: The Phillips Curve and the Inflation-Unemployment Trade-off **400**

21.1   Introduction   400

21.2   The Original Phillips Curve   400

21.3   The Revised Phillips Curve   406

21.4   The Accelerationist Theory of Inflation   409

21.5   Deflation, Expectations and Credibility   412

21.6 The Augmented Phillips Curve: Evidence from the Eurozone 416
21.7 Conclusion 420

Chapter 22: The Labour Market and Unemployment 421
22.1 Introduction 421
22.2 The Labour Force 421
22.3 Employment Trends 425
22.4 The Dynamics of Unemployment 427
22.5 Who Are the Unemployed? 430
22.6 Why Doesn't the Labour Market Clear? 432
22.7 Factors Affecting the Incentive to Work 439
22.8 Reducing Unemployment 441
22.9 Conclusion 442

Chapter 23: Measuring the Economy's Performance: Introduction to National Income Accounting 443
23.1 Introduction 443
23.2 The Circular Flow of Income Model 443
23.3 Measuring the Nation's Output 447
23.4 Reconciling the Income and Expenditure Approaches 449
23.5 The Disposable Income of the Nation 452
23.6 Public and Private Saving 456
23.7 Saving, Investment and the Balance of Payments 457
23.8 Conclusion 460
Appendix: Adjusting for changes in the terms of trade 460

Chapter 24: The Performance of the Irish Economy in the Long Run 462
24.1 Introduction 462
24.2 The Record 462
24.3 Real Convergence 466
24.4 Interpreting the Record: 1922–61 468
24.5 Interpreting the Record: after the 1950s 471
24.6 The 'Celtic Tiger' Period: 1994–2001 478
24.7 Graphical Representation 483
24.8 Conclusion 487

Index 489

Preface

In the late 1980s we believed there was a need for a book that allowed Irish students to study modern macroeconomic theory and policy based on data and illustrations from the Irish economy. The first edition of the authors' *Macroeconomy of Ireland* appeared in 1990 and our belief was vindicated by the feedback from students and colleagues. In response to popular demand a second edition was published in 1992, a third in 1995, and a fourth 'EMU edition' in 1998.

In the preface to that fourth edition we vowed (at least one of us vowed!) that it would be the last on the grounds that Ireland as a member of the Eurozone no longer merited a separate macroeconomic textbook. We pointed out that Ireland's entry into EMU and the adoption of the single currency in 1999 radically altered the Irish macroeconomy. Ireland could no longer exercise control over interest rates or the exchange rate and fiscal policy would be constrained by the Stability and Growth Pact. As a result, after 1999, there was little or no need for a macroeconomics textbook at a national, Irish level.

We have adhered to the letter, if not the spirit, of that resolution. What convinced us of the need for the present book was the continued strong demand for the fourth edition even after Ireland adopted the euro. The present textbook is not a fifth edition of the earlier text. Over a period of nearly two years, it has been thoroughly updated, rewritten and reoriented towards Ireland's situation as a full member of a common currency area–the Eurozone. It contains new material on, for example, the functions and operations of the European Central Bank (ECB), the Stability and Growth Pact, the costs and benefits of participating in Economic and Monetary Union (EMU) and how economies adjust to economic shocks given the constraints of EMU membership. The book also provides a considerable amount of reference material on the origins and evolution of EMU.

The book does not purport to be a comprehensive primer on the Eurozone or European economies. Instead the intention is to provide Irish students with the theory and data they need to understand how the Irish economy functions as a member of the Eurozone.

We hope that our new book will serve the current generation of Irish economics students as well as the four editions of our previous book served earlier generations.

As usual, we are indebted to our many colleagues at University College, Dublin and the University of Limerick for comments and advice on earlier editions and drafts. We would like to thank Ailbhe O'Reilly, formerly at Gill & Macmillan, whose insistence, perseverance and encouragement contributed in no small way to the completion of the transcript within the agreed timeframe. Our greatest debt, however, is to successive generations of students in our economics courses in Limerick and Dublin who helped us improve the exposition of the theories and policies contained in this book. The authors alone are responsible for the views expressed and any remaining errors.

Plassey, Limerick   A.J.L.
Belfield, Dublin   B.M.W.
                                                                      April 2003

CHAPTER 1

Introduction to Macroeconomics

1.1 INTRODUCTION

Macroeconomics is concerned with the study of the economy as a whole. It deals with topics that are never far away from the front pages of the newspapers: inflation, interest rates, unemployment, growth and exchange rates. In this chapter, the goals of macroeconomic policy are outlined. These goals may be summarised as attempting to achieve:

1. An improvement in the *standard of living* of the population
2. A low *unemployment* rate
3. Price stability or a low *inflation* rate.

These three objectives have to be achieved subject to two important constraints:

*   Maintaining a long-run balance in the public finances and the balance of payments.

In this chapter, these objectives and the associated constraints are discussed.

1.2 A RISING STANDARD OF LIVING

In order to evaluate the performance of an economy over time and to compare it with other economies, we have to measure the output of all the goods and services being produced. This is no easy feat. Imagine that you have a bird's eye view of Ireland. Think of the hundreds of thousands of different goods and services being produced in the country. If we add together the value of all the goods and services produced in the country over the course of a year, we obtain the value of the total output of the economy. One measure of this is known as *Gross Domestic Product* (GDP). The Central Statistics Office (CSO) estimates that GDP in Ireland in 2000 was €103,470 million or €27,322 per person (or per capita).

Closely related to GDP is the concept of *National Income*. This is the total amount of income received by residents in the country. The nation's output is closely linked to the nation's income. If a person works harder at his or her job and produces more, then he/she would expect their income to rise accordingly. The same is true at national level: the more the nation produces, the more income is generated. An important policy goal is to ensure that a satisfactory growth rate is maintained in the level of GDP.

If this objective is achieved, then the standard of living of the population rises. There is more income for the country as a whole to use and in principle this means that everyone could be made better off.

Table 1.1
Per capita GDP, 2000

	Population ,000 A	GDP $ billion B	GDP/capita $ B/A
Austria	8,092	189	23,443
Belgium	10,222	226	22,168
Finland	5,165	121	23,543
France	60,273	1,294	21,472
Germany	82,087	1,873	22,817
Greece	10,534	112	10,632
Ireland	3,745	94	25,100
Italy	57,630	1,074	18,636
Luxembourg	438	18	43,151
Netherlands	15,807	364	23,072
Portugal	9,969	105	10,543
Spain	39,418	558	14,171
Eurozone	303,380	6,032	19,884
United Kingdom	59,237	1,415	23,880
USA	272,878	9,896	36,265
Japan	126,686	4,750	37,491

Source: OECD Main Economic Indicators

Table 1.1 shows per capita GDP (that is, GDP divided by the population) for the twelve counties making up the Eurozone (that is, the countries that adopted the single European currency — the euro — in 1999) and the UK, US and Japan in 2000. It can be seen that the US, Japan and Luxembourg are among the richest countries in the world. The standard of living in Ireland is now above the average of the Eurozone and is ahead of countries such as Italy, UK, Spain and Portugal. In contrast, some of the poorest countries are to be found in Africa (Ethiopia, Congo, Burundi and Sierra Leone all had a per capita GDP of less than $150 in 1999).

Note:
The following countries are members of the Eurozone (2002): Austria, Belgium, Finland, France, Germany, Greece, Ireland, Italy, Luxembourg, the Netherlands, Portugal and Spain. In the UK, Eurozone membership is a subject of intense political and economic debate.

It is important to emphasise at the outset that some serious problems are encountered in calculating the nation's output and there are major limitations to its use as a measure of welfare or the standard of living. Many countries' GDP may be exaggerated or under-estimated. Some of these measurement problems are discussed in box 1.1.

Box 1.1
Problems encountered in estimating GDP

Double counting In calculating GDP it is important to include only *final* goods and not *intermediate* goods. If intermediate goods are included then there is double-counting and GDP will be overestimated. For example, suppose the only good produced in the economy is bread. Bread is a final good because it is consumed and not used to produce any other goods. Wheat and flour, on the other hand, are intermediate goods as they are inputs in the production of bread and should not be included in calculating GDP.

Household production and non-market activities National income accounting is primarily concerned with activities that are bought or sold. Non-market activities, such as 'do-it-yourself' repairs or cooking and cleaning in the home, are not included in GDP as it is measured in most countries.

Spillover effects Spillover effects can be either positive or negative. An example of a negative spillover or external diseconomy is the pollution caused by a factory for which the affected parties receive no compensation. (The environmental effect on the Irish Sea by the nuclear reprocessing plant in Cumbria is a pertinent example for Irish readers!) An example of a positive spillover or external economy is the grounds of a university campus that yield positive benefits to local residents. These spillover effects are not bought and sold and are therefore not included in the national income accounts.

The underground or 'black' economy The underground economy consists of unreported or undetected economic activity. There are, in general, two types of unrecorded transactions: illegal transactions, such as drug trafficking and prostitution, which are not reported for obvious reasons; and legal transactions (such as small building jobs) that are kept hidden to avoid paying taxes on them. It is estimated that the black economy in Ireland could be between 3 and 10 per cent of GDP.

Multinational companies The activities of multinational companies (MNCs) in Ireland distort the GDP estimates. Some of these companies are believed to engage in transfer pricing, selling components and raw materials at artificially low prices to subsidiary companies in order to maximise profits in low tax countries. This has the effect of artificially boosting the Irish GDP figures.

GDP AND GNP

Gross *Domestic* Product (GDP) is a measure of the total output of final goods and services produced in the country. Not all of the output or income generated in a country goes to people resident in that country. Gross *National* Product (GNP) is a measure of the income accruing to the country's residents. The difference between GDP and GNP is *net factor income from the rest of the world* (F). ('Net' here refers to the difference between the gross inflows and outflows.) In Ireland there is a substantial outflow of money for a variety of reasons. For example, the repatriation of profits by multinational firms operating in Ireland and the interest on foreign (external) debt paid to non-residents. As a result, for several years now, F, has been negative in Ireland. In 2000:

$$GNP = GDP - F$$
$$€95,012m = €103,470m - €8,457m$$

Although GDP is generally used in international comparisons of economic activity, GNP is a better guide to the trend in Ireland's living standards. Throughout this book we refer to GNP when discussing the Irish economy.

1.3 REAL GROWTH AND INFLATION

GNP measures the level of output for a given year. However, as GNP changes from year to year, it is important to distinguish between changes in *nominal* and *real* GNP. Nominal GNP is equal to real GNP multiplied by the price level.

   Nominal GNP = Real GNP × Price level

An increase in real GNP means that a greater *volume* or quantity of goods has been produced. In terms of improving the country's standard of living, it is the change in volume GNP or real GNP that matters. Also changes in real GNP are closely associated with changes in both employment and unemployment.

   Consider the hypothetical data in table 1.2, which assumes that bicycles are the only good produced in the economy. In 1980, 3,000 bicycles were produced at a price of €10 each. Hence nominal GNP was €30,000. By 2003, production has increased to 5,000 bicycles at a price of €120 each. Nominal output in 2003 has increased to €600,000.

Table 1.2
Hypothetical example where the only good produced is bicycles

	Real GNP	×	Price level (€)	=	Nominal GNP (€)
	Quantity of bicycles produced	×	Price of bicycles	=	Value of bicycles produced
1980	3,000	×	10	=	30,000
2003	5,000	×	120	=	600,000

In calculating real GNP, the *price level is held constant*. Hence, real GNP in 2003 (based on 1980 prices) is €50,000 (5,000 × €10). Real output has increased by 66 per cent over the period 1980 to 2003:

   [(€50,000 − €30,000)/€30,000] × 100 = 66%

The important point is that improvements in a country's standard of living only come about through changes in real GNP. If increases in nominal GNP are due to price increases only, people are not becoming any better off.

   The *real growth rate* measures the percentage change in real GNP from one year to the next. A high and stable rate of economic growth is one of the principal goals of macroeconomic policy.

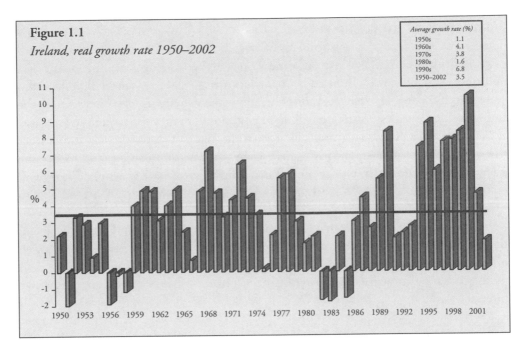

Figure 1.1

Ireland, real growth rate 1950–2002

Average growth rate (%)	
1950s	1.1
1960s	4.1
1970s	3.8
1980s	1.6
1990s	6.8
1950–2002	3.5

1.4 THE BUSINESS CYCLE

Figure 1.1 maps out the real growth rate in Irish GNP for each year from 1950 to 2002. The variability of the real growth rate over time is referred to as the *business cycle*. It can be seen that the Irish growth rate has fluctuated widely from year to year. The average real growth rate over the period 1950 to 2002 was 3.5 per cent. The average real growth rate for the US and UK over the same period was 2.9 and 2.3 respectively. The Irish economy has, therefore, been growing, on average, slightly faster than either of these two economic blocs.

The following terms are useful when describing the business cycle. A *peak* describes the upper turning point, and a *trough* is the lower turning point. A downturn in the business cycle is referred to as a *contraction* in output, and an increase in the growth rate is referred to as an *expansion*. There is no hard and fast definition of a recession. In the US, if a contraction lasts for two or more consecutive calendar quarters, the economy is said to be in a *recession*. If a recession is prolonged and deep, it may be called a *depression*. The distinction between recession and depression is not always clear-cut. President Harry S. Truman remarked that a recession was when your neighbour was out of work and a depression was when you were out of work!

Using this terminology, the Irish economy experienced a boom in the 1960s, 1970s and the 1990s. Between 1994 and 2000, the average growth rate was 8.0 per cent considerably above the long-run average. The exceptional growth recorded over these years gave rise to the label the 'Celtic Tiger'. The real growth rate fell significantly in 2001 and 2002. The growth rate was low or even negative during periods in the 1950s, 1960s, 1970s and 1980s. The recession (depression) of the mid-1980s was particularly severe and this was associated with a significant rise in unemployment.

SIGNIFICANCE OF THE BUSINESS CYCLE

The business cycle acts as a barometer of business activity. During periods of rapid growth, firms find that sales rise and order books fill up. As a result, employment rises and unemployment falls. In periods of slow growth or decline, sales fall and unsold stocks accumulate. During recessions, unemployment tends to rise. Because of the importance to business, firms are willing to pay a lot of money for economic forecasts. If slow growth is predicted, firms will 'tighten the belt' and adopt policies to weather the storm. They will postpone investment plans, cut back production, and reduce the size of their workforce. If, on the other hand, a high growth rate is expected, they will contemplate investing in new machinery and hire additional workers so as to be able to meet the demand for their product as the economy expands.

If the economy were to grow at a steady 3.5 per cent per annum, real output would double every twenty years. Each successive generation would be more than twice as well off as the preceding one. In fact, real income per person in Ireland is now more than double what it was at the beginning of the 1960s. Such is the power of compound interest!

1.5 UNEMPLOYMENT

Although unemployment is a topic of grave public concern, its definition and measurement are fraught with difficulties. The general principle is that a person is regarded as being unemployed if he or she is looking for work and willing to accept a job at the going wage rate for the type of work that he or she is qualified to do. If someone is only casually looking for a job or holding out until a 'suitable' position with a high wage becomes available, then they may not be classified as unemployed.

The *labour force* is defined as the sum of the numbers employed and unemployed:

Labour force = the employed + the unemployed

The *unemployment rate* is defined as the number unemployed as a percentage of the labour force:

Unemployment rate = unemployed/labour force

In 2002, the Irish labour force totalled 1,825,400, of whom 1,745,500 were employed and 80,000 unemployed. The unemployment rate was therefore 4.4 per cent.

Note:
There are two principal measures of unemployment in Ireland. The first is a survey of households which used to be called the *Labour Force Survey* but is now called the *Quarterly National Household Survey* (QNHS). The second is the *Live Register*, which records the number of people registered for unemployment benefits and assistance. In mid-2002 the number registered as unemployed was 162,252, compared to 80,000 unemployed in the QHNS. The QHNS data are regarded by economists as a more reliable measure of 'genuine' unemployment. In a survey carried out by the CSO in 1996, a sample of people claiming on the live registrar was selected for interview. About 25 per cent could not be located at their stated address. Only 50 per cent of those that were located would have been classified as 'unemployed' according to the QHNS definition. The data in this chapter are based on International Labour Office (ILO) definitions used in the QHNS.

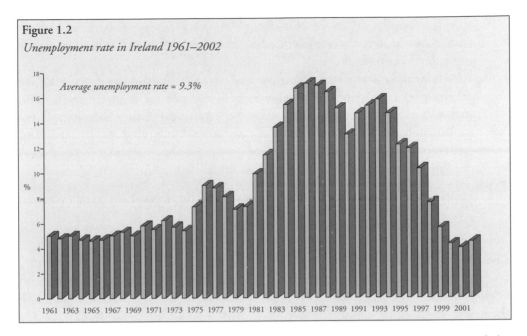

Figure 1.2

Unemployment rate in Ireland 1961–2002

Average unemployment rate = 9.3%

Figure 1.2 shows the unemployment rate in Ireland from 1961 to 2002. Until the mid-1970s it remained between 4 and 6 per cent. It rose to 9 per cent in 1976 and to 17.5 per cent in 1987 as the rate of economic growth slowed. However, due to rapid growth in the 1990s, the unemployment rate fell to 4.4 per cent in 2002. There is a marked difference in unemployment rates between the advanced industrial nations. In 2002, the unemployment rate in Luxembourg was only 2.4 per cent compared to 13 per cent in Spain. Having once been the highest in the EU, the Irish rate is now well below the Eurozone average of 8.6 per cent.

COSTS OF UNEMPLOYMENT

The costs of unemployment to individuals and society are very serious.

- Most unemployed people feel a low level of self-esteem and this can lead to personal stress and suffering. It has been found that the unemployed are much more likely to suffer high levels of psychological distress than people at work, and that this distress increased with the duration of unemployment.
- The unemployed suffer a loss of income. In developed countries this loss is shared between the employed and unemployed through transfer payments such as unemployment benefits, which are paid for by taxes levied on the working population. However, these transfers do not make up all of the income lost through unemployment, and as a result there is a close relationship between the rate of unemployment and the incidence of poverty in a country.
- The budgetary implications of high unemployment are serious. In 1998, spending on unemployment benefit and unemployment assistance amounted to €1,070 million, down from a peak of €1,331 million in 1993. In addition, high unemployment results in a loss of tax revenue. A country with a high rate of unemployment therefore faces the unpalatable prospect of having to impose a

heavy tax burden on the employed population to help support those without work. As we shall see, a heavy burden of taxation makes it harder to alleviate the unemployment problem.

- The national economy loses the output and income that would be produced if the unemployed could find work. However, in the present Irish situation, with unemployment close to a record low, the big problem is to find people to fill the available jobs. A 4 per cent unemployment rate no longer represents much lost output.

TYPES OF UNEMPLOYMENT

It is customary to talk about different types of unemployment, even though it is never possible to identify who falls into each category.

Cyclical unemployment

During the contractionary phase of the business cycle, firms lay off workers and unemployment rises. In principle, many of these workers should be hired back during the recovery phase of the business cycle.

Structural unemployment

Structural unemployment arises when there is a permanent decline in employment in the industries located in a particular region or country. If enough people do not migrate between regions there will be growing disparities between rates of unemployment. Jobs may be available in one region while there is a high level of unemployment in another region. Similarly, job vacancies may not match the skills or the occupations of the unemployed. There may be job vacancies for carpenters, but this will do little to alleviate unemployment among coalminers. Long-term unemployment of this type is the worst feature of unemployment. Cyclical unemployment can turn into structural unemployment if the recession is prolonged or the recovery weak.

Frictional unemployment

In a dynamic economy people's preferences or tastes are ever changing, new technologies are constantly being introduced and relative prices vary. As a consequence, some firms go out of business, while others open up. There are always people losing their jobs, switching between one job and another, and entering and leaving the labour force. Unemployment that arises because of changes or friction in particular markets is referred to as *frictional unemployment*. A particular type of frictional unemployment is *seasonal* unemployment. Some industries, such as tourism and fishing, are seasonal in nature. During the off-season, people engaged in these industries become temporarily unemployed.

1.6 INFLATION

Microeconomics is concerned with the relative prices of goods and services. Macroeconomics, on the other hand, is concerned with the *aggregate* price level. This is measured using a price index, which is a weighted average of the individual prices included in it. The most widely used price index in Ireland is the *Consumer Price Index* (CPI). To construct the CPI, the CSO employs 200 people to collect approximately 45,000 prices relating to a basket of 985 goods and services. Prices are obtained at a fixed panel of retail and services outlets in 82 towns and cities around the country. Pricing takes place on the first Tuesday of each month. In deriving the index, prices are averaged on the basis of their relative importance (the weight) in the typical household budget.

The CSO uses the *Household Budget Survey* to ascertain consumers' expenditure patterns. Based on a sample of 7,705 private households around the country, the CSO calculates expenditure (the weight) on categories such as food, drink, clothing, fuel, housing and so on. Table 1.3 shows the commodity group and the associated weights currently employed by the CSO.

Table 1.3
Commodities and weights used to calculate the CPI, January 2000

Commodity group	Expenditure weights (%)
Food	22.8
Services and related expenditure	16.7
Alcoholic drink	12.6
Transport	13.9
Housing	8.1
Other goods	6.4
Clothing and footwear	6.2
Fuel and light	4.9
Tobacco	4.8
Durable household goods	3.6
All items	100.0

Source: Central Statistics Office, Dublin.

The value of the price index in the base year is set equal to 100. Changes in the index are then monitored relative to this base year. CPI quarterly data are available back to 1922. (Monthly data were introduced from January 1997.) Over the period 1922 to 2002, the CPI index increased from 100 to 4,046, or by 3,946 per cent.

The CSO also publishes the EU *Harmonised Index of Consumer Prices* (HICP). This index, which is used by the European Central Bank to monitor inflation in the Eurozone, excludes approximately 8 per cent of the expenditure items in the CPI. Mortgage interest and building materials, for example, are excluded. As a result the expenditure weights are different from those used to calculate the CPI. All the countries of the Eurozone collect and publish data on the trend in their HICPs.

Note:

There are other important price indexes. *The GDP price deflator*, for example, is used to calculate real GDP. There are other price indexes relating to particular sectors in the economy. The most commonly cited indexes are the *manufacturing industry output price index*, the *wholesale price index*, and the *agricultural output price index*. These indexes do not necessarily follow the exact same trend, but they do tend to move together over time.

INFLATION RATE

The annual inflation rate is defined as being equal to the percentage change in the price index over a year:

$$\text{Inflation rate} = [(P_t - P_{t-1})/P_{t-1}] \times 100$$

where P_t and P_{t-1} are the price indices in the current and previous year, respectively. Table 1.4, for example, shows the CPI data for 2000 and 2001 and the associated inflation rate. In this case, P_t is the current price index and P_{t-1} is the index twelve months previously. Hence the inflation rate in January 2001 is derived as:

$$[(112.5 - 106.9)/106.9] \times 100 = 5.24.$$

Figure 1.3 displays the annual rate of inflation (measured by the CPI) since the formation of the state. There were periods of *deflation* or falling prices in the 1920s and 1930s, but since 1951 there was only one year (1959) when there was no inflation. High rates of inflation were recorded in the late 1930s, and there was a significant rise in prices between the late 1960s and the mid-1980s. Between 1970 and 1985 the annual average rate of inflation was over 13 per cent. After entry into the European Monetary System (EMS) in 1979, and the collapse of world oil prices in 1985, however, inflation subsided.

EFFECTS OF INFLATION

Most contemporary Irish students of economics have never experienced high inflation first hand. Since the mid-1980s inflation in Ireland and most advanced countries has been relatively low, well below 5 per cent on average, but in many poorer countries — especially in Latin America — very high inflation is still a serious problem. And there is always the danger that inflation could return to haunt us, as it did in the 1970s.

Should we worry about inflation? Should we be willing to squeeze inflation out of the economy if this entails high unemployment and slow growth? To answer these questions we need to consider the costs of inflation.

VALUE OF MONEY

Inflation lowers the purchasing power of money and people living on fixed incomes (such as pensioners) suffer a decline in their living standards as a result. For example, suppose you go to a supermarket at the start of the year and spend €100 on a basket of goods. If the inflation rate is, say, 10 per cent, €100 will not be able to buy the same amount of goods at the end of the year. Prices have risen by 10 per cent and some goods will have to be omitted from the basket. In other words, because of inflation, money has lost some of its purchasing power.

In this context, inflation will also erode the value of wage increases. Consider, for example, table 1.5 which shows the percentage change in average hourly earnings and

Table 1.4
Consumer price index (CPI) and the rate of inflation

		CPI	Inflation Year on Year Rate
2000	January	100.0	
	February	100.8	
	March	101.5	
	April	102.2	
	May	103.0	
	June	103.6	
	July	103.9	
	August	104.5	
	September	104.9	
	October	105.6	
	November	106.0	
	December	106.1	
2001	January	105.2	5.2
	February	106.2	5.3
	March	107.0	5.4
	April	108.0	5.6
	May	108.6	5.4
	June	109.2	5.3
	July	108.9	4.8
	August	109.3	4.6
	September	109.7	4.6
	October	110.1	4.3
	November	110.0	3.8
	December	110.6	4.2

Source: Central Statistics Office, Dublin.

Figure 1.3
Inflation in Ireland 1922–2002

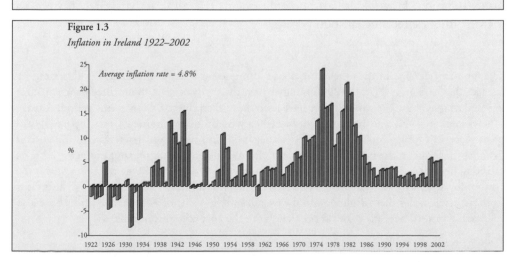

Table 1.5
Deriving real wages
Annual percentage charges

	Average Hourly Earnings A	Inflation B	Real Wages (A-B)
1991	6.0	3.2	2.8
1992	3.8	3.1	0.7
1993	6.4	1.4	5.0
1994	1.7	2.3	−0.6
1995	2.5	2.5	0.0
1996	4.1	1.7	2.4
1997	3.1	1.5	1.7
1998	4.6	2.4	2.2
1999	5.8	1.6	4.3
2000	6.9	5.7	1.2
2001	8.4	4.9	3.5

Source: Central Statistics Office, Dublin.

the associated inflation rate from 1991 to 2001. The (percentage change) in the *real* wage is roughly the (percentage change) in the nominal wage minus inflation:

$$\%\Delta\text{Real wage} = \%\Delta\text{Nominal wage} - \text{inflation}$$

It can be seen that inflation has a serious impact on workers' real earnings over the period. There were years when real earnings declined (1994), remained stagnant (1995) or increased only very marginally (1992 and 2000). Real wages did, however, increase significantly in 2001. Over the longer run, people will tend to anticipate inflation and make appropriate adjustments. Interest rates will rise to reflect the loss of purchasing power of borrowed money. Incomes, including pensions, will be indexed to allow for future inflation. However, all of these adjustments take time and are rarely perfect, so that the unfair effects of inflation persist.

Note:
The long-run decline in the purchasing power of money as a result of inflation is illustrated by the fact that one pound (£1) in 2000 is only worth the equivalent of about three pence (£0.03) in 1922 money. In other words, prices have risen more than thirty-fold over this period. A wage of £3 a week in 1922 was the equivalent of £100 a week in today's money. James Joyce's Ulysses takes place in Dublin on 16 June 1904. Readers will find numerous references to the cost of living at that time in the book. For example, a pint of milk and a pint of stout both cost 2d. The morning newspaper cost 1d. A domestic servant was paid £12 a year. (Remember that d. was the symbol for a penny and there were 240 pence in the pound in pre-decimal currency.) It is clear from these examples that in addition to the overall inflation since 1904, relative prices have also changed: a pint of beer now costs more than twice the cost of a pint of milk!

INTERNATIONAL COMPETITIVENESS

Inflation can have very serious implications for an economy's international competitive position. That is, the ability of domestic firms to compete with their international rivals. If, for example, Ireland has an inflation rate of 10 per cent while foreign inflation is only 5 per cent, Irish goods and services will be progressively priced out of both the domestic and export markets. (This assumes that the currency is not allowed to depreciate — an option no longer available to Eurozone countries.) As a result, the real growth rate and employment will fall and unemployment will rise. The cost of excess inflation will be a loss of output and increased unemployment. It is therefore desirable that a country keeps its rate of inflation lower than that of its main trading partners. Several studies have shown that low inflation countries tend to grow more rapidly than those countries experiencing relatively high inflation.

TRANSPARENCY VERSUS CONFUSION

Price stability improves the transparency between relative prices. This can improve the allocation of resources that in turn can increase the productive capacity of the economy. High inflation, on the other hand, introduces confusion and a possible misallocation of resources. Furthermore, price stability reduces the risk premium inherent in interest rates. Price stability, therefore, can result in lower interest rates that can stimulate growth and investment. This issue is discussed in chapter 8.

HYPERINFLATION

Once inflation becomes entrenched, the risk is that the rate of inflation will increase. This can lead to astronomical rates of inflation or hyperinflation, as experienced in Germany after World War I, in several Latin American countries during the 1980s and, most recently, in some of the former communist economies of Europe. Serbia probably holds the record, where inflation reached 100,000 per cent a *month* towards the end of 1993. The national currency, the Serbian dinar, became worthless. Faced with this situation, people will try to spend their money as fast as they can before rising prices further reduce its value. They will also seek to be paid in a stable currency, such as dollars or euro, while trying to use the local currency to pay their debts, especially their taxes! This response to inflation is known as 'dollarisation'. In 2002 Ecuador officially abandoned its own currency and adopted the dollar. Hyperinflation undermines the economic life of a country and can destabilise it both socially and politically. The case of Argentina in 2002 is a frightening example of how the failure to maintain a stable monetary system reduced a once-prosperous country to deep poverty.

MENU AND SHOE LEATHER COSTS

Price increases impose costs on firms and shops, which have to reprint price lists etc. to convey the new prices to their customers. Customers have to go to some trouble to find out about price changes in order to keep up to date. Economists call these the 'menu costs' of inflation. Also during periods of high inflation people will hold less currency. As a result they will make more trips to the bank to withdraw cash. This is referred to as the 'shoe leather' costs of inflation. While these effects may not be very large, they are a nuisance. It is also likely that if the rate of inflation varies over time, consumers may get confused by the way prices are changing. This reduces the efficiency of the price system.

EFFECTS ON INCOME DISTRIBUTION

Inflation can result in a redistribution of income between different groups in society. Consider, for example, a person who saved and put money in a bank in Ireland in the 1970s. The interest received on the bank deposit (8 per cent in interest [before tax]) was less than the inflation rate (15 per cent). Savers were therefore penalised by inflation. Conversely, borrowers paid an interest rate that was lower than the inflation rate and benefited by going into debt and repaying the loan in money whose value had declined. Thus one effect of inflation has been to transfer real wealth from savers to borrowers. In general, inflation (when it is not fully anticipated) acts like a tax on the weaker groups in society: the elderly living on fixed incomes, people with small savings receiving only fixed-interest payments, and others who are not able to act to offset the effects of rising prices on their income and wealth.

1.7 MACROECONOMIC POLICY

Policy makers would like to raise incomes and achieve more rapid growth, but they are constrained in how effective they can be in this area. The constraints they face are two-fold, real and financial.

REAL CONSTRAINTS

A nation's income depends on what its population can produce and sell. The key factors used to produce output are labour, physical capital (plant, machinery and infrastructure), human capital (education, skills and training of the labour force) and technology. The efficiency with which they are combined to produce output is a key determinant of a country's standard of living.

Labour, capital, and technology are constraints on the value of what an economy can produce. The rate of growth of the economy's GNP depends on the rate at which these inputs are growing. Ireland has achieved a very rapid rate of growth of GNP in recent years because we have been able to increase employment by over 3 per cent a year — much higher than would be possible in other European countries. Moreover, the rising educational standard of the Irish workforce is also a key factor in maintaining a high growth rate. Finally, our stock of physical capital has been rising and its quality improving. There has been a large inflow of foreign investment, much of it in very high-tech sectors. The transfer of technology from other, more advanced economies (such as the US) has been a key ingredient of our recent success.

FINANCIAL CONSTRAINTS

All too often policy makers are impatient with the achievements of their country in regard to economic growth. In order to increase their popularity they would like to see the economy growing faster. But they should be aware that they face important financial constraints when pursuing the goals of high growth and low unemployment. The first is the country's *fiscal deficit*; the second is its *balance of payments*. These can act as constraints on the authorities' freedom of action in trying to achieve growth and employment objectives.

THE FISCAL DEFICIT

From time immemorial governments have found it hard to live within their means and have been tempted to run fiscal deficits. This is particularly true in times of recession when output is stagnant and unemployment is rising. Governments come under pressure to increase spending in order to stimulate the economy.

The fiscal deficit is the balance between government revenue (mainly from taxation) and government expenditure. Cumulative borrowing to finance the fiscal deficit leads to an increase in the *national debt*. The problem with the national debt is that it has to be serviced. Interest must be paid on the outstanding balances. Furthermore, with so much money committed to debt service, the burden of taxation is heavy and the government's ability to spend in other areas, such as education or job creation, is severely constrained. If the national debt does increase significantly then this will undermine the government's ability to intervene in the economy. A government may end up introducing policies to cut the fiscal deficit, regardless of the consequences for growth and unemployment, if the debt grows at an unsustainable rate.

As we shall see in chapter 5, this is essentially what happened in Ireland in the 1980s. In 1998 Ireland's national debt stood at €39,370 million. Of this, €9,365 million is external debt owed to foreigners or non-residents. In 2000 interest payments on the national debt amounted to €2,847 million or 36 per cent of the yield of income tax. Although these numbers are large, relative to GDP the burden of the national debt is falling very rapidly. There has been a vast improvement from the dark days of the 1980s when we wondered whether or not the country was going bankrupt and collapsing under the weight of its national debt.

THE BALANCE OF PAYMENTS

The balance of payments is a record of a country's transactions with the rest of the world. It imposes another constraint on the country's ability to increase its living standards.

Ireland used to be considered a classic example of a *small open economy*. In this context, 'small' relates to the very small size of Irish firms in relation to the overall world market, and 'open' refers to the importance of international trade to the economy. One measure of 'openness' is exports as a percentage of GDP. Table 1.6 shows that using this yardstick, Ireland is considerably more open than Germany, the UK, the US and, perhaps surprisingly, Japan. However, since Ireland joined the Eurozone it essentially became a region of the larger European economy.

Note:
In the case of Luxembourg, exports as a percentage of GDP amount to 147.7 per cent. At first sight, this may seem odd. How could a country export more than its total output of goods and services? The answer is that *net* exports (exports minus imports) are used to calculate GDP. While the total export figure may be very large, the net export figure can be relatively small.

Table 1.6
Open economies

	Exports as % of GDP (2002)
Austria	53.2
Belgium	84.9
Finland	40.3
France	29.0
Germany	35.1
Ireland	93.2
Italy	28.8
Luxembourg	147.7
Netherlands	64.1
Portugal	32.1
Spain	30.4
United Kingdom	27.1
USA	9.8
Japan	11.0

Source: European Commission, *European Economy*, 2001, No. 73, Table 36.

Figure 1.4
Current account of balance of payments
% of GDP, 1960–2002

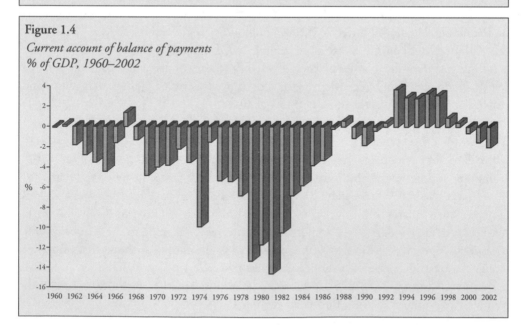

In the past, due to the openness of the Irish economy, we paid particular attention to the country's balance of payments. Figure 1.4 shows the current account of the balance of payments (as a percentage of GDP) over the period 1960 to 2002. The current account includes merchandise trade, tourism and travel, royalties and investment income among other items. Throughout the 1970s and 1980s, a very sizeable deficit (an excess of payments over receipts) was recorded. In 1992 the balance of payments had moved into a surplus (an excess of receipts over payments) position. However, a deficit re-emerged on the balance of payments in 2000.

As explained in chapter 9, the balance of payments summarises the supply and demand for a country's currency. A balance of payments deficit could lead to a depreciation of the exchange rate. Conversely, a balance of payments surplus can lead to an appreciation. This consideration imposes a constraint on the policy makers' ability to achieve the macroeconomic objectives. For example, a policy that increases real GNP could result in a rapid increase in imports and a balance of payments deficit. This, in turn, could lead to a depreciation of the exchange rate which could increase inflation. The rise in inflation could undermine the policy of increasing real GNP. The international dimension of macroeconomic theory and policy is very important in an analysis of the Eurozone economy.

Note:
Ireland is now a member of European and Monetary Union (EMU). We abandoned the Irish pound as a separate currency on 1 January 1999. The euro is now the country's legal tender. Early in 2002 the Irish pound ceased to serve as legal tender and was phased out of circulation. Since Ireland no longer has a separate currency, it no longer has a genuine balance of international payments. What matters now is the Eurozone balance of payments. Because Ireland is so small in relation to the rest of EMU, it is not possible for an Irish balance of payments deficit to result in a depreciation of the euro exchange rate. If the EMU countries as a whole were to record a balance of payments deficit then this could undermine the value of the euro on international exchanges.

1.8 SUMMARY

In the introduction to this chapter we outlined the main objectives of macroeconomic theory and policy. The goals of macroeconomics may be generally stated as attempting to increase the real growth rate and keep unemployment low. With regard to inflation, the goal here is generally to achieve 'price stability'. The European Central Bank has defined 'price stability' as an inflation rate of less than 2 per cent. This target is applicable to the Eurozone and should therefore be taken as the goal for Ireland and the other countries participating in the system. In fact Irish inflation ran significantly above this level in 2001 and 2002.

The three goals are inter-linked. In chapter 2, and on numerous other occasions in this book, these inter-relationships will be discussed.

The goals of macroeconomics also have to be achieved subject to the government's budget and balance of payments constraints. In 1978, for example, the government incurred a large budget deficit in an attempt to boost the real growth rate. Unfortunately, the result was a large increase in the balance of payments deficit that had serious long-run consequences for the economy. It is imperative that equilibrium is achieved on both the budget and balance of payments accounts over the longer run.

Looking back over the charts in this chapter it can be seen that the performance of the Irish economy was very favourable during the 1990s. The economy recorded exceptionally rapid growth, unemployment fell sharply, and inflation remained subdued. The fiscal budget moved into surplus. We were the best performing economy in the Organisation for Economic Co-operation and Development (OECD), if not in the world, in these years. Things were rarely, if ever, so good in Ireland. A glance at figures 1.1 and 1.2 will show that during the depression of the mid-1980s unemployment reached unprecedented levels.

A central issue in this book is to identify the policy instruments that are most effective in achieving the goals of macroeconomics. It should be noted at the outset, however, that some economists are of the opinion that the best results will be achieved if the economy is left to itself. Market economies have proved remarkably capable of raising living standards and reducing poverty around the world. Centrally planned or socialistic economies have failed dismally to deliver remotely comparable results.

1.9 Conclusion

In this chapter we:

- Introduced the main topics to be dealt with in a course on macroeconomics
- Outlined the concepts of gross domestic product (GDP), gross national product (GNP), national income, unemployment and inflation
- Provided data on Ireland's real growth rate, unemployment and inflation, and some international comparisons
- Discussed the principal goals of macroeconomic policy, which are to maintain over the long run a high rate of growth of real GNP and low rates of unemployment and inflation
- Discussed the costs associated with unemployment and inflation
- Discussed the manner in which the fiscal deficit and the balance of payments act as constraints on policy makers in a small open economy such as Ireland.

CHAPTER 2

Introduction to the Theory of Income Determination

2.1 INTRODUCTION

We saw in chapter 1 that the primary objectives of macroeconomic policy are to achieve a high and stable growth rate in real GNP and to maintain a low level of unemployment. A low rate of inflation is also desirable, both in its own right and because it helps to achieve the growth and unemployment objectives. In pursuing these objectives policy makers are constrained by the need to avoid excessive fiscal and balance of payments deficits.

In this chapter we turn to the issue of the interaction between the real GNP, unemployment and the price level. A macroeconomic model of how the economy behaves is outlined. This is referred to as the *theory of income determination*. That is how the policy maker can influence output (national income), unemployment, and the price level. This model is then used to explain how the economy adjusts to economic 'shocks', that is, unexpected events that throw it off course. The concluding sections discuss two broad schools of thought, Keynesian and classical, and explain how they differ in regard to their conclusions about the workings of the economy and the scope for an active macroeconomic policy.

2.2 MACROECONOMIC MODELS

Macroeconomic theory uses models to explain how the economy works. Model building consists of setting out the way in which variables such as GNP, unemployment and the price level are interrelated. A model can be used to explore how policy variables, such as government expenditure, taxation, interest rates and the exchange rate affect the economy's performance. A macroeconomic model should help us to:

- Explain economic events
- Prescribe solutions to economic problems
- Forecast correctly long-term economic trends.

It is important to bear in mind that models are based on theories. It is necessary to keep testing economic theories against the facts to make sure that they are consistent with reality. A theory of the Irish economy would not be much use if, for example, it could not explain the fall in unemployment in the late 1990s.

Note:
Economists use econometric theory to estimate economic models. This involves using statistical techniques to estimate the parameters or coefficients of a model and to carry out various diagnostic

tests. Lawrence Klein developed one of the first large-scale macro econometric models at the University of Pennsylvania in the 1950s. In Ireland, the two most widely used models have been developed by the Central Bank of Ireland and the Economic and Social Research Institute (ESRI).

2.3 THE GENERAL THEORY

Modern macroeconomics essentially commenced with the publication of the book *The General Theory of Employment, Interest and Money* in 1936 by the British economist John Maynard Keynes (1883–1946). He was not entirely modest about what he was attempting to achieve. In a letter to George Bernard Shaw in 1935 he wrote: 'I believe myself to be writing a book on economic theory which will largely revolutionise — not, I suppose, at once but in the course of the next ten years — the way the world thinks about economic problems.'

The inspiration for the book was that Keynes felt that the orthodox or classical model of the day was unable to explain the reality of the Great Depression of the 1930s. At the time he was writing, the industrial countries of the world were in the severest depression in modern history. In the US, over the period 1929 to 1933, real output *fell* by 30 per cent, unemployment increased from 3.2 per cent to 25 per cent and the price level fell by 25 per cent. On Tuesday 29 October 1929, stock prices in New York fell by 12 per cent. By June 1932 stock prices had fallen by 85 per cent from their peak. By the time Franklin Delano Roosevelt (FDR) took office in March 1933, the depression was much more severe than anything experienced in the past. Unemployment in Britain increased from 10.4 per cent in 1927 to a peak of 22.1 per cent in 1932. In Ireland, unemployment increased from only 22,858 in 1929 to a peak of 133,319 in 1933.

However, not all of the European countries remained mired in depression throughout the 1930s. In Italy, the Fascist regime had embarked on a public works programme in the 1920s and averted the worst effects of the Great Depression. After Hitler's accession to power in Germany in 1933, government expenditure was increased and there was a rapid expansion in output and employment. In Sweden a Social

Democratic government had maintained a high level of employment by increasing its public works programmes.

Note:
Keynes, in a lecture delivered in University College, Dublin, in 1933, mentioned with approval the fact that several European countries 'have cast their eyes or are casting them towards new modes of political economy'. He praised the protectionist policies of the recently installed Fianna Fáil government as an alternative to the *laissez-faire* recommendations of classical economics. (J. M. Keynes, 'National Self-Sufficiency' [the first Finlay Lecture at University College, Dublin,] reprinted in *Studies*, June 1933, 184.) Keynes went on to decry 'decadent international capitalism' which, he said, 'doesn't deliver the goods'.

Policy makers in the English-speaking democracies at this time did not have a macroeconomic model that justified action by governments to move the economy out of the Depression. Keynes's *General Theory* was devoted to developing such a model. At its crudest, what he proposed was relatively simple. If the economy is in a depression, with high unemployment and plenty of unused capacity, government should increase spending or reduce taxation. This would lead to a higher level of economic activity and lower unemployment.

In fact Keynes's ideas had little immediate impact on policy. The Establishment in America, as well as in Britain, remained intellectually committed to the tenets of orthodox or classical economics, which predicted that in due course the economy would right itself. Their main concern was with balancing the budget. In fact, in the early 1930s tax rates were raised and expenditure cut, which had the effect of exacerbating the Depression. Only when government spending on armaments soared and vast numbers were mobilised into active military service, as World War II loomed, did unemployment begin to fall rapidly.

For Keynes the problem was to break away from the tenets of classical theory and develop an entirely new model of the economy. Keynes remarked in the preface to *The General Theory*: 'The composition of this book has been for the author a long struggle to escape ... The difficulty lies, not in the new ideas, but in escaping from the old ones, which ramify ... into every corner of our minds.' (*op. cit.* p. viii.)

In the following sections, we outline the basic Keynesian theory of income determination. This model will be extended at various stages throughout this book.

2.4 THE GOODS AND SERVICES MARKET

At the heart of all macroeconomic models are the concepts of *aggregate demand* (AD) and *aggregate supply* (AS). Expenditure on output is demand. If someone spends money on a cup of coffee, they contribute to the demand for coffee. *Total expenditure* is referred to as aggregate demand (AD). This is a particularly important concept in macroeconomic analysis. Like any demand schedule in microeconomics, the AD schedule relates total spending to the price level. In a later section we explain why AD is inversely related to the price level.

When someone buys a good someone else must have produced and delivered it. It takes two to complete a transaction. Looked at from the other side of the market, the total amount of goods and services produced by firms, that is *Gross National Product* (GNP), is referred to as aggregate supply (AS). Once again, as in microeconomics, the AS schedule is a positive function of the price level. As we shall see, the inter-action between total expenditure (demand) and GNP (supply of goods and services) determines, real GNP, unemployment and the price level.

There are three possibilities here:

GNP = TE   or   AS = AD Equilibrium
GNP > TE   or   AS > AD Excess supply
GNP < TE   or   AS < AD Excess demand

If AS equals AD, the economy is said to be in *equilibrium*. If AS exceeds AD, there is an *excess supply* of goods and services. If AS is less than AD, there is an *excess demand* for goods and services. This allows for a disequilibrium relationship to exist between the two variables. An excess supply means that firms are producing too much output and this is a signal to cut back on production. Similarly, excess demand means that firms are producing too little output and this is a signal to increase production.

As will become apparent in due course, the policy maker can attempt to influence either the supply or demand sides of the economy and thereby influence the key macroeconomic objectives. We now develop in more detail the crucial concepts of aggregate demand and aggregate supply.

Note:

An important role is played by changes in stocks or inventories in this process. Unplanned changes in stocks arise if the economy is not in equilibrium. *Unplanned* changes in stocks send signals to firms whether to increase or decrease production. In particular if GNP > TE, stocks build up and this indicates to firms to cut production. Conversely, if GNP < TE, stocks will be run down this indicates to firms to increase production. See Appendix 1 to this chapter for a more formal treatment of the role played by changes in stocks.

2.5 AGGREGATE DEMAND

We start from the premise that total expenditure (TE) in the economy can be divided into five categories:

		As a per cent of total expenditure
Private consumer expenditure	C	48
Investment	I	24
Government current expenditure	G	13
Exports	X	98
minus Imports	− M	83
Total		100

In short:

$$\text{Total expenditure} \equiv C + I + G + X - M \tag{1}$$

Consumer expenditure (C) refers to household expenditure on a whole range of goods and services and accounts for just over 50 per cent of TE. Investment (I) refers to firms' expenditure on new machinery and buildings. Thus, households do not buy all of the goods and services produced by firms. Some firms purchase machines and materials from other firms. Included in I is government capital expenditure on roads, buildings, and other forms of physical infrastructure. Government current expenditure (G) is expenditure of a day-to-day nature such as civil servants' salaries and so on. No asset is created with this type of expenditure, although spending on teachers' salaries, for example, presumably raises the national educational level, which constitutes part of its human capital. Exports (X) are expenditure by foreigners on Irish-produced goods and services. Imports are expenditure by Irish people on goods produced in other countries. Imports are deducted from total expenditure to arrive at expenditure on domestically produced goods and services. C, G, X and I include expenditure on both domestic and imported goods and services. Subtracting M leaves us with expenditure on the domestically produced goods. The difference between exports and imports (X − M) is referred to as *net exports*, NX, so we can rewrite (1) as

$$\text{Total expenditure (TE)} \equiv C + I + G + NX \tag{2}$$

The symbol $\equiv$ denotes an *identity* or something that is true by definition. Note that while exports and imports are individually very large, net exports are relatively small.

Note:
The letters or symbols we are using to describe macroeconomic variables have become standard. It was not always so. In a paper entitled, 'Mr Keynes and the Classics' (*Econometrica*, April 1937) which reviewed *The General Theory*, the Nobel prize-winning economist John Hicks (1904-89) used the symbol I for GNP or national income. In a letter to Hicks, Keynes wrote: 'I regret that you use the symbol I for income. One has to choose, of course, between using it for income and investment. But, after trying both, I believe it is easier to use Y for income and I for investment. Anyhow we ought to try and keep uniform in usage.' This letter is reproduced in J. R. Hicks, *Economic Perspectives: Further Essays on Money and Growth* (Oxford University Press, 1977, 145).

AGGREGATE DEMAND SCHEDULE
A demand curve shows the relationship between the price a firm charges and consumers' demand for that product. The higher the price, the lower the demand for the product. The rationale for a downward demand schedule for individual products is explained in courses in microeconomics. Similar but somewhat different considerations apply in macroeconomics.

On the demand side of the macroeconomy there is an inverse relationship between the price level (P) and real GNP. This is reflected in the downward-sloping aggregate demand (AD) curve in figure 2.1. In microeconomics it is easy to understand why a change in price would affect the demand for a firm's output. If a firm lowers its price, consumers will switch their spending from alternative products with a higher price. The demand for the firm's product will increase and the demand for the substitute product will fall. But why should a change in the *overall* price level affect the aggregate level of output? The theoretical explanation for this is given in box 2.1.

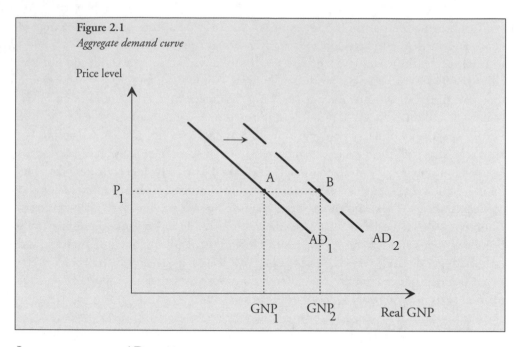

Figure 2.1
Aggregate demand curve

LOCATION OF THE AD CURVE

Let us consider now the factors that determine the *location* of the AD curve. For a given price level, an increase in any component of AD, such as C, I, G or NX, will shift the AD curve upwards to the right. A fall in any of the components of AD will shift the curve downwards to the left. To see how, consider the point A in figure 2.1, which corresponds to a price level P_1 and a real GNP level of GNP_1. An increase in, say, C moves the AD curve out to the right. B is a point on the new aggregate demand curve, AD_2. At this point the level of output has risen to GNP_2. By moving the AD curve outwards to the right in this fashion, we can examine the relationship between the old price level and the new higher level of real GNP. Conversely a fall in C will shift the AD back to the left.

Examples of 'economic shocks' and how they impact on the AD curve are given in box 2.2. The first example relates to an increase in oil prices that leads to higher imports and a fall in net exports. As a consequence, the AD curve moves to the left. The second example shows that a decrease in tax rates (such as the cut of $1.6 trillion — that is $1,600,000,000,000 — introduced by George W. Bush in 2001) boosts consumer expenditure (C). The AD curve moves to the right.

The third example is based on a change in government expenditure, which also influences the position of the AD curve. Changes in government expenditure and/or tax rates that influence total expenditure are examples of discretionary *fiscal policy*. Increases in expenditure and cuts in taxes are *expansionary*, decreases in expenditure and taxes hikes are *contractionary*. Finally, the adverse effects of 11 September would shift the AD curve left and an increase in exports would shift the AD curve right.

The main point to note, at this stage, is that an increase in C, I, G, X or a decrease in M will shift the AD curve up to the right and vice versa.

Box 2.1
The slope of the aggregate demand curve

There are basically three reasons why the aggregate demand curve slopes downwards.

International substitution effect A fall in the domestic price level relative to the foreign price level will increase the price competitiveness of domestic firms (assuming a fixed exchange rate). As a result, domestic firms will capture a greater share of both domestic and foreign markets. In terms of equation (2), net exports (NX) rise, and this leads to an increase in AD and subsequently to an increase in real GNP.

Real balance effect This refers to the effect of the price level on the real value of assets and subsequently on the level of consumption. If you hold some of your savings in cash, a fall in the price level will increase the real value (or purchasing power) of your wealth. Because you are now richer, you are likely to feel that you can afford to consume more out of your income. Hence, a decrease in the price level increases households' wealth, which, in turn, increases consumption (C) and aggregate demand (AD). The real balance effect is known as the Pigou effect because it was first suggested by Keynes's contemporary at Cambridge University, Arthur C. Pigou (1877–1959).

Inter-temporal substitution Briefly, the argument here is that high interest rates *(i)* encourage consumers to postpone or abandon expenditure plans because of the high cost of borrowing money. For example, suppose you intend to finance the purchase of a CD player by borrowing from a bank. If interest rates increase, you may decide to make do with your old music system as the cost of finance is too high. On the other hand, low interest rates encourage people to spend as the cost of borrowing is cheap.

As explained in detail in later chapters, there is a relationship between the price level (P) and the interest rate *(i)*. A fall in the price level leads to a fall in the rate of interest. The fall in the interest rate, in turn, leads to increased spending on interest-sensitive components of AD, such as consumer expenditure (C) and investment (I). Conversely, a higher price level increases the interest rate. The higher interest rate should lower C and I and, therefore, aggregate demand.

Box 2.2
Examples of 'economic shocks' and their impact on AD curve

Shock	AD curve shifts
Increase in consumer expenditure	Left
Decrease in taxes	Right
Increase in government expenditure	Right
September 11th	Left
Increase in exports	Right

2.6 AGGREGATE SUPPLY

Figure 2.2 shows an upward-sloping aggregate supply (AS) curve. The price level (P) and real GNP are measured on the vertical and horizontal axes, respectively. An upward-sloping AS curve indicates that an increase in P will lead to an increase in the supply of goods and services. Conversely, a decrease in the price level will lead to a fall in the supply of goods and services.

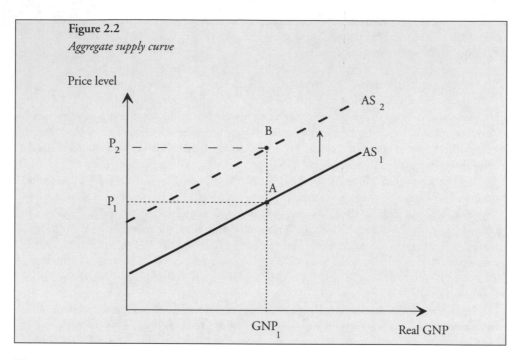

Figure 2.2
Aggregate supply curve

THE SLOPE OF THE AGGREGATE SUPPLY CURVE

Why should a firm increase its output when all prices are rising? To answer this, consider the fact that a firm's profit is equal to total revenue minus total cost:

$$\text{Profit} = \text{total revenue} - \text{total cost} \qquad (3)$$

In turn, total revenue equals the price of output (P_q) multiplied by the volume of output (Q). Total cost equals the price of inputs (P_z) multiplied by the volume of inputs (Z), such as raw materials and labour. (Wages are the price of labour.) Substituting into equation (3):

$$\text{Profit} = (P_q \times Q) - (P_z \times Z) \qquad (4)$$

It is assumed that the firm's output price increases as the general price level rises. An increase in output prices will increase profits *if input prices remain constant*: the firm enjoys higher revenue for the same cost. Higher profits, in turn, act as an incentive for firms to increase the volume of output. This positive relationship between the price level and the volume of output supplied is reflected in an upward-sloping AS curve.

This result depends crucially on the assumption that input prices, and wages in particular, remain constant as output prices change. Obviously if wages remain constant as prices rise, workers will be worse off. Hence, the assumption that wages are constant is certainly not valid in the long run. The AS schedule depicted in figure 2.2 is therefore a *short-run* relationship.

LOCATION OF THE AS CURVE

As mentioned, the AS curve is drawn for a given level of input prices or total costs. If input prices (costs) change, the AS curve will shift. To see this, consider the point A in figure 2.2, where the price level, P_1, corresponds to the real output level, GNP_1. Suppose that costs increase and firms, in order to maintain profits, pass these higher costs on to customers in the form of higher prices for their products. In terms of equation (4), the increase in input prices is reflected in an increase in output prices in order to maintain profit levels. The increase in output prices is shown in figure 2.2 as a movement from A to B. At B, real GNP is unchanged, but the price level has increased from P_1 to P_2. The supply schedule has shifted upwards to the left, from AS_1 to AS_2. By moving the AS curve upwards in this way, we can examine the relationship between the new, higher price level and the original level of real GNP. Conversely, lower input prices will be reflected in a shift downwards to the right of the AS curve.

An important influence on the location of the AS curve, which we have not yet mentioned, is *productivity*, defined as the ratio of output to inputs. (Total output divided by the quantity of labour employed is referred to as *labour productivity*.) If more output is obtained from the same, or fewer, inputs, productivity has increased. This occurs as technology improves or there is an improvement in working practices. An increase in productivity reduces costs as more output can be produced with a given amount of inputs. Hence, increases in productivity shift the AS curve down to the right, whereas decreases in productivity shift the AS curve upwards to the left.

Box 2.3 gives some examples of 'economic shocks' that impact on the AS curve. In the first example, an increase in oil prices increases the price of a whole range of raw materials and, as a result, the AS curve moves left. This is an example of an adverse supply-side shock. A decrease in wages, on the other hand, reduces costs and shifts the AS to the right. Similarly, a decrease in electricity charges will move the AS curve right. These are examples of positive supply-side shocks.

Box 2.3
Examples of 'economic shocks' that imapct on AS curve

Shock	AS curve shifts
Increase in the price of oil	Left
Decrease in wages	Right
Decrease in electricity charges	Right
Rise in the price of raw materials	Left
Increase in productivity	Right

The key point to note at this stage is that an increase in input prices (costs) or a fall in productivity will shift the AS curve to the left. Conversely, a fall in input prices or a rise in productivity will shift the AS curve to the right.

2.7 EQUILIBRIUM

In figure 2.3, the AS and AD curves are brought together, and we see that the equilibrium price (P_1) and real output (GNP_1) combination is at the point A. When the AS and AD curves intersect, GNP equals total expenditure. That is:

$$GNP = TE \equiv C + I + G + NX \qquad (5)$$

Output equals total expenditure, which, in turn, can be broken down into consumer expenditure, investment, government expenditure and net exports.

Recall that changes in stocks act as a signal to firms as to whether production should be increased, reduced, or left unchanged. At A there are no unplanned (unanticipated) changes in stocks. This is the key to the concept of equilibrium in the market for goods and services.

If the price level is lower than P_1, as at P_2, AS is less than AD and there is excess aggregate demand. This excess demand will lead to an unplanned reduction in stocks. In order to ration the available supply among those trying to buy it, firms will raise prices. As the price level rises, this encourages firms to increase production (along the AS curve) and reduces the demand for goods (along the AD curve). Eventually equilibrium will be restored at the point A.

Similarly, if the price level is greater than P_1, as at P_3, AS exceeds AD and there is an excess supply of goods and services. There will be an unplanned increase in stocks. Firms will lower prices in order to clear unwanted stocks. As the price level falls, firms will cut production (along the AS curve) and the demand for goods and services will increase (along the AD curve). Again equilibrium will be reached at A.

In what follows we assume that equilibrium is quickly re-established following some disturbance. This is certainly true of the financial markets where excess supply or

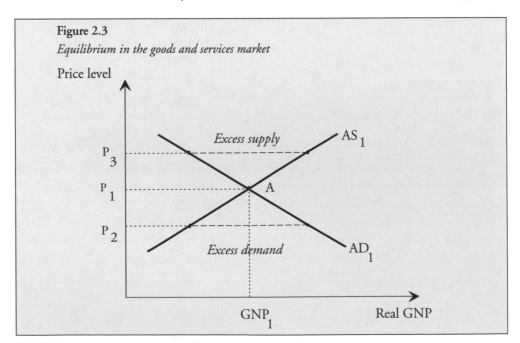

Figure 2.3

Equilibrium in the goods and services market

Price level

demand positions are eliminated in a matter of minutes. Goods or service markets tend to be more sluggish. However, we will not consider this possibility at this early stage.

ALTERNATIVE REPRESENTATION

An alternative representation is to replace 'levels' with 'rates of change' in figure 2.3. This entails replacing the price level with the inflation rate and real GNP with the real growth rate. Hence the model is also suitable for examining the relationship between growth and inflation. This is perhaps a more realistic framework to use as the price level and real GNP rarely fall. However, it is more complicated to explain why AD should be a positive function of the rate of inflation. In what follows, we shall use the 'level' version of the AS/AD model throughout the remainder of this chapter.

2.8 DEMAND-SIDE AND SUPPLY-SIDE SHOCKS

Recall from chapter 1 that the main goals of macroeconomics are to:

1. Increase real GNP
2. Keep unemployment low
3. Achieve 'price stability'.

In figure 2.4 the price level is given along the vertical axis and real GNP along the horizontal axis. In the background, a change in real GNP is associated with a change in the unemployment rate. Hence, the intersection of the AS and AD curves influences three of the key macroeconomic variables.

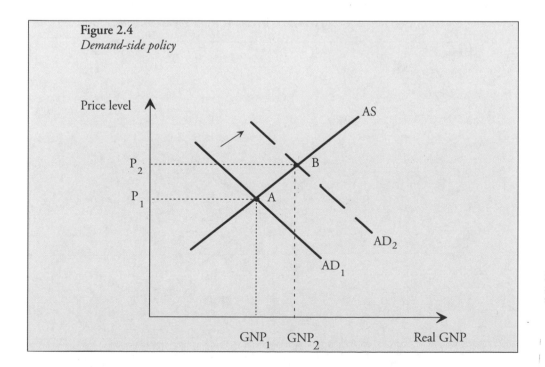

Figure 2.4
Demand-side policy

Starting from the point A in figure 2.4, suppose the government embarks on an expansionary fiscal policy (increases government expenditure and/or cuts taxation). The AD curve shifts to the right and a new equilibrium is established at the point B. Consider now what has happened to real GNP and the price level. Along the horizontal axis, real GNP has increased and unemployment falls. Hence, we are closer to attaining objectives 1 and 2. However, the price level has increased along the vertical axis so that we are further from attaining objective 3.

Note:
As explained in section 2.9, the reason for the inverse relationship between changes in real GNP and unemployment is that firms must hire more labour to produce more output. As employment increases, unemployment falls.

Similarly, if the government introduced a deflationary fiscal policy the AD curve would shift down to the left (not shown). In this case, real GNP falls and unemployment rises. Objectives 1 and 2 are further away. However, the price level falls so that we move closer to achieving objective 3. What this serves to illustrate is that demand-side policies result in a *policy dilemma*. It is possible to move closer to objectives 1 and 2 at the expense of objective 3 or vice versa — in the short run at least. But it is not possible, using demand-side policies, to achieve all three objectives simultaneously.

SUPPLY-SIDE POLICY
Consider now figure 2.5 where the economy is initially at the point A. Suppose the government negotiates a favourable national wage agreement with the trade unions and the employer groups. There have been a number of such agreements in Ireland over the period 1987 to 2002. The latest agreement is called the *Programme for Prosperity and*

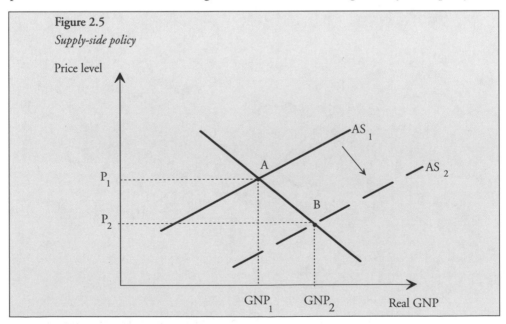

Figure 2.5
Supply-side policy

Fairness and is due to expire in December 2002. The effect of these agreements should be to shift the AS curve down to the right. The result is an increase in real GNP and a fall in unemployment. However, on this occasion prices also fall. Hence all three macroeconomic objectives move in the desired direction and no policy dilemma exists. In this regard, a favourable supply-side policy is very effective.

Note, however, that an adverse supply-side shock (such as an increase in oil prices) is a particularly harmful development. If the AS curve shifts up to the left, all of the key macroeconomic variables are adversely affected. There will be a fall in real GNP and a rise in unemployment. The price level also increases. Clearly, adverse supply-side shocks are to be avoided if at all possible.

The combination of rising prices and falling output has been labelled *stagflation*. A leftward shift of the AS curve occurred when the price of energy inputs rose sharply in the 1970s, and again, although only briefly, during the Gulf War of 1990–91. The collapse of oil prices in 1986 was a very favourable supply-side shock.

Versions of supply-side economics became popular in the 1980s in the US during the Reagan administration and in Britain during the Thatcher era. It was widely believed that the key to greater prosperity lay in shifting the AS curve to the right by increasing the incentives for the unemployed to accept whatever jobs were available and encouraging people to work harder and take greater risks by lowering the top rates of income tax. Demand-side policies were considered to be less effective.

2.9 REAL GNP AND UNEMPLOYMENT

How does unemployment fit into the above analysis? In the short run, if a firm wishes to expand its output, it will tend to hire more workers. Recall from chapter 1 that:

Labour force = employed + unemployed   (6)

Assuming the labour force is relatively constant, an increase in real GNP (along the horizontal axis in figure 2.3) will lead to an increase in employment and this, in turn, will be associated with a fall in unemployment. Conversely, a fall in real GNP should lead to a decrease in employment and a rise in unemployment. Hence, changes in real GNP impact on the unemployment rate. This assumes, of course, that the labour force is reasonably constant. Such an assumption is not valid in the Irish case as we have a long history of emigration and more recently of substantial net immigration. We shall ignore the possibility of changes in the labour force for the moment. This relationship between real GNP and unemployment is now examined more formally under the heading of *Okun's law*.

Note:
Firms use the *factors of production*: labour, physical and human capital and technology to produce the goods and services in an economy. We are assuming that in the short run, capital and technology are relatively constant. If this is the case, firms must use more labour (employment) to generate more output.

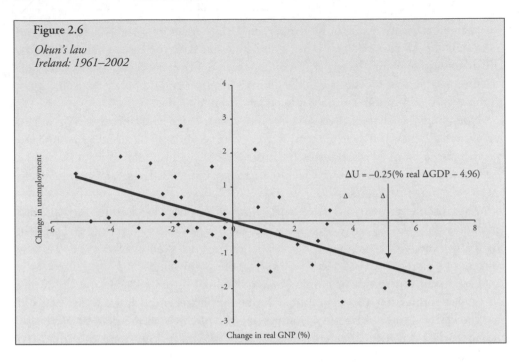

Figure 2.6

Okun's law
Ireland: 1961–2002

$\Delta U = -0.25(\% \text{ real } \Delta GDP - 4.96)$

Change in unemployment

Change in real GNP (%)

OKUN'S LAW

In this section we examine the relationship between the rate of growth in real GNP and unemployment. The link between these two variables may be seen from a comparison of figures 1.1 and 1.2 in chapter 1. These two diagrams suggest that there is a relationship between cyclical swings in the business cycle and the rate of unemployment in Ireland. During periods of rapid growth, the 1960s, 1977–79 and the 1990s, for example, more jobs were created and this led to a fall in unemployment. Conversely, during periods when output is falling, such as the mid-1980s, employment falls and unemployment rises. The American economist Arthur Okun first investigated this relationship between growth and unemployment in the 1960s. This relationship has become known as Okun's law.

Note:

Arthur Okun (1929–79) became Professor of Economics at Yale in 1963. He was made a member of John F. Kennedy's Council of Economic Advisors in 1964 and became chairman of this council in 1968. He joined the Brookings Institution, in Washington D.C. in 1969 where he remained until his death in 1979. Using 1950s' data for the US economy, he found that a one-percentage point increase in the unemployment rate was associated with three-percentage points fall in real GDP. He later commented 'This "rule of thumb" held up so well over the next decade that some of my professional colleagues called it Okun's Law'.

The relationship between growth and unemployment can be examined more formally by plotting the *percentage change* in real GDP (the growth rate) against the *change* in the unemployment rate. (We switch here from GNP to GDP to facilitate international comparison.) Figure 2.6 shows the relationship between these two variables from 1961 to 2002. Each point shows the growth/change in unemployment combination for that year. The regression line running through the scatter diagram illustrates this relationship. The line slopes downwards, indicating that as the growth rate increases along the horizontal axis, the unemployment rate falls on the vertical axis. In estimating the regression line the average real growth rate over the period 1961–2000 (which was 4.96 per cent) is deducted from the actual growth rate. Hence the estimated equation is:

$$\Delta U = \alpha[\%\Delta\text{real GDP} - 4.96] \qquad (7)$$

The α coefficient is calculated to be -0.25. The regression results therefore suggests, that for every 1 per cent increase in real growth, over the average of 4.96 per cent, unemployment falls by 0.25 percentage points (one-quarter of a per cent). The reason why the average growth rate is deducted is to allow for changes in productivity (output per worker) and also changes in the labour force participation rate (the proportion of the population participating in the labour force).

Table 2.1 shows the estimated α coefficient for the Eurozone countries. (The coefficients were estimated using data from European Commission, *European Economy*, No. 73, 2002.) The Irish labour market is very open and as a result the supply of labour is relatively elastic. We would therefore expect the α coefficient to be smaller in Ireland than in some of the larger Eurozone countries. But this does not seem to be the case. The estimated α coefficient is much lower in Germany and France. There would also seem to be a weak relationship between economic growth and unemployment in Austria, Italy and

Table 2.1
Okun's law

	Estimated α coefficient
Austria	-0.11
Belgium	-0.18
Finland	-0.37
France	-0.13
Germany	-0.19
Greece	-0.07
Ireland	-0.25
Italy	-0.07
Luxembourg	-0.01
Netherlands	-0.23
Portugal	-0.10
Spain	-0.27
Eurozone	-0.17

Source: Authors' estimates, based on data over the period 1961–2002.

Portugal. This points to the difficulties of reducing unemployment in these countries. It would seem that it is much easier to reduce unemployment in Spain and Finland where the α coefficient is relatively high. The downside is that during periods of recession, there will be a significant upsurge in unemployment in these countries.

Okun's law makes it clear that the macroeconomic objectives of growth and unemployment are closely associated. If the policy maker is successful in maintaining a strong real growth rate, then over time the unemployment rate should fall to a low level. Okun's law also illustrates why a boom cannot last forever. Rapid growth pushes the unemployment rate down, but sooner or later the economy reaches or passes 'full employment'. Shortages of workers will also lead to higher wage demands that will increase inflation and slow the economy down.

2.10 NATURAL REAL GNP AND THE LONG-RUN AS CURVE

As mentioned, one of the main goals of macroeconomics is to increase real GNP and raise the standard of living in the country. In this regard it is important to introduce the concept of *natural real GNP*. Natural real GNP is defined as that level of output that could be produced with a stable rate of inflation in a fully employed economy, given the size of the labour force, the physical and human capital stock, and the available technology.

The capital stock includes all the plant and machinery and the education and skills of the labour force. If the economy is operating at this level, firms are operating at capacity and there is full employment in the labour market. This level of output is also referred to as *potential GNP*, or *full-employment GNP*, and the underlying level of unemployment is referred to as the *natural rate of unemployment*. Box 2.4 outlines the main factors that influence the growth of natural real GNP over time.

Box 2.4
Factors influencing natural real GNP

Labour force The bigger the labour force the more goods and services that can be produced. Between 1994 and 2001, the Irish labour force increased by 30 per cent to 1,819,000 people. This was due to the growth of the population and a rise in the labour force participation rate (the proportion of the population that is in the labour force). Due to the age structure of the population and the high rate of immigration, Ireland's labour force could grow by about 1.5 per cent over the immediate future. This contrasts with the near-stagnation of most European labour forces.

Capital stock The capital stock consists of physical and human capital. Physical capital relates to the plant and machinery and the infrastructure in the economy. Human capital relates to the experience, skills and education of the labour force. The greater a country's stock of physical and human capital, the more output that can be produced. Investment in education is an important determinant of a country's human capital.

Technology A firm which employs the latest technology will produce more output than a firm using out-of-date machinery. Investment in research and development is a key factor influencing advances in technology. This investment, in turn, is largely financed from domestic savings. Because of this link between savings and investment, economists have always attributed a very important role to thrift among the sources of economic progress.

The supply of raw materials If a country has an abundance of natural resources, such as oil and gas fields, then this will increase the country's potential output. Likewise, scarcities of key raw materials could hinder the growth of the economy. Such scarcities have not, however, been much of a constraint on growth over the years. New sources of supply are always opening up and new technologies are constantly finding ways of economising on raw materials, whose long-run price has tended to fall relative to the general cost of living.

Note:

The significance of the 'natural rate' concept, is that the economy contains an 'automatic' or 'self-correcting mechanism' which tends to move actual output towards its natural rate. The natural rate of unemployment is not zero. Due to frictions in the labour market it is never possible to achieve zero unemployment. It is difficult, however, to actually define the natural rate of unemployment. The rate depends on the flexibility of the workforce and the efficiency with which the labour market functions.

In figure 2.7 natural real GNP is denoted as GNP* and is represented by the vertical line. The reason why the line is vertical is because natural real GNP is *independent* of the price level. Changes in the price level along the vertical axis will not affect natural real GNP. Only changes in the labour force, the capital stock or advances in technology can change natural real GNP. A decrease in the available levels of these factors shifts the natural GNP line to the left, an increase shifts it to the right. For this

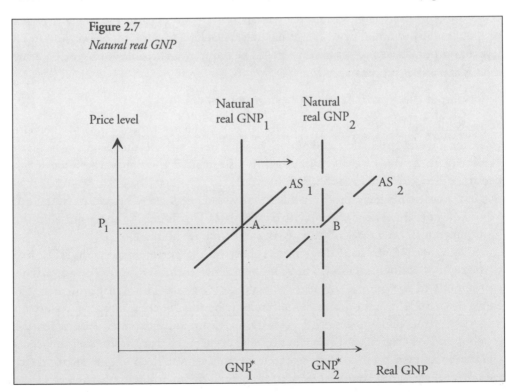

Figure 2.7
Natural real GNP

reason the natural real GNP line is sometimes referred to as the *long-run aggregate supply curve* (LAS).

The diagram also shows the upward-sloping *short-run AS curve* derived earlier. Along the short-run AS curve, changes in the price level will give rise to changes in the supply of goods and services and this is reflected in the upward sloping AS curve. It should be noted that a change in natural real GNP will also lead to a change in the short-run AS curve. If a firm can produce more output in the long run, it can also produce more output in the short-term. As shown in figure 2.7, a shift in natural real GNP to the right also brings forth a shift of the short-run AS curve to the right and vice versa.

AGGREGATE DEMAND AND NATURAL REAL GNP

If the aggregate demand curve is now re-introduced we obtain equilibrium in the goods and services market. However, changes in either the AD curve or the short-run AS curve can cause the economy to move away from natural real GNP. At any particular point in time the economy could be in *recession, over-heating* or at natural real GNP.

For example, the three diagrams at the top part of figure 2.8, show the economy in recession (left-hand side), at natural real GNP (centre) and over-heating (right-hand side). In the left-hand diagram, the short-run AS curve intersects the AD curve to the left of natural real GNP. The economy is operating below capacity and unemployment is above its natural rate. It is important to be able to relate this to the business cycle discussed in chapter 1.

The diagram in the bottom part of figure 2.8 shows the actual real growth rate swinging above and below the natural real growth rate (horizontal line). When the economy is to the left of natural real GNP, this is equivalent to the point A in the diagram at the bottom of figure 2.8. When the actual level of output is below the natural level of output, an *output gap* has emerged. The economy is capable of producing more than it actually is producing.

$$\text{Output gap} = \text{actual real GNP} - \text{natural real GNP} \qquad (8)$$

When actual real GNP is below natural real GNP, unemployment tends to rise. The economy is not producing enough to provide jobs for all the people who seek employment. In this case, the output gap is also referred to as an *unemployment gap* because unemployment is above its natural rate.

In the centre diagram, the short-run AS curve intersects the AD curve at natural real GNP and unemployment is also at its natural rate. This is akin to the point B in the lower diagram. The actual growth rate is equal to the natural rate.

Finally, in the right-hand diagram, the short-run AS curve intersects the AD curve to the right of natural real GNP. The economy is now in an over-heating position. This corresponds to the point C in the business cycle diagram. The actual growth rate is above the natural rate. In this case, the economy booms. There is upward pressure on wages and firms pass-on the rising costs by increasing output prices. Also when the economy is over-heating firms may not be able to meet the demand for their products and this encourages them to raise prices. Hence, in the lower diagram, the inflation rate rises. In this case, the output gap is referred to as an *inflation gap*.

Figure 2.8

Linking the AS/AD model to the business cycle

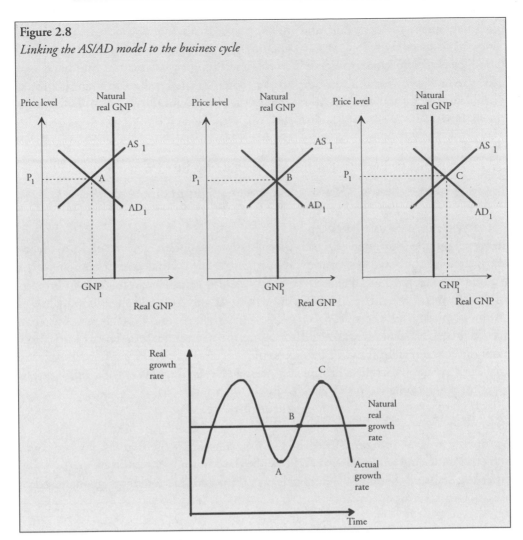

Note:

A major difficulty is that both the natural real growth rate and the natural rate of unemployment may vary over time. For example, it is estimated that the natural real growth rate fell significantly in Ireland in 2001 due to labour shortages. (This issue is discussed in chapter 24.) Similarly, due to emigration the Irish labour market is very open and, as a result, the natural rate of unemployment tends to vary. When jobs become available in Ireland, people return to the country and fill the positions. Conversely, people tend to emigrate when jobs become scarce. Furthermore, the natural rate of unemployment varies between countries (see chapter 21). Many Eurozone economies — notably Spain — appear to have high natural rates of unemployment. This means that when unemployment falls below about 12 per cent, inflationary pressures quickly build up. A high natural rate of unemployment is a major defect of many European economies and a major contrast with the US economy.

POLICY IMPLICATIONS

At any point in time, the short-run AS and the AD curves are buffered by various shocks that move the economy away from natural real GNP. If the economy is operating above potential, unemployment falls and inflation speeds up. On the other hand, if the economy is operating below capacity, unemployment rises while the inflation rate falls. Good macroeconomic management avoids increasing prices on the one hand and excessive unemployment on the other, by keeping the actual real growth rate as close as possible to the natural real growth rate over time. This raises the question: Following a shock, how does the economy adjust back to natural real GNP?

2.11 ADJUSTING TO ECONOMIC SHOCKS IN THE LONG RUN

In this section we illustrate the way the economy adjusts to various shocks.

AN ADVERSE DEMAND-SIDE SHOCK

In figure 2.9, the (short-run) AS and AD curves initially intersect at the point A. Hence the price level is P_1 and the economy is operating at the natural rate. Suppose now the economy is subjected to an adverse demand-side shock such as an increase in imports or a fall in investment. The AD curve shifts from AD_1 to AD_2 and the economy moves to the point B. Both the price level and real GNP fall. Actual GNP is now less than natural real GNP and unemployment is above the natural unemployment level. How does the economy adjust out of this recession?

The key variable in the adjustment process is the *real wage* (W/P). This real wage is equal to the nominal wage (W) divided by the price index (P).

$$\text{Real wage} = \text{Nominal wage/Price index} \tag{9}$$

At the point A in figure 2.9, there is a particular real wage that is consistent with the economy being at natural real GNP. When the economy moved to the point B, the price level fell and, because the nominal wage is unchanged, the real wage increased.

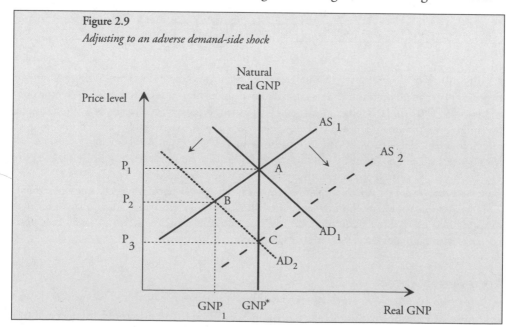

Figure 2.9

Adjusting to an adverse demand-side shock

Recall that nominal wages are one of the main determinants of the location of the AS curve. If workers recognise that real wages have risen and accept a cut in nominal wages (W), (to restore the original real wage), the AS curve will shift down to the right. The economy now moves from the point B to the point C and the economy is back to natural real GNP. At the point C, the original real wage is restored because the fall in nominal wages is exactly equal to the fall in the price level.

This analysis indicates an important difference between the long-run (natural real GNP) and short-run AS curves. Along the natural real GNP line the *real wage is constant*. As the economy moved from the point A to C, the change in nominal wages exactly offsets the change in the price level and the real wage is constant. However, along the short-run AS curve the *real wage varies*. Because the nominal wage is constant, changes in the price level are reflected in changes in the real wage.

EXPANSIONARY FISCAL POLICY

Consider now figure 2.10 where the economy is initially at the point A and is operating at natural real GNP. The government – facing an election – may pursue an expansionary fiscal policy (increasing expenditure or cutting tax rates) in the belief that real GNP can be increased and unemployment reduced. The AD curve shifts out to the right and the economy moves to the point B. The price level has risen to P_2 and actual real GNP is above natural real GNP^*. How does the economy adjust from this inflationary situation?

Along the short-run AS_1 curve nominal wages are constant. Hence, the increase in the price level from P_1 to P_2 reduces the real wage (W/P). After a time, workers will recognise that real earnings have fallen and will increase their wage demands. As nominal wages increase the AS curve shifts up to the left. The economy now moves to

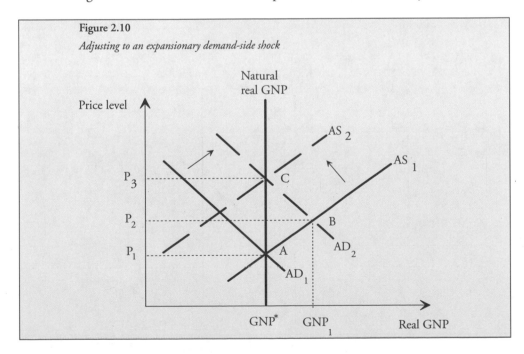

Figure 2.10

Adjusting to an expansionary demand-side shock

the point C and back to natural real GNP. At the point C, the original real wage is restored because the change in the price level from P_1 to P_3 is exactly equal to the increase in nominal wages. The effect of the expansionary fiscal policy has been a temporary increase in real GNP and a permanent increase in the price level.

INCREASE IN OIL PRICES

Consider now the effect of an adverse supply-side shock such as an increase in the price of oil. Suppose the economy is initially at the point A in figure 2.11. The economy is at natural real GNP and the price level is P_1. The Organisation of Petroleum Exporting Countries (OPEC) — the cartel of oil producing countries — increased oil prices from $3 to $12 a barrel in 1974 and from $12 to $30 a barrel in 1979. How do increases in oil prices impact on the economy?

Higher oil prices affect a whole range of raw materials and increase firms' costs. Electricity charges, heating bills, telephone charges, and so on, all increase. In an attempt to maintain profit levels, firms pass-on the higher costs in higher output prices. In figure 2.11, the short-run AS curve shifts up to the left.

The increase in oil prices also shifts the AD curve. Imports increase and higher oil prices will adversely affect firms' investment decisions. The AD curve shifts down to the left. As drawn in figure 2.11, the movement of the AS curve is greater than the movement of the AD curve and, as a result, equilibrium is re-established at the point B. At the point B, the price level has increased and real GNP has fallen. Because the nominal wage is unchanged, the rise in the price level reduces real wages. In the background, unemployment will also have increased.

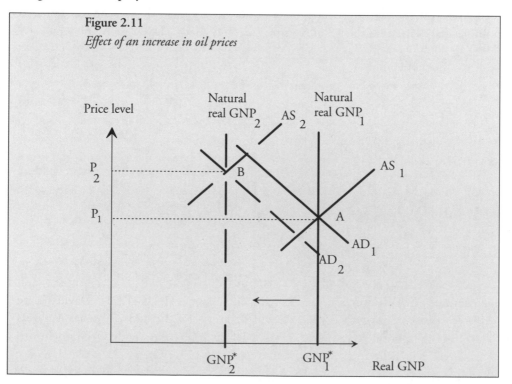

Figure 2.11
Effect of an increase in oil prices

It is clear from figure 2.11 that higher oil prices have a particularly adverse impact on the economy. All of the key macroeconomic variables have deteriorated. It is also possible that the economy may not adjust back to the original natural real GNP but will in fact stay at the point B. The reason for this is that the lower real wage leads to a reduction in the labour force. Fewer people are willing to work at the lower real wage. As a consequence, the natural real GNP line itself shifts to the left and intersects the short-run AS and AD curves at the point B. Hence, not only does natural real GNP decrease but the associated natural rate of unemployment also rises. In this case, an increase in oil prices affects the performance of the economy in both the short and long run.

2.12 Keynesian Economics

Consider again figure 2.9, which showed the economy moving from natural real GNP to the point B following an adverse demand-side shock. At the point B, the economy is in recession and unemployment is above the level defined as 'full employment'. The real wage has also increased and a cut in nominal wages is required if the economy is to revert back to natural real GNP. Keynesian economists argue the point B represents equilibrium because aggregate supply equals aggregate demand and there is no unwanted or unintended accumulation of stocks. Most importantly, Keynes argued that nominal wages are inflexible in a downward direction and the economy could remain at the point B for quite a long time. If nominal wages do not fall, the AS curve will not move down to the right and the economy will remain at the point B.

Because of the inflexibility of nominal wages, Keynes argued that output gaps could persist and that the economy could get stuck at levels of output below natural real GNP. This would be very costly over time in terms of lost output and excess unemployment. Examples of this problem are the Great Depression of 1929–39 and Ireland in the mid-1980s. In both cases the economy remained in recession for several years and the unemployment rate was considerably above any reasonable definition of full employment.

To deal with the problem, Keynes recommended an *interventionist* fiscal policy stance. Starting at the point B in figure 2.9, an increase in government expenditure and/or a cut in tax rates would shift the AD curve back to its original position. As a result the economy would revert to natural real GNP and the recession would quickly end. Keynesian economics advocated an *active* policy stance.

2.13 Classical Economics

Classical economics emerged gradually from the writings of the great eighteenth- and nineteenth-century economists, such as François Quesnay (1694–1774), David Hume (1711–76), Adam Smith (1723–90), David Ricardo (1772–1823), Thomas Malthus (1766–1834), and John Stuart Mill (1806–73). Classical economics has its foundations in the Physiocrat movement of the seventeenth century. (Physiocrat comes from a French word of Greek origin meaning the 'rule of nature'.) This school of thought provided a strong intellectual justification for a non-interventionist, *laissez-faire* political economy. Members of the school argued that government intervention advocated by earlier economists was grossly inefficient.

Note:
Ironically, the first account of economics to be labelled 'the classical model' is given in chapter 2 of Keynes's *General Theory*. (See 'The Postulates of the Classical Economics', *op. cit.*)

Classical economists tend to take a long-run perspective on how the economy operates. They argue that if there is no government interference, the economy will automatically revert back to full employment following an adverse shock. The only long-run equilibrium is where aggregate demand intersects the natural real GNP line. Points such as B in figures 2.9 and 2.10 are only 'temporary' equilibrium points. In due course, nominal wages will adjust to move the economy to natural real GNP.

But what about the Keynesian argument that nominal wages are inflexible in a downward direction? While it is true that it is most unusual for absolute nominal wages to fall, this is not the case when rates of change are considered. For example, if equation 9 above is totally differentiated we obtain:

$$\Delta RW = \Delta W - \pi \tag{10}$$

That is, the percentage change in real wages (ΔRW) is equal to the percentage change in nominal wages (ΔW) minus inflation (π). To bring about a cut in real wages all that is required is for inflation to exceed the change in nominal earnings. There are plenty of examples of this occurring in Ireland. For example, in 1994, real wages fell by –0.6 per cent because a 1.7 per cent increase in nominal earnings was more than offset by 2.3 per cent inflation (see table 1.5 in chapter 1). From this perspective, a fall in real earnings may not be so implausible.

To some extent, the argument is about how long it takes for the adjustment to take place. In response to the classical argument that in the long run real wages would adjust, Keynes famously retorted, 'In the long run we are all dead'.

Similarly, classical economists predicted that the government could not increase GNP beyond natural real GNP for any length of time. We saw in figure 2.10, for example, that attempts by the government to do so resulted in a permanent hike in the price level leaving real GNP unchanged. All that was achieved was a surge in inflation.

The policy conclusion that emerges from this is that there is no need for intervention on the part of the authorities. Governments should pursue a *non-interventionist* policy stance and not try to use fiscal policy to influence the macroeconomy. The greater is wage and price flexibility, the faster the economy will revert to natural real GNP. Unemployment or inflation gaps will as a consequence be short-lived. Governments therefore should introduce policies to deregulate the markets so as to make wages and prices more flexible.

The only way to increase real output is by increasing natural real GNP, which requires a rightward shift of the long-run AS curve. This comes about through growth in the skills and expertise of the labour force and investment in new and better capital equipment. Thus, classical economists place the emphasis on supply-side measures rather than on the manipulation of aggregate demand, as the way to achieve lasting increases in the level of output.

2.14 MODERN MACROECONOMICS

After World War II Keynesian policy eventually became the new orthodoxy, especially in English-speaking countries. The appeal of the theory lay in the way it seemed to show governments how to reduce unemployment without enkindling inflation. At the theoretical level the whole profession debated the validity of Keynes's ideas. One influential part of the economics profession attempted to refine Keynes's model and explain it within the basic classical framework. Paul Samuelson — the US Nobel prize-winner in economics who wrote the first modern textbook of economics aimed at university students — labelled this the 'neoclassical synthesis'. Between 1940 and the mid-1970s, the neoclassical synthesis was accepted by the majority of economists and much work was carried on refining some of the main theories or concepts identified by Keynes.

During the 1960s the most important debate was between the Keynesians and the monetarists whose intellectual leader was Milton Friedman. The Keynesian/monetarist debate centred on issues such as the relative effectiveness of fiscal and monetary policy and whether or not there is a trade-off between inflation and unemployment.

However, in the 1970s, following the lead set by the monetarists, a classical counter-revolution gained ground. First, as economies began to experience stagflation (rising inflation and rising unemployment), there was increasing scepticism about the Keynesian model and in particular the effectiveness of macroeconomic policy in achieving lasting increases in employment and output.

Secondly and most importantly, new sophisticated versions of the classical model emerged that emphasised the role of rational expectations. The chief exponents of this new theory were the American economists Robert Lucas (who was awarded the Nobel prize in 1995), Thomas Sargent and Robert Barro. This school of thought, which is known as *New Classical* or *Rational Expectations* macroeconomics, argues that there is no trade-off between inflation and unemployment and that policy makers cannot use large-scale macroeconomic models to evaluate policy decisions (the Lucas critique).

It is probably fair to say that a new synthesis has now emerged which involves the acceptance of the rational expectations theory set in a Keynesian framework. This new rational expectations synthesis is now accepted by most mainstream economists.

Many of the Nobel prize winners in economics (listed in an appendix to this chapter) based their writings on topics first raised by Keynes. While they may have strongly disagreed with his views, their intellectual debt to him was enormous.

There is still a good deal of disagreement between economists, especially in regard to the effectiveness of policies to alleviate the problem of unemployment. It is our task in the chapters that follow to outline the various issues and to identify the different strands to the arguments in this ongoing debate.

2.15 CONCLUSION

In this chapter we have introduced the broad themes of macroeconomics. These included:

- The idea of a macroeconomic model
- The Keynesian theory of income determination
- The concepts of aggregate supply and aggregate demand
- Equilibrium in the goods and services market
- The distinction between demand-side and supply-side policies
- Okun's law
- The concept of natural real GNP and the natural unemployment rate
- Output gaps and how these related to changes in unemployment and inflation
- How economies adjust to demand-side and supply-side shocks
- How changes in wages automatically move the economy to natural real GNP
- The debate between Keynes and the classical school
- Developments in modern macroeconomics.

APPENDIX 1
THE ROLE OF STOCKS IN ESTABLISHING EQUILIBRIUM

The basic assumption is that firms have a *planned* or *desired* stock level and they set aside a proportion of their output for stock building. If, however, sales fall short of what was anticipated, the firm will have produced too much output and there will be an unplanned accumulation of stocks. Conversely, if sales exceed expectations, the firm will have produced too little output and there will be an unplanned reduction in stocks.

In any given period, therefore, total stock changes (ΔSK) will consist of a planned component (ΔSK_p) and an unplanned component (ΔSK_u):

$$\Delta SK = \Delta SK_p + \Delta SK_u \tag{11}$$

Now ΔSK_p is classified as a part of investment. However, ΔSK_u is classified as part of GNP and is not included in investment or total expenditure. This means that if GNP exceeds aggregate demand, ΔSK_u is positive and firms will cut production until GNP equals aggregate demand. Conversely, if GNP is less than aggregate demand, ΔSK_u is negative and firms will expand production until GNP equals aggregate demand. Thus changes in unplanned stocks play a crucial role in modern macroeconomics, sending signals to managers on which they base their production plans. The macroeconomy is said to be in equilibrium when GNP equals aggregate demand and $\Delta SK_u = 0$.

APPENDIX 2
NOBEL PRIZE IN ECONOMIC SCIENCES WINNERS AND THEIR CONTRIBUTIONS TO ECONOMICS: 1969–2002

1969	Ragnar Frisch and Jan Tinbergen (joint award) For the development and the application of dynamic models for the analysis of economic processes.
1970	Paul Samuelson The development of static and dynamic economic theory and his contribution to raising the level of analysis in economic science.
1971	Simon Kuznets For his empirically founded interpretation of economic growth which led to a new insight into the economic and social structure and process of development.
1972	John Hicks and Kenneth Arrow (joint award) For their pioneering contributions to general economic equilibrium theory and welfare theory.
1973	Wassily Leontief For the development of the input-output method and for its application to important economic problems.
1974	Gunnar Myrdal and Friedrich August Von Hayek (divided equally) For their pioneering work in the theory of money and economic fluctuations and for their analysis of the interdependence of economic, social and institutional phenomena.
1975	Leonid Kantorovich and Tjalling Koopmans (joint award) For their contributions to the theory of optimum allocation of resources.
1976	Milton Friedman For his achievements in the fields of consumption analysis, monetary history and theory and for his demonstration of the complexity of stabilisation policy.
1977	Bertil Ohlin and James Meade (divided equally) For their contribution to the theory of international trade and international capital movements.
1978	Herbert Simon For his pioneering research into the decision-making process within economic organisations.
1979	Theodore Schultz and Arthur Lewis (divided equally) For their contribution to economic development research with particular consideration of the problems of developing countries.

1980   Lawrence Klein
        For the creation of econometric models and the application to the analysis of economic fluctuations and economic policies.

1981   James Tobin
        For his analysis of financial markets and their relations to expenditure decisions, employment, production and prices.

1982   George Stigler
        For his seminal studies of industrial structures, functioning of markets and cause and effect of public regulation.

1983   Gerard Debreu
        The incorporation of new analytical methods into economic theory and a reformulation of the theory of general equilibrium.

1984   Richard Stone
        His contribution to national income accounting and improving the basis for empirical economic analysis.

1985   Franco Modigliani
        His analysis of saving and financial markets.

1986   James Buchanan
        His development of the contractual and constitutional basis for the theory of economic and political decision-making.

1987   Robert Solow
        For his contribution to the theory of economic growth.

1988   Maurice Allais
        For his contribution to the theory of markets and efficient utilisation of resources.

1989   Trygve Haavelmo
        His clarification of probability theory foundations of econometrics and his analysis of simultaneous economic structures.

1990   Harry Markowitz, Merton Miller and William Sharpe (one third each)
        For their work in the theory of financial economics.

1991   Ronald Coarse
        For his discovery and clarification of the significance of transaction costs and property rights and for the institutional structure and functioning of the economy.

1992   Gary Becker
        For extending the domain of microeconomic analysis to a wide range of human behaviour and interaction, including non-market behaviour.

1993   Robert Fogel and Douglass North (joint award)
        Renewed research in economic history by applying economic theory and quantitative methods in order to explain economic and institutional change.

1994	John Harsanyi, John Nash and Reinhard Selten (joint award) For their analysis of equilibria in the theory of non-cooperative games.
1995	Robert Lucas The development and application of the hypothesis of rational expectations, and thereby having transformed macroeconomic analysis and deepened the understanding of economic policy.
1996	James Mirrlees and William Vickrey Their contribution to the economic theory of incentives under asymmetric information.
1997	Robert Merton and Myron Scholes For a new method to determine the value of derivatives.
1998	Amartya Sen For his contributions to welfare economics.
1999	Robert A. Mundell For his analysis of monetary and fiscal policy under different exchange rate regimes and his analysis of optimum currency areas.
2000	The prize was shared between James J. Heckman For his development of theory and methods for analysing selective samples and Daniel L. McFadden For his development of theory and methods for analysing discrete choice.
2001	The prize was shared between George A. Akerlof, A. Michael Spense and Joseph E. Stiglitz For their analyses of markets with asymmetric information.
2002	The prize was shared between Daniel Kahneman for having integrated insights from psychological research into economic science, especially concerning human judgment and decision-making under uncertainty and Vernon L. Smith for having established laboratory experiments as a tool in empirical economic analysis, especially in the study of alternative market mechanisms.

Source: The Nobel Prize Internet Archive

CHAPTER 3

The Consumption Function and Income Determination

3.1 INTRODUCTION

In chapter 2 we discussed the role of aggregate demand or domestic expenditure in determining output and employment in the economy. In this chapter we focus on the largest component of aggregate demand, namely, consumer expenditure. The first part of the chapter examines the *consumption function*, which plays a key role in macroeconomic theory and policy. This is followed by a discussion of the multiplier model. This is an integral part of Keynesian theory and has an important bearing on the effectiveness of fiscal policy in regulating the business cycle. The concluding sections of the chapter examine two important theories of consumer behaviour, the life-cycle hypothesis and the permanent-income hypothesis.

3.2 DISPOSABLE INCOME, CONSUMPTION AND SAVING

Personal consumption expenditure (C) in Ireland accounts for just over 50 per cent of domestic expenditure or aggregate demand (AD). The study of consumption is therefore important not just in its own right but for our understanding of the determination of output, income, and employment.

Although we are primarily concerned with consumption expenditure aggregated over all types of consumer goods and services, it is of interest to look at the composition of this expenditure. Table 3.1 shows the breakdown of personal consumption between the different categories of expenditure. The largest components are transport and communications, food, recreation and entertainment, and alcoholic beverages. (By international standards, Irish households spend an unusually large proportion of their income on alcoholic beverages and tobacco.)

The data given in table 3.1 are an average for all the households in the country. When households are classified by income group, important differences in consumption patterns are apparent. In particular, people on low incomes spend a higher proportion of their income on necessities such as food and housing. As income increases, the proportion of income spent on clothing, transport, and leisure activities rises. High-income households buy better quality food, but they spend a smaller proportion of their income on it.

THE CONSUMPTION FUNCTION

Given the importance of consumer expenditure in total expenditure, an important issue is to identify the factors that influence it. We start with two important definitions. First *disposable income* (Y^d) is equal to gross income (Y) minus taxation (T).

Table 3.1
Composition of personal consumption expenditure, 2000

Category	€ millions	%
Transport and communication	7,329	14.5
Food and non-alcoholic beverages	6,497	12.8
Housing	8,232	16.2
Alcoholic beverages	4,980	9.8
Recreation, entertainment and education	4,655	9.2
Household equipment	3,642	7.2
Clothing and footwear	3,372	6.7
Tobacco	1,869	3.7
Fuel and power	1,481	2.9
Miscellaneous	9,169	18.1
Net expenditure by non-residents	−540	−1.1
Total consumer expenditure	*50,685*	*100.0*

Source: National Income and Expenditure Accounts, 2000, Table 13, Central Statistics Office, Dublin, 2000.

$$Y^d = Y - T \qquad (1)$$

Secondly, disposable income is used for consumer expenditure (C) or is saved (S).

$$Y^d = C + S \qquad (2)$$

On average, consumption, saving and taxation accounted for 70, 20 and 10 per cent of personal income, respectively, over the period 1958–2000. In the 1950s and 1960s, consumption accounted for a much higher proportion of income with correspondingly lower saving and taxation rates.

The British economist John Maynard Keynes in his book, *The General Theory of Employment, Interest and Money* (Macmillan, 1936), argued that the main determinant of consumer expenditure was current disposable income, Y^d. This function plays a central role in modern macroeconomic theory. The *consumption function* may be written as:

$$C = \alpha + mpc \times Y^d \qquad (3)$$

where α is the intercept term and mpc is the *marginal propensity to consume*. Equation (3) reads 'consumption expenditure is a function of disposable income'. The direction of causation is running from Y^d to C. Because Y^d *causes* changes in C, Y^d is referred to as the *explanatory* (or independent) variable, and C as the *dependent* variable.

In order to explain how the consumption function is derived, consider the data on Y^d, C and S given in table 3.2 for a hypothetical cross-section of households. That is, the data relate to income and expenditure for a variety of households at a particular point in time. Household A has an income of €10,000 and consumption of €9,000 per annum. Household B has an income of €15,000 and spends €12,000, and so on for the richer households, C to G. Table 3.2 shows that as disposable income increases, households spend less and save more as a proportion of income.

Figure 3.1 plots the relationship between disposable income and consumption given in table 3.2. Consumer expenditure is shown on the vertical axis and disposable income on the horizontal axis. Point B in figure 3.1 corresponds to consumer expenditure of €12,000 and income of €15,000. The remaining points in figure 3.1 correspond to the other households in table 3.2.

The line joining the points A, B, C etc. is the consumption function for this cross-section of households. The *intercept* is the point where the consumption function cuts or intercepts the vertical axis. It corresponds to the α term in equation 3 above. The intercept can be thought of as the level of consumer spending that is independent of the level of Y^d, and is referred to as autonomous consumption.

Table 3.2
Household disposable income, consumption and saving

Households	Disposable Income (Y^d) €	Consumption (C) €	Saving (S) €	APC	APS
A	10,000	9,000	1,000	0.90	0.10
B	15,000	12,000	3,000	0.80	0.20
C	20,000	15,000	5,000	0.75	0.25
D	25,000	18,000	7,000	0.72	0.28
E	30,000	21,000	9,000	0.70	0.30
F	35,000	24,000	11,000	0.68	0.32
G	40,000	27,000	13,000	0.67	0.33

Figure 3.1
Consumption function

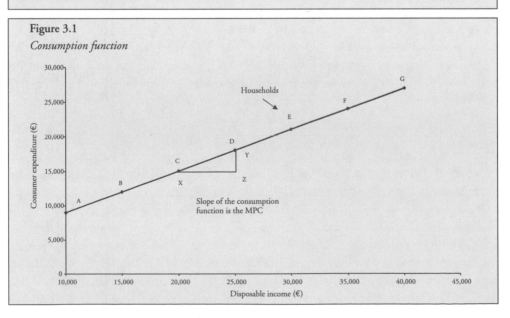

How does consumer expenditure *react* to a change in disposable income? The *slope* of the consumption function, which is given by the marginal propensity to consume (mpc), answers this question. It tells us by how much a household's consumption will increase as a result of a given increase in income. (In economics, the word 'marginal' means 'extra' or 'additional'.)

Consider again equation 3. Taking first differences we can write:

$$\Delta C/\Delta Y^d = mpc \tag{4}$$

where Δ denotes change. The mpc shows how C reacts to a given change in Y^d. The mpc is a positive number which is generally greater than zero but less than 1: $0 > mpc > 1$. An mpc of 0.9 means that for every €1 increase in income, spending increases by €0.90.

The hypothetical data on income and consumption in table 3.2 may be used to calculate the mpc. As household income increases from €10,000 to €15,000, consumption expenditure increases from €9,000 to €12,000. The mpc is therefore 0.6.

$$mpc = \Delta C/\Delta Y^d = (€12,000 - €9,000)/(€15,000 - €10,000) = 0.6 \tag{5}$$

The mpc may also be represented graphically as the slope of the consumption function. Consider the triangle labelled XYZ in figure 3.1. The distance XZ represents the change in disposable income, and the distance ZY represents the change in consumption expenditure. The slope of the consumption function XY is the ratio ZY/XZ and equals $\Delta C/\Delta Y^d$, which we defined as the mpc.

Note:
Because the consumption function in figure 3.1 is linear, the mpc is the same at all points on the line. (The reader can confirm this by calculating the mpc for the range of income and expenditure given in table 3.2.) We have presented a linear consumption function simply for illustrative purposes. In reality, it is possible that the mpc would decrease at higher levels of income because the richer a household becomes, the larger the proportion of any further increase in income it is likely to save. If a line is non-linear, then each point on the line has a different slope. The slope at a particular point on the curve can be calculated by drawing a line tangent to the curve at that point. The slope of the tangent line gives the slope of the curve at that point.

THE SAVING FUNCTION

Consumer expenditure and saving sum to disposable income. Because C depends on Y^d, it follows that S also depends on Y^d. The relationship between S and Y^d is referred to as the *saving function*. Mathematically, the relationship may be written as:

$$S = \beta + mps \times Y^d \tag{6}$$

where β represents the intercept term and mps the *marginal propensity to save*. The mps shows what proportion of an increase in Y^d is saved. To see this, differentiate equation 6 to obtain:

$$\Delta S/\Delta Y^d = mps \tag{7}$$

An mps of 0.2, for example, indicates that households save €0.20 for every €1 increase in disposable income. In terms of table 3.2, note that as household B's income increases from €15,000 to €20,000, its savings increase from €3,000 to €5,000. Hence, the mps for this household is 0.4:

$$\text{mps} = (€5{,}000 - €3{,}000)/(€20{,}000 - €15{,}000) = 0.4$$

Because income is either spent or saved, the mpc and the mps must also sum to one.

$$\text{mpc} + \text{mps} = 1 \tag{8}$$

If the mpc equals 0.6, then the mps must equal 0.4. That is, if a household receives one extra euro in income, 60 per cent is spent and 40 per cent is saved.

The consumption and saving functions are very important building blocks in macroeconomic theory. As we shall see later in this chapter, the consumption function partly determines the effectiveness of fiscal policy.

3.3 EVIDENCE FROM THE IRISH ECONOMY

In figure 3.2 we examine the aggregate Irish data over a number of years, plotting the percentage change in disposable income and consumption over the period 1959–99. It can be seen that there is a close correlation between the two series. However, there are some years when the two series are out of synch. For example, in 1980 and 1986, consumption increased more rapidly than income implying a fall in the savings rate. Conversely, in 1979 and 1982, consumption lagged behind the change in income.

Using the same data set it is possible to calculate the mpc for the Irish economy as follows: defining ΔC and ΔY as:

$$\Delta C^* = \Delta C_t - \Delta C_{mean} \tag{9}$$

Figure 3.2

Disposable income and consumption Ireland, 1959–99

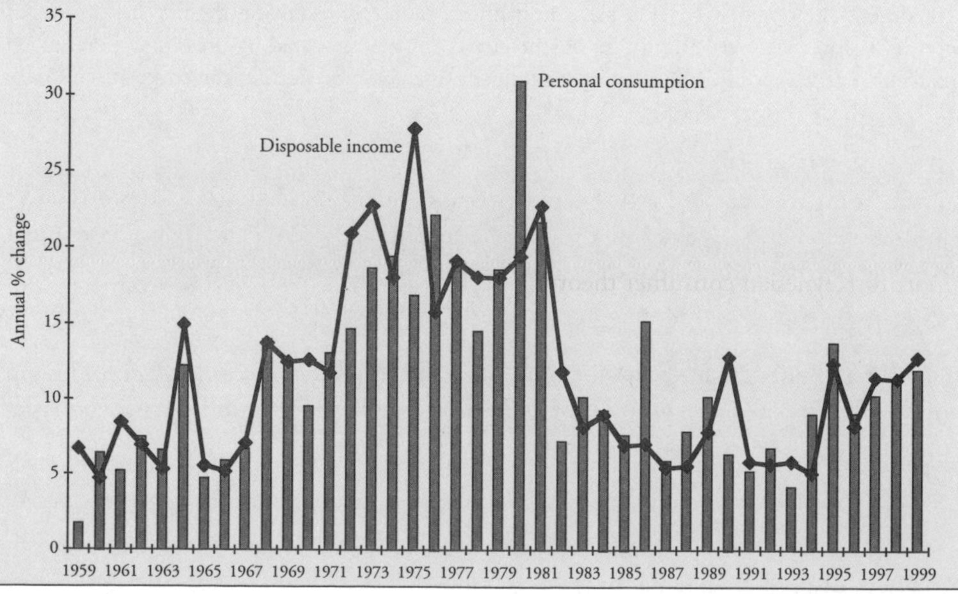

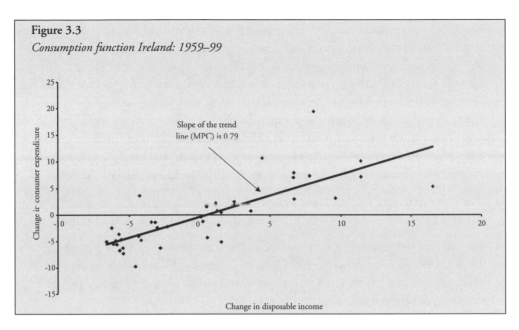

Figure 3.3

Consumption function Ireland: 1959–99

$$\Delta Y^* = \Delta Y_t - \Delta Y_{mean} \tag{10}$$

ΔC^* is the change in consumption adjusted for the average or mean change over the period. It calculates the change in consumption over and above the average change over the period. Similarly, ΔY^* is the change in disposable income again adjusted for the mean change over the period.

The two variables, ΔC^* and ΔY^* are then plotted as a scatter diagram as, for example, in figure 3.3. Each point in the diagram corresponds to the ΔC^*, ΔY^* combination for a particular year. A trend or regression line can now be fitted to this scatter diagram and the slope of this line is the marginal propensity to consume.

Applying this procedure to the Irish data, the mpc is estimated to be 0.79. This suggests that a change in disposable income (over and above the mean change) leads to a corresponding 79 per cent change in consumer expenditure. Put another way, the equation states that a €1 change in disposable income leads to a €0.79 change in current consumption. The implied marginal propensity to save (mps) is 0.21.

This consumption function is a relatively simple one. It does not take into account any of the influences on consumption other than current year's income. Yet it gives a reasonably good account of the year-to-year variations in consumption and it offers support to Keynesian consumer theory.

3.4 THE KEYNESIAN MULTIPLIER

In chapter 2 we defined total expenditure (aggregate demand) as being equal to consumer expenditure (C), investment (I), government expenditure (G) and net exports (NX). Net exports are the difference between exports and imports. When the economy is in equilibrium, GNP will equal total expenditure. Hence:

$$GNP = TE \equiv C + I + G + NX \tag{11}$$

An important issue in macroeconomic analysis is to assess by how much does an increase in total expenditure raise GNP. On first thought, GNP might be expected to rise by an equal amount. However, according to Keynesian multiplier theory, equilibrium GNP will actually increase by a multiple of the initial increase in spending. This concept of the *multiplier* is an integral part of Keynesian economics.

For example, suppose government expenditure (G) was to increase by €1 billion. If this resulted in an increase in GNP of, say, €5 billion, then the multiplier is 5. If GNP was to increase by, say, €2 billion, the multiplier is 2. The multiplier is simply a number that relates the initial change in expenditure to the ultimate change in equilibrium GNP. In general:

Change in equilibrium GNP = Initial change in expenditure × multiplier

The idea of the multiplier increased the appeal of Keynesian theory in the 1950s and 1960s. After all, if every additional €1 billion spent by the government boosts GNP by some multiple of €1 billion, additional spending would appear to be justified as long as there are unemployed resources in the economy.

AN INTUITIVE EXPLANATION

In order to explain the multiplier effect let us make two simple adjustments to equation (11) and to the consumption function (equation 3). With regard to equation (11) note that national income (NI) is very closely related to GNP (see chapter 23). If an individual works longer hours and produces more output, he or she would expect their income to rise accordingly. Similarly at the macro level, if firms produce more output they must increase employment, which will generate more income. Hence we can re-write (11) above as:

$$NI = GNP = TE \equiv C + I + G + NX \qquad (12)$$

The second extension relates to the consumption function. Earlier we expressed consumer expenditure (C) as a function of disposable income (Y^d). To simplify matters let us replace Y^d by NI in the consumption function. Hence:

$$C = \alpha + mpc \times NI \qquad (13)$$

Suppose now there is an increase in government expenditure (G). This will increase total expenditure by definition. Firms respond to the higher level of demand by producing more goods and services, and GNP and NI both increase. At the end of this first round, GNP and NI have increased by exactly the amount of the initial increase in G.

However, that is not the end of the process. In the second round we take account of the fact that the increase in NI raises C via the consumption function. This leads to another increase in total expenditure and GNP. In other words, the consumption function leads to a *feedback effect* that leads to further increases in GNP and NI. This process will continue into third, fourth and successive rounds because the economy has entered into a rising income-consumption spiral. The process and the feedback from NI to C are depicted in box 3.1. The numbers in the top row indicate the sequence of events.

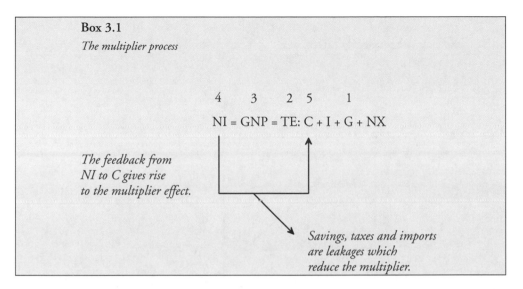

Box 3.1

The multiplier process

$$4 \quad 3 \quad 2\ 5 \quad 1$$
$$NI = GNP = TE: C + I + G + NX$$

The feedback from NI to C gives rise to the multiplier effect.

Savings, taxes and imports are leakages which reduce the multiplier.

Two important points need to be made relating to the multiplier process. First, the process eventually comes to an end because the mpc is less than 1. In each successive round the increase in consumption is the mpc times the increase in NI. If the mpc is equal to 0.8, an increase of €1 billion in NI will lead to a €0.8 billion increase in consumption. In the next round, NI rises by €0.8 billion and C rises by a further €0.64 billion (that is, the €0.8 billion increase in NI times the mpc). Thus the increases in consumption taper off in successive rounds. The expansion therefore comes to a halt sooner, the smaller the mpc. Conversely, it lasts longer the higher the mpc.

The second point is that the multiplier largely relates to a situation where the aggregate supply (AS) curve is *horizontal*. That is, additional output is forthcoming in response to increased demand, without any rise in the aggregate price level. For this to be true, there must be significant unutilised resources (especially labour) in the economy. Keynes argued that the slope of the AS curve is not uniform at all levels of real GNP but is actually kinked. That is it takes on different slopes depending how close the economy is to natural real GNP (GNP*). When there is a great deal of excess capacity in the economy and the unemployment rate is high, the AS curve is likely to be horizontal. A shift to the right in the AD curve leads to an increase in real GNP without having a marked increase in the price level.

As GNP* is approached, the AS curve becomes steeper. Any further shift of the AD curve to the right will lead to both an increase in the price level and real output. As the economy moves to the right of GNP*, the AS curve becomes vertical. A shift of the AD curve to the right will now result only in higher prices and have no impact on real GNP.

Figure 3.4 shows the kinked AS curve suggested by Keynes. (Included in the diagram is a vertical line indicating natural real GNP.) If the economy is initially at the point A, an increase in government expenditure will shift the AD curve to the right and the economy moves to the point B. The increase in real GNP along the horizontal axis is greater than the initial increase in government expenditure. This is the multiplier effect. Note that the price level remains unchanged. After the point B, however, the AS curve becomes upward sloping. This means that a further shift of the AD curve to the

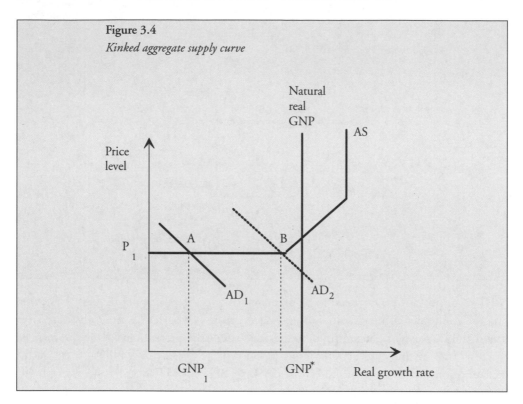

Figure 3.4
Kinked aggregate supply curve

right results in both an increase in real GNP and the price level. On this upward-sloping section of the AS curve, the impact on real GNP would be considerably less. Hence, the multiplier really relates to a situation where the *aggregate price level (P) is fixed* due to the overhang of spare capacity in the economy. This may be realistic in a situation where there are considerable unemployed resources in the economy, and rising prices is not a factor to be reckoned with, which of course was the case when Keynes was writing in the 1930s, but is less obviously true for later periods.

CALCULATING THE MULTIPLIER FORMULA

In order to derive the multiplier formula, consider the following equations:

$$GNP = TE \qquad\qquad \text{Equilibrium condition} \qquad\qquad (14)$$

$$TE \equiv C + I + G + NX \qquad\qquad \text{Aggregate demand} \qquad\qquad (15)$$

$$C = \alpha + (mpc \times GNP) \qquad \text{Consumption function} \qquad\qquad (16)$$

Note that in equation (16) to minimise the notation we have replaced NI with GNP. Since GNP and NI are very closely related this should not present any complication but it will make the algebra less complicated. To derive the multiplier formula, substitute (15) into (14) to obtain:

$$GNP = C + I + G + NX \qquad\qquad\qquad (17)$$

Now substitute (16) into (17):

$$\text{GNP} = \alpha + (\text{mpc} \times \text{GNP}) + I + G + NX \qquad (18)$$

Bring the (mpc × GNP) term over to the left-hand side:

$$\text{GNP}(1 - \text{mpc}) = \alpha + I + G + NX \qquad (19)$$

Divide both sides by $(1 - \text{mpc})$ to obtain:

$$\text{GNP} = [1/(1 - \text{mpc})](\alpha + I + G + NX) \qquad (20)$$

We see that if any of the terms (α, I, G or NX) change, the level of equilibrium GNP changes by $1/(1 - \text{mpc})$ times this change. The multiplier therefore equals $1/(1 - \text{mpc})$. For example, if the mpc equals 0.8, the multiplier is:

$$\text{Multiplier} = 1/(1 - 0.8) = 5$$

An increase in G of €1 billion would raise GNP or national income by €5 billion. If the mpc were 0.9, the multiplier would be 10. We see immediately that the higher the marginal propensity to consume, the larger the multiplier.

We know from our earlier discussion that the mpc and the mps must sum to 1 (see equation 8 above). It follows that $(1 - \text{mpc})$ is equal to mps and the multiplier formula can be rewritten as:

$$\text{Multiplier} = 1/\text{mps}$$

An mpc of 0.8 implies an mps of 0.2. Inserting this value for the mps into the above formula, the multiplier again equals 5. The higher the mps, the lower the multiplier; the lower the mps, the higher the multiplier.

Saving is, however, only one of the three possible *leakages* from the multiplier process. The other two leakages, which we have ignored in this section, are taxes and imports. It is the sum of these leakages that determines the size of the multiplier. We now turn to a more generalised version of the multiplier formula that takes all three leakages into account.

GENERALISING THE MULTIPLIER

The size of the multiplier depends on how much of an initial increase in GNP or NI is passed on through an increase in C. In the simplified model we have just presented, there was only one possible leakage out of domestic expenditure, namely, saving. However, in a more complete model, with a foreign sector and taxes, there are other important leakages.

In an open economy, much of any increase in expenditure will leak abroad in the form of additional imports (M). That is, a significant proportion of increases in income is spent on the output of some other economy. Clearly, this does nothing to stimulate further increases in the level of output in the domestic economy. Similarly, we should take account of the fact that taxes on income and expenditure divert a sizeable proportion of additional consumer income to the government. This is another leakage from the multiplier process. These additional leakages tend to bring the multiplier process to a halt sooner than would be the case in the simple model we discussed above.

We now consider how these leakages affect the value of the multiplier. The algebra is set out in the appendix.

TAXES

If there is a single flat rate of tax on income, the relationship between tax revenue (T) and GNP is given by the following equation:

$$T = \text{mpt} \times \text{GNP} \tag{21}$$

where mpt is the marginal tax rate or *marginal propensity to tax*, and $0 < \text{mpt} < 1$. If the flat rate of tax was 30 per cent, the mpt would equal 0.3. Allowing for a tax of this type, the multiplier formula becomes:

$$\text{Multiplier} = 1/(\text{mps} + \text{mpt}) \tag{22}$$

Note that the formula has the sum of the 'marginal propensities to leak' (that is, to tax and save) in the denominator. Hence, the larger these leakages from extra income, the smaller the multiplier. This general principle holds true even for the most complicated models.

IMPORTS

The third possible leakage is due to the relationship between GNP and imports. The relationship may be expressed as:

$$M = \delta + (\text{mpm} \times \text{GNP}) \tag{23}$$

where δ is an intercept term, and mpm is the *marginal propensity to import*, and $0 < \text{mpm} < 1$. If, for example, mpm equals 0.4, then equation (23) states that 40 per cent of any increase in GNP is spent on imports. As shown in the appendix, the multiplier with saving, taxation and import leakages is:

$$\text{Multiplier} = 1/(\text{mps} + \text{mpt} + \text{mpm}) \tag{24}$$

Once again, the denominator is the sum of all the leakages from the multiplier process. We apply this to the Irish economy below.

SUMMARY

Any change in the level of investment (I), government expenditure (G), net exports (NX) or the intercept terms of the consumption and import functions affects the equilibrium level of GNP and NI. The final change in GNP is greater than the initial change in TE. The ratio between the two is defined as the multiplier. The larger the leakages from the multiplier process, the smaller the multiplier and, conversely, the smaller the leakages, the larger the multiplier.

Many more complex multiplier formulas can be derived. The models outlined here do not include a financial or money market, which we have not yet discussed. When the model is expanded to include a money market, the multiplier formula becomes even more complex. As a consequence, in recent years simple multiplier analysis of the type presented here has lost much of its prominence in economics.

Another formula that is of some interest is the *balanced budget multiplier*. This shows that an equal decrease (or increase) in tax revenue and government expenditure has a multiplier of one, and not zero as might be expected. That is, suppose the government cuts taxation and this, in turn, boosts consumer expenditure (C) by €1 billion. If the government simultaneously cuts government expenditure (G) by €1 billion, it could be expected that the increase in C would be offset by the fall in G. However, it can be shown that total expenditure and GNP will increase by €1 billion.

Some textbooks elaborate multiplier formulas, presumably in the belief that a bit of algebra is good for the student's soul! However, it is far more important that the student understands the basic concepts, and the issues at stake, in the application of the Keynesian model, than that he or she spends a lot of time deriving complicated multiplier formulas.

THE MULTIPLIER IN THE IRISH ECONOMY

Ireland is a small economy that is extremely open to international trade. Furthermore, the marginal rate of income tax and the indirect tax rates applied to discretionary spending are high. These considerations would lead us to expect that the multiplier would be low. A survey of the available research confirms this. There is widespread agreement that mps = 0.26, mpt = 0.24 and mpm = 0.4 are realistic values for the parameters that enter into the calculation of the multiplier. Inserting these values into the formula given above yields the following result:

$$\text{Multiplier} = 1/(0.26 + 0.24 + 0.4) = 1.11 \tag{25}$$

This implies that an increase in G, C, I, or X, or a reduction in M of €1 billion would raise GNP by €1.11 billion. Under these conditions 'multiplier' is somewhat of a misnomer. The leakages are so large that GNP only increases by marginally more than the initial increase in TE itself. In addition to the fact that large tax and import leakages give rise to small multipliers, there are other considerations, which we shall explore in subsequent chapters, that suggest that fiscal policy will not have any long-lasting effect on GNP. Thus one of the alluring features of the simple Keynesian model, the idea that an increase in government spending results in an increase in the equilibrium level of GNP equal to a multiple of the original stimulus, has to be modified to take account of Irish conditions. None the less, increased total expenditure does tend to increase the equilibrium level of GNP.

3.5 AVERAGE PROPENSITY TO CONSUME AND SAVE

The data on a cross-section of households presented in table 3.2 indicate that as disposable income increases, households spend less and save more as a proportion of income. That is, the low-income households save very little of their income, whereas the high-income groups save a large proportion of income.

This point can be made more formally by calculating the *average propensity to consume* (APC) and the *average propensity to save* (APS). The APC is defined as being equal to consumption expenditure divided by disposable income, C/Y^d. For example, in table 3.2, the APC for household B is calculated as follows:

$$APC = C/Y^d = €12,000/€15,000 = 0.8 \qquad (26)$$

An APC of 0.8 indicates that the household spends 80 per cent of its disposable income on consumption goods and services. Similarly, the average propensity to save (APS) is defined as being equal to saving divided by disposable income, S/Y^d. Again for household B in table 3.2:

$$APS = S/Y^d = €3,000/€15,000 = 0.2 \qquad (27)$$

An APS of 0.2 indicates that 20 per cent of disposable income is saved. Because disposable income is either spent or saved, the APC and the APS must sum to 1:

$$APC + APS = 1 \qquad (28)$$

Keynes argued, on the basis of his own intuition rather than a detailed study of the data, that the APS would decline as income rose. Keynes put it as follows in the *General Theory*:

> The fundamental psychological law, upon which we are entitled to depend with great confidence both *a priori* from our knowledge of human nature and from the detailed facts of experience, is that men are disposed to increase their consumption as their income increases, but not by as much as the increase in income.'
>
> (Keynes, *General Theory*, 96.)

This led Keynes to worry about the problem of the economy absorbing an increasing stream of saving as income increased. As explained in later chapters, household saving in banks and other financial institutions is used to finance new investment (I) by firms. Keynes worried that it would be difficult to find new profitable investment outlets in line with the rise in saving and that, in certain circumstances, this could push the economy into recession.

In a famous passage he praised the ancient Egyptians for building pyramids and the people in the Middle Ages for building cathedrals, because these activities used up their savings and provided employment. Furthermore, because there was no tendency for the *rate of return* from building pyramids to fall: 'Two pyramids, two masses for the dead, are twice as good as one; but not so two railways from London to York.' (Keynes, *General Theory*, 131.)

The Japanese economy has been in the doldrums since the 1980s and a high propensity to save, with few profitable outlets for saving, has contributed to this stagnation.

A modern example of the problem of finding profitable outlets for saving is provided by the over-investment in electronics/telecommunications technology in the late 1990s. It is said that there is enough fibre optics cable now lying idle to stretch from earth to the moon and back! The first generation of mobile phone technology was highly profitable, but the third generation has yet to yield any pay-off to the enormous sums invested in acquiring licences.

The evidence for a declining APC was, however, shaky. In the mid-1940s Nobel

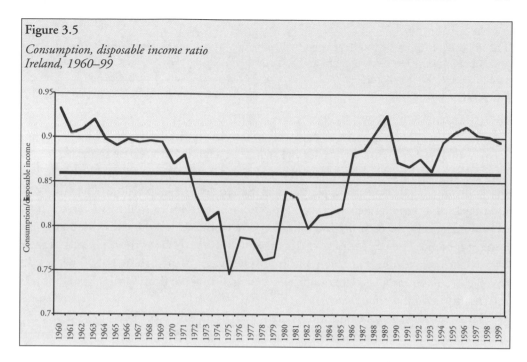

Figure 3.5

Consumption, disposable income ratio
Ireland, 1960–99

prize-winner Simon Kuznets (1901–85) presented evidence that the APC was equal to 0.87 throughout the periods 1869–98, 1884–1913 and 1904–33. This meant that the ratio of consumption to income was relatively stable and that the APC did *not* decline as disposable income increased. Note here that Kuznets evidence is 'over time' whereas the data in table 3.2 are cross-section data at a 'particular point in time'.

Figure 3.5 shows the ratio of consumer expenditure to disposable income for the Irish economy over the period 1960–99. Inserting a trend line confirms that the APC has in fact been stable over the period (the slope of the line is +0.0003). The average APC is 0.86, very close to Kuznets figure of 0.87. It is evident, however, the ratio has fluctuated significantly from year to year. In 1960 the ratio was 0.93 compared to 0.75 in 1973.

In the 1950s, the apparent conflict between Keynes's intuition and Kuznets' findings led to the refinement of theories of consumer behaviour. Two of the most influential contributions have been, first, the *life-cycle hypothesis* and, second, the *permanent-income hypothesis*.

3.6 THEORIES OF CONSUMER BEHAVIOUR

We now turn to a discussion of two of the most influential long-run theories of consumer behaviour.

THE LIFE-CYCLE THEORY OF CONSUMPTION

The life-cycle theory of consumption was developed by the 1985 Nobel prize-winning economist Franco Modigliani. He argued that a household's consumption does not depend only on its current disposable income, as in the Keynesian consumption function, but rather on its lifetime income.

Note:
The life-cycle hypothesis was developed by Modigliani in conjunction with Richard Brumberg and Albert Ando. (See F. Modigliani and R. Brumberg, 'Utility Analysis and the Consumption Function', in K. Kurihara (ed.) *Post-Keynesian Economics*, New Brunswick, N.J.: Rutgers University Press, 1954.)

Disposable income changes over the life-cycle. Typically, an individual has no income in the first eighteen years of life, while at school. Once he or she starts work, income rises rapidly reaching a peak in mid-life. On retirement at, say, 65 there is a sharp decline in income as the individual has to live on a pension. The life-cycle hypothesis assumes that people prefer to maintain a constant or slightly increasing flow of consumption over their lifetime to one where consumption depends completely on current income. They can achieve this if they are willing to save at those periods in their lives when their earnings are high and to dissave when their income falls. This would involve dissaving early and late in life, and saving during the peak earning years. This is referred to as *consumption smoothening*.

This pattern of consumption is depicted in figure 3.6. The upward-sloping consumption line depicts a steadily rising expenditure stream; the inverted U-shaped disposable income line depicts how the typical individual's income might vary over his or her lifetime. Areas A and C in figure 3.6 are associated with *dissaving*. In area B the individual saves a proportion of income. The saving of one period is used to finance consumption in other periods so that over the life-cycle consumption equals income. The dissaving in areas A and C equals the saving in area B.

This theory predicts that changes in current disposable income (Y^d) have much less influence on consumption expenditure (C) than would be expected from the Keynesian

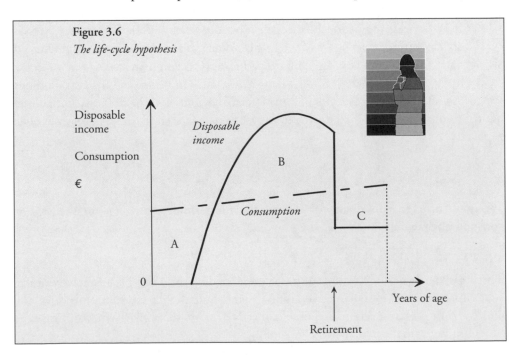

Figure 3.6
The life-cycle hypothesis

consumption function we introduced above. Individuals are supposed to take the long view and set their consumption targets in line with their expected lifetime income, rather than simply adjusting consumption to day-to-day fluctuations in income.

EXTENSIONS TO THE LIFE-CYCLE HYPOTHESIS

The life-cycle hypothesis can be extended in a number of ways. Consumption can be expressed as a function of disposable income and *wealth*. The greater a person's wealth the higher will be consumption, and vice versa. This means that changes in wealth brought about by a stock market crash can lead to a fall in consumption and thereby help push the economy into recession. This was a feared effect of the stock market crash in October 1987. But the feared slump in consumption did not materialise. The stock market crash was short-lived. But even the longer stock market slump of recent years has not depressed consumption as much as feared. Studies have found that house prices have a far bigger wealth effect than stock prices; more people own their houses than own stocks and shares. The booming housing market of the 1990s underpinned consumer confidence regardless of what happened to stock prices.

Note:

Income, consumption, saving, and investment are *flow* variables. They measure how much is earned, consumed, saved and invested over a period of time. Wealth and the capital stock are, on the other hand, *stock* variables. They measure the value of assets at a point of time.

The introduction of wealth also reconciles the apparent disagreement between Keynes and Kuznets. Consider, for example, figure 3.7. Wealth determines the *intercept* (or location) of the short-run consumption function. Over the long run, wealth increases significantly and this shifts the short-run consumption function upwards. As the short-run consumption functions shift up, the points A, B and C in the diagram

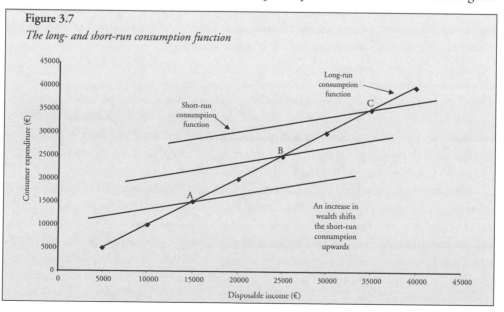

Figure 3.7

The long- and short-run consumption function

map out the long-run consumption function. Thus, even if each short-run consumption function displays a declining APC (as advanced by Keynes), the long-run consumption function cuts through a series of *upward shifting* short-run consumption functions. Hence, the long-run consumption function is much steeper than the short-run consumption functions. The long-run APC can be constant (as Kuznets' data suggested), even though the short-run APC is declining.

From the life-cycle hypothesis it also follows that changes in the retirement age and the presence of social welfare or a state pension have an impact on saving and therefore consumption. A lower retirement age suggests that people will save more during their working years and lifetime consumption will, as a result, be lower. In contrast, the existence of social welfare or a state pension means that people do not need much saving to maintain consumption in their retirement period. Hence, the saving rate will be lower.

Finally, the age distribution of the population can have an important bearing on aggregate saving and consumption. A stationary or declining population, such as that of many European countries today, implies a high proportion of elderly. This, in turn, implies that many people are living off past savings, which will depress the aggregate savings ratio.

The permanent-income hypothesis

The permanent-income hypothesis was developed by Milton Friedman, 1976 Nobel prize-winner in economics (*A Theory of the Consumption Function*, Princeton University Press, 1957). The permanent-income hypothesis is similar in many respects to the life-cycle hypothesis. The permanent-income hypothesis argues that current consumption depends on *permanent* income (YP):

$$C = f(YP) \tag{29}$$

The equation reads: consumer expenditure is a function of permanent income. In Friedman's original exposition of the theory, no precise definition of permanent income was given. However, we can think of permanent income as being equal to a weighted average of *current* and *past* incomes. An example is:

$$YP_t = 0.6Y^d_t + 0.3Y^d_{t-1} + 0.1Y^d_{t-2} \tag{30}$$

where Y^d_t is disposable income in time t, Y^d_{t-1} is disposable income in time t-1 and Y^d_{t-2} is disposable income in time t-2. Equation (30) says that today's permanent income is equal to 60 per cent of this year's disposable income plus 30 per cent of last year's income plus 10 per cent of income two years ago. Note that the weights used in the calculation tend to get smaller the further we go back in time.

The basic idea underlying equation (30) is that people base their consumption patterns on income averaged over good and bad times. Irish farmers, for example, do not splurge the proceeds of an exceptionally good harvest because they know from experience that there will be bad harvests in the future! Because permanent income is based on long-run average income, it is similar to lifetime income. The permanent-income hypothesis does, however, have the advantage in that it can easily be applied to aggregate time series data for income, whereas the concept of lifetime income is difficult to measure using aggregate data. The life-cycle hypothesis, on the other hand, allows for a greater role for saving and initial wealth.

Friedman's basic hypothesis is that there is a constant proportional relationship between consumption and permanent income. This means that the APC out of permanent income is constant (that is the long-run consumption to income ratio is constant). This squares well with Kuznets' findings. Hence, the permanent income hypothesis can explain why the APC is supposedly constant over time.

However, actual income is highly variable and the proportion of it that is consumed also varies. Income that is not expected to be repeated in the future is referred to as *transitory* (or temporary) income (YT). A good example of such income would be a once off legacy or a Christmas bonus that is not expected to be repeated. According to Friedman's theory this type of unexpected windfall gain should have a weak effect on consumption — most of it will be saved. A numerical example may help.

Suppose an individual starts working life at 18, works until she is 65 and dies at 90. If annual average income is €30,000, lifetime income will be €1,410,000:

€30,000 × working years (65 – 18)) = €1,410,000

Spreading this income over her lifetime (90 – 18 years) allows for annual consumption of €19,583.3.

C = €1,410,000/72 years = €19,583.3

Suppose now that permanent income was to rise by €5,000 per year. Lifetime income now rises by €235,000.

€5,000 × 47 working years = €235,000

Spreading this over 72 years of her lifetime enables her to increase consumption by €3,263.8.

C = €235,000/72 years = €3,263.8

The marginal propensity to consume (mpc) out of permanent income is 0.652.

$\Delta C/\Delta YP$ = €3,263.8/€5,000 = 0.652

If, on the other hand, transitory income (YT) was to increase by €5,000 in one year only, lifetime consumption would increase by only €69.4.

C = €5,000/72 years = €69.9

The mpc is now only 0.0138.

$\Delta C/\Delta YP$ = €69.4/€5,000 = 0.0138

This example illustrates that the marginal propensity to consume is much higher out of permanent income than it is out of transitory income.

The permanent — transitory distinction is important in the context of tax cuts. If a government tries to stimulate spending by cutting taxes, consumers may not respond if they believe the tax cuts will be only temporary. If eventually the government has to revise its tax cuts, households will have enjoyed only a transitory rise in disposable income that will not have much effect on consumption.

3.7 CONCLUSION

The main points discussed in this chapter were:

- The relationship between household disposable income, consumption and saving
- The consumption and saving functions
- The multiplier effect and how its size depends on the saving, tax and import leakages
- The multiplier under Irish conditions
- The average and marginal propensities to consume and save
- Life-cycle and permanent-income theories of consumption.

APPENDIX

DERIVING THE MULTIPLIER FORMULA WITH SAVING, TAXATION AND IMPORT LEAKAGES

The notation c, s, t and m is used to denote the marginal propensity to consume (mpc), the marginal propensity to save (mps), the marginal propensity to tax (mpt) and the marginal propensity to import (mpm), respectively. The equilibrium condition is:

$$GNP = C + I + G + X - M \qquad (1)$$

The behavioural relationships underlying the equilibrium condition are:

$$C = \alpha + (c\,NI) - T \qquad \text{Consumption function} \qquad (2)$$

Note that taxation (T) is deducted from NI to obtain disposable income.

$$T = t\,NI \qquad \text{Taxation function} \qquad (3)$$

$$M = \beta + m\,NI \qquad \text{Import function} \qquad (4)$$

The letters α and β denote the intercept term in the consumption and import equations respectively. The coefficients c, t and m show how C, T and M react to changes in NI. The consumption function here differs from the over-simplified multiplier formula given in section 3.4 in that consumer expenditure is determined by gross income and by taxation. Previously, consumer expenditure depended only on gross income. Here the consumption function states that a change in gross income affects consumer expenditure via c, whereas a change in taxation has a direct effect on consumer expenditure.

Substitute equation (3) into equation (2).

$$C = (\alpha + c\,NI) - (t\,NI) \qquad (5)$$

or

$$C = \alpha + (c - t)NI \qquad (6)$$

Substitute equations (6) and (4) into the equilibrium condition (1).

$$GNP = \alpha + (c - t)NI + I + G + X - \beta - (m\,NI) \qquad (7)$$

Bring the terms involving NI over to the left-hand side and assume GNP = NI.

$$GNP - (c - t - m)GNP = \alpha - \beta + I + G + X \qquad (8)$$

or

$$GNP(1 - c + t + m) = \alpha - \beta + I + G + X \qquad (9)$$

Recall that s $^{-}$ 1 $-$ c

$$GNP(s + t + m) = \alpha - \beta + I + G + X \qquad (10)$$

Divide both sides by the term in brackets:

$$GNP = [1/(s + t + m)] \times (\alpha - \beta + I + G + X) \qquad (11)$$

The term $[1/(s + t + m)]$ is the multiplier formula when saving, taxation and import leakages are allowed for. Note that the minus sign on the import intercept term, β, indicates that an increase in imports, not brought about by a change in national income, will decrease GNP via the multiplier formula. As before, an increase in α, I, G or X will increase GNP via the multiplier formula, and vice versa.

It is clear that taking taxation and imports into account lowers the value of the multiplier. For example, if s, t and c equalled 0.26, 0.24 and 0.4, respectively, the crude multiplier that ignored taxes and imports would be equal to 3.84. However, the more realistic multipliers that include taxes and imports would be equal to only 1.11. The latter value is more relevant in Ireland's very open and taxed economy.

CHAPTER 4

Fiscal Policy and the Business Cycle

4.1 INTRODUCTION

The Keynesian theory of income determination discussed in chapter 2 suggests that governments can use fiscal policy to smoothen the business cycle. We saw in chapter 1 that the growth rate of Irish real GNP has been very erratic over the years. For example, the recession of the 1980s was followed by the boom of the 1990s. One of the principal tenets of Keynesian economics is that governments can adjust their spending and taxation (fiscal policy) to stabilise the rate of growth of real GNP. This chapter begins by outlining what is meant by stabilisation policy. This is followed by a discussion of the problem of assessing the stance of fiscal policy, that is distinguishing between 'automatic' and 'discretionary' changes in government expenditure and tax receipts. The concluding sections identify the problems encountered in implementing a stabilisation policy and examine how changes in tax rates affect the supply-side of the economy.

4.2 STABILISATION POLICY

According to Keynesian theory, fiscal policy can be used to keep the actual real growth rate close to the natural real growth rate over time.

Note:
We refer to the level of output the economy could produce with a fully-employed labour force, the available physical (machinery and plants) and human (education and experience) capital stock, and technology as natural real GNP. The rate of change in natural real GNP over time depends on increases in population, physical and human capital accumulation, and advances in technology. The long-run determinants of natural real GNP are the subject of that branch of economics labelled growth theory.

In figure 4.1, the *natural real growth rate* is indicated by a horizontal line. This assumes that the economy is capable of averaging a steady 4.5 per cent annual growth rate over the long run. A higher growth rate would not be sustainable in the long run due to shortages of skilled labour, capacity constraints and other bottlenecks.

The *actual real growth rate* is shown crossing and re-crossing the natural real growth rate line. When the actual growth rate is above the natural rate, firms are operating at above full capacity, labour shortages emerge and there is upward pressure on wages. These wage increases tend to be passed-on by firms in higher output prices. The result is a rise in the inflation rate. For this reason, the distance from the actual growth rate down to the natural rate is referred to as an *inflation gap*. Conversely, when the actual

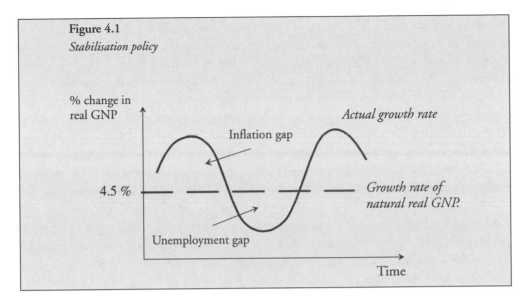

Figure 4.1
Stabilisation policy

growth rate is below the natural rate, firms find they have excess capacity and workers will be laid off. Employment decreases and unemployment increases. The distance from the actual growth rate up to the natural rate is called the *unemployment gap*.

Note:
The 'output gap' is widely used to refer to the gap between actual and natural rate of output in levels, that is, GNP – GNP*. When this is negative, the economy is operating below capacity.

The objective of stabilisation policy is to keep actual growth rate as close as possible to the natural rate so as to avoid inflation or unemployment gaps. Figure 4.2 shows the

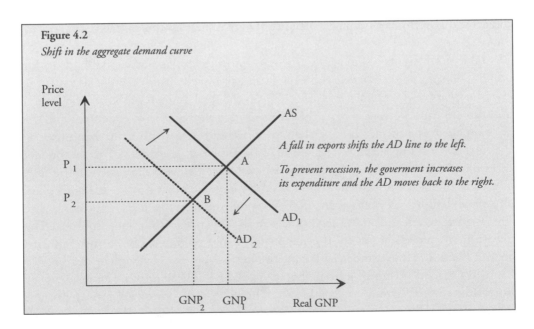

Figure 4.2
Shift in the aggregate demand curve

aggregate demand (AD) and aggregate supply (AS) model developed in chapter 2. (We assume an upward-sloping AS curve and not a horizontal or vertical AS curve as is sometimes the case.) The position or *location* of the AD is determined by consumption expenditure (C), investment (I), government expenditure (G), exports (X) and imports (M). An increase in C, I, G, X or a fall in M will shift the AD curve out to the right and vice versa. Stabilisation policy is an attempt by government to offset the instability caused by fluctuations in the private sector components of aggregate demand. For example, if the economy begins to move into a recession because of, say, a fall in X, the government could counter this fall in demand by increasing G. Alternatively, it could stimulate C by reducing tax rates and/or increasing transfer payments or providing incentives to stimulate I.

Similarly, if prices are rising because of an excess demand for goods and services, the Keynesian prescription is for government to cut expenditure and/or raise tax rates, thereby dampening the inflationary pressure. These *discretionary* fiscal measures should be *counter-cyclical* — injecting additional spending when the economy goes into recession, and withdrawing it when the economy is booming. If properly implemented, an active fiscal policy will keep the actual growth rate close to the natural rate, than would be the case if the government ignored the business cycle.

4.3 THE BUDGET

In Ireland, the government's budget is divided into a *current* and a *capital* account. Current expenditure is of a day-to-day nature. It does not result in the creation of fixed assets. Current revenue is income from taxes and state-owned enterprises. A *current budget deficit* (CBD) arises if current expenditure exceeds current revenue.

Capital expenditure involves the creation of assets such as schools, hospitals and roads. Capital revenue consists of interest on stocks owned by the government, loan repayments and capital grants received from the European Union (EU). The excess of the central government's capital expenditure over capital revenue is called the *capital budget deficit*.

Table 4.1 presents a summary of the government's current and capital budgets for 2000. The sum of the current and capital budget deficits (subtotals A and B) is the *exchequer borrowing requirement* (EBR). This is the total amount of money the central government must borrow to cover the excess of its spending over revenue. In 2000, the government had a surplus because the capital account deficit was more than offset by the current account surplus. The *general government surplus* (deficit) is the budget measure used by the EU in judging fiscal policy. This is a broader measure than the EBR as it takes into account cash flows of local authorities and other grant-aided bodies and also some definitional changes. In 2000 this was projected to be a small surplus.

If government incurs a deficit, it can be financed from four sources. The government can sell bonds to (i) general (non-bank) public, it can borrow from (ii) central bank, or (iii) commercial banks, or alternatively the government can borrow from (iv) abroad. Borrowing from abroad involves selling bonds to non-residents or borrowing directly from foreign banks. The source of borrowing has important implications. We return to this issue at various stages in the book.

Table 4.1
The government's budget: 2001

	€ millions	% of GNP
A1. Current expenditure	24,248	
A2. Current revenue	28,738	
A = A2 − A1. *Current budget balance*	4,490	4.7
B1. Exchequer capital expenditure	6,036	
B2. Exchequer capital revenue	1,880	
B = B2 − B1. *Capital budget balance*	−4,156	−4.3
(C) *Exchequer surplus* (A + B)	334	0.3

Source: Budget 2002.

One further important point, if the government does increase expenditure in order to influence real GNP, this expenditure should be productive and yield a return to the community. In other words, the expenditure should not be of a current nature that yields little or no return. Also the yield should be high enough to justify the burden that servicing the debt will impose on future taxpayers.

CURRENT EXPENDITURE

Table 4.2 shows the main headings underlying total government current expenditure in 2000. The largest headings are health, social welfare, national debt service and education. Over the period 1986 to 2000 spending on health increased significantly, whereas spending on education declined. The cost of servicing the national debt has fallen from 25 per cent of GNP in 1986 to 11.5 per cent in 2000. This is a very favourable trend, but the absolute amount of debt servicing illustrates the problems attributable to heavy borrowing in the past.

Table 4.2
Principal heads of government current expenditure

	1986		2000	
	€ m	%	€ m	%
Service of the public debt	2,524	24.5	2,339	11.5
Social welfare	1,949	18.9	3,498	17.1
Health	1,389	13.5	4,119	20.2
Education	1,878	18.2	3,150	15.4
Gárda Síochána	333	3.2	818	4.0
Defence	321	3.1	607	3.0
Total current expenditure	10,268		20,402	

Source: Receipts and Expenditure, 1986 and Budget 2001.

Government current expenditure has been growing at a very rapid pace in the 1990s. Some categories of spending have risen very rapidly. Many commentators have drawn attention to the fact that the extremely buoyant tax revenue in the late 1990s has allowed current spending to race away, almost out of control. The main contributory factor to this has been the very rapid growth of spending on public sector pay and pensions.

PUBLIC CAPITAL EXPENDITURE

Government capital expenditure accounted for 7.6 per cent of GNP in 2000. Although somewhat higher than in recent years, this is much lower than the 17.4 per cent of GNP that went on public capital spending in 1981. This figure was exceptionally high by international standards at the time. With the rapid growth of the economy in the 1990s, however, it was recognised that spending on infrastructure (roads, railways, ports etc.) had to be raised to try to keep pace with growing demands. Under the current *National Development Plan* (NDP) the government proposes spending €51.5 billion (€6.7 billion per annum) over the period 2000–06 on a whole range of development projects.

Note that changes in capital expenditure have a disproportionate effect on the level of activity in the building and construction sector. This sector is inherently prone to wide cyclical fluctuations and changes in the government's capital budget amplify these fluctuations.

GOVERNMENT REVENUE

Figure 4.3 shows that total taxation is broken down into taxes on *income and wealth*, *expenditure*, *capital*, and 'other' taxes. The first two are by far the most important sources of revenue for the government. With regard to taxes on income and wealth, *income tax* and *social insurance contributions* are the largest components. This indicates the heavy burden of taxation on employees.

In the case of taxes on expenditure, *value added tax* (VAT) and *excise duties* are by far the biggest contributors. There are heavy excise taxes on cars, alcoholic drinks, tobacco, petrol and a wide range of consumer goods.

Note that VAT is an *ad valorem* tax, levied as a percentage of the price of the good or service. The VAT yield rises automatically with inflation. Excise duties, on the other hand, are mostly specific taxes (that are levied in terms of so much per unit) and have to be adjusted to prevent inflation eroding their real value. This is why successive ministers for finance have imposed higher excises on the 'old reliables' (tobacco, drink and petrol) in their budgets in order to maintain this source of revenue.

RECENT TRENDS IN TAXATION

Figure 4.4 show that the burden of taxation increased from 22 per cent of GNP in 1962 to a peak of 45 per cent in 1988. It dropped to 37 per cent of GNP in 1999. The increase in the tax burden in the 1980s had serious adverse effects on the economy. It fuelled inflationary wage claims that impaired the country's international competitiveness. The falling burden of taxation in the 1990s has been a positive factor, contributing to Ireland's rapid economic growth. It is in marked contrast to the trend

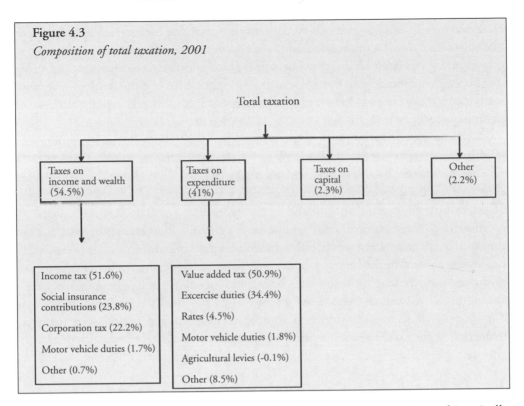

Figure 4.3

Composition of total taxation, 2001

Total taxation

Taxes on income and wealth (54.5%)

Taxes on expenditure (41%)

Taxes on capital (2.3%)

Other (2.2%)

Income tax (51.6%)

Social insurance contributions (23.8%)

Corporation tax (22.2%)

Motor vehicle duties (1.7%)

Other (0.7%)

Value added tax (50.9%)

Excercise duties (34.4%)

Rates (4.5%)

Motor vehicle duties (1.8%)

Agricultural levies (-0.1%)

Other (8.5%)

of the continental EU countries, where the burden of taxation remains at historically high levels.

Taxes on income and wealth trebled as a percentage of GNP from 7.2 per cent in 1962 to 20.5 per cent in 1999. Within this category, the yield of *income tax* has

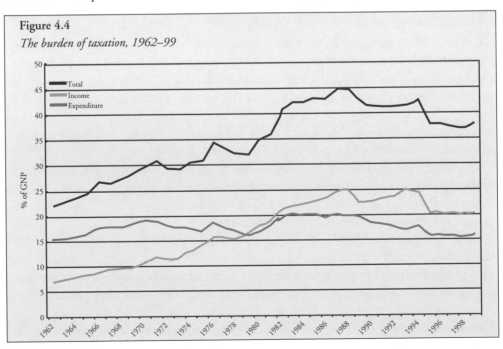

Figure 4.4

The burden of taxation, 1962–99

increased significantly. Income tax receipts rise automatically as incomes increase if the tax allowances and bands are not adjusted to compensate for inflation. The fastest growth of all has been recorded in social insurance contributions, as more and more income has been made subject to this levy and higher rates of contribution have been introduced. Also the yield of *corporate profits* tax has increased very rapidly as many of the tax concessions given to firms in the 1970s were phased out.

Taxes on expenditure rose over the period, but their share in total taxation fell. Within this category, revenue from VAT and excise duties has been very buoyant.

The narrow tax base in Ireland remains a problem. It is argued that the PAYE sector contributes a disproportionate amount of total tax revenue, and a fairly narrow range of goods bear high rates of VAT and excise taxes. The result is that the burden of taxation is particularly heavy on groups such as PAYE workers who spend a high proportion of their income on petrol, tobacco and alcoholic drinks. It has been widely suggested that it would be fairer, and more economically efficient, if a larger proportion of the tax burden were borne by taxes on wealth, especially land and property, which cannot be moved out of the country. From this perspective, the abolition of rates on domestic dwellings in 1978 and of the Residential Property Tax in 1997 were perverse, increasing as they did Ireland's dependence on income taxes.

4.4 ASSESSING THE STANCE OF FISCAL POLICY

We have dealt with government spending and taxation as if they were completely *exogenous*, that is, as if they could be set precisely at a level decided by the government. In reality, the levels of government spending and taxation are strongly influenced by the business cycle.

AUTOMATIC STABILISERS

During a recession government tax receipts fall and government expenditure automatically increases. For example, as unemployment rises households and companies pay less income tax and VAT receipts decline. Similarly, as unemployment rises, the government pays out more money in social welfare and other transfer payments. The process goes into reverse during an expansion. In this case, tax revenue rises and government expenditure on social welfare falls. As a result, the budget deficit automatically increases during recessions and falls during booms.

Because the government is automatically injecting money into the economy in times of recession and withdrawing money in boom periods, cyclically-induced changes in the fiscal budget act as *automatic stabilisers* on the economy. That is, changes in the budget automatically act to stabilise the business cycle.

GRAPHICAL REPRESENTATION

The government's budget surplus is equal to taxes (T) minus government expenditure on current goods and services (G) plus social welfare and other transfer payments (SW).

Budget surplus = T − [G + SW]   (1)

Defining net taxes (NT) as being equal to T minus SW:

$$NT = T - SW \hspace{4cm} (2)$$

NT is that portion of government tax revenue and spending that varies with fluctuations in nominal GNP. Current expenditure (G), on the other hand, is assumed to be constant and does not vary with changes in GNP. In figure 4.5, NT and G are shown along the vertical axis. Nominal GNP is shown on the horizontal axis. As government expenditure, G, is assumed to be constant at all levels of GNP, it is represented as a horizontal line. The net taxes (NT) line, on the other hand, is positively sloped. This is because more tax revenue is collected and less is paid out in social welfare as GNP increases. Conversely, as GNP falls, less is collected in taxes and more paid out in social welfare and NT decreases.

In figure 4.5, a vertical line has also been included to indicate natural GNP. This reference line will become useful in assessing the stance of fiscal policy. Consider the point A in the diagram, corresponding to natural nominal GNP, denoted GNP*. Government expenditure equals net taxes and the budget is balanced. To the left of GNP* there is a budget *deficit* (expenditure exceeds revenue), and to the right a budget *surplus* (expenditure is less than revenue). It is clear from the diagram that the budget balance automatically changes as GNP changes. If, for example, we start from GNP_1 and move to GNP_2, then net taxes move up along the NT line and the government's budget swings automatically from deficit to surplus. This means that as the economy moves out of a recession, the government's budget surplus will automatically increase. Conversely, as the economy contracts, the budget surplus automatically falls.

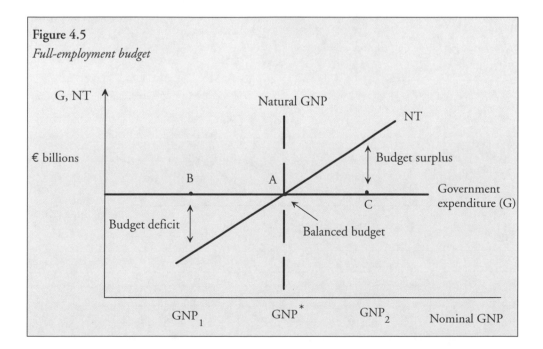

Figure 4.5
Full-employment budget

DISCRETIONARY FISCAL POLICY

The diagram allows us to clarify the distinction between *automatic* and *discretionary* changes in the budget balance. Discretionary budget changes arise when the government deliberately changes the stance of fiscal policy by changing tax rates, the level of social welfare benefits, or the level of its expenditure on goods and services. For example in figure 4.6 an increase in taxes or/and a cut in SW shifts the NT line upwards to the left. This initially gives rise to a budget surplus. GNP would now have to fall to GNP_1 for the budget to be balanced (point B in the diagram). Conversely a cut in taxes or/and an increase in SW shifts the NT line downwards to the right. GNP would now have to rise to GNP_2 for the budget to balance (point C in the diagram). Similarly, a cut in government consumption shifts the government expenditure (G) line downwards and vice versa.

Each of these changes represents a policy decision by the government. They are discretionary policy changes that result in the budget being balanced at different levels of GNP. At what level of GNP should the government attempt to balance the budget?

THE FULL-EMPLOYMENT BUDGET

It can be argued that the relevant budget balance from a policy perspective is the *natural GNP budget surplus* or deficit (also referred to as the *full-employment, structural, high-employment,* or *cyclically adjusted* budget surplus or deficit). The government should choose a combination of tax rates and levels of expenditure that would result in a balanced budget *if the economy were at natural GNP*.

As mentioned, in figure 4.5, the vertical line represents natural GNP. At this point, NT = G and the budget is balanced. To the left of natural GNP, the economy is in recession and the government should tolerate the resultant budget deficit. In contrast,

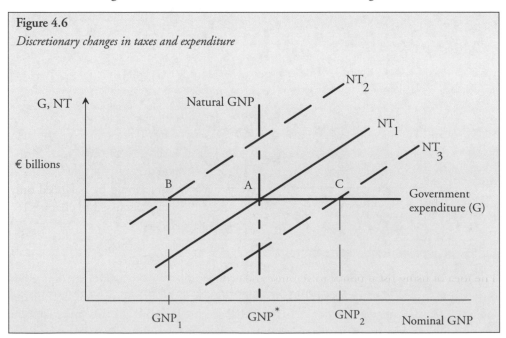

Figure 4.6
Discretionary changes in taxes and expenditure

to the right of natural GNP the economy is over-heating (working above capacity) and the government should run a surplus.

The problem is that in many cases, governments pursue a policy of *always* trying to balance the budget. Suppose, for example, in figure 4.5 GNP falls from GNP^* to GNP_1. The economy is in recession and a budget deficit emerges. If the government, in an effort to balance the books, responded by cutting expenditure or raising taxes, this would push the economy further into recession. This is what happened in many countries in the 1930s: governments that wanted to balance the budget pushed their economies deeper into recession.

On the other hand, suppose that in figure 4.5 the economy moved from GNP^* to GNP_2. Now the economy is in a boom phase and a surplus emerges. If the government attempts to eliminate this surplus by cutting taxes or increasing expenditure, the result will be to add further fuel to the boom. In general, a policy of always balancing the budget can lead to policy being *pro-cyclical*. That is, government policy exacerbates the swings in the business cycle.

In evaluating fiscal policy, economists attempt to gauge if government policy is expansionary, neutral or deflationary and whether policy is appropriate to the needs of the economy. In attempting to assess the stance of fiscal policy, the natural GNP budget balance is more relevant than the actual budget balance. An examination of the actual budget balance without adjustment for built-in stabilisers can give a misleading picture of the direction of fiscal policy. However, in practice it is not easy to identify the natural GNP budget because natural GNP is itself changing over time. This point should be borne in mind in any assessment of the effectiveness of fiscal policy in Ireland.

Note:
For an analysis of the stance of Irish fiscal policy see I. Kearney, D. McCoy, D. Duffy, M. McMahon and D. Smyth, 2000, 'Assessing the Stance of Irish Fiscal Policy,' in A. Barrett (ed.), *Budget Perspectives*, Dublin: The Economic and Social Research Institute. See also P. R. Lane, 1998, 'On the Cyclicality of Irish Fiscal Policy', *The Economic and Social Review*, Vol. 29, No. 1, 1–16. These studies give Irish discretionary fiscal low marks. They find that the tendency has been pro-cyclical — expansionary during boom times and contractionary during recessions — exactly the reverse of what would have been appropriate from the point of view of stabilising the economy.

It should also be noted that under the *Stability and Growth Pact* (agreed in Dublin in 1996), member states of the Eurozone are required to balance their budgets by 2004. This deadline applies regardless of market conditions or where a country is on its business cycle. That is, it takes no account of the notion that budgets should be balanced only when the economy is at natural real GNP. The Stability Pact is discussed in chapter 16.

4.5 PROBLEMS IN IMPLEMENTING STABILISATION POLICY

The idea of using fiscal policy to stabilise the economy is appealing, but experience has shown that it is in practice very difficult, if not impossible, successfully to fine-tune the economy in this manner. In fact, we noted that the Irish record on this front is poor. Let us consider why it is difficult to use fiscal policy successfully.

LAGS

If the economy experiences an adverse shock and is going into recession, the government should adopt an expansionary fiscal stance. But the timing of this response is likely to be delayed. It takes time to recognise what is happening to the economy (the *recognition lag*). Only a limited amount of timely economic data is available. Information on key variables becomes available gradually — in Ireland no quarterly GNP estimates are published. While numerous unofficial estimates are prepared, economists often disagree about the direction in which the economy is moving.

Secondly, policy makers have to decide on whether to change taxes or expenditure (the *decision lag*). If more money is to be spent should it go on roads or education? In which part of the country should the money be spent?

Thirdly, there is an *implementation lag*. This too takes time. More money cannot be spent on road building until project documents have been drawn up, planning permission obtained and tenders approved. Tax changes are usually introduced only once a year, at budget time, and do not take effect until after they have been passed into law. The tax reductions announced in the budget of December 2000 were not reflected in higher take-home pay until April 2001.

These lags are referred to as *inside lags*. There is also the *outside lag* between implementing a policy and when it actually affects aggregate demand. The impact of the large income tax cuts in the 2000 budget that went into effect in April 2001 built up over the second half of the year.

The problem with these lags is that by the time the fiscal policy takes effect economic conditions in the country may have altered. The implication is that the policy could be inappropriate by the time it becomes effective and end up *destabilising* instead of stabilising the business cycle.

A good example of getting fiscal policy wrong was Minister for Finance Charlie McCreevy's decision to launch the Special Saving Incentive Scheme, to boost saving and dampen consumer expenditure. This scheme was thought up during the inflationary boom of 2000, launched in 2001, and really took effect in 2002, when the economy was no longer growing rapidly.

Figure 4.7 shows the economy adjusting back towards the natural real growth rate after it is hit by an adverse 'economic shock'. The economy moves below the natural real growth rate and into recession. After a time the government recognises the downturn and sets about implementing an expansionary fiscal policy. Because of the recognition, decision, implementation and outside lags, this policy will take some time to impact on the economy. Nine months later the economy automatically rights itself. There may, for example, be an up-turn in consumer confidence and the actual growth rate starts to move back to the natural rate. Six months later, the expansionary fiscal policy kicks in and pushes the economy into an over-heating position. The timing of the fiscal policy destabilises the business cycle.

HOW BIG A RESPONSE?

Another difficulty arises from the problem of deciding how much additional demand the government should inject into or withdraw from the economy. The appropriate

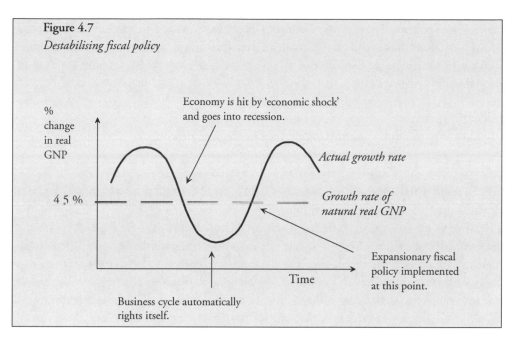

Figure 4.7
Destabilising fiscal policy

% change in real GNP

Economy is hit by 'economic shock' and goes into recession.

Actual growth rate

4 5 %

Growth rate of natural real GNP

Time

Expansionary fiscal policy implemented at this point.

Business cycle automatically rights itself.

amount to spend to counter a fall in aggregate demand can only be calculated on the basis of an exact knowledge of how the 'shock' hits the economy and the relevant multipliers. But calculating multipliers entails estimating a model of the economy, which is a far from exact science.

POLITICAL ECONOMY

Policy makers are not disembodied technicians, unaware of political realities. In all countries economic policy is influenced by the desire of politicians to get re-elected, which depends on delivering results such as low inflation and unemployment. The relative importance of these objectives differs between countries. German politicians, for example, have believed that low inflation is crucial, while until recently Italian politicians were willing to condone high inflation giving priority to the unemployment problem. Thus economic policies are *endogenous*, a reflection of policy makers' and the public's preferences.

The *timing of elections* also has an important influence on policy. During the general election of 1978, for example, Irish political parties vied with one another in their extravagant promises to the electorate. After the election, increases in expenditure and cuts in taxation were implemented when the economy was already booming. Furthermore, politicians find it much easier to implement expansionary policies as opposed to deflationary policies. Hence there is an asymmetric effect where politicians are very keen to deal with recession but are very reluctant to introduce the measures to curb an over-heating economy.

One way around the problem created by the political cycle is to create independent economic policy-making institutions. Following the American and German examples, many European governments, including Britain, have given their central banks increased autonomy and the independence to withstand demands for inflationary financing of government deficits. Countries like Ireland that participate in the European Monetary Union have relinquished control over their monetary policy to the European Central Bank and agreed to observe the Stability and Growth Pact in the conduct of their fiscal policy.

CROWDING-OUT

Consider the equilibrium equation derived in chapter 2.

$$GNP = TE \equiv C + I + G + NX \qquad\qquad (3)$$

GNP equals total expenditure, which in turn can be broken down into consumer expenditure, investment, government expenditure and net exports. Suppose the government increases G in order to boost total expenditure and raise GNP. Assuming the government incurs a budget deficit, the extra spending will have to be borrowed in financial markets. This increase in the demand for funds on the money markets can cause interest rates to rise (this effect will be elaborated upon in chapter 8). The higher interest rates, in turn, can reduce consumer expenditure (C) and private sector investment (I). As C and I fall, the level of aggregate demand decreases. In terms of equation (3), the initial increase in G is completely offset by the fall in C and I and GNP is unchanged. Government expenditure has *crowded-out* consumption and investment. In this case, there is 100 per cent crowding-out and fiscal policy has no impact on aggregate demand.

In practice, the degree of crowding-out is likely to be considerably less than 100 per cent. Fiscal policy would therefore affect aggregate demand although by less than the increase in G. The important point is that the ultimate effect on GNP is smaller than that suggested by the multipliers we derived in chapter 3, which took no account of crowding-out.

BARRO-RICARDO EQUIVALENCE THEOREM

A second issue relates to the effect of government deficits on the behaviour of households. In an influential article published in 1974, the Harvard economist Robert Barro proposed the idea that increases in government debt could result in a fall in private sector consumption. In terms of equation (3), the increase in G is offset by a fall in C. The classical economist David Ricardo (1772–1823) appeared to have entertained the same idea, hence it is now known as the *Barro-Ricardo equivalence theorem*.

The bones of the proposition are as follows. Suppose the government lowers taxes without cutting its spending and finances the deficit by selling bonds to the public. These bonds must be redeemed (with interest) at some time in the future. Households' *current* disposable income rises due to the tax cut, but *future* disposable income will fall by an equivalent amount because of the necessity of repaying the debt. Thus, households' long-run or permanent income (see chapter 3) is not increased by the tax cut. If households are rational and care about future generations, their consumption should remain unchanged. However, if the present generation is willing to pass the increased debt on to future generations they would feel better off as a result of the tax cut and their consumption would increase.

The Irish experience offers some support for the Barro-Ricardian equivalence theorem. When the fiscal deficit was very large in the first half of the 1980s, the private sector saving ratio was very high; when the public sector deficit was brought under control in the later 1980s, the private sector saving ratio fell.

SUPPLY-SIDE SHOCKS

Another problem is that fiscal policy entails the government counter-acting shifts in either the aggregate demand (AD) or aggregate supply (AS) curves using only fiscal policy. However fiscal policy is not an effective policy response to dealing with an adverse supply-side shock.

For example, in figure 4.8 the economy is initially at the point A. The price level is P_1 and real GNP is GNP_1. Suppose now the economy is hit by a supply-side shock which shifts the AS curve up to the left. As the economy moves to the point B real GNP falls and the price level increases to P_2. If the government now introduces an expansionary fiscal policy to increase real GNP, the AD curve moves up to the right and a new equilibrium is achieved at the point C. The difficulty, however, is that there is a further increase in the price level. So while the fiscal policy can (in certain circumstances) deal with the fall in real GNP it cannot simultaneously counter-act the increases in prices. This example illustrates that a demand-side policy is not an effective policy response to a supply-side shock.

SUMMARY

From the above discussion it should be clear that in practice the use of fiscal policy to stabilise the economy is not an easy task. While the basic idea seems simple, its implementation is fraught with difficulties. Moreover, economists have become

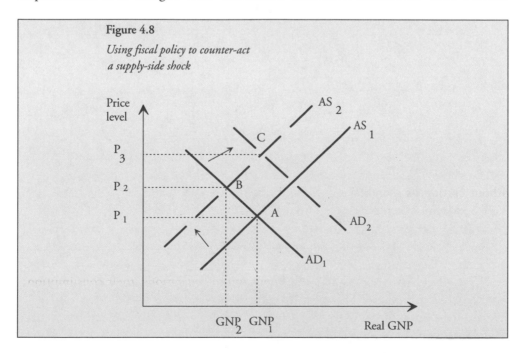

Figure 4.8

Using fiscal policy to counter-act a supply-side shock

increasingly sceptical of some of the assumptions underlying the basic Keynesian model. None the less, policy makers continue to try to use budgets to reduce the fluctuations in economic output.

4.6 TAXATION AND THE SUPPLY-SIDE OF THE ECONOMY

Up to this point, our emphasis has been on how taxation affects the demand-side of the economy. But ever since Adam Smith, economists have recognised that taxation also affects the supply-side of the economy by affecting the *incentives to work* and *save*. This affects the level and composition of output and income. If these effects are large they can have surprising results. Under certain conditions, it could be that tax cuts increase, rather than decrease, tax revenue. This argument has been put forward by the University of Southern California economist Arthur Laffer, who reputedly first drew the *Laffer curve* on a napkin in a Washington restaurant to explain the point to a reporter.

The Laffer curve depicts the relationship between the average tax rate (vertical axis) and the tax revenue to the government (horizontal axis). This is illustrated in figure 4.9, which shows how much revenue is obtained from different average rates of income tax. There are two rates where no tax revenue is collected: zero and 100 per cent. In the first case, there is no tax and therefore no revenue. In the second case, all income would be taken in tax and there would be no incentive to work. If no one works there is no income to tax and revenue is zero. Between these two extremes, it is argued, revenue first increases and then decreases as the tax rate rises.

Figure 4.9 shows that there is a revenue maximising tax rate, T^*. Moreover, the same amount of tax revenue can be obtained at high or low tax rates: T_1 and T_2 generate the same revenue, R_1. It follows, therefore, that government could cut the tax rate from T_1 to T_2 without suffering any loss of revenue. More generally, if the tax rate is below T^*

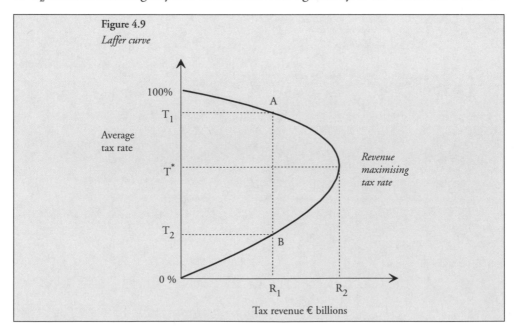

Figure 4.9
Laffer curve

an increase in the tax rate leads to an increase in revenue. This is what is normally expected. However, if the tax rate is above T*, we have the surprising result that an increase in the tax rate leads to a reduction in revenue. In the latter situation, the government raises the tax rate in order to generate extra revenue and finds that its tax receipts fall. If it lowered the tax rate it would generate extra revenue.

WORK INCENTIVES

The explanation for the paradoxical result that above T*, an increase in the tax rate reduces revenue centres on work incentives. High tax rates discourage people from working. If people work less, their taxable income falls and so do tax receipts. In 1986 the marginal income tax rate in Ireland was 65 per cent. The rate for evening teaching at a university was €30 per hour. For every €30 earned, the government took €19.50 in income taxes and the lecturer received €10.50. When this after-tax income is spent a further 20 per cent or so was taken in indirect taxes. If the lecturer decided that the after-tax purchasing power of the lecture fee was not worth the time and effort involved, (s)he would stay at home in the evenings instead of going out to teach an extra course. If enough people reacted in this way, the course would not go ahead and the government would lose tax revenue. A reduction in the marginal tax rate would make it more worthwhile to put on the course and tax receipts would rise.

In addition to discouraging work effort, high tax rates create many other undesirable incentives. People are encouraged to switch from the formal economy into the informal or 'black' economy, to take money out of the country and place it in foreign tax havens ('capital flight'), and even to emigrate. High tax rates also encourage people to shop in countries where indirect taxes are low. Tax rates in Ireland, for example, cannot move too far out of line from the tax rates that obtain in the UK. High tax rates on spirits, petrol and electrical goods led shoppers from the Republic to purchase these items in Northern Ireland in the mid-1980s. When the tax rates were cut towards the end of the decade, more was spent in the Republic and revenue rose. These effects of high tax rates are consistent with the existence of a Laffer curve.

When marginal tax rates are high it may therefore be argued that a reduction in tax rates would have a stimulating effect on the economy by encouraging people to work harder leading to a rise in real GNP and ultimately to higher tax revenue.

Note:
There are a number of reasons, however, why tax cuts may not have the dramatic effects predicted by this theory. It is possible, for example, that lower taxes might encourage people to work less because after the tax cut they can obtain the same level of take-home pay with less effort; they may decide to enjoy more leisure at the same income, which they can now earn by working less. This would offset the effects predicted by Laffer. Moreover, for the Laffer curve to be bell shaped, the reduction in taxes has to boost real GNP by an amount sufficient too more than compensate for the initial loss of tax revenue.

TAX RATES AND THE AD, AS DIAGRAM

Economists are generally agreed that changes in taxation impacts on the supply-side of the economy. Disagreement, however, arises on the extent of this impact. In figure 4.10,

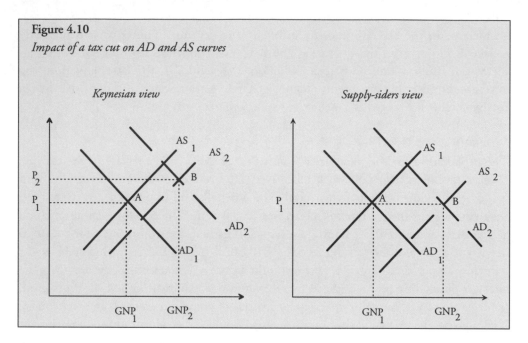

Figure 4.10

Impact of a tax cut on AD and AS curves

left-hand diagram, Keynesian economists agree that a tax cut will shift both the aggregate demand (AD) and aggregate supply (AS) curves to the right. The AD curve moves because the tax cut leads to an increase in consumer expenditure (C) and therefore aggregate demand. On the supply-side, the tax cut increases the incentive to work and more people enter the labour force. This expands the supply-side of the economy and the AS curve shifts to the right (natural real GNP also increases). The Keynesian view is that the shift in the AD curve will be greater than the movement of the AS curve. As shown in the diagram, the economy moves from the point A to B and both the price level and real GNP increase. (Note that the greater the movement of the AS curve, the lower the change in the price level and the greater the increase in real GNP.) Hence, we obtain the standard Keynesian result, that an expansionary fiscal policy generates more real GNP but also increases the price level.

Supply-side economists such as Arthur Laffer, on the other hand, assert that the shift of the AS curve to the right will be approximately equal to the movement of the AD curve. As can be seen in the right-hand diagram in figure 4.10, the result is a much bigger increase in real GNP and little or no effect on the price level. Some supply-side economists go further and argue that the movement of the AS curve will be greater than the movement of the AD curve. In this case, the increase in real GNP will be accompanied by a fall in the price level.

The dispute between the Keynesians and the supply-siders is therefore one of quantifying the effect of the tax change on the AS curve. In the context of stabilisation policy, it is clear that the Laffer curve and the effect of tax changes on the AS curve create more uncertainty about the effects of fiscal policy on the economy.

4.7 CONCLUSION

The main points discussed in this chapter were:

- Stabilisation policy
- The government's budget and the characteristics of government expenditure and taxation
- Automatic fiscal stabilisers
- The natural GNP budget deficit
- The difficulties in the way of implementing such a stabilisation policy
- The Laffer curve
- Taxation and the supply-side of the economy.

CHAPTER 5

Fiscal Policy in Ireland

5.1 INTRODUCTION

In this chapter we examine the role of stabilisation policy in Ireland since the 1950s. We also look at the various approaches to economic planning that have been adopted. As we saw in chapter 4, stabilisation policy relates to discretionary changes in fiscal policy in an attempt to stabilise the economy by minimising the business cycle. An economic plan, on the other hand, is a medium-term plan designed to achieve specific targets relating to growth, employment, and other key macroeconomic variables. Ambitious plans of this sort have gone completely out of fashion now, but they were considered important in Ireland in earlier decades. The first part of the chapter discusses the various economic plans introduced since the 1950s. The second half of the chapter is concerned with stabilisation policy and its effectiveness. We hope that our interpretation of events will help identify the main difficulties or limitations of implementing fiscal policy in a small open economy such as Ireland.

5.2 ECONOMIC PROGRAMMING AND PLANNING

There was a long tradition of economic planning or programming in Ireland. Numerous government documents set targets for the future growth of real GNP usually with little success. Figure 5.1 shows the *projected* or target growth rates in GNP cited in each of the economic programmes since the 1950s, with the *actual* growth rate recorded in the relevant period. It can be seen that the projections bear little resemblance to the actual outcome. This highlights the point that large-scale planning of the sort attempted in Ireland in the past has a poor track record. None the less, it is of some interest to review these plans in an historical perspective.

THE ORIGINS OF ECONOMIC PLANNING IN THE 1940S AND 1950S

The Public Capital Programme was introduced after World War II in an attempt to systematise the public sector's annual spending on capital and development projects. This was linked to our participation in the Marshall Plan because, as a condition of receiving aid, the US authorities wanted to see integrated proposals for spending it. The Department of Finance was opposed to borrowing, even on very favourable terms, for ambitious new projects, but the Department of Foreign Affairs, where Seán MacBride was minister, prepared a long-term development plan.

These tentative steps towards 'planning' were overtaken by the stagnation of the early 1950s and the crisis of 1955–56, when living standards and employment fell and emigration soared. T. K. Whitaker, who was secretary of the Department of Finance at

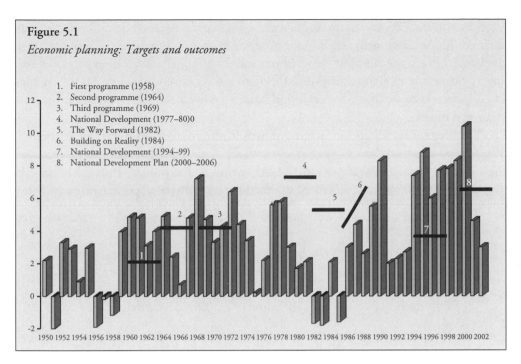

Figure 5.1

Economic planning: Targets and outcomes

1. First programme (1958)
2. Second programme (1964)
3. Third programme (1969)
4. National Development (1977–80)0
5. The Way Forward (1982)
6. Building on Reality (1984)
7. National Development (1994–99)
8. National Development Plan (2000–2006)

the time, commented: 'The mood of despondency was palpable. Something had to be done or the achievement of national independence would prove to have been a futility. Various attempts were made to shine a beam forward in this dark night of the soul.'

In early 1958, a survey of the economy was prepared in the Department of Finance and was published in November under the title *Economic Development*. This survey provided the basis for the *First Programme for Economic Expansion*, which was published soon afterwards. To escape from the recession, the *First Programme* proposed three main policies.

• Public expenditure should be switched from non-productive to productive projects. In particular, capital spending on local authority housing and hospitals was to be reduced and spending on agriculture and industry increased.

• Priority was to be given to a significant reduction in taxation, particularly income taxation, because 'high taxation is one of the greatest impediments to economic progress because of its adverse effects on saving and on enterprise'.

• It was also suggested that the increase in wages and salaries in Ireland should lag behind that in Britain.

• The hope was that agriculture would still serve as the engine of growth for the economy.

Note:

Out of a total of 212 pages of text in the *First Programme*, 100 were devoted to a detailed discussion of agriculture, forestry and fisheries. (The headline in the *Irish Independent* proclaimed 'Easier credit schemes for farmers proposed'!) The same emphasis on rural development was apparent in the reports of the Commission on Emigration published in 1954, which looked mainly to agriculture to halt the outflow of population.

The conflict between trying to increase agricultural output while at the same time maintaining exceptionally high protective tariffs on industrial products was not discussed. In fact, the failure of *protectionism* and the need to move to an export-oriented strategy were not explicitly addressed. Although it was acknowledged that tariffs 'might impair the incentive to reduce costs and increase efficiency', the enthusiasm for free trade was muted.

The *Programme* set an 11 per cent growth in the volume of GNP over the period 1959–63, but growth of 23 per cent was actually achieved (figure 5.1). However, the improved performance was *not* attributable to any of the policies introduced in the *Programme* for the reason that few of its recommendations were implemented.

- The burden of taxation was not eased. Instead, income tax in particular rose inexorably.
- There is no evidence of a rise in the level of manufacturing investment.
- Agriculture did not prove to be an engine of growth. Even after entry into the EEC and a massive injection of subsidies from the Community, agriculture's share of GNP declined steadily and the number employed on family farms continued to fall.
- The role of economic locomotive was assumed by industry, as the scale of the inflow of foreign capital far exceeded that in the *First Programme's* projections.
- Growth resumed in 1958–59, before any of the new policies could have taken effect.

In reality, due to the rapid expansion of the world economy during the 1960s the Irish economy recovered more or less spontaneously from the protracted recession of 1954–58. This was helped by the opening up of the economy, the dismantling of protectionism, which was not emphasised in the *Programme*.

There is, however, no doubt that the *First Programme* captured the imagination of a much wider population than would normally be aware of a detailed discussion of economic policy. It served to gain acceptance of the importance of economic development as a policy objective, and the need to look outward rather than inward in order to generate this development.

ECONOMIC PLANNING: 1960s AND 1970s

It was inevitable that the dramatic improvement in the performance of the Irish economy in the years following the publication of the *First Programme* would be attributed to the *Programme* itself. It is not surprising that the planning exercise was repeated in a much more ambitious form in subsequent years. A *Second Programme 1964–70* was published in 1964 and a *Third Programme, Economic and Social Development 1969–72* in 1969. These contained much more detailed statistical analyses of the Irish economy than had been attempted in 1958.

Both of these programmes projected a growth rate of 4 per cent a year in real GNP, which was the actual growth rate during the recovery from the deep recession of the 1950s. However, as may be seen from figure 5.1, the projections of the growth of the economy proved as wide of the mark during the *Second* and *Third Programmes* as they had been in the *First*. The greater sectoral detail contained in the later documents drew attention to their increasing lack of relevance as the planning periods progressed. The *Second Programme* was based on the assumption that Ireland would be a member of the EEC by 1970. France's veto of British entry shortly after its publication provided a rationale for abandoning the *Programme*. It also became clear, after the publication of the *Third Programme* in 1969, that the targets contained in this, especially those relating to employment, would not be achieved. Thus the exercise in planning that was a central feature of Irish economic policy in the 1960s seemed to end in failure.

The degree of disillusionment with the process of planning in the turbulent economic circumstances of the 1970s is reflected in the words of the Minister for Finance, Richie Ryan, in his 1975 budget speech: '...of all the tasks that could engage my attention, the least realistic would be the publication of a medium- or long-term economic plan based on irrelevancies in the past, hunches as to the present and clairvoyance as to the future...'.

ECONOMIC PLANNING: 1970S AND 1980S

Irish economic planning enjoyed renewed popularity after the formation of a new government in 1977. A Department of Economic Planning and Development was created. A plan called *National Development 1977–80* was published, containing specific targets for the growth of output and employment and the reduction in unemployment. It was envisaged that the public sector would provide an initial boost to the economy, after which the private sector would take up the running. This required increased government spending and recruitment in the public sector. The optimistic projections on which the plan was based were rendered irrelevant by the second oil-price crisis in 1979. With hindsight it is evident that the plan hindered, rather than helped, the adjustment of the economy to this shock.

Subsequent government statements on national development focused on the constraints facing the economy, rather than on specific targets for sectoral output. Following entry into the European Monetary System in 1979, it was recognised that pay moderation was essential if competitiveness was to be improved. In 1981 the coalition government established a *Committee on Costs and Competitiveness*. Its report set out calculations of a wage norm based on forecast increases in our competitors' wage costs and likely changes in exchange rates. The idea was that if this norm were adhered to, there would be no deterioration in the country's competitiveness. Unfortunately, the norm proposed in October 1981 was rendered inappropriate by a weakening of sterling almost as soon as it was published. (The fall in sterling meant that greater wage moderation was required if Ireland was to maintain its competitiveness with the UK.)

A planning document, *The Way Forward*, was prepared by the Fianna Fáil government during 1982 and became the manifesto on which the party fought (and lost) the second general election of 1982. This document contained optimistic forecasts of economic growth based on a dramatic improvement in our international competitiveness, to be achieved by 'moderate pay increases combined with increases in productivity'.

In March 1983 the new coalition government established an independent National Planning Board to prepare a study that would form the basis for a new plan. (One of the authors of the present book, Brendan Walsh, was a member of the Committee on Costs and Competitiveness and of the National Planning Board.)

Proposals for Plan 1984–87 was published in April 1984. This document differed fundamentally from its immediate predecessors, and in some ways returned to the spirit of the *First Programme*, by presenting very detailed sectoral policy recommendations. It contained no fewer than 241 recommendations, ranging over many aspects of economic and social policy. The recommendations included:

- The need to reduce the level of public sector borrowing by expenditure cuts rather than increased taxation.
- To increase the efficiency of the public sector through privatisation and deregulation. The high costs of monopolistic state companies were acting as a drag on the ability of the private sector to compete internationally.
- Special targeted measures to alleviate the problem of long-term unemployment.
- The plan emphasised the goal of stabilising the debt/GNP ratio and reducing the level of taxation.

In many respects the package proposed resembled a *structural adjustment programme* of the type supported by soft loans from the International Monetary Fund and World Bank in numerous developing countries in the 1980s.

The coalition government's plan, *Building on Reality*, was published in autumn 1984. This generally endorsed the policy recommendations contained in *Proposals for Plan*. It forecast that total employment would increase over the next three years as employment in private sector services grew rapidly and industrial employment began to recover from the recession. These projections proved too optimistic. The public finances continued to deteriorate until 1987 and employment did not begin to recover until 1988.

NATIONAL WAGE AGREEMENTS

Ambitious, large-scale economic plans of the type described in the previous section faded away in the mid-1980s. Economists were increasingly sceptical of the relevance of such exercises in a small, open economy like Ireland. This was, in turn, partly influenced by a renewed belief in market forces and the harmfulness of government interference in the economy in countries like the UK and the US. In Ireland, however, one issue that remained prominent was how to deal with the evolution of pay.

In Britain in the 1980s the power of the unions was undermined by confrontations such as the one that crushed the mineworkers' strike in 1984 and subsequent legislative changes. However, in Ireland there was no explicit agenda to curb union power. Instead there was a return to the centralised approach to wage bargaining adopted in the 1970s.

The minority Fianna Fáil government that was formed in 1987 published a *Programme for National Recovery 1987–90* in October 1987. This model was influenced by the successful experience of countries like the Netherlands, Austria, Norway and Sweden. At its core was an agreement between employers, trade unions and the government to adhere to specified increases in wages and salaries over a three year period. A reduction in the rate of income taxation was promised, and the prospect of increases in employment in selected state-sponsored enterprises was held out.

A similar wage formula was accepted in the *Programme for Economic and Social Progress (PESP)*, 1991–94, the *Programme for Competitiveness and Work*, 1994–96, *Partnership 2000*, 1997–99 and the *Programme for Prosperity and Fairness* 2000–03.

These national agreements have been hailed as examples of co-operation between the social partners (trade unions, employers, farmers and government) and are referred to as corporatism (see Lars Calmfors and John Driffill, 'Bargaining Structure, Corporatism, and Macroeconomic Performance', *Economic Policy*, 1988, 6 (1), 13–61). The agreements have been credited with maintaining industrial peace, providing a stable framework for business and moderating wage costs. As such they have been identified by a number of commentators as one of the reasons underlying the economic boom in Ireland during the 1990s.

However, wage agreements can also be criticised for imposing a uniform wage increase on all sectors of the economy and being tailored to the needs of stronger unionised sectors (including the public sector), rather than those of small and medium-sized firms facing severe international competition.

RECENT YEARS

Although ambitious centralised planning gave way to more modest national wage agreements, there was still a role for planning the government's capital spending. Increased funding for infrastructure projects became available from the European Union in the 1990s, but this required a more systematic approach to project evaluation. The EU was not prepared to give the Irish government lots of money to spend on projects unless it could be shown that these had a sound economic and social justification. The response was to prepare more detailed public capital programmes, based on serious cost-benefit appraisals. Although called 'plans' these capital programmes differed fundamentally from the discredited attempts at macroeconomic planning of the 1960s and 1970s.

In October 1993 the coalition government published the *National Development Plan: 1994–99*. This plan envisaged spending €28 billion between 1993 and 1999 on a whole range of areas including industry, natural resources, tourism and transport. Expenditure was funded by the EU (39.4 per cent), the public sector (42.2 per cent) and the private sector (18.4 per cent). The basic objective was to create jobs by developing the agricultural, industrial and services sectors, by improving infrastructure and by developing the skills of the workforce through education and training. The plan anticipated an annual real growth rate of 3.5 per cent from 1994–99. This target proved too pessimistic. As figure 5.1 shows, the period since 1994 has been characterised by an unprecedented growth of output and employment that was not anticipated at the time this plan was drafted. This provides yet another illustration of the inability of policy makers to foresee the behaviour of a small open economy.

The *National Development Plan 2000–06* proposes spending €51.5 billion over the seven years of the plan. Most of the money is going into what is perceived to be weak aspects of the Irish economy. This includes upgrading national roads and public transportation, environmental pollution and housing shortages. A considerable portion of the total expenditure is to be spent developing human resource skills and tackling deprivation and poverty.

Note:

An interesting example of the need for systematic cost-benefit appraisal of public capital spending proposals is provided by the history of the plans for a National Sports Campus in north Dublin labelled the 'Bertie Bowl', because it was favoured by the Taoiseach Bertie Ahern. This was not included in the National Development Plan and controversy raged over its eventual cost as well as over its potential benefits. After much disagreement it was finally shelved in September 2002.

SUMMARY

Economic planning of the type undertaken by successive Irish governments since the 1950s is now unfashionable. With the collapse of the planned socialist economies of the Soviet Union and Eastern Europe in the 1980s, and the success of the *laissez-faire* American economy in the 1990s, little credibility now attaches to the notion that governments can direct their economies towards desired goals.

Successive Irish governments moved from ambitious macroeconomic plans that were inherently incapable of being successfully implemented, to looser 'indicative plans', which also achieved very little, and then to a more successful approach based entirely on centralised wage negotiations. This at least had the merit of bringing some order to the rates of pay negotiated between employers, unions and the government. Finally, due to the stimulus of increased inflows from the EU, a more systematic approach has now been adopted to prioritising public capital spending.

5.3 THE IRISH EXPERIENCE WITH STABILISATION POLICY

Stabilisation policy is concerned with the short-run fluctuations in the business cycle. Even if we accept the conclusion of the foregoing review of economic planning and programming, it is still possible to believe that government fiscal policy has a role to play in smoothing the economy's growth path by manipulating aggregate demand along the lines described in chapter 4. In this section we review the Irish experience with stabilisation policy.

To facilitate the discussion figures 5.3, 5.4 and 5.5 show respectively the *current budget deficit*, the *exchequer borrowing requirement* (EBR) and the *national debt* all expressed as a percentage of GNP. (See chapter 4 for a definition of these concepts.) Changes in these budget balances give a rough indication of the direction of fiscal policy. However, the reader should bear in mind the discussion of automatic built-in stabilisers in chapter 4. The point is that rapid growth in the economy automatically reduces the budget deficit through tax buoyancy and reduced social welfare spending. Conversely, a recession automatically increases the budget deficit. Hence, an examination of the unadjusted deficit gives a misleading picture of the stance of fiscal policy. In order to assess the stance of fiscal policy, it is desirable to net out the automatic effects (due to tax buoyancy and social welfare spending) and to isolate the discretionary changes in fiscal policy. An examination of the data in figures 5.3, 5.4 and 5.5, therefore, only gives a crude indication of the stance of fiscal policy.

Before the 1970s, Irish finance ministers did not consciously attempt to implement an active fiscal policy. (Box 5.1 below identifies the various finance ministers since the foundation of the state.) Annual budgets were framed primarily to raise the money needed to finance the government's day-to-day spending. In 1924, for example, Ernest Blythe infamously reduced the old age pension by a shilling a week. Although borrowing was incurred to finance the Public Capital Programme, fiscal policy was not consciously used as an instrument of demand management or to try to reduce the level of unemployment. This situation changed radically after the first oil shock in 1973. During the 1970s Irish public finances were transformed by the attempt to use government spending to achieve macroeconomic objectives.

Box 5.1

Finance ministers since the foundation of the state

1.	Eoin MacNeill	22–1–1919
2.	Michael Collins	2–4–1919
3.	William T. Cosgrave	26–8–1922
4.	Ernest Blythe	6–12–1922
5.	Seán MacEntee (1)	9–3–1932
6.	Seán T. Ó Ceallaigh	16–9–1939
7.	Frank Aiken	19–6–1945
8.	Patrick Mc Gilligan	18–2–1948
9.	Seán MacEntee (2)	14–6–1951
10.	Gerard Sweetman	2–6–1954
11.	James Ryan	20–3–1957
12.	Jack Lynch	21–4–1965
13.	Charles J. Haughey	16–11–1966
14.	George Colley (1)	9–5–1970
15.	Richie Ryan	14–3–1973
16.	George Colley (2)	5–7–1977
17.	Michael O'Kennedy	12–12–1979
18.	Gene Fitzgerald	16–12–1980
19.	John Bruton (1)	30–6–1981
20.	Ray MacSharry	9–3–1982
21.	Alan Dukes	14–12–1982
22.	John Bruton (2)	14–2–1986
23.	Ray MacSharry (2)	10–3–1987
24.	Albert Reynolds	25–11–1988
25.	Bertie Ahern	14–11–1991
26.	Ruairi Quinn	15–12–1994
27.	Charlie McCreevy	26–6–1997

1972–77: Departure from Fiscal Rectitude

The year 1973 was a watershed in Western economic history. The Organisation of Petroleum Exporting Countries (OPEC) raised crude oil prices from $3 to $12 a barrel. This was a severe shock to both the demand and the supply-sides of economies dependent on imported energy. On the demand-side, the enormous price rise greatly increased expenditure on imports because there was little scope in the short run for reducing dependence on imported energy.

As figure 5.2 illustrates, (see also figure 2.11 in chapter 2) an increase in imports shifts the aggregate demand (AD) schedule down to the left. On the supply-side, the increase in the cost of a basic input has the effect of shifting the aggregate supply (AS) schedule up to the left. Putting the two effects together we see that output falls, but whether the price level rises or falls depends on the slopes and the relative size of the shifts in the AD and AS schedules. In figure 5.2 the shift in AS is larger than that in AD. The economy moves from A to B, an *output gap* opens up between actual and natural real GNP, unemployment rises sharply and the price level increases. This combination of rising unemployment and higher inflation is known as *stagflation*. This is what happened throughout the developed economies in 1973–74 and again in 1979.

The immediate policy response to the oil crisis was to try to maintain the level of aggregate demand by increasing government spending without any corresponding increase in the level of taxation. However, an expansionary fiscal policy is not an adequate response to the oil price shock. An expansionary fiscal policy will shift the AD curve in figure 5.2 upwards to the right (not shown). The result will be an increase in real output but also an increase in the price level. Hence the fiscal policy exasperates the inflation problem.

In 1975 the government recognised the need to dampen the inflationary pressures that were building up. Food subsidies and tax cuts were introduced in a mini-budget in

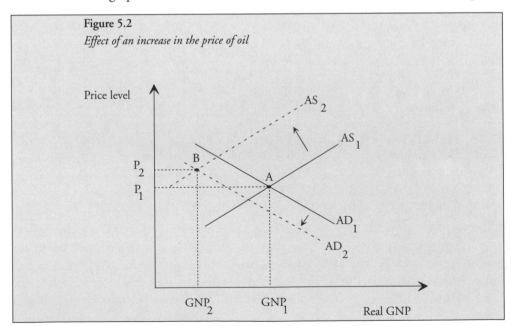

Figure 5.2

Effect of an increase in the price of oil

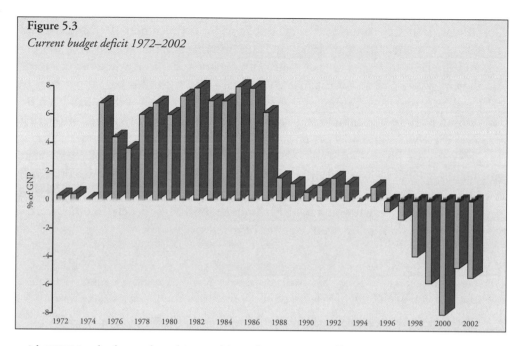

Figure 5.3
Current budget deficit 1972–2002

mid-1975 in the hope that this would moderate wage inflation. In fact it increased the current budget deficit and added to inflationary pressures. By 1975, the current budget deficit and the EBR increased to 6.8 per cent and 15.8 per cent of GNP respectively (figures 5.3 and 5.4). The national debt/GNP ratio increased from 54 to 70 percent (figure 5.5).

In a reversal of policy in 1976 the finance minister (Richie Ryan) raised taxes and curbed expenditure as the economy began to recover. A wealth tax was introduced, the upper income tax band was raised to 80 per cent and VAT on wine, spirits and petrol were introduced. (This earned him the title 'Minister for Hardship' and 'Red Richie' in the media.) As a result of these corrective measures, combined with a recovery in economic growth, the current budget deficit fell to 3.6 per cent of GNP, and the EBR to 9.7 per cent, in 1977. It appeared that the economy had weathered the oil crisis and the public finances were moving in the right direction.

In fact the structural problems created by the oil price shock remained unresolved and Ireland, like most other OECD countries, was still vulnerable to further increases in the price of oil. It was not until after the second oil price shock, at the end of the 1970s, that investment in energy conservation began in earnest.

1977–81: GOING FOR BROKE
The General Election of 1977 destroyed the chances of maintaining progress towards restoring order in the public finances. The political parties vied with one another in promising to cut taxes and raise expenditure. (Both major parties claimed credit for proposing the idea of abolishing rates on private houses.) The incoming Fianna Fáil government exceeded their manifesto commitments to tax cuts and increased expenditure.

Minister for Finance, George Colley, in his 1978 budget, increased income tax allowances, public sector pay and rates and the wealth tax were abolished. A total of

11,250 new posts were authorised in the public sector between mid-1977 and the end of 1978. As a result of these measures, the current budget deficit increased to 6.3 per cent and the EBR to 13 per cent of GNP. This occurred at a time when the economy was already growing at an unsustainable rate: real GNP expanded by 7.0 per cent in 1977 and was forecast to continue to grow rapidly in 1978 even if there had been no fiscal stimulus. Employment and real earnings were increasing rapidly and for the first time ever there was substantial net immigration to Ireland.

The rationale for the 1978 budget was, firstly, the need to reduce unemployment which, although falling, was still above its 1973 level. Secondly, the policy was described as a 'self-financing fiscal boost'. That is, the increase in the real growth rate would generate extra taxes, which would quickly eliminate the budget deficit. In other words, the expansionary fiscal policy would 'pump-prime' the economy.

Note:

This period in economic policy has been the subject of much criticism, some of it quite colourful. For example, Kevin Myers, in a profile of the civil servant Tom Barrington wrote,

> Fortunately for his mental health, his retirement came in 1977, the year in which Irish politics lurched from mere slovenly venality and genial incompetence to outright criminality. The economy of the country was debauched and local government effectively destroyed: the most brilliant civil service cannot stop credulous electorates choosing recidivist delinquents to represent them, nor prevent the consequences of malfeasant policy.
>
> (*The Irish Times*, 20 April 1991)

Events between 1978 and 1980 confounded the hope that the budget deficit would be quickly eliminated. A second oil price shock occurred in 1979 and the price of crude oil rose to over $40 a barrel. The rate of growth of real GNP fell to 2.7 per cent in 1979

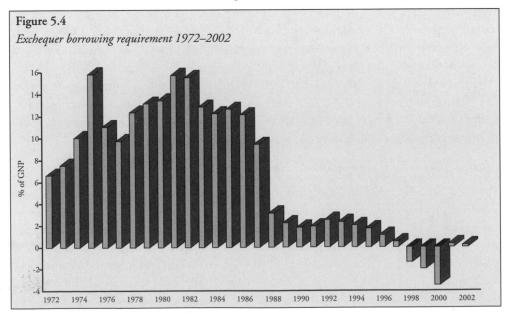

Figure 5.4

Exchequer borrowing requirement 1972–2002

and remained at that level in 1980. By 1981, the current budget deficit rose to 7.3 per cent and the EBR to 15.7 per cent of GNP. The national debt/GNP ratio increased to 93 per cent.

Of even greater significance was the fact that the real growth rate had fallen to 2 per cent, unemployment was up to 10 per cent and inflation rose to 20 per cent. Also the current account balance of payments deficit rose to 11 per cent of GNP. The Irish economy was in crisis.

The fiscal deficit was already so large and the level of the national debt was growing so rapidly that no scope remained for trying to offset the deflationary impact of the oil price increase through an expansionary fiscal policy.

Note:

The budget deficits incurred after 1973 and our resort to external borrowing to finance them had turned us into a net debtor country by 1980: the level of our external public debt had reached £2,207 million, whereas our official external reserves were only £1,346 million.

This episode illustrates many of the points made in chapter 4 concerning the problems of successfully implementing a stabilisation policy.

- There was confusion about how rapidly the economy was growing.
- The policies that were implemented began to take effect long after the conditions they were designed to address had changed.
- The desire of politicians to be elected prevailed over economic realities.

There was little general awareness of the speed with which the country was being plunged into debt and the implications for the future tax burden. Some economists argued that there was no need to worry about further external borrowing because our international credit rating was still sound and additional borrowed money could be used

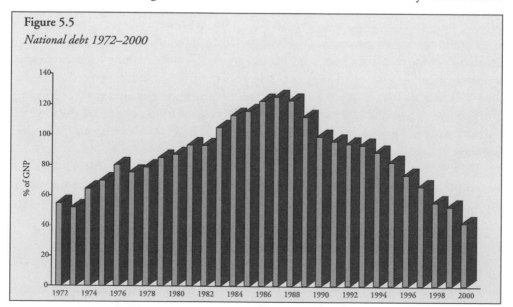

Figure 5.5
National debt 1972–2000

to generate employment and create valuable assets. But in reality much of the borrowed money was wasted; it went to finance day-to-day expenditure or projects with a rate of return that was much lower than the rate of interest. Further borrowing for such purposes was not warranted, regardless of the willingness of international bankers to lend to the country. Moreover, the growth of public sector debt throughout Eastern Europe, Africa and Latin America was to trigger off an international crisis in 1982, which completely changed the attitude of international creditors to countries in Ireland's situation.

1981–86: PICKING UP THE PIECES

In mid-1981 a new coalition government consisting of Fine Gael and the Labour Party was elected and in early 1982 a deflationary budget was introduced to try to correct the deteriorating fiscal situation. The Minister for Finance, John Bruton promised to phase out the budget deficit over four years. A VAT rate of 18 per cent was imposed on children's clothing and footwear. Excise duties, income tax, postal and phone charges were all increased and income tax allowances were reduced. The independent socialist TD for Limerick East, Jim Kemmy, could not support the tax on children's footwear and he defected to the opposition benches. The budget was defeated by 82 votes to 81 votes. John Bruton remains the only finance minister not to have his budget ratified by the Dáil.

This led to another general election and a minority Fianna Fáil government supported by the Workers Party was returned to office. In November 1982, the Workers Party withdrew their support and another general election saw the return of a Fine Gael, Labour Party coalition.

The emphasis was placed on tax increases, rather than cuts in current expenditure, to reduce the deficit. This set the pattern for several subsequent attempts to restore order to the public finances. However, in 1982 due to the absence of revenue buoyancy the current budget deficit actually increased to 7.9 per cent of GNP and the EBR to 15.5 per cent of GNP. This outcome (higher taxation leading to larger rather than smaller current budget deficits) was to be repeated in subsequent years.

The financial and economic crisis continued to intensify. By 1983, the national debt/GNP ratio reached 113 per cent, the real growth rate was a minus 1.8 per cent and unemployment was up to 14 per cent. The gravity of the economic crisis facing the country was now widely appreciated. The main political parties agreed that restoring order to the public finances had to take precedence over trying to reduce the level of unemployment. The policy *instrument* (fiscal policy) had taken over from the policy *objectives* (growth, unemployment and inflation).

The coalition government tried to tackle the problem over the period 1982–86 both by raising the level of taxation and reducing current expenditure, but without much success for the following reasons.

- A ban on public sector recruitment did not bring the wage bill under control.
- Rising unemployment caused social welfare (transfer payments) to increase.
- The accumulating national debt and rising interest rates caused debt interest payments to increase.

Higher tax rates did not yield more revenue due to the stagnation of the economy and the Laffer-type effects we discussed in chapter 4. The most striking illustration of the failure of the tax strategy was provided by Minister for Finance, Alan Dukes' 1983 budget. This set a record for tax increases but produced hardly any reduction in the current budget deficit.

The result was that by 1986 the current budget deficit rose to 8.3 per cent and the EBR had fallen to 12.1 per cent. The coalition government obviously found it easier to reduce the capital budget deficit than the current deficit. The debt/GNP ratio also rose from 105 to 128 per cent.

In the autumn of 1986, disappointing exchequer returns led to further loss of confidence in the economy, which was manifested in nervousness on the foreign exchange markets and a 3 per cent increase in Irish relative to UK interest rates. This episode marked the beginning of the end of the attempt to reduce the level of borrowing through higher taxation.

It had become clear to all but a small minority that this strategy was self-defeating. The economy was shrinking under the increasing burden of taxation and capital was fleeing the country for more benign environments. (It is estimated that the private capital outflow reached over £1 billion in 1986 despite exchange controls.) The public finances were on a downward spiral due to falling revenue and rising transfer payments. It was generally accepted that the problem had to be tackled through drastic cuts in expenditure rather than further tax increases, but the coalition government split and fell on this issue. The cuts in current expenditure proposed by the Minister for Finance, John Bruton, in the draft *Book of Estimates* in October 1986 were not acceptable to his Labour Party partners in government, who still favoured maintaining a high level of expenditure and trying to reduce the deficit by increasing taxation.

1987–91: ORDER RESTORED

The formation of a minority Fianna Fáil government in January 1987 initially increased the economic uncertainty. While in opposition the party had vehemently attacked what they had labelled the 'monetarist' or 'Thatcherite' policies of the coalition government. They fought the election with promises of *increased* government spending. However, once in office the new government, with the support of the main opposition parties, tackled the problem of curbing government expenditure head-on. In the 1987 budget, the Minister for Finance, Ray MacSharry, reduced current government spending by more than had been proposed by Fine Gael in the draft *Book of Estimates* that had led to the downfall of the coalition government (earning him the nickname 'Mac the Knife'). There were cuts in public spending, a public sector pay freeze, an embargo on public sector recruitment and the tax burden increased by 9.5 per cent.

The restoration of order in the public finances gained momentum in the January 1988 budget when an unprecedented 3 per cent reduction in government spending was passed. This cut in expenditure was with the support or abstention of the main opposition parties and came to be known as the *Tallaght Strategy*. (So called after a speech supporting the cuts was made by the opposition leader Alan Dukes in Tallaght,

Co. Dublin.) By the end of 1988, the current budget deficit fell to 1.6 per cent and the EBR to 2.9 per cent of GNP (figures 5.3 and 5.4).

The 1988 budget also proposed a tax amnesty (known as the *Tax Incentive Scheme*), with the objective of collecting £30 million in unpaid taxes. In fact, during 1988 over £500 million was raised from this source and from the application of a new system of self-assessment of income tax to the self-employed. These amounts far exceeded the most optimistic forecasts. In addition, other sources of revenue (VAT and excises) were buoyant and expenditure was held below the level projected in the budget.

Expansionary fiscal contraction

The performance of the Irish economy during the period 1987 to 1990 was extraordinary. Despite the deflationary fiscal policy, the rate of growth of GNP increased markedly. The fact that a reduction in the fiscal deficit was associated with an increase in economic growth seemed to refute the conventional Keynesian view of fiscal policy.

It has been claimed that the Irish experience during these years is an example of an *expansionary fiscal contraction* (EFC). (The phrase 'expansionary fiscal contraction' was first coined by F. Giavazzi and M. Pagano, 'Can Severe Fiscal Contraction be Expansionary? Tales of Two Small European Countries', *Macroeconomics Annual*, eds. O. Blanchard and S. Fischer, National Bureau of Economic Research, 1990). To explain the EFC argument consider the equilibrium condition in the goods and services market:

$$GNP = TE \equiv C + I + G + NX \tag{1}$$

That is, GNP equals total expenditure which, in turn, can be broken down into consumer expenditure (C), investment (I), government expenditure (G) and net exports (NX).

According to EFC, the contraction in G is more than offset by increases in C or I, with the result that there was a net *increase* in aggregate demand. Briefly, the EFC argument is that the economy was facing a crisis of confidence arising from the lack of credibility of the government's commitment to restoring order to the public finances. This had led to capital flight and a widening interest rate differential between Ireland and Britain. Once the financial markets became convinced that the government was intent on reducing the borrowing requirement, the capital outflow subsided, and this facilitated a reduction in domestic interest rates. Increased confidence and lower interest rates led to a recovery in C and I, which helped offset the contractionary effects of fiscal retrenchment.

However, other factors also played a role in the recovery. These included the collapse of world oil prices, higher farm prices, and the accelerating growth in the UK economy. These were reinforced by an improvement in our international competitiveness following the successful 8 per cent devaluation of the Irish pound in August 1986. This devaluation contributed to an upsurge in net exports in 1987. Moreover, interest rates began to fall in the wake of the devaluation, *before* the 1987 budget.

The 1990s

During the 1990s, especially after 1993, Ireland experienced an unprecedented combination of rapid growth and low inflation. The stance of fiscal policy moved away from the failed stabilisation policies of earlier years. Policy became dominated by the objective of qualifying for membership of European Monetary Union (EMU) in 1999. This entailed achieving a government deficit of less than 3 per cent of GDP and a debt/GDP of 60 per cent. In May 1998, Ireland was deemed to have met the entry criteria and was invited to join the single currency club.

Another dimension to fiscal policy was the various national wage agreements introduced in 1987. This is an agreement between government, employers and trade unions, whereby in return for low wage increases, the government gives a commitment to cut taxes at budget time. For example, the *Programme for Prosperity and Fairness* (PPF), is a three-year agreement signed in 2000. It covers approximately 500,000 workers out of total employment of 1,819,000. It was amended in late 2000 following an unanticipated rise in inflation and a special 2 per cent inflation-compensation award was paid in April 2001.

As a result of the wage agreements, tax rates have fallen quite significantly. In 1987, for example, there where three rates of tax: standard rate of 35 per cent, middle rate of 48 per cent and a higher rate of 58 per cent. In 2002, there are two rates of tax, a standard rate of 20 per cent and a higher rate of 42 per cent. It is estimated that these lower tax rates combined with increases in tax allowances have added approximately 1.8 per cent per annum to real (inflation adjusted), disposable (after tax) income.

EARLY 2000S

In 1997, the real growth rate was 7.7 per cent, unemployment was at 10.3 per cent and inflation was down to 1.5 per cent. As the economy continued to boom, the Minister for Finance, Charlie McCreevy in his 1997 budget reduced income and corporation tax, increased spending on social welfare, education, health and infrastructure. This was repeated in subsequent years. In his 1999 budget the minister introduced tax cuts of €1.89 billion and the 2000 budget involved injecting €5 billion in expenditure and tax cuts into the economy. Despite this fiscal stimulus, in 2000 a current budget *surplus* of 7.1 per cent and an exchequer balance (negative EBR) of 2.5 per cent of GNP were recorded. Such is the power of a booming economy and the built-in stabilisers. The national debt/GNP ratio had also fallen to 54 per cent.

There was considerable controversy over the so-called *individualisation* measures introduced in the 1999 budget. This is where the tax allowance for a married couple, two persons working, is greater than the allowance for a married couple, one person working. The second working person in a marriage can earn €14,000 and pay tax at the standard rate. Normally, the second working person would pay tax at the higher rate. However, this tax allowance cannot be claimed if there is only one person working. The main purpose of the individualisation measure was to increase the incentive for people working at home to join the labour force. That is, increase the labour force participation rate (the proportion of the population in the labour force). Opponents of the scheme felt it discriminated against people working at home and that the scheme was not backed by other measures such as subsidies for child care facilities.

The stance of fiscal policy was relatively expansionary in the second half of the 1990s. It was *pro-cyclical*, tending to fuel the flames of the strong expansion that is already under way. This shortcoming of fiscal policy was a source of concern. However, the Minister for Finance, Charlie McCreevy, argued in 2002 that the measures in his five budgets would increase the supply-side of the economy and facilitate the expansion of the demand-side of the economy.

Mr McCreevy's *supply-side enhancing fiscal policy* was justified on two grounds. First, the tax cuts increase the incentive to work and thereby encourage more people into employment. Lower tax rates, increased allowances, a widening of the tax bands and the 'individualisation policy' made accepting a job a more attractive proposition. This strategy may be given some credit for the 15% rise in employment between 1997–2002.

The tax cuts also underpinned the moderate pay increases provided for in national wage agreements, which contributed to industrial peace and improved international competitiveness.

The second argument relates to capital expenditure. This type of expenditure increases the physical and human capital stock and the productive capacity of the economy. By 2000 capital spending had risen by 237 per cent since 1997. Within this, capital spending on education increased by 271 per cent, health by 191 per cent and the environment by 182 per cent. In contrast, current expenditure rose by 52 per cent and public sector pay and the pensions bill by 54 per cent.

Despite the tax cuts and expenditure increases, the minister was still able to show a substantial surplus in 2000 and 2001. However in 2002 the approach ran into trouble. The sharp fall in the economy's growth rate and the effect of the cuts in income tax in earlier years led to a slump in tax revenue. Instead of projected growth of 14 per cent receipts rose by only 1 per cent. Even allowing for the conjuring trick in Budget 2002 of obtaining €610 million from the Central Bank of Ireland, €500 million from the Capital Services Redemption Account (used to repay the national debt) and €635 million from the Social Insurance Fund (used to pay social welfare payments), the outturn was a deficit.

Mr McCreevy's expansionary Budget 2001 provoked a reprimand from the European Commission and from the finance ministers of EU member states. Newspaper headlines announced, 'Guardians of euro give best pupil a serious dressing down' (*The Irish Times*, 25 January 2001). The EU Commission points out that real GNP growth in Ireland in 2000 was 10.4 per cent, unemployment was down to 4.3 per cent and inflation was at 5.6 per cent. Their view is that the Irish economy was over-heating. Fiscal policy, they argue, is primarily a demand-side phenomenon, which, in the short-term, will exasperate the inflation problem.

Mr McCreevy was not, however, without his own supporters. At the Davos summit in January 2001, the 'spiritual father of the euro', Nobel prize-winning economist Robert Mundell endorsed the strategy by saying the tax cuts were 'exactly correct'.

This debate has become less meaningful as events transpired and the slowdown in the American economy in 2001 reduced the Irish economic growth rate to 4.6 per cent in 2001 and 1.8 per cent in 2002. But as the economy slowed down there was little scope for adopting expansionary fiscal policies. Critics of Mr McCreevy argue that it would have been better to have used the exceptional period of the late-1990s to prepare for less favourable times in the future.

5.4 CONCLUSION

In this chapter, we have reviewed the stance of fiscal policy since the 1970s. We showed that:

- The timing of fiscal policy has been pro-cyclical, i.e. it has tended to amplify rather than dampen the business cycle
- The most conspicuous effect of deficit spending was to increase the burden of the national debt
- Since the late 1980s we succeeded in reducing the debt/GDP ratio and meeting the fiscal criteria required to gain admission to the Eurozone.

None the less, recent fiscal policy has continued to be pro-cyclical, fuelling the fires of an already fast-growing economy and paying too little attention to the need to keep something in reserve for less favourable times in the future.

CHAPTER 6

Money and Banking

6.1 INTRODUCTION

The initial sections in this chapter discuss the functions of money and the types of money used in modern economies. We outline the role of the banking system in the money creation process. This is followed by an account of the role and functions of a central bank. The concluding section explains how the central bank controls the money supply.

6.2 WHAT IS MONEY?

Money performs four basic functions. The most important of these is its role as a *medium of exchange*. It also serves as a *unit of account*, a *standard of deferred payment*, and a *store of value*. We discuss each of these functions in turn.

MEDIUM OF EXCHANGE

Without money an economy would have to operate on a *barter* system: all transactions would involve the exchange of goods and services directly for other goods and services. A farmer, for example, would have to exchange the output of his farm for clothes and other necessities. A doctor, in return for medical services, would receive goods or services from her patients. Such a system would involve enormous transaction costs. To complete a transaction there would have to be a *double coincidence of wants*: each party to a deal would have to want what the other was offering. A hungry doctor and a sick farmer, for example, would be able to do business. If an economics lecturer wanted a haircut he would have to find a hairdresser who wanted an economics lecture. Clearly, in practice, most people would find it difficult to complete a transaction. As a result, intermediaries would tend to become involved and the cost of transactions would increase.

Adam Smith in *The Wealth of Nations* (1776) gave a famous illustration of the benefits of the division of labour based on the working of a pin factory. By *specialising* in the production of a single item, the workforce became very efficient and output increased significantly. However, under a barter system the cost of transactions would deter people from specialising. They would be forced to be *self-sufficient* and prevented from concentrating on a particular skill or trade. Occupations requiring a high degree of specialisation such as engineering, accountancy and teaching would not come into existence. As a consequence, productivity would remain low. Barter is costly and inefficient and almost all societies have abandoned it in favour of money.

In a money economy, goods and services can be sold for money that can be used to purchase other goods and services. The use of money as a *medium of exchange* is a very significant progression away from barter. It greatly reduces the cost of doing business and encourages people to specialise and trade. It allows people to specialise in what they do most efficiently, selling the output that is surplus to their needs and buying what they want with the proceeds. This is an infinitely more efficient arrangement than a barter system. Far from being 'the root of all evil', the use of money is of major benefit to all societies!

UNIT OF ACCOUNT

Once people become involved in trading, they need a *unit of account* in which to quote prices and compare whether something is dear or cheap relative to other items. Money serves this important function. Usually the same currency is used as a medium of exchange and a unit of account. It is possible, however, to use a unit of account that is not actually in circulation as money. The International Monetary Fund (IMF), for example, uses SDR's (special drawing rights) in its dealings with member states. A number of multinational firms operating in Ireland use dollars as their unit of account. In horse racing, the One Thousand Guineas is a classic race but no bets are accepted or paid out in guineas any more.

STANDARD OF DEFERRED PAYMENT AND STORE OF VALUE

These functions allow us to link the present with the future when doing business. Loans, leases and other contracts can specify amounts of money to be paid in the future (standard of deferred payment). People can save some of their income as cash (store of value) and use it to purchase things in the future. This is useful, but there are risks involved. In inflationary periods money loses its value over time. If inflation gets out of control, people will learn to specify contracts in a manner that takes account of inflation (this is called indexation). Similarly, people will look to other assets (foreign currencies, land, works of art, old stamps) to use as a store of value. However, all these ways of coping with inflation involve costs. Thus inflation is a threat to the efficiency of a modern economy.

6.3 TYPES OF MONEY

Over the centuries, money has taken many forms in different countries. Whales' teeth in Fiji, feather money in Santa Cruz, dogs' teeth in the Admiralty Islands, boar tusk in New Guinea, beeswax in Borneo, tea brick currency in Mongolia, reindeer in Asiatic Russia, salt money in Ethiopia, silk and salt in China, and cocoa beans in Mexico, to mention a few. There are two basic types of money, namely, *commodity* money and *token* money.

Note:
The origins of the 'pound sterling' go back over 900 years as the following letter published in *The Irish Times* points out:

> Sir, I am afraid your correspondent (name withheld) has got the wrong end of the stick. He disdains the use of the term 'sterling' to mean the British pound on the grounds that this is just a propaganda term meaning 'the real thing'. On the contrary, English silver penny coins were called 'sterlings' as much as 900 years ago.

Thus the pound sterling was, originally, a pound weight of sterlings. It was because of the high quality of these sterlings that — from the late 17th century on — the term came to mean something like 'the real thing'. Soon thereafter the gold guinea, and then the sovereign, wholly replaced silver coins in England, but the term 'sterling' survived. The connotation of excellence has, of course, been rather tarnished in more recent times. What's in a name? Mention of the guinea brings to mind the currency of Guinea, called the Syli, and which had the misfortune to live up to its name, before it was eventually replaced. When it comes to our own currency, I confess to a preference (unless *as Gaeilge*) for 'pound' rather than 'punt', if only to avoid the connotation of something small and flat-bottomed, prone to sinking if not looked after properly.

(Patrick Honohan, *The Irish Times*, 7 December 1997)

COMMODITY MONEY

It was natural that intrinsically valuable commodities would be the first money. Cattle were used in many early societies, including Ireland. (The Latin word for cattle is *pecus* and for money *pecunia*, whence the English word 'pecuniary'.) Over the centuries silver and gold emerged as the preferred form of commodity money. Their durability, divisibility and scarcity ensured that their value would remain stable. The main disadvantage of commodity money is that it ties up the commodity used as money and diverts it from other uses. When silver is used to make coins, the supply of silver to jewellers and other users is reduced.

TOKEN MONEY

This is money that does not have any intrinsic value. The notes and coins in circulation in Ireland today fall into this category. Their intrinsic value is very small compared to their value as a medium of exchange. For example, the paper in a €50 note is almost valueless as paper. Our so-called silver coins (used up until 2002) are in fact made from a cheap cupro-nickel alloy. No silver is wasted in making them. However, even though the 'silver' coins are made of very cheap metal, the process of minting them is quite expensive.

In the past, bank notes were convertible into something of intrinsic value, such as gold or silver, but this is generally no longer the case today. Inconvertible notes and coins made from paper and cheap metals are issued by governments and decreed to be the only legal tender that may circulate in their country. (Legal tender refers to the currency that must be accepted in payment of debts and taxes.) Because it derives its value ultimately from a government decree, it is known as *fiat money*.

CIRCULARITY IN ITS ACCEPTANCE

Whatever commodity, paper or coin is used as money, it must first achieve circularity in its acceptance. The only reason people accept paper money is because they are certain that they can use it to purchase goods and services at a later stage. If people had the slightest suspicion that paper money could not be spent, they would not accept it as payment. If token money is to be accepted it must not be easily reproduced or *counterfeited*. Counterfeiting can be a serious problem for a government because if it were practised on a large scale it would undermine the economy. As the following quote from John Maynard Keynes indicates, Vladimir Lenin asserted that the best way to undermine a society was to debauch the currency.

> Lenin is said to have declared that the best way to destroy the Capitalist System is to debauch the currency. Lenin was certainly right. There is no subtler, no surer means of overturning the existing basis of society than to debauch the currency. The process engages all the hidden forces of economic law on the side of destruction, and does it in a manner that not one man in a million is able to diagnose.

During World War II, the Germans attempted to flood Britain with forged currency in order to disrupt the war economy.

Note:

Forged currency can be very sophisticated and bears a close resemblance to the real thing. Soon after the new Irish £20 notes were issued in 1993, forged look-alikes were found in circulation. In Italy, forged euro notes appeared on the market *before* the new currency was officially issued in 2002. Shopkeepers in the US are often suspicious of being paid even moderate amounts in cash as opposed to credit cards. But not all forgery is sophisticated. Prior to the introduction of the euro, one of the authors discovered in his change a 10 pence coin battered down to look like a 50 pence coin. The forged coin has, however, six sides instead of the normal seven. It took a lot of hard work to make 40 pence profit!

When gold and silver coins were in circulation, debasing them in one way or another was brought to a fine art. Clipping referred to clipping small pieces off the edges of coins. The authorities responded by milling the circumference of coins. A second practice was sweating. People put gold coins into a bag and shook the bag vigorously. The dust at the bottom of the bag that flaked off the coins was the profit. Governments and monarchs were not above cheating by adding a cheap metal alloy to the precious metals in the manufacture of legal tender.

GRESHAM'S LAW

Sir Thomas Gresham (1519–79) was Queen Elizabeth I's currency dealer in Antwerp. He noticed that bad money tended to drive out good. This is known as *Gresham's law*. To understand the idea, consider what would happen if a country originally had coins minted with a high silver content (as was the case with the Irish florins and half-crowns until the 1940s). If the government puts into circulation coins of substantially lower silver content but with the same face value (as happened in the 1940s) the latter will quickly replace the former: anyone coming across an older coin, with a high silver content, will hoard it. As a result you will never receive an old two-shilling piece in change today: it is worth far more than 10 pence for its silver content.

In the US in the nineteenth century both gold and silver coins circulated as legal tender (this system is known as bimetallism). The ratio of the value of gold to silver was set at various ratios to try to ensure that both types of coins remained in circulation, but in 1873 silver was demonetised, leaving America on the gold standard. However, a

Whence it came and where it went

shortage of gold (restriction of the money supply) led to falling prices and recession. William Jennings Bryan ran for election to the Senate for the silver-producing state of Nevada in 1896 on the slogan 'We shall not crucify mankind on a cross of gold.' He lost! The new goldmines in the Klondike and South Africa provided enough gold to meet the demand for monetary purposes by the end of the nineteenth century.

6.4 THE BANKING SYSTEM IN A MODERN ECONOMY

Banks are deposit-taking institutions. They accept funds from the public and place them in accounts. There are two principal types of accounts: current (checking) and deposit (savings) accounts. In Ireland, prior to joining the European Monetary Union (EMU), there were two definitions of the money supply. The *narrow* definition was M1 = currency plus current accounts. The *broad* definition was called M3 = M1 plus deposit accounts. However, following EMU membership in 1999, the old definition of the Irish money supply was terminated. Instead, the term used is Ireland's *contribution* to the Eurozone's money supply.

Note:
No interest is paid on a current account, but cheques can be drawn on it. Interest is paid on money in a deposit account, but cheques cannot be drawn on it, and notice may be required before money can be withdrawn.

Table 6.1
Money supply, August 2001

	€ billions	% of M3
Currency	318.5	6.0
+ Overnight deposits	1,744.7	32.7
= M1	= 2,063.2	38.7
+ Deposits with agreed maturity up to 2 years	+ 1,091.5	20.5
+ Deposits redeemable at notice up to 3 months	+ 1,292.5	24.3
= M2	= 4,447.1	83.5
+ Repurchase agreements	223.1	4.2
+ Money market fund shares	497.6	9.3
+ Debt securities up to 2 years	149.8	2.8
= M3	5,327.6	100.0

Source: European Central Bank, *Monthly Bulletin*, October 2001, Table 2.4.

In the Eurozone, the definition of the money supply is different from what was previously used in Ireland. As table 6.1 shows there are now three measures of the money supply: M1, M2 and M3. These represent narrow and wide definitions of the money supply respectively. Instead of making a distinction between current and deposit accounts, the new Eurozone definition distinguishes between the *maturity* of various deposit accounts. The *overnight deposits* are very short-term deposits that attract little or no interest rate but are very liquid. These accounts are equivalent to current accounts in the old definition. M1 is equal to these overnight deposits plus currency in circulation.

'Deposits with an agreed maturity of two years' relates to accounts where the money is locked in for up to two years. These accounts are less liquid but they generally pay a higher rate of interest. 'Deposits redeemable at notice up to three months' is the equivalent of the old demand deposit accounts. Most banks do not insist on notice before a withdrawal is made. These accounts pay a lower rate of interest but are more liquid. When these two types of deposit accounts are added to M1 we obtain M2. Finally, adding repurchase agreements (an agreement to buy back government bonds and other securities), fund shares and debt securities to M2 gives M3.

A fundamental difference between the old Irish and the new Eurozone definitions of the money supply relates to Eurozone residents. The old Irish money supply related to Irish residents only. However, the new series includes Eurozone deposits in Ireland. Hence if a German firm or a Spanish bank or a French person has an account in Ireland, that money is now part of Ireland's contribution to the Eurozone's money supply.

Figure 6.1 shows the annual percentage change in M1, M2 and M3, since January 1999. It can be seen that the M1 series is more volatile than the other two series. This poses the question: which measure of the money supply should the central bank try to control?

The European Central Bank (ECB) has decided that the M3 definition should be used for policy purposes. As we shall see in chapter 7, changes in the money supply can

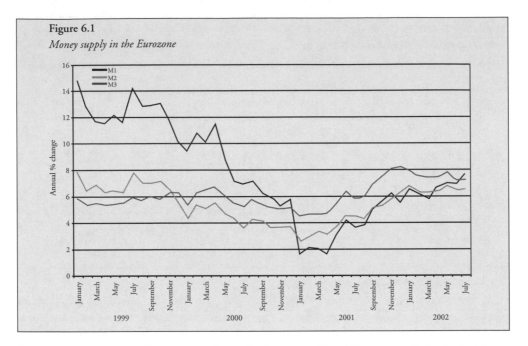

Figure 6.1
Money supply in the Eurozone

have an important influence on the inflation rate. For this reason, it is desirable to control the money supply in the economy.

THE FRACTIONAL RESERVE BANKING SYSTEM

Banks act as *financial intermediaries*; that is, they channel funds from savers to borrowers. This function gives them a key role in the money-creation process. To see this, consider the balance sheet of the European commercial banks (table 6.2). (To simplify the analysis, we use hypothetical data.) The important entry on the liability side is the deposit accounts. This money is owed to depositors and hence is a liability from the banks' perspective. On the asset side, there are entries for bank reserves, loans and advances. Reserves consist of the banks' holdings of currency, deposits with the ECB and government stock. Deposits with the ECB can be converted into cash immediately and used to meet depositors' demands. Government stock can be sold at short notice. Loans and advances consist of banks lending to the private sector, the government and other financial institutions. These loans cannot be called at short notice: the banks have to wait for them to mature in order to obtain cash for them.

Modern banking is based on a system of *fractional reserves*. The banks operate on the basis that it is not necessary to keep 100 per cent of deposits in cash. When €1 is deposited, the bank need keep only a fraction in reserve. The rest can be either lent out or used to purchase interest-bearing securities such as government stock or corporate bonds. Over time, new deposits are likely to match withdrawals so that all that is really necessary is to keep a small amount of 'till money' to meet occasional net outflows. If a bank has sufficient reserves to meet normal requirements, the public's confidence in it will remain high and the fractional reserve system will work well. The bank will earn interest from its loans and advances, and the public will enjoy the convenience of having money on deposit.

Table 6.2
Commercial banks' balance sheet, (hypothetical data) euro billions

Assets		Liabilities	
Reserves	900	Deposit accounts	30,000
Lending	21,000		
	30,000		30,000

Note:
The fractional reserve system was developed by the goldsmiths of the Middle Ages. People used to place gold and other valuables with them for safe-keeping. At first they simply stored the gold in a vault for a small fee and issued receipts that could be used at a later stage to reclaim the gold. However, it soon became apparent that it was most unlikely that all of the depositors would withdraw all of their gold at the same time. It was therefore possible to make profits by lending out money (gold) and charging interest on the loans. Of course, a certain proportion of the gold had to be kept on hand to meet any withdrawals that would arise. This would reassure depositors, and as long as they had confidence in the system, only a small proportion of the gold would actually be withdrawn. The rest could be put to work to earn interest for the goldsmiths turned bankers.

RESERVE REQUIREMENTS
To minimise the risk of default and failure, in most countries banks are required by law to keep minimum reserves in relation to deposits. They can keep excess reserves if they wish, but since they earn less on their reserves than on other assets, they tend not to do so.

In Europe, the ECB sets a required liquidity ratio known as the *minimum reserve*. This ratio applies to all banks and financial institutions. In 2002 the minimum reserve stipulates that 2 per cent of 'relevant resources' must be kept in reserve.

Minimum reserve ratio = 2 per cent of relevant resources

'Relevant resources' comprise of mainly short-term deposits (overnight and up to two years agreed maturity). The reserve requirement does not apply to deposits with over two years maturity. Thus, for every €100 the banks have in current and deposit accounts, a minimum of €2 must be kept in notes and coins plus deposits at the ECB. The purpose of the minimum reserve ratio is to ensure that the banks have adequate liquid assets to meet demands for cash by their depositors.

BANK PROFITS AND BAD DEBTS
The rate of interest paid by banks on deposits is lower than the rate they charge on loans. For example, in 2001 the commercial banks in Ireland paid 0.1 to 1.0 per cent on deposits less than €5,000 and charged 11.5 12.75 per cent to category A borrowers (i.e. personal and retail borrowings) on term loans. This *interest differential* is the main source of bank profits. (Banks charge for all transactions to cover their day-to-day operating costs. There are nearly thirty different types of charges relating to a current account.)

Note:
Bank profits were the subject of much criticism by the public. The Irish Banks' Standing Committee (IBSC) was set up in 1920, comprised of representatives of both southern and northern banks, to agree common interest rates and bank charges. This suggested that a cartel had been formed with the objective of making supra-normal profits from bank customers. Criticism focused, in particular, on the spread between deposit and lending rates. It was pointed out that deposit rates were lower and lending rates higher than similar rates in the UK. The concern at the outflow of large deposits from Ireland to the UK added weight to this argument. The IBSC continues to exist, but it no longer sets interest rates for the banks, and its influence has been eroded by the entry of new financial institutions into the banking market.

Bank profits are reduced by bad debts, that is, loans that are not repaid. Obviously, the lower the provision that has to be made for bad debts, the higher bank profits will be. As the economy booms, the banks suffer less from bad debts, but during a slump bad debts mount.

To minimise bad debts, banks screen and monitor borrowers very carefully. Yet bankers are influenced by the psychology of the moment, and when a boom in property or land starts they lend to speculators to buy at prices that are unjustified by the underlying value of the assets being bought. When boom turns to bust, the value of the assets used as collateral falls, and even if a bank forecloses it cannot realise its loans. There has been much criticism of bankers in several countries for the role they played in the property boom of the 1980s. In several countries — the US and France, for example – these booms ended in the banks being bailed out at taxpayers' expense. In Japan the big banks loaned money for office properties that fell sharply in value in the 1990s, resulting in large-scale panics and bank failures.

When very large banks become insolvent governments feel they must be rescued because otherwise they might bring the whole financial system crashing down. This is known as the 'Too Big To Fail' syndrome. But if governments bail out banks that have lent money recklessly there is a *moral hazard*: why should the banks worry about taking risks? If things go right they will make big profits; if things go wrong someone else will pick up the cost! The risk that bailing out banks encourages them to take imprudent risks is known as a moral hazard.

6.5 MONEY CREATION IN A MODERN ECONOMY

In a modern economy, where bank money is the most important type of money and the banks operate on fractional reserves, an inflow of cash will cause a *multiple expansion* of the money supply. This process is illustrated by the simplified example in table 6.3. It is assumed that (a) there is only one bank in the country, (b) that the minimum reserve requirement is 10 per cent, and (c) that the bank does not keep any excess reserves. On the liability side of the balance sheet are deposits. On the asset side, there are entries for bank reserves and bank lending.

Let us explore what happens when there is a net inflow of reserves (cash) to the bank. Suppose someone receives €1,000 from abroad in return for some service and

Table 6.3
Money creation with fractional reserve banking

				Commercial banks' balance sheet			
Assets				*Liabilities*			
Increases in round:	1	2	3		1	2	3
Reserves	100	90	81	Deposits	1,000	900	810
Loans	900	810	729				

deposits it in the bank. Given the 10 per cent reserve requirement, the bank will keep €100 in reserve and can make a loan of €900. Suppose the loan of €900 is used to purchase a car. A local garage receives €900 in exchange for the car and lodges it with its bank. Hence the car loan has, in the second round, resulted in the creation of a deposit of €900. The bank again keeps 10 per cent (€90) of the new deposit in reserve and loans out the remainder (€810). The process need not end there. The borrower of €810 from the bank purchases a CD player from a local store. The store, in turn, deposits the €810 with its bank. Once again the bank will keep 10 per cent in reserves and lend out the rest. This process will go on, but the amount loaned out at each successive stage dwindles.

Table 6.4 shows what happens to M3 as this process unfolds. As bank deposits increase in each round, so too does the money supply. Given a minimum reserve ratio of 10 per cent, the initial €1,000 deposit will eventually lead to a €10,000 increase in the money supply. However, if somewhere along the line someone hoarded the money and kept it out of the banking system, then the expansion of the money supply would halt. The money-creation process only works when the money lent out finds its way

Table 6.4
The process of money creation with fractional reserve banking

Round	ΔM	=	Δ Deposits
	€		€
1	1,000		1,000
2	900		900
3	810		810
4	729		729
.	.	.	
n	.	.	
Total	10,000		10,000

Note: The symbol Δ denotes the change in the magnitude.

back into a bank as a deposit. (Of course, the process also works in reverse. If a bank loses reserves, there will be a multiple contraction of credit.)

MONEY MULTIPLIER

The final increase in the money supply can be calculated using a formula for the money multiplier.

Money multiplier (m) = 1/minimum reserve requirement

In the above example, m = 1/0.1 = 10, so that

Change in M3 = (m) × (initial increase in reserves)

€10,000 = 10 × €1,000

Note that the higher the minimum reserve requirement, the lower the money multiplier. A reserve requirement of 20 per cent (0.2), for example, gives a money multiplier of five, but a reserve requirement of 3 per cent (0.03) gives a money multiplier of 33.3. The less money that has to be held in the form of reserves, the greater the final increase in the money supply following an initial increase in reserves. However, we must bear in mind that this example is based on a very unrealistic example in which people do not increase their holdings of currency. In section 6.7 a more realistic example, which allows for currency leakage, is worked out.

Note:

The money multiplier should not be confused with the *fiscal* multiplier discussed in chapter 3. The fiscal multiplier relates increases in aggregate demand to increases in real GNP, whereas the money multiplier relates a change in a bank's reserves to the final change in the money supply.

6.6 THE ROLE OF A CENTRAL BANK

With the launch of European Monetary Union (EMU) in 1999 the monetary policy of the participating countries has been taken over by the European Central Bank (ECB), located in Frankfurt. The Central Bank of Ireland no longer sets Irish monetary policy. The ECB decides what the policy should be for the Eurozone as a whole. This is often referred to as a 'one size fits all' monetary policy. In chapters 15 and 16, we discuss the ECB's monetary policies in more detail.

The main functions of a central bank are:

* To issue the currency in the economy
* To act as banker to both the commercial banks and the government
* To supervise the orderly operation of the financial system
* To conduct monetary and exchange rate policies so as to safeguard the integrity of the country's money.

Table 6.5 shows the structure of the ECB's balance sheet using hypothetical data. The liability side of the balance sheet contains euro currency in circulation. The ECB has the sole authority to issue currency. The ECB also accepts deposits from both the commercial banks and the government. In effect, the ECB serves as a 'bankers' bank'

Table 6.5
European Central Bank balance sheet: (hypothetical data) € billions

Assets		Liabilities	
External reserves	500	Currency	350
Loans:		Commercial bank reserves	300
Banks	130		
Government	20	Government deposits	300
Government securities	140		
Other	10	Other	50
Total	1,000	Total	1,000

and the government's banker. (The national central banks act as the ECB's agent in each member state.)

On the asset side, the most important entry is the *official external reserves*. These are the Eurozone's official holdings of foreign currency, gold and other reserves. This is in effect what backs the euro currency. The ECB is willing to exchange foreign currency, such as sterling, dollars and yen, for euro and, conversely, to buy back euro with these currencies. It is the fact that euro can be converted into other currencies that maintains confidence in the currency.

Complementing its deposit-taking role, the ECB also provides loans to both the commercial banks and the government. The other important entry on the asset side is the ECB's holdings of government bonds. As discussed below, the ECB can influence the money supply in the Eurozone through buying and selling government bonds.

Two important issues relating to the above functions are *seigniorage* and *lender of last resort*. Consider first seigniorage. A central bank is a profitable institution. The surplus of the income earned on Europe's official external reserves and from net lending over the ECB's operating expenses (profit) is turned over to the national governments. However, the ECB is also able to raise revenue (or reduce its liabilities) by printing money. This, and the related concept of an *inflation tax*, is explained in box 6.1.

An important function related to its role as banker to the commercial banks is the role of lender of last resort. To understand what this entails, recall that commercial banks do not have all of their depositors' money available on demand. Most of it is given out in short- and medium-term loans that cannot be called in immediately. However, the central bank is ready to lend to banks that need cash to redeem their obligations to depositors. This ultimately ensures that the banks can operate on fractional reserves and still retain the confidence of their depositors. But while the central bank can act as a lender of last resort in times of crisis and provide the liquidity that stops a run on the banks, it is important that it should not encourage the banks to lend money recklessly. Monitoring the solvency of the banks is therefore an important responsibility of the central bank.

Box 6.1
Seigniorage and the inflation tax

Seigniorage refers to the revenue raised by a government or central bank through issuing money. The inflation tax refers to the revenue accruing to government as a result of inflation. The two concepts are closely linked.

Let us first define seigniorage. The term comes from the French word *seigneur*, meaning lord. In the Middle Ages, feudal lords had the right to mint coins on their estates. Today, central banks have a monopoly on this right. A central bank can issue money by purchasing bonds, for example, on the open market and paying for them with a cheque drawn on itself. Anyone selling a bond to the central bank is happy to accept the bank's cheque because they can lodge it with their bank without any difficulty. (The bank gains reserves by accepting the lodgement of a cheque drawn on the central bank, and the money supply increases.) The central bank has now gained an interest-earning asset (the bond) in exchange for an increase in its non-interest-earning deposits. The profit the central bank makes by expanding the money supply in this way is eventually transferred to the government.

Consider now what is meant by an inflation tax. As we shall see in our discussion of the quantity theory of money in chapter 7, an increase in the money supply will increase the inflation rate. This reduces the *real* value or the purchasing power of money. For example, if the annual inflation rate is 10 per cent, then €100 today will buy 10 per cent less goods and services in a year's time. Hence, inflation acts as a form of tax on holders of money. The fall in the real value or purchasing power of the money supply benefits the central bank and government by reducing the real value of their liabilities. The losers are, of course, the public who hold money and see its purchasing power decline.

BANK SOLVENCY

If a rumour got around that the bank had made unsound loans, depositors would converge on the bank and ask to withdraw their money. The bank would not be able to meet depositors' demands and would have to close its doors to get time to convert its loans and other assets into cash. If it could not do so, it might have to cease trading. When a bank fails like this the depositors only receive a certain proportion of their money back. Bank failures were rare in the 1950s and 1960s, but have become more frequent recently. Examples include:

- Continental Illinois Bank of Chicago, one of America's largest banks, collapsed in 1984 as a result of losses on its loans.
- Bank of Credit and Commerce International (BCCI) in 1991 had its banking licence revoked first in the United States, then in Britain. Worldwide depositors lost billions of pounds in the largest bank collapse in history.
- Irish Trust Bank and Merchant Banking closed in 1976 and 1982, respectively. Depositors with these banks lost a significant proportion of their money.
- The Private Motorists Protection Association and the Insurance Corporation of Ireland (ICI), a wholly owned subsidiary of Allied Irish Banks were placed under administration in 1983 and 1985, respectively. It is believed that in the ICI case losses of around €127 million were incurred. These large losses were paid for by a levy on other insurance companies and by subventions from the Irish taxpayer.

(For an account of this episode see Patrick Honohan and Jane Kelly, 'The Insurance Corporation Collapse: Resolving Ireland's Worst Financial Crisis', *Administration*, Vol. 45, No. 3 (Autumn 1997), 67–77.)

6.7 HIGH-POWERED MONEY AND THE MONEY MULTIPLIER

The central bank's liabilities are referred to as *high-powered money* or the *monetary base*. The reserves of the commercial banks are included in this total. It is called high-powered because changes in reserves have a multiple or expanded impact on the money supply. Ignoring, for simplicity, government deposits and 'other liabilities' on the liability side of the central bank balance sheet (see table 6.5), high-powered money (H) is equal to currency (CU) plus commercial bank reserves at the Central Bank (RE).

$$H = CU + RE \qquad (1)$$

Using this definition we can now present a more complete version of the money multiplier than the simple one introduced earlier in section 6.5. We assume that people hold currency in proportion to their current and deposit accounts (D):

$$CU = c_p D \qquad (2)$$

where $0 < c_p < 1$. If c_p was equal to, say, 0.1, this means that for every €1 held in current and deposit accounts, the public holds 10 cent in currency.

Because of the minimum reserve ratio, commercial bank reserves at the central bank are also related to current and deposit accounts.

$$RE = r_b D \qquad (3)$$

Again, $0 < r_b < 1$. If the minimum reserve ratio were 10 per cent, r_b would be at least 0.1. The banks can, however, keep excess reserves if they wish. If equations (2) and (3) are inserted into equation (1), we obtain:

$$H = (c_p + r_b)D \qquad (4)$$

Recall now that M3 is equal to currency plus current and deposit accounts.

$$M3 = CU + D \qquad (5)$$

Substitute equation (2) into equation (5):

$$M3 = (c_p + 1)D \qquad (6)$$

The final step in deriving the relationship between M3 and H is to take the ratio of equation (6) to equation (4):

$$M3/H = (c_p + 1)/(c_p + r_b) \qquad (7)$$

or

$$M3 = (c_p + 1)/(c_p + r_b)H \qquad (8)$$

This version of the money multiplier relates high-powered money to the overall money supply and allows for currency leakages. If $c_p = 0$ (the public does not increase currency holdings as deposits increase) we obtain the earlier version of the multiplier.

We can calculate the money multiplier in the Eurozone August 2001. At that time, currency = €318 billion, bank reserves = €10.6 billion and deposits €6,250 billion.

$$c_p = CU/D = 318/6,250 = 0.05$$

$$r_b = RE/D = 125/6,250 = 0.02$$

The money multiplier is equal to

$$(c_p + 1)/(c_p + r_b) = (0.05 + 1)/(0.05 + 0.02) = 15$$

This means that an increase of €1 in high-powered money would lead to an increase of €15 in the money supply. An increase in currency holdings in relation to deposits (c_p) will reduce the money multiplier. Similarly, as we noted earlier, an increase in r_b will decrease the money multiplier.

High-powered money is increased whenever the ECB increases its assets or its liabilities. It follows, therefore, that if the ECB can control currency in circulation and bank deposits with the ECB, it should be able to control the money supply. In practice, however, controlling the money supply has proved to be a very difficult task. During the early 1980s UK economic policy relied heavily on trying to control sterling M3 by controlling the stock of high-powered money. However, control of high-powered money did not translate simply into control of the money supply. It was found that the money multiplier was very unstable, perhaps because the UK banking system was undergoing a profound transformation under deregulation.

There is also the possibility that if the ECB tries to control one definition of the money supply, the public will switch into near substitutes outside this definition to sidestep the control. This tendency has been called *Goodhart's law*, after Professor Charles Goodhart of the London School of Economics who drew attention to this problem.

Despite the problems of fine-tuning the money supply, international experience shows that it is not possible to have a sustained expansion of the money supply without an increase in the monetary base. Hence the ECB's balance sheet is at the centre of the stage of monetary policy in the Eurozone.

6.8 INSTRUMENTS OF MONETARY POLICY

The key role of a central bank is to 'protect the integrity of the nation's currency'. The key to success in this objective lies in maintaining price stability, that is, keeping inflation low. Central banks are judged successful if they achieve a low rate of inflation and, linked to this, prevent the currency from falling in value (depreciating) relative to other currencies.

The key to success in this area is generally seen as independence from political interference. That is, central bankers have to be free to take unpopular decision – such as raising interest rates — even if this is awkward for politicians facing elections. For that reason, the governors of central banks in Europe and the US are appointed for long-terms and cannot be removed by politicians.

Most central banks are of the opinion that there is a close link between changes in the money supply and inflation. This relationship is based on the *Quantity Theory of Money* (see chapter 7). If central banks can control the money supply, they can control the inflation rate.

Note:

We shall show in chapter 8 that here is a close relationship between the interest rate and the quantity of money the pubic wishes to hold. In practice, the main instrument of monetary policy relied on by modern central banks is the interest rate.

However, central banks can use a range of instruments to control the money supply or, more broadly, liquidity in the economy. These include the following devices.

OPEN MARKET OPERATIONS

This is by far the most important and most frequently used instrument of monetary policy. Open market operations consist of buying and selling government stock (bonds) on the 'open market' in order to influence the money supply. If the central bank buys government stock, it writes a cheque on itself that it gives to the seller of the bond. The bond seller then lodges this cheque in a bank deposit and the money creation process starts to unfold.

In terms of the ECB's balance sheet (table 6.5) the entry for government securities increases on the asset side and bank reserves increase on the liability side. The monetary base or high-powered money now increases and this sets off a multiple expansion in the money supply. Hence, by buying government stock, the central bank increases the money supply.

On the other hand, if the ECB sells government bonds, it reduces the money supply in the system. The person buying the bond pays the ECB by writing a cheque against his or her commercial bank's deposit account. In terms of the ECB's balance sheet, government securities go down on the asset side and bank reserves fall on the liability side. The fall in high-powered money leads to a multiple contraction in the money supply. Hence by selling stock, the central bank causes a reduction in the reserves of the banking system and in the money supply.

The American banking system represents a good example of how a central bank conducts open market operations. The principal asset held by the Federal Reserve Board is US government bonds. Purchases and sales of these through the Fed's *Open Market Committee* is the most important monetary policy-making instrument in the world. American interest rates have a major influence on interest rates all over the world, but foreign interest rates do not have much effect on them, so the Fed is relatively free to conduct an independent policy in this area.

THE MAIN REFINANCING INTEREST RATE

The interest rate a central bank charges on its lending to the commercial banks and the government has different names in different countries. In Britain it used to be known as the bank rate, then the minimum lending rate, but now the only rate set by the Bank of England is the bill discounting rate. In the US the rate charged by the Federal Reserve Board (Fed) to the commercial banks is known as the discount rate and the key interest rate targeted by the board is known as the Federal funds rate. The Fed influences this rate through its open market operations, that is it drives the market rate down by buying bonds and drives it up by selling them. In Germany the rate set by the Bundesbank was called the Lombard rate. In Ireland the rate set by the Central Bank of Ireland was called the short-term credit facility (STCF). The main ECB rate is known as the *main refinancing* (MRIR) interest rate.

The MRIR has a very important effect on all the interest rates (deposit and lending) set by the commercial banks in Europe. An increase in the MRIR discourages the banks from borrowing from the ECB and thus restricts lending throughout the economy. Conversely, a reduction in the MRIR encourages the banks to borrow from the ECB and this enables them to expand lending.

Moreover, the banks will pass an increase in the MRIR through to their customers. This allows the central bank to influence the whole structure of interest rates in the economy. More often than not, a central bank uses the MRIR to indicate its intentions or 'send a signal' to the commercial banks. When it raises the MRIR, this is taken as a signal to the commercial banks to curtail credit.

SETTING RESERVE REQUIREMENTS

The ECB sets the reserve requirements that apply to all the banks in Europe. The banks have to comply with these requirements or be penalised. The minimum reserve ratio is set well above the level deemed prudent from the banks' point of view and it ensures that they have sufficient liquid assets on hand to meet day-to-day withdrawals. If the central bank increases the reserve ratio the banks have to contract their lending in order to meet the new requirement. In fact, because it is a relatively blunt instrument that could lead to severe changes in liquidity, the reserve ratio is changed only infrequently.

CREDIT GUIDELINES

A central bank can try to dictate to the banks by how much they can increase their lending over a specified period of time. If the banks exceed the guideline, then they can be subject to penalties. Credit guidelines are asymmetrical in the sense that banks can be restrained from exceeding the ceiling but cannot be forced to go up to it. If the demand for credit is weak, banks will not be able to reach the ceiling. Credit guidelines were first used in Ireland in the mid-1960s and were abandoned in the 1980s. There are not used by the ECB and are not an important instrument of monetary policy.

6.9 CONCLUSION

In this chapter we introduced the subject of money and banking and reviewed their history in Ireland from the earliest times to the present. The main points discussed included:

- Money performs a number of functions. The most important is its role as a medium of exchange
- Fractional reserve banking
- How bank lending results in an increase in bank deposits
- How money is created
- The money multiplier
- The role of a central bank
- High powered money and the money multiplier
- How central banks control the money supply.

CHAPTER 7

The Price Level and the Money Supply in the Long Run

7.1 INTRODUCTION

We begin this chapter by outlining the quantity theory of money, which is the classical theory of how the price level and the rate of inflation are determined in a closed economy. This is followed by a discussion of the causes and consequences of inflation. We then discuss the Keynesian perspective on the quantity theory and present some evidence on the theory from the Eurozone countries. In the concluding sections of this chapter, we explain the development of the Irish currency up until the introduction of the euro in 1999 and the evolution of central banking in Ireland.

7.2 THE QUANTITY THEORY OF MONEY

The quantity theory of money explains the price level and hence the rate of inflation. In its simplest form, it states that the larger the quantity of money in the economy, the higher the price level. Alternatively, the more rapid the rate of increase in the money supply, the higher the rate of inflation.

Note:
The discovery of large silver mines in Mexico, Bolivia and Argentina led to a vast increase in the stock of silver coins in circulation in Europe from the sixteenth century onwards. The rise in the price level experienced at the same time was attributed by many observers to the increase in the quantity of money. This is the origin of the modern quantity theory. The quantity theory was first outlined by Richard Cantillon, who was from County Kerry, in his *Essai Sur la Nature du Commerce en Général* (published in 1755 but written 20 years earlier) and by David Hume in *Political Discourses* (1752).

To set out the quantity theory in algebraic terms, we define the *velocity of circulation of money* (V) as nominal GNP divided by the stock of money:

$$V \equiv GNP/M^s \qquad (1)$$

For example, if GNP equals €100 billion and the money supply is €50 billion, then the velocity of circulation is 2.

$$V \equiv €100 \text{ billion}/€50 \text{ billion} = 2$$

GNP is the total amount of goods and services sold during the course of the year. Since it takes two to make a transaction, this is also the amount of goods and services purchased during the year. Given a money supply of €50 billion, this means that the average monetary unit financed €2 worth of expenditure on final goods and services. In other words, the average monetary unit was used twice during the year. This is what is meant by 'velocity'.

If nominal GNP is divided into the price level (P) and real GNP, identity (1) can be written:

$$V \equiv (P \times \text{real GNP})/M^s \qquad (2)$$

Multiply both sides of (2) by M^s:

$$M^s \times V \equiv P \times \text{real GNP} \qquad (3)$$

This is the *equation of exchange*. It is an identity or something that holds true by definition. It simply states that the money supply multiplied by velocity must equal nominal GNP (or the price level multiplied by real GNP).

To get from the equation of exchange to the *quantity theory*, we make two assumptions:

- V is relatively stable.
- Natural real GNP is not affected by a change in the money supply.

Given these assumptions, it is clear that if the money supply, M^s, is increased the brunt of the adjustment must come through an increase in P, the price level. This, in a nutshell, is the explanation of inflation that follows from the quantity theory of money: increases in the money supply lead to higher prices. The quantity theory is a cornerstone of that school of economics that has come to be known as *monetarism*.

Figure 7.1 illustrates how an increase in the money supply impacts on the economy. Suppose the economy is initially at the point A, which is on the natural real GNP line.

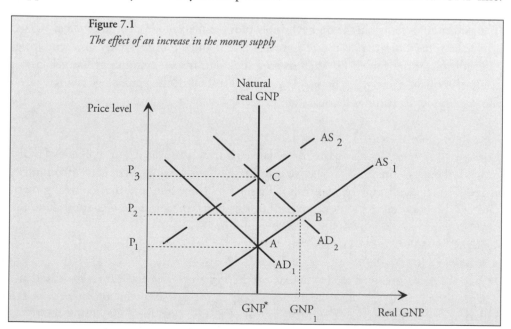

Figure 7.1

The effect of an increase in the money supply

An increase in the money supply will shift the AD curve up to the right and the economy moves to the point B. In the short run, the effect of the increase in the money supply is to increase *both* the price level and real GNP. However, at the point B, real wages have fallen. This is because the price level has increased while nominal wages remain unchanged. Workers will now demand an increase in nominal wages to restore the original real wage and the AS curve shifts up to the left. Eventually, the economy reverts to the point C and natural real GNP. In the longer-term, the effect of the increase in the money supply has been a proportionate increase in the price level and no change in real GNP.

Note:
As explained in chapter 8, the money supply is another variable that determines the position or location of the AD curve. This is because an increase in the money supply leads to lower interest rates. A change in the interest rate, in turn, affects consumer expenditure, investment and net exports and therefore the AD curve.

This gives rise to the so-called *classical dichotomy*. This relates to the distinction or separation between real and nominal variables. Examples of real variables are real GNP, unemployment, exports and employment. Nominal variables are the price level and the money supply. The classical school argue that a change in the money supply does not impact on real variables but only affects nominal variables such as the price level. This proposition is also know as *monetary neutrality*. A change in the money supply has a neutral effect on real variables.

Another way or representing the quantity theory is to totally differentiate equation (3) above to obtain:

$$\Delta M^s + \Delta V = \Delta P + \Delta \text{real GNP} \tag{4}$$

The percentage change in the money supply plus the percentage change in velocity must equal the inflation rate plus the real growth rate. Notice that in totally differentiating, the multiplication sign in (3) changes to a plus sign in (4). Assuming that velocity is relatively constant and the economy is at natural real GNP, the percentage change in the money supply determines the inflation rate.

THE QUANTITY THEORY AND MONETARY POLICY

Equation (4) provides the basis for pillar 1 of the European Central Bank's (ECB) monetary policy. The ECB's objective is to keep inflation below 2 per cent. Economists at the ECB forecast that velocity will fall by 0.5 to 1 per cent and that the real growth rate will be between 2 to 2.5 per cent. On this basis, the ECB's target is to allow the money supply to grow by 4.5 per cent per annum.

$$\Delta M^s + \Delta V = \Delta P + \Delta \text{real GNP}$$
$$4.5\% - (0.5 - 1\%) = (2 - 2.5\%) + (0 - 2\%)$$

Hence the steps involved are (1) decide on the inflation target, (2) forecast V and the real growth rate and (3) allow the money supply to increase at a rate consistent with the inflation target. In this way, the quantity theory can be used for policy purposes.

Monetarists believe there should be no *discretionary* monetary policy. The authorities should simply maintain the growth in the money supply to achieve the inflation objective. If this *monetary rule* is followed, the growth in the money supply will support the growth in the real economy without inflation.

As support for the quantity theory, monetarists point to the close correlation between inflation and the growth in the money supply over the long run in different countries and at different periods of time. Milton Friedman's *A Monetary History of the United States: 1867–1960*, Princeton University Press, 1963 (written with his wife Anna Schwartz) found support for the monetarist point of view in the experience of the United States since the nineteenth century. Friedman also found support for the quantity theory in inflation-prone countries such as Brazil, Bolivia and Israel. These countries have had high growth rates in their money supplies and rapid inflation. This led Friedman to conclude: 'Inflation is always and everywhere a monetary phenomenon'.

7.3 HYPERINFLATION

Hyperinflation is the label given to extremely high inflation rates, say in excess of 1,000 per cent a year. Because the annual inflation rates are so high, it is easier to state monthly rather than annual inflation rates. Hence, in Germany and Austria in 1922–23, the average inflation rate was 322 per cent per month. The peak was in October 1923 when the monthly inflation rate touched 29,000 per cent. A good that cost €1 at the beginning of the month cost €290 at the end of the month. Box 7.1 shows how the price of a newspaper changed between January 1921 and November 1923.

Although the German/Austrian case is probably the best known there are numerous other examples of hyperinflation. In Greece in 1943, the inflation reached 365 per cent per month. In Hungary in 1945–46, inflation went to 3,170 per cent per month. In Bolivia in 1985, a monthly inflation rate of 3,170 per cent was recorded. The highest rate we are aware of was Serbia in 1993 when the monthly inflation rate reached 100,000 per cent. It took 6 million dinars (the local currency) to buy one Snickers bar.

Box 7.1
Change in the price of newspapers during German hyperinflation

	Marks
January 1921	0.3
May 1922	2
October 1922	8
February 1923	100
September 1923	1,000
1 October 1923	2,000
15 October 1923	20,000
29 October 1923	1,000,000
9 November 1923	15,000,000
17 November 1923	70,000,000

THE CONSEQUENCES OF HYPERINFLATION

There are numerous illustrations of what hyperinflation does to an economy. Here are some examples.

> Argentines went on a buying spree yesterday in a race against soaring prices. In a whirl of hyperinflation, supermarkets are sometimes marking up prices twice a day while the Argentine currency, the austral, plunges in value. Customers overturned trolleys full of goods at one supermarket after the management announced over loudspeakers that all prices were being immediately raised by 30 per cent.
>
> (*The Irish Times*, 26 April 1989)

John Maynard Keynes noted that if you went into a bar in Germany during the hyperinflation of 1922–23, it would be worth your while to buy two pints of beer rather than one. The reason was that the rate of inflation was higher than the rate at which the second pint went stale! Another story goes that a woman went to buy bread with a basket full of money. A mugger snatched the basket from her and ran off throwing the worthless paper money on the roadside. It has also been pointed out that if you take a taxi ride in a hyperinflation period it is important to pay when you enter the taxi. The fare will be considerably higher by the time you reach your destination.

Countries with high inflation rates inevitably have weak or depreciating exchange rates. For example, in Bolivia the exchange rate fell from peso 500,000/\$1 to peso 900,000/\$1 in a single day. In Argentina, soaring inflation also undermined the exchange rate of the country's currency. The austral was introduced in 1985 when it was worth \$1.25. By mid-1991, there were 10,000 australs to \$1. The government announced plans to replace it with a new currency, which would be called the (new) peso. This was only the most recent in a series of new currencies introduced as inflation undermined the old ones: one new peso would be worth 10,000 *billion* of the old pesos that were in use in the 1960s.

As inflation soars and the exchange rate depreciates, there is a flight from domestic money. Salaries and wages denominated in the local currency are falling rapidly and people attempt to switch into a stable currency such as the dollar or the euro. This process is called *dollarisation*.

A nation of 'money-changers' emerges and wages have to be paid several times during the day. Bribes, strikes, stealing and smuggling become the norm. Eventually, the inflation becomes so disruptive that the country's social and political culture becomes undermined. How then can a government stop hyperinflation?

CAUSES OF HYPERINFLATION

The quantity theory of money comes into its own in explaining hyperinflation. Such high rates of inflation are simply not possible without equally high rates of increase in the money supply. But this, of course, simply pushes the explanation back a stage and provokes the question: Why is the money supply increasing so rapidly? Obviously there is no single answer to this: each situation is unique in its own right. However, one of the most common contributing factors is *an excessive fiscal deficit*. That is, the government's budget deficit lies at the root of the problem. Suppose a government is running a deficit in the region of 30 per cent of GNP. The government is unable or unwilling to cover its expenditure through taxation, so it has to borrow this much each year to balance the books. The public and the foreign banks may refuse to lend to the government possibly anticipating a default on the loan in the future.

The government is now forced to borrow from its own central bank. Table 7.1, for example shows the balance sheet of the central bank. Loans to government increase on the asset side (+ €1 million) and government deposits increase on the liability side (+ €1 million). The government can now run down its deposits by obtaining currency or by writing a cheque on its account. Either way, the stock of high-powered money (the monetary base) increases and there is a multiple expansion of the money supply. This is the equivalent of printing money and is referred to as *debt monetisation*.

According to the quantity theory, as the money supply increases the inflation rate starts to accelerate. However, as inflation takes off, the budget deficit automatically gets worse. This is because:

1. People and firms will delay paying their taxes. Inflation is reducing the real value of the domestic currency and so the longer people hold out paying taxes the less they have to pay in real terms.
2. Governments usually attempt to curtail inflation by charging low prices for public services. But this, in effect, means greater subsidies for public services, which adds to the budget deficit.
3. Nominal interest rates tend to rise in line with inflation and, as a result, the interest payments on the public debt increases.

Overall, with the tax revenue falling and public spending increasing the budget deficit gets worse. To stop the hyperinflation, the government must stop printing money to finance the budget deficit. But fiscal reform entails both cuts in government spending and higher taxes. Hence, ending the hyperinflation is both a fiscal and a monetary phenomenon. The credibility of both the government and the central bank is crucial to the process. Usually most governments find that it is beyond their powers to introduce the necessary measures and resort to calling-in the International Monetary Fund (IMF).

Table 7.1
Central Bank balance sheet: € millions

Assets		Liabilities	
External reserves		Currency	
Loans:		Commercial bank reserves	
Banks			
Government	+1	Government deposits	+1
Government securities			
Total	+1	Total	+1

It is then left to the IMF the unsavoury task of implementing the necessary reforms to stop the hyperinflation.

7.4 KEYNESIAN PERSPECTIVE ON THE QUANTITY THEORY

Keynesian economists disagree with the monetarists and argue that the quantity theory cannot be used for policy purposes. (For a quirky view, see N. Kaldor, *The Scourge of Monetarism*, Oxford University Press, 1982.) They advance a number of arguments to support this proposition. Firstly, it is argued that velocity is not constant and that an increase in the money supply will lead to a fall in velocity. If this is the case, an increase in the money supply may have little or no effect on nominal output. In terms of equation (4), if the increase in M^s is matched by a fall in V, then the right-hand side of the equation is unchanged. The implication is that monetary policy will be ineffective.

Secondly, Keynesians argue that there is a long and variable lag between changes in the money supply and inflation. Milton Friedman himself admits that this lag could be as much as two years. This suggests that a deflationary monetary policy, which is intended to curb inflation, may instead push the economy into recession. In other words, a decrease in M^s on the left-hand side of equation (4) may result in a lower real growth rate leaving inflation unchanged.

Note:
In terms of figure 7.1 this involves the AD curve shifting down to the left. The result is an increase in real wages and recession. It is now necessary for nominal wages to fall to restore the original real wage. If this happens the AS curve will shift down to the right. Keynesians point to the inflexibility of nominal wages in a downward direction and argue that the economy could remain in recession for a long period of time.

A third serious criticism of the quantity theory is that causation may run from nominal GNP to the money supply and not the other way round. In other words, the money supply is 'demand-led'. As we shall explain in chapter 8, an increase in nominal GNP will increase the demand for money for transaction purposes. That is, as the economy expands, more money is required as a 'medium of exchange'. Also as the economy grows and more jobs are created, people will be willing to borrow more from the banks and lending increases. If this happens then the causation in equation (4) is running from right to left. Changes in nominal GNP have resulted in an expansion of the money supply and not the other way around

A fourth problem with the quantity theory is the difficulty in controlling the money supply. We mentioned in chapter 6 that the money multiplier is not constant. Hence the relationship between high-powered money and the overall money supply tends to vary. This makes the central bank's job of regulating the money supply very difficult. Furthermore, the narrow and broad definitions of the money supply do not move in tandem. This raises the question of which definition of the money supply the central bank should attempt to control?

7.5 Evidence from the Irish Economy and the Eurozone

The quantity theory of money is essentially a theory of inflation in a closed economy. In a small, open economy like Ireland external factors such as foreign inflation and movements in the exchange rate have an important bearing on domestic inflation. Nevertheless, it is of interest to review the relationship between the change in the money supply and inflation in Ireland.

Figure 7.2 shows the relationship between the growth in the Irish money supply (M3) and Irish inflation over the period 1961 to 1998 (when the money supply series was terminated). The money supply series has been lagged one year in order to allow for the time it takes for changes in the money supply to translate into inflation. (For example, the rate of growth of the money supply in 1996 would be expected to affect inflation in 1997.) It can be seen that there is a weak relationship between the two series. This is particularly evident after 1991 when the money supply increased significantly while the inflation rate remained low. The lack of a relationship between the money supply and the rate of inflation is important even in a small open economy such as Ireland.

An alternative way of examining the two series is to present a scatter diagram. This is done in figure 7.3 where the percentage change in the money supply is given along the horizontal axis and the inflation rate is on the vertical axis. Each point in the scatter diagram shows the change in the money supply (lagged one year) and the inflation rate for a particular year. The slope of the trend line (called the regression coefficient) going through the scatter diagram is estimated to be 0.46. This means that a 1 per cent increase in the money supply this year leads to 0.46 per cent increase in inflation the following year. In contrast to Figure 7.2 this seems to indicate a strong relationship between the two series.

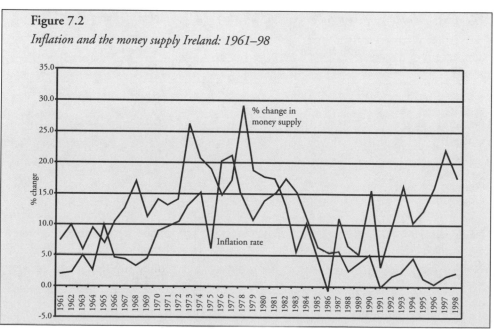

Figure 7.2

Inflation and the money supply Ireland: 1961–98

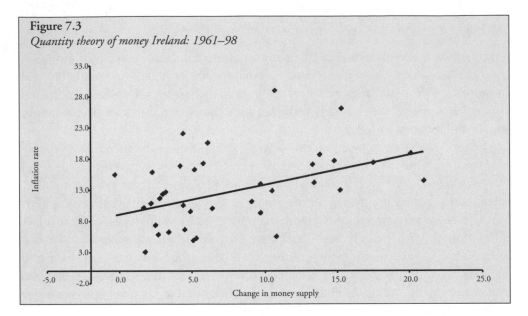

Figure 7.3
Quantity theory of money Ireland: 1961–98

A similar calculation was done for the other countries in the Eurozone. The estimated coefficients are given in table 7.2. Countries with a high coefficient are Greece, Spain, Italy and Portugal. For the Eurozone as a whole the coefficient is estimated to be 0.61. Hence a 1 per cent increase in the money supply translates into a 0.61 percent increase in inflation in the following year. Table 7.2 also shows the estimated coefficient between the change in the money supply (lagged one year) and the real growth rate. It can be seen that the coefficients are generally much smaller than in the inflation case. This is also evidence in favour of the Quantity Theory.

Table 7.2
The effect of a change in the money supply on inflation and the real growth rate

	Estimated coefficient Inflation	Estimated coefficient Real Growth Rate
Austria	0.36	0.22
Belgium	0.31	0.11
Finland	0.43	0.08
France	0.41	0.15
Germany	0.26	0.31
Greece	0.73	0.08
Ireland	0.46	0.05
Italy	0.59	0.19
Netherlands	0.31	0.08
Portugal	0.66	0.04
Spain	0.72	0.09
EU12	0.61	0.19

Source: Authors' estimates.

Finally, figure 7.3 shows the velocity of circulation of money for Ireland over the period 1971–98 (the year the Irish money supply series was terminated). Velocity is defined as nominal GNP divided by M3 (broad money supply). It can be seen that velocity varied within a fairly narrow range up to 1992 but since then it declined significantly. This tends to bear out the Keynesian argument that velocity is inversely related to changes in the money supply. Figure 7.2 showed a large increase in the money supply after 1992 and this is associated with a decline in velocity. The average velocity figure over the period was 1.73.

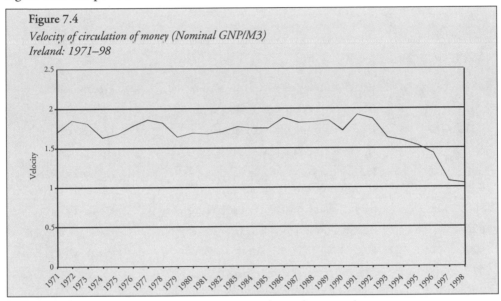

Figure 7.4

Velocity of circulation of money (Nominal GNP/M3)
Ireland: 1971–98

7.6 The Development of the Irish Currency

We now turn to a discussion of the development of an Irish currency up until its withdrawal in 2002. This section provides a brief history of Irish money.

Early history

Gold and silver were used in Ireland as a medium of exchange in ancient times, although the units took the form of rings and bracelets rather than coins. Money, however, took many other forms as the following quote suggests: 'The Annals of the Four Masters, originating from A.D. 106, state that the tribute (Boroimhe meaning literally 'cow-tax') paid by the King of Leinster consisted of 150 cows, 150 pigs, 150 couples of men and women in servitude, 150 girls and 150 cauldrons.' (P. Einzig, *Primitive Money*, New York: Pergamon, 2nd edition, 1966, 239.)

The first coinage in Ireland can be traced to the Norse settlement in Dublin in the 990s. The amount of coinage in circulation was relatively small and largely confined to the main trading towns. The use of coinage increased after the arrival of the Normans in 1169. In 1460 the Irish parliament met in Drogheda and established the first separate Irish currency. This currency was subsequently devalued relative to the English currency. The exchange rate was 15:12 or 15 Irish pence were worth 12 English pence (that is one

English shilling). Over the centuries the exchange rate between the Irish and English currencies has varied considerably. A summary of the fortunes of the Irish pound is given in table 7.3.

Table 7.3
A brief history of the Irish pound

Date	Exchange rate	Movement of Irish currency in terms of sterling relative to previous date
1200	Par	
1487	IR 1.5 silver coins/ UK 1 silver coin	Depreciation
1561	IR 1.3 silver coins/UK 1 silver coin	Appreciation
1601–1602	IR 4 silver coins/UK 1 silver coin	Depreciation
1603	IR 1.3 silver coins/UK 1 silver coin	Appreciation
1650	Par	Appreciation
1689	IR 13 pence/UK 12 pence	Depreciation
1797–1826	Irish currency floated against UK currency	Depreciation
1826	Abolition of independent Irish currency	Par
1927	Creation of Saorstát pound	Parity with sterling
1979	The Irish currency depreciated following Ireland's entry into the Exchange Rate Mechanism (ERM) of the European Monetary System. Followed by appreciation.	Depreciation
1990–1992	Entry of Britain into the ERM Stability at about IR£ = STG£0.92	
1992 (September)	Sterling is devalued on foreign exchanges and drops out of the ERM.	
1993 (August)	Margins of fluctuation in ERM widened to 15 per cent.	
1993–99	Irish pound the strongest currency in the ERM.	
1998 (March)	Irish pound revalued by 3 per cent in ERM realignment.	
1999 (January)	Irish pound permanently fixed to the euro. Irish pound ceases to be a currency and becomes a unit of account.	
2002	Irish currency withdrawn from circulation and replaced by euro notes and coins.	

In the sixteenth century the English monarchy allowed the so-called Harp coinage (sometimes referred to as 'white money') to be issued. In doing so, the monarchy acknowledged the existence of a separate Irish currency unit. This was followed in 1601 by an issue of copper coinage by Queen Elizabeth I.

By the 1680s, when banking-type activities first began to emerge, the currency situation in Ireland was unsatisfactory for a number of reasons. Firstly, there was a general shortage of coins and the economy still operated partly on a barter system. So bad was the currency situation that James II melted down cannons to manufacture coins. This became known as 'gun money' and gave rise to the expression 'not worth a brass farthing'.

Generally, the coinage in circulation consisted of a mix of Spanish, French, Portuguese and English coins, which were of different quality and design, and this lack of uniformity impaired its ability to function as a medium of exchange (recall our discussion of Gresham's law in chapter 6).

In the early 1720s a Mr Wood received a patent to issue coinage (Wood's halfpence) which would have increased the copper coinage in circulation by about a quarter. However, this patent was withdrawn two years later, partly because of the argument used by Jonathan Swift in *The Drapier's Letters* that the increase in currency would raise prices (the quantity theory argument discussed earlier). A general shortage of coinage continued in Ireland, but as the poorer people in the country areas still lived in a subsistence and semi-barter economy, this had little effect on them. Merchants also issued their own coins in order to facilitate trade.

FROM THE EIGHTEENTH CENTURY TO INDEPENDENCE

Throughout the eighteenth century, the Irish currency was at a discount of about 8 per cent relative to the English currency: 13 Irish pence equalled 12 English pence. In 1797, during the turmoil of the Napoleonic Wars, the convertibility of Irish and British coins to gold was suspended, and in 1803 the Irish currency depreciated sharply. A parliamentary inquiry was established which issued a report known as the *Irish Currency Report* (1804). This *Report* argued that excessive credit expansion caused the depreciation and that the exchange rate could be stabilised if the growth of credit were controlled.

After 1804 the Irish currency gradually stabilised at a 13:12 exchange rate against sterling. By the time gold convertibility was resumed in 1821, this rate was sufficiently re-established for the Bank of Ireland (a commercial bank) to accept responsibility for maintaining the Irish currency at this rate. Following the implementation of the monetary provisions of the 1800 *Act of Union* in 1826, the Irish currency was abolished and full political and monetary union was established between Ireland and Great Britain. Thereafter British coins and notes circulated freely in Ireland.

Note:
The *Irish Currency Report* influenced thinking in the 'bullionist controversy' in England (1796–1821) and is an important document in the history of monetary economics. The key issue it addressed was whether there could be an 'excessive' growth in the money supply. The *Report* set out what came to be the orthodox view that an 'excess' increase in the money supply

would lead to an increase in the price level and this, in turn, would make exports less competitive and cause the exchange rate to depreciate. This reasoning was influential in the development of the modern quantity theory of money.

DEVELOPMENTS SINCE INDEPENDENCE

Following the foundation of the Irish Free State in 1922, the *Coinage Act* of 1926 was passed in order to enable the finance minister to issue new Irish coins. These coins were used in Ireland until 1971, when a new design was introduced and the coinage decimalised.

Note:

Until the 1950s the 'silver' coins minted for Ireland contained significant amounts of silver. Some of them became very valuable as the price of silver rose. The two-shilling and half-crown coins from the early 1940s are now worth hundreds of pounds. Hence, following Gresham's law, they have entirely disappeared from circulation.

A banking commission was set up in 1926 to advise the government on the establishment of an Irish pound. This was known as the Parker-Willis Commission, after its chairman, Professor Henry Parker-Willis (1874–1937) of Columbia University, a former secretary of the Federal Reserve Board (the US Central Bank). The commission's final report was signed in January 1927. It recommended that a new currency unit, the Saorstát pound, be created. In order to ensure public confidence in the new currency, it should be backed 100 per cent by sterling reserves, British government stock and gold reserves and freely convertible into sterling. Also its value in terms of sterling could not be changed without the introduction of additional legislation. Thus the new currency would, in effect, be sterling with an Irish design. This would ensure that it would be acceptable alongside sterling as a medium of exchange. The commission also recommended the establishment of a new body, confusingly called the *Currency Commission*, to oversee the issue of the new legal tender notes.

The recommendations of the Parker-Willis Commission were incorporated into law in the *Currency Act 1927*. The Currency Commission was established and remained in existence until 1942, when its powers were transferred to the new Central Bank. Its only chairman was Joseph Brennan (1887–1976), who became the first governor of the Central Bank of Ireland. The first Irish notes were issued in September 1928.

Note:

Under the new arrangements the commercial banks were allowed to issue a certain quantity of private bank notes which bore the banks' names. These were called the consolidated bank note issue and the notes were known as ploughman notes because of their design. These notes were finally withdrawn from circulation in 1953.

The share of Irish legal tender notes in the total supply of money in circulation is believed to have reached about two-thirds by the beginning of World War II. This represents another example of the benefits of seigniorage. To understand how seigniorage profits arise, consider the following example. In 1928 the Irish public exchanged their holdings of sterling for the new Irish currency. The Currency Commission (which issued the new Irish notes) received sterling in return and this sterling was placed on the London money markets and earned interest. The interest received by the Currency Commission (allowing for expenses) represented seigniorage profits. It has been estimated that the value of the seigniorage amounted to about 0.2 per cent of national income at the time. (Cormac Ó Gráda, *Ireland 1780–1939: A New Economic History*, Oxford University Press, 1994, 42.)

7.7 THE EVOLUTION OF CENTRAL BANKING IN IRELAND

In this section, we present an overview of the development and the demise of central banking in Ireland. In nineteenth-century Ireland there was no central bank. In particular, there was no lender of last resort to bail out the commercial banks when they got into trouble. A key date in Irish banking history is 1783 when the Bank of Ireland was founded by royal charter. It performed some of the functions of a central bank. It issued notes and managed the government's account. Because of its size it was able to lend money to banks that were in distress, but it was not always willing or able to provide enough support to avert bank failures. Greater competition in the banking sector following the *Bankers' (Ireland) Act* of 1845 forced the Bank of Ireland to evolve along commercial lines. This reduced its willingness to help out other banks in times of crisis.

Also following the Act of Union in 1801 and the abolition of the Irish currency in 1826, the Bank of England was given some responsibility for supervising banking in Ireland.

The banks at this time were primarily involved in facilitating the trade of agricultural produce. Merchants borrowed from the banks to pay farmers for crops that were sold on the domestic market and exported. With their receipts, the merchants repaid their bank loans. The farmers used the bank notes given to them by the merchants to pay the landowners' rent. The landowners then returned the notes to the private banks in exchange for gold, silver or foreign currency. Hence the private banks facilitated a transfer of resources from tenant farmers to landowners.

Note:

Because there was no lender of last resort, the Irish private banks were very vulnerable in times of crisis. In 1820, for example, at the end of the Napoleonic Wars there was a slump in agricultural prices and widespread bankruptcy among the merchants to whom the banks had loaned money. When depositors got wind of this there was a 'run on the banks'. However, the banks did not have enough cash on hand to meet the demand and could not call in their loans from bankrupt clients. They had to close their doors and call in liquidators. In Munster the 'run' started in Cork city and quickly spread throughout the province. In Limerick, the four private banks (Maunsells' Bank, Furnell and Company, Bruce's Bank and Roche's Limerick bank) all ceased trading. In one month thirty banks failed in Munster alone and the crisis spread throughout the rest of the country, leaving only ten banks solvent outside Dublin. (See Eoin O'Kelly, *The Old Private Banks and Bankers of Munster*, Cork University Press, 1959). As the banks were private companies, when they failed the partners who owned them lost their capital and frequently had to sell off their town houses and country estates as well. Depositors were lucky if they got back half the money they had lodged with the banks.

The private banks were superseded by joint stock banks following the banking crises of the 1820s. These had at least six major shareholders (who accepted unlimited liability) and they were therefore better able to withstand crises.

THE CURRENCY COMMISSION

The question of the appropriate way to regulate the banking system emerged as an issue after Independence. It was recognised that a serious conflict of interest would have emerged if the Bank of Ireland were asked to act as the central bank in the Free State. None the less, the Minister for Finance in the new provisional government asked the Bank of Ireland to continue to manage the government's account. The Banking Commission, which reported in 1927, did not intend that the *Currency Commission* would become a fully-fledged central bank. It was not given the power to act as a lender of last resort, nor could it set reserve requirements for commercial banks. It did not gain control over the commercial banks' sterling assets, which continued to be kept in London. Furthermore, the commission did not manage the government's account, nor did it advise the government on monetary matters.

Perhaps the main reason a central bank was not established in the 1920s was that there was little such an institution could usefully do as long as the country remained in a monetary union with Great Britain. There was a fixed exchange rate between the Irish currency and sterling and there was no money market in Ireland. Under these circumstances, a central bank could not control the money supply or have any influence on the price level, output or employment. All that was needed was some type of *currency board*, to issue local currency in exchange for approved assets such as sterling. This function was discharged by the Currency Commission.

Another possible reason why a central bank was not established after Independence was, '…a conviction that central banks were being promoted as antidotes to backward or unduly risk-adverse commercial banking systems. Accordingly, creating an Irish central bank might be seen as both a slight and a threat to the long-established commercial banks'. (Ó Gráda, *op. cit.*, 27.)

In the same vein, when government asked the commercial banks to underwrite a flotation of government stock in the 1930s, the banks were reluctant and wished to know how the government intended to spend the proceeds.

When in September 1931 the UK terminated the gold standard and sterling was devalued by 25 per cent against gold, there were misgivings in some quarters in Ireland that the Irish currency was automatically devalued due to the link with sterling. The Fianna Fáil government established a second *Banking Commission* in 1934 to report on money and banking in Ireland. The new commission included Joseph Brennan (chairman of the Currency Commission), George O'Brien (professor of national economics at University College, Dublin) and the Swedish economist Per Jacobsson who later became president of the International Monetary Fund. (John Maynard

Keynes was considered but was not invited, possibly because of his support for the Irish government's protectionist policies in a lecture in Dublin in the previous year.) A bishop was included, but Dr McNeely was '...unaware of any reasons why he should have been appointed, except to add an atmosphere of respectability to the Conference'. (Ó Gráda, *op. cit.*, 42.)

This second Banking Commission deliberated for nearly four years and reported in 1938. As one commentator put it, 'The opinion of the majority report on the system of banking and currency may be summarised as a recommendation to leave things as they were'. (James Meenan, *The Irish Economy since 1922*, Manchester University Press, 1970, 222.)

The creation of an Irish central bank, as such, was not recommended, but it was suggested that the Currency Commission be allowed to engage in open market operations and that its name be suitably altered to 'indicate that the monetary authority envisaged in these recommendations is a central banking organisation'. Thus, the commission tried to steer a course between outright advocacy of a central bank and the status quo. In the days before the start of World War II, the Bank of Ireland approached the Bank of England to see if it would act as a lender of last resort to the Irish banks in an emergency. The Bank of England replied that it was not in a position to provide assistance and suggested that 'as Eire was a separate political entity it should have a central bank of its own'. (Ó Gráda, *op. cit.*, 39.)

Perhaps in the light of this rebuff the Irish commercial banks, which had been heavily represented on both banking commissions and had staunchly opposed the creation of a central bank, had second thoughts on the issue. In any event,

> The government chose to ignore the Report, and used the threat of war to produce central banking legislation. In the end, the Central Bank Act of 1942 was a compromise between, on the one hand, Brennan and the Department of Finance [who did not wish to establish a Bank], and the majority of ministers [who did] on the other.'
>
> (Ó Gráda, *op. cit.*)

The *Central Bank Act* was passed in 1942 and soon afterwards the Central Bank of Ireland was established, with Joseph Brennan, the former chairman of the Currency Commission, as the first governor.

THE CENTRAL BANK OF IRELAND

Since its launch in 1942, there have been eight governors of the Central Bank (see box 7.2). The primary function of the new Central Bank was to 'safeguard the integrity of the currency'. Its powers were, however, limited. It could act as lender of last resort and use open market operations to influence liquidity in the money market, but it could not set reserve requirements or act as a banker to either the government or the commercial banks. The government continued to hold its account with the Bank of Ireland and the commercial banks held most of their reserves in the London money markets. Thus, little changed in Irish banking immediately following the establishment of the Central Bank of Ireland.

Box 7.2
Governors of the Central Bank of Ireland

Joseph Brennan	1943–53
James J. McElligott	1953–60
Maurice Moynihan	1961–69
T. Kennedy Whitaker	1969–76
Charles H. Murray	1976–81
Tomás Ó Cofaigh	1981–87
Maurice F. Doyle	1987–94
Maurice O'Connell	1994–2001
John Hurley	2001–

The 1960s, however, was a period of rapid development in Irish banking. A number of new banks began operations in Ireland and there was a wave of mergers among the established ones. The Bank of Ireland acquired the Hibernian Bank in 1958 and the National Bank in 1965. The Allied Irish Bank group was formed with the merger of the Munster and Leinster Bank, the Provincial Bank and the Royal Bank of Ireland in 1966. Appendix 1 to this chapter discusses the structure of the banking sector in Ireland today.

In 1965, the Central Bank of Ireland first issued 'letters of advice' (or credit guidelines) to the banks, telling them to restrain credit expansion in order to curtail the growing balance of payments deficit. The Central Bank began to promote new markets in foreign exchange, government stocks and money. Because of these developments, it was becoming increasingly clear that the 1942 Central Bank legislation was inadequate. In response the *Central Bank Act, 1971*, was passed. This act significantly increased the powers of the Central Bank. Its main features were:

- The Central Bank became the licensing authority for banks.
- The government's account was transferred from the Bank of Ireland to the Central Bank.
- The commercial banks were required to keep their reserves with the Central Bank.
- The Central Bank was given the power to issue primary and secondary reserve ratios (these were first issued in August 1972).
- The new legislation made it possible to break the sterling link by government order. This power was exercised in March 1979, following Ireland's entry to the European Monetary System.

The *Central Bank Act, 1989*, brought money brokers, financial futures traders and companies associated with the new International Financial Services Centre (IFSC) under the supervision of the Central Bank. In addition, commercial bank charges were brought under its control and, as mentioned earlier, a deposit protection scheme was established to protect the savings of small depositors. Under the *Building Society Act, 1989*, and the *Trustee Savings Bank (TSB) Act, 1989*, the Central Bank gained responsibility for supervising the building societies and the Trustee Savings Banks.

In 1978 the Irish government decided to participate in the European Monetary System, even as Britain decided to stay out. In the 1990s, the Irish government took the decision to participate in European Monetary Union when it commenced in 1999. This involved replacing the Irish currency with the euro and surrendering monetary independence to the ECB. The governing council of the ECB, which will include the governors of the central banks of the participating countries, formulates monetary policy in the Eurozone.

In effect Ireland had an independent currency for less than twenty years: between breaking the link with sterling in March 1979 and the fixing of the value of the Irish pound to the euro in January 1999. The Irish pound ceased to exist as a legal currency on 9 February 2002.

7.8 Conclusion

In this chapter we discussed the quantity theory of money and reviewed the history of money and banking in Ireland from the earliest times to the present. The main points discussed included:

- The concept of the velocity of circulation of money
- The equation of exchange
- The quantity theory of money
- Hyperinflation
- The Keynesian argument that the quantity theory cannot be successfully used for policy purposes
- The evolution of currency and banking in Ireland
- The origins of the Central Bank of Ireland.

APPENDIX
The structure of the Irish financial sector

Although small, the Irish financial sector is quite complex. For historical reasons, a variety of different categories of banks exist and different regulations, including reserve requirements, are applied to them. The various types of financial institutions specialise in different segments of the market, attracting their deposits from different types of depositors and lending to different types of borrowers. The main categories of financial institutions are as follows:

Associated banks
(Allied Irish Bank, Bank of Ireland, National Irish Bank and the Ulster Bank). These banks are public quoted companies which provide a full range of lending and deposit facilities and together they constitute the backbone of the Irish retail banking system which meets the banking needs of the general public. The term 'associated banks' comes from the Central Bank Act, 1942, and indicates that a special relationship exists between these banks and the Central Bank. It should be noted that the associated banks have important subsidiaries operating in other segments of the banking market and in hire-purchase finance. The Irish retail banking system is characterised by a few large banks

with hundreds of branches. In this it resembles the British and Canadian systems. Banking in the US, on the other hand, is still characterised by thousands of small, independent and localised banks, although regional and national banking networks are being established.

Non-associated banks

This category is subdivided into:

1. Merchant and commercial banks (Allied Irish Investment Bank, ABN Ambro, Guinness and Mahon, the Bank of Nova Scotia, Citibank, etc.). These banks cater to the wholesale end of the market, which includes large personal and corporate accounts. They also provide investment management and consultancy services.
2. Industrial banks (Allied Irish Finance, Bank of Ireland Finance, Bowmaker Bank, Lombard and Ulster, UDT Bank, etc.). These specialise in providing fixed interest loans to the personal sector for consumer durables and to industry for machinery and other equipment. Note that the associated and non-associated banks comprise the licensed banks.

The interest rate charged by the industrial banks is roughly double that charged by the associated banks. A rough rule is:

Industrial interest rate $=$ (associated bank rate $\times$ 2) $-$ 1

This is because the associated banks charge interest on the reducing principal. The industrial banks charge interest on the original sum borrowed regardless of what is outstanding on the loan.

To counter-act financial institutions quoting misleading interest rates, the annual percentage rate (APR) must now be displayed on all advertisements for loans, hire-purchase arrangements, etc. This is the true interest rate changed for a loan.

State-sponsored financial institutions

The Industrial Credit Corporation and the Agricultural Credit Bank are state-owned banks which were established to act as development banks in industry and agriculture, respectively.

The post office savings bank

This is a government-owned savings bank. All deposits are used to purchase government securities. The post office also administers an instalment savings scheme and issues savings certificates on favourable tax terms.

Trustee savings banks

Approximately 80 per cent of the deposits of these banks are lent to the government and the remainder is lent to the public. These banks are owned by trustees on behalf of their depositors.

Building societies (First National Building Society, Educational Building Society, Irish Permanent Building Society, etc.)

Building societies now act very much like banks, but they were founded as mutual societies (owned by members or policy shareholders) to help small savers acquire money for house purchase against the security of the property. The 1989 legislation has brought them more into line with ordinary banks. There has been a wave of demutualisation in many countries in recent years. In Ireland, there are now just two mutual building societies down from fourteen some twenty years ago.

Hire-purchase finance companies (Allied Finance, Advance Finance, etc.)

These companies are similar to the industrial banks in that they provide fixed interest loans for the purchase of consumer durables and machinery for industry. Many of them are subsidiaries of the associated banks.

Credit unions

Credit unions are localised, co-operative banks whose main business is lending to their members on a non-profit basis. The following data indicates the growth of the credit unions over the last forty years.

	1959	2001
Number of credit unions	3	535
Members	200	2.7 million
Savings	€525	€7 billion

CHAPTER 8

Money and Interest Rates in a Closed Economy

8.1 INTRODUCTION

We begin this chapter by outlining the theory of the demand for money. We then show how the supply and demand for money determines the rate of interest. The money market is then combined with the goods and services market to create a more realistic model of the macroeconomy. The link between the money market and the goods and services market is the relationship between the rate of interest and interest-sensitive expenditure. Using the expanded model, issues such as the relative effectiveness of fiscal and monetary policy are discussed. In particular, the concept of 'crowding-out' is discussed.

8.2 MONETARY POLICY

The main purpose of this chapter is to explain how changes in the money supply impact on aggregate demand, output and employment. Figure 8.1 presents an overview of the key diagrams underlying the analysis. The lower diagram shows equilibrium in the *money market*. In this market, the supply (M^s) and demand (M^d) for money determine the *nominal* interest rate (i). An increase in the money supply, for example, will shift the M^s line out to the right and this reduces the interest rate.

The centre diagram shows the interest-sensitive expenditure (IE) line. This line illustrates an inverse relationship between the *real* interest rate (r) and interest-sensitive expenditure such as consumer expenditure, investment and net exports (exports minus imports). An increase in interest rates leads to a reduction in expenditure and vice versa. The IE line acts as the link or bridge between the money market and the goods and services market.

Finally, the upper diagram represents *equilibrium in the goods and services market*. This is the familiar aggregate supply (AS) and demand (AD) developed in chapter 2. The vertical line represents the long-run AS curve or the natural real GNP line. The main point is that changes in interest-sensitive expenditure (brought about by changes in the interest rate) shift the AD line. An increase in interest-sensitive expenditure will shift the AD line up to the right and vice versa.

Taking the three diagrams together, the central bank can influence real output and the price level as follows.

- An increase in the money supply leads to a fall in interest rates.
- Via the IE line, this leads to an increase in expenditure.
- The rise in expenditure shifts the AD curve out to the right and in the short run both real GNP and the price level increase. However, in the longer-term, the

Figure 8.1
Goods and money markets

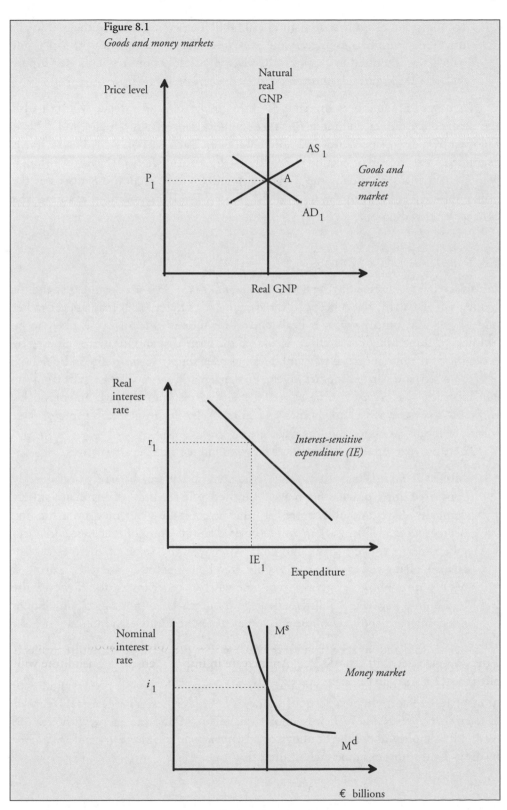

economy will revert back to natural real GNP. The overall effect of the increase in the money supply is to increase the price level. This is the quantity theory result which was discussed in chapter 7. Conversely, a reduction in the money supply will, in the long run, lead to proportionate decrease in the price level.

We now examine the various strands of this analysis in more detail. We start with the demand for money and money market equilibrium (sections 8.3 and 8.4). This is followed by a discussion of real and nominal interest rates (section 8.5). The IE line is examined in section 8.6. Section 8.7 outlines the transmission mechanism through which changes in the money supply affect nominal GNP. Section 8.8 discusses the policy differences between Keynes and the classics. Finally, section 8.9 examines the concept of crowding-out.

8.3 THE DEMAND FOR MONEY

In this section we discuss the Keynesian *theory of liquidity preference* or the demand for money. At first sight, the concept of the demand for money (M^d) may appear rather odd. If you ask someone what is her 'demand for money', the answer is likely to be 'infinite' or something to that effect. However, the term 'demand for money' is used by economists in a rather special way and does not refer simply to the desire to be rich.

To understand what economists mean by the demand for money, we start from the consideration that *wealth* can be stored in many forms: money, government stocks, company shares, works of art, houses and so on. Why do people keep some of their wealth in money as opposed to the alternatives?

There are two important differences between money and the alternatives.

- Money is *liquid*, that is, its value is known and it can be easily and quickly converted into purchasing power. On the other hand, government stocks, company shares and other stores of value give a return, but they are in varying degrees *illiquid*. That is, they cannot be used as a medium of exchange and it can take time to convert them into cash. Moreover, the value of these assets can change, giving rise to some uncertainty as to how much they are really worth.
- Money does not give a *return* over time whereas other assets do. However, the borderlines between the different categories of assets are not rigid. Some liquid assets such as deposit accounts and some current accounts earn interest.

These considerations shed light on the reasons why people forgo the return available on interest bearing assets and keep some of their wealth in money or cash.

Keynes developed his theory of liquidity preference (why people prefer liquidity or money) to explain why people hold money. (J. M. Keynes, *The General Theory of Employment, Interest and Money*, London: Macmillan, 1936.) He analysed the reasons for holding money under the headings of the *transaction*, *precautionary* and *speculative* motives. Let us now examine each of these in turn.

TRANSACTION AND PRECAUTIONARY MOTIVES

People need money for transaction purposes, that is, to do their shopping, buy lunch, pay bus fares, etc. No matter how rich one is, it is hard to purchase a meal or a suit of clothes without paying with money or a cheque. Keynes described the transaction motive for holding money as the need 'to bridge the interval between the receipt of income and its disbursement' (Keynes, *General Theory*, 195).

The precautionary motive is the desire to hold money to cater for unexpected contingencies (accidents, illness, etc.) or opportunities that may arise. According to Keynes, people hold money to 'provide for contingencies requiring sudden expenditure and for unforeseen opportunities of advantageous purchases' (Keynes, *General Theory*, 196).

It is reasonable to assume that the amount of money demanded for transactions and precautionary reasons depends on the level of income. The richer a person is, the more expensive her lifestyle and the more money she needs for transaction and precautionary reasons. The same is true at the macro level. As national income or nominal GNP increases, there is an increase in the demand for money for transaction and precautionary purposes. An increase in nominal GNP leads to an increase in the demand for money and a fall in nominal GNP reduces the demand for money. The transaction and precautionary motives for holding money may therefore be written as:

$$M^d = f(\text{nominal GNP}) \qquad f_1 > 0 \qquad\qquad (1)$$

Equation (1) states that the demand for money is a function of nominal GNP. The f_1 > 0 indicates that an increase in GNP increases the demand for money.

Note:
Causation runs from the variable inside the brackets to the variable on the left-hand side. As a result, the variables inside the bracket are referred to as *explanatory* or *independent* variables and the variable on the left-hand side is the *dependent* variable.

THE SPECULATIVE DEMAND FOR MONEY

In addition to the desire to hold money to finance day-to-day transactions and eventualities, Keynes believed that people hold money with the 'object of securing profit from knowing better than the market what the future will bring forth' (Keynes, *General Theory*, 170). He called this the speculative motive. To understand the speculative motive we need to look at the workings of the bond market.

THE BOND MARKET

Bonds issued by a company differ from shares in the company in a number of important ways.

- Shareholders own a proportion of the company and have voting rights that give them some control over the operations of the company. This ownership entitles them to an uncertain dividend that depends on the profits of the company.

- In contrast, bondholders lend money to a company for a specific period of time and do not have any control over the company's affairs; bonds pay a fixed monetary return (*coupon*) until the maturity date, so the bondholder knows with certainty how much income she will receive from the bond. For example, a bond with a face value of €2,000 and a coupon of €100 that matures in the year 2010 entitles the bondholder to a sum of €100 every year until 2010 and repayment of the €2,000 principal in 2010. A bond which is never redeemed but which pays an income indefinitely is known as a *perpetuity*.

Table 8.1
The relationship between interest rates and bond prices

1. Interest rate on bank deposit	20%	10%	5%
2. Fixed bond coupon	€10	€10	€10
3. Price of bonds	€50	€100	€200
4. Yield on bonds (= coupon/price)	20%	10%	5%

The government is the largest issuer of bonds in most modern economies, and government bonds provide a convenient medium for speculators trying to make *capital gains*. To see how this may be done, we need to consider what determines bond prices and bond yields. Consider the data in table 8.1.

- Line 1 displays three rates of interest on bank deposits.
- Line 2 shows the *fixed coupon* payable on a government bond. This is assumed to be €10.
- *Arbitrage* should now ensure that the yield (per cent) on the bond is the same as that on bank deposits. The yield on a bond is defined as the coupon divided by the price of the bond. If the coupon is €10 and the price of the bond is €100 then the yield is 10 per cent. (See box 8.1 for a discussion of the concept of arbitrage.) The price of the bond required to ensure that the bond yield is the same as the interest rate is given in line 3.
- The only way for the yield on bonds to change, given that the coupon is fixed, is for the *price of the bond* to vary. (We assume that it is a perpetuity, so that what matters to an investor is its current and future yields, rather than its value at maturity.) Line 4 shows the yield on bonds that is equalised with that on bank accounts.
- Notice what happens when the interest rate falls from 20 to 10 to 5 per cent. Arbitrage will ensure that the yield on government bonds also falls from 20 to 10 to 5 per cent. For this to happen, the price of the bond must rise from €50 to €100 to €200. Therefore, as interest rates *fall*, bond prices *rise* and, conversely, as interest rates *increase*, bond prices *fall*.

Note:
There are many different interest rates, for example, the rates on short- and long-term government stocks, on low- and high-risk company bonds (the latter became known as 'junk bonds' during the 1980s), as well as the rates charged by the banks on loans and paid on deposits. All these rates tend to move together, allowing us to refer to an average or representative interest rate as 'the' interest rate.

> **Box 8.1**
> *Arbitrage*
>
> Arbitrage is defined as buying a commodity or a currency in one market and selling it in another with a view to making a profit. The effect of arbitrage is to equalise returns across markets. For example, if the price of gold was lower in London than in New York, speculators could make a profit by buying in London and selling in New York. But the increased demand for gold in London would drive up the London price, while simultaneously the increased supply in New York would drive down the New York price. In a short space of time the two prices would converge. Arbitrage is particularly effective in financial markets because information on prices and yields all over the world can be readily obtained. As a result, investors will buy and sell comparable assets until their yields are equal. We are assuming that arbitrage ensures that the yield on the bond is equal to the interest rate obtainable from a bank deposit. In reality, risk, transaction costs and other factors have to be taken into account, and strict equality between the yields on different types of assets will not exist.

SPECULATION

The inverse relationship between interest rates and bond prices means that bondholders stand to make a capital *gain* when interest rates *fall*. Conversely, bondholders incur a capital *loss* when interest rates *rise*. Investors should therefore buy bonds if they expect interest rates to fall and sell them if they expect interest rates to rise. This strategy provides the basis of the Keynesian speculative motive for holding cash.

KEYNES'S 'NORMAL RATE OF INTEREST'

Keynes believed in the existence of a 'normal' rate of interest. He argued that departures from this rate are viewed as temporary. If interest rates rise above the normal rate, the expectation will be that they will eventually fall. Similarly, if interest rates fall below the normal rate, the expectation will be that they will rise.

Suppose, for example, that the normal rate of interest is considered to be 5 per cent and interest rates increase from 5 to 8 per cent. Investors holding bonds suffer a capital loss. However, the *expectation* now is that interest rates will fall back to the normal level of 5 per cent sometime in the future. Investors should therefore reduce their money holdings and purchase bonds in anticipation of making a capital gain. Hence the rise in the interest rate from 5 to 8 per cent is associated with a fall in the demand for cash balances.

Conversely, a fall in the interest rate from 5 to 3 per cent gives rise to the expectation that interest rates will rise in the future. Investors should get out of bonds and into money to avoid making a capital loss. The fall in the interest rate is, therefore, associated with an increase in the demand for money.

The relationship between the interest rate (i) and the demand for money can be written:

$$M^d = f(i) \qquad f_1 < 0 \tag{2}$$

where $f_1 < 0$ indicates that an increase in the interest rate causes a fall in M^d and vice versa.

Note:

The inverse relationship between the interest rate and the demand for money could also be explained in terms of the *opportunity cost* of holding cash. As we saw above, wealth held as cash does not earn a return, whereas wealth held as bonds or in other assets does. By holding cash, a person is therefore forgoing the interest that could have been earned on bonds, for example. Thus, when the interest rate is high, the opportunity cost of holding cash balances is also high, and it is to be expected that the public will economise on their holdings of cash. It is therefore only realistic to include the rate of interest among the determinants of the demand for money.

COMBINING THE TRANSACTION, PRECAUTIONARY AND SPECULATIVE MOTIVES

Combining equations (1) and (2) we can account for all the motives for holding money and write the demand for money function as:

$$M^d = f(\text{nominal GNP}, i) \quad f_1 > 0, f_2 < 0 \qquad (3)$$

Equation (3) states that the demand for money is a function of nominal GNP and the interest rate. As before, f_1 and f_2 indicate how the explanatory variables influence the dependent variable. Separating nominal GNP into its real and price components, equation (3) can also be rewritten as:

$$M^d = f(\text{real GNP}, P, i) \qquad f_1 > 0, f_2 > 0, f_3 < 0 \qquad (4)$$

Equation (4) states that the demand for money is positively related to both real GNP and the price level (P), but negatively to the rate of interest.

A demand for money schedule is drawn in figure 8.2. The nominal rate of interest is on the vertical axis and the demand for money on the horizontal axis. The relationship between the interest rate and the demand for money is shown by movements along the line. A decrease in interest rate from i_1 to i_2 leads to an increase in the demand for money. Conversely, an increase in the interest rate reduces the demand for money.

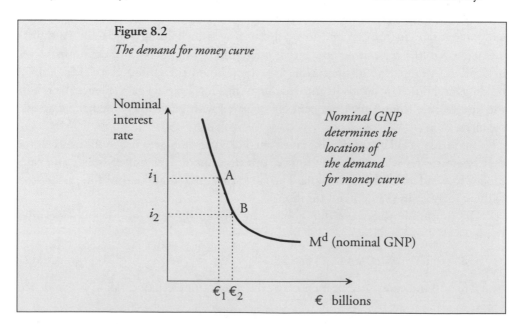

Figure 8.2

The demand for money curve

Nominal GNP determines the position (or location) of the demand for money curve. An increase in nominal GNP shifts the M^d schedule to the right; a fall in nominal GNP shifts it to the left. (This is why nominal GNP is put in brackets after M^d.)

Note that the slope of the demand for money curve is not linear. At low interest rates the curve is flat or horizontal. The reason for this is that at low interest rates there may be unanimity among investors that interest rates will rise in the future. That is, investors expect bond prices will fall. In order to avoid speculative losses in the bond market investors therefore keep their wealth in money. At low rates of interest, the demand for money is virtually infinite as no one wants to hold bonds. This is reflected in the diagram in the flat portion of the demand for money curve.

8.4 MONEY MARKET EQUILIBRIUM

In figure 8.3 the money supply (M^s) schedule is combined with a demand for money (M^d) schedule. The money supply is shown as a *vertical* line, which indicates that changes in the interest rate do not affect the supply of money. This assumes that the money supply is completely controlled by the monetary authorities or central bank. Put another way, we are assuming that the money supply is exogenous. (If changes in interest rates had a positive effect on the money supply, the M^s curve would slope upwards to the right.)

The rate of interest is the price of money and, like other prices, it is determined by the forces of supply and demand. At an interest rate of i_1, the supply and demand for money are equal. The money market is in equilibrium.

Note:

If the interest rate is above i_1, there is an excess supply of money and the interest rate will fall towards the equilibrium rate. If the interest rate is below i_1, there is an excess demand for money and the interest rate will rise to the equilibrium rate.

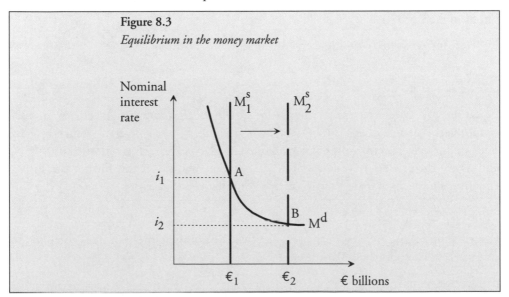

Figure 8.3
Equilibrium in the money market

Figure 8.3 also illustrates what happens to the interest rate when the central bank increases the money supply through, for example, open market operations (see chapter 6). The money supply (M^s) line moves out to the right and the interest rate falls from i_1 to the new equilibrium level, i_2. An increase in the money supply therefore reduces the nominal interest rate. Conversely, a reduction in the money supply leads to an increase in the interest rate.

As mentioned in the previous section, the demand for money schedule is horizontal at low interest rates. An increase in the money supply along the flat portion of the demand for money curve would not lower interest rates and monetary policy is in this case ineffective. This situation is known as the *liquidity trap*. An example of a liquidity trap is Japan in the 1990s and perhaps the US in autumn 2001. Nominal interest rates are close to zero in Japan and below 2 per cent in the US. Since nominal interest rates cannot be set below zero, there is little or no scope for the monetary authorities to further stimulate the economy.

Shifts in the demand for money curve

As mentioned, an increase in nominal GNP will shift the demand for money (M^d) curve upwards to the right. As shown in figure 8.4, if the money supply is held constant, the result will be an increase in the interest rate from i_1 to i_2. Similarly, a fall in nominal GNP will shift the M^d curve downwards and, assuming the money supply is constant, interest rates will fall. This effect is important when we come to discuss the 'crowding-out' effect later in this chapter.

8.5 Nominal and Real Interest Rates

At this point it is important to make a distinction between real and nominal interest rates. The nominal interest rate, i, is the rate quoted in the newspapers or by banks and issuers of bonds. The real rate, r, is defined as the nominal interest rate minus the inflation rate, π.

Real interest rate = nominal interest rate − inflation rate

or
$$r = i - \pi \tag{5}$$

Equation (5) is referred to as the *Fisher equation* after one of America's greatest economists, Irving Fisher (1867–1947), who taught at Yale University. Since interest rates are forward looking (interest is paid or charged over the next six months or a year), and as we do not know what the rate of inflation will be in the future, the Fisher equation should be stated in terms of *expected* inflation, that is, π^e

$$r = i - \pi^e \tag{6}$$

Rearranging equation (6), we can also state that the nominal interest rate is equal to the real interest rate plus the inflation rate.

$$i = r + \pi^e \tag{7}$$

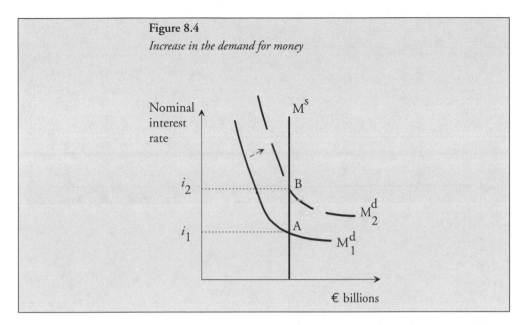

Figure 8.4

Increase in the demand for money

According to this equation, if the real interest rate is stable, a rise in the expected rate of inflation will lead to a one-to-one increase in the nominal interest rate. This is known as the Fisher effect.

Figure 8.5 shows the nominal interest rate and the inflation rate in Ireland between 1970 and 2001. The difference between the two series is the real interest rate. Figure 8.6 shows the real interest rate. It can be seen that in the 1970s, early 1980s and since 1999, the real interest rate was negative, while a high positive real rate was recorded in the late 1980s and 1990s. The average real interest rate in the 1970s, 1980s and 1990s was −2.97, 4.45 and 4.51 per cent respectively. The average over the entire period 1971–2001 was 1.89 per cent.

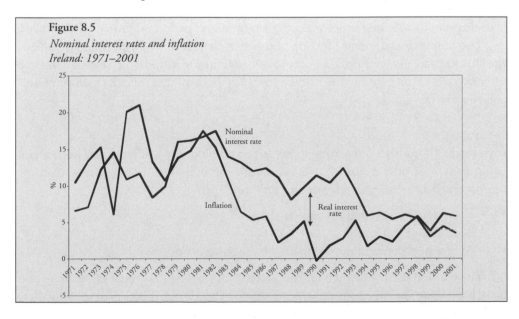

Figure 8.5

Nominal interest rates and inflation
Ireland: 1971–2001

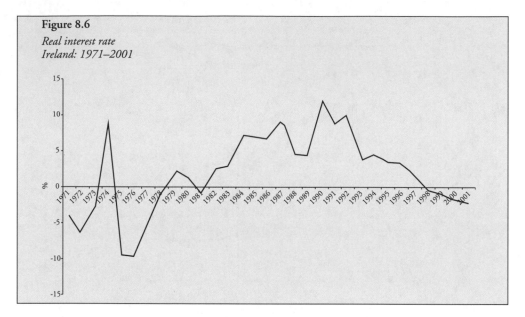

Figure 8.6

Real interest rate
Ireland: 1971–2001

8.6 Aggregate Demand and Interest Rates

In this section we explain how changes in the interest rate impacts on interest-sensitive expenditure (IE) which, in turn, affects the aggregate demand (AD) curve. Changes in the AD curve will affect real GNP, the price level and unemployment.

Consumer expenditure

Changes in the interest rate can be expected to influence consumer expenditure (C), which is a key determinant of aggregate demand. A decrease in the interest rate could be expected to increase C and vice versa. The fall in interest rates in the late 1990s, for example, as Ireland joined the European Monetary Union, encouraged more people to take out loans and increase expenditure. Conversely, if interest rates were to rise to a high level this would encourage people to cut expenditure and pay off expensive existing loans.

The simple consumption function outlined in chapter 3 can be extended to include the interest rate. In this case, C becomes a function of disposable income and the interest rate. A change in the interest rate can be expected to affect autonomous consumer expenditure.

Investment

Investment (I) consists of creating assets such as building roads, factories, houses and equipment. Consider a firm that is contemplating investing in, say, a new plant or machinery. It has three possible ways of financing this:

- Using retained earnings or profits
- Borrowing from a bank
- Selling new shares in the company on the stock exchange.

The main sources of finance for private sector investment are retained earnings and bank borrowing. Because banks charge interest on their loans, it is easy to see why there is an inverse relationship between investment and the interest rate. A higher rate of interest will tend to discourage borrowing for investment. Conversely, a lower interest rate will tend to encourage borrowing for investment.

But the rate of interest should also be taken into account when retained earnings are being considered to finance an investment project. Firms should take account of the *opportunity cost* of using retained profits. Retained earnings could be used to purchase government bonds and thereby earn a rate of return. The investment project should offer a rate of return that at least matches the return from bonds.

Similarly, a firm's ability to raise money through the stock market depends on whether it can convince investors that the investment project will generate a return that is comparable to what they could earn from investing in bonds. Thus, the rate of interest will affect a firm's investment plans, *regardless of which of the three sources of funds it uses*.

In an appendix to this chapter we explain the concept of net present value and show how it is used to evaluate the profitability of an investment project.

NET EXPORTS
Changes in the interest rate also affect net exports (exports minus imports). As explained in chapter 9, changes in the interest rate will affect the *exchange rate* and this, in turn, will impact on net exports. In particular, a rise in Eurozone interest rates, *ceteris paribus*, will lead to an appreciation of the euro exchange rate. This, in turn, will make Eurozone exports more expensive and imports cheaper. The result will be a fall in net exports (NX).

Conversely, a fall in Eurozone interest rates, *ceteris paribus*, will lead to a depreciation of the euro exchange rate. This will make Eurozone exports cheaper or more competitive and imports dearer. The result is a rise in NX.

THE INTEREST RATE AND INTEREST-SENSITIVE EXPENDITURE

This inverse relationship between the real interest rate, on the one hand, and consumer expenditure, C, investment, I, and net exports, NX, is known as the *interest-sensitive expenditure* (IE) schedule and it is illustrated in figure 8.7. The interest rate is measured along the vertical axis and expenditure (C, I and NX), along the horizontal axis. If changes in the rate of interest have a weak effect on expenditure, then the IE curve will be *steep* (inelastic). If, on the other hand, changes in the rate of interest have a strong effect on expenditure, the IE curve will be *flat* (elastic). As we shall see, the slope of this IE schedule has an important bearing on the relative efficiency of fiscal and monetary policy.

8.7 MONETARY POLICY IN A CLOSED ECONOMY

We now incorporate our model of the money market and the IE curve into the AS/AD model developed in chapter 2. The expanded model of the economy contains two markets: the *goods or product market* and the *money market*. In the goods market, the interaction of the AS and AD curves determines real GNP and the price level. In the

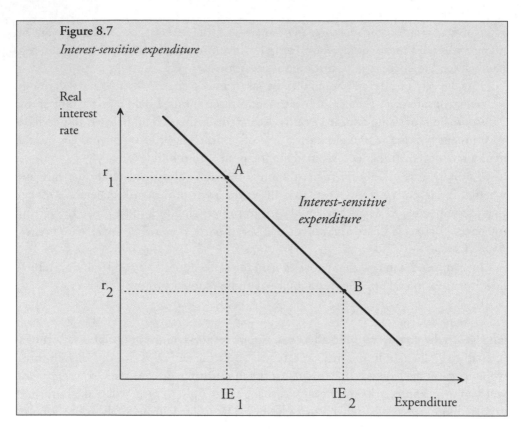

Figure 8.7
Interest-sensitive expenditure

money market, the supply and demand for money determines the nominal interest rate. The link or bridge between the goods and money market is the IE curve.

The authorities have *two policy instruments*, government expenditure and taxation (fiscal policy) and the money supply and interest rates (monetary policy), with which to influence real GNP and the price level.

Figure 8.8 illustrates the effect of an increase in the money supply. In the lower diagram, the central bank increases the money supply from M^s_1 to M^s_2. The nominal interest rate falls from i_1 to i_2. This fall in the nominal interest rate also leads to a fall in the real interest rate via the Fisher equation. In the centre diagram, the fall in the real interest rate leads to an increase in interest-sensitive expenditure (IE).

In the top diagram, the increase in IE shifts the aggregate demand schedule upwards to the right and the economy moves from the point A to the point B. In the short run, real GNP increases from GNP_1 to GNP_2 and the price level from P_1 to P_2. This increase in real output also leads to lower unemployment.

In the short run the sequence of events is:

$$\uparrow M^s \rightarrow \downarrow i \rightarrow \downarrow r \rightarrow \uparrow IE \rightarrow \uparrow AD \rightarrow \uparrow GNP \text{ and } \uparrow P$$

Note:
Fiscal policy is much more direct in its effects than monetary policy: an increase in G increases aggregate demand directly, whereas an increase in M^s operates indirectly through its effect on the rate of interest.

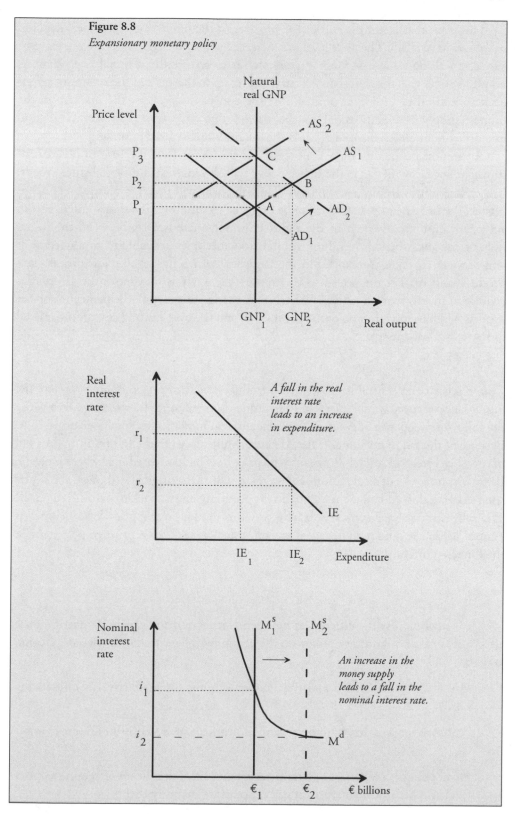

Figure 8.8
Expansionary monetary policy

However, that is not the end of the process. At the point B in the upper diagram, *real wages* have fallen. The price level has increased while nominal wages are unchanged. Workers will now increase their wage demands to restore the original real wage. As nominal wages rise, the short-run AS curve moves up to the left and the economy reverts back to natural real GNP at point C. At the end of the process, the increase in the money supply is exactly equal to the rise in the price level and real GNP and unemployment are unchanged. This is the quantity theory prediction.

An important qualification is necessary at this point. The increase in investment (brought about by the fall in the interest rate) will also increase the capital stock (roads, factories, equipment and technology). This, in turn, will increase natural real GNP. Hence, the increase in investment can be expected to shift both the short- and long-run aggregate supply curves out to the right. However, there is a lag between the initial investment and when the resultant capital stock becomes available to produce goods and services. It takes time to build the factories, set-up the production process and produce and market the product. To simplify the analysis we ignore the effect of a change in investment on natural real GNP. A change in consumer expenditure or net exports will have no effect on natural real GNP and the over-heating situation depicted in figure 8.8 will emerge.

DEFLATIONARY MONETARY POLICY

Conversely, if the central bank was to introduce a *deflationary* monetary policy, the money supply curve would shift left. (The reader is urged to re-draw figure 8.8 to verify the following sequence of events.) Nominal and real interest rates increase and IE falls. Because of the fall in investment, the AD curve shifts down to the left resulting in a fall in the price level and real GNP. Because the price level has decreased, real wages increase. If workers now accept a cut in nominal wages to restore the original real wage, the short-run AS curve shifts down to the right and the economy reverts back to natural real GNP. The fall in the money supply is exactly equal to the fall in the price level. Money is neutral in that it does not affect real variables such as real GNP or unemployment in the longer-term.

8.8 MONETARY POLICY AND THE KEYNESIAN, CLASSICAL DEBATE

We shall now discuss the differences between Keynes and the classics concerning the effects of fiscal and monetary policy on the economy. The extreme Keynesian position is that:

- Fiscal policy is effective and that monetary policy is ineffective in influencing GNP.

In contrast, neoclassical economists and monetarists such as Milton Friedman argue that:

- Fiscal policy is ineffective and monetary policy has a significant effect on the price level and little or no impact on real output (the quantity theory).

The disagreement between Keynesian and neoclassical economists essentially revolves about two relationships, namely, those between:

- The interest rate and the demand for money. This is referred to as the *interest elasticity of the demand for money*.
- The interest rate and interest-sensitive expenditure, that is, the *IE curve*.

KEYNESIAN POSITION

Keynesians argue that:

- The demand for money curve is relatively *flat*. This means that an increase in the money supply leads to a small decrease in the interest rate.
- The IE curve is relatively steep (inelastic). Changes in the interest rate have a weak effect on expenditure. With regard to the effect of the interest rate on investment, Keynes emphasised factors such as changes in the level of business confidence, uncertainty and expectations about the future. 'Dark forces, of time and ignorance which envelop our times.' For Keynes the problem was to examine 'the economic behaviour of the present under the influence of changing ideas of the future'.

The effect of these two assumptions is that monetary policy has a weak effect on real GNP and unemployment. A given increase in the money supply leads to a small change in the nominal and real interest rates. This, in turn, will have a weak effect on expenditure. Overall, the AD curve will not move very much to the right and there will be little or no change in real output and the price level. (Again we suggest that the reader experiments with figure 8.8 in order to verify that this is the case.)

Note:
If the demand for money curve is horizontal at low interest rates, an increase in the money supply along this portion of the M^d curve will have no effect on the interest rate. In this case, monetary policy cannot be used to increase output and employment. This is the liquidity trap.

CLASSICAL POSITION

Neoclassical economists, on the other hand, argue that:

- The demand for money curve is *steep* (inelastic). An increase in the money supply will lead to a large fall in the nominal interest rate.
- The IE curve is relatively *flat* (or elastic). Changes in the interest rate have a strong effect on expenditure (aggregate demand).

Note:
An early exposition of the classical position is given in Irving Fisher's *The Purchasing Power of Money*, New York: Macmillan, 1911. An early and very influential paper is Milton Friedman, 'The Quantity Theory of Money: A Restatement', in Milton Friedman (ed.) *Studies in the Quantity Theory of Money*, University of Chicago Press, 1956.

Taking these two assumptions together, an expansionary monetary policy leads to a significant fall in interest rates, which, in turn, provokes a large rise in expenditure (C, I and NX). However, as demonstrated in figure 8.8, the classical school point out that the long-run AS curve is *vertical* at natural real GNP. The result is that the expansionary monetary policy leads to a proportionate increase in the price level and has no effect on real output and unemployment.

Neoclassical economists also believe that fiscal policy has little or no effect on GNP. At first sight this appears rather odd. After all, an increase in government expenditure (G) boosts aggregate demand and GNP. Hence changes in government expenditure must influence GNP. Neoclassical economists, however, point to *crowding-out* as a reason why fiscal policy is ineffective.

8.9 CROWDING-OUT

An expansionary fiscal policy (changes in government expenditure and taxation) shifts the AD curve to the right and both real GNP and the price level increase. (We ignore here the possibility that changes in tax rates could affect the supply-side of the economy.) Hence, it seems certain that fiscal policy will increase nominal GNP (price level multiplied by real GNP). However, neoclassical economists dispute this conclusion by pointing to the crowding-out effect.

First, recall that total expenditure is equal to:

$$\text{Nominal GNP} = \text{Total expenditure} \equiv C + I + G + X - M \tag{8}$$

Where C is consumer expenditure, I is investment, G is government expenditure, X is exports and M is imports. An expansionary fiscal policy (increase in G) will increase total expenditure (aggregate demand) and nominal GNP. In short:

$$\uparrow G \rightarrow \uparrow AD \rightarrow \uparrow \text{nominal GNP}$$

However, the increase in nominal GNP increases the demand for money (M^d) via the transactions motive. If there is no increase in the money supply this will push up interest rates. The rise in interest rates will, in turn, lower interest-sensitive expenditure (IE). In terms of equation (8), the G element is going up and the IE components are going down. The initial increase in government expenditure thus leads to a reduction in IE. In other words, interest-sensitive expenditure has been crowded-out by government expenditure:

$$\uparrow \text{nominal GNP} \rightarrow \uparrow M^d \rightarrow \uparrow i \rightarrow \uparrow r \rightarrow \downarrow IE$$

If $\uparrow G = \downarrow IE$, there is 100 per cent crowding-out. In this case, AD and nominal GNP revert back to their original level and fiscal policy is completely ineffective. This is the extreme neoclassical position.

Figure 8.9 illustrates the crowding-out effect. The expansionary fiscal policy increases GNP (not shown). The increase in GNP, in turn, shifts the demand for money curve upwards from M^d_1 to M^d_2 (left-hand diagram). The interest rate rises from i_1 to i_2 along the vertical axis. In the right-hand diagram, the increase in the real interest rate

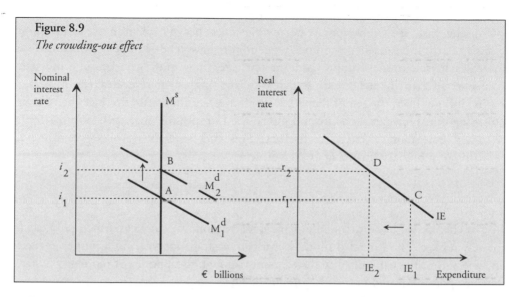

Figure 8.9
The crowding-out effect

reduces IE. In terms of the components of aggregate demand, the fall in IE offsets the initial increase in government expenditure and aggregate demand may revert back to its initial level.

The elasticity of the IE schedule is what determines the degree of crowding-out. The neoclassical contention that the IE is flat (elastic) at the current interest rate means that a small increase in the interest rate will have a relatively *large* effect on expenditure. If this is the case, crowding-out will be important. If, however, as the Keynesians argue, the IE curve is steep (inelastic), crowding-out will not be important, as changes in interest rates have little or no effect on expenditure.

Note:

In the course of our discussion of fiscal policy in Ireland, we mentioned 'expansionary fiscal contraction' in 1987. One possible explanation of this episode is that a form of 'reverse crowding-out' or 'crowding-in' occurred. According to this view, the reduced pressure on the domestic money market due to the lower budget deficits led to a reduction in interest rates, which stimulated IE. For this interpretation of events to be valid, IE would have had to increase by more than the reduction in public sector spending. This is more extreme than the case of complete crowding-out on which the classical case for the ineffectiveness of fiscal policy is based.

MONETARY FINANCING

It is important to note that the crowding-out effect only occurs when the money supply remains unchanged in the face of a fiscal expansion. If the money supply increases as the demand for money rises, the interest rate need not rise and crowding-out need not occur. In this context, the method of financing government expenditure is important. In the past, a government could finance its borrowing requirement from four sources: (i) abroad; (ii) central bank; (iii) commercial banks; and (iv) domestic non-bank public. Sources (i), (ii) and (iii) are referred to as *government monetary financing* (GMF). Borrowing from these sources increases the money supply. Borrowing from source (iv) does not affect the money supply.

In the past, Irish government borrowing relied heavily on monetary financing. Consequently, increases in government expenditure have tended to be accompanied by increases in the money supply and interest rates have not been unduly affected. Moreover, in a small open economy such as Ireland, higher interest rates tend to attract capital inflows from the rest of the world. Both these considerations reduce the risks of crowding-out. However, once Ireland joined the European Monetary Union in 1999, it signed the Stability and Growth Pact. This Pact severely restricts governments resorting to monetary financing of budget deficits.

8.10 Conclusion

In this chapter we have extended our basic macroeconomic model by incorporating a money market. The extended model consists of a goods market and a money market and the authorities can influence the economy through fiscal policy or monetary policy. The key points covered in this chapter included:

- The demand for money. Changes in nominal GNP and interest rates affect the demand for money
- The interaction of the supply and demand for money determine the nominal rate of interest
- The Fisher equation that distinguishes between nominal and real interest rates
- The link between interest rates and interest-sensitive expenditure is known as the IE schedule
- Monetary policy. Changes in the money supply affect aggregate demand and GNP via the real rate of interest and its influence on expenditure
- The differences between Keynes and the classics with regard to fiscal and monetary policy and the concept of crowding-out.

APPENDIX

NET PRESENT VALUE

The concept of the *net present value* (NPV) is used to demonstrate the effect of a change in the interest rate on the profitability of an investment project. The NPV technique is now routinely used in the evaluation of investment projects by firms, banks and governments.

The significance of the 'net' in NPV is that the income stream is net of costs. We are calculating the net income or profit from the investment project.

To illustrate its use, let us suppose that you have the opportunity of investing in a project that is forecast to generate profits over a three-year period. For simplicity, we assume that no assets remain at the end of the three-year project. We also ignore inflation, so that the above income flows are given in constant (year 1) prices.

How much would you be prepared to pay to buy into such a project? To answer this, we must discount the projected profit stream to calculate its NPV. Discounting is the inverse of the more familiar concept of *compounding*, according to which a sum of money, €x, invested today at r per cent is worth €x(1 + r) at the end of the year. Hence, €1,000 invested at 10 per cent generates a total return of €1,100: (€1,000(1 + 0.1) = €1,100).

Discounting inverts this process and asks: how much is €x to be paid at the end of a year worth today? What is its present value? The answer is $€x/(1 + r)$. Extending this logic, a sum paid at the end of two years has a present value of $€x/(1+r)^2$. Similarly, a sum of money paid at the end of three years has a NPV of $€x/(1+r)^3$.

Assuming a real interest rate of 5 per cent (r = 0.05), table 8.2 shows how the NPV of a hypothetical profit stream is calculated. (Note that what matters for investment projects is the real, not the nominal, rate of interest.)

Table 8.2
Calculating net present value using a 5 per cent discount rate

Year	Net profit at end of year	Discount factor	Present value
	€	€	€
	(1)	(2)	(3) = (1) × (2)
1	100,000	$1/(1.05) = 0.9524$	95,238
2	110,000	$1/(1.05)^2 = 0.9070$	99,773
3	105,000	$1/(1.05)^3 = 0.8638$	90,703
	Total = €315,000		Project's NPV = €285,714

These calculations tell us that while this project yields an undiscounted profit stream of €315,000, the NPV of this profit stream is €285,714, given an interest rate of 5 per cent.

Table 8.3
NPV and the interest rate

Interest rate (%)	NPV (€)
0.0	315,000
2.5	299,763
5.0	285,714
7.5	272,731
10.0	260,706

Table 8.3 shows how the NPV of the hypothetical investment project falls as the interest rate increases. As, for example, the interest rate rises from 5 to 10 per cent, the NPV falls from €285,714 to €260,706. The higher the rate of interest, therefore, the lower the value of the project to a prospective investor. As a consequence, a rise in the interest rate can make a previously profitable project unprofitable. A fall in the interest

rate can make an unprofitable project profitable. This then explains the inverse relationship between interest rates and investment.

Note that the interest rate has a greater effect on the NPV of projects that are long-lived: some very capital-intensive investments that have a very long life, such as electricity-generating projects, can only be profitable at low rates of interest.

CHAPTER 9

The Foreign Exchange Market and Exchange Rates

9.1 INTRODUCTION

In this chapter we expand out study of macroeconomics by introducing international trade, capital flows and exchange rates. We move away from the closed economy models of earlier chapters and introduce open economy macroeconomics. We begin by explaining the balance of payments and its relationship with the foreign exchange market. This leads to a discussion of the factors that influence exchange rates in the short- and medium-term.

9.2 THE BALANCE OF PAYMENTS

The balance of payments is a record of a country's economic transactions with the rest of the world. It tracks all transactions that involve the exchange of domestic currency for foreign currencies and vice versa. The basic rules in drawing up the balance of payments accounts are:

- Items, such as exports, that lead to a *receipt* of foreign exchange are *positive* entries or inflows.
- Items, such as imports, that lead to *payments* of foreign exchange are *negative* entries or outflows.

Table 9.1 presents a simplified version of the Eurozone balance of payments for 2000. There are three main sub-headings:

- Current account
- Capital account
- Financial account, that is, changes in central bank external reserves.

Of course it is not possible to keep exact track of the myriad dealings between countries so that there is always an entry at the end of the accounts referring to errors and omissions. This ensures that everything adds up!

Note that since 1999 Ireland has not had a separate national currency but is using the euro along with eleven other EU countries. While we still tend to think of the 'Irish balance of payments' it is largely irrelevant now because it does not track the supply and demand for a separate currency. In what follows we focus on the Eurozone accounts.

THE CURRENT ACCOUNT

Within the current account there are four further sub-accounts, showing the balance on:

Table 9.1
Euro billions, net flows

	€ billions
Current account	
1. Goods	52.2
2. Services	−15.3
3. Income	−20.2
4. Current transfers	−51.4
5. Balance on current account	−34.7
Capital account	
6. Balance	10.4
Financial account	
7. Direct investment	−22.8
8. Portfolio investment	−128.9
9. Financial derivatives	−1.1
10. Other investment	142.0
11. Reserve assets	17.5
12. Balance on capital account	6.8
13. Errors and omissions	17.5

Source: European Central Bank, *Monthly Bulletin*, October, 2001, Table 8.1, 57.

- Trade in goods
- Trade in services
- Net income from abroad
- Current transfers.

Each of these sub-accounts is now considered briefly.

Trade in goods (or merchandise trade) refers to exports and imports of goods. In 2000, there was a surplus of exports over imports equivalent to €52.2 billion. The Irish economy also had a surplus on the trade account in 2000. In that year, Irish merchandise exports exceeded imports by €14,680 million. This substantial surplus reflects the very strong export performance of Irish industry in recent years.

Figure 9.1 shows exports and imports as a percentage of GDP for the Irish economy over the period 1960–2000. The difference between the two series is the balance of trade. Note that both exports and imports have increased substantially as a percentage of GDP over the years. Exports now amount to 95 per cent of GDP compared to only 30 per cent in 1960. This documents the extreme openness of the economy. Ireland's trade account was in deficit up to 1985, but since then it has recorded a trade surplus.

The *services* sub-account records transactions such as international freight, tourism and travel. In the Eurozone, there was a deficit of €15.3 billion in 2001. In Ireland there has also been a significant deficit on this sub-account in recent years. This is in part due

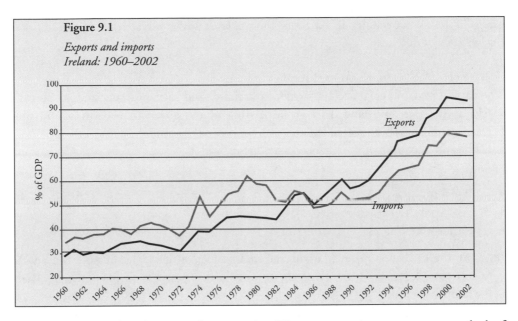

Figure 9.1

*Exports and imports
Ireland: 1960–2002*

to the dealings of multinational companies. These companies export a great deal of goods, but they have to pay significant amounts for services they buy from abroad. These service payments are usually under the heading of royalties and licenses.

The *income* sub-account records dividends and interest on foreign and domestic investments. This represented a deficit of €20.2 billion for the Eurozone in 2000. Similarly in Ireland, the income sub-account was in deficit in 2000. This reflects the importance of *profit remittances* by the multinational companies and the external payments on our national debt.

Finally, the *current transfers* sub-account reflects payments and receipts that are made but not in return for services rendered or goods purchased. Examples are aid to less developed countries and remittances from emigrants. In Ireland, this entry is positive due to the transfers from the European Union.

Putting these sub-accounts together, the result was an overall deficit of €34.7 billion for the Eurozone in 2000.

MULTINATIONAL COMPANIES AND THE BALANCE OF PAYMENTS

It is important to stress how the operation of multinational companies in Ireland affects the current account. These companies account for much of the enormous surplus in merchandise exports, but their payments of royalties, interest, and dividends to parent companies and shareholders are recorded as outflows in the other sub-accounts of the current account. Most of the effects of *transfer pricing* cancel out in the overall current account. This point has been much misunderstood in recent discussion of the issue.

Note:
Transfer pricing occurs when multinational firms try to maximise the profits in a low tax country. Ireland, with its 12.5 per cent corporate profits tax on manufacturing industry and internationally traded services is such a location. A subsidiary company in a high tax country can sell inputs at a low book cost to a subsidiary company in a low tax country. The effect is to boost

profits in the low tax country. In due course most of these profits will be remitted abroad from the low tax country.

THE CAPITAL AND FINANCIAL ACCOUNTS

The capital and financial accounts record purchases and sales of assets such as bonds, stocks and shares, and land. Foreign borrowing by the government, banks, and the private sector are also included here.

The sub-accounts of the financial account record:

- Direct investment
- Portfolio investment
- Financial derivatives
- Other investments

In 2000, the Eurozone recorded an overall financial account surplus of €6.8 billion. A very substantial deficit on the portfolio account was offset by a surplus on the 'other investments' account.

The financial account also includes changes in *reserve assets*. This is the (official) reserve of the European Central Bank (ECB). It consists of the holdings of foreign currency (dollars, sterling and yen) and a small amount of gold. In January 1999, €40 billion was transferred from the national central banks of the Eurozone to the ECB. This money consisted of 15 per cent gold (750 tons) and 85 per cent in dollars and yen. In August 2001, the total external reserves of the Eurozone came to €382.2 billion of which €45.9 was held by the ECB and the remainder of €336.3 was held by the national central banks.

Finally, errors and omissions refer to unexplained flows through the balance of payments. This is the inflow and outflow of funds on which the authorities have no information. In the following section we explain how we arrive at the figure for errors and omissions.

ERRORS AND OMISSIONS

The overall balance of payments should sum to zero. In order to explain this statement note that:

- A *receipt* by a Eurozone resident from abroad leads to a *demand for euro* on the foreign exchange market. (This market is discussed below.) Suppose, for example, a Eurozone exporter sells goods in the UK and receives sterling in return. The sterling receipts are exchanged for euro in a bank and this leads to a demand for euro.
- A foreign *payment* by a resident leads to a *supply of euro* on the foreign exchange market. If an Irish importer needs to obtain sterling to pay his UK supplier, euro are exchanged for sterling in a bank. The importer is in effect supplying euro and demanding sterling.

Now the overall balance of payments should *sum to zero* because it takes two parties to complete a transaction. If someone is supplying (selling) euro on the foreign exchange market, then someone else must be demanding (buying) them. Hence, referring to table 9.1, the current account (CA) deficit, the capital account (CP) surplus and the financial account (FA) surplus should sum to zero:

$$CA + CP + FA = 0 \tag{1}$$

Independent estimates provide data of these three magnitudes. Using the data in table 9.1 we find that:

$$-€34.7 + €10.4 + €6.8 \neq 0.0$$

A current account deficit of $-€34.7$ billion, a capital account surplus of €10.4 billion and a financial account surplus of €6.8 give an overall balance of payments deficit of $-€17.5$ billion. To reconcile the accounts, it is necessary to include the errors and omissions entry.

This reflects unrecorded transactions, and errors and omissions in the current, capital and financial accounts. It includes money that is being moved illegally into and out of the country and similar 'hidden economy' transactions.

Inserting a residual item (NR) into equation 1:

$$CA + CP + FA = NR \tag{2}$$

Using again the data from table 9.1 we have:

$$-€34.7 + €10.4 + €6.8 = -€17.5$$

Note that when the NR ($-€17.5$ billion) is taken over to the left-hand side in equation 2, it appears with a positive sign. This is why it is given as a positive €17.5 billion in table 9.1.

THE SIGNIFICANCE OF THE BALANCE OF PAYMENTS

It is easy to think of a current account surplus as good and a deficit as bad. This reflects the *mercantilist fallacy* according to which a country should maximise its exports. Named after the seventeenth-century economists who believed that a country grew powerful by amassing gold obtained from running balance of trade surpluses. In fact exports are only valuable in that they allow us to purchase imports. There is nothing inherently bad in a current account deficit provided there is a capital account surplus to offset it.

However, it should be noted that a capital account surplus is akin to foreign borrowing. Foreign investors are, in effect, lending us money. This increases a country's future debt service obligations. The money has to be repaid with interest at some stage in the future. As a result, sooner or later foreign exchange markets tend to take a dim view of a country that pays for current account deficits with large capital account surpluses. There were crises in Mexico in 1994–95 and in Malaysia, Thailand and several other South Asian countries in 1997 due to panics over their ability to continue to borrow abroad to finance balance of payments deficits. The other side of the coin is to offset a current account surplus by having a capital account deficit. This can be achieved by accumulating foreign assets and reserves. However, beyond a certain level it does not make sense to continue exporting just to accumulate foreign assets. Perhaps the best advice is that given by Polonius in *Hamlet*: 'Neither a lender nor borrower be...'.

Certainly, over time a country should think of balancing its books instead of running large and cumulative surpluses or deficits. This simply follows from the idea that no person and no country can get away with borrowing indefinitely. Trying to 'pass the buck' to future generations in this manner is known as a Ponzi Game, named after the notorious Boston conman, Charles Ponzi. In the space of eight months he raised nearly $15 million from 40,000 investors by promising to double their money in ninety days by investing in stamps. In fact he was running a financial chain letter, using new money to pay off previous investors. Sooner or later this process has to stop. The FBI arrested Ponzi in 1920 and he spent three and a half years in jail. A similar scheme operated from Dun Laoghaire, Co. Dublin in the 1960s, known as Shanahan's Stamp Auctions. Financing an ever larger current account deficit through a capital inflow resembles a Ponzi scheme.

9.3 THE FOREIGN EXCHANGE MARKET

Most countries have their own national currencies. The *foreign exchange market* is the market where these currencies are bought and sold. This market is essential for trade between countries that use different currencies. Consider, for example, an Irish firm sending a shipment of computers to the US. If the US importer pays the Irish exporter in dollars, the Irish exporter will exchange these dollars for euro on the foreign exchange market. This completes the transfer of purchasing power from the US importer to the Irish firm.

The foreign exchange market spans the globe by means of telephones, computers and telex machines, and is open twenty-four hours a day. It is possible to sell, for example, dollars for euro in Tokyo and buy sterling for euro in Dublin. The main markets are in Sydney, Tokyo, Hong Kong, Singapore, Bahrain, Frankfurt, London, New York, Chicago and San Francisco. The opening hours of these markets overlap so it is possible to buy or sell currencies at any time of the day or night.

EXCHANGE RATES

The exchange rate is the price of one currency in terms of another. In Ireland, the exchange rate is defined as the foreign price per unit of the domestic currency. This is referred to as an *indirect quote*. In the middle of 2002, a euro was worth about $0.98, Stg£0.63 and Yen118. Those were the foreign currency prices of the euro. This way of quoting exchange rates is the British convention, used in Ireland, the UK, Australia and New Zealand. The alternative (American and European) convention is known as a *direct quote*. This expresses the domestic currency (the euro) in terms of the foreign currency. Following this convention, the euro exchange rate was €1.02 per $1, €1.59 per Stg£ and €0.008 per ¥1.

The reason why Ireland and the UK use indirect quotes was that it was awkward to express the price of foreign currencies in the old pounds, shillings and pence (£. s. d.) used up to the early 1970s in Ireland and the UK.

If a currency falls in value relative to the foreign currency, it *depreciates*; if it rises, it *appreciates*. For example, as the dollar moves from \$0.88/€1 to \$0.98/€1 this is an appreciation of the euro. Irish residents would obtain more dollars than before. If sterling moved from €0.62/€1 to Stg£0.52/€1, this would be a depreciation. Less sterling would be obtained for every euro.

An advantage of the British convention is that when a currency appreciates, its exchange rate rises, when it depreciates its exchange rate falls. This is more natural than what happens under the American convention, with a rise in the exchange rate implying a depreciation, and a fall an appreciation. We follow the British convention in this book.

BID AND OFFER EXCHANGE RATES

Bureaux de change and banks charge hefty commissions for small transactions in foreign currencies. As a result, converting small amounts of currency is expensive. In addition to commission charges, banks earn a profit by quoting different exchange rates for buying and selling foreign currency. These rates are known as the *bid rate* (the rate at which banks will buy euro or sell foreign currency) and the *offer rate* (the rate at which banks sell euro or buy foreign currency). The difference between the bid and offer rates is known as the spread. Table 9.2 shows bid and offer \$/euro rates quoted by the banks for December 2001. Note that the exchange rates quoted relate to transactions less than €1,000. The spread decreases on transactions greater than €1,000.

Table 9.2
Bid and offer rates for the dollar, euro exchange rate: December 2001

Bid	Offer
0.8758	0.8998

Source: Allied Irish Banks, International Department.

For example, the bank will pay you €1,111.35 for \$1,000. Later the bank will sell \$1,000 to another customer for €1,141.81. The profit to the bank from this transaction is €30.46.

9.4 THE RISE AND FALL OF THE IRISH FOREIGN EXCHANGE MARKET

Up to the early 1970s there was virtually no foreign exchange market in Ireland. The sterling/Irish pound exchange rate was fixed at a one-to-one parity, a very large proportion of Irish trade was with the UK, and the commercial banks held their reserves in sterling in London. The Irish demand for currencies such as dollars and francs was easily dealt with on the London foreign exchange market. In 1969, the Money Market Committee set up by the Central Bank of Ireland under the chairmanship of Professor W. J. L. Ryan, recommended that the Central Bank of Ireland (CBI) should encourage the development of a foreign exchange market. In line with this recommendation, in the early 1970s the commercial banks reserves were transferred from London to the CBI and the banks were requested to conduct their foreign exchange business directly with the CBI. In 1976 the CBI quoted for small amounts of foreign exchange. This encouraged the banks to hire and train dealers and to conduct more of their business directly between themselves and on world foreign exchange markets.

Up until 1979 the exchange rate of the Irish pound was fixed to sterling on a one-to-one basis. (Fixed exchange rate systems are discussed in chapter 10.) On 13 March 1979, Ireland entered the exchange rate mechanism (ERM) of the European Monetary System (EMS) but the pound sterling did not. The potential now existed for a breaking of the sterling link and the birth of a new currency: the Irish pound. *The Irish Times* economics correspondent tells the story.

> Finally, the day came. On March the 29th, sterling went on a strong run . . . and things were happening. After the close (of business) that day, the pound was trading outside the EMS limits and I called a New York bank several times for rates of sterling against the DM (Deutsche Mark). It was the makings of a scoop. None of the other papers had been on to the story to the same degree — and I hoped that they were not on to the goings on that night. Finally, at about 7.30 p.m. I rang the governor of the Central Bank (Charles Murray) at home and reported on the latest rates from New York. I didn't need to. What would happen if the same rates applied in the morning? Without any equivocation he said: 'we'll break the link', and I had my story. We had the scoop on the front page the next morning — and within hours of the paper appearing, history had been made.'
>
> (Ken O'Brien, 'Anatomy of a "scoop"', *Finance*, March, 1989)

On the morning of 30 March 1979 the sterling exchange rate fell and for a time the one-to-one exchange rate held. However, sterling then rose to a level that was incompatible with holding the Irish pound in the EMS band and soon afterwards the link was broken. The first deal was done at 10.15 a.m. when Stg£500,000 was purchased at an exchange rate of IR£1 = Stg£0.9975. With the termination of the sterling link, Irish foreign exchange dealers moved from being 'price-takers' to being 'price-makers'. Many firms with large sterling debt lost heavily as the Irish pound unexpectedly depreciated against sterling. However, the banks coped very well with the new arrangements.

Over the next two decades the Irish foreign exchange market grew at a significant pace. By the late 1990s, the daily turnover was in excess of £2.5 billion. About 80 per cent of the deals involve exchanging one foreign currency for another. For example, exchanging sterling for Deutsche Marks or dollars. This is because an Irish firm might be selling into the US (dollar receipts) and buying its raw materials in the UK (sterling payments). The firm would then exchange dollars for sterling in order to pay its bills in the UK. Only a small proportion of the dollar receipts would be exchanged for Irish pounds.

From early in 2002, the national currencies of the twelve countries participating in European Monetary Union (EMU) ceased to exist and were replaced by the euro. New euro notes and coins were put into circulation and the old national currencies withdrawn. The twelve countries that comprise the Eurozone (2002) are: Austria, Belgium, France, Finland, Germany, Greece, Ireland, Italy, Luxembourg, the

Netherlands, Spain and Portugal. The foreign exchange dealers in Ireland have again become price-takers when they quote exchange rates for the euro. The introduction of the euro entailed a considerable loss of business for the banks. The numbers employed in foreign currency dealing fell.

9.5 THE EXCHANGE RATE OF THE IRISH POUND AND THE EURO

Figures 9.2 and 9.3 show the exchange rate of the Irish pound to sterling and the dollar over the period 1955–2000. These were the most important bilateral rates of the Irish pound. As already mentioned, up to March 1979, the sterling/IR£ rate was fixed on a one-to-one basis. Between 1979–99 this exchange rate moved fairly widely in both directions but it did not drift far from the original parity. Some of the main trends in the value of the Irish pound since 1979 now follow.

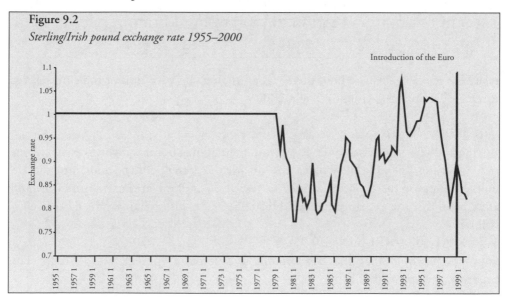

Figure 9.2
Sterling/Irish pound exchange rate 1955–2000

After the break in the link with sterling, the Irish pound depreciated sharply, falling as low as Stg£0.72 in 1981. In the later half of the 1980s it gained relative to sterling, culminating in the crisis of 1992, when sterling depreciated sharply against the EMS currencies and the Irish pound rose to Stg£1.10. Following the 10 per cent devaluation of January 1993 the Irish pound traded at lower levels, depreciating sharply as sterling strengthened in 1997–98.

The US$/IR£ exchange rate has fluctuated widely, reflecting the movement of the dollar against the European currencies, as well as the fluctuations of the Irish pound relative to the latter. The dollar was weak in 1980 but climbed to a peak in 1985 (when for a brief period the IR£1 was worth less than $1), but in the latter half of the 1980s it weakened considerably. The dollar strengthened in the mid-1990s. The absence of a clear trend in the value of the dollar is sometimes referred to as the 'dance of the dollar'.

Figures 16.4, 16.5 and 16.6 in chapter 16 shows the exchange rate of the euro to dollar, sterling and the yen. It can be seen that whereas the exchange rate has been

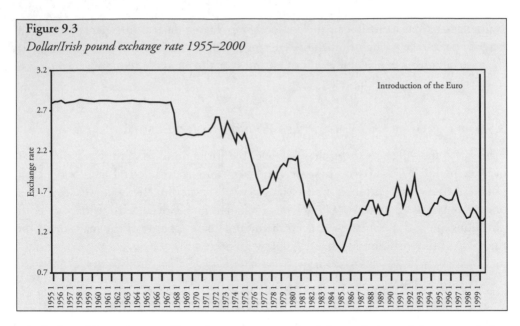

Figure 9.3

Dollar/Irish pound exchange rate 1955–2000

relatively stable against sterling, there was a sustained depreciation of the euro relative to the dollar and the yen until late in 2000.

IMPORTANCE OF THE EXCHANGE RATE

Buying and selling goods and services across international borders involves *exchange rate risk*. Consider, for example, the case of an Irish exporter selling goods into the US market. Suppose the exporter expects to receive $1 million in one month's time and anticipates that the exchange rate will be $0.96/£1. At this exchange rate, euro receipts will be:

€1,041,667 = ($1 million/0.96)

Suppose, however, that the Irish pound unexpectedly appreciates to $0.98. The exporter's receipts will only be:

€1,020,408 = ($1 million/0.98)

This is €21,259 less than was anticipated and could render the deal unprofitable. Hence, even small changes in the exchange rate can result in large profits or losses. Note that when exporters lose, importers gain. The importer has to pay less euro for US goods and services.

Traders naturally wish to minimise this type of risk. In chapter 19 we outline a number of different *hedging techniques* that have been developed for this purpose. However, these hedging techniques only offer short-term protection against exchange rate risk. In the longer-term the firm will have to accept the consequences of exchange rate movements.

From a *macroeconomic perspective*, a change in the exchange rate will affect a country's competitive position. This, in turn, affects the aggregate demand curve and, therefore, inflation, the real growth rate and unemployment. A misaligned exchange rate is economically damaging. At least over the short run, an overvalued currency adversely affects a number of key macroeconomic variables, while an undervalued currency will have some beneficial effects. Over-valuation leads to a loss of competitiveness and makes it difficult to export, while imports become more attractive. This is like an adverse shock to the aggregate demand curve.

9.6 EXCHANGE RATE DETERMINATION

As discussed in section 9.2:

- Any transaction that gives rise to a receipt (export) of foreign currency leads to a *demand* for euro.
- Conversely, any transaction that gives rise to a payment (import) by Irish residents abroad leads to a *supply* of euro.

A graphical representation of the supply and demand for euro is given in figure 9.4. The exchange rate, e, is expressed as the foreign currency price of a euro (for example, $/€) on the vertical axis and the number of euro supplied/demanded is shown on the horizontal axis. The demand curve is downward sloping and the supply curve is upward sloping. Consider first the demand curve.

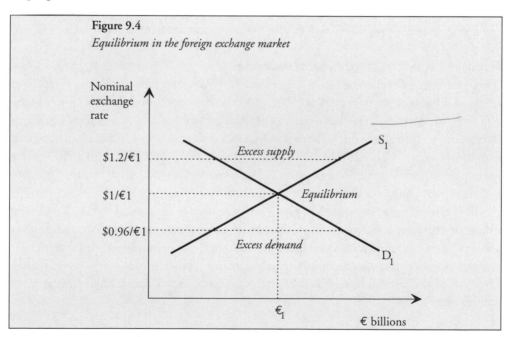

Figure 9.4
Equilibrium in the foreign exchange market

THE DEMAND FOR EURO

A downward-sloping demand schedule implies that a depreciation increases the demand for euro. When the euro depreciates Irish exporters can reduce their prices abroad. Irish exports become more competitive and, as a result, more are demanded. The demand for euro increases. Start from an exchange rate of $1.2 = €1. Ignoring transport costs, taxes and other factors, if the price of a sweater is €40 in Dublin, at this exchange rate the price in New York would be $48. If the euro depreciates to $1/€1, and Irish prices and costs do not change in the short run, the sweater will still cost €40 in Dublin but the exporter could afford to lower the New York price to $40. At the lower price in New York more sweaters are sold and as a result the demand for euro increases.

Alternatively, the exporter could decide to leave the New York price at $48 and allow her profits to benefit in full from the depreciation. Assuming no change in the number of sweaters sold, the demand for euro would still increase because the euro equivalent of $48 would rise from €40 to €48. Thus a devaluation must increase the value of exports denominated in the home currency. This is why the demand curve for the home currency slopes downwards.

THE SUPPLY OF EURO

An upward-sloping supply curve for euro indicates that a depreciation reduces the supply of euro on the foreign exchange market and an appreciation increases it. The logic behind this is that a depreciation makes imports more expensive and consequently less are sold. For example, at an exchange rate of $1.2/€1, a pair of jeans selling for $30 in New York would sell in Dublin for €25. If the euro depreciates to $0.95, the Dublin price would rise to €31.58 unless some of the depreciation was absorbed as lower profits by the US exporter. As the price increases the quantity of imports falls. Provided the demand for imports is price elastic the euro value of imports will fall, leading to a reduction in the supply of euro to the foreign exchange market.

EQUILIBRIUM IN THE FOREIGN EXCHANGE MARKET

The equilibrium exchange rate is determined by the intersection of the supply and demand schedules. In figure 9.4 at a rate of $1/€1 the supply and demand for euro are equal. At an exchange rate higher than this, say, $1.2/€1, there is an excess supply of euro. This is equivalent to a balance of payments deficit on the combined current and capital accounts. The value of payments is greater than that of receipts. At a lower exchange rate, say $0.96/€1, there is an excess demand for euro which, under a floating exchange rate regime, leads to an appreciation.

The crucial point is that the foreign exchange market must clear. When there is an excess demand for a currency, its value rises (the exchange rate appreciates) and when there is an excess supply, its value falls (the exchange rate depreciates). Appreciation or depreciation continues until supply equals demand. Hence under a floating exchange rate system the current and private capital accounts of the balance of payments must sum to zero.

EXCHANGE RATE REGIMES

There are different ways of organising the foreign exchange market for a currency. The dominant arrangement, which currently applies to the world's main currencies, is *floating exchange rates*. This means that currencies are free to move up or down in response to shifts in the supply and demand for currencies.

When the exchange rate is floating, in principle governments and central banks do not intervene to *peg* or *fix* the value of currencies. As a consequence, exchange rates may be very unstable or volatile. But in fact it is difficult to find a situation where exchange rates are allowed to float completely free of central bank intervention. Central banks buy and sell foreign exchange in order to stabilise the market and keep currencies in informal *target ranges*. Even when there is no formal target range, central bankers and ministers for finance may believe that their currencies are 'too high' or 'too low' and try to nudge the rate up or down by intervening. This is known as *dirty floating*.

The alternative to floating is a fixed exchange rate regime. Under this arrangement the values of currencies are fixed or pegged relative to each other. Governments and central banks are committed to maintaining the declared parities. The gold standard and the post-war Bretton Woods system were examples of such a regime. Between 1979 and 1993 the EMS was a *quasi-fixed exchange rate regime*. Exchange rates were not rigidly fixed, but formal target (or central) rates were set and currencies were expected to be kept within a ± 2.25 per cent band round these rates. In mid-1993 this system was greatly weakened. The margin of fluctuation was widened to ± 15 per cent in recognition of the strains caused by trying to maintain narrower bands. Fixed exchange rate systems are explained in chapter 11.

Note:

The terms depreciation and appreciation are used for changes in a floating exchange rate. Devaluation and revaluation are applied when a fixed or pegged exchange rate is moved down or up.

9.7 THE J CURVE

The foreign exchange market does not always adjust in the well-behaved manner described above. It is possible that a depreciation increases the Irish pound value of imports and the supply curve slopes down. To see how this could happen note that:

Value of imports $= P_m \times Q_m$

where P_m and Q_m are the price and quantity of imports. A depreciation leads to a rise in P_m and a fall in Q_m, but whether the value of imports (in euro) rises or falls depends on the price elasticity of demand for imports.

If the price elasticity is less than one (inelastic), then as P_m increases following a depreciation, Q_m will fall less than proportionately and $(P_m \times Q_m)$, will increase. This could happen if a large proportion of imported goods have no domestically produced substitutes. An example of such imports would be petroleum products in Ireland. Under these circumstances the supply curve of euro is downward sloping and the foreign exchange market unstable. This is illustrated in figure 9.5. The market is initially in equilibrium at an exchange rate of $1.2/€1$. If the exchange rate fell to $1/€1$ there would be an excess supply of euro, leading to further depreciation. The exchange rate would move away from equilibrium.

The slope of the supply curve for the domestic currency has implications for the effect of a depreciation or devaluation on the current account of the balance of payments. If there is a downward-sloping supply curve for the home currency, as in figure 9.5, then a depreciation will lead to a deterioration, rather than an improvement, in the current account.

In figure 9.6 the current account is shown along the vertical axis and time along the

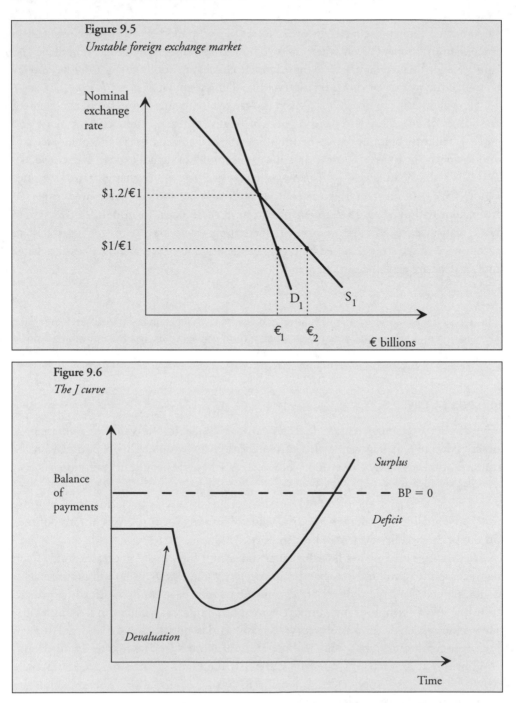

Figure 9.5
Unstable foreign exchange market

Figure 9.6
The J curve

horizontal axis. We have also inserted a line labelled CA = 0. Along this line the current account is zero. Points above the line are associated with a current account surplus and points below with a deficit. Suppose that the country is experiencing a current account deficit and the government decides to devalue the currency in order to correct this. If the supply curve of domestic currency is downward sloping, the devaluation initially leads to a deterioration in the current account. In due course, however, the price effects work in the correct direction (the long-run elasticity of demand for imports is greater than one), so there is eventually an 'improvement' in the current account. The curve that maps out how the current account reacts to a devaluation under these assumptions, it is known as the J-curve.

9.8 Shifts in Supply and Demand

The equilibrium exchange rate changes due to shifts in the demand and supply schedules. These are caused by changes in the factors such as income, world prices and preferences. The following are some examples of developments that would shift these schedules:

- A fall in the demand for exports due to a recession in Europe's trading partners would shift the demand for euro to the left.
- The fall in tourism from the US to Europe due to the September 11, 2001 atrocity shifted the demand for euro down to the left.
- The restrictions on movements introduced in response to the foot and mouth epidemic in 2001 reduced the flow of tourists into the UK and the demand for sterling fell.
- An increase in foreign borrowing by Irish banks or the government in the London money market would shift the demand for euro to the right.

If the exchange rate is floating, the first two events would cause a depreciation, the second two an appreciation. Figure 9.7 illustrates an increase in the demand for imports due, for example, to higher oil prices. This shifts the supply schedule of euro to the right. If the exchange rate is floating it will depreciate from $1.2/€1 to $1/€1. The lower panel shows an increase in the demand for Irish exports brought about, for example, by a successful marketing campaign for Irish exports, and the exchange rate appreciates from $1/€1 to $1.3/€1.

9.9 Factors Influencing Exchange Rates in the Medium-term

Factors influencing exchange rates in the medium-term include inflation, interest rates and growth rates. A rise in Irish inflation relative to that in other countries will lead to a loss of competitiveness. As a result, exports will tend to decline and imports to increase. In the foreign exchange market, the fall in exports shifts the demand curve down to the left and the rise in imports shifts the supply curve down to the right. As shown in figure 9.8, the result is a depreciation of the exchange rate. Countries with relatively high inflation rates tend to have weak or depreciating currencies, while those with relatively low inflation rates tend to have strong or appreciating currencies. The link between inflation and exchange rates is one version of the theory known as *purchasing power parity* (PPP). This theory is discussed in detail in chapter 10.

Governments or central banks frequently use *interest rates* to influence capital inflows or outflows from a country and thereby attempt to influence the exchange rate. For example, if interest rates are higher in the Eurozone than the US this could lead to a capital inflow as investors take advantage of the higher returns. The inflow of funds

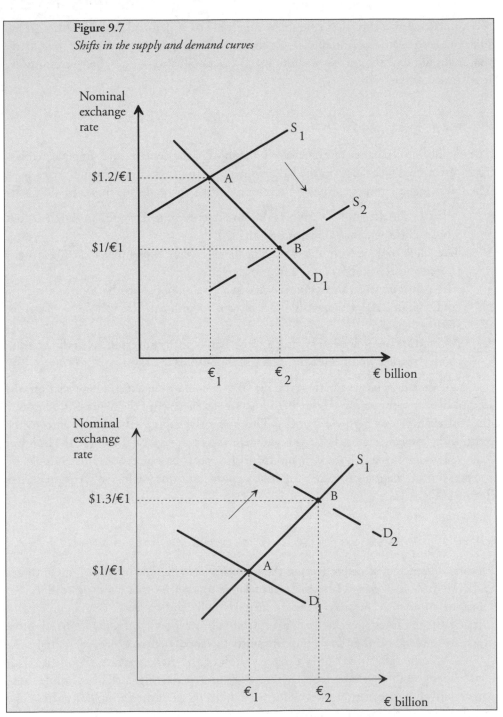

Figure 9.7
Shifts in the supply and demand curves

shifts the demand curve up to the right and the exchange rate tends to appreciate. Conversely, relatively lower interest rates in the Eurozone could lead to a capital outflow as investors move funds into the US. This outflow of capital shifts the supply curve down to the right and the exchange rate falls. Generally, central banks use interest rates in an attempt to prevent a depreciation of the exchange rate.

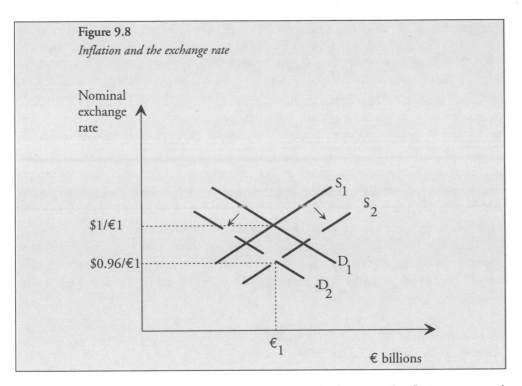

Figure 9.8
Inflation and the exchange rate

But more fundamentally, countries with relatively high expected inflation rates tend to have relatively high nominal interest rates (recall our discussion of the Fisher effect in chapter 8). As we shall see, a high nominal interest rate is a price that investors extract before they are prepared to hold currencies that are likely to depreciate.

The *real growth rate* has two effects on the balance of payments. First, a rapid rate of economic growth leads increases the demand for imports (via the marginal propensity to import) and this will lead to a trade deficit. Second, a rapid rate of economic growth may be reflected in high company profits, a rising stock market, and high share dividends. This could lead to a capital inflow as investors attempt to take advantage of the profit opportunities offered by the boom. The result will be a capital account surplus. As long as the capital account surplus is greater than the current (trade) account deficit, the exchange rate will appreciate. This has been the situation in the US in the 1990s and into the twenty-first century. Despite massive current account deficits, the dollar appreciated against most other currencies due to a capital account surplus.

9.10 SPECULATION

When discussing the balance of payments in section 9.2, we assumed that the demand and supply of foreign exchange arise because people wish to import and export goods and services or to deal in assets such as stocks and shares across national boundaries. However, the reality of foreign exchange markets today is that in the short run they are dominated by speculative flows, that is, individuals and institutions trying to make money by dealing in currencies. This can be done by correctly anticipating movements in exchange rates.

Speculators can shift vast amounts of money from one currency to another in the course of a few minutes. A speculator tries to buy a currency cheap and sell it dear. The profit is derived from correctly anticipating an exchange rate movement. A simplified example would be if a speculator believed today's exchange rate of $0.96/€1 is too high. He expects the dollar to appreciate; that is, the euro to depreciate. If he buys €1 million worth of dollars at $0.96 he obtains $960,000. If the euro depreciates to $0.89 he can sell these dollars and obtain €1,078,651: a profit of 12.3 per cent. Not all of this will be pure profit, however, because the speculator probably had to borrow the money used in this deal. The net profit depends on the interest rate paid on the loan, the interest rate earned on the dollars, and the length of time the speculator had to wait for the anticipated devaluation to materialise. Of course, if the devaluation did not materialise he would have made a loss due to the cost of the borrowed funds.

Note that under a floating exchange rate regime there is no scope for this type of speculation: because as soon as dealers begin to sell the currency, it depreciates. Fixed or pegged exchange rates offer speculators opportunities of gains that are absent under floating exchange rate systems.

SELLING SHORT

Speculators frequently sell a currency short, that is, they sell the currency on the *forward market* (for delivery sometime in the future) and hope to be able to complete the contract by buying the currency at a lower price when the time comes. We discuss the forward foreign exchange market in chapter 19.

Speculative attacks developed on the currencies of the European Monetary System (EMS) during the crisis of 1992–93. Speculators took the view that the value of sterling was too high and begin to sell it short in anticipation of making a profit when it is devalued.

In September 1992 the Hungarian-born financier George Soros, among others, became convinced that the British government would not be able to maintain sterling at its level in the EMS. He speculated that the pound would be devalued and is estimated to have made a profit of £1 billion on 'Black Wednesday' when sterling withdrew from the system and fell sharply on the foreign exchanges. There is a sense in which speculators can create a self-fulfilling prophecy — by heavy selling of a currency they help force its devaluation. That is the supply curve for the currency shifts down to the right. However, it does not always work that way. Mr Soros speculated against the French franc during the currency crisis, but eventually became convinced that concerted action by France and Germany would be sufficient to maintain the parity set in 1987.

Note:
During the East Asian currency crisis of 1997, politicians blamed Mr Soros, amongst others, for undermining confidence in the fixed exchange rates of the currencies.

Speculation may make exchange rates volatile. Following the outbreak of the Gulf War, in January 1991, the US dollar rose on the foreign exchange markets. Dealers, suddenly expert in military matters, read the results of the first day's air strikes as an indication that Saddam Hussein's forces could not put up any real resistance. As the week went on and the battlefield situation became less clear, the dollar lost all its gains. Later in the month, as the military defeat of Iraq became inevitable, the dollar began to appreciate again. Speculators respond almost instantaneously to any news that is likely to affect the long-run value of a currency.

LEADING AND LAGGING

Countries sometimes introduce exchange controls to try to prevent speculative inflows or outflows. Since 1992 this is no longer permissible between EU states. Moreover, speculation is very difficult to stop. It can take many forms. Leading and lagging by companies has been an important type of speculation in Ireland. It works as follows: if an exporter to the UK expects the euro to depreciate relative to sterling in the near future, he will delay (lag) converting his sterling receipts into euro because they will be worth more after the depreciation has taken place. Similarly, an importer may speed up (lead) payments to his UK supplier in order to avoid paying more after the depreciation. Because of the size of Ireland's trade in relation to GNP, leads and lags in payments and receipts can put tremendous pressure on the exchange rate.

TOBIN TAX

Speculators must base their expectations on the underlying 'fundamentals'; they must have reasons for believing a currency is over- or under-valued. When they act to correct a misalignment of a currency, that is, to force down a currency that is over-valued or to force up an under-valued currency, speculation is beneficial. If, however, speculation is uninformed it can destabilise a currency, increasing volatility and uncertainty in the market. This is undesirable. Some economists, including the Nobel prize-winning James Tobin, have proposed that taxes be imposed on speculative gains to curb the level of speculation, but most reject the notion of a 'Tobin tax' as unworkable, because it would be impossible to distinguish between 'speculative' and 'non-speculative' deals. It may also be unnecessary because there is no agreement that speculation is harmful to any significant degree. Countries that are really concerned about speculation can always allow their currency to float. This deprives speculators of a target to attack.

9.11 THE TRADE-WEIGHTED EXCHANGE RATE INDEX

It is useful to have a single statistic that summarises a currency's external value. The summary statistic that is most widely used for this purpose is the *trade-weighted exchange rate index* (TWERI), also referred to as the *effective exchange rate index*. This is an index of the average value of the euro in terms of the other main international currencies. Each of the currencies in the calculation is 'trade-weighted'. In other words, if a particular country, such as the US, has a large proportion of it's trade with the Eurozone, then the dollar has a correspondingly large weight in the calculation.

In table 9.3 we show how the trade-weighted exchange rate index is calculated. Column one lists the Eurozone's trading partners according to their share in exports. Column two shows the trade weight for each country. The UK has the largest weight

Table 9.3
Trade-weighted exchange rate index for the Eurozone (hypothetical data)

	Trade weight	Bilateral exchange rate index		Trade weighted exchange rate index	
		2002	*2003*	*2002*	*2003*
Country	*1*	*2*	*3*	*4*	*5*
United Kingdom	0.19	100	96.1	19	18.26
Sweden	0.04	100	102.1	4	4.08
Denmark	0.02	100	95.3	2	1.90
Candidate countries	0.13	100	97.3	13	12.65
Switzerland	0.06	100	104.1	6	6.24
United States	0.17	100	95.0	17	16.15
Japan	0.03	100	100.2	3	3.01
Asia excluding Japan	0.15	100	97.5	15	14.62
Africa	0.06	100	94.5	6	6.67
Latin America	0.05	100	103.2	5	5.16
Other countries	0.10	100	102.1	10	10.21
	1.00			**100**	**97.96**

of 0.19 (19 per cent of the Eurozone's exports is with the UK), the US has a weight of 0.17, and so on down to Denmark which has a weight of 0.02. These weights sum to 1.0.

The first step in deriving the TWERI is to express the bilateral exchange rates as indices. The exchange rates are set equal to 100 in a base year and the index for subsequent years is calculated with reference to this base. For example, if the $/€ exchange rate was $1.2/€1 in 2002 and $1.14/€1 in 2003, the dollar exchange rate index would be 100 in 2002 and 95 in 2003. Hypothetical exchange rates for 2003 are given for each country in column three of table 9.3. It is assumed that over the year the euro depreciated against, for example, sterling and the dollar but appreciated against the currencies of Sweden and Switzerland.

The trade-weighted exchange rate index is calculated by multiplying each exchange rate index by its trade weight and summing for all countries. This is done in columns four and five for 2002 and 2003 respectively. Column five shows that in 2003 the trade-

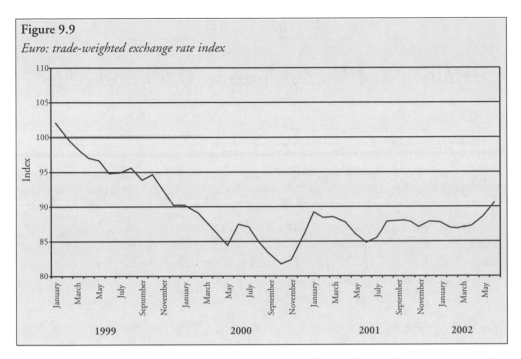

Figure 9.9

Euro: trade-weighted exchange rate index

weighted exchange rate index had fallen to 97.96. This indicates that, on average, the euro depreciated by over 2 per cent over the period.

Figure 9.9 shows the euro's trade-weighted exchange rate index (1999 = 100) over the period 1999–2001. It can be seen that the euro depreciated by approximately 13 per cent since its launch in January 1999.

9.12 CONCLUSION

In this chapter we have discussed a number of topics relating to the balance of payments and the determination of exchange rates. The main issues and concepts covered included:

- The balance of payments is a record of a country's economic transactions with the rest of the world. Apart from errors in measurement, the current, capital, and official external reserves accounts must sum to zero
- The foreign exchange market
- How supply and demand for foreign exchange determine the nominal exchange rate
- The trend in the exchange rate of the dollar, and sterling relative to the Irish pound
- How inflation, real growth rate, interest rates and speculation influence exchange rates
- The nominal trade-weighted exchange rate index.

CHAPTER 10

Inflation and Interest Rates in Open Economies

10.1 INTRODUCTION

In this chapter we discuss the factors that influence inflation, interest rates, and exchange rates in open economies. We begin by outlining the theory of purchasing power parity (PPP). This entails a discussion of real exchange rates and other indicators of international competitiveness. We then explain the relevance of PPP theory under both fixed and flexible exchange rates. This is followed by a discussion of uncovered interest rate parity (UPT). We conclude the chapter by linking together some of the key relationships in international monetary economics.

10.2 PURCHASING POWER PARITY

The theory of purchasing power parity (PPP) is based on the idea that the prices of similar goods, *expressed in a common currency*, should be the same in all countries. Purchasing power parity means *equal value for money* for goods and services in different countries. Using the Eurozone and the United States for the purpose of illustration, the strong version of PPP, referred to as *absolute* PPP, can be stated as:

$$P_{EUR} \times e = P_{US} \tag{1}$$

where P_{EUR} and P_{US} are the Eurozone and US price levels, respectively, and e is the nominal exchange rate (expressed as the dollar per unit of the euro, \$/€). This states that Eurozone prices equal US prices when converted using the current exchange rate. Put another way, if PPP holds prices in the two countries (converted at the exchange rate) are equal.

LAW OF ONE PRICE

The reason why Eurozone and US price levels, expressed in a common currency, should be equal is based on the *law of one price*. This is the tendency for the same price to prevail for a good everywhere in the world. This tendency depends on the *arbitrage* of internationally traded goods, which occurs when people take advantage of the opportunity of making a profit by buying cheap in one market and selling dear in another. Suppose, for example, a pair of Levi jeans cost \$30 in New York and €30 in Dublin. If the exchange rate were €1 = \$1, then PPP holds and a person would be indifferent between buying in Dublin or New York. If, however, the exchange rate were €1 = \$1.5, then the New York price is much lower. In this case, traders could make a profit by buying in New York and selling in Dublin. The increased demand would drive up the price in New York and the increased supply would drive the Dublin price down. Arbitrage would ensure that the prices in the two cities would converge.

An illustration of how the prices of internationally traded goods tend to equalise is provided by the Irish experience in the 1980s. Due to movements in the exchange rate and higher rates of indirect taxation in the Republic, a whole range of goods, including petrol, drink and electrical appliances, became cheaper (in Irish pounds) in Northern Ireland than south of the border. Excursions were organised throughout the Republic for shoppers to go to Newry and Belfast in search of bargains. Similarly, people living in border areas bought all their petrol and drink in the North. Garages and supermarkets in the Republic, unable to cut their prices because of high taxes, went out of business and those in the North expanded. The Irish finance minister was forced to reduce indirect taxes on selected items in the Republic.

This was an example of arbitrage forcing prices to converge. It simply was not possible for major price discrepancies to persist north and south of the border.

REASONS WHY ABSOLUTE PPP MAY NOT HOLD

There are, however, many factors that impede the operation of the law of one price and ensure absolute PPP does not hold. These include:

- National income or GDP. Differences in the standard of living, as measured by national income or GDP, plays an important role in explaining why price differences persist. The explanation for this is known as the Balassa-Samuelson effect. This is explained in section 10.7.
- Macroeconomic policy. Different macroeconomic policies can result in countries being on different phases of the business cycle. This, in turn, can influence relative prices.
- Transportation costs. It takes time and money to shop across national borders or to transport goods. In the Eurozone, these costs should decrease over time due to euro credit cards and virtual shopping on the internet. One of the reasons for introducing the euro was to increase price transparency within the Eurozone.
- National preferences. Market conditions and prices may also be affected by cultural and linguistic preferences.
- Trade restrictions. Tariffs and quotas drive a wedge between prices in different countries. Even under the European Single Market, it is still the case that when you import wine or beer into Ireland from the Continent you must demonstrate to customs that it is for personal consumption and not for re-sale.
- Different indirect taxes. If you import a car into Ireland you must pay a vehicle registration tax (VRT) of over 20 per cent of the Irish retail price. But since the retail price already contains value added tax (VAT), the VRT is a tax on a tax and it makes the retail price of Irish cars among the highest in Europe, even though the net-of-tax price is one of the lowest. Up until the end of September 2002, the car industry was exempt from EU competition rules. The new directives are likely to increase cross-border and national competition in the future.
- Exchange rate fluctuations. Firms do not immediately adjust prices as exchange rates fluctuate. This is no longer a factor for countries participating in the Eurozone.

- Market structure. Generally, perfectly competitive markets are perceived to be the most efficient as they result in optimal prices. However, in most cases, manufacturers have some form of control over the market and, therefore, can influence prices. Firms can influence the market through product differentiation (a VW car sold in Germany is very different from the model sold in Ireland), after-sales service, regulating distribution networks and market entry, strategic price setting and collusive behaviour, to mention a few.

- Competitive environment. Market competition is changing constantly due to government deregulation, advances in new technologies and changes in patent rules and technical standards. This can have a significant bearing on relative prices.

TRADED AND NON-TRADED GOODS

PPP is only expected to operate for traded goods. An increasing proportion of consumer expenditure is on non-traded services, such as building and construction, personal services, hotel rooms, restaurants and healthcare. It is quite possible for inflation in non-traded items and indeed traded goods to differ between countries and even between regions of a country.

EVIDENCE FROM THE EUROZONE

Given the obstacles to the operation of absolute PPP it is hardly surprising that PPP may not hold in the short-term. Table 10.1 gives an indication of the degree of disparity in prices in the Eurozone when the euro notes and coins were introduced in January 2002. Finland is one of the most expensive countries. A can of coke costs 3.5 times more in Helsinki than in Madrid. Greece, Portugal, and the Netherlands offer the best value for money. Euro pricing highlights other, rather odd, discrepancies. For example, a Renault car costs less in Italy than in France. On the basis of the figures, absolute PPP does not appear to hold. Clearly, there is some way to go before absolute PPP is established in the Eurozone.

Table 10.2 shows price indexes for particular products across the Eurozone countries (the Eurozone average is set equal to 100). The table confirms that countries like Finland, the Netherlands, Luxembourg and Ireland are high price countries whereas Spain, Portugal and Greece are low priced countries. Ireland comes out worse in the case of alcohol, tobacco and house rents.

Using the coefficient of variation (the ratio of the standard deviation to the mean) as an indicator of price dispersion, the table also shows that traded goods (food, clothing and furnishings) have a lower price differential than non-traded goods (house rents, communications, education and health). This suggests that absolute PPP theory performs better for traded goods than non-traded goods.

10.3 THE PPP EXCHANGE RATE

While PPP theory can be traced back to the sixteenth century to studies at the University of Salamanca in Spain, the term 'purchasing power parity' was first coined by the Swedish economist Gustav Cassel. He wrote '(the exchange rate) between two

Table 10.1
Price inequality in the Eurozone

	One litre of milk	Four-door 1.6 litre Renault Megane	McDonald's Big Mac	Stamp for postcard to Eurozone country	Compact disc in national top 10	Can of Coca-Cola
	€	€	€	€	€	€
Austria	0.86	15,650	2.50	0.51	19.95	0.50
Belgium	0.84	13,100	2.95	0.47	21.99	0.47
Finland	0.71	21,700	2.90	0.50	21.99	1.18
France	1.11	15,700	3.00	0.48	22.71	0.40
Germany	0.56	17,300	2.65	0.51	17.99	0.35
Greece	1.04	16,875	2.11	0.59	15.99	0.51
Ireland	0.83	17,459	2.54	0.36	21.57	0.70
Italy	1.34	14,770	2.50	0.41	14.96	0.77
Luxembourg	0.72	12,450	3.10	0.52	17.50	0.37
Netherlands	0.79	16,895	2.60	0.54	22.00	0.45
Portugal	0.52	20,760	2.24	0.54	16.93	0.44
Spain	0.69	14,200	2.49	0.45	16.80	0.33

Source: Reuters, January 2002.

countries is represented by the ... purchasing power of money in one country and the other. I propose to call this parity "The Purchasing Power Parity".' (See 'Abnormal Deviations in International Exchanges', *Economic Journal*, 28 December 1918.)

Between 1870 and World War I, the world's major currencies had been fixed to gold and, therefore, to each other. This fixed exchange rate system was called the *gold standard*. However, during World War I the system broke down and, in the aftermath of the war, countries attempted to re-establish the system. Given that prices had risen very unevenly in different countries during the war years the issue that concerned Cassel was to calculate the appropriate exchange rate on which to re-establish the gold standard. Cassel proposed using PPP theory to derive the correct exchange rates. This involved calculating the exchange rate that equated prices in the various countries. For example, rearranging equation (1) above, we can define the *PPP exchange rate*, as:

$$e_{PPP} = P_{US} / P_{EUR} \tag{2}$$

Table 10.2
Comparative prices indices for products in the Eurozone, 2000

Product category	Highest	Lowest	Coefficient of variation
Food and non-alcoholic beverages	115 (Finland)	87 (Spain)	9.2
Recreation and culture	122 (Finland)	87 (Greece)	9.6
Clothing and footwear	117 (Luxembourg)	79 (Portugal)	9.9
Furnishings, household equipment	115 (Netherlands)	78 (Portugal)	10.6
Restaurants and hotels	126 (Finland)	84 (Portugal)	11.9
Transport	129 (Finland)	75 (Greece)	13.9
Electricity, gas and other fuels	132 (Netherlands)	66 (Greece)	16.3
Health	137 (Finland)	62 (Greece)	18.8
Education	169 (Luxembourg)	63 (Portugal)	29.4
Communications	159 (Finland)	68 (Greece)	29.7
Alcoholic beverages, tobacco	175 (Ireland)	72 (Spain)	30.2
Rentals for housing	141 (Ireland)	33 (Portugal)	30.9

Source: European Central Bank, 'Price Level Convergence and Competition in the Euro Area', *Monthly Bulletin*, August, 2002, p. 43.

This is the exchange rate that ensures that PPP holds. Britain was one country that did not avail of this calculation. In 1925, sterling went back on the gold standard at the old pre-war parity level. However, since Britain has experienced much more inflation than the US since 1914, sterling was overvalued and this contributed to recession in the UK.

ILLUSTRATION USING BIG MAC PARITIES

As an example of deriving the purchasing power parity exchange rate, consider the price of a McDonald's Big Mac in Dublin and New York. In January 2002, the Dublin price was €2.5 and the New York price was $2.75. Inserting these prices into equation (2) above:

$$e_{PPP} = \$2.75/€2.5 = 1.1$$

If the exchange had been at this level a Big Mac would have been the same price (in a common currency) in Dublin and New York. To the extent to which this is not the case an exchange rate can be said to be over- or undervalued. In January 2002, the actual or market exchange rate was \$0.8787/€1 compared with a PPP exchange rate of \$1.1/€1. On the basis of Big Macs, at least, we could claim that in Ireland the euro was 25.2 per cent $[((1.1 - 0.8787)/0.8787) \times 100]$ per cent *undervalued* relative to the dollar. European tourists to New York must feel a little 'cheesed off' at local prices!

Note:
Since it was first published by *The Economist* in the 1980s the Big Mac standard has received a lot of attention. Economists find it difficult to digest the standard! After all, McDonald's offer a fast food service that has a high labour content. As a result of wage differentials, the price could vary considerably from country to country. None the less, the standard has stood up well to criticism and earned grudging respect from academics. Currencies that appear overvalued on the Big Mac standard seem to revert to it over time.

10.4 PPP AND THE REAL EXCHANGE RATE

The real exchange rate (ϵ) is simply the ratio of domestic and foreign prices expressed in a common currency. If in equation (1), the US price level is brought over to the left-hand side, we can write:

$$\epsilon = (P_{EUR} \times e)/P_{US} \tag{3}$$

The real exchange rate is the nominal exchange rate adjusted for relative prices. The importance of the real rate is that it is a measure of whether a country is becoming more or less *price competitive* relative to its trading partners over time.

- A *rise* in the real exchange rate implies a *loss* of competitiveness because either the domestic price has risen relative to foreign price and/or the nominal exchange rate has appreciated.
- Conversely, a *fall* in the real exchange rate implies a *gain* in competitiveness. Either the domestic price has fallen relative to foreign price and/or the nominal exchange rate has depreciated.

Equation (3) is normally expressed as an index with the base year set equal to 100. It can be seen that PPP holds if the real exchange rate is constant. If, for example, an increase in the Eurozone price level is offset by an equal depreciation of the euro exchange rate, PPP will continue to hold and the real exchange rate will be constant. Similarly, if a rise in the US price level is offset by an appreciation of the euro exchange rate, PPP holds and the real exchange rate is again constant. Hence, one way of determining if absolute PPP holds is to calculate real exchange rates and examine the trend over time.

EVIDENCE FROM THE IRISH ECONOMY
Figure 10.1 shows Ireland's real exchange rates relative to the Deutsche mark (the nominal exchange rate has, of course, been fixed since January 1999) and sterling over the period 1955 to 2001 based on indices equal to 100 in 1955.

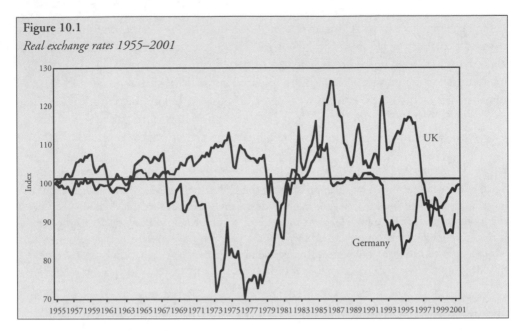

Figure 10.1
Real exchange rates 1955–2001

With regards to sterling, the real exchange rate increased steadily up to 1975 suggesting a loss of competitiveness in Ireland. As the sterling/Irish pound nominal exchange rate was fixed, this increase in the real exchange rate was due to a rise in Irish prices relative to UK prices.

From 1979 to 1984, the real exchange rate index fell sharply suggesting an improvement in Ireland's competitive position. This was due to the depreciation of the nominal exchange rate soon after the link with sterling was broken.

However after 1984, the real exchange rate index increased, showing deterioration in Ireland's competitive position. This was due to the appreciation of the nominal exchange rate and the rise in the relative price level in Ireland. In 1997 there was another sharp fall in the real sterling exchange rate brought about by nominal exchange rate depreciation. At the end of the forty-five year period, the real exchange rate index was nearly back to where it was in the mid-1950s.

Against the Deutsche mark (DM), the Irish economy enjoyed a competitive gain during the 1970s, but this gain was subsequently eroded during the 1980s. Despite much short-term volatility, the competitive position between Ireland and Germany is almost exactly the same in 2002 to what it was in the mid-1950s.

The relatively stability of the real exchange rate over the long run illustrates the power of the PPP idea — the nominal exchange rate has moved in line with relative prices. Put another way, the real exchange rates tend to revert to a stable long-run average. This is called the property of *mean reversion* and it is an implication of purchasing power parity. But the Irish experience also shows that there can be significant deviations from absolute PPP in the short run.

Note:
The real exchange rate index only monitors movements in competitiveness relative to the base year. This can give rise to misleading interpretations. For example, if you choose 1986 as the

base year for sterling, then by 2001 the index would have fallen indicating a gain in Irish competitiveness. Again if you choose 1977 as the base year for Germany then by 2001 the index had risen implying a loss of competitiveness from an Irish perspective. We have used quarterly data going back to the mid-1950s to avoid this problem of base year misinterpretation.

ALTERNATIVE PRESENTATION

A problem with using the real exchange rate to evaluate absolute PPP is that the index fails to bring out the underlying dynamics. That is we are not sure if changes in the real exchange rate are due to movements in the nominal exchange rate or relative prices. An alternative presentation that gets around this problem is to graph the nominal exchange rate against relative prices. For example, consider again the absolute PPP relationship equation (1):

$$P_{EUR} \times e = P_{US}$$

Taking P_{EUR} over to the left-hand side we have:

$$e = P_{US}/P_{EUR}$$

If, over time, the trend in the exchange rate is equal to the trend in relative prices, absolute PPP holds (the real exchange rate will also be constant). If the exchange rate line is above the relative price line, then this indicates a *loss* of competitiveness from an Irish perspective. Conversely, if the exchange rate line remains below the relative price line, this indicates a *gain* in Irish competitiveness.

Figure 10.2 illustrate the Irish experience relative to the US from 1955 to 2001. It can be seen that the nominal exchange rate is much more volatile than the relative price series. Up to 1985, the exchange rate and price series tend to move in tandem as PPP

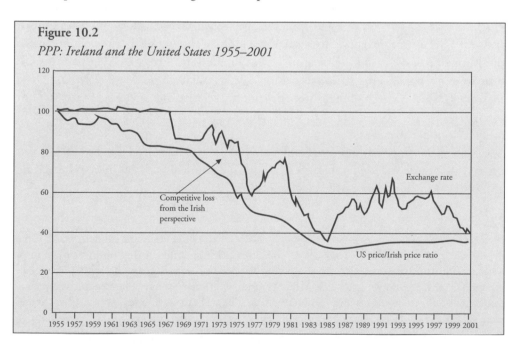

Figure 10.2

PPP: Ireland and the United States 1955–2001

would suggest. As the dollar/Irish pound exchange rate depreciates, the Irish price rises relative to US price. Throughout this period, Ireland suffered a competitive loss relative to the US. By 1985, however, the absolute PPP relationship had been re-established. The experience after 1985 is quite different. The Irish pound appreciates relative to the dollar but this brings forth little or no change in the relative price series. It is remarkable that the 1955 PPP relationship is re-established in 2001.

Note:
Evidence from other countries would seem to support this view. PPP appears to be a poor guide to the behaviour of exchange rates in the short run. Persistent deviations from PPP have been documented in studies of the major industrial countries. One study concluded after a review of the literature that the hypothesis that arbitrage quickly equates goods prices internationally has probably been rejected more decisively by empirical evidence than any other hypothesis in the history of economics. (M. Obstfeld and K. Rogoff, 'Mirage of Fixed Exchange Rates', *Journal of Economic Perspectives*, Fall 1995, 73–96.) However, this does not detract from the force of the theory as a theory of exchange rates in the long run. To be convinced of this, just ask yourself what would happen if the exchange rate between the US dollar and the euro was roughly 10:1 instead of 1:1 and the price levels in the two regions remained as they are.

10.5 AN ALTERNATIVE MEASURE OF COMPETITIVENESS

In chapter 9, the trade-weighted exchange rate index (TWERI) was defined as the average movement of the euro against the other main international currencies. The real trade-weighted exchange rate index is calculated by trade-weighting *real* exchange rates over time. The calculation is the same except that nominal exchange rates are replaced by real exchange rates.

Since the Irish pound no longer exists, the Central Bank of Ireland discontinued the TWERI series at the end of 1998. The European Central Bank does publish nominal and real TWERI for the euro. However, these indices ignore trade between countries in the Eurozone and instead use weights based on euro-area external trade patterns. To overcome this problem, national central banks calculate *national competitiveness indicators* (NCI) for each of the Eurozone countries. These indicators take into account internal trade patterns in the Eurozone and give a better indication of changes in national competitiveness.

Figure 10.3 shows the nominal and real NCI for Ireland since January 1999. It can be seen that there has been a slight fall in both the nominal and real indices indicating a slight gain in competitiveness since January 1999.

Note:
In deriving the real exchange rate index, the choice of the price index to be used poses some problems. It is possible to use an index of consumer prices, manufacturing output prices, or of wholesale prices. These usually move closely together but sometimes a different picture can emerge depending on which price index is used. National competitiveness indicators are published for both consumer and producer prices. The real exchange rates given in this chapter were calculated using the consumer price index.

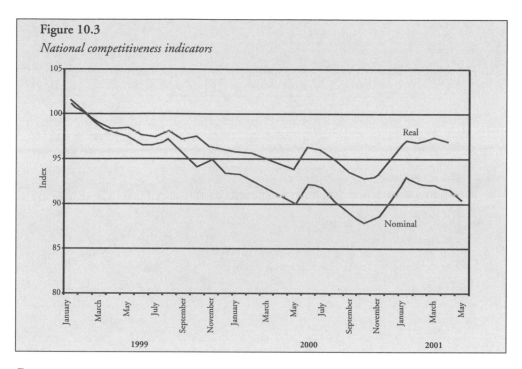

Figure 10.3

National competitiveness indicators

REAL UNIT LABOUR COSTS IN A COMMON CURRENCY

An alternative measure of competitiveness is an index of real unit labour costs in a common currency (RULC). This measures the inflation adjusted, labour cost of producing a unit of output in Ireland relative to its trading partners. This allows for (A) the trend in relative real wages (nominal wages adjusted for inflation), (B) the trend in relative labour productivity, and (C) movements in the exchange rate. By taking all these factors into account, the RUWC index provides an indication of the competitiveness of the Irish labour force.

Figure 10.4 shows that since the mid-1980s there has been a sharp and almost uninterrupted decline in Ireland's index. Since 1990, for example, the index has fallen by 57 per cent. This reflects the rapid growth of labour productivity in Irish manufacturing industry, the small increase in real wages and the depreciation of the Irish pound and the euro. On the basis of this index the country has enjoyed a steady and quite exceptional improvement in labour competitiveness over the last ten years.

The RUWC has been criticised as an indicator of labour competitiveness as it includes the high productivity levels of an 'entrepôt economy' (entrepôt comes from the French word for 'warehouse'). Companies in pharmaceuticals, computer software and certain food sectors have very high productivity levels and it is this that is driving down the RUWC index. For example, in 2002, output per employee in the chemical sector was €510,000 compared to €100,000 in the rest of manufacturing industry.

If these entrepôt industries are excluded, Irish output and productivity levels are much more subdued and the RUWC index tells a rather different story. Excluding the chemicals sector, the International Monetary Fund (IMF) calculates that Ireland's competitive position stagnated between 1995 and 2001 (IMF, *Country Report on Ireland*, August, 2002).

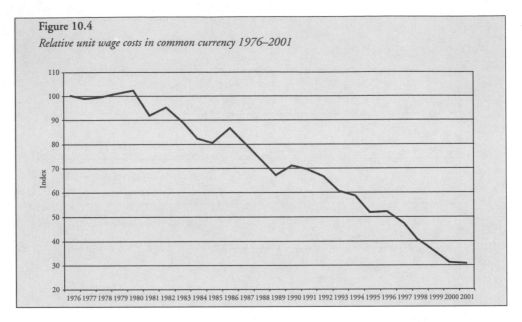

Figure 10.4

Relative unit wage costs in common currency 1976–2001

10.6 PPP: GRAPHICAL REPRESENTATION

The way in which PPP is expected to operate is illustrated in figure 10.5. The Irish price level is measured on the vertical axis and the \$/€ exchange rate is on the horizontal axis. A PPP line is drawn for a constant foreign price level. For illustrative purposes, we use the US price level, P_{US}, to indicate the foreign price level.

At all points on the PPP line the real exchange rate is constant. To see this, consider the movement from A to B in the upper diagram. The increase in the Irish price level from P_1 to P_2 is exactly matched by a depreciation of the \$/€ exchange rate from €$_1$ to €$_2$. As P_{US} is constant, the real exchange rate is unchanged between A and B.

The real exchange rate is overvalued at all points above the PPP line. For example, at the point C, we have a combination of P_2 and €$_1$. The Irish price level is higher than that consistent with PPP and the real exchange rate is overvalued. Conversely, the exchange rate is undervalued at all points below the PPP line. At the point D, we have the combination of P_1 and €$_2$. The Irish price level is lower than the level consistent with PPP and the real exchange rate is undervalued.

The foreign price level determines the *location* or position of the PPP line. An increase in P_{US} shifts the PPP line out to the right. Conversely, a decrease in P_{US} shifts the PPP line to the left. Suppose, for example, that a rise in the US price level is offset by an appreciation of the \$/€ exchange rate (as predicted by absolute PPP). In the lower diagram in figure 10.5, an increase in P_{US} shifts the PPP line to the right and the economy moves from X to Y. This movement from the point X to Y entails an appreciation of the \$/€ exchange rate from €$_1$ to €$_2$. PPP holds at the point Y (the real exchange rate is unchanged) because the rise in the US price is offset by the appreciation of the \$/€ exchange rate. We have used figure 10.5 to illustrate the policy implications of PPP theory.

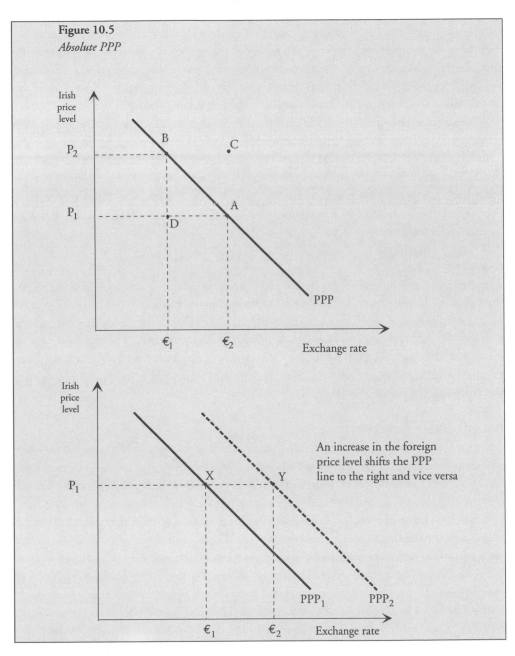

Figure 10.5
Absolute PPP

10.7 RELATIVE PPP

Absolute PPP is often referred to as the hard version of PPP because, for the reasons mentioned earlier, prices are unlikely to be the same in different countries at any particular time. An alternative version of PPP is *relative PPP*. This weaker version of PPP expresses equation (1) in terms of percentage rates of change. That is, differentiating equation (1) gives:

$$\pi_{EUR} + \Delta e = \pi_{US} \qquad (4)$$

where π_{EUR} and π_{US} are the rates of inflation in the Eurozone and the US respectively and Δe is the percentage change in the nominal exchange rate. Equation (4) allows for the possibility that prices in different countries may not be the same in any particular period. However, given the initial difference, the change in relative prices should be similar and, therefore, prices should not diverge any further over time.

However, even with this weaker version of PPP, there are reasons why the hypothesis may not hold. Firstly, due to different macroeconomic policies and other factors, countries may be on different phases of the business cycle. For example, at the end of the 1990s, the Spanish economy was booming whereas the German economy was in recession. As a consequence, inflation was relatively higher in Spain. We now discuss two other reasons why relative PPP may not hold: the 'convergence effect' and the 'Balassa-Samuelson' effect.

CONVERGENCE EFFECT

The introduction of the euro will lead to greater price transparency which, in turn, should contribute to the completion of the internal market in the EU. The result should be a convergence of prices to a common level. As such, countries with low prices, for example Spain, will tend to experience relatively high inflation. On the other hand countries with high prices, for example Germany, will experience relatively low inflation as part of the convergence process. The result is that relative PPP may not hold during the convergence period.

BALASSA-SAMUELSON EFFECT

There are two basic findings that PPP theory needs to explain. Firstly, it has been observed that prices are much lower in poorer or less developed countries. For example, services are considerably cheaper in Bratislava, Slovakia than they are in Vienna, Austria even though the two cities are only a few miles apart. A closer examination tends to suggest that this difference in prices can be accounted for by differences in non-traded goods and services. Secondly, it has been observed that countries that have high growth rates in productivity and standards of living tend to experience higher inflation.

The Balassa-Samuelson theory attempts to explain these two findings by linking growth rates in productivity to non-traded prices. Bela Balassa was a Hungarian born economist at Johns Hopkins University and Paul Samuelson is a Nobel Prize winner from MIT. Working separately, these economists found that countries with high productivity growth in the traded goods sector tend to experience relatively higher inflation rates. Hence, if two countries experience different rates of growth of productivity, these countries will have different inflation rates and the relative PPP hypothesis will not hold. Box 10.1 gives a more detailed explanation of the Balassa-Samuelson effect.

There is some evidence to suggest that this type of effect has been in operation in Ireland in recent years as more and more multinational companies have become established here. An example would be where a hi-tech multinational like Dell Computers, using the latest technology, achieve a high level of labour productivity (the number of computers produced per day). Accordingly workers at Dell command high rates of pay. If, say, a dentist decides that his or her pay should rise in line with what is

---

Box 10.1
The Balassa-Samuelson effect

On the basis of a few straightforward assumptions it can be shown that:

$$\pi_{NT} - \pi_T = \Delta PROD_T - \Delta PROD_{NT} \qquad (1)$$

The equation states that if the growth in productivity in the traded sector ($\Delta PROD_T$) is greater than the growth of productivity in the non-traded sector ($\Delta PROD_{NT}$), non-traded inflation (π_{NT}) will rise relative to traded inflation (π_T).

Briefly, the argument is that the growth in productivity in the traded goods sector results in higher wages. However, because the higher wages are offset by the rise in productivity, traded prices remain unchanged. The higher wages in the traded sector are, however, transmitted to the non-traded goods sector. Workers are generally mobile between the two sectors and, as a result, wage differentials cannot get too far out of line. But because the opportunities to increase productivity in the non-traded sector are limited, the higher wages are passed-on in higher non-traded prices.

By definition, the overall inflation rate is the sum of the inflation rates in the traded and non-traded sectors:

$$\pi = \alpha\pi_T - (1 - \alpha)\pi_{NT} \qquad (2)$$

where π is the overall consumer price inflation and α is the weight showing the contribution of traded and non-traded inflation to overall inflation. From this equation, it is clear that the rise in non-traded inflation results in an increase in the overall inflation rate.

By adding and subtracting π_T to equation (2) and rearranging, we can re-write the equation as:

$$\pi = \pi_T - (1 - \alpha)(\pi_{NT} - \pi_T) \qquad (3)$$

Substituting in equation (1) above we have:

$$\pi = \pi_T - (1 - \alpha)(\Delta PROD_T - \Delta PROD_{NT}) \qquad (4)$$

A similar calculation can be done for country B.

$$\pi^B = \pi_T^B - (1 - \alpha)(\Delta PROD_T^B - \Delta PROD^B{}_{NT}) \qquad (5)$$

Subtracting equation (5) from (4) we obtain the following equation:

$$\pi - \pi^B = (1 - \alpha)(\Delta PROD_T - \Delta PROD_T^B) \qquad (6)$$

This equation states that the inflation differential between two countries will depend on the difference in the growth in productivity in the traded goods sectors. High relative productivity results in high relative inflation. Pulling the strands of the theory together, the high productivity in the traded goods sector results in higher wages and higher prices in the non-traded sector. This results in a higher overall inflation rate. Hence, differences in productivity are reflected in different rates of inflation between countries.

---

happening at Dell, dental charges will have to be raised because the dentist can see only so many patients per day and so the opportunity to increase productivity is very limited. The increase in the dental changes will feed through to the overall Consumer Price Index (CPI). The high Irish inflation rate in 2001–02 is largely due to high inflation in services such as healthcare, meals in restaurants and so on.

10.8 PPP UNDER FLEXIBLE EXCHANGE RATES

Rearranging equation (4) above we can write:

$$\Delta e = \pi_{US} - \pi_{EUR} \tag{5}$$

Equation (5) states that changes in the nominal exchange rate will be offset by differentials in inflation rates between countries. If, for example, the rate of inflation in the Eurozone exceeds the US rate, the euro should depreciate.

$$\pi_{US} < \pi_{EUR} \Rightarrow \downarrow \Delta e$$

Conversely, if Eurozone inflation is less than US inflation, the euro should appreciate:

$$\pi_{US} > \pi_{EUR} \Rightarrow \uparrow \Delta \epsilon$$

Figure 10.6 illustrates the case where a rise in Eurozone inflation leads to exchange rate depreciation. (Note that, in contrast to figure 10.5, the price level and the exchange rate have been replaced by the inflation rate and the percentage change in the exchange rate.) In this case, relative PPP continues to hold. Another example would be where a rise in the US inflation rate leads to an appreciation of the exchange rate. This would entail the relative PPP line shifting out to the right (not shown in the diagram).

Hence, PPP theory implies that price or inflation differentials are the most important determinant of exchange rates. Countries with low inflation, such as the US, will generally have strong, appreciating currencies. Conversely, countries with high inflation rates will have weak or depreciating currencies.

History shows that relative PPP is a good general guide to the behaviour of exchange rates. When exchange rates are free to adjust, it is invariably true that high inflation currencies tend to depreciate sharply relative to low inflation currencies.

To take some extreme examples, in 1921 the dollar/German mark exchange rate was $1 = Reichsmark 270, but by October 1922 the mark had depreciated to $1 = Reichsmark 25,000 million reflecting the hyperinflation in Germany. In the early 1990s hyperinflation in Russia and many of the former socialist economies, such as Yugoslavia and the Ukraine, rendered their currencies worthless on foreign exchanges. For example, at the beginning of 1992 there were 300 roubles to the dollar; by the end of 1998 there were 6,000. This reflected high inflation in Russia relative to the US. The same is true of the Latin American countries that have experienced hyperinflation: their currencies have become worthless on the foreign exchange markets.

10.9 PPP UNDER FIXED EXCHANGE RATES

Fixed exchange rate systems are discussed in the following chapter. For the moment all that is necessary to note is that central banks can enter into an agreement to lock or fix the value of their currencies so that the exchange rate is held constant. For a small economy with a fixed exchange rate, PPP becomes a *theory of inflation*. Suppose that instead of comparing the Eurozone and the US, we instead compare the Czech Republic and the Eurozone. Rearranging equation (4) so that the Czech Republic plays the role of the small country 'price taker' we can write:

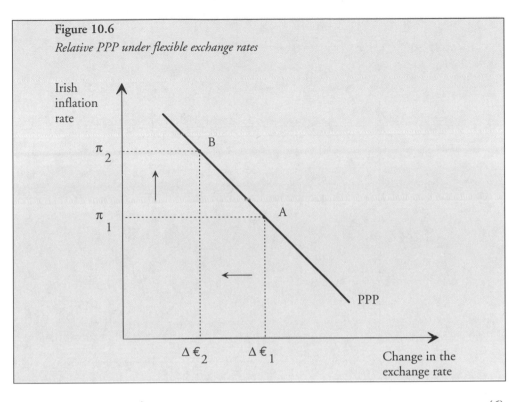

Figure 10.6

Relative PPP under flexible exchange rates

$$\pi_{CZ} = \pi_{EUR} - \Delta e \tag{6}$$

where π_{CZ} is the inflation rate in the Czech Republic and Δe is the percentage change in the crown/euro exchange rate. If the exchange rate is constant ($\Delta e = 0$), then Czech inflation should equal Eurozone inflation. Because of the smallness of the Czech economy relative to the Eurozone, Czech firms are in general price-takers with little or no market power. Hence, the causation must run from Eurozone to Czech inflation. This view of inflation is very important in a small open economies all around the world. The theory is also very relevant for those countries participating in the European Monetary Union. When the national exchange rates were irrevocably fixed at the start of 1999, the Δe term in equation (6), went to zero and can be omitted. If relative PPP held, the inflation rates across all the Eurozone countries should have converged. This was perceived as being one of the important benefits to emanate from EMU membership.

As shown in figure 10.7, the nominal exchange rate, e, is fixed on the horizontal axis. In this case, an increase in Eurozone inflation shifts the relative PPP line upwards and the economy moves from A to B. If PPP holds, the Czech inflation rate will rise along the vertical axis until relative PPP is restored. Conversely, a fall in Eurozone inflation would shift the PPP line downwards and this would lead to a fall in Czech inflation along the vertical axis (not shown in the diagram).

We discuss this theory in greater depth once we have explained how fixed exchange rate systems work. Note, however, that relative PPP under fixed exchange rates states that domestic inflation is primarily caused by foreign inflation and changes in the

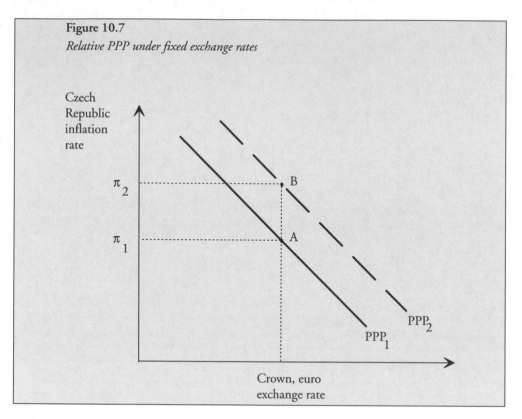

Figure 10.7
Relative PPP under fixed exchange rates

exchange rate. This means that domestic variables (such as changes in firm costs and wages) have no, or very little, effect on domestic inflation. This is an issue that has attracted much attention from Irish economists.

10.10 UNCOVERED INTEREST RATE PARITY (UIP)

In this section we switch the emphasis away from inflation to nominal interest rates. In a later section we shall reconcile the two analyses. The theory of uncovered interest rate parity (UIP) is concerned with how interest rate differentials between countries give an indication of how exchange rates will vary in the future.

Consider the case of an investor who is trying to decide whether to invest in the Eurozone or the US. A straightforward comparison of interest rates in the two areas would be misleading. The investor has to take into account expected changes in the exchange rate. To see why, compare the return from an investment in government bonds in the Eurozone to a similar investment in the US. The return from the *domestic* (Eurozone) investment is given by:

$$(1 + i_{EUR})$$

For example, if the interest rate in the Eurozone, i_{EUR}, is 10 per cent then an investment of €1,000 will yield a total return of €1,100.

$$€1,000(1 + 0.1) = €1,100$$

The return from the *foreign* (US) investment is more complicated. The steps involved are as follows:

1 January 2003

- Convert euro into dollars using today's spot exchange rate, e_t.
- Invest the dollars in US and receive a total return of $(1 + i_{US})$.

31 December 2003

- Convert the total dollar return back into euro using the spot exchange rate $(1/e^e_{t+1})$. The term e^e_{t+1} denotes the *expected* exchange rate twelve months from now. We have to use the expected exchange rate as we have no way of knowing the future spot exchange rate. The euro could rise or fall relative to the dollar over the period. If t denotes January, the subscript t+1 indicates the spot rate next December. We also use $1/e^e_{t+1}$ because we are converting from dollars into euro.

The US return, expressed in euro, is given by:

$$(1 + i_{US})e_t/e^e_{t+1}$$

Example

Consider an investment of €1,000 in US treasury bills.
- The spot exchange in January is e_t = $0.8787/€1. Hence, €1,000 will translate into $878.7.
- If that money is invested in the US at an interest rate of i_{US} = 8.25 per cent, the return will be $72.49. The total return (principal *plus* interest) will be $951.19.
- Suppose, next December, the actual spot exchange rate turns out to be e_{t+1} = $0.8647/€1. Using this exchange rate, the total return in euro is €1,100.

Note that the US investment gave a return of €100 or 10 per cent (the same as in the Eurozone) despite the fact that the interest rate in the US was only 8.25 per cent. The reason for this is that there are two parts to foreign investment:
- The interest rate in the currency.
- Gain or loss on the foreign exchange market. In the example the euro depreciated from $0.8787/€1 to $0.8647/€1. Hence the investor made a gain as he or she was holding dollars.

ARBITRAGE

The basic theorem of UIP is that investors will move money between countries so as to obtain the best return on their money. However, this movement of funds should ensure that the total returns from investment in different places are equalised. Suppose, for the moment, that this is the case then the Eurozone investment should equal the US investment. That is:

$$(1 + i_{EUR}) = (1 + i_{US})e_t/e^e_{t+1}$$

Bring e^e_{t+1} and e_t over to the right-hand side.

$$(e^e_{t+1}/e_t) \times (1 + i_{EUR}) = (1 + i_{US})$$

Now bring $(1 + i_{EUR})$ over to the right-hand side.

$$(e^e_{t+1}/e_t) = (1 + i_{US})/(1 + i_{EUR})$$

Subtract 1 from both sides and rearrange to obtain:

$$(e^e_{t+1} - e_t)/e_t = (i_{US} - i_{EUR})/(1 + i_{EUR}) \qquad (7)$$

This is the equation underlying *uncovered interest parity* (UIP) theory. This condition is readily interpretable. Ignoring for simplicity the terms in the denominator, the equation states that if US interest rates exceed Eurozone rates $[(i_{US} - i_{EUR})$ is positive] the market expects the exchange rate to appreciate $[(e^e_{t+1} - e_t)$ is positive)] in the future.

• US interest rate > Eurozone interest rate ⇒ expect appreciation of \$/€ exchange rate.

Conversely, if the Eurozone interest rates is greater than the US interest rate, the \$/€ exchange rate is expected to depreciate.

• US interest rate < Eurozone interest rate ⇒ expect depreciation of \$/€ exchange rate.

The important implication resulting from equation (7) is that *interest rate differentials* give an indication of how the market expects the *exchange rate to move in the future*. This is a handy way of formulating expectations about the future movement of exchange rates.

Consider now the case where equation (7) does not hold. Suppose, for example, that the US offered the best rate of return on an investment. In terms of equation (7) and ignoring the denominator:

$$(e^e_{t+1} - e_t) < (i_{US} - i_{EUR})$$

This would set the forces of arbitrage in motion. Consider what this would do to the variables in equation (7). Investors would withdraw their funds from the Eurozone (i_{EUR} increases) and rush to invest in New York (i_{US} decreases). Hence, the term on the right will fall. Secondly, the exchange of euro for dollars would drive down the spot exchange rate. The term on the left-hand side will increase. With the right-hand side term decreasing and the left-hand side term increasing, UIP will be quickly established. Only the fast movers would benefit as the arbitrage forces will equalise the returns in Europe and New York.

SPECULATION

The UIP theorem is very relevant to the phenomenon of speculative attacks. If a speculator expects a currency to depreciate he or she will only hold it if the interest rate earned is high enough to compensate for the currency's expected loss of value. If a currency comes under speculative attack, the central bank can try to fend off this attack by raising interest rates above those prevailing abroad. While this is unpopular at home, it may persuade speculators to hold the currency and abandon their attack on it. However, we shall see that this strategy failed repeatedly in the history of the European Monetary System (EMS).

COVERED AND UNCOVERED INTEREST PARITY

We used the word 'uncovered' to describe the situation in equation (7) because the investor is exposed to exchange rate risk. He or she does not know with certainty what the future exchange rate will be. An investor can *hedge* against exchange rate risk by entering into a *forward rate agreement*. A forward rate agreement is a contract to buy or sell foreign currency at a specified date in the future but at an exchange rate agreed today.

The investor is now 'covered' in the sense that he or she is no longer exposed to unexpected movements in the exchange rate. If the forward exchange rate (f_t) is inserted into equation (7) in place of the expected exchange rate, then we have an alternative version of the theory called *covered* interest rate parity (CIP) theory.

$$(f_t - e_t) = (i_{US} - i_{EUR})$$

Hedging and the forward exchange rate are discussed in chapter 19.

10.11 THE IRISH, UK EXPERIENCE WITH UIP

THE EXPERIENCE UP TO 1979

Between 1826 and 1927, Ireland was in a monetary union with the UK, and between 1927 and 1979 the Irish pound was rigidly fixed to sterling on a one-to-one, no margins basis. There was no possibility of this sterling link being terminated and, as such, the expectation was no change in the sterling, Irish pound exchange rate. In fact, it was not until the *Central Bank Act of 1971* that the government possessed the legal authority to break the sterling link.

Given the size of the UK money market relative to the Irish market, Irish interest rates were dictated by UK rates. In terms of equation (7), if the term on the left-hand side is zero (the expected change in the exchange rate) then Irish interest rates must equal UK rates.

An early illustration of this emerged in 1955 when the Irish banks were prevailed on by political pressure not to follow an increase in London interest rates. A gap opened up between Dublin and London interest rates. The net external assets of the Irish banking system fell by about 8 per cent of GNP during the year, as capital flowed out of the country in response to the higher returns available abroad. This led to panic among the Irish authorities and forced them to take corrective action, which contributed to the recession that followed.

Figure 10.8 shows the trend in Irish, UK and German interest rates between 1970 and 1998 when the euro was introduced. (Interest rates are three-month inter-bank interest rates.) It is evident that Irish interest rates were more or less the same as UK rates *up to 1979*. On the other hand, a significant gap existed between Irish and UK interest rates, on the one hand, and German rates, on the other. As an example of UIP, note that between 1973 and 1977, the Irish-German interest rate gap was positive. This differential reflected an expectation that sterling (and the Irish pound) would depreciate relative to the DM. This is what happened as the pound fell from about DM8/IR£1 in the early 1970s to DM4/IR£1 in 1976.

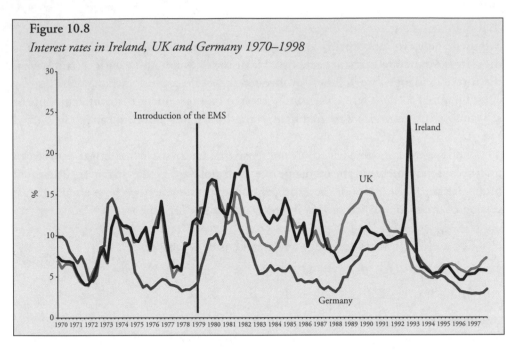

Figure 10.8

Interest rates in Ireland, UK and Germany 1970–1998

THE EXPERIENCE BETWEEN 1979 AND 1998

Following Ireland's entry into the EMS and the termination of the sterling link in 1979, exchange rate uncertainty became an extremely important consideration for an investor comparing returns in Dublin and London. The difference between Irish and UK interest rates now reflected exchange rate expectations.

Figure 10.8 also shows Irish, UK and German interest rates for the period 1979 to 1998. The contrast in the interest rate differential pre-and post-EMS is evident. As an illustration of the hypothesis, note that in 1982 the Irish rate was above both the UK and German rates. This indicates that the market expected the Irish pound to depreciate against both sterling and the DM. This is indeed what happened. However, the interest rate's differential more than compensated investors for this risk. Buying Irish bonds would have been a good decision for a German investor to have taken as the overall return (interest rate minus currency depreciation) was higher than that available from German bonds. The relatively high interest in Ireland over this period was one of the disadvantages of the EMS.

CURRENCY CRISIS

On three occasions — in 1983, 1986 and 1992 — there was a sharp widening of the Irish-German interest rate differential. On each occasion, the Irish pound appreciated relative to sterling and speculators took the view that the Irish pound exchange rate could not be maintained and would be devalued.

On the first two occasions — in 1983 and 1986 — the Irish authorities reacted quickly and devalued the Irish pound. This restored confidence in the Irish pound and the Irish-German interest rate differential narrowed.

In 1992, however, the Irish Government resisted devaluing the Irish pound for a period of four months. Interest rates in the Dublin money market were raised to unprecedented levels: in November 1992 and January 1993 the Central Bank raised the overnight rate to 100 per cent. The one-month rate peaked at 44 per cent.

Despite these drastic measures it was clear that the Irish currency was overvalued and that devaluation was inevitable. Eventually, the Irish pound was devalued by 10 per cent in January 1993 and this restored confidence in the Irish currency. Money flowed back to Dublin and the Irish-German interest rate differential narrowed.

The 1983, 1986, and 1992 episodes illustrate the importance of the sterling/Irish pound exchange rate as an indicator of the sustainability of the Irish exchange rate within the EMS. However, now that the Irish pound has been replaced by the euro, movements in the sterling exchange cannot result in speculative flows against the Irish pound exchange rate. It is still the case, however, that swings in the sterling exchange rate can have serious implications for the Irish economy.

10.12 THE EURO AND UIP

With the introduction of the euro in virtual form in January 1999 and in physical form in January 2002, the expected change in the exchange rates of Eurozone currencies relative to each other became zero and the term on the left-hand side of equation (7) should be set at zero. According to UIP, if follows that there can only be one interest rate in the Eurozone. It simply is not possible for interest rates to differ between Limerick, Ireland, Coimbra, Portugal, Santander, Spain or any other town or city in the Eurozone.

Figure 14.2 in Chapter 14 shows the interest rates in the twelve Eurozone countries from 1979 to 2002. In the early 1980s there was a notable divergence between interest rates among the twelve countries. However, as the date for the introduction of the euro came closer, rates stated to converge. Following the introduction of the euro in 1999, nominal interest rates converged across the Eurozone. By mid-2002 the rate was close to 3.25 per cent in all Eurozone countries. This represented a significant fall for the traditionally high inflation/high interest rate countries like Ireland, Portugal, Spain, Finland and Italy. A low nominal interest rate was combined with relatively high inflation in Ireland, especially in 2000, and this contributed to the exceptionally high growth rate and reinforced the inflationary pressures at that time.

10.13 EXCESS RETURNS AND THE PESO PROBLEM

The UIP theory outlined above was based on the notion that arbitrage tends to equalise expected returns between markets. If this is combined with the idea that expectations are on average correct, then there should be *no excess returns* to be earned from investing in one financial centre rather than another. The movement of the exchange rate should, on average, cancel out higher or lower interest rates.

In reality, this has not been found to hold *ex post*. Many countries have had much higher interest rates than were warranted after the fact by the weakness of their currency.

THE EMS EXPERIENCE

One of the arguments put forward in favour of Ireland's entry into the EMS was that Irish interest rates would quickly converge to the lower German rates. It was argued that given a fixed Irish pound/DM exchange rate, Irish interest rates could not remain above German rates without causing a capital inflow into Ireland. In fact this outcome did not materialise, at least until the early 1990s. Markets were not convinced of the Irish commitment to holding the exchange rate within the EMS: they consistently anticipated devaluation. However, they were too pessimistic on this score. The high relative interest rates in Ireland more than compensated for the depreciation of the Irish pound. As a result, Ireland offered a better return on investments than Germany over the period 1979 to 1987. This episode indicates that UIP does not always hold and that investors can, on occasions, make speculative profits from the market.

When UIP does not hold, and nominal interest rates more than compensate for the exchange rate risk, excess returns are said to obtain. These prevailed in Ireland during the 1980s and have been noted for many other currencies, including several in Latin America in recent years.

What is the explanation for this apparent breakdown of economic theory? One explanation that is given is called the *peso problem*. This refers to the risk, associated with Mexico and other Latin American countries, of a radical change in policies (due to a revolution, perhaps), which results in a major fall in the value of the currency. In the 1980s there was some risk that Ireland's economic crisis would become so bad that it would have defaulted on its foreign debt or dropped out of the EMS. Although such events were not observed, the risk that they could occur was present and taken into account by investors. A *risk premium* was, in effect, attached to the currency.

10.14 THE OPEN ECONOMY MONETARY MODEL

In this section, we introduce the open economy monetary model. Essentially, the model links together the goods and services market with PPP theory. This model will be developed at different stages in the course of this book and this section offers only a cursory introduction.

The model is outlined in figure 10.9. The right-hand diagram shows equilibrium in the goods and services market. This diagram was first outlined in chapter 2. The interaction of the aggregate supply (AS) and aggregate demand (AD) curves determine the real growth rate and inflation. The left-hand diagram shows the relative PPP relationship developed earlier in this chapter. At the point A, the economy is operating at the natural growth rate and unemployment is also at its natural level. At the point M, relative PPP holds between the Eurozone and the US. We can use the model to examine what factors influence inflation, interest rates and exchange rates in open economies.

In the course of our discussion of inflation and exchange rates we developed the following key theories:

$$\Delta M^s + \Delta V \equiv \Delta \text{real GNP} + \pi \qquad \text{(The quantity theory of money)}$$
$$\Delta e_t = \pi_{US} - \pi_{EUR} \qquad \text{(Purchasing power parity)}$$

$$i = r + \pi^e \qquad \text{(The Fisher equation)}$$
$$(e^e_{t+1} - e_t)/e_t = (i_{US} - i_{EUR})/(1 + i_{EUR}) \qquad \text{(Uncovered interest parity)}$$

PPP and UIP are discussed in this chapter. The quantity theory of money and the Fisher equation were explained in chapters 7 and 8.

Suppose that a central bank relies on the monetarist approach to achieve a target of low inflation. Using the quantity theory of money, its main instrument will be to control the rate of growth in the money supply (ΔM^s) in order to control inflation (π). In terms of figure 10.9, the inflation rate, π_1, could be as low as 1–2 per cent. Assuming that the change in velocity (ΔV) is small and that the real growth rate (Δreal GNP) is equal to the natural rate (point A), it follows that a small, steady increase in the money supply should result in price stability.

If a country's rate of inflation is low compared to other countries then this will have the following important effects.

- Firstly, via PPP theory, it will result in a stable or appreciating spot exchange rate. In the left-hand diagram of figure 10.9, if Eurozone inflation is equal to US inflation, the \$/€ exchange rate will be constant along the horizontal axis.
- Secondly, via the Fisher equation, the low inflation will result in low nominal interest rates (i). We assume here that the real interest rate (r) remains constant.
- Low nominal interest rates will, via UIP theory, lead to the expectation that the exchange rate will be stable or appreciate in the future.

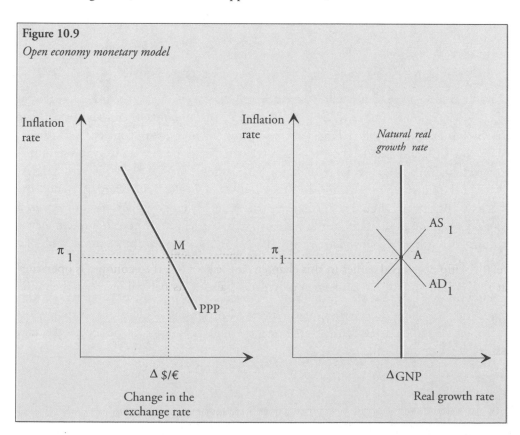

Figure 10.9
Open economy monetary model

In summary, control of the money supply and low relative inflation bring forth the benefits of low nominal interest rates and a stable or appreciating exchange rate. The central banks of countries such as Germany and the United States are examples of institutions that have successfully implemented such a policy and have achieved good anti-inflation reputations. It is hoped that the new European Central Bank (ECB), which is modelled on the Bundesbank, will be able to emulate this performance.

The other side of the coin are central banks who are subservient to governments and forced to bank-role large budget deficits. For example, the former Soviet Union, several Latin America countries, and many countries in Africa have governments that run huge budget deficits and expect the central bank to finance them. In these countries large annual increases in the money supply are associated with high rates of inflation, as predicted by the quantity theory. This, in turn, results in weak, depreciating currencies (via PPP theory) and high nominal interest rates (via the Fisher equation and UIP).

CURRENCY PEG

An alternative approach to achieving low inflation that has often been adopted in small open economies is to peg the exchange rate to a hard currency. In terms of figure 10.9, the exchange rate is fixed along the horizontal axis. The most frequent choices are the euro and the US dollar. In this case, the quantity theory is no longer relevant and can be omitted from the analysis. The relative PPP relationship must also be arranged as:

$$\pi_{EUR} = \pi_{US} - \Delta e_t \qquad \text{(Purchasing power parity)}$$

$$i = r + \pi^e \qquad \text{(The Fisher equation)}$$

$$(e^e_{t+1} - e_t)/e_t = (i_{US} - i_{EUR})/(1 + i_{EUR}) \qquad \text{(Uncovered interest parity)}$$

This amounts to the central bank announcing that the change in the exchange rate in the PPP equation will be zero ($\Delta e = 0$). If the PPP theory holds, then the inflation rate in the small economy will, in large part, be determined by the Eurozone or US inflation. This low inflation should then translate (via the Fisher equation) into low nominal interest rates. Also because the term on the left-hand side of UIP should be zero, interest rates in the small country should converge to the rate in the large country. Hence, the currency peg policy should result in the small country's inflation and nominal interest rates converging to the rates in the large country. This approach to economic policy is known as borrowing *anti-inflationary credibility* or reputation from a central bank of a large country.

The launch of the EMU goes a stage further than the attempt to borrow the reputation of a 'hard-nosed' central bank through an exchange rate peg. It entails twelve countries replacing their national currencies with the single European currency, the euro, and handing over control of monetary and exchange rate policy to the new European Central Bank.

10.15 CONCLUSION

In this chapter we have discussed a number of topics relating to the determination of inflation and interest rates in open economies. The main issues and concepts covered included:

- The theory of absolute and relative purchasing power parity
- Reasons why PPP theory may not hold
- The real exchange rate and other measures of international competitiveness
- Evidence from the Irish economy
- The operation of PPP theory under both fixed and flexible exchange rates
- Uncovered interest rate parity theory. This is the link between expected changes in the exchange rate and the difference between foreign and domestic interest rates
- The concept of excess returns and the peso problem
- The open economy monetary model and link between key relationships, such as the quantity theory of money, PPP and UIP theories
- An exchange rate peg as an anti-inflation commitment.

CHAPTER 11

Fixed Exchange Rate Systems: Theory and History

11.1 INTRODUCTION

Proponents of fixed exchange rates believe that freely floating rates create uncertainty and discourage international trade and investment. It is claimed that speculative flows may drive exchange rates significantly above or below their equilibrium levels, distorting the pattern of trade and investment between countries. When exchange rates are fixed, so the argument goes, uncertainty is reduced and trade and investment are promoted. This in turn should increase output and employment. These arguments have been very influential as justifications for establishing a single currency in the Eurozone.

In this chapter we first explain how a fixed exchange rate system works. This is followed by a discussion of the 'automatic adjustment mechanism' and the concept of 'sterilisation'. We then explain why policy co-ordination is essential if a fixed exchange rate system is to endure. The final sections discuss the gold standard, the Bretton Woods system and the snake system. We conclude by discussing the advantages and disadvantages of fixed and floating exchange rates.

11.2 HOW A FIXED EXCHANGE RATE SYSTEM WORKS

As we saw in chapter 9, when exchange rates are allowed to float the foreign exchange market is just like any other market. The price (exchange rate) adjusts automatically to equate supply and demand. There is no need for central banks or governments to become involved. Fixed exchange rate systems, on the other hand, require countries to observe elaborate 'rules of the game'.

Fixed exchange rate systems generally involve central banks agreeing on *central* exchange rates and on *upper* and *lower* limits within which the market rate should be maintained. The Exchange Rate Mechanism (ERM) of the European Monetary System (EMS) is such a system.

A fixed exchange rate system entails central banks intervening on the foreign exchange markets to support a currency. The *official external reserves* play a key role in central bank intervention.

The official foreign exchange reserves or 'reserve assets' are a central bank's holdings of foreign currencies and other external monetary assets. Table 11.1 gives a breakdown of the European Central Bank's (ECB) 'reserve assets' as of December 2000. The external reserves are primarily made-up of currencies other than the euro, for example, dollars, sterling and yen.

In addition to foreign currencies and gold, the reserve's assets also consist of assets created by international agencies like the International Monetary Fund (IMF). *Special*

Table 11.1
European Central Bank's reserve assets, December 2000

	€. billions	%
Foreign exchange	234.1	59.5
SDR	4.3	1.1
Reserve position at IMF	20.8	5.3
Gold	117.8	29.9
Other claims	16.4	4.2
Total	393.4	100.0

Source: European Central Bank, *Monthly Bulletin*, November 2001, Table 8.7.

Drawing Rights (SDRs), sometimes referred to as 'paper gold', are reserve assets created by the IMF in order to supplement the world's monetary reserves. SDRs were first issued in 1970 to member countries in return for subscriptions in their own currencies. The SDR is a basket of the currencies of five of the main industrial nations.

Figure 11.1 illustrates the principles underlying central bank intervention to stabilise an exchange rate. Participating central banks agree on a central exchange rate and on upper and lower limits within which the exchange rate should be maintained. We can illustrate this using the narrow band exchange rate mechanism (ERM) of the EMS that operated between 1979 and 1993. In 1992 the central rate of the Irish pound against the Deutsche mark was DM2.67. The permissible fluctuation margin was a range of ± 2.25 per cent around this rate. The upper limit to this band would be DM2.73 = IR£1 and the lower limit DM2.61 = IR£1. The Irish and German Central Banks were committed to intervene if these limits were about to be breached.

In Figure 11.1 the market is in equilibrium at DM2.67 = IR£1. Suppose now there is an increase in imports that shifts the supply schedule for Irish pounds to the right (S_1 to S_2). At the new equilibrium B the Irish pound has depreciated to DM2.50 = IR£1. This exchange rate is below the agreed lower limit of DM2.61. To prevent the pound falling outside the target zone, the Central Bank of Ireland (CBI) and the Bundesbank must *buy* Irish pounds and *sell* Deutsche marks on the foreign exchange market. In effect, they create an *artificial demand* for Irish pounds and an *artificial supply* of Deutsche marks. The CBI must use up some of its external reserves for this purpose, whereas the Bundesbank acquires additional reserves in the form of Irish pounds. The purchase of Irish pounds would have the effect of shifting the demand curve for Irish pounds to the right (D_1 to D_2). The new equilibrium would be at C and the exchange rate would have been kept within the agreed band.

Conversely, central banks can keep the exchange rate from rising above the upper limit of the agreed band by selling pounds and buying marks. The CBI sells Irish pounds and the Bundesbank buys them. This will keep the exchange rate within the band.

When a currency is depreciating a central bank's ability to support it is limited by its holdings of reserves of foreign exchange. Were reserves to fall below the minimum

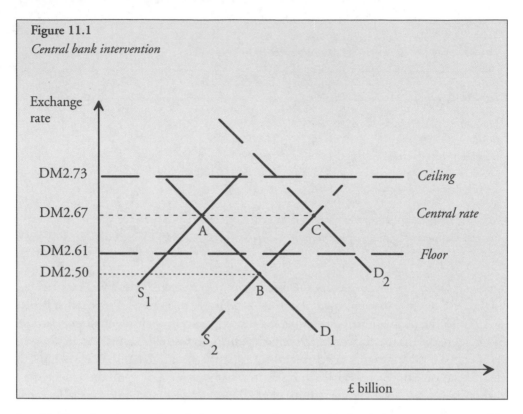

Figure 11.1
Central bank intervention

level believed to be prudent (often expressed as a multiple of the country's monthly import bill), the bank would be unable to continue to support the exchange rate. More damaging is the fact that central banks will also raise interest rates to encourage speculators to hold the currency and to compensate them for losses due to further depreciation. The combination of falling reserves and penal interest rates have time after time forced the abandonment of the target exchange rate.

11.3 THE MONETARY ADJUSTMENT MECHANISM

The theory of fixed exchange rates relies on the concept of a *monetary adjustment mechanism*. To illustrate how this is supposed to operate, consider the case of a country with a relatively high inflation rate. Because its inflation rate is high, its goods become expensive on world markets and a deficit emerges on the current account of its balance of payments. If it adheres to a fixed exchange rate there is, in theory, a mechanism that will reduce its inflation rate and move its current account back into equilibrium.

   Recall from chapter 6 that high-powered money (H) is the sum of the central banks assets or liabilities. Table 11.2 shows that on the liability side, H is equal to currency (CU) plus commercial bank reserves at the central bank (RE) plus government deposits (GD). On the assets side H is equal to the external reserves (R), plus central bank credit to the government (CCG) and the commercial banks, (CCB) and its holdings of government securities (GS). Hence on the asset side we have:

$$H \equiv R + CCB + CCG + GS \tag{1}$$

Table 11.2
Central Bank balance sheet: (hypothetical data) € billions

Assets		Liabilities	
External reserves	−1	Currency	
Loans:		Commercial bank reserves	−1
Banks			
Government		Government deposits	
Government securities			
Total	H	Total	H

In chapter 6, we also showed that high-powered money affects the money supply (M^s) via the money multiplier (m).

$$Ms = mH \qquad (2)$$

It follows from these two equations that changes in external reserves affect high-powered money which, in turn, causes a change in the money supply.

$$\Delta R \rightarrow \Delta H \rightarrow \Delta M^s$$

For example, if the central bank buys €1 billion and pays for this out of its external reserves, in table 11.2, R falls on the asset side and RE on the liability side. (People and firms who sell Irish pounds to the central bank take the money from their deposit accounts in the commercial banks.) The fall in R leads to a fall in H and, via the multiplier, a decrease in the money supply.

Conversely, if the central bank sells domestic currency to the foreign exchange market to avert an appreciation, R increases on the asset side and RE on the liability side. As H increases, the money supply expands. A key conclusion from this is that when a country adheres to a fixed exchange rate it loses control over its money supply. Hence, it is not possible to participate in a fixed exchange rate and simultaneously follow a monetary policy of controlling the money supply.

THE QUANTITY THEORY OF MONEY

Taking the analysis one stage further, we recall that changes in the money supply affect the inflation rate. The quantity theory (see chapter 7) is written as:

$$\Delta M^s + \Delta V = \Delta \text{real GNP} + \pi \qquad (3)$$

The percentage change in the money supply plus the percentage change in velocity must equal the real growth rate plus the inflation rate. Assuming that velocity is relatively constant and the economy is at natural real GNP, the percentage change in the money supply determines the inflation rate.

Now consider the case of a country with relatively high inflation and an associated current account deficit. How does that economy adjust back towards equilibrium?

(Under flexible exchange rates, the balance of payments deficit would result in depreciation.) Under a fixed exchange rate, the central bank intervenes by buying its currency on the foreign exchange market and the external reserves fall. This leads to a fall in H and M^s, which in turn leads to a fall in the rate of inflation.

$$\text{Current account deficit} \rightarrow \downarrow R \rightarrow \downarrow H \rightarrow \downarrow M^s \rightarrow \downarrow \pi$$

The decline in inflation improves the country's competitive position, exports increase and imports fall, leading to the elimination of the current account deficit. Conversely, a country with a current account surplus sees its external reserves and money supply rise. This increases the rate of inflation, making the country less competitive. Exports fall, imports rise and the current account surplus is eliminated.

This adjustment mechanism is a key feature of fixed exchange rate systems.

11.4 STERILISATION

Central banks, even if they are participating in a fixed exchange rate system, are often unwilling to surrender control over the money supply and inflation. *Sterilisation* is a way of breaking the link between changes in the external reserves and the money supply. To see how sterilisation works, consider again the central bank's balance sheet in table 11.3.

Suppose the central bank is intervening in the foreign exchange market to prevent the exchange rate depreciating. This intervention will lead to a fall in the external reserves (R) on the asset side and a fall in commercial bank reserves (RE) on the liability side. This in turn will reduce high-powered money (H) and, via the multiplier, the money supply (M^s).

The sterilisation strategy involves trying to keep H constant. This can be done by buying government securities (GS) and by paying for them by issuing new currency (CU). Hence on the asset side of the balance sheet, GS rises and on the liability side CU rises. If the rise in GS is exactly equal to the fall in R, the monetary base or high-powered money remains constant. The central bank has broken the link from changes in R through to M^s.

Table 11.3
Central Bank balance sheet: (hypothetical data) € billions

Assets		Liabilities	
External reserves	−1	Currency	+1
Loans:		Commercial bank reserves	−1
Banks			
Government		Government deposits	
Government securities	+1		
Total	H	Total	H

One difficulty is when the central bank buys bonds, it tends to drive their price up. But this implies lower interest rates, which will encourage an outflow of funds. This could lead to a capital outflow, which on top of the current account deficit will put even more pressure on the central bank.

Consider now the case where a country is experiencing an inflow of foreign exchange that threatens to increase the domestic money supply and eventually increase the rate of inflation. R increases on the asset side and RE on the liability side of the central bank's balance sheet. If the central bank now sells bonds, both GS and CU will fall. If the rise in R is equal to the fall in GS, H will remain unchanged and the sterilisation policy will be complete.

However, selling bonds to the public could mean a fall in their price. This implies that interest rates would have to rise. However, higher interest rates would tend to attract a capital inflow from abroad that would augment the current account surplus. Given that higher interest rates would also be harmful to the domestic economy, the central bank would sooner or later find it more attractive to allow its exchange rate to rise rather than to continue with its sterilisation policy.

History shows that sterilisation is of limited effectiveness. It is usually abandoned after a short trial period. A good example is provided by the response of the German Central Bank to the inflow of dollars when the Bretton Woods system was breaking down in the early 1970s.

MONETARY APPROACH TO THE BALANCE OF PAYMENTS

Another method of conducting monetary policy under fixed exchange rates is the *monetary approach to the balance of payments* (MAB). This theory involves issuing credit guidelines on commercial bank credit in order to achieve an external reserves target. We defer to Appendix 1 in this chapter for an explanation of this theory.

11.5 WHY FIXED EXCHANGE RATE SYSTEMS DO NOT ENDURE

In chapter 9 we discussed the determinants of exchange rates and we pointed out that there are many factors that impinge on a country's exchange rate. For example, differences in growth rates and adverse economic shocks such as the foot and mouth disease in Ireland in 2001. Inflation rate differentials, in particular, have a very important impact on exchange rates. (This effect is also known as purchasing power parity theory.) Countries with high relative inflation rates will tend to have weak or depreciating exchange rates and visa versa. Hence, for a fixed exchange rate system to succeed, the chosen exchange rates must accurately reflect the inflation and growth rates in the participating countries. If inflation or growth rates are out-of-line then this will give rise to a *fundamental misalignment* that will force a change in the agreed exchange rates.

POLICY CO-ORDINATION

Going one stage further, it is also essential that the participating countries pursue similar macroeconomic policies so as to achieve similar inflation and growth rates. If the currencies are misaligned to start with, or divergent policies create misalignments with the passage of time, persistent balance of payments current account deficits and surpluses will arise. These symptoms of disequilibrium will eventually lead to realignments and the possible breakdown of the fixed exchange rate system.

An example of the tensions caused by uncoordinated policies is provided by the early years of the EMS. In 1983 France was pursuing an expansionary fiscal policy, while Germany was implementing a deflationary monetary policy, but both were committed to maintaining stable exchange rates within the EMS. The result was an increasing balance of payments deficit in France and a surplus in Germany. Speculators, anticipating a devaluation of the French franc, converted large amounts of money from francs into Deutsche marks. Eventually the French franc was devalued, rewarding the speculators. It was only after France abandoned its expansionary fiscal policy that the speculation subsided.

The lesson to be learned is that fixed exchange rate systems can only reduce exchange rate uncertainty if macroeconomic policy in the individual states is consistent. This can be achieved by explicit or implicit *policy co-ordination*.

SPECULATION — A ONE-WAY BET UNDER FIXED EXCHANGE RATES?

A problem with fixed exchange rates is that they offer speculators opportunities for making a killing. Consider the case of the Irish pound participation in the EMS. If foreign exchange dealers became convinced that the currency is overvalued, each dealer (or speculator, if you prefer) would have an incentive to speculate against the currency. Suppose, for example, a dealer believed the Irish pound would be devalued by 10 per cent, from DM2.67 to DM2.41. He could borrow IR£1 million pounds and convert them to Deutsche marks (DM) at an exchange rate of DM2.67. Total Deutsche mark receipts are DM2.67 million. If the devaluation now occurs you can convert back from Deutsche marks to Irish pounds at an exchange rate of DM2.41. Total Irish pound receipts are IR£1,107,884. The dealer now repays the bank £1 million and the speculative profit is £107,884.

Since he borrowed the money with which to speculate, the only cost has been the interest charges incurred over the month. Unless the central bank pushes interest rates very high, these interest charges will not eat up much of the profit. If the devaluation fails to materialise, the dealer would lose on the difference between the interest earned on Deutsche marks and the interest paid on Irish pounds.

To avert this sequence of events, the central bank — committed to the fixed exchange rate — will increase interest rates in an attempt to persuade investors to hold the domestic currency and discourage them from selling it on the foreign exchange market. The process of defending the exchange rate can become very painful. During the currency crisis of 1992–93, for example, central banks around Europe raised interest rates to astronomical levels to defend their currencies. The Swedish Central Bank raised its rate to 500 per cent, in January 1993 the Central Bank of Ireland raised its rate to 100 per cent and the Danish Central Bank did likewise in February. But these high interest rates were not sufficient to prevent speculators from continuing to sell the currencies short. All the currencies that were attacked were eventually devalued and the speculators made handsome profits. One of these speculators was the billionaire George Soros, who was credited (or blamed) for having forced Britain out of the EMS in 1992.

The level of official external reserves sets a limit to how long a central bank can continue to intervene to support its currency. However, the rise in interest rates and the adverse affect on consumer and investor confidence tends to break governments' resolve to support fixed exchange rates. In Ireland and Britain, high interest rates are particularly unpopular because so many households hold variable rate mortgages. Politicians quickly decided that the possible benefits of a fixed exchange rate do not merit the unpopularity and economic costs of the measures needed to defend it. Speculators are aware of this weakness in the commitment to the exchange rate target and are encouraged to continue to sell the currency in order to make a speculative profit.

On 16 September 1992 (ten years ago from the time of writing) Britain left the EMS. This was labelled Black Wednesday at the time, but since then it has been hailed as the start of an economic renaissance in Britain. Freed from the constraints of the quasi-fixed exchange rate system, the Bank of England and Treasury focussed on an inflation target of 2.5 per cent and over the following ten years the UK enjoyed low inflation, rapid economic growth and low unemployment. In fact, even the exchange rate was relatively stable, although not committed to any particular target against the euro or the dollar.

One of the difficulties highlighted by the turbulence of the EMS was that 'half-way-houses' between rigidly fixed exchange rates and free floating create problems of the type experienced in Europe 1992–93. The extreme alternative of abolishing the national currency — by adopting a common currency such as the euro or through out-and-out 'dollarisation' — avoids these problems, but at the cost of completely abandoning an independent monetary policy.

Having outlined how fixed exchange rate systems operate and the difficulties of sustaining them, we turn now to a brief account of the most important historical examples of fixed exchange rate systems, the gold standard, the Bretton Woods system and the precursor to the EMS. (We discuss the EMS in chapter 12.)

11.6 THE GOLD STANDARD

The most famous example of a system of fixed exchange rates is the gold standard, which was in full force from 1870 to the outbreak of World War I in 1914. Over this period the values of the world's major currencies were fixed in terms of gold. This determined their value relative to each other. For example, a US dollar was worth 23.22 grains of gold and a pound sterling 113 grains, so the parity between the pound and the dollar was £1 = 113/23.22 = $4.8665 or roughly 1:5. (The two-shilling piece was commonly known as 'half a dollar' because there were ten to a £1.)

Note:
As there are 480 grains in a Troy ounce, an ounce was worth $20.66 or £4.25. The ounces used in buying and selling gold are 'Troy ounces', which are slightly heavier than the more familiar (avoirdupois) ounces. One Troy ounce = 1.097 avoirdupois ounce.

The gold standard relied on the automatic adjustment mechanism to correct current account balance of payments surpluses and deficits. If, for example, a country were experiencing a current account deficit, gold would flow out of the country. This reduction in the money supply (gold) would put downward pressure on the price level. Lower prices, in turn, improved competitiveness, increased exports and reduced imports. The incipient current account deficit would be automatically eliminated by this redistribution of the world's gold supply. Similarly, a country with a current account surplus would experience an increase in its money supply and rising prices. The loss in competitiveness would choke off the current account surplus. The monetary authorities in these countries should not intervene to prevent these flows or their effects on the price level: this was an essential part of the 'rules of the game'.

In addition to the gold flows labour and capital could also be expected to flow from the deficit to the surplus country. This is what happens today between the regions of a country. In the United States, for example, cut-backs in the defence industry hit California hard, its current account went into deficit, the state went into a severe recession and resources flowed out. A rise in oil prices, on the other hand, would lead to a current account surplus in Texas, money and resources would flow into the state and the economy would boom. A similar adjustment mechanism will operate throughout the Eurozone following the introduction of the euro.

THE DEMISE OF THE GOLD STANDARD

During World War I, France and Britain suspended convertibility of their currencies into gold and, although the United States maintained limited convertibility of the dollar, this marked the end of the full-blown gold standard. At the time the suspension of convertibility was regarded as temporary, like the suspension of gold payments during the Napoleonic Wars, and a major aim of British post-war policy was to return to the gold standard at the pre-war value of sterling.

In 1925 Winston Churchill, then Chancellor of the Exchequer, put the pound back on the gold standard at the pre-war parity. Orthodox financial opinion in Britain was gratified at the thought that the pound was once again worth $4.8665. However, since 1914, Britain has experienced considerably more inflation than the United States with the result that sterling was overvalued.

The adjustment to this mistake was slow and painful. It has always been difficult for countries to adjust to an overvaluation, because it requires price and wage cuts. Unemployment and cuts in wages in England in the late 1920s led to riots and widespread social unrest.

Hence one of the main reasons the gold standard broke up was due to differences in inflation rates in member states. In contrast to Britain, France went back on the gold standard in 1928 but at a realistic, lower exchange rate that more than compensated for the inflation that had occurred since 1914.

There were, however, other fundamental problems with the gold standard.

• As international trade increased there was an associated increase in the demand for gold to act as reserve backing for currencies. Increases in the gold supply, however, depended on new discoveries and these occurred erratically in the course of the nineteenth century, in California, South Africa and Australia. Consequently there was a tendency for periodic shortages of international liquidity to develop.

- Governments were not willing to abide by the 'rules of the game', which were the equivalent of the automatic monetary mechanism we described earlier. For example, the United States had a surplus on its balance of payments and this led to an inflow of gold. However, the Federal Reserve System, created in 1913, prevented these inflows from increasing the US money supply because of the risk to inflation. It operated a sterilisation policy, which thwarted the automatic adjustment mechanism on which the gold standard rested.

GREAT DEPRESSION

When recession hit Germany in 1928 and then America in 1929 it was quickly transmitted throughout the world. It is now widely agreed that the restoration of the gold standard in the 1920s was one of the reasons why this recession intensified into the Great Depression. In any event, the financial panics and bank failures that followed in the wake of the stock market crash of 1929 led to the collapse of the gold standard.

Britain suspended sterling convertibility to gold in 1931 and in 1933 dollar convertibility was suspended, to be restored in 1934 at the higher gold price of $35 an ounce. Most other countries abandoned the gold standard completely.

John Maynard Keynes regarded the financial world's obsession with gold as a 'barbarous relic'. He thought Mr Churchill's decision to re-establish the pre-war gold value of sterling in 1925 was a quixotic blunder that imposed a severe deflation on the British economy. When Britain abandoned the gold standard Keynes wrote, 'There are few Englishmen who do not rejoice at the breaking of our gold fetters. We feel that we have at last a free hand to do what is sensible. The romantic phase is over, and we can begin to discuss what policy is for the best'. (J. M. Keynes, 'The End of the Gold Standard' in *Essays in Persuasion*, Rupert Hart-Davis, London, 1952)

Note:
Keynes was visiting Ireland, to give the Finlay Lecture at University College, Dublin, in March 1933, when the news arrived that the dollar's convertibility had been suspended. The lecture was followed by a dinner and some of the best-known wits of Dublin were invited. The dinner was a total failure. Keynes was called to the telephone in the middle of the meal. When he came back, he said 'You may be interested to know that the United States has just left gold'. The short silence that was felt appropriate was broken by [Oliver St John] Gogarty: 'Does that matter?' (James Meenan, *George O'Brien: A Biographical Memoir*, Dublin: Gill and Macmillan, 1980, 171.)

As the recession of 1929 intensified into the Great Depression, governments abandoned the commitment to fixed exchange rates, adopting instead a policy of 'beggar thy neighbour' devaluations. They devalued in order to secure a competitive gain over their rivals in trade, but the countries that were adversely affected retaliated by devaluing in turn. The result was that no country gained a lasting advantage. The instability of the floating exchange rate system during the 1930s caused policy makers to attach a high priority to re-establishing a fixed exchange rate system after World War II.

11.7 THE BRETTON WOODS SYSTEM, 1945–71

In Bretton Woods, a mountain resort town in New Hampshire, representatives of forty-four nations met in July 1944 (three weeks after D-Day) to discuss the arrangements for the post-war world monetary system. They hoped that when the war ended there would be no going back to the chaotic international financial system that had prevailed after the gold standard broke down in the 1930s. They believed that only a system of fixed exchange rates could provide the stable framework required for economic reconstruction.

By 1945, the United States held most of the western world's gold reserves. Consequently it was natural that the dollar should assume the role of the new reserve currency for the western world. The agreement was that the dollar would remain fixed at its 1934 value of $35 per ounce of gold and that all other countries would keep their exchange rates within a 1 per cent band of an agreed parity with the dollar. Central banks would buy or sell currencies as appropriate to keep exchange rates within the agreed band. This dollar exchange standard was, therefore, an attenuated form of the old gold standard.

The principal architects of the new system were J. M. Keynes and an American economist, Harry Dexter White. Mr White may or may not have been a Soviet spy; it seems that every night he informed the Soviet Embassy of the details of the negotiations! (See Robert Skidelsky, *John Maynard Keynes: Fighting for Britain 1937–46*, Macmillan, 2000.) This was Keynes's last major contribution to public affairs before his death on Easter Sunday, 1946.

THE INTERNATIONAL MONETARY FUND AND THE WORLD BANK

The International Monetary Fund (IMF) was set up to assist countries experiencing balance of payments difficulties and to help maintain fixed exchange rates. *The International Bank for Reconstruction and Development* (IBRD or the *World Bank*) was set up to help finance post-war reconstruction. (The IMF and World Bank are still known as the 'Bretton Woods Institutions'.) Central banks could borrow foreign exchange from the IMF and use it to support their currency on the markets. If, however, a country was experiencing a 'fundamental disequilibrium' in its balance of payments it could devalue. The IMF could not veto a devaluation if it was less than 10 per cent, but its permission was required for devaluation in excess of 10 per cent.

Figure 11.2, illustrates how a 10 per cent devaluation of the pound, relative to the dollar, would work. The initial central rate against the dollar is $2.8/£1 and, given the ± 1 per cent band, the ceiling rate is $2.828 and the floor rate $2.772. Following the 10 per cent devaluation, the new central rate is $2.52 and the ceiling and floor rates are $2.5452 and $2.4948 respectively. This devaluation should remove Britain's balance of payments deficit and the fixed exchange rate system can proceed as normal.

The provision for devaluation marked a crucial difference between the Bretton Woods system and the old gold standard. No longer did countries have to suffer the protracted deflation of the automatic adjustment mechanism in order to correct a balance of payments problem. Instead they could obtain international agreement on devaluation.

Figure 11.2

Exchange rate realignment

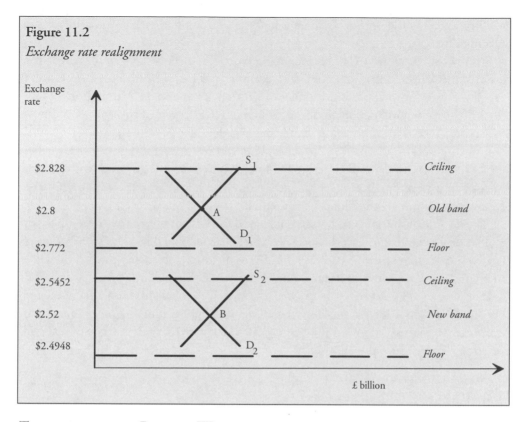

THE DEMISE OF THE BRETTON WOODS SYSTEM

The Bretton Woods system worked well during the 1950s and into the 1960s. The major currencies held to fixed exchange rates for long periods of time. For example, between 1949 and 1967, sterling was worth $2.80 (and because the Irish pound was fixed at one-to-one parity with sterling it too was worth $2.80). For eighteen years this was a fact of economic life and no one bothered to look up the newspapers to see if there had been any change. Trade and investment between the nations of the western world expanded rapidly under the fixed exchange rate regime.

However, strains began to be felt in the late 1960s. The US began running huge fiscal budget deficits to fight a 'war on poverty' at home and a 'war on communism' in south-east Asia. This, in turn, led to massive US current account deficits and undermined confidence in the dollar. The increase in government spending also increased US inflation.

The other main industrial countries were unwilling to revalue their currencies to help eliminate the US deficit. For a while, central banks were glad of additional dollars to augment their reserves, but the continued loose US monetary and fiscal policies soon created an excess supply of the currency.

By 1970 the German and Japanese Central Banks held so many dollars that if they had been allowed to obtain gold in exchange for them, American gold reserves would have been completely depleted. In 1969 the German money supply grew by 25 per cent in a week due to the inflow of dollars and the Bundesbank proved powerless to offset this through sterilisation. There was growing reluctance to continue to absorb the dollars flooding on to world foreign exchange markets. The dollar exchange standard was breaking down.

Finally, in August 1971 President Richard Nixon officially terminated the convertibility of the dollar into gold. In December 1971, the Smithsonian Agreement (which was concluded at the Smithsonian Institution, a museum in Washington, D.C.), raised the price of gold to $38 an ounce, which in effect devalued the dollar by almost 8 per cent. Most of the other major currencies also devalued in terms of gold. This final attempt to patch up the Bretton Woods system did not succeed. There was a further devaluation of the dollar in February 1973 (which raised the price of gold to $42.22 an ounce), but instead of restoring confidence in the system, this encouraged the countries of Europe to terminate their links with the dollar and to float their currencies.

The decline of the dollar relative to gold paved the way for one of the greatest periods of inflation in the history of the world. As the dollar fell in value, the *Organisation of Petroleum Exporting Countries* (OPEC) decided to quadruple the dollar price of oil when the opportunity presented itself during the Arab-Israeli War late in 1973.

The rise in oil prices in turn fuelled the massive global inflation that occurred between 1973 and 1985. It is understandable, in the light of this chain of events, that governments yearned for a return to some form of backing for their currencies that will prevent a recurrence of this experience.

11.8 THE EUROPEAN SNAKE, 1972–74

Instability in the foreign exchange markets was unsettling for the European Economic Community (as it then was). It made it very difficult to operate the Common Agricultural Policy, whose goal was to establish a common price for agricultural products throughout the Community. How could this be done if the currencies of Europe were fluctuating wildly on the foreign exchange markets? But it also undermined the long-standing aim of the Community to establish a common European currency and a single European market for goods and services.

In 1972 the EEC central banks agreed to intervene in the foreign exchange markets to minimise fluctuations. Countries were expected to hold their currencies in a band $\pm$ 1.125 per cent around a central rate (the 'snake'). They also had to maintain their exchange rates in a $\pm$ 2.25 per cent band against the dollar (the 'tunnel'). This system became known as the 'snake in the tunnel' because the European currencies slid up and down within the 'tunnel' as they followed the movements of the dollar.

In March 1973, the European currencies decided to float against the dollar and the 'tunnel' part of the system came to an end. The remaining snake had a short life. The UK joined at the start, but left after two months because it proved impossible to maintain the value of sterling at the target level. (The Irish pound entered and left the snake along with sterling.) France left and rejoined as the franc rose and fell against the DM. By the mid-1970s the snake was dead.

The main reason for the failure of the snake was the same as that which led to the downfall of the gold standard and the Bretton Woods system, namely, the lack of economic policy co-ordination between the participating countries and differences in inflation rates. If countries do not have similar monetary policies, leading to similar rates of inflation, they cannot hope to maintain their balance of payments in equilibrium under a system of fixed exchange rates. During the 1970s France and the UK pursued much more expansionary fiscal and monetary policies than Germany. As a result they tended to run chronic current account deficits, while Germany ran surpluses. These imbalances eventually forced exchange rate changes and killed off the snake.

The renewed currency instability increased the awareness of the need for a system that would stabilise exchange rates in Europe and led to the initiatives that culminated in the launch of the EMS in 1979.

CO-ORDINATED EXCHANGE RATES

Since the collapse of the Bretton Woods system in the 1970s, the United States has proclaimed that it is committed to a floating dollar. An important change in US policy took place in September 1985, however, when the world's seven main industrialised nations (known as G7) met in the Plaza Hotel in New York City to co-ordinate a depreciation of the dollar against the other currencies. This approach can restore stability to the foreign exchange markets for a while, but does not remove the potential for further tensions. Because of its importance in world trade and because it is the most widely held reserve currency, the dollar always occupies centre stage. This is despite its periodic weaknesses and the long-run decline in its value relative to the Deutsche mark and the Japanese yen. So far the dollars status has not been undermined by the introduction of the euro. Following the euro launch in January 1999, it fell almost 30 per cent over the next two years, but recovered some ground in 2002.

11.9 WHICH EXCHANGE RATE REGIME IS BEST?

In principle, countries have a choice between fixed exchange rate systems and floating, or various compromises between these two systems. Orthodox economic opinion has varied as to the relative merits of the alternatives. In this section we examine the arguments on both sides of this debate.

ADVANTAGES OF FLOATING EXCHANGE RATES

The basic argument in favour of floating is that the foreign exchange market should be allowed to function free of government intervention and find its own equilibrium through the interaction of the forces of supply and demand. Attempts by governments to set targets and peg exchange rates are, according to this view, as misguided in this market as they would be in the market for apples or shoes. How do governments know what the 'correct' exchange rate is? How can they distinguish a temporary fluctuation in the supply and demand for foreign exchange (which should be smoothed out) from a fundamental adjustment (which should not be resisted)? How can they avoid handing speculators sure bets by merely delaying a devaluation or revaluation?

Even if governments are successful in maintaining a fixed exchange rate, the result can be a misalignment. This gives rise to *problems of adjustment*. If, for example, the exchange rate is overvalued, but the government is committed to a fixed exchange rate, measures will have to be taken to reduce domestic costs and prices. The required deflationary policies will have an adverse effect on output, employment and unemployment, in the short run at least, and are politically difficult to implement.

Furthermore, it is unrealistic to expect employees and trade unions to understand that they should accept cuts in nominal wages so as to restore the country's international competitiveness. The best that can be hoped for is to hold domestic costs down while foreign costs rise, but it can take a long time to achieve the desired result. Floating exchange rates avoid all these adjustment problems.

DISADVANTAGES OF FLOATING EXCHANGE RATES

The most frequently made argument against allowing currencies to float freely is that left to its own devices the foreign exchange market tends to be dominated by speculative flows. In principle, this should not be a problem if speculators base their actions on the 'fundamentals' that ultimately determine the relative value of currencies. However, at times speculators' expectations appear to lack an anchor. In the short run, currencies can gyrate widely in response to all sorts of news and rumours. As a consequence many small countries, although proclaiming that their currencies are floating, in fact intervene in the foreign exchange markets and try to maintain fairly stable exchange rates. This has been referred to as a 'fear of floating'. (See Guillermo A. Calvo and Carmen M. Reinhart, 'Fear of Floating', *NBER Working Paper*, No. 7993, November, 2000.)

An argument in favour of fixed exchange rates is that they avoid the uncertainty and volatility that occur when currencies are allowed to float freely. However, there is surprisingly little evidence that this volatility actually reduces the level of international trade and investment.

A further potential disadvantage of flexible exchange rates is that depreciation may provoke a depreciation-inflation spiral. This occurs when an initial depreciation increases domestic costs and prices and generates pressure for further depreciation and so on. Why do we have such high inflation? Because the exchange rate is depreciating. And why is the exchange rate depreciating? Because we have high inflation. The experience of a number of South American countries illustrates how difficult it can be to stop this spiral.

There is no consensus as to which exchange rate regime is the best. In fact, it is unlikely that any one regime is ideal in all circumstances. The UK has shown since 1992 that a large, well-managed economy can use a floating currency combined with disciplined domestic policies to deliver high growth and low inflation. Countries with a history of high inflation can use a peg to a strong currency such as the dollar or the euro to win the fight against inflation, but only if the peg is supported by tight fiscal and monetary policies. The more inflation-prone Eurozone countries: Italy, Ireland, Greece, Spain and Portugal, got their houses in order before they adopted the common currency. It is still too early to say whether the common currency will be of long-run benefit to them. We discuss these topics at greater length in chapter 14.

The Argentine case is instructive. In 1991 a new Argentine peso was launched and rigidly pegged to the US dollar at 1:1 through a currency board that could only issue currency that was fully backed by dollars. During the 1990s Argentina enjoyed a sharp fall in inflation and a resumption of economic growth. But by 2001 the contradictions between the currency peg and the lack of domestic economic discipline led to a collapse. By mid-2002 the peso had fallen to almost 4:1 and the country was plunged in a dire economic crisis.

11.10 CONCLUSION

In this chapter we have discussed the following topics:

- The operation of a fixed exchange rate system
- The official external reserves and their composition
- The automatic adjustment mechanism and sterilisation
- The importance of policy co-ordination
- The limitations to central bank intervention on foreign exchange markets
- The gold standard
- The Bretton Woods system
- The European snake
- The question of the best exchange rate regime
- We have left a discussion of the EMS and the move towards a single currency to the following chapters.

APPENDIX
THE MONETARY APPROACH TO THE BALANCE OF PAYMENTS (MAB)

From the consolidated balance sheet of the banking system it can be shown that:

$$\Delta M^3 \equiv \Delta NGL + \Delta BLG + \Delta R \tag{1}$$

where

M^3 = The broad money supply

NGL = Bank lending to the non-government sector

BLG = Bank lending to the government

R = External reserves

The symbol Δ denotes rate of change. The sum of NGL and BLG is often referred to as domestic credit expansion (DCE). This is the increase in bank lending to the private sector and to the government.

A key assumption underlying MAB theory is that the supply of money is determined by the demand for money (M^d). That is, the money supply is assumed to respond to demand. This assumption is consistent with the fact that the central bank cannot control the money supply when the exchange rate is fixed. However, the MAB suggests that it can influence the composition of the money supply by restricting domestic credit expansion. For any given growth in the demand for money, the slower the rate of domestic credit expansion, the faster the rate of accumulation of external reserves. This suggests that *credit guidelines* can be used to achieve an external reserves target.

Note:
Credit guidelines may be issued by central banks as a means of curtailing the growth in bank credit. Typically, these guidelines stipulate by how much the banks can collectively increase their lending over a period such as a year. If the banks exceed the guideline they have 'excess' lending, while if the growth of bank lending falls short of that specified by the guideline they have a 'deficiency' in lending relative to the guideline. Since loans are the principal component of the banks' assets, credit guidelines are equivalent to placing a ceiling on the assets of the banking system. If a borrower is refused a loan because of a credit guideline, he is said to have experienced *credit rationing*. Banks have a profit incentive to meet a demand for credit provided they have the necessary reserves, even if this involves breaching a credit guideline. As a result, central banks are normally obliged to accompany credit guidelines with some form of enforcement measure. The Central Bank of Ireland has imposed *special deposits* on the banks for this purpose. These try to ensure that a bank makes a loss on excess lending.

The following steps illustrate how a credit guideline can be used to achieve an external reserves target:

1. Estimate the growth in the demand for money for the forthcoming year, which gives the target for the growth in the money supply. Typically this estimate is based on a forecast of the change in nominal GNP and the interest rate.
2. Decide on the external reserves target. Usually some rule of thumb such as building up a certain number of months' import cover is used.
3. Estimate the growth in Central Bank and commercial bank lending to the government (ΔBLG).
4. Issue a credit guideline to ensure that the change in bank lending to the private sector (ΔNGL) is consistent with the external reserves objective.

Suppose, for example, that the Central Bank predicts that the demand for money will increase by €100 billion and that bank lending to the government will increase by €25 billion. If the objective is to increase the external reserves by €25 billion, from the MAB identity the growth in commercial bank lending to the private sector should be restricted to €50 billion. Given the various estimates and the external reserves objective, the credit guideline is in effect calculated as a residual.

MAB is a theory of the balance of payments because changes in the external reserves equal the overall balance of payments. A balance of payments deficit leads to a fall in the external reserves. Hence, an external reserves target is tantamount to a balance of payments target.

It is important to note that a key assumption implicit in the MAB theory is that the demand for money is a *stable* function of a few variables such as nominal GNP and the interest rate. If, however, the demand for money fluctuates unpredictably over time, so too will the amount of additional money that can be absorbed by the economy, and an identity like (i) will be of little value for policy purposes.

CHAPTER 12

The European Monetary System:
Precursor to the Euro

12.1 INTRODUCTION

After the collapse of the Bretton Woods system and the snake system in the 1970s there was a desire to re-establish fixed exchange rates between the major European currencies. The next initiative was the launch of the European Monetary System (EMS) in 1979. The EMS survived several setbacks during its existence and has now been superseded by the European Economic and Monetary Union (EMU).

In this largely historical chapter we explain how the EMS operated and how the ECU evolved into the new euro. This is followed by an explanation of how EMS membership involved a convergence of inflation rates and the risks associated with this strategy. The following sections discuss the EMS experience and, in particular, the currency crisis of 1992–93. The concluding section examines the response to the currency crisis and how this influenced the subsequent decision to forge ahead with a monetary union in Europe.

12.2 THE EUROPEAN MONETARY SYSTEM, 1979–98

It has been argued that exchange rate stability is regarded as essential for the proper functioning of the Common Market. Despite the failure of the snake, during the second half of the 1970s the EC Commission pressed ahead with plans for a European monetary union. The interim goal was to create a 'zone of monetary stability' in Europe. Following an initiative by the then President of the European Union, Lord Roy Jenkins, an agreement was reached in 1978 between the French President, Valéry Giscard D'Estaing, and the German Chancellor, Helmut Schmidt, to fix exchange rates and eventually push for a common currency in Europe. After long and difficult negotiations the EMS commenced on 13 March 1979. More details of the chronology of events surrounding the EMS are provided in Appendix 1 to this chapter.

THE EUROPEAN CURRENCY UNIT AND THE OPERATION OF THE EMS
At the heart of the EMS was a system of quasi-fixed exchange rates, known as the *Exchange Rate Mechanism* (ERM). The ERM was based on the *European Currency Unit* (ECU), a basket of currencies. (The écu was a medieval French coin. There was ambiguity as to whether 'ECU' refers to this or is simply an acronym of European Currency Unit.)

Table 12.1 shows that the ECU was a basket of currencies: it contained 0.6242 Deutsche marks, 1.332 French francs, 0.2197 Dutch guilders and so on. The amount

Table 12.1

The European currency unit (ECU): November 1993

	Units of currency	Weight	(%)
1.	Deutsche mark (DM)	0.6242	30.1
2.	French franc (FF)	1.332	19.0
3.	Dutch guilder (HFL)	0.2197	9.4
4.	Belgian franc (BFR)	3.301	
5.	Luxembourg franc (LFR)	0.13	7.9
6.	Italian lira (LIT)	151.8	10.15
7.	Danish krone (DKR)	0.1976	2.45
8.	Irish pound (IR£)	0.0085	1.1
9.	Pound sterling (STG£)	0.0878	13.0
10.	Spanish peseta (PTA)	6.885	5.3
11.	Greek drachma (DR)	1.15	0.8
12.	Portuguese escudo (ESU)	1.393	0.8
		1 ECU	**100.0**

of each currency in the ECU was based on a country's intra-EC trade. The Deutsche mark (DM) had by far the largest weight, reflecting the size of the German economy and its dominant role in European trade. The Irish pound accounted for only 1.1 per cent of the value of an ECU. It may be seen that the Deutsche mark, French franc and pound sterling together accounted for over 60 per cent of the ECU value.

Note:

The basket of currencies comprising the ECU was first defined when the EMS commenced in 1979. It was redefined in 1984, 1989, and a final set of weights was agreed in November 1993. Hence the data in table 12.1 relates to November 1993.

The ECU as given in table 12.1 is an artificial currency in that it is made up of a number of different European currencies. In order to make the ECU operational we have to calculate the exchange rate of the various national currencies to the ECU. For example, to calculate the Irish pound/ECU exchange rate we convert each currency in the basket to Irish pounds and sum. Table 12.2 shows how this is done using exchange rates prevailing in 1998. At an exchange rate of DM2.4046/IR£1, the DM0.6242 in the basket translates into IR£0.2596. Similarly, at an exchange rate of FF8.2158/IR£1, the FF1.332 in the basket converts to IR£0.1621. And so on for the other currencies making up the ECU. Summing over all the various currencies gives an exchange rate of IR£0.7969/ECU1. A similar calculation is done to derive the ECU exchange rate to any other currency.

At the start of the EMS, each participating currency declared a *central rate* against the ECU. These rates were then used to calculate the *parity grid*. That is the ceiling and the floor relative to the central rate. The idea is that a central bank would not intervene to influence a particular exchange rate while it remains inside the band. The central

Table 12.2
Calculating the ECU exchange rate for the Irish pound

November 1997

	Basket (1)	Exchange rate (2)	Converted to IR£ (3) = (1)/(2)
DM	0.6242	2.4046	0.2596
FF	1.332	8.2158	0.1621
HFL	0.2197	2.6982	0.0804
BFR	3.301		
LFR	0.13	49.49	0.0693
LIT	151.8	2,408.59	0.0630
DKR	0.1976	9.4537	0.0209
IR£	0.0085	1	0.0085
STG£	0.0878	0.9835	0.0893
PTA	6.885	197.73	0.0348
DR	1.15	362.79	0.0032
ESU	1.393	244.43	0.0057
Total =	1 ECU		0.7969

bank will only intervene if an exchange rate threatens to go through the ceiling or fall through the floor of the system.

Given the ECU central rates, it was then possible to calculate the *cross rates* between participating currencies. For example, if we know the central rate between the IR£/ECU and the DM/ECU, then we can calculate the central rate between the DM/IR£.

Table 12.3 shows the central rates at which each currency was locked to the ECU in 1998. Technically, each exchange rate can fluctuate by ± 15 per cent relative to the central rate up to that date. For example, this gives an upper and lower boundary for the DM/Irish pound exchange rate of 2.8554 and 2.1105 respectively relative to a central rate of 2.483.

But why this round about way of calculating central rates between participating currencies? Why not just declare the central rates between participating currencies and do away with the ECU? The answer is that the authorities were anxious to introduce

Table 12.3
Central rates and intervention margins for IR£: May 1998

	HFL	B/LFR	DM	PTA	FF	LIT
Central Rate + 15 %	3.2177	58.903	2.8554	242.995	9.5783	2827.85
Central Rate	2.798	51.22	2.483	211.3	8.329	2459.00
Central Rate −15 %	2.3783	43.537	2.1105	179.605	7.0796	2090.15

the concept of a single currency at an early stage. The ECU was always seen as the forerunner of the new single currency (the euro) in Europe.

European Monetary Co-operation Fund

The *European Monetary Co-operation Fund* (EMCF) was an important part of the EMS. It was designed to help countries maintain their central rates in the ERM. In 1979 it received 20 per cent of all members' foreign reserves. In return, each member was credited with an equivalent amount in ECUs. The EMCF provided ECU credits to countries experiencing current account balance of payments deficits. It operated a 'Very Short-Term Financing Facility' (VSTFF) which allowed central banks to borrow ECUs for the purpose of defending a currency in the ERM. These credits had to be repaid in due course.

Flexibility in the EMS

There were two important features of the EMS that conveyed a degree of flexibility to the system. The first was that *realignments* were permitted. A realignment was an adjustment of a currency's central rates against the other ERM currencies. Thus if circumstances warranted it, the parity grid was altered. Between 1979 and 1998 there were twenty-one changes in the ERM central rates. The dominant trend was for the Deutsche mark and the Dutch guilder to be revalued upwards, and the French franc, Italian lira and the other smaller currencies to be devalued. The exception was a 3 per cent revaluation of the Irish pound against all the other currencies, including the DM, in March 1998.

The second source of flexibility in the EMS was the *margin of fluctuation* around the central rates. Until August 1993 the maximum permissible deviation of the strongest and weakest currencies in the ERM from their central rates was ± 2.25 per cent. (The Spanish peseta, the Portuguese escudo and the pound sterling were allowed a ± 6 per cent fluctuation margin.) The combination of periodic realignments and the margin of fluctuation round the central rate meant that the EMS was a compromise between a rigidly fixed exchange rate system like the gold standard or the Bretton Woods system and free floating.

The euro

In Madrid in 1995 it was decided that the currency to be adopted by the countries joining EMU in 1999 would be called the euro. At the start of EMU in January 1999, one ECU was set equal to one euro and thereafter the ECU ceased to exist. This is because the basket of currencies comprising the euro is not the same as the ECU. The euro only contains the currencies participating in the single currency system. Sterling and the Danish krone are not included in the calculation of the euro. These currencies have been replaced by the Austrian schilling and the Finnish markka.

12.3 Inflation Convergence in the EMS

Since the early 1950s, the Bundesbank had established itself as one of the world's most anti-inflationary central banks. By controlling the money supply, the Bundesbank had succeeded in keeping German inflation to a low level and this, in turn, resulted in a 'hard' or appreciating DM and low nominal interest rates. One reasons why countries wanted to participate in EMS was to 'feed off' Germany's success in maintaining low inflation.

This policy can be explained by referring to the *purchasing power parity* (PPP) theory developed in chapter 10. Consider, for example, the case of Ireland and Germany. According to PPP

$$\pi_{IRL} = \pi_G - \Delta e_{DM} \tag{1}$$

where π_{IRL} and π_G are the Irish and German inflation rates respectively and Δe_{DM} is the change in the DM/Irish pound exchange rate. If the exchange rate is fixed so that $\Delta e_{DM} = 0$, then PPP theory predicts that German inflation will be transmitted to Ireland so that $\pi_{IRL} = \pi_G$. This is because Ireland is a small economy relative to the large German economy and the causation is running from Germany to Ireland. Hence, PPP theory predicted that as long as the Irish pound was pegged to the Deutsche mark we had to experience the same rate of inflation as Germany.

A similar argument applies to the other countries participating in the EMS. Implicit in this policy is the belief that the EMS countries (other than Germany) had little faith in their own central banks to control their money supplies and inflation. They preferred the alternative approach of fixing their currencies to the DM thereby inheriting the low German inflation rate.

THE SPEED OF ADJUSTMENT

A country with initially high inflation may hope to achieve a rapid disinflation by pegging to the Deutsche mark. The speed of this convergence is a key issue. If it takes a relatively long time to bring about a convergence of inflation rates, then the cost in terms of lost output and rising unemployment could be very high.

Figure 12.1 uses the PPP diagram developed in chapter 10 to illustrate the issues. The right-hand diagram shows equilibrium in the goods and services market. The Irish inflation rate is on the vertical axis and the real growth rate is on the horizontal axis. The left-hand diagram shows the PPP relationship. The Irish inflation rate is on the vertical axis and the DM/IR£ exchange rate is on the horizontal axis. The German inflation rate determines the position of the PPP line.

Taking the case of Ireland and Germany, suppose the Irish economy is initially at the point A where the actual growth rate is equal to the natural real growth rate. Suppose, however, the Irish inflation rate is at π_1 which is above the German inflation rate. Given the fixed DM/IR£ nominal exchange rate, the Irish economy would be at a point such as X which is above the PPP line. At the point X, the Irish economy experiences a loss of competitiveness relative to Germany. How does the Irish inflation rate converge to the lower German inflation rate?

The loss of competitiveness results in a decrease in Ireland's net exports (exports minus imports). This causes the AD curve in the right-hand diagram to shift down to the left moving the economy from the point A to B. The real growth rate is now below the natural growth rate and unemployment will start to increase. The Irish economy is now experiencing the costs associated with its deflationary policy.

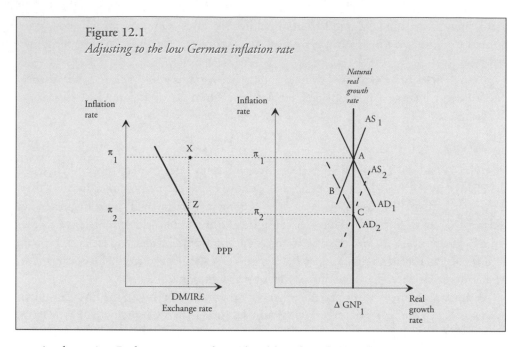

Figure 12.1
Adjusting to the low German inflation rate

At the point B, however, workers should realise that real wages (nominal wages adjusted for inflation) have increased. This is because inflation has fallen while nominal wages are, so far, unchanged. If workers now accept a cut in the (rate of change of) nominal earnings, so as to restore the original real wage, the AS curve will shift down to the right. The economy now moves to a point such as C. At this point, the Irish economy is back to the natural real growth rate, and the PPP relationship has been established between Ireland and Germany. The Irish inflation rate has converged to the lower German rate.

POLICY CREDIBILITY

If it takes a relatively short period of time to move from points A to C, the cost of adjustment, as measured by the lost output and employment, will be small. If, however, it takes a long time to adjust, the costs of joining the EMS will be high. The behaviour of wages plays a crucial role in determining the adjustment period. The speed at which the rate of inflation falls depends on how quickly workers reduce their nominal wage demands and firms reduce the rate of increase in output prices.

Much here depends on the *credibility* of the government's commitment to the EMS. If the Irish government is running large fiscal deficits or is pursuing fiscal or monetary policies inconsistent with what is happening in Germany, the EMS commitment will lack credibility. In this case, disinflation would only come through the effect of high unemployment on wage and price expectations and the deflationary effect of an overvalued exchange rate working its way through the economy. These forces would take time to operate and an output gap would persist during this interval.

If, on the other hand, the government's commitment to the EMS is credible because it is backed up by appropriate fiscal and monetary measures and the policy is communicated effectively to the public, the rate of change of wages and inflation could adjust downwards relatively quickly and the disinflation policy would be relatively painless.

We discuss the Irish EMS experience with disinflation in chapter 13.

12.4 HISTORY OF EMS

1979–87

The EMS was launched in March 1979 as a system of quasi-fixed exchange rates that relied on *indirect policy co-ordination* for its success. There was no mechanism to force the participating countries to harmonise their fiscal or monetary policies. Yet it was recognised that stable exchange rates could not be maintained unless all the countries participating in the system pursued similar economic policies.

In the early years of the EMS countries like Germany pursued a tight monetary policy whereas France under President Mitterrand implemented expansionary socialist measures. The result was that realignments were frequent: two in every year from 1979–83. Italy, for example, devalued the lira eight times between 1979–87. If realignments had continued at this frequency the EMS would have been undermined.

A major change occurred in 1983 when the Mitterrand administration abandoned its attempt at domestic expansion in favour of a programme of austerity and stabilisation. Between 1983–86 the system became more stable and transformed into a more rigidly fixed exchange rate system.

1987–92

Between 1987–92 there were no major realignments and the margin of fluctuation between the main currencies narrowed to a *de facto* ± 1 per cent. Spain, Portugal and Britain entered the ERM, and Italy moved from the broad to the narrow band. Stability was helped by the participating countries pursuing consistent economic policies and their rates of inflation were much lower and more uniform than was the case during the early 1980s. These were the golden years of the EMS.

The trajectory of inflation in the various member states is shown in figure 12.2. The chart illustrates the dramatic narrowing of inflation differentials between the beginning and the end of the 1980s. In 1979 countries like Italy, Ireland and France had much higher inflation rates than Germany, but by the end of the 1980s this was no longer the case.

The convergence of inflation rates may be cited as evidence of the achievement of the EMS, but it should be borne in mind that inflation fell in all OECD countries during the 1980s. The major reasons were the collapse of energy prices in 1986 and tighter monetary policies.

12.5 THE CURRENCY CRISIS OF 1992–93

The apparent stability of the EMS in 1992 was deceptive. A number of factors were soon causing serious tensions and would lead to the eventual breakdown of the system.

GERMAN UNIFICATION IN 1990

In the Autumn of 1989, the Berlin wall came down. In July 1990, after more than forty years of separation, the economically strong Federal Republic of Germany (West) was

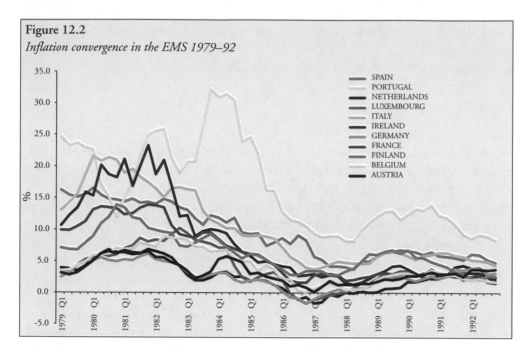

Figure 12.2

Inflation convergence in the EMS 1979–92

united with the economically weak German Democratic Republic (East) in an economic, monetary and social union. In October 1990, German economic integration was made irreversible by political unification.

The immediate effect of reunification was a significant increase in the government's fiscal deficit. Investment in East Germany's infrastructure and its ailing industries, social welfare payments to the unemployed and subsidies to loss-making and inefficient firms ensured a massive increase in government expenditure. On the other hand, the government did not raise taxes to any significant degree to finance this expenditure. Higher taxes would have made it more difficult to sell the reunification policy to the electorate.

The effect of the expansionary fiscal policy was to increase economic growth and inflation in the West. In response to this over-heating, the German Central Bank, the Bundesbank, tightened monetary policy in order to reduce the inflationary pressures. The combination of an expansionary fiscal policy and a tight monetary policy resulted in a three-percentage point increase in German interest rates to 9.7 per cent.

Furthermore, European and US monetary policy became markedly out of sync in the early 1990s. To stimulate the US economy, the Federal Reserve Bank lowered short-term interest rates in 1992 to their lowest levels for twenty-nine years. In Germany, on the other hand, interest rates were rising in the wake of reunification. The combination of lower interest rates in the US and higher rates in Germany caused a capital outflow from the dollar into the Deutsche mark, leading to an appreciation of the DM.

Note:

A recurrent problem with the EMS was the fact that when money flows into Europe from the rest of the world, European currencies — even those participating in the EMS — were not regarded as perfect substitutes. The Deutsche mark was favoured over other currencies, putting upward pressure on it and generating strain in the ERM.

The reunification episode illustrates that the Bundesbank's commitment to EMS parities was secondary to its concern for the domestic economy. In other words, the Bundesbank was prepared to implement policies to deal with domestic problems even if these policies were wholly inappropriate for Europe as a whole.

DANISH REFERENDUM

Another factor frequently blamed for precipitating the currency crisis was the Danish 'No' vote in a referendum on the Maastricht Treaty (2 June 1992). At the same time opinion polls predicted a 50/50 split in the French referendum, which was to be held in September. Since the Maastricht Treaty contained the timetable for moving forward to 'irrevocably' fixed exchange rates and the adoption of a single European currency, its rejection by a major European country would have caused a full-scale political as well as monetary crisis.

The French voted 'yes' by a narrow margin but the uncertainty caused by the referendum drew attention to the shaky political foundations on which the project rested.

EXCHANGE RATE POLICY IN THE UK

Between 1986 to 1989 the Chancellor of the Exchequer in the UK, Nigel Lawson, adopted the policy of sterling 'shadowing' the DM. Sterling was pegged unofficially in the range STG£1 = DM2.94 to DM3.00. According to Mrs Thatcher's autobiography, this policy was pursued unknown to her. Apparently it was not until Treasury officials highlighted the stability of the sterling/DM exchange rate that she confronted Lawson about this policy.

This exchange rate eventually proved unsustainable due to the excessive monetary expansion that Mr Lawson permitted, and by December 1989 sterling had fallen to DM2.80. This depreciation led to pressure for sterling to formally join the ERM. Mrs Thatcher remained entrenched in her view, and stated at the Madrid Summit in June 1989, that sterling would participate 'only when the time is right'. In this she was supported by her unofficial economic adviser, Professor Alan Walters. Disagreement on this issue eventually led to Lawson's resignation in October 1989.

Mrs Thatcher finally brought sterling into the ERM, albeit only into the wide (± 6 per cent) band on 8 October 1990. She argued that this would add credibility to the fight against inflation and she urged unions to accept modest wage increases in order to maintain UK price competitiveness. (This proved to be one of her last important decisions as prime minister. She resigned on 22 November 1990.)

Between 1990 and 1992 the British experience in the ERM was reasonably favourable. Inflation fell from 10.8 per cent in October 1990 to 4.3 per cent in August 1992, and short-term interest rates fell from 15 per cent to 10.2 per cent. However, the real growth rate remained low and by 1992 the economy was in recession.

THE EXTERNAL EFFECTS OF GERMAN UNIFICATION

Because of the commitment to fixed exchange rates, higher German interest rates were transmitted to the other EMS countries. Rising interest rates and appreciating exchange rates were painful for countries such as Italy, the UK and Spain, which were in recession. What these countries needed was lower interest rates and currency depreciation to kick-start their economies.

The conflict between the tight German monetary policy and the needs of the rest of Europe was clearly causing tension in the ERM. With hindsight it is now clear that the lira, sterling and the peseta were vulnerable to a speculative attack in the early 1990s.

Despite massive intervention by central banks, a number of currencies quickly fell below their permitted ERM floors. Early in September, the Finnish markka abandoned its unofficial peg to the Deutsche mark. Despite the Bank of Italy raising short-term interest rates to defend its currency, the lira was devalued by 7 per cent on 12 September.

Speculators noticed that Britain, in particular, appeared to have entered the ERM at too high an exchange rate. In late summer 1992 the conviction grew that the sterling/DM central rate was unsustainable. Massive amounts of sterling were dumped on the foreign exchanges. On 16 September, 'Black Wednesday', the Bank of England spent an estimated £10 billion supporting sterling and the Bank of France and the Bundesbank bought sterling heavily. British interest rates were raised from 10 to 15 per cent.

Matters were not helped by an apparent personality clash between the Prime Minister, John Major and the Chancellor of the Exchequer, Norman Lamont. At one stage during the crisis Lamont arrived at 10 Downing Street to discuss with Major the option of devaluating sterling. However, Major refused to leave an unimportant meeting with a delegation of local authority councillors from northern England to talk to Lamont. The Chancellor was forced to leave Downing Street without any clear instruction or mandate from his prime minister.

Lamont took the decision to suspend sterling's membership of the ERM on 16 September. Sterling depreciated by 15 per cent and interest rates in London fell from 15 per cent to 8 per cent. Despite the large-scale intervention, the speculators had clearly won out. The Hungarian-born financier George Soros, is estimated to have made a profit of £1 billion on 'Black Wednesday' and became dubbed as 'the man who broke the Bank of England'. Soon afterwards, Lamont resigned as Chancellor of the Exchequer.

Note:
As discussed in the following chapter, these developments had a profound effect on Irish money markets. Despite the extreme pressure on the Irish pound following sterling's departure from the ERM and depreciation in autumn 1992, the Irish authorities resisted a devaluation of the Irish pound until January 1993.

On the following day the Italian government withdrew the lira, and the Spanish peseta was devalued by 5 per cent. Pressure then switched to the French franc, the Danish krone, the Irish pound, the Portuguese escudo and the peseta. The Banque de France raised short-term interest rates to 13 per cent and with the help of the German authorities fought off the attack on the franc. The successful defence of the franc was the only achievement of central bank intervention during the crisis, but it was an important one for it preserved the commitment of France and Germany to continue to peg their currencies.

Pressure in the system gradually lessened late in 1992, especially after the peseta and the escudo were devalued in November and the Swedish krone (which had been informally pegged to the Deutsche mark) was floated.

In the UK, lower interest rates and the competitive gain from the devaluation were instrumental in making the UK economy's recovery from recession more rapid than that of the continental European countries. The Bank of England was allowed to pursue a 2.5 per cent inflation rate free from political interference. (The independence of the Bank was formalised by Tony Blair's new Labour government in 1999.) Britain's experiences with a floating exchange rate have been very favourable; it has been the fastest growing *major* economy in Europe, with low inflation and unemployment, and a relatively stable exchange rate! On the tenth anniversary of 'Black Wednesday' commentators were wondering if 'White Wednesday' would not be a better label. The speculators, it seems, had given the British establishment a lesson in macroeconomics.

By early 1993 virtually all the currencies of the ERM had been devalued relative to the Deutsche mark. After a long and painful period of turbulence, the result was much the same as would have followed from a unilateral revaluation of the German currency in 1992. It is believed that the German authorities offered to revalue the mark in mid-1992 but the French and British authorities resisted this because they did not wish to see their currencies devalued. If this was the case, then this is another example of irrational pride in the nominal value of currencies overriding sound economic policy.

Note:
The way speculators moved from one currency to another during the crisis of 1992–93 is an interesting example of 'contagion'. Having profited from the vulnerability of one currency to an attack, speculators were quick to realise that other currencies were also vulnerable.

There was a period of stability in the first half of 1993 when the ERM appeared to have weathered the storm and settled back into a stable parity grid. But by the summer renewed speculative pressures emerged as markets came to view the Spanish peseta and French franc as overvalued. The EU finance ministers finally threw in the towel in August 1993 and announced that the ERM fluctuation margins were being widened to $\pm$ 15. To all intents and purposes the ERM was dismantled. It is important to note, however, that the French franc survived the crisis without devaluation and with its peg to the Deutsche mark intact. Although the franc came under heavy selling pressure on several occasions during the 1992–93 crisis the central rate remained DM1 = FF 3.35, the level that was adopted at the beginning of 1987. The market rate between these currencies at times dipped below the intervention level but by and large remained within the $\pm$ 2.25 per cent fluctuation margin. Thus since 1987, the two key currencies in the ERM were kept within a target zone.

12.6 THE RESPONSES TO THE 1992–93 CRISIS

There were two possible responses to the effective demise of the ERM. The first, perhaps most obvious, reaction would have been to abandon the notion of fixed exchange rates and allow all the currencies of Europe to float freely, following the example of sterling. The second possible reaction was to push ahead for a full monetary union involving a single currency.

The second option was the one preferred by 'convinced Europeans'. It was argued that the reliance of the EMS on indirect policy co-ordination was one of the reasons for its demise. As a 'half-way-house' between freely floating and rigidly fixed exchange rates, it was inherently vulnerable to speculative attacks. A better option would be a single European currency and a European Central Bank, conducting monetary policy in the interests of all member states. Also a single European currency would eliminate the possibility of future speculative attacks. It is not possible to speculate against the Irish pound if it no longer exists!

These arguments were attractive to countries other than Germany. However, Germany would have to be convinced that it stood to gain something by participating in the proposed EMU. Given that the Deutsche mark had been the lowest-inflation currency in Europe for decades, what gain was there to Germany in replacing it with the euro and aligning itself with a number of countries that had been highly inflation prone in recent years? To assuage German fears on this front, strict convergence criteria were included in the Maastricht Treaty, complemented by the Stability and Growth Pact. These would have to be met by countries hoping to qualify for entry to EMU.

Another argument to recommend the EMU to Germany was the prospect that the mark would no longer attract speculative inflows during currency crises. These inflows had repeatedly driven up the value of the Deutsche mark in the past, rendering the economy less competitive. This problem would be removed by replacing the Deutsche mark with the euro.

A further argument for pushing ahead towards a full-blown monetary union was that the completion of the internal market could never be accomplished as long as prices were quoted in national currencies. The costs and benefits associated with EMU membership are discussed in more detail in chapter 14.

These were the immediate arguments that provided the impetus for the Commission of the EU to bring forward plans for an Economic and Monetary Union in the 1990s. While the blueprint that was proposed was a descendant of the prototype outlined in the *Werner Report* of 1970, it was more radical than anything that was deemed possible when the EMS was launched in 1979.

12.7 CONCLUSION

In this chapter we have discussed the following topics:

- The design of the EMS
- The ECU and how it evolved into the euro

- How inflation rates were expected to converge in the EMS and the risks associated with this policy
- The EMS experience and the currency crisis of 1992–93
- The response to the currency crisis and the decision to forge ahead with a monetary union in Europe.

APPENDIX
CHRONOLOGY OF MAIN EVENTS RELATING TO THE EMS

- European Monetary Co-operation Fund (EMCF) established in April 1973. It is designed on the lines of a European IMF, to help countries maintain fixed exchange rates by supplying them with credits during currency crises.
- European unit of account (EUA) — a basket of currencies — introduced in 1975. The ECU was subsequently based on the same basket of currencies.
- At the European Council meeting in Copenhagen in April 1978, the German Chancellor Schmidt and the French President Giscard d'Estaing propose the creation of an EMS. The EMS is intended to create a zone of monetary stability in Europe. This was the beginning of the Franco-German co-operation that was behind the push for monetary union in Europe.
- July 1978: EC heads of state and governments meet in Bremen and agree on the structure of the EMS.
- December 1978: The European Council meeting in Brussels agrees on the mode of operation of the EMS. Ireland is committed to joining.
- The EMS commences operation in March 1979. Within the narrow band of the Exchange Rate Mechanism (ERM) currencies are to fluctuate within a maximum of ± 2.25 per cent of the central rates. All the currencies of the member states as of 1979 entered the narrow band ERM, except the Italian lira, which was put in a wider band (± 6 per cent), and sterling, which did not join. The Spanish peseta joined the wide band in June 1989. In January 1990 the lira came into the narrow band and in September sterling joined the wide band. The Portuguese escudo joined the wide band in April 1992.
- September 1992: Following intense speculative pressure, UK and Italy leave the ERM. The Finnish markka, which had been informally pegged to the ERM, is floated.
- September 1992–January 1993: After prolonged speculative attacks, the peseta, the escudo, and the Irish pound are all devalued and the Swedish and Norwegian krona abandon their ERM pegs.
- August 1993: Renewed speculative pressure against the French franc, the Belgian franc and Danish krone force a decision to widen the ERM band to ± 15 per cent for all except the Deutsche mark and Dutch guilder. The Irish Finance Minister Bertie Ahern states that the plan to create a single currency in Europe is 'now on the back-burner'.
- 1995–96: Following the enlargement of the EU, the Austrian schilling joined the ERM in January 1995 and the Finish markka in October 1996.

- 1997: Of the currencies of EU countries, only the Greek drachma and the Swedish krona have never been in the ERM. The Swedish government commissioned a study of the proposed single currency that recommended that Sweden should not enter in the first wave. The new Irish government, with Mr Ahern as Taoiseach, endorses the policy of Ireland adopting the single currency even if Britain does not.

CHAPTER 13

Irish Exchange Rate Policy from the Sterling Link to EMU

13.1 Introduction

In this chapter we examine Irish exchange rate policy from Independence to the decision to join the European Economic and Monetary Union in 1998. The most important event during this period was the decision, taken at the end of 1978, to enter the Exchange Rate Mechanism (ERM) of the European Monetary System (EMS). This eventually led to the decision to participate in EMU.

The chapter deals with the sterling link period from 1922–79, the decision to enter the EMS in 1979 and the Irish experience as a member of EMS, with particular reference to the crisis of 1992. The concluding section discusses exchange rate policy in the run-up to joining EMU.

13.2 The Sterling Link, 1922–79

A link with sterling was the logical policy for Ireland in the 1920s. Sterling had been the strongest currency in the world until World War I, and in the 1920s was still regarded as a reliable store of value, despite the wartime inflation and suspension of convertibility into gold. Ireland's trade was predominantly with Britain, and the Irish and British banking systems were closely linked. Preserving the sterling link minimised transaction costs for Irish importers and exporters.

Furthermore, there was no other real alternative to the sterling link in the early years of the state. Doubts were expressed about the merits of maintaining the sterling link at the time of the devaluations of 1949 and 1967, but the debate remained academic in the absence of a realistic alternative arrangement.

The rationale for maintaining the sterling link can also be understood by referring to absolute and relative purchasing power parity (PPP) theory developed in chapter 10. *Absolute PPP*, can be stated as:

$$P_{IRL} \times e_{UK} = P_{UK} \tag{1}$$

where P_{IRL} and P_{UK} are the Irish and UK price levels, respectively, and e_{UK} is the nominal exchange rate (expressed as sterling per unit of the Irish pound). This states that Irish prices will equal UK prices when converted using the current exchange rate. A weaker version of this theory is *relative PPP*, which can be written as:

$$\pi_{IRL} = \pi_{UK} - \Delta e_{UK} \tag{2}$$

where π_{IRL} and π_{UK} are the Irish and UK inflation rates respectively and Δe_{UK} is the percentage change in the sterling/Irish pound exchange rate. If the exchange rate is fixed so that $\Delta e_{UK} = 0$, then relative PPP theory predicts that UK inflation will be transmitted to Ireland so that $\pi_{IRL} = \pi_{UK}$. This is because Ireland is a small economy relative to the larger UK economy and the causation is running from the UK to Ireland. Hence, relative PPP theory predicted that as long as the Irish pound was pegged to sterling we had to experience the same rate of inflation as Britain.

THE IRISH EXPERIENCE UNDER THE STERLING LINK

Figure 13.1 shows the ratio of the Irish and UK price (P_{IRL}/P_{UK}) levels, in a common currency, from 1922 to 2001. It is evident that over the period 1922–40 and again between 1945–79 the two price levels moved closer together. They diverged significantly only during World War II, when rationing and price controls were in operation in Britain and distorted the comparison. Thus, up until 1979 and with the exception of the war period, the evidence does seem to support the absolute PPP hypothesis rather strongly.

However, following the termination of the sterling link in March 1979, the series becomes much more volatile due to movements in the sterling/Irish pound exchange rate, which of course had previously been fixed at 1:1. But given that the price ratio in 2001 is back to its level in 1922, the evidence seems to suggest that absolute PPP holds in the long run, even though there can be significant divergences in the short run.

Figure 13.2 compares inflation rates in Ireland (adjusted for exchange rate movements) and the UK over the period 1922 to 2001. With the exception of the war years, the inflation rates in the two countries were very similar. After entry into the EMS in 1979, the Irish inflation rate, adjusted for movements to the exchange rate, becomes much more volatile. However, at no point in time does the Irish inflation rate get widely out of line with the UK rate. Hence, the data does tend to offer support for the relative PPP hypothesis particularly in the pre-EMS period.

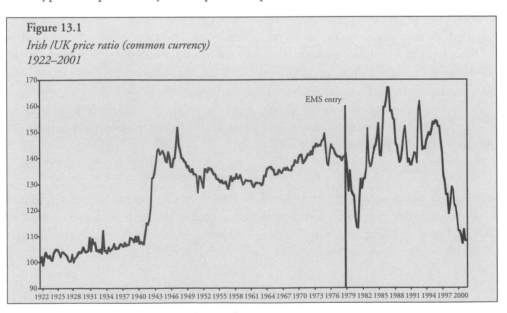

Figure 13.1

Irish /UK price ratio (common currency)
1922–2001

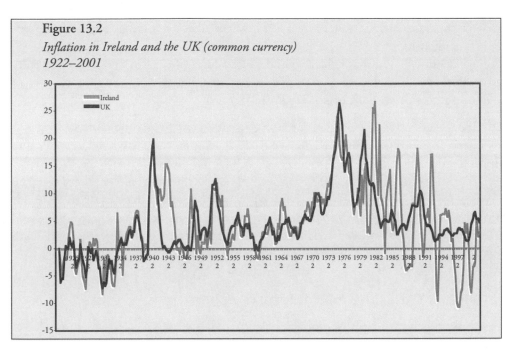

Figure 13.2

Inflation in Ireland and the UK (common currency)
1922–2001

13.3 THE RATIONALE FOR JOINING THE EMS

The problem with the sterling link was that for most of the 1960s and 1970s, the German inflation rate was much lower than the UK rate. As predicted by PPP theory, this resulted in a depreciation of the Deutsche mark (DM)/sterling exchange rate from DM11 = £1 in 1964 to DM4 = £1 in 1978. Since the Irish pound was pegged to sterling, its value in terms of the DM fell at the same rate.

An argument in favour of breaking with sterling and switching to a low inflation or 'hard' currency, such as the DM, was that Ireland would then enjoy the low German inflation rate. Equation (2) would now be replaced by:

$$\pi_{IRL} = \pi_G - \Delta e_{DM} \tag{3}$$

where π_G and Δe_{DM} are the German inflation rate and the percentage change in the DM/Irish pound exchange rate respectively. If e_{DM} is fixed so that $\Delta e_{DM} = 0$, then the German inflation rate should be transmitted to the Irish economy.

Another factor predisposing Ireland to contemplate breaking the sterling link was the proposal to launch the European Monetary System (EMS) in 1979. The Governor of the Central Bank, Charles Murray, justified Ireland joining in the following terms (see The Central Bank of Ireland, *Annual Report*, 1979):

- The inappropriateness of continuing the sterling link. He believed '. . . that a floating, unstable (but generally depreciating) pound [sterling], and a steady fall in (the relative importance of) Ireland's trade with the UK, had diminished the attractiveness and appropriateness of the link'.

- The benefits in terms of a reduction in inflation to be obtained from adherence to a hard currency regime. 'It would be prudent to assume that, in the longer run at any rate, membership of the EMS involves a harder currency regime than non-membership.'

- He also believed that Ireland should make a commitment to a major Community initiative, and that support would be forthcoming in the form of a 'transfer of resources' from the Community.

However, it was a major leap of faith to assume that when the currency peg was switched from sterling to the DM a new PPP relationship between Germany and Ireland would quickly become established. Britain had been our main trading partner for centuries, the two banking systems were closely interwoven, and there were no barriers to the movement of money between the two countries. In contrast, in 1979 our financial links with the EMS countries were relatively weak, exchange controls hindered the flow of money between Ireland and the Continent, and the narrow-band EMS countries accounted for only about one-third of our trade.

13.4 POLICY CREDIBILITY AND THE SPEED OF ADJUSTMENT

A key issue is how long it would take Ireland's inflation rate to converge to the lower German rate. As already discussed in chapter 12, section 12.3, if the adjustment period is relatively short, the cost as measured by the lost output and employment, will be small. If, however, the adjustment period is prolonged, the costs of joining the EMS are high.

At the time, it was widely expected that disinflation would be relatively painless once we were members of the EMS. 'The Central Bank's calculations suggest that, given sensible domestic policies, the adjustment problems will be manageable and of relatively short duration.' (The Central Bank of Ireland, *Annual Report*, 1979, 106.) Also: 'After a decade of inflation, we can now contemplate the prospect of an early and sustained return to inflation rates comfortably back into single figures.' (*Annual Report*, 1979, 109.)

However, others cautioned that the adjustment would not be instantaneous. In the White Paper on EMS membership published in December 1978 (9–10) it was stated: '... in the initial period of operation of the EMS, the parity of our currency might be higher than it otherwise would be. This could impose severe strain on Ireland's competitiveness, leading to a possible loss of output and employment'.

This prospect gave the Irish government grounds for seeking additional aid from the Community to finance an enlarged programme of infrastructure and industrial development in order to help the economy adjust to the new hard currency regime.

WAGE RATE ADJUSTMENT

As explained in chapter 12, the behaviour of wages plays a crucial role in the adjustment. The speed at which the rate of inflation falls depends on how quickly workers reduce their nominal wage demands and firms reduce the rate of increase in output prices. If the government's commitment to the ERM had been credible in 1979, wage and price increases would have immediately moderated and disinflation would have been rapid and relatively painless. On the other hand, if the commitment to the EMS lacked credibility, disinflation would only come through the effect of high unemployment on wage and price expectations and the deflationary effect of an overvalued exchange rate working its way through the economy. These forces would take time to operate and an output gap would persist during this interval.

13.5 THE EXPERIENCE IN THE EMS

During the discussions leading to the launch of the exchange rate mechanism (ERM) of the EMS, Ireland was committing to joining when it learned on 5 December 1978 that the British Government would *not* participate. This involved holding our exchange rate within ± 2.25 per cent of the central rates against all the other participating currencies, while sterling continued to float relative to them. This raised the prospect that the Irish pound/sterling exchange rate could not be held at 1:1. To the surprise of most forecasters, within weeks of the launch of the EMS, sterling strengthened sharply relative to the DM. The prediction that joining the ERM would peg the Irish pound to a strong currency had been falsified almost as soon as it was made. As a consequence of the rise of sterling, it proved impossible for Ireland to maintain the sterling link and remain in the narrow band of the ERM simultaneously. The break with sterling came on 30 March 1979. For the first time since Independence the Irish pound and sterling diverged in value. Furthermore, for the first time ever, Northern Ireland and the Republic were separated by an exchange rate.

Note:
One of the witnesses to the Banking Commission (1934–38) claimed that there were only two catastrophes that Ireland had been spared, earthquakes and an exchange rate. We got an independent exchange rate with sterling in March 1979. Five years later, on the morning of 19 July 1984, an earthquake measuring 5.4 on the Richter scale was recorded in Dublin!

Ireland has remained a member of the narrow band ERM from 1979 until the bands were widened to 6 15 per cent in summer 1993. The UK did eventually join the ERM in October 1990 but left in September 1992. Let us now review how Ireland fared as a participant in the narrow band ERM.

INFLATION
Figure 13.3 shows Irish, UK and German inflation in the years following the launch of the EMS. The initial experience was at variance with the predictions based on the PPP model. Instead of a rapid convergence of Irish inflation to German levels, the divergence between the two rates widened. In 1980 Irish inflation was 10.25 per cent higher than the German rate. Once again, economists' predictions were quickly proved wrong!

Even more disappointing was that Irish inflation was higher than UK inflation in the early 1980s. Britain was having more success in curbing inflation outside the ERM than Ireland in it. The assumption that sterling would remain a weak, inflation-prone currency, although widespread in 1978, proved invalid. The adoption of monetarist policies by the UK Labour government in 1978 and a Conservative Party victory under Mrs Thatcher in the 1979 election were not given due weight. The Thatcher government opted to curb inflation by controlling the money supply rather than by

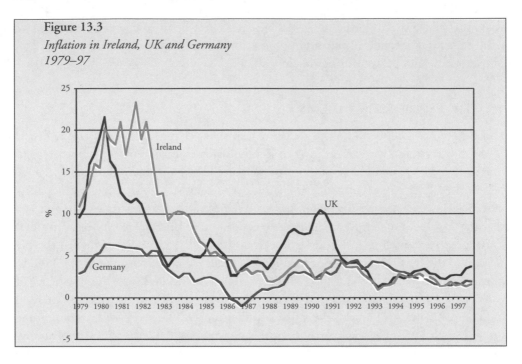

Figure 13.3

Inflation in Ireland, UK and Germany 1979–97

participating in the ERM. UK inflation fell from 18 per cent in 1980 to 4.5 per cent in 1983, but the cost of this disinflation in terms of lost output and unemployment was considerable. Output fell by nearly 3 per cent in 1981 and 1982, and unemployment increased from 1.1 million in 1979 to three million in 1984.

After 1982 the Irish rate of inflation fell and the gap between Irish and German inflation gradually narrowed. However, it was not until the third quarter of 1990, more than ten years after joining the system, that Irish inflation finally fell to the German level. This indicated a slow and protracted adjustment to the lower German rate.

INTEREST RATES

Figure 13.4 shows the behaviour of nominal interest rates following our entry into the ERM was similar to that of inflation. Convergence of Irish interest rates to the German rates occurred only after 1988. In line with the discussion of uncovered interest rate parity (UIP) in chapter 10, the relatively high Irish interest rates reflected the market's belief that the Irish pound was overvalued and would be devalued.

However, the differential between German and Irish interest rates more than compensated for the fall in the value of the Irish pound over time. Over the period 1979–92 an investor would have earned 40 per cent more in Irish than in German bonds. This over-compensation for the depreciation of the currency is known as *excess returns*.

THE YIELD CURVE

Further evidence of the failure of membership of the ERM to bestow low interest rates and inflation is provided by the behaviour of the yield curve over the period since 1979. Box 13.1 explains what is meant by the yield curve (see also chapter 19) and why it indicates the future direction of both interest rates and inflation.

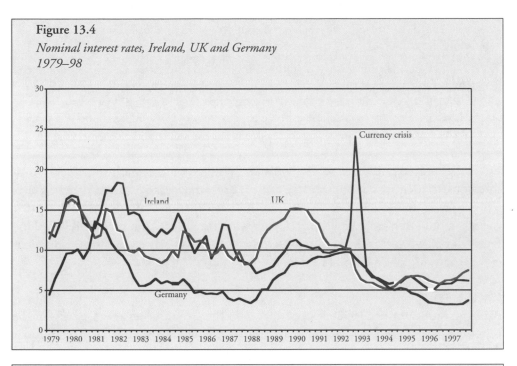

Figure 13.4
Nominal interest rates, Ireland, UK and Germany 1979–98

Box 13.1
The yield curve

The yield on bonds of different maturities varies. Short-dated bonds, such as exchequer bills which are redeemable within three months, may not have the same yield as medium or long-dated securities that do not mature for five or ten years. If investors expect interest rates to rise, bonds with long maturities will tend to have higher yields than bonds with short maturities. A graph showing yields on the vertical axis and maturities (from short to long) on the horizontal axis is called the *yield curve*. The yield curve reflects the term structure of interest rates. If longer-dated securities have higher yields than short-dated ones, the yield curve will be positively sloped. This is the normal situation, because there is always some risk that the rate of inflation will rise over the longer run.

Consider, for example, the yields on a range of Irish government stock in 1997 and 1998 (since joining EMU, Irish interest rates are determined at a European level and do not reflect market conditions in Ireland).

Irish government securities' yields: % per annum

Maturity	Yield November 1997	Yield October 1998
6 months	8.33	10.95
1 year	8.81	10.30
5 years	8.68	9.63
10 years	7.97	9.20
20 years	7.62	8.73

In 1997 the yield curve had an inverted U shape: the yield on a one-year bond was higher than that on a six-month bond, but yields on higher maturities were lower. In 1998 yields were lower the longer the maturity, that is, the yield curve was inverted or negatively sloped at all maturities.

The slope of the yield curve provides information on the public's expectations about interest rates in the future. Interest rates are, in turn, related to the inflation rate via the Fisher equation. If inflation is expected to rise then this will lead to higher interest rates and vice versa. Hence, if the EMS policy were credible, the expectation of lower interest and inflation rates should have led to a negatively sloped yield curve. This was not the case until the late 1980s.

In Ireland, over the period 1979–88, the yield curve was, with the exception of three-quarters, either flat or positively sloped. Thus the market expected interest rates either to remain unchanged or to rise. This indicates that investors did not believe that a sharp disinflation would follow from entry into the ERM. Only after 1988 did long rates fall below short rates. This indicated that that investors were at last revising their expectations of nominal interest rates (and inflation) downwards.

Capital flight

A further indicator of the public's confidence in the government's management of the economy is provided by the flow of private capital into or out of the country. Anticipation of higher inflation and a loss of confidence in the currency will lead to a movement of funds out of the country, i.e. *capital flight*. To minimise these flows the government imposed exchange controls on the movement of funds between Ireland and the UK following our entry into the EMS. (They already existed between Ireland and the rest of the world.) However, such measures are never watertight.

The residual in the balance of payments reflects unrecorded flows across the foreign exchanges and tends to be dominated by illicit private capital flows. This residual rose to nearly £1 billion (equivalent to 6 per cent of GNP) in 1986, probably largely due to capital flight as investors contravened the exchange controls and moved money out of Ireland. This reflected a loss of confidence in the currency and a lack of credibility in the government's commitment to holding its value in the ERM.

Following the devaluation of the Irish pound in 1986 and the restoration of order to the public finances, capital flight subsided. By the end of the decade there was a positive inflow of capital into Ireland.

13.6 Why Ireland Did Not Initially Benefit from the ERM

Several factors contributed to the disparity between the expected benefits of membership of the EMS and the outcome during the first half of the 1980s.

Fiscal and monetary policy

Fiscal policy in Ireland during the years 1979–82 was inconsistent with German policy and this undermined the currency peg to the DM. Between 1979–86, fiscal policy in Ireland resulted in a continuous rise in government borrowing, the national debt and debt service. This, in turn, led to concerns that Ireland's international credit rating was deteriorating. If Ireland could not continue to borrow abroad, or could only do so at penal interest rates, the external reserves would have been rapidly depleted and maintaining the exchange rate within the ERM would have become impossible. These uncertainties undermined credibility in the EMS policy.

EXCHANGE RATE POLICY IN THE EMS

During the early years of the EMS there were frequent currency realignments, usually involving a revaluation of the DM and a devaluation of the French franc and other weak currencies. Irish policy during these years was to 'go through the middle' at realignments.

However, this 'middle-of-the-road' policy made no allowance for Ireland's relatively high inflation rate. The failure to devalue the nominal exchange rate by a sufficient amount ensured that the high Irish inflation rate resulted in a significant appreciation of the *real* exchange rate.

Table 13.1 shows the real exchange rate against selected currencies in 1979 and 1986 (which was when the Irish pound real exchange rate peaked). It can be seen that there was a significant real appreciation of the Irish pound against all the ERM currencies, the most pronounced being the 58 per cent rise relative to the Belgian franc. Due to the relatively high Irish inflation rate, the DM/IR£ real exchange rate *appreciated* by almost 40 per cent despite the 30 per cent *fall* in the nominal exchange rate.

This rise in the real exchange rate clearly indicated that the Irish currency was overvalued and was, therefore, a candidate for devaluation. This further undermined confidence in the DM peg.

Note:

In the ERM without Britain, Ireland was vulnerable to swings in the sterling exchange rate. The Irish pound was devalued on three occasions, in 1983, 1986 and 1993, and each time was a

Table 13.1
Change in the Irish pound real exchange rate relative to selected currencies

	1979	1986
Belgium	100	158
Netherlands	100	147
Germany	100	140
Denmark	100	147
France	100	136
US	100	100
Japan	100	147
UK	100	113
Italy	100	109
Weighted average	100	119

Source: Derived using consumer prices obtained from the OECD, *Main Economic Indicators*, and nominal exchange rates obtained from the Central Bank of Ireland, *Quarterly Bulletin*.

response to sterling weakness. These devaluations illustrated that there had not been a clean switch from the sterling link to a DM peg.

WAGES

ERM membership appeared to have little or no effect on workers' wage demands. Quite the opposite: the expansionary fiscal policy in 1978 fuelled workers' expectations and led to an increase in wage demands. As the Central Bank of Ireland commented in April 1979:

> The industrial relations situation does not appear to have adjusted yet to the changed circumstances implicit in our adherence to the EMS. There have been several pay claims in excess of 20 per cent and some union leaders have suggested that 15 per cent would be an appropriate minimum. Such high settlements do not recommend themselves in a situation where price inflation seems likely to decelerate well into single figures fairly quickly.
>
> (The Central Bank of Ireland, *Annual Report*, 1979, 119.)

Obviously the social partners did not share the Central Bank's view of the speed with which inflation would fall. This failure of wages to adjust ensured that the economy would remain in recession for a long period of time. Only after the stance of fiscal policy altered in the mid-1980s, and wage moderation was established (partly by a soaring unemployment rate), did Irish wages and inflation start to converge to the lower German rates.

ASSESSMENT

The evidence does not support the view that EMS entry conferred a credibility bonus on Irish economic policy in the period up to 1986. Ireland's inflation rate did not converge rapidly to the German inflation rate. The Irish pound real exchange rate rose and remained above its 1979 level. The yield curve continued to suggest that inflation would accelerate. There was evidence of large-scale capital flight. Only after a very large rise in unemployment did inflationary pressures moderate. None of these developments were consistent with the existence of a credibility bonus as a consequence of having joined the ERM.

The late Professor Rudi Dornbusch (1942–2002) summed up the situation as follows:

> A policy that uses a fixed exchange rate to disinflate and at the same time requires fiscal consolidation can easily run into difficulties. The fixed exchange rate policy stands in the way of a gain in competitiveness and in fact easily becomes a policy of overvaluation. The overvalued currency then needs to be defended by high real interest rates. The combination of budget cutting, high real interest rates and an overly strong currency creates unemployment on each score. There is no offsetting crowding-in mechanism unless money wages are strongly flexible downwards or productivity growth

is high. Neither was the case in Ireland and hence the country is locked into a high unemployment and high debt trap.

> (Rudiger Dornbusch, 'Credibility, Debt and Unemployment: Ireland's Failed Stabilization', *Economic Policy*, April 1989, 174–209.)

It also seems clear that the PPP model, which was the one underpinning our decision to participate in the ERM, may not have been appropriate for short-run policy analysis in Ireland.

13.7 THE IRISH POUND AND THE CRISIS OF 1992–93

THE CURRENCY CRISIS

One of the most dramatic episodes in recent Irish economic history centred on the turmoil in the world currency markets that started in September 1992. This episode has a potentially important lesson for how Ireland will fare in the EMU.

In chapter 12 we explained how German unification and other factors caused tension in the ERM. Speculators noticed that Britain appeared to have entered the ERM at too high an exchange rate. In late summer 1992 the conviction grew that the sterling/DM central rate was unsustainable. Massive amounts of sterling were sold on the foreign exchanges. Despite large-scale, but short-lived, intervention by the Bank of England, the speculators won. Sterling's membership of the ERM was suspended on 16 September and the currency depreciated by 15 per cent on the foreign exchange markets. This development had a profound effect on Irish money markets.

From the decision to join the EMS in 1979, the sterling exchange rate had been the Achilles' heel of Ireland's commitment to the ERM. In March 1983 the weakness of sterling prompted a 3 per cent devaluation of the Irish pound. A similar situation occurred in August 1986 when the Irish pound was devalued by 8 per cent (the largest of any currency in the ERM up to then). These devaluations were reluctantly undertaken by the Irish authorities as a means of reconciling our ERM membership with our economic dependence on the UK market.

Not surprisingly, the foreign exchange markets formed the view that the Irish pound was likely to be devalued when sterling was weak. Hence, when sterling devalued in September 1992, funds flowed out of Ireland in anticipation of a devaluation of the Irish pound. Figure 13.5 shows that the Irish pound rose from Stg£0.94 to well over parity. (It hit Stg£1.105 on 6 October 1992, the highest rate ever recorded.) Despite this severe misalignment, the government decided on this occasion to resist devaluation.

Note:

The so called currency crisis war cabinet consisted of Maurice O'Connell, Department of Finance, Maurice Doyle, Governor of the Central Bank, Adrian Kearns, National Treasury Management Agency (NTMA), Bertie Ahern, Minister for Finance, and Michael Somers, Chief Executive NTMA.

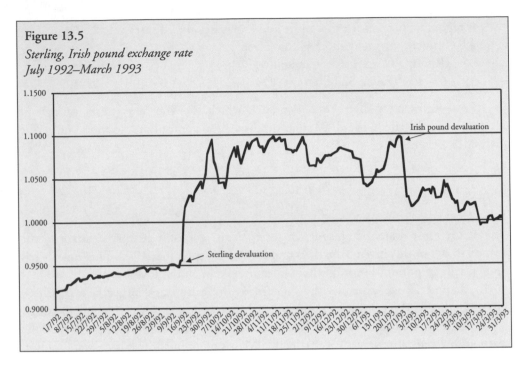

Figure 13.5

*Sterling, Irish pound exchange rate
July 1992–March 1993*

IMPLICATIONS OF THE NO DEVALUATION STANCE

It is estimated that well over a billion pounds flowed out of Irish financial markets in a few days in September 1992. This outflow of funds had the following effects:

- The Central Bank's external reserves fell from £3.05 billion at the end of August to £1.07 billion at the end of September, despite significant foreign borrowing.

- Short-term interest rates were raised to unprecedented heights to defend the currency from speculative attacks. Figure 13.6 shows that one-month inter-bank interest rates peaked at 57 per cent on 12 January 1993. However, the government was able to break the link between inter-bank rates and mortgage and commercial lending rates. As a result, mortgage and bank commercial interest rates only increased by 3 per cent. This separation of inter-bank and commercial lending rates was not sustainable in the medium-term.

- Overnight interest rates on the Euro-Irish pound market rose to 1,000 per cent. Central Bank lending to the money market increased from £74 million at the end of August to £1.8 billion at the end of September. Without this support, interest rates would have been much higher.

- The Central Bank was required to enforce exchange controls to prevent further speculation.

The combination of an overvalued currency and penal interest rates was seriously damaging the Irish economy.

WHY DID THE GOVERNMENT RESIST DEVALUATION?

In a statement issued in January 1993, on the weekend before the devaluation, the government argued that a devaluation would be inappropriate on the grounds that:

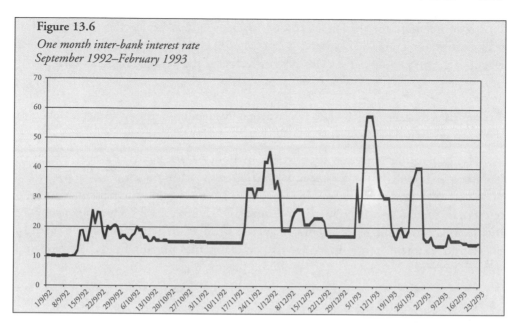

Figure 13.6

One month inter-bank interest rate
September 1992–February 1993

- There was no guarantee that the devaluation would be accepted by the markets. In this case, there would be no significant inflow of funds and interest rates would not fall.

- The currency was not overvalued. As evidence of this they pointed to the surplus on the trade account of the balance of payments.

- Speculators could not be allowed to destroy the ERM, which was regarded as the stepping stone to EMU.

- It was the government's desire to break our dependence on the UK and become a hard-core EMS country.

- Devaluation was ineffective as it resulted in only a short-term competitive gain. PPP theory predicts that devaluation will result in an increase in import prices. This, in turn, will push up the general price level. If the price increase is equivalent to the devaluation, then the competitive gain from the devaluation is short-lived. (In terms of the real exchange rate, the fall in the nominal exchange rate (e) would be offset by an increase in P_{IRL} and the real exchange rate (ϵ) would return to its previous level.)

- The rise in prices could lead to higher wage demands resulting in a wage-price spiral. This would erode competitiveness over the medium-term and have an adverse effect on growth and employment.

- The foreign debt would increase by £100 million for each 1 per cent the Irish pound is devalued. This would also increase the debt/GNP ratio and make it more difficult to achieve the Maastricht criteria for participation in EMU.

- The cost of servicing the foreign debt would increase by £8.5 million for each 1 per cent the Irish pound is devalued.

- The significant foreign debt of the state agencies would also increase. The higher cost of servicing this debt would lead to higher charges and price increases for the consumer.

To compensate for the loss of competitiveness caused by the sharp appreciation relative to sterling after September 1992, a 'Market Development Fund' was launched which paid £50 per job per week to firms affected by the devaluation of sterling.

Note:

If there was no foreign debt, and PPP theory did not hold in the short run, the arguments cited above for not devaluing the currency lose much of their substance.

The government received support for its policy from many quarters. The Irish Congress of Trade Unions, for example, presented the Minister for Finance with a list of names of banks and stockbrokers believed to be engaging in speculation, and referred to their actions as sabotage and unpatriotic. Table 13.2 shows the outflow of Irish pounds since the crisis began. It can be seen that the largest outflow related to sales of government bonds by foreigners and companies moving funds for trade and investment.

Table 13.2
Outflow of funds September 1992–January 1993

	£ billions
Sales of government stock by foreigners	1.80
Companies moving funds for trade and investment	1.25
Speculation on devaluation	0.50
Small scale buying of foreign currencies	0.45

Bishops joined in the denunciation of the speculators. Editorial writers warmed to the theme:

> It is the duty of a sovereign government to defend its currency as it would its national territory. It is the final determinant of a nation's wealth. It represents the accumulated value of its industry, its productiveness, its labour. It is a statement of a country's worth, its reliability, its intrinsic economic soundness ... The long-term consequences of devaluation would be little short of catastrophic for the economy. Ireland would be consigned to the outer ring of monetary union, its currency most likely linked to the anaemic pound sterling. High inflation would be introduced once again. And none of this would guarantee even the short-term palliative of lower interest rates.
>
> (*The Irish Times*, 9 January 1993)

DEVALUATION OF JANUARY 1993

During the last weekend of January 1993, following a renewed weakness of sterling, the government was not prepared to guarantee the exchange rate risk on a proposed plan to borrow £1.1 billion of foreign currency. The plan was to channel this money to the building societies and to business to help alleviate the crisis. If the exchange rate was devalued by 10 per cent after the money was borrowed, this would have cost the government an immediate £100 million.

The government requested an emergence meeting of the EC monetary committee in Brussels. The committee met on Saturday 30 January and at 7.00 p.m. a press release was issued announcing a 10 per cent devaluation of the Irish pound. This was the largest unilateral devaluation ever of a currency in the ERM.

In the aftermath of the devaluation, Irish politicians blamed our European partners, and the German authorities in particular, for their half-hearted support for the Irish pound during the crisis. The Bundesbank could have intervened on a scale that would have beaten off the speculators, but they did not regard the level of the Irish pound in the ERM as sustainable in view of the depreciation of sterling.

As can be seen from figure 13.6, in the months after the devaluation the decline in Irish interest rates was dramatic. The fear that we would suffer a long-lasting penalty in the form of a risk premium due to the possibility of further devaluations proved unfounded. The size of the devaluation was sufficient to restore our competitive position vis-à-vis the UK and convince the markets that the Irish pound might appreciate in the medium-term. Money flowed back into the country and confidence in the economy was restored. There was no resurgence in inflation, and for several years after the event we enjoyed a competitive gain.

It is estimated that the Central Bank of Ireland purchased £8,000 million Irish pounds during the defence of the exchange rate. This entailed using up the external reserves and engaging in foreign borrowing. It is estimated that the cost of intervening in the foreign exchange market during the crisis was between £350 million and £500 million (P. Honohan, 'Costing the Delay in Devaluing 1992–93', *The Irish Bank Review*, Spring 1994).

13.8 WAS THERE AN ALTERNATIVE TO DEVALUATION?

There was an alternative to devaluation. To understand what it entailed, consider figure 13.7, which shows the open economy monetary model first developed in chapter 10. (Note that we focus on inflation rather than the price level and as a result the analysis relates to the relative PPP hypothesis.) The diagram on the right shows equilibrium in the goods and services market. The diagram on the left shows a PPP relationship between Ireland and the UK and the centre diagram represents a PPP relationship between Ireland and all our other trading partners. We use the DM exchange rate to represent the 'all other trading partners' exchange rate.

Suppose the economy is initially at the points A, M and X. The inflation rate is π_1 and the economy is at the natural real growth rate. The effect of the Irish pound appreciation against sterling is to move the economy from the point X to Y in the left-hand diagram. At the point Y, the sterling/Irish pound exchange rate is overvalued. The Irish pound exchange rate relative to the DM (centre diagram) is unchanged because sterling has also fallen against the DM.

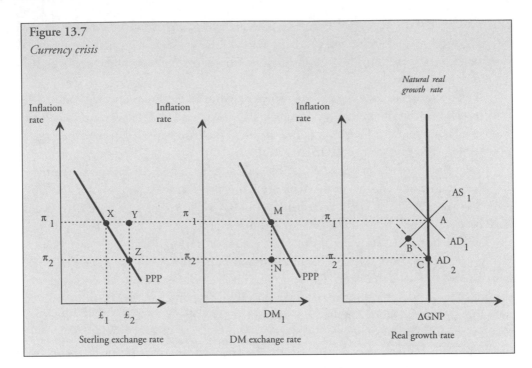

Figure 13.7
Currency crisis

The overvaluation of the sterling/Irish pound exchange rate results in a loss of competitiveness relative to the UK and this reduces Irish exports and increases imports. In the right-hand diagram, this shifts the aggregate demand (AD) curve down to the left and the economy moves to the point B. At the point B, real wages have increased because the inflation rate has fallen while the nominal wage has remained unchanged. If trade unions were to accept a cut in the rate of change of nominal wages so as to restore the original real wage, this would be reflected in the right-hand diagram as a shift of the aggregate supply (AS) curve down to the right. The economy would move to the points C, N and Z.

At the point C, the economy has returned to the natural real growth rate. Workers are not any worse off because the original real wage has been restored. The PPP relationship has been re-established against the UK. However, the DM/Irish pound exchange rate is now undervalued. This undervaluation could result in a further shift of the AD curve up to the right (not shown) and possibly give rise to overshooting of the natural real GNP level.

Note:
One difficulty with this analysis is that it takes no account of the observed reluctance of Irish firms to pass on price reductions following the appreciation of the Irish pound exchange rate. Many firms apparently engaged in profit-taking. This has the effect of slowing down the adjustment process.

ADVANTAGES OF THE WAGE ADJUSTMENT OPTION
A cut in the rate of growth in nominal wages has several advantages over the devaluation option.

- Firstly, the original level of output and employment is restored at a lower inflation rate.
- Secondly, and most importantly, the adverse effects of devaluation on the foreign debt and debt servicing are avoided.
- Thirdly, the social partners would be seen to have responded to the sterling devaluation in a positive and effective way without resorting to an EMS realignment, and this would help restore confidence in the Irish economy. Capital would be expected to flow into the economy and interest rates to decline.

One of the obstacles to this policy response was that the *Programme for Economic and Social Progress* (PESP) was in place in 1992. The trade unions, which supported the strong exchange rate policy, none the less indicated that they would not renegotiate this agreement. The refusal of the trade unions to renegotiate PESP, even though prices were falling due to the sudden appreciation of the currency, showed a lack of realism — if nothing worse — at a time when major job losses were threatened.

The sterling crisis illustrates how damaging the combination of a fixed exchange rate and rigid wages can be for an economy. If the exchange rate is fixed, nominal wages must be flexible so as to accommodate external shocks. Ireland's experience in the ERM raises questions about our membership of European Monetary Union (EMU) particularly when our most important trading partner, Britain, is not a member.

Note:

Note from figure 13.7 the implications of the devaluation option. Devaluation against sterling moves the economy from the point Y back to X but, in doing so, it improves competitiveness relative to our other trading partners. Perhaps this is why the devaluation was so successful. In other words, against all our trading partners, there was an 'excess' devaluation which exceeded investors' expectations. The semi-official interpretation of why the devaluation was so successful is that markets were impressed by the determination of the authorities to hold out for as long as they did: an interpretation without support in theory or evidence!

IMPLICATIONS FOR PPP THEORY

The experience of 1992–93 shows that the PPP model was a bad guide to the short-run behaviour of the economy. If PPP had held in the short run, Irish costs and wages would have fallen as our exchange rate rose in the second half of 1992. As we have seen this did not happen. While the required adjustment might have occurred in the 'long run', by then large segments of Irish industry would have been shut down and unemployment would have soared.

A rigid application of PPP theory also lay behind the dire predictions that if we devalued in 1992 the result would be no more than a wave of inflation that would rapidly erode the competitive gain. The evidence from the aftermath of the 1986 and 1993 devaluations of the Irish pound shows that it is possible to use the exchange rate to restore a loss in competitiveness. By joining EMU we have renounced this instrument of economic policy.

13.9 IRISH EXCHANGE RATE POLICY AFTER THE 1992–93 CRISIS

Germany's continued insistence that domestic policy considerations (such as maintaining price stability in the face of the fiscal expansion that followed German unification) took precedence over European considerations resulted in further turmoil on the foreign exchanges in the summer of 1993. This time the speculators targeted the French franc, the Danish krone and the Belgian franc. After large-scale intervention by European central banks it was finally decided to widen the ERM bands from ± 2.25 per cent to ± 15 per cent for currencies except the Deutsche mark and Dutch guilder. This effectively meant that EU currencies were floating and that the ERM had ceased to exist in all but name.

It is instructive to consider how Irish exchange rate policy was conducted after 1993 now that the narrow band ERM had collapsed. For the first time ever, the Irish currency was in effect floating, without a meaningful peg to another currency or basket of currencies.

What was remarkable about the period 1993–98 was how successfully the economy performed in the new environment. This was the period when the 'Celtic Tiger' economy emerged. Inflation remained extraordinarily low, the real growth rate soared, and unemployment fell steadily. Fears that we would suffer from the devaluation of 1993 or from the difficulty of coping with a floating exchange rate proved groundless. What accounts for the success of Irish exchange rate policy over these years?

After the widening of the ERM bands in mid-1993, the Central Bank of Ireland appeared to follow a policy of trying to stabilise the *effective* exchange rate index, that is, a weighted average of the value of the Irish pound relative to its main trading partners. In practice this involved playing off the strength of sterling against the weakness of the Deutsche mark. The Central Bank, in effect, attempted to find a middle ground by allowing the Irish pound to rise against the DM and simultaneously fall against sterling.

Figure 13.8 shows the trend in the DM and sterling exchange rates (presented in an index form) from April 1996 to May 1998 (when the exchange rates of currencies participating in the single currency area were locked). It can be seen that up to August 1997, the Irish pound drifted down against sterling and strengthened against the DM. The effective exchange rate was quite stable over this period.

After August 1997, the DM exchange rate was allowed to drift down towards the ERM central rate of DM2.41. While this depreciation conferred a competitive advantage on the Irish economy ahead of entry to EMU, it gave rise to the fear that inflation would accelerate. This fear led to a 3 per cent revaluation of the Irish pound's central rate to DM2.48 in March 1998. This was the last adjustment of the Irish pound's value in the ERM. This is perhaps the sporting equivalent of scoring a goal in extra time!

From the launch of EMU in 1999, the flexible exchange rate policy, so successfully pursued by the Central Bank in the run-up to EMU entry, ceased to be an option. It is ironic that what was probably the Central Bank of Ireland's 'finest hour' immediately preceded the termination of the Irish currency and the adoption of the euro.

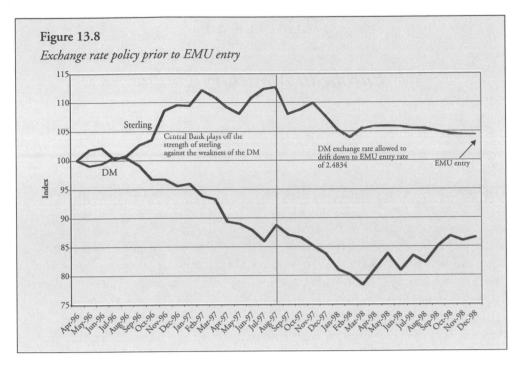

Figure 13.8

Exchange rate policy prior to EMU entry

13.10 CONCLUSION

In this chapter we have examined the Irish experience in the EMS in the light of our earlier discussion of macroeconomic policy in an open economy. The topics discussed included:

- Inflation and the exchange rate prior to EMS entry
- The anticipated benefits from EMS entry
- Evidence from inflation differentials, interest rates and the yield curve that suggests the EMS policy, in the first ten years of membership, was not a success
- The reasons underlying Ireland's unsuccessful EMS policy
- The currency crisis of 1992–93 and the government's response
- Irish exchange policy after the 1992–93 crisis.

CHAPTER 14

European Monetary Union

14.1 INTRODUCTION

European Monetary Union (EMU) is an experiment without parallel in economic history. Never before has a group of sovereign, independent nations surrendered their currencies and adopted a new currency, the euro. The experiment is truly a leap in the dark. We begin this chapter by outlining what is meant by EMU. We then discuss the costs and benefits of EMU. It is argued that EMU offers the promise of considerable benefits in terms of lower inflation and interest rates, increased efficiency and closer economic union between the countries of Europe. On the cost side, the main problem relates to how countries, constrained by EMU membership, adjust to economic shocks. An open economy monetary model is used to illustrate how a country might adjust to an adverse demand-side shock and an adverse supply-side shock.

14.2 THE RUN-UP TO ECONOMIC AND MONETARY UNION

My annals have it so:
A thing my mother saw,
Nigh eighty years ago
With happiness and awe.

Sight never to forget:
Solemn against the sky
In stately silhouette
Ten emus walking by.

M. Fullerton, 'Emus' in Douglas Stewart (ed.)
Poetry in Australia, Vol. 1, University of California Press, 1965, 193.

European Monetary Union (EMU) was launched in Europe in January 1999. A detailed account of the chronology of events leading to its formation is contained in Appendix 1. The design of the EMU dates back to a meeting of the European Council in June 1988 in Hanover, when a committee was given the task of 'studying and proposing concrete stages leading towards [economic and monetary] union'. (Committee for the Study of Economic and Monetary Union, *Report on Economic and Monetary Union in the European Community*, Office for the Official Publications of the European Communities, 1989, foreword.) The committee was chaired by the Commission President Jacques Delors and consisted of the governors of the central banks of the twelve member states (including Ireland's Maurice Doyle), a Commission representative and three invited experts. The committee published its report (known as the *Delors Report*) in April 1989.

Time *magazine welcomes the Eurozone*

The concept of EMU can be divided into two parts: 'economic' and 'monetary'. We now summarise what is meant by these two terms.

ECONOMIC UNION

- A single market within which persons, goods, services and capital can move freely (the four freedoms). The implementation of the 1987 *Single European Act* went a considerable way towards achieving this objective.
- A common competition policy. To establish a 'level playing field' governments are required not to subsidise firms and to reduce state aid to industry. Following reunification, Germany became one of the main offenders on this front. Ireland's special 12.5 per cent profit tax rate on industry has come in for increased criticism although it is not officially regarded as a state aid to industry.
- Structural and regional convergence. It was understood that a monetary union between countries at very different levels of development was unlikely to succeed. In acknowledgment of the difficulties faced by 'peripheral regions' a Cohesion Fund was established to help in the transition to a single market. Because Ireland lagged behind the average standard of living in the EU in the 1990s, we received considerable subsidies from this fund.

Newsweek *magazine welcomes the Eurozone*

MONETARY UNION

- The complete liberalisation of capital transactions and full integration of banking and other financial markets. A directive passed in June 1988 provided for complete liberalisation by 1992.

- The introduction of a single currency. Following the abortive attempts to achieve a 'zone of monetary stability' in Europe (the snake and EMS discussed in previous chapters), it was decided in the 1990s to press ahead for the adoption of a single European currency. It was decided in Madrid in 1995 to call this the euro. The *Delors Report* actually called for a system of rigidly fixed exchange rates. It was later decided that a single currency was a better option.

- Monetary (money supply and interest rates) and exchange rate policies to be conducted by the European Central Bank (ECB). Its basic objective is to ensure price stability in Europe. The participating countries surrender control over their monetary and exchange rate policy to the ECB.

Note:

The EMU concept is closely related to the theory of an *Optimum Currency Area* (OCA), which was first outlined by the Nobel prize winning economist Robert A. Mundell. (See 'A Theory of

Optimum Currency Areas' in *American Economic Review*, Vol. 51, [Sept. 1961], 657–65.) As its name implies, this theory was developed to assess the optimum size of an area that uses the same currency.

The framers of the Maastricht Treaty were very conscious of the fact that before full EMU could be launched the participating countries should first have achieved a high degree of 'nominal convergence'. That is, the key nominal (price) indicators should be aligned before the single currency was adopted. Accordingly they laid down several convergence criteria that would have to be met by any country that wanted to join EMU. These criteria related to inflation and interest rate differentials, the levels of the fiscal deficit, and the national debt.

The actual criteria proposed were originally framed for the purpose of excluding traditionally inflation-prone countries such as Italy from the EMU, but as circumstances changed during the 1990s, it became difficult for even France and Germany to meet them. Consequently in May 1998 the criteria were loosely applied and eleven countries were deemed eligible to participate in EMU. These countries were: Austria, Belgium, France, Finland, Germany, Ireland, Italy, Luxembourg, the Netherlands, Spain and Portugal. Greece initially failed to meet the criteria but then joined in January 2001. Sweden, Britain and Denmark opted out for domestic political reasons and because of their misgivings about the soundness of the project. A more detailed account of these criteria and how they were applied is contained in Appendix 2 to this chapter.

The fact that twelve EU countries are in and three outside implies that the process of economic and monetary integration is now progressing at different speeds in Europe. This will become even more apparent when the EU is enlarged to include Poland, the Czech Republic, Hungary, Slovenia, and other East European countries. Some of these potential new members have already fixed their exchange rates to the euro.

THE STEPS TOWARDS ESTABLISHING EMU

The *Delors Report* envisaged Europe evolving towards the EMU in three stages. These stages were subsequently modified by the Maastricht Treaty which was drafted in 1992 and at a number of inter-governmental conferences, in particular, the summit meeting in Madrid in December 1995. Stages I and II were concerned with completing the internal market and launching the European Monetary Institute (EMI) (the precursor of the ECB).

The final stage, Stage III, of EMU was over the period January 1999 to March 2002. This involved:

- May 1998: the conversion exchange rate from national currencies to the euro was agreed.
- 1 July 1998: the EMI was replaced by the ECB.
- 1 January 1999: the euro was introduced in 'virtual' form, that is, exchange rates were irrevocably fixed but the new currency was not yet put into circulation.
- 1 January 2002: euro notes and coins were introduced. All notes and coins denominated in national currencies were withdrawn by mid-2002. This completed the transition to the EMU.

PROSPECTS FOR EMU

The evidence of history is that systems of fixed exchange rates do *not* endure. From the gold standard to the EMS, previous attempts to stabilise the world's currency markets have eventually collapsed. The most important reason has been that sovereign countries have retained the right to implement independent economic policies. Sooner or later incompatibilities between national economic policies have led to strains, speculative attacks, and ultimately the abandonment of fixed exchange rates.

The collapse of the EMS in 1993 convinced many that the best way forward would be to abolish national currencies and adopt a single European currency. They argued that only when the commitment to fixed exchange rates is made 'irrevocable' in this manner will the full benefits of a stable international financial system be enjoyed in Europe. Others interpret the history of the EMS since 1979 as evidence of the dangers inherent in trying to fix exchange rates between sovereign countries. They point to the risks involved in the single currency project. We now turn to an assessment of the cost and benefits of participating in the EMU.

14.3 THE POLITICAL BENEFITS OF EMU TO IRELAND

On the positive side of the ledger, numerous benefits have been claimed for the adoption of a single European currency. These should be considered under two broad headings, political and economic. In this section we examine the political benefits and in the following section the economic benefits.

Some of the most important potential benefits from the adoption of a single European currency are political in nature. This is because it is very possible that EMU is only a prelude to a fully-fledged federal European Union.

If a federal Europe were to emerge, then it is argued this would ensure peace in Europe. The former French President François Mitterrand is quoted as saying 'Nationalism – that is war'. Similarly, the German Chancellor Kohl has stated that EMU would 'free Europe from war in the twenty-first century'. While another war in Europe is inconceivable, it is clear that EMU could lead to a more effective EU foreign policy. It could be expected that Germany would play a key role in the design and implementation of such a policy. In addition, it is claimed that a single currency will increase solidarity between participants and reduce the risks of trade disputes. The EU is frequently compared to a bicycle: it must either move forward or stall, and EMU was the next logical step toward deeper integration.

The political argument that Ireland must be seen to move forward with Europe appears to be very influential in official circles. Failure to do so, it is claimed, would have serious adverse repercussions such as less favourable treatment in future allocations of structural funds and exclusion from key economic decision-making processes.

Also by participating in EMU from its inception Ireland had a voice in the formulation of European monetary policy. The Governor of the Central Bank of Ireland has a seat on the Governing Council of the ECB. While European monetary policy clearly will not be tailored to Irish problems, our influence has been none the less disproportionate to the size of our economy.

14.4 The Economic Benefits of EMU to Ireland

In this section we outline the main economic benefits that have been advanced for adopting the euro.

Completing the internal market

One economic benefit of adopting the euro will be the extent to which it will help complete the single, or internal, European market. There are a number of ways in which the abolition of national currencies will increase economic integration.

Firstly, the use of a common currency increases the *transparency of prices and costs* across countries. Since all prices are now denominated in euro, price differentials are more obvious. This should encourage arbitrage which, in turn, should lead to a convergence of prices across Europe (see chapter 10). Using the internet and a euro credit card, it is possible to go on a virtual shopping spree across Europe. However, we spend a large and growing proportion of our income on non-traded services. Significant price differentials persist between the cost of educational, medical and personal services around Europe. Ireland has become a relatively expensive country for tourists, as you can confirm on your next holiday in Spain, Portugal or Greece.

However, the single currency is not a prerequisite for cross-border shopping: at present there is more use of the internet by Irish subscribers to purchase from the US and the UK rather than from the Eurozone. Indirect taxes and red tape are a more serious obstacle to price convergence across Europe than are national currencies, as anyone interested in buying a car in Belgium for use in Ireland will appreciate.

Secondly, the euro eliminates *exchange rate transaction costs* between Eurozone countries. These costs are estimated to be about one-half of 1 per cent of GDP. While the cost of converting currencies is high for small transactions, such as tourist purchases, they are smaller for larger business deals.

The more important trade is, relative to GDP, the greater the savings in transaction costs from adopting the euro. While Ireland is very small and its economy is very open to international trade, a substantial proportion of its international transactions involve sterling and the dollar. Hence, the reductions in overall transaction costs that followed from adopting the euro were not as great as was the case for other Eurozone countries. On the other hand, the savings on transaction costs within the Eurozone resulted in a significant fall in foreign exchange earnings in the financial sector.

Reduction in exchange rate uncertainty

As discussed in chapter 9, exchange rate fluctuations can result in large profits or losses for importers and exporters. Hedging techniques offer only short-term protection against exchange rate risk. It is argued that doing away with the risk of exchange rate fluctuations will stimulate trade and investment between Eurozone countries. Uncertainty regarding exchange rate movements is seen as a deterrent to planning long-run investment across international frontiers.

Plausible though this seems, the empirical research has found little evidence that floating exchange rates depress international trade and investment. Trade between Japan and the United States and Europe has grown rapidly even though their exchange rates are not pegged.

Note:

One of the strongest proponents of the benefits of a common currency is Professor Andrew Rose of the University of California, Berkeley. He has argued that otherwise similar countries that use a common currency end up trading three times as much with one another as they would if they used separate currencies. Many believe these estimates are exaggerated. A counter-example is provided by the Irish experience. When we broke the sterling link there was no significant adverse effect on the volume of Anglo-Irish trade. (See Rodney Thom and Brendan Walsh, 'The Effect of a Currency Union on Trade: Lessons from the Irish Experience', *European Economic Review*, 46, 2002, 1111–1123.)

It should be recalled that in Ireland exchange rate risk continues to exist in relation to sterling, the dollar and the other currencies outside the Eurozone. The adoption of the euro did not remove the risk relating to a substantial proportion of Irish international transactions.

SCALE ECONOMIES

Prior to the introduction of the euro, firms had an incentive to spread their plants around Europe to protect their profits or assets from sudden movements in exchange rates. For example, suppose an Irish firm had a plant in Ireland and another in Spain. An appreciation of the peseta/Irish pound exchange rate would have increased the value of the Irish plant and decreased the value of the Spanish plant. If the gain offset the lost, the assets of the overall firm would not be adversely affected. If, however, the firm had only one plant in Spain, the assets of the group, measured in Irish pounds, would decline.

Now that the euro has removed the exchange rate risk in the Eurozone, firms make location decisions on genuine considerations of comparative costs rather than as part of a strategy of hedging against sudden currency movements. That is, firms can locate their plants so as to reap *economies of scale*, ignoring national boundaries. Economies of scale lead to an efficiency gain, lower costs and higher company profits.

The downside is that peripheral regions like Ireland could suffer a decline in their share of European economic activity as firms move to the main market in the core or centre of the Eurozone.

INFLATION

Adopting the euro should allow formerly inflation-prone countries to enjoy a degree of price stability that they were unable to attain on their own. According to *purchasing power parity* (PPP) theory, the inflation rate in the smaller Eurozone countries should converge to the rate in the larger countries or the average of the Eurozone.

The magnitude of this gain depends on how successful the ECB is in controlling inflation. The ECB is designed as a clone of the German Bundesbank and has been given a mandate to achieve price stability in the Eurozone. It interprets this to be a rate of inflation below 2 per cent. In 2001 and 2002 it missed this target, but only by a small margin. If the ECB is successful over time in achieving its low inflation target, then formerly inflation-prone countries like Ireland should also enjoy low inflation. It is argued that relying on the strength and anti-inflation reputation of the ECB will be more beneficial for smaller countries than relying on their own national central banks to maintain low inflation.

Figure 14.1 shows the inflation rate in each of the Eurozone countries from 1979 to 2002. Back in the early 1980s, at the commencement of the EMS, there was considerable divergence in inflation rates. Rates then started to converge as global inflation declined and then as countries strove to meet the Maastricht inflation criteria. The convergence of inflation rates in the late 1990s shows that it is possible for independent central banks — firmed up by the goal of meeting the Maastricht criteria — to deliver price stability. The UK experience since it left the EMS in 1992 also shows how an independent national central bank can deliver low inflation *outside* the Eurozone.

However, after 1997 Eurozone inflation rates started to diverge. In 2002, the inflation rates in the Netherlands (5.1 per cent), Ireland (4.4 per cent), Portugal (3.9 per cent), Greece (3.5 per cent) and Spain (2.9 per cent) were well above the rate in Germany (1.5 per cent), as well as exceeding the ECB target of 2 per cent.

Various factors have contributed to relatively high inflation in Ireland since we joined the Eurozone. The weakness of the euro against sterling and the dollar has had a larger inflationary impact on Ireland than on the rest of the Eurozone. Secondly, the low *real* interest rates experienced in Ireland since 1999 contributed to an unprecedented real growth rate of 10.4 per cent in 2000. This rate of growth contributed to an upsurge in the inflation rate. Also recent Irish budgets have imposed significant increases in excise taxes on tobacco and alcohol and higher VAT.

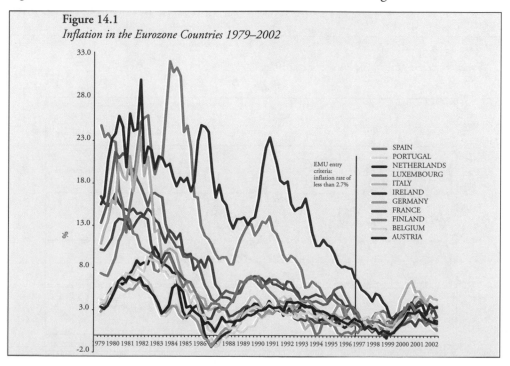

Figure 14.1
Inflation in the Eurozone Countries 1979–2002

It should also be mentioned that the anti-inflation stance necessary to achieve EMU membership in 1997 appeared to wane in a number of Eurozone countries once that objective was accomplished. The experience is similar to an athlete observing a special diet to qualify for an event. But once the event is over, the athlete reverts to a less demanding lifestyle.

With hindsight we now realise that adopting the euro does not guarantee that exactly uniform inflation will prevail in all countries, but the size and persistence of the differentials have been surprising.

INTEREST RATES

Under the EMS arrangement that operated from 1979–93 European currencies were pegged but adjustable. For most of the period this did not deliver low interest rates in countries like Ireland due to the perceived risk that the pound would be devalued. However, in line with uncovered interest rate parity theory, the introduction of the euro means that there can be only one interest rate in the Eurozone.

Figure 14.2 shows interest rates for each Eurozone country from 1997 to 2002. Reflecting the trend in inflation rates, there was considerable divergence of interest rates in the early 1980s. Interest rates started to converge in the run up to the euro in January 1999 and thereafter there is only one uniform rate across the Eurozone. The rate of 2.75 per cent in 2003 represents a significant fall for the historically high interest rates countries like Ireland, Portugal, Spain, Finland and Italy.

But while lower interest rates will benefit investors and borrowers, they will hurt savers. In 2003, inflation rates in countries such as Spain, Ireland and the Netherlands are higher than the interest rate and, as a result, savers experience *negative* real interest rates. This results in a transfer of resources away from savers to borrowers. Also, these

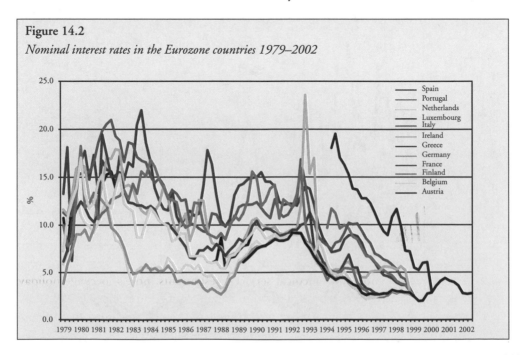

Figure 14.2

Nominal interest rates in the Eurozone countries 1979–2002

negative real interest rates have important implications for how countries adjust within the Eurozone.

As already mentioned, the low inflation and interest rates, associated with adopting the euro, undoubtedly contributed to the boom in Ireland in the late 1990s. We discuss these and other developments related to the 'Celtic Tiger' period in chapter 24.

14.5 The Economic Costs of EMU to Ireland

We now discuss the main costs associated with adopting the single currency.

Transition costs

Let us first consider the least important aspect of the changeover: the costs associated with the mechanics of the conversion from national currencies. On 28 February 2002, the transition to the euro was finally completed. From that date, national banknotes and coins ceased to be legal tender. Among the currencies made obsolete was the Greek drachma, the world's oldest currency.

Note:
The drachma was first introduced in 600 B.C. and is mentioned in both the *Old* and *New Testaments*. It comes from the word *drás-somai* meaning 'to grip'. Originally one drachma was equal to a handful of grain. During the Greek hyper-inflation in 1945 the exchange rate depreciated to 70 trillion drachmas to one British sovereign.

While the euro changeover has been described as an enormous success, there were considerable costs involved in the process. It has been estimated that the cost to the banks, government and the non-bank corporate sector of switching to the euro could run into hundreds of millions of euro. The costs include:

- Staff training (10 per cent)
- Stationary, marketing and public relations (20 per cent)
- Changes to information technology (50 per cent).

Other costs include adapting both the domestic and international payments system to take account of the euro, storing large volumes of euro prior to their introduction, withdrawing domestic notes and coins and designing euro notes and coins.

From the consumer's perspective, the main cost is the price rounding associated with the conversion from national currencies to the euro. In the Irish case, the conversion rate is IR£1 = €1.2697 or €1 = IR£0.787564. At this rate, the euro does not convert exactly into units of the old Irish pound and this results in rounding-up or down. The Consumers Association of Ireland, in a nationwide survey, found that in January 2002 the euro resulted in a rise in prices in a whole range of products and services. These included leisure activities, pub food and drink, medical services, restaurants, hotels, package holidays, nightclubs and gardening. This pushed the annual rate of inflation in January 2002 to 4.9 per cent up from 4.2 per cent in December 2001. The survey concluded that the euro was not brought in on the concept of 'new currency — same price'.

14.6 FACTORS CONSTRAINING ADJUSTMENT WITHIN THE EUROZONE

We now turn to one of the most serious costs associated with EMU membership, namely the problem of adjusting to economic shocks in the absence of a national exchange rate.

ASYMMETRIC SHOCKS

We live in a dynamic world where the economy is constantly buffered by different types of shocks. These shocks can take many forms. For example, fluctuations in the sterling, yen or dollar exchange rates, the September 11 terrorist attack, the foot and mouth crisis in 2001 or the reunification of Germany in the early 1990s. These shocks can potentially affect all nations, but not equally. A shock that has a disproportionate impact on a particular economy is referred to as *country-specific* or *asymmetric shock*.

Some economists argue that the risk of an asymmetric shock within Europe is now minimal because the EU economies are highly integrated and structurally similar. A shock to one would be a shock to all. Countries have not become highly specialised in narrow branches of economic activity but more diversified with increasingly similar industrial structures. A fall in the demand for, say, electronic engineering or tourism would affect many European countries equally seriously.

However, this argument should not be pushed to the point of denying the possibility of region-specific shocks. A sudden strengthening of the sterling/euro exchange rate would have a disproportionate effect on the Irish economy. Our exposure to a weakening of sterling is the biggest risk to which we exposed the economy by joining a EMU from which Britain is absent.

RELINQUISHING THE EXCHANGE RATE OPTION

Adopting the euro means that a member state can no longer resort to exchange rate devaluation or appreciation as an instrument of macroeconomic policy. There is no unanimity among economists on the costs of relinquishing this policy instrument. On one side, it is argued that the exchange rate tends to be less effective as a policy instrument in open as opposed to closed economies. A devaluation may quickly feed through to higher inflation and the effect on the real exchange rate tends to be quickly eroded. If this is the case, the costs of relinquishing the exchange rate instrument should be small for Ireland.

The counter-argument is that PPP does not hold in the short run and changes in the exchange rate can result in important competitive gains or losses. For example, the currency crisis of 1992–93 demonstrates the difficulty of dealing with a shock (in this case the sudden depreciation of sterling) while trying to maintain a pegged exchange rate. The Irish pound devaluations of 1983, 1986 and 1993, were all triggered by a weakening of sterling. If the Irish authorities did not have recourse to the exchange rate option at these times, the economic consequences for the overall economy could have been very serious.

There are numerous other examples from all around the world. Overvalued exchange rates were part of the reason for the Mexican crash of 1994–95, the crisis in East Asia in 1997 and Argentina in 2002. These examples indicate that in the absence of an exchange rate movement, adjustment can be slow and incomplete.

It is difficult to ignore the evidence provided by these, and many more, examples and to maintain that abandoning the exchange rate as a policy instrument will be virtually cost-free.

Another important issue relating to the adjustment process is the movement of the euro exchange rate. Normally, a particular country's exchange rate could be expected to reflect economic fundamentals. For example, if a country is experiencing a balance of payments deficit or a relatively high inflation rate, the exchange rate could be expected to depreciate. The movement of the exchange rate should help adjust the economy back to natural real GNP.

However, the Irish economy, which accounts for 1 per cent of Eurozone GDP, is too small to have any effect on the euro exchange rate. This means that fluctuations of the euro could facilitate or exacerbate the adjustment process.

For example, if the Irish economy was over-heating, an appreciation of the euro exchange rate might be advantageous, as it would help slow the economy. However, the euro could just as easily move in the opposite direction and add an unwelcome stimulus into the economy. This, in effect, is what happened between January 1999 and the end of 2000. The Irish economy was growing at an unprecedented rate and was clearly over-heating. Yet the real exchange rate depreciated by 7.1 per cent against sterling, by 14.9 per cent against the dollar and the real trade-weighted competitiveness indicator fell by 5.7 per cent. This is an example of an unfavourable movement of the euro exchange rate adding to the burden of adjustment.

MONETARY POLICY

Without a national currency a country is also deprived of an independent monetary policy. An independent central bank would reduce interest rates in times of recession or increase interest rates when the economy is over-heating. Changes in interest rates would affect interest-sensitive expenditure and thereby impact on the demand-side of the economy. Ireland has no affect on Eurozone interest rates except through Ireland's representative on the Governing Council of the ECB. Adopting the euro therefore entails surrendering the monetary policy option.

The monetary policy of the ECB is designed to achieve price stability in the whole of the euro area. But this in effect means that its policy stance is strongly influenced by the inflation rates in Germany, France, and Italy whose economies account for over 70 per cent of the euro area's output and have correspondingly high weights in the Eurozone inflation rate. Only when the Irish economy is moving in tandem with these three large countries will the ECB's monetary policy be appropriate for the Irish economy. If the Irish economy is out of synch with the larger Eurozone economies, as was the case in the early years of the Eurozone, the ECB's monetary policy could be a source of instability for Ireland.

In 2001, for example, responding to the low inflation rates in Germany and France, the ECB cut interest rates on three occasions to 3.25 percent. However, countries like Spain, Greece, Ireland, Portugal and the Netherlands were experiencing relative high inflation rates and the fall in nominal interest rates resulted in negative real interest rates in those countries. This was the opposite of what was required to curtail inflation and slow the real growth rate.

CONSTRAINTS ON FISCAL POLICY

Keynesian theory recommends an expansionary fiscal policy in times of recession and a deflationary policy in times of over-heating. In principle these options are still open to countries in the Eurozone. However, the Stability and Growth Pact can result in fines on countries whose budget deficit exceeds 3 per cent of GDP. The Stability Pact acts as a constraint because when an economy goes into recession, the budget deficit automatically worsens. While there are various let-out clauses, it is still the case that a government, in an attempt to avoid penalties, might be forced to raise taxes and cut expenditure at a time when the economy is in recession. That is, the Stability Pact could result in a government being forced to introduce a *pro-cyclical* fiscal policy that would intensify the recession.

In Germany in 2003 the economy was growing at a mere 1 per cent. Because the budget deficit had risen close to the Stability Pact penalty threshold, the government came under considerable pressure from the European Commission to reduce it. In this situation, the government was constrained from using an expansionary fiscal policy to move the economy out of recession. At the same time, the ECB was concerned that Eurozone inflation was slightly above the target 2 per cent and held interest rates at 2.75 per cent. This was in marked contrast to the US Federal Reserve which had cut rates to 1.75 per cent.

WEAK FISCAL FEDERALISM

Within federal political systems a process known as *fiscal federalism* helps regions to adjust to shocks. After an asymmetric shock the depressed regions pay less in taxes to the central government and receive more in transfer payments from it. Booming regions, on the other hand, pay more in taxes and receive less in transfer payments. These automatic stabilisers help soften the impact of regional-specific shocks.

Even the United States, with its relatively flexible labour markets and high mobility of capital and labour, relies on fiscal federalism to help dampen the effects of shocks on its regions. Similarly, in Ireland a region that suffers job losses and increased unemployment pays less in taxes and receives more in unemployment benefit and other transfer payments.

The Eurozone is not such a federal political system. The EU budget is very small (less than 2 per cent of GDP) and there are no automatic mechanisms for transferring funds to areas that experience adverse shocks. The money paid from specific funds, notably FEOGA, the agricultural fund, does not increase in response to cyclical downturns. Nor is there any EU tax whose yield automatically falls during a recession.

LACK OF FACTOR MOBILITY

Faced with persistent unemployment it is likely that Irish emigration to Britain and elsewhere would increase; this was an important part of the adjustment mechanism in the 1950s and again in the 1980s. Migration would help ease labour shortages elsewhere and reduce unemployment in Ireland. However, this channel of adjustment entails personal and social costs for Ireland. In fact, politicians in any country have never welcomed large-scale emigration, but adopting the euro implies accepting that it will become a more important component of the adjustment process.

While the EU has made considerable progress towards establishing the free movement of labour between member states, it is still far from an integrated single market. Labour mobility is low by comparison with that between the regions of the United States. Differences in language and culture, rigidities in housing markets and ethnic discrimination present significant barriers to the movement of labour between member states. The mobility of labour from Ireland to the UK and the US is much higher than it is within the EMU area.

14.7 Adjusting to Economic Shocks within the Eurozone

In this section we examine how a country, constrained by EMU membership, adjusts to an adverse demand-side and an adverse supply-side shock. The model used for analytical purposes is the open economy monetary model (OEMM) first developed in chapter 10.

Open economy monetary model

Figure 14.3 outlines the open economy monetary model. The right-hand diagram shows how aggregate demand (AD) and aggregate supply (AS) interact to determine the real growth rate and the inflation rate. The vertical line indicates the natural real growth rate. To the right of this reference line, the economy is over-heating and to the left, the economy is in recession.

The centre diagram in figure 14.3 shows a relative PPP relationship between Ireland and the other Eurozone countries. The euro ensures that the exchange rate is fixed along the horizontal axis. Relative PPP holds between Ireland and the other Eurozone countries along the PPP line. If the economy is above the PPP line, the Irish economy experiences a *loss* of competitiveness relative to the other Eurozone countries. Below the PPP line the Irish economy experiences a *gain* in competitiveness. Note that a fall in inflation in the other Eurozone countries will shift the PPP line downwards and vice versa.

The diagram on the left-hand side of figure 14.3 shows a relative PPP relationship between Ireland and its non-EMU trading partners, mainly the US and the UK. The change in the dollar/euro exchange rate is shown along the horizontal axis and, as before, the Irish inflation rate is given on the vertical axis. (It is assumed here that sterling and the dollar move in tandem.)

This presentation points to a *dualism* in determining the competitive position of the Irish economy. It is possible for the Irish economy's competitive position to be under-valued relative to the Eurozone countries and overvalued relative to the US and the UK or some other combination.

The points A, X and M represent a long-run sustainable position for the Irish economy. At these points, the actual growth rate equals the natural rate and relative PPP holds against the other Eurozone countries and also against the non-EMU trading partners.

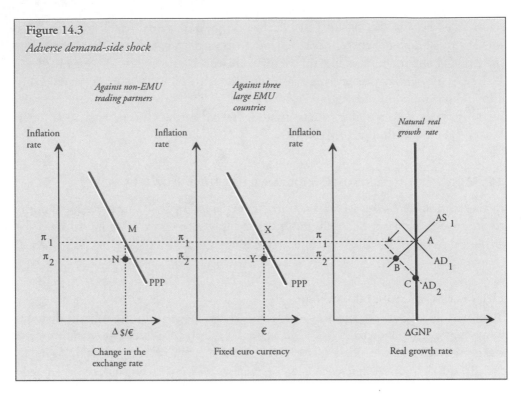

Figure 14.3
Adverse demand-side shock

ADVERSE DEMAND-SIDE SHOCK

Suppose there is an adverse demand-side shock that shifts the aggregate demand (AD) curve down to the left. This could be due to a crisis in the agricultural sector. The economy moves from the points A to B, X to Y and M to N. At the point B both the inflation rate and the real growth have fallen. At the points Y and N, the Irish economy experiences a gain in competitiveness relative to the other Eurozone countries and to the non-EMU countries. How does the economy return to the natural real growth rate?

In the pre-EMU entry period, Irish policy makers had the option of resorting to an expansionary monetary or fiscal policy. Note that the devaluation option would not be appropriate as the economy is already experiencing a gain in competitiveness. A reduction in interest rates, or an increase in government expenditure, and/or a cut in taxation (fiscal policy) would shift the AD curve back up to the right and the economy would return to the points A, X and M. However, as discussed in the previous section, in the post-EMU entry era, implementing such a policy may not be an option.

However, there are *two automatic adjustment mechanisms*, a 'PPP effect' and a 'real wage effect' which should move an economy back to the natural growth rate and long-run equilibrium.

At the points N and Y in figure 14.3, the Irish economy experiences a gain in competitiveness relative to our main trading partners. This 'PPP effect' should increase net exports and shift the AD curve back up to its original position thereby eliminating the output gap. If the 'PPP effect' works quickly then the output gap will not persist and the costs in terms of lost output and high unemployment are small. If, on the other hand, relative PPP does not hold in the short run, the economy could remain at the point B for some time. In this case, the costs of adopting the euro are high.

Taking the analysis a stage further, suppose that the 'PPP effect' does not work effectively in the short run, because relative PPP itself does not hold. In this situation, the 'real wage effect' takes on a prominent role in the adjustment process. At the point B in figure 14.3, the real wage has increased because inflation has decreased while nominal wages are unchanged. The percentage change in the real wage, ΔRW, is defined as:

$$\Delta RW = \Delta W - \pi \qquad (1)$$

where ΔW is the percentage change in the nominal wage and π is the inflation rate. If workers accept a cut in the growth of nominal wages, so as to restore the original real wage, the AS curve will shift down to the right (not shown) and the economy moves towards the point C. This 'real wage effect' can be expected to move the economy back towards the natural growth rate.

Note:

If it were the case that *absolute* nominal wages had to fall to move the economy from the point B to C in figure 14.3, then it is likely that the economy would remain in recession for some time. This is because workers are very resistant to cuts in nominal earnings. However, all that is required for the adjustment process to work quickly is for the rate of change in nominal wages to fall short of the inflation rate. This would reduce the rate of growth of real earnings. This suggests that, to facilitate the adjustment process, a certain amount of inflation may be both necessary and desirable.

The point C in figure 14.3 is not, however, a long-run equilibrium point. This is because PPP does not hold between Ireland and its main trading partners. At some point the 'PPP effect' will take effect and move the AD curve up to the right. With the AS curve shifting down to the right and the AD curve shifting up to the right, there is a distinct possibility that the economy will over-shoot the natural real growth rate. The degree of over-shooting could be expected to depend on the relative strength of the 'PPP effect' and the 'real wage effect'.

Adverse supply-side shock

Consider now figure 14.4 which illustrates the case of an adverse supply-side shock. This could be an increase in the price of raw materials or an increase in electricity, telephone or heating charges. The short-run AS curve shifts up to the left and the economy moves from the points A to B, X to Y and M to N. In the right-hand diagram, the real growth rate decreases and the inflation rate rises. At the points Y and N, the Irish economy is above the relative PPP lines and suffers a loss of competitiveness relative to its main trading partners. In short, at the points B, Y and N, the economy is operating below its natural growth rate and the real exchange rate is overvalued.

Note that at the point B, the real wage rate has *decreased*. This is because the inflation rate has risen while nominal earnings have remained unchanged. (It is assumed here that it was not an increase in wage demands which shifted the AS curve left in the

Figure 14.4
Adverse supply-side shock

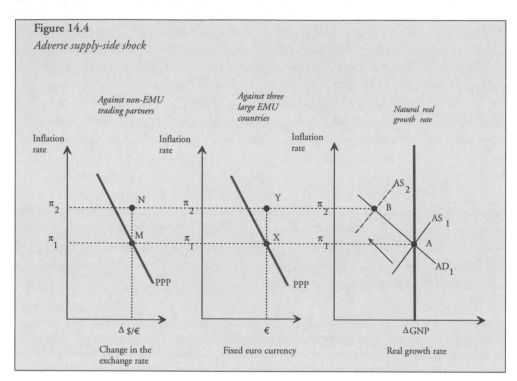

first instance.) For the economy to return to natural real GNP, it is necessary for the AS curve to shift back down to the right. This could come about if workers accepted a cut in the rate of growth of nominal earnings so as to reduce the real wage. However, since workers already experienced a fall in real earnings in the movement from the point A to B, such a development is likely to be resisted.

If a fall in nominal earnings is not forthcoming, it is possible that the economy would remain at the point B for some time. In this case, the cost in terms of lost output and high unemployment would be high.

Note that an expansionary monetary or fiscal policy cannot resolve the problem. Such a policy would shift the AD curve up to the right but, in doing so, increases inflation and the real exchange rate. After a time, the loss of competitiveness will shift the AD curve back down to the left. This illustrates the point that a demand-side policy cannot be used to resolve a supply-side shock.

KEYNES EFFECT

There is another factor that should work to ensure the economy does not remain at the point B in figure 14.4 indefinitely. At the point B, unemployment has increased above the natural unemployment rate. This rise in unemployment could be expected to put downward pressure on the growth in nominal wages and this, in turn, will shift the AS schedule down from AS_2 to AS_1. The economy reverts back to natural real GNP.

The fall in inflation increases aggregate demand along the AD curve and this leads to a rise in the real growth rate. In short:

Unemployment $\rightarrow \downarrow \Delta W \rightarrow \downarrow \pi \rightarrow \uparrow AD \rightarrow \uparrow \Delta$real GNP

Equilibrium will be achieved at the point A where the output gap has been eliminated.

This sequence of events linking unemployment to an increase in the real growth rate is sometimes known as the 'Keynes effect'. However, this whole process could take some considerable time and the costs in terms of lost output and employment are likely to be high.

If the 'Keynes effect' is slow to bring about the necessary adjustment, then it is possible that the 'PPP effect' will act to compound the problem. Note that at the points Y and N in figure 14.4, the real exchange rate is overvalued. If relative PPP holds, the associated loss of competitiveness could shift the AD curve down to the left moving the economy even further away from the natural growth rate. This is a potential source of instability which intensifies the recession and puts an even greater adjustment burden on the 'real wage' adjustment mechanism.

SUMMARY

Our analysis highlights a number of points. Firstly, EMU membership has the fundamental effect of shifting the burden of adjustment away from the money and foreign exchange markets to fiscal policy and on to the labour market ('real wage effect') and price convergence ('PPP effect'). The monetary sector (interest rates) and the euro exchange rate are no longer fast and efficient clogs in the adjustment process but are instead a potential source of instability.

Secondly, given that the burden of adjustment falls on the labour market and price convergence, it is possible that the economy will find it much harder to adjust than in the pre-EMU period. Thirdly, comparing figures 14.3 and 14.4, it is evident that the 'PPP effect' is the correct stabilising factor in the case of a demand-side shock and that the 'real wage effect' is the correct stabilising factor in the case of a supply-side shock. The implication is that if the 'PPP effect' dominates the 'real wage effect', it will be a destabilising factor in the case of a supply-side shock. On the other hand, if the 'real wage effect' dominates the 'PPP effect', it will be a destabilising factor in the case of a demand-side shock.

This suggests that there are no guarantees that the adjustment process will arrive at a long-run equilibrium point. The 'real wage effect' and the 'PPP effect' could interact in such a way as to intensify a recession or cause the economy to over-shoot the natural real growth rate.

14.8 CONCLUSION

In this chapter we have outlined what economic and monetary union means and discussed the main benefits and costs of adopting the euro. Among the main benefits discussed were:

- Political benefits
- Economic benefits, such as reduced transaction costs, reduced risk, scale economies, low inflation and low interest rates.

The main costs discussed included:

- Transition costs
- The loss of exchange rate and monetary policy in adjusting to economic shocks

- The shift in the burden of adjustment from monetary and fiscal policy to a 'PPP effect' and a 'real wage effect'
- We also discussed how an economy like Ireland constrained by EMU membership might adjust to an adverse demand-side and an adverse supply-side shock.

APPENDIX 1
CHRONOLOGY OF THE EU AND EMU

- April 1951: France, West Germany, Italy, Belgium, the Netherlands and Luxembourg sign the Treaty of Paris, which establishes the European Coal and Steel Community (ECSC).
- March 1957: These six countries sign the Treaty of Rome, which establishes the European Economic Community (EEC). One of the objectives of the Treaty is to establish a customs union where there is free movement of goods, services and capital. The Treaty also refers to the desirability of achieving international monetary stability. The EEC and the ECSC constitute the European Communities (EC).
- January 1962: The EC Common Agricultural Policy (CAP) commences with the aim of establishing a common market and prices for agricultural produce.
- October 1962: A Commission report to the Council proposes to form a monetary union by 1971. Germany objects on the grounds that the Bretton Woods system is working well.
- February 1969: Barre Report on the co-ordination of economic and monetary policies is published.
- December 1969: At a conference of European governments in The Hague, the German Chancellor Brandt called for establishing economic and monetary union in stages. This followed the devaluation of sterling in 1967 and the realignment of the French franc and German mark in 1969. His proposal was based on the Barre Report and was adopted by the European Council and a working party chaired by Pierre Werner (Prime Minister of Luxembourg) was set up to examine the issues.
- October 1970: The Werner Report is published. The Report calls for the creation of a monetary union, in stages, by 1980. Monetary union will entail (i) fixing European currencies irrevocably or introducing a single currency, (ii) free movement of capital, (iii) the establishment of a ECB, and (iv) co-ordination of macroeconomic policy. The Report called for 'parallel progress' towards monetary union, involving co-ordination of fiscal and monetary policies at the same time as progress was being made towards fixing exchange rates. The Report suggested that economic policies are co-ordinated and exchange rate fluctuations reduced so that after a period of ten years exchange rates could be irrevocably fixed.
- March 1971: The Council adopts a resolution to achieve economic and monetary union by 1980.
- March 1972: As the Bretton Woods system collapses, European governments agree to maintain exchange rates within a $\pm$ 2.25 per cent band relative to each other

(the snake). The snake did not succeed in stabilising European exchange rates and the remaining stages proposed in the Werner Report were postponed.

- January 1973: Denmark, Ireland and the UK join the EC.
- March 1979: The European Monetary System (EMS) commences operation.
- February 1986: Signing of the Single European Act which came into force in July 1987, after its adoption by referendum in Ireland. Its aim is to complete the internal market.
- June 1988: Council of Ministers directive to liberalise capital movements by July 1990. Transition period extended for Ireland, Portugal, Greece and Spain.
- June 1988: A committee of central bank governors and other experts is formed at a meeting of the European Council in Hanover to study how economic and monetary union could be achieved. EC Commission President Jacques Delors chairs the committee.
- April 1989: The *Delors Report* is published.
- June 1989: European Council at a meeting in Madrid agrees to implement the first stage of the *Delors Report* starting July 1990.
- December 1989: European Council meeting in Strasbourg agrees to establish the institutional changes necessary to implement Stages 2 and 3 of the *Delors Report*.
- July 1990: Beginning of Stage 1 of the process leading to EMU.
- October 1990: European Council meeting in Rome agrees to start the second stage of EMU in January 1994.
- December 1991: At a meeting in Maastricht, in the Netherlands, the heads of state of the EC countries agree to create a single currency by 1997 or 1999 at the latest. Details contained in the Maastricht Treaty. Britain obtains an 'opt out' from the proposed single currency.
- May 1992: Ireland votes 'yes' in a referendum to adopt the Maastricht Treaty
- June 1992: Denmark rejects the Maastricht Treaty by a narrow margin.
- August 1992: France passes the Maastricht Treaty by a narrow margin.
- January 1994: The second phase of the EMU commences with the establishment of the European Monetary Institute (EMI).
- June 1994: Norway, Sweden, Finland and Austria sign treaties of accession to the EU on 1 January 1995. Austria (July 1994), Finland (October 1994) and Sweden (November 1994) vote 'yes' in referendums on accession. Norway (November 1994) votes 'no'.
- 1996: Swedish government appoints an independent commission of economists to examine the merits of joining the EMU. The Commission favours a 'wait and see' policy. In 1997 the Swedish government endorses this view, partly because of the growing unpopularity of the EU in Sweden.
- December 1996: At the Dublin Summit the Growth and Stability Pact was drafted. This constrains fiscal policy in countries that join the EMU.
- 1997: The new British Labour government unveils its policy on the EMU. Unlike its Conservative predecessor it is not in principle opposed to the project.
- 1997: Despite the declaration that sterling will remain outside the EMU, the new Irish government reaffirms the intention of joining the EMU in the first wave.

- May 1998: At a meeting of heads of governments in Brussels eleven EU countries — Austria, Belgium, France, Finland, Germany, Ireland, Italy, Luxembourg, the Netherlands, Spain and Portugal — were deemed eligible to join the EMU. The exchange rates at which national currencies will be converted to the euro were announced and the deadline for a January 1999 launch of Stage III was reaffirmed.
- July 1998: The European Monetary Institute (EMI) is replaced by the ECB.
- January 1999: The euro is introduced in virtual form.
- January 2001: Greece joins the Eurozone bringing the total number of countries in the system to twelve.
- January 2002: The euro is introduced as a day-to-day currency.
- 28 February 2002: All national currencies of the Eurozone countries are withdrawn from circulation. This completes the transition to EMU.

APPENDIX 2
THE MAASTRICHT CONVERGENCE CRITERIA AND THEIR APPLICATION

The Maastricht convergence criteria stipulated that to be eligible to participate in the EMU:

- A country's rate of inflation should be within 1.5 per cent of the average of the three lowest inflation rates in the Community.
- Its long-term interest rate should be within 2 per cent of the average interest rate of the three lowest inflation countries in the Community.
- Its fiscal budget deficit should not exceed 3 per cent of GDP.
- The country's public debt/GDP ratio should be no more than 60 per cent or falling rapidly to that level.

As the deadline for EMU qualification approached countries indulged in a certain amount of financial window dressing or creative accountancy. Privatisation plans were speeded up and the proceeds used to lower the budget deficit. In France, a £5 billion France Telecom pensions rebate to the government was used to improve the budget figures. Many countries postponed expenditure to 1998 and accelerated receipts in 1997. Italy imposed a once-off EMU tax to 1997. The Belgian government was accused of selling churches! Even the German government indulged in creative accounting, postponing tax refunds until 1998, and at one stage proposing the use of the Bundesbank's gold reserves to reduce the fiscal deficit.

The decision on eligibility to participate in the EMU was taken over the 1998 May Day weekend at a summit held in Brussels. It was based on data for the fiscal outcomes for 1997.

The outcomes for each member state are shown in table 14.1. It may be seen that all countries, with the exception of Greece, met the deficit/GDP criterion. There was much less success in meeting the debt/GDP criterion, however, with countries like Belgium, Greece, Italy, the Netherlands, Spain and Sweden far outside the limit. It would seem that little attention was paid to the failure of several countries to meet this

Table 14.1
EMU qualification criteria, 1997

EU member	Deficit (Surplus)/GDP	Debt/GDP ratio	Inflation
Target	**3%**	**60%**	**2.7%**
Austria	2.5	66.1	1.1
Belgium	2.1	122.2	1.4
Denmark	(0.7)	65.1	1.9
Finland	0.9	55.8	1.3
France	3.0	58.0	1.3
Germany	2.7	61.3	1.4
Greece	4.0	108.7	5.4
Ireland	(0.9)	66.3	1.2
Italy	2.7	121.6	1.8
Luxembourg	(1.7)	6.7	1.4
Netherlands	1.4	72.1	1.8
Portugal	2.5	62.0	1.8
Spain	2.6	68.8	1.9
Sweden	0.8	76.6	1.9
UK	1.9	53.4	1.9

criterion. With regard to inflation, all states, with the exception of Greece, were inside the target. Greece was the only country deemed not to have satisfied the criteria. Denmark and the UK decided not to adopt the euro. Greece did eventually join the EMU on 1 January 2001.

CHAPTER 15

The European Central Bank and Economic Policy in EMU

15.1 INTRODUCTION

On 1 January 1999, the European Central Bank (ECB) assumed responsibility for monetary policy within the Eurozone. The countries that joined the EMU (collectively known as 'the Eurozone') surrendered their powers to make independent monetary policies to the ECB. Situated on Kaiserstrasse in Frankfurt some three miles away from the Bundesbank (the German Central Bank), the ECB formulates monetary policy for the Eurozone as a whole. This unprecedented experiment in supranational economic policy co-ordination is the subject of this and the next chapter. In this chapter we outline the design of the ECB, its policy objectives and how it formulates monetary policy. We conclude the chapter by outlining some potential problems in implementing monetary policy and by examining the experience up until the end of 2002.

15.2 THE DESIGN OF THE ECB

The Treaty on European Union was agreed in December 1991 and signed on 7 February 1992 in Maastricht. It entered into force on 1 November 1993. The *Maastricht Treaty* contains the statutes establishing the European Monetary Institute (EMI) and the European System of Central Banks (ESCB). The EMI was founded in January 1994 as a precursor of a fully-fledged ECB. The national central banks of the EU contributed ECU615 million to the EMI and the income from this was used to finance its running costs. (An ECU was the equivalent of one euro in January 1999.) In July 1998, the EMI was replaced by the ECB. The ECB will remain a relatively small institution relying on national central banks to perform functions such as bank supervision and regulation at national level.

The new *European System of Central Banks* (ESCB) consists of the ECB and the national central banks of the Eurozone countries (figure 15.1). The ECB is managed by an *Executive Board*, comprising of the president and vice-president of the ECB and four other members, appointed by 'common accord' by the heads of the Eurozone states for an eight-year non-renewable term. Table 15.1 lists the names of the people appointed to the inaugural executive board in May 1998.

The Executive Board is responsible for the day-to-day implementation of monetary policy and giving instructions to the national central banks. The most important decision-making body of the ECB is the *Governing Council*, comprising the governors of the national central banks of the Eurozone countries plus the members of the

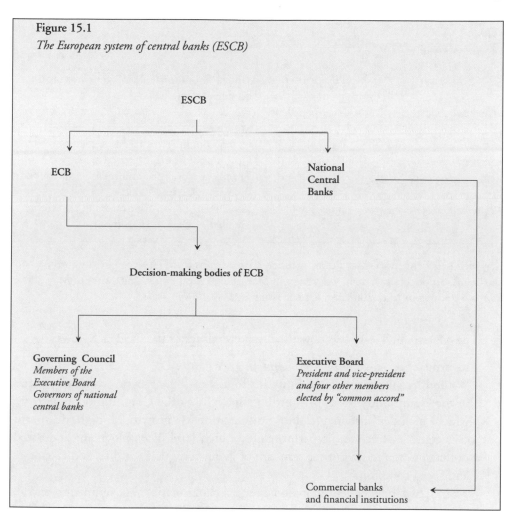

Figure 15.1

The European system of central banks (ESCB)

ESCB

ECB

National Central Banks

Decision-making bodies of ECB

Governing Council
Members of the Executive Board Governors of national central banks

Executive Board
President and vice-president and four other members elected by "common accord"

Commercial banks and financial institutions

Executive Board of the ECB. The Governing Council is responsible for formulating all aspects of monetary policy within the Eurozone. Decisions are taken by simple majority voting, with the president having a casting vote. The Executive Board implements the decisions of the Governing Council and, when appropriate, sends instructions to the national central banks.

Note:

Selecting four members by 'common accord' can prove difficult. There was disagreement about who should be the president of the ECB. The Germans favoured the Dutch former finance minister, Willem (or Wim) Duisenberg, (who was the president of the EMI from 1997–98) but the French put forward their own central banker Jean Claude Trichet. Over an 'eleven-hour lunch' at the Brussels summit in May 1998, a compromise was reached. Wim Duisenberg was appointed president but only after he announced that he would not serve his full eight-year term. He has said he will step down in August 2003 and may be replaced by the French Central Bank Governor Jean Claude Trichet. At the time of writing Mr Trichet is involved in a court case. He is accused of knowing that the French bank Crédit Lyonnais falsified accounts and did nothing to rectify the situation. Only if acquitted will Mr Trichet succeed Mr Duisenberg. The

Table 15.1
Executive board of ECB

Wim Duisenberg	President	Dutch Economist, IMF governor, former president of the EMI.
Christian Noyer	Vice-president	French Civil servant in French finance ministry.
Otmar Issing	German	Chief economist at the Bundesbank.
Sirkka Hamalainen	Finnish	Governor of Finnish Central Bank.
Eugenio Domingo Solans	Spanish	Academic economist and member of council of Spanish Central Bank.
Tommaso Padoa-Schioppa	Italian	Economist, Italian Central Bank and former member of Delors committee.

new vice-president (until May 2006) will be G. Papademos from Greece. The only woman on the board, Sirkka Hamalainen, will resign in May 2003, Domingo Solans retires in May 2004, Padoa-Schioppa in May 2005 and Otmar Issing in May 2006.

The Maastricht Treaty lays down the responsibilities of the ECB as follows:

- Its primary responsibility is to *maintain price stability*.
- Without prejudice to price stability, it also supports 'the general economic policies in the Community' so as to contribute to realising the Community's objectives, which include 'sustainable and non-inflationary growth, a high degree of convergence of economic performance, a high level of employment and social protection, the raising of the standard of living and quality of life, and economic and social cohesion.'
- The ECB is independent of national central banks, national governments, and all other bodies in formulating policy: 'Neither the ECB, nor a national central bank, nor any member of their decision-making bodies shall seek or take advice from Community institutions or bodies, from any government of a member state or from any other body.'
- The ECB may not lend to any Community institution or government.

In practice, price stability is the ECB's overriding objective. The commitment to promoting the general economic policies of the Community is too vague to be of much significance. We now turn to a discussion of what is meant by 'price stability'.

15.3 WHAT IS 'PRICE STABILITY'?

The economist Milton Friedman suggested the 'price stability' should mean an inflation rate of zero. However, there are a number of problems with this definition of 'price stability'. Firstly, there is the problem of accurately measuring the 'true' rate of inflation with conventional indices such as the Consumer Price Index (CPI) or the EU Harmonised Index of Consumer Prices (HICP). The Boskin Commission in the US reported in 1996 that indices of this sort tend to overestimate the 'true' rate of inflation

---

Box 15.1
The Fed and the ESCB

There are close parallels between the structure of the US Federal Reserve System (the Fed) and the ESCB. The Federal Reserve System consists of twelve Federal Reserve Districts (each with its own Federal Reserve Bank) and the Federal Reserve Board of Governors in Washington, D.C. The President of the United States appoints the seven members of the board for fourteen-year terms of office. The chairman of the board is appointed for a four-year term and considered to be the most powerful monetary policy maker in the world. (The current chairman is Alan Greenspan.) The twelve-member *Federal Open Market Committee* (FOMC) comprises five of the twelve presidents of the Federal Reserve District Banks and the seven members of the Federal Reserve Board. This Committee has been described as the 'most powerful group of private citizens in America' because it formulates America's monetary policy.

The relationship of the national central banks of the Eurozone to the Governing Council of the ESCB will be similar to that of the Federal Reserve Districts (Boston, New York, Chicago, San Francisco, Philadelphia, Cleveland, St. Louis, Kansas City, Atlanta, Richmond, Dallas and Minneapolis) to the Federal Reserve Board and the FOMC. It remains to be seen if the president of the ECB will come to rival the global influence of the chairman of the Fed.

---

by 1 to 2 per cent a year. Research in Germany arrived at a similar conclusion regarding their measure of inflation. This overstatement is due to the failure to allow for shifting patterns of expenditure, for improvements in the quality of consumer goods, and for the growing importance of shopping at discount retail outlets and in sales.

Consider, for example, the effect of changes in 'quality' on a price index. The price of a personal computer in 2003 is much the same as it was in 1988. A price index would therefore suggest no change in its price over the period and a zero inflation rate for this item. However, the power of computers has increased a thousand-fold since 1988. In this sense the quality of the machine has improved dramatically. The price of a *constant quality* computer (assuming it were available) would have fallen dramatically. Conventional price indexes do not take improvements in quality fully into account and therefore overestimate inflation.

A second issue is that it is not possible to maintain inflation equal to zero at all times. This suggests that it could be appropriate to set an *inflation band* as the target. That is an upper and lower limit for inflation. So long as the inflation rate remains within the specified band, it could be deemed that the 'price stability' had been attained. However, the use of an inflation band introduces a degree of subjectivity as some economists may argue for a narrow band and others might favour a wide band. Note that it is undesirable to allow the inflation rate to fall too low as well as to rise too high. A negative rate of inflation — deflation — could pose serious problems for a modern economy.

A third issue is that there is no uniform inflation rate in the Eurozone countries. As may be seen from table 15.2, there were significant differences in inflation in 2002. The rate of inflation in Ireland, Greece and the Netherlands is more than twice the rate in France, and Germany; the differential between the highest (Ireland) and lowest (Germany) inflation rates was about 3.5 percentage points. The ECB target is a weighted average of inflation rates in the Eurozone and ignores regional differences.

Table 15.2
Inflation rates in the Eurozone, March 2001 to March 2002

	%
Austria	1.7
Belgium	2.5
Finland	2.6
France	2.1
Germany	1.9
Greece	4.4
Ireland	5.1
Italy	2.5
Luxembourg	1.7
Netherlands	4.3
Portugal	3.3
Spain	3.3
Average	2.5

Source: Central Statistics Office, Dublin, 2002.

The ECB has opted for an *inflation target of 0–2 per cent*. We discuss the ECB's record in achieving this target later in this chapter.

15.4 CENTRAL BANK INDEPENDENCE

The Maastricht Treaty contains several provisions that make the ECB extremely free from political interference. It is only required to present an annual report on its activities to the European Parliament, the Council of Ministers and the Commission. The parliament may decide to hold a debate on the report, but it has no powers to sanction the members of the ECB's Governing Council. This means that the ECB is not directly accountable to elected politicians or the public. This level of independence is even greater than that of the Bundesbank and the US Federal Reserve Bank. The Bundesbank is ultimately subject to the German parliament and the Fed to the US Congress. However, neither the European parliament nor the national parliaments can interfere with the ECB. It would require a revision of the Maastricht Treaty — ratified by referendum in all the EU member states — to alter this.

Furthermore, unlike the Bank of England, the ECB does not publish the minutes of governing council meetings. It is argued that this would create a 'false transparency' and force all important decisions to take place 'in the corridor'. This lack of accountability, however, gives rise to the accusation that there is a 'democratic deficit'. That is, a small number of non-elected individuals have control over key macro-economic policy instruments and are not accountable to parliament or the public. This is part of the reason why the British, Danes, and Swedes decided not to join EMU in the first wave.

Why should the ECB have such exceptional autonomy? The answer is that independence from political pressure is seen as essential in achieving low inflation. There are two main dimensions to the argument: the historical record and the problem of 'time inconsistent and inflation bias'.

THE HISTORICAL RECORD

Figure 15.2 shows the relationship between central bank independence and inflation for a sample of countries. Measured along the horizontal axis is the average annualised inflation rate for each country over the period 1960–90. An index of central bank dependence is measured along the vertical axis. This index is compiled by reference to legal provisions relating to:

- Appointment and dismissal of the governor
- Procedures for the formation of monetary policy
- Objectives of the central bank
- Limitations on lending by the central bank.

The minimum score of zero indicates no independence and a maximum score of one indicates complete independence.

Note:

The data in figure 15.2 is derived from D. Williams and R. Reid, 'A central bank for Europe', in P. Temperton (ed.), *The Euro*, John Wiley and Sons, 1997.

The trend line running through the scatter plot shows an inverse relationship indicating that the greater the independence of the central bank, the lower the average inflation rate. The Bundesbank, the Swiss and Austrian central banks are reckoned to be very independent of political influences and to have delivered low inflation. In

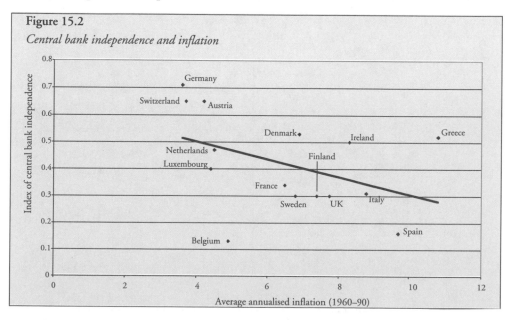

Figure 15.2

Central bank independence and inflation

contrast, the Banco de Espána is at the other end of the spectrum. The central banks of Belgium and Greece appear to be the two most obvious out-liners. While there are a number of misgivings about the validity of this type of analysis, particularly in relation to the construction of the 'independence index', the findings tend to confirm that independence is a prerequisite for the attainment of low inflation.

INFLATION BIAS AND TIME INCONSISTENCY

A second rationale for central bank independence is the problem of *inflation bias* and *time inconsistency*. To understand this problem, consider figure 15.3, which shows the aggregate supply (AS) and aggregate demand (AD) model developed in earlier chapters. Suppose the economy is initially at the point A, which is on the natural real GNP line. An increase in the money supply will shift the AD curve up to the right and the economy moves to the point B. In the short run, the effect of the increase in the money supply is to increase *both* the price level and real GNP. However, at the point B, real wages have fallen. This is because the price level has increased while nominal wages remain unchanged. Workers will now demand an increase in nominal wages to restore the original real wage and the AS curve will shift up to the left. Eventually, the economy reverts to the point C and natural real GNP. In the long-term, the effect of the increase in the money supply has been a proportionate increase in the price level and no change in real GNP.

    This means that monetary policy has no long-run effect on the real economy. A monetary expansion will increase the price level but will have no effect on real variables such as the growth rate and the rate of unemployment. In the *short run*, however, a

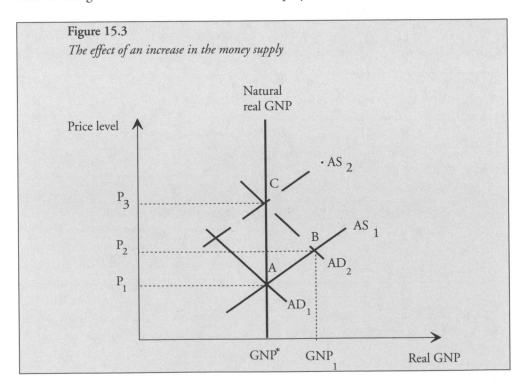

Figure 15.3
The effect of an increase in the money supply

surprise expansionary monetary policy could be used to boost output and employment at the expense of higher inflation.

The problem is that politicians are (time) inconsistent in their commitment to curbing inflation. On assuming office it makes sense for them to declare that they are committed to price stability, but sooner or later and especially at election time, they will opt for lower unemployment (*time inconsistency*) and become biased against curbing inflation (*inflation bias*). That is, they may try to get re-elected by exploiting the movement along the short-run AS curve. If policy makers are subservient to politicians they will be obliged to engineer the desired surprise inflation.

An early example of this occurred in March 1999 when the German finance minister of the day, Oskar Lafontaine, put pressure on the ECB to cut interest rates in order to stimulate the stagnant EU economy. Relations between Lafontaine and the ECB president Wim Duisenberg became very heated and the episode only ended when Lafontaine was removed from office. The existence of inflation bias and the time inconsistency problem is a reason for *institutionalising* central bank independence.

WILL ECB INDEPENDENCE ENSURE PRICE STABILITY?

Most of the countries joining EMU believe that handing control of monetary policy to the ECB will increase their anti-inflation commitment. This is part of the rationale for abandoning independent national monetary policies and adopting the single currency.

Note:

In the case of Germany, however, this rationale does not apply because initially at least the ECB will not enjoy anti-inflation credentials as strong as the Bundesbank's. This explains why the EMU project is not popular with the German public. It also raises the question of why German politicians are so committed to EMU. One explanation is that it allows Germany to shed the burden of being the economy that sets European monetary policy.

For this hope to be realised, the ECB must be seen to be independent of all political interference. Its independence and commitment to fighting inflation will also be enhanced by the fact that hard-nosed men (and women) will be appointed to its decision-making bodies, the Executive Board and Governing Council. The appointees will all be European central bankers who have presided over the implementation of the Maastricht convergence criteria in their own countries and they may be expected to be even more hard-nosed when moved from their national sphere to Frankfurt.

However, while independence is a necessary condition for achieving low inflation it is not a guarantee of success. Firstly, it assumes that the ECB can effectively control inflation through its policy instruments, principally its willingness to raise interest rates to reduce inflationary pressures, regardless of how unpopular this proves to be with the general public. The ECB has shown considerable resolve on this front, holding interest rates relatively high in the course of 2002 despite the slowdown in the major European economies. They have been clearly anxious to establish their anti-inflationary reputation from the start.

Secondly, while the present ECB President and board are clearly committed to tough anti-inflation policies, there is no guarantee that their successors will be as hard-nosed.

A third and potentially more serious problem is that the Eurozone countries have different social and political structures, and their politicians have different preferences concerning the short-run trade-off between price stability and unemployment. Some may not be as willing as others to allow unemployment to rise in order to avert or reduce inflation. A situation could arise in which the Governing Council wished to prevent a rise in inflation after an adverse supply-side shock. The resultant increase in unemployment would be extremely unpopular and would be blamed on the ECB. Politicians in member states may find a faceless international bank in Frankfurt a suitable target for their rhetoric when the economic going gets tough. It remains to be seen if the independence of the ECB would survive this sort of crisis.

15.5 Monetary Policy in the EMU

The ECB's monetary policy is referred to as the *Eurosystem's Stability Orientated Monetary Policy Strategy*. This policy, described by the ECB as a 'new and distinct strategy', involves the interaction between two pillars. These pillars are the *quantity theory of money* and *inflation targeting*.

Pillar 1: the quantity theory of money
As discussed in chapter 7, the formula for the quantity theory is:

$$\Delta M^s + \Delta V = \Delta \text{real GNP} + \pi \tag{1}$$

$$4.5\% - (0.5 - 1\%) = (2 - 2.5\%) + (0 - 2\%)$$

In using the quantity theory for policy purposes, the starting point is to first decide on the inflation (π) objective. As already mentioned, the ECB's target is to keep inflation inside a band of 0–2 per cent. The second step is to forecast the percentage change in velocity (ΔV) and the real growth rate (Δreal GNP) for the coming year. For 2002, economists at the ECB forecast that velocity will fall by 0.5 to 1 per cent and that the real growth rate will be between 2–2.5 per cent. On the basis of the inflation target and the forecasts, it follows from equation (1) that the ECB should strive to keep the percentage change in the money supply to 4.5 per cent per annum. This is the growth in the money supply consistent with the inflation target.

Note:
The ECB does not attempt to control the money supply 'mechanistically'. To allow for temporary fluctuations, the ECB focuses on 'a three month moving average of a twelve month growth in the broad money supply'.

If the ECB achieves its inflation target, then European, British and US inflation rates should be very similar — all close to 2 per cent. It follows that over the long run the euro, dollar and sterling exchange rates should be relatively stable. Secondly, from the Fisher equation, low inflation should lead to low nominal interest rates. Price stability, therefore, is the key to a strong currency and low nominal interest rates.

DISCLOSURE AND FINANCIAL SPECULATION

Note that the ECB has announced a specific reference rate for the growth in the broad money supply. Hence, if the actual growth in the money supply is above the 4.5 per cent target, the ECB could be expected to reduce the money supply. Conversely, if the growth in the actual money supply is below the 4.5 per cent target, the ECB could be expected to act to increase the growth of the money supply. As illustrated in figure 15.4, (see also chapter 8) the supply (M^s) and the demand (M^d) for money determines the interest rate (i). The location, or position, of the M^d curve is determined by nominal GNP. An increase in GNP shifts the M^d curve upwards and vice versa. Given the demand for money, changes in the money supply will result in opposite changes in nominal interest rates (i). As shown in figure 15.4, an increase in the money supply leads to lower interest rates.

Pulling the two strands together, a comparison of the actual growth in the money supply relative to the 4.5 per cent target, may give an indication, *ceteris paribus*, of how interest rates might move in the future.

Going a stage further, there is also an inverse relationship between interest rates and bond prices (see table 8.1, chapter 8.) An increase in interest rates will lead to a fall in bond prices. Conversely, a fall in interest rates will lead to a rise in bond prices. Using the ECB's pillar 1, it is therefore possible that a treasury manager or a speculator could formulate a 'rule' to make capital gains or avoid capital losses on the bond market.

For example, if the actual growth in the money supply is above the 4.5 per cent reference rate, the expectation is that the ECB will cut the money supply thereby raising interest rates. A treasury manager should therefore sell bonds, before this happens, in order to avoid incurring a capital loss. Conversely, if the growth in the money supply is below the 4.5 per cent reference rate, the likelihood is that interest rates will fall in the future. A speculator should, in this instance, buy bonds in the hope of making a capital gain.

If the ECB's money supply and inflation targets can be used to formulate 'rules' to profit from the bond market, this raises the question as to why the ECB is divulging

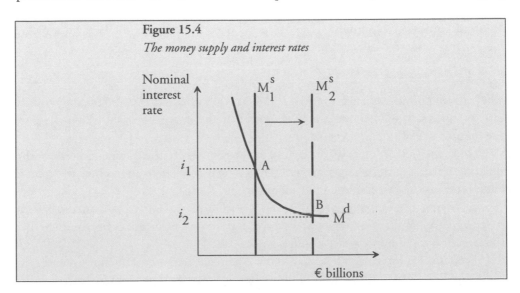

Figure 15.4
The money supply and interest rates

such information? The answer is that the ECB's wants its inflation policy to be *transparent* in the hope that the inflation target provides an *anchor* for the public's inflation expectations. In addition, the ECB is a new institution, managing a new currency and it has to establish a reputation for being hard-nosed and committed to fighting inflation. By outlining its inflation target and policy, the ECB increases its accountability and allows the public to evaluate its performance. In this way it can establish its reputation over time.

THE EVIDENCE

As discussed in chapter 7, there are a number of problems with using the quantity theory for policy purposes. As shown in figure 15.3, for example, a change in the money supply can effect real output and unemployment in the short run. The ECB is, however, taking a long-run perspective and comments that 'One of the most remarkable empirical regularities in macroeconomics is the stable long-run relationship between the price level and money' ('The Monetary Policy of the ECB', *European Central Bank*, 2001, 47).

However, empirical tests of the quantity theory are by no means conclusive (see section 7.5 in Chapter 7). In general, the results suggest that the relationship between changes in the money supply and interest rate, on the one hand, and inflation and real growth rates, on the other hand, is unpredictable and uneven across the Eurozone. Furthermore, there appears to be a much stronger relationship between the change in money supply and the real growth rate and between interest rates and the real growth rate especially in the short run. None the less, the German Bundesbank relied heavily on monetary targeting and the influence of the Bundesbank on the ECB assures that this approach will be used for the foreseeable future.

PILLAR 2: INFLATION TARGETING

Although not explicitly mentioned by the ECB, pillar 2 of the ECB's monetary policy is very similar to the 'inflation targeting' approach that has become fashionable in recent years. This approach can be explained by reference to the so-called *Taylor rule* (after the Stanford University economist, John Taylor). Taylor showed that the behaviour of the US Federal Reserve Bank could be closely modelled by the following rule:

$$i = i^T + \alpha\,(\pi^F - \pi^T) - \beta(U^F - U_N) \qquad (2)$$

where i is the nominal interest rate, π is the inflation rate and U is the unemployment rate. A super-script F denotes a *forecast* variable and T a *target* variable. U_n represents the natural rate of unemployment.

The α coefficient indicates the central bank's response to the difference between the inflation forecast and the target rate ($\pi^F - \pi^T$). The β coefficient shows how the central bank reacts to the forecast unemployment gap ($U^F - U_N$).

In arriving at its interest rate target (i^T) the ECB may assume a *real* interest rate of 3 per cent and an inflation target of 2 per cent. It follows from the *Fisher equation* that the target nominal interest rate would be 5 per cent.

If inflation is forecast to be equal to the 2 per cent target and unemployment is at the natural rate, then the bank would leave interest rates at 5 per cent.

If, however, the inflation rate is forecast to rise above the target rate of 2 per cent, the central bank will increase the interest rate. This rise in interest rates could be expected to reduce aggregate demand, which, in turn, would reduce inflation. Conversely, if inflation were forecast to fall below the target rate of 2 per cent, interest rates would be reduced. This should inject a stimulus into the economy.

Note:

This α coefficient can be expected to be greater than one because the rise in interest rates must be greater than the predicted rise in inflation so as to ensure an increase in the real interest rate. If, for example, inflation was forecast to rise by 1 per cent (above target) and the central bank reacted by raising interest rates by, say, 1.5 per cent, the real interest rates would increase by 0.5 per cent. This would deflate the economy and curtail inflation.

The emphasis here is very much on the future or forecast inflation rate. Even if the current inflation rate is very close to the target rate, the ECB may still raise interest rates if it forecasts a rise in inflation in the future. In this sense, the policy is a *pre-emptive strike*, which is designed to prevent deviation from its target rate of inflation.

As mentioned, the coefficient, β, determines the response of the central bank to the forecast unemployment gap. However, because the ECB is primarily concerned with price stability, the forecast unemployment gap may not have an important bearing on its decision to change interest rates. In this case, the β coefficient might be expected to be near zero. The more hard-nosed or inflation-adverse the central bank, the larger will be α and the smaller β.

The inflation targeting approach was adopted in the 1990s in Canada, New Zealand, Australia, Israel, Sweden, Finland, Spain and the UK among other countries. New Zealand pioneered the approach by signing a Policy Targets Agreement in 1990, setting the target inflation rate in the range between 0–3 per cent and raising the possibility that the governor of the Central Bank would be fired if this target was not met. (The target was missed during the 1990s. The governor was not dismissed.)

The UK adopted a target of 2.5 + 1 per cent in 1992. Similar targets were subsequently adopted by the other countries listed above, except for Israel, which set a target range of 8–11 per cent.

As with pillar 1, it is intended that this inflation targeting approach will act as an anchor for the public's inflation expectations. By making the policy clear, understandable and transparent, the ECB is hoping the policy will be credible and the public will adopt it in formulating inflation expectations. If this is the case, the inflation target may be a self-fulfilling prophecy. This would be the case if the inflation target had a strong bearing on wage demands. If the trade unions anticipate a low inflation rate next year, then they may settle for a low nominal wage increase. If, on the other hand, a high inflation rate is anticipated then this could lead to high wage demands. It is essential, therefore, that the public believes the inflation target will be achieved as this will minimise the rise in costs and wages.

PROBLEMS WITH INFLATION TARGETING

One of the major problems with the inflation targeting approach is to accurately forecast inflation. Inflation is very difficult to forecast even over a short-term horizon. Different economic models may result in different forecasts and there is no agreement on which economic model is best. In addition there is the problem of identifying external shocks and projecting their influence on inflation.

A second problem is that to successfully forecast inflation, the structure of the economy must be stable and easily modelled. The Eurozone, however, represents a *regime shift* creating behavioural, institutional and structural uncertainties. This means that there could be a breakdown of old empirical relationships and this makes forecasting difficult. Furthermore, there is no long-run HICP data and this introduces a measurement bias into the forecast.

The ECB has stated that it will use a 'broad base assessment' in forecasting inflation. This means that the ECB will use 'leading indicators' such as the trend in price indices, labour costs, exchange rates, bond prices, measures of real economic activity, fiscal policy indicators, business and consumer surveys.

A third problem with the inflation targeting approach is that changes in interest rates may have a long and variable effect on the inflation rate. Given that the inflation rate itself is changing over time, the ECB is aiming at a moving target. As the late American economist Rudiger Dornbusch commented: 'Shooting at a moving target in the fog is no easy task.' Skill and luck are required if the inflation target is to be achieved.

CONSISTENCY BETWEEN THE TWO PILLARS

Pillar 1 involves controlling the growth rate of money whereas pillar 2 entails targeting the nominal interest rate (the i^T variable in equation [2]). One potential problem with this is that it is not possible to simultaneously target *both* the money supply and the interest rate and, as such, pillar 1 and 2 may not be entirely consistent.

To see this, consider figure 15.5, which shows equilibrium in the money market. In the left-hand diagram, the central bank pursues a money supply target approach. This involves keeping the M^s curve constant in order to achieve an inflation target. However, because the M^d curve shifts up (due to higher GNP), the interest rate rises. Conversely, if the M^d curve moved down, interest rates would fall. Hence, if the central bank pursues a constant M^s target, it loses control over interest rates.

In the right-hand diagram, the central bank opts for an interest rate target which, from the Taylor rule, it deems appropriate. In this instance, the central bank varies the money supply in order to accommodate changes in the demand for money and thereby keeps interest rates constant. As the M^d curve shifts up, the central bank increases M^s and interest rates remain at i_1. In this case, the central bank loses control over the money supply.

The two approaches to achieving an inflation target are therefore independent of each other. In practice, the central bank may opt for some compromise between them. Note, however, if the demand for money is very volatile or unpredictable, the central bank's job is considerably more difficult. Considerable research has gone into determining whether or not the M^d curve is a stable function of a few variables, such as nominal GNP. If the M^d curve is unstable, it may not be possible to use either the money supply or interest rate targeting approaches to achieve an inflation objective. It

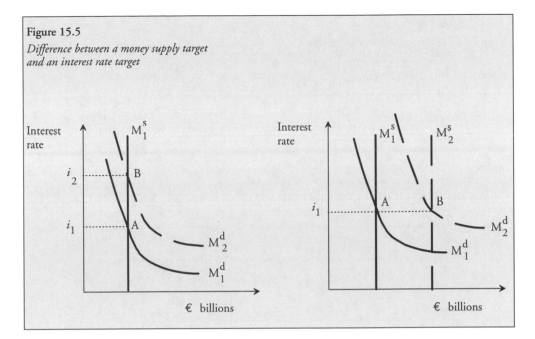

Figure 15.5

Difference between a money supply target and an interest rate target

is far from clear whether there will be a stable demand for money function across the EMU as a whole.

A second problem is that the quantity theory approach (pillar 1) and the inflation targeting approach (pillar 2) may give opposing signals. For example, in April 1999, the ECB cut interest rates by 0.5 per cent because the 'leading indicators' were pointing to a slowdown in inflation. However, the growth in the money supply was well above the target rate of 4.5 per cent and hence the cut in interest rates was inconsistent with pillar 1. In November 1999, the ECB raised interest rates by 0.5 per cent. On this occasion the two pillars were consistent as the growth in the money supply was above target and the 'leading indicators' were pointing to an increase in inflation. It is the prospect of opposing signals that raises the question of which pillar has priority? The inconsistency issue also has the potential to undermine the credibility of the overall policy.

THE RECORD UNTIL THE END OF 2002

Figure 15.6 shows the growth in the money supply in relation to the 4.5 per cent target. At no time since the start of EMU has the money supply been below the announced target. (In late 2001, the money supply expanded by 8 per cent but this was explained by the ECB as a 'rush into liquidity' following the September 11 attacks.)

Figure 15.7 shows the inflation rate relative to the 0–2 per cent band. Generally, the inflation record is reasonably good. A comparison of figures 15.6 and 15.7 raises the point made earlier in this chapter about the poor relationship between the growth in the money supply and inflation in the short-run. If the growth in the money supply has been well above target (figure 15.6) how is it that the inflation rate has been so close to target (figure 15.7)? If there was a strong relationship between money and inflation, the two series could be expected to move (allowing for lags) in tandem. But this does not seem to be the case and this raises doubts about the ECB's underlying monetary strategy.

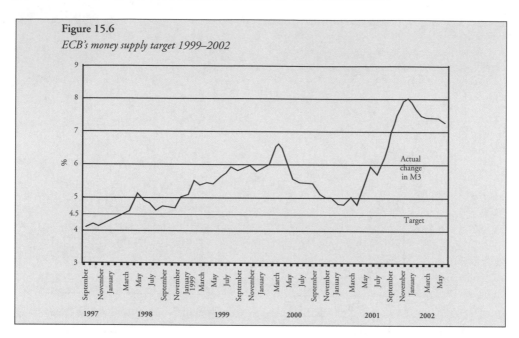

Figure 15.6

ECB's money supply target 1999–2002

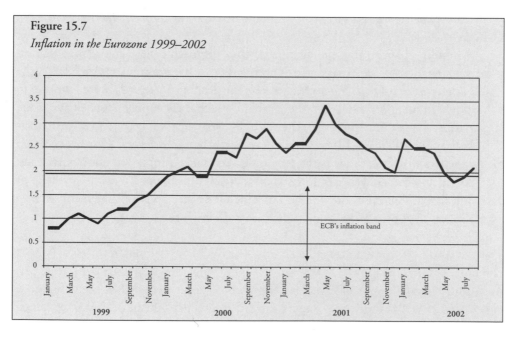

Figure 15.7

Inflation in the Eurozone 1999–2002

15.6 CONCLUSION

In this chapter we discussed the framework within which monetary policy is formulated in the Eurozone. Among the main points discussed were:

- The constitution and structure of the ECB
- The independence of the ECB from political pressures
- The main objective of the ECB — to maintain price stability
- The two pillars underling the formulation of monetary policy.

CHAPTER 16

Interest Rate, Exchange Rate and Fiscal Policy in the Eurozone

16.1 INTRODUCTION

In this chapter we study the conduct of monetary and fiscal policy in the Eurozone. We begin by explaining how a variable money multiplier can make it difficult for the European Central Bank (ECB) to control the money supply. This is followed by a discussion of the various ECB interest rates and how these rates are used to influence commercial interest rates. We then discuss the determinants, other than the ECB, of commercial interest rates in the Eurozone. We then turn to a discussion of the euro exchange rate and how the ECB must engage in 'sterilisation' if it intervenes to support this exchange rate. The final sections of the chapter examine fiscal policy in the Eurozone and, in particular, the Stability and Growth Pact.

16.2 CONTROLLING THE MONEY SUPPLY

Earlier in chapter 6 we defined *high-powered money* (H) or the *monetary base* as being equal to currency in circulation (CU) plus commercial bank reserves at the central bank (RE).

$$H = CU + RE \tag{1}$$

The money supply (M3) was defined as being equal to currency in circulation (CU) plus deposits in commercial banks (D).

$$M^s = CU + D \tag{2}$$

Using these two definitions, we derived the following equation:

$$M^s = [(c_p + 1)/(c_p + r_b)]H \tag{3}$$

The term c_p is a coefficient $(0 < c_p < 1)$ which relates currency holdings (CU) to current and deposit accounts (D).

$$CU = c_p D \tag{4}$$

Similarly, the term r_b is a coefficient $(0 < r_b < 1)$ which shows the relationship between commercial bank reserves at the Central Bank (RE) to current and deposit accounts (D).

$$RE = r_b D \tag{5}$$

The term $[(c_p + 1)/(c_p + r_b)]$ is the money multiplier and it provides the link between high-powered money and the money supply. The smaller the c_p and r_b coefficients the larger will be the money multiplier and vice versa. This suggests that the public, the banks and the central bank (the ECB) all play a role in determining the money supply.

It follows from equation (3) that the ECB can control the money supply providing the money multiplier is stable and the terms CU and RE (and therefore H) can be regulated. In practice, however, controlling the money supply is no easy task. Earlier in chapter 6 we mentioned some of the problems involved. Here we identify another problem, namely instability in the money multiplier. In particular, if the c_p and the r_b coefficients change over time so too will the multiplier and this makes the relationship between H and M^s unstable.

FACTORS INFLUENCING THE MONEY MULTIPLIER

The c_p coefficient is generally stable and predictable but, from time to time, the coefficient can be influenced by external developments. In late 2001, for example, following the September 11 terrorist attack there was a 'rush to liquidity' and currency holdings as a proportion of deposits increased significantly. The increase in c_p would have the effect of reducing the money multiplier.

Of greater concern is the r_b coefficient because this is a function of a number of factors. These include:

- The interest rate foregone in holding excess reserves (i). The higher this rate the less inclined banks will be to hold excess reserves and vice versa.
- The cost of borrowing when a bank is short of reserves (i_d). The higher this rate the more likely banks will be to hold reserves.
- The minimum reserve ratio stipulated by the ECB (rr). The higher this minimum reserve, the more reserves the banks must maintain.
- The uncertainty of net deposit flows (σ). The more volatile deposit flows are, the greater the excess reserves a bank will tend to keep.

Taking these factors together:

$$r_b = f(i, i_d, rr, \sigma) \tag{4}$$

Equation (4) indicates that the r_b coefficient is itself a function of interest rates. The more volatile interest rates are, the greater is the variability of the r_b coefficient and the money multiplier, and the more difficult it will be to control the overall money supply.

16.3 THE ECB'S INTEREST RATE POLICY

The key interest rates in the Eurozone are EONIA (Euro overnight index average) and the 1, 3, 6, and 12 month EURIBOR (Euro inter-bank offer rates). EONIA is described as a 'weighted average of overnight loans made by a panel of banks most active in the money markets'. These rates are determined on the European inter-bank market. This is a market where banks and other financial institutions lend (supply) and borrow (demand) money from each other for periods ranging from a day to a year. This inter-bank market has no exact location. It is a market conducted through computers, telephones, fax and telex machines. The forces of supply and demand in this market determine the EONIA and EURIBOR interest rates.

These inter-bank interest rates are crucially important because of their influence on all the other interest rates in the banking system. When EONIA changes, the commercial banks and building societies quickly change their lending and deposit interest rates because they are heavily dependent on the inter-bank market as a source of funds.

The ECB exercises an important influence on the inter-bank rate through the rate at which it is willing to lend to the banks. As the ECB points out, 'The euro area banking system — due to its needs for banknotes and the obligation to fulfil reserve requirements — has an aggregate liquidity deficit and is reliant on refinancing from the Eurosystem.' (*The Monetary Policy of the ECB*, European Central Bank, 2001, 73.)

Because the ECB is a supplier of funds to the money markets, it is in a position to steer interest rates (EONIA), signal the stance of monetary policy and manage the liquidity position in the money market.

Note:
TARGET (Trans-European Automated Real-time Gross Settlement Express Transfer) is a cross-border payments system in central bank money. The system enables payments or debts to be settled quickly and this increases the integration of the Eurozone money market and the implementation of monetary policy. Each country has a RTGS (real-time gross settlement) system at the national central bank (NCB). Each national RTGS is then linked through TARGET. The use of the NCB's means that TARGET is a decentralised system and this minimises the administrative structure at the centre, which would be required to manage 8,000 financial institutions in the Eurozone. In 2001, the system catered for transfers of €1,500 billion per day, 90 per cent of which were inter-bank payments.

INSTRUMENTS OF MONETARY POLICY

The ECB has a number of techniques that it uses to influence liquidity and interest rates. These include:

1. Open-market operations
This instrument consists of:
    (a)   Main refinancing operations
    (b)   Longer-term refinancing operations
    (c)   Fine-tuning operations
    (d)   Structural operations
    (e)   Standing facilities
2. Compulsory deposits held at the ECB (required reserves)
3. Outright purchase or sale of government bonds or securities

We now explain briefly each of these instruments.

1. OPEN-MARKET OPERATIONS

Main refinancing operations

This involves the purchase of marketable public or private debt instruments or the provision of credit against eligible assets (collateral). In terms of the ECB's balance sheet (table 16.1), loans to the commercial banks increase on the asset side and commercial bank reserves increase on the asset side. Overall, high-powered money and the money supply will increase.

Table 16.1
European Central Bank balance sheet

Assets	Liabilities
External reserves	Currency
Loans:	Commercial bank reserves
Banks	
Government	Government deposits
Government securities	
Other	Other
High-powered money (H)	High-powered money (H)

The purchase of debt is under a reverse agreement. That is a *repurchase agreement*, or REPO, which provides funds for a limited period (usually two weeks). This technique is 'liquidity-providing' only. It cannot be used to absorb liquidity. It is executed in a decentralised manner by the NCBs and the interest rate charged on this source of funds is called the *main refinancing interest rate* (MRIR). By raising or lowering this rate, the ECB sends a signal about the direction in which it wants interest rates to move throughout the Eurozone.

Note:
A repurchase agreement involves the ECB lending money to the commercial banks at a fixed rate of interest for a fixed period. In return, a commercial bank transfers government stock or some private debt instrument to the ECB with an agreement that the banks will buy them back (repurchase) at the end of the period. This provides the banks with temporary additional reserves.

Longer-term refinancing operations

This source of finance is also 'liquidity-providing' and gives the commercial institutions access to longer-term finance, usually three months. This source of funds accounts for approximately 26 per cent of total open market operations.

Fine-tuning operations

This technique consists of 'reverse transactions', 'foreign currency swaps' or 'out-right purchases or sales'. It can be liquidity-providing or liquidity-absorbing and is designed to smooth the effects on interest rates of unexpected liquidity fluctuations in the money markets.

Note:
Commercial banks' holdings of foreign exchange are not included in banks' required reserves. If a bank has foreign exchange (e.g. dollars, sterling, yen) for use at a later date and is short of reserves, the foreign exchange can be temporarily swapped for funds at the ECB. This 'foreign currency swap' can be used both to inject liquidity into the market (the ECB swaps euros for foreign currency) or remove liquidity (the ECB swaps foreign currency for euros).

Structural facilities
This facility is aimed at changing the structural liquidity position of the Eurozone. This is the amount of liquidity in the market over the longer-term. This facility can be liquidity-providing or liquidity-absorbing. So far, the ECB has not made use of this facility.

Standing facilities
This is intended to restrict interest rate volatility by providing a *corridor* within which the overnight interest rate, EONIA, can fluctuate. There are two types:

- Marginal lending facility

Used for liquidity-providing only. It provides overnight funds at an interest rate higher than the market rate. The commercial institutions, therefore, only use it as a last resort and this acts as an interest rate ceiling. The interest rate charged on this facility is the *marginal lending rate*.

- Deposit facility

This facility absorbs liquidity only. Commercial institutions can make overnight deposits at a predetermined interest rate called the *deposit rate*. This rate is much lower than the market interest rate and is used by the commercial institutions only if funds cannot be put to any other use. The deposit interest rate acts as a floor for interest rates.

2. COMPULSORY DEPOSITS HELD AT THE ECB
The ECB can also influence liquidity in the money market by changing the required reserve ratio. A reduction in the required reserve ratio increases the liquidity of the banking system; an increase in the ratio lowers it. In 2002, the reserve requirement was set at 2 per cent of the 'reserve base' (mostly short-term deposits). Each financial institution is permitted to deduct an allowance of €100,000 to cover administrative costs. Compliance with the reserve base is based on the average of daily balances over a one-month maintenance period.

Figure 16.1, for example, shows how the reserve system works. If the banks were required to maintain the reserve on a daily basis this would lead to volatile interest rates. By allowing banks to average over a one-month period, reserve deficiencies at any particular time can be offset by a surplus at a later stage. The overall effect is to stabilise

Figure 16.1
The ECB's minimum reserve ratio

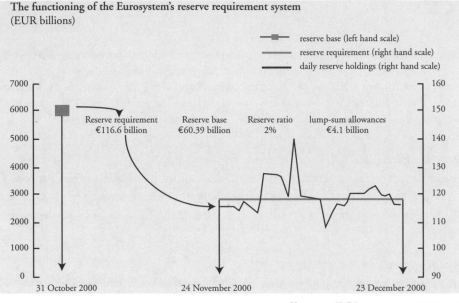

(Source: ECB, op. cit., 2001, 71)

interest rates because the banks do not have to borrow from, or lend to, the inter-bank market on a daily basis. The ECB pays the main refinancing interest rate on required reserves. An important side effect of the reserve ratio is that it makes the commercial institutions beholden to the ECB for refinancing. That is, it creates a demand for ECB funding and this enables the ECB to dictate interest rates.

3. OUTRIGHT PURCHASE OR SALE OF GOVERNMENT BONDS OR SECURITIES

This technique involves the ECB buying or selling government securities on the money market. Suppose, for example, the ECB purchases €1 billion government bonds from a commercial bank. In terms of the ECB's balance sheet (table 16.1) the entry for government securities increases on the asset side and bank reserves increase on the liability side. The result is that the monetary base or high-powered money increases and this sets off a multiple expansion in the money supply. Hence, by *buying* government stock, the central bank *increases* the money supply. Similarly by *selling* government stock, the central bank *decreases* the money supply.

Generally, when the ECB engages in the purchase or sale of government securities, it will back this up by also changing its own interest rates in the required direction.

INTERACTION BETWEEN THE VARIOUS INTEREST RATES AND OPEN MARKET OPERATIONS

Figure 16.2 shows the relationship between the key interest rates using daily data over the period January 1999 to December 2000. It can be seen that the ECB's main refinancing interest rate (MRIR) and EONIA move closely together. The reason for this is that the commercial institutions can get funding from either the inter-bank market or the ECB and hence the rates cannot differ very much. If, for example, EONIA was lower than MRIR, the banks would seek to borrow in the inter-bank market and this would soon drive EONIA upwards. Conversely, if EONIA was greater than MRIR, the banks would borrow from the ECB thereby reducing the demand for inter-bank funding. It also follows from this that changes in the MRIR will impact on EONIA and this, in turn, will affect all the commercial interest rates in the Eurozone.

The ECB's marginal lending rate and deposit rate act as a ceiling and a floor for MRIR and EONIA. It is only as a last resort that the commercial institutions will avail of these upper and lower rates and hence they act as a corridor for MRIR and EONIA.

It is clear from the foregoing that the ECB can have a major impact on interest rates' trends in the Eurozone. If, for example, it forms the view that European rates have fallen too low in relation to its objective of price stability, it may wish to nudge interest rates up on the inter-bank market. It can do this by increasing MRIR, the marginal lending rate and the deposit rate. Changes in these rates will quickly impact on the EONIA and EURIBOR rates. In addition, the ECB would back this up by creating a *liquidity shortage* by buying government securities. These measures will force up inter-bank interest rates, which, in turn, will raise interest rates across the Eurozone.

If, on the other hand, the ECB feels that a reduction in interest rates is warranted because of the possibility of deflation in Europe, interest rates can be lowered by doing the opposite to the above. In this way the ECB can use its interest rates and open market operations as a means of achieving its ultimate objective of price stability.

Figure 16.2
The ECB's interest rates and EONIA

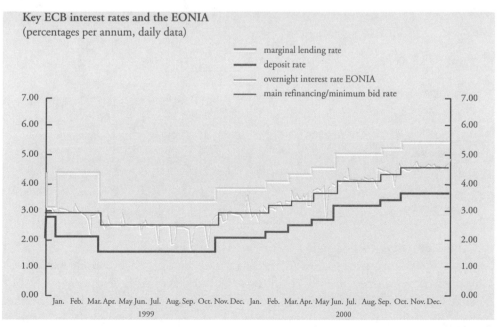

(*Source: ECB, op. cit., 2001, 64*)

16.4 OTHER FACTORS INFLUENCING INTEREST RATES IN THE EUROZONE

To understand how factors, other than the ECB, impact on Eurozone interest rates it is necessary to study the relationship between the balance sheets of the ECB and the commercial banks and how these interact with the European inter-bank money market. Figure 16.3 gives an overview of the inter-action between the ECB, the financial institutions and the inter-bank market.

The required reserve ratio is a crucial link in the determination of interest rates. The important point is that if a bank has a *deficiency* of reserves, it will borrow (*demand*) funds on the inter-bank market. Conversely, a bank with *excess* reserves will lend (*supply*) funds to the inter-bank market and earn interest on them. There is therefore a direct link between the adequacy of the banks' reserves (their liquidity) and the supply and demand for funds on the inter-bank market. If supply exceeds demand, EONIA will fall and, conversely, if supply is less than demand, EONIA will rise. Changes in EONIA will quickly impact on the whole spectrum of commercial bank interest rates.

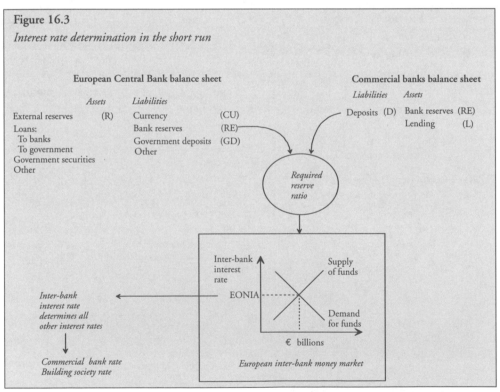

Figure 16.3

Interest rate determination in the short run

The alternative to borrowing in the inter-bank market is, of course, the ECB. Hence, if inter-bank interest rates are tending to rise, and the ECB considers this to be a desirable development, the ECB will raise its rates. As mentioned earlier it is not possible for the EONIA and the main refinancing interest rate to get too far out of line. Conversely, if the EONIA rate is tending to fall, the ECB will lower its rates if this is deemed to be consistent with the goal of maintaining price stability. In what follows, we examine the main factors impacting on the inter-bank market and the EONIA rate on the assumption that the ECB reacts passively to market trends.

The main influences on liquidity in the inter-bank market are:

- The balance of payments
- Changes in the public's holding of cash (CU)
- Bank lending
- Savings by the public
- Government borrowing.

We now examine how these variables influence liquidity in the money market and the EONIA interest rate.

THE BALANCE OF PAYMENTS

If the ECB pursues a fixed or 'dirty floating' exchange rate policy, a balance of payments deficit or surplus will be reflected in a change in the external reserves. This is because the ECB is intervening in the foreign exchange market: either buying or selling the euro. These changes in the external reserves (R) have an important influence on high-powered money and interest rates. In general, a change in the external reserves on the asset side of the ECB's balance sheet (table 16.1) will be reflected in changes in commercial banks' reserves (RE) on the liability side. In general:

$$\downarrow R \Leftrightarrow \downarrow RE \text{ (and vice versa)}$$

Note:
To illustrate this, consider a firm in Europe importing €1 million worth of computer parts from the US. When the importer first withdraws money from his or her account, deposits (D) and reserves (RE) decrease on the commercial bank balance sheet. The importer is now holding €1 million in currency. On the ECB's balance sheet, RE falls and CU increases. The importer now exchanges the domestic currency for dollars at the foreign exchange desk of the bank. The commercial bank holds only a small amount of foreign currency and is, in effect, only acting as an intermediary between the individual and the ECB. This foreign exchange transaction is reflected in the ECB balance sheet as a fall in CU (liability side) and a fall in the external reserves (R) on the asset side. Overall, on the ECB balance sheet, the fall in R is matched by an equal fall in RE (the change in CU was only temporary).

Suppose now that prior to the withdrawal of funds the banks had the correct reserves/deposit ratio to meet the required reserve ratio. Following the decrease in its reserves the bank will have a *deficiency* of reserves and to redress the situation will borrow from the inter-bank market (we ignore the possibility of borrowing from the ECB). This will put upward pressure on the EONIA and EURIBOR interest rates. Thus in general:

- A balance of payments *deficit* will reduce the commercial banks' reserves and lead to an increased *demand* for funds on the inter-bank market. Eurozone interest rates will rise.
- A balance of payments *surplus* will increase commercial banks' reserves and lead to an increase in the *supply* of funds on the inter-bank market and a reduction in interest rates.

As we pointed out in chapter 9, there are numerous short-run influences on the balance of payments and therefore the level of the external reserves. Among the main influences are:

- Inflation
- Currency speculation
- Interest rates
- Real growth rates.

If, for example, speculators expect a depreciation of the dollar/euro exchange rate, capital is transferred from euro to foreign currencies in anticipation of making a capital gain. This will be reflected in the ECB's balance sheet as a fall in R and RE, and the banks will have a deficiency of reserves. The demand for funds on the inter-bank market will increase and Eurozone interest rates will rise.

Up until the end of 2002, changes in the external reserves were not a major factor impacting on interest rates. This is because the ECB has pursued a flexible exchange rate policy with regard to the euro. That is, with the exception of a few instances, the ECB has not intervened in the foreign exchange market to influence the euro exchange rate. We discuss this issue in more detail in section 16.6.

CHANGES IN HOUSEHOLDS' CASH BALANCES

Net changes in cash balances or currency holdings (CU) by the public tend to be seasonal and reasonably predictable. For example, there is always a significant increase in currency holdings in the weeks leading up to Christmas. This involves withdrawals of money from commercial banks' deposit accounts. In this case:

$\downarrow D \Leftrightarrow \downarrow RE$ (*commercial banks'* balance sheet)

The increase in currency holdings will be reflected in:

$\uparrow CU \Leftrightarrow \downarrow RE$ (*ECB's* balance sheet)

If the increase in CU was unexpected, and banks were maintaining only the exact ratio of reserves to deposits, they would be forced to borrow on the inter-bank market and interest rates would tend to rise. Conversely, a fall in currency holdings would tend to reduce inter-bank interest rates.

PRIVATE SECTOR DEPOSITS

A similar analysis applies in the case of private sector deposits. An increase in private sector deposits, due to, say, an increase in savings, would lead to excess reserves. The supply of funds to the inter-bank market would increase and interest rates would tend to fall. Conversely, a slow down in the growth of bank deposits would be associated with a rise in Eurozone interest rates.

COMMERCIAL BANK LENDING

An upsurge in commercial bank lending, not brought about or matched by an increase in deposits, will reduce reserves and the banks may encounter a deficiency in relation to the reserve requirement. This will increase the demand for funds on the inter-bank market and interest rates will start to nudge upwards. Conversely, a fall-off in bank lending may be consistent will a decline in interest rates.

GOVERNMENT BORROWING

The financing of national governments' borrowing requirements has traditionally been a major influence on the liquidity of the commercial banks. However, in the context of the restrictions placed on the countries participating in EMU, it will be much less significant in the future.

Generally, governments can borrow from:

1.   Abroad
2.   The central bank
3.   The commercial banks
4.   The non-bank public.

A government can borrow abroad either by borrowing directly from a foreign (non-Eurozone bank) or by selling bonds to non-Eurozone residents. When a government borrows from abroad, it is, in effect, borrowing foreign currency such as dollars or sterling. This foreign currency has to be exchanged for euro at the NCB. The balance sheet transaction is similar to that of an increase in any other inflow across the balance of payments. In terms of table 16.1, the external reserves (R) rise on the asset side and government deposits rise on the liability side. The government can now spend the money by writing a cheque on its account. Because high-powered money has increased there will be a multiple expansion of the money supply. It should be noted that this type of financing is unlikely to occur under the rules of the single currency.

Government borrowing from the central bank also increases high-powered money (H) and therefore has a multiple effect on the overall money supply. Under the provisions in the Maastricht Treaty, the ECB and national central banks can act as agents for government but they cannot lend them money, provide credit or buy bonds directly from them. This source of funding is ruled out by the terms of the Maastricht Treaty.

As the ECB can no longer provide credit, it is possible that governments will rely more on commercial financial institutions. Hence, borrowing from commercial banks (source 3) is likely to become much more important in the future. If the government borrows from a commercial bank, the effects are similar to what happens when a firm or individual borrows from the bank. Because the loan is only one step in the money creation process, this form of funding only has a *once-off* effect on the money supply. In contrast, borrowing from abroad and the central bank have a *multiplier* effect on the money supply.

If the banks had no excess reserves to begin with, there would be a deficiency in reserves following the increase in lending to the government. This would lead to an increased demand for funds on the inter-bank market and interest rates would rise.

The most important source of funds for a government in the EMU will be borrowing from the non-bank public by selling government securities. Purchases of government stock will lead to a fall in commercial bank deposits as money is withdrawn to pay for the stock. When the government spends the money, a large part of it will find its way back to the banks and deposits will return to their original level. In the long-term, therefore, there will be little change in bank deposits, bank reserves, high-powered money or interest rates. Borrowing from the non-bank public has little or no effect on the money supply or Eurozone interest rates.

This is why the provisions in the Maastricht Treaty are designed to constrain government borrowing to the non-bank public. Since this type of borrowing does not affect the money supply, it makes it much easier for the ECB to achieve its primary goal of price stability.

16.5 THE EURO AS A GLOBAL CURRENCY

The US dollar is the most widely used currency in global commerce today. It is used outside the United States as a store of value in countries where hyperinflation has led to a distrust of the local currency ('dollarisation'). It is also widely used as a medium of exchange throughout the world. Many international contracts and the prices of most major commodities, such as oil, are specified in dollars. Finally, because of its general acceptability and good anti-inflation reputation, the dollar is the most important reserve currency held by central banks round the world as backing for their national currencies.

How will the euro perform relative to the dollar as a global currency? Prior to the introduction of the euro in January 1999, some economists predicted that it would appreciate strongly against the dollar (one forecast put the appreciation at 40 per cent). This view was based on the belief that the euro would at least partly replace the dollar in some of its functions as a global currency. (These consist of the use of the dollar as

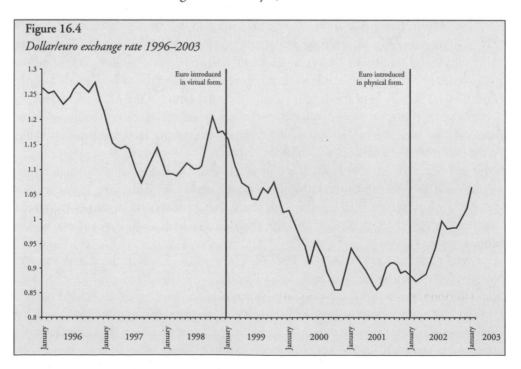

Figure 16.4
Dollar/euro exchange rate 1996–2003

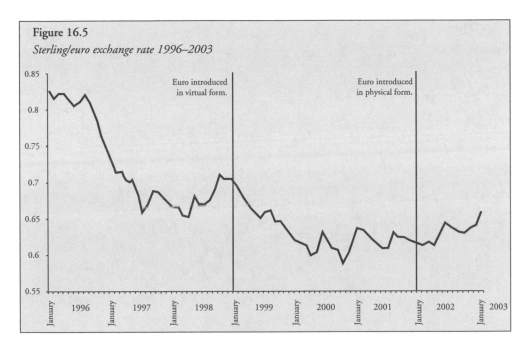

Figure 16.5

Sterling/euro exchange rate 1996–2003

an international store of value, medium of exchange, and as a reserve currency by almost all central banks.) It was estimated that the euro could become the unit of account for up to a quarter of world trade. By early 2003, however, there was little evidence that these predictions were proving correct. The initial demand for the euro outside the Eurozone has been weak. The dollar had not even begun to be displaced from its dominant role in world trade and finance.

Contrary to expectations there was a significant fall in the value of the euro relative to the dollar, sterling and the yen from 1999 through 2000. Figures 16.4, 16.5 and 16.6 show the euro exchange rate relative to the dollar, sterling and yen respectively, using monthly data over the period 1996 to 2003.

Note:

This data is taken from a valuable website maintained by Prof. Werner Antweiler at the University of British Columbia, from which a wealth of exchange rate information can be easily downloaded: http://pacific.commerce.ubc.ca/xr/data.html. Readers may find it informative to update figures like 16.4, 5 and 6 from this site.

Between January 1999 and April 2002, the euro fell by 24 per cent relative to the dollar and by 12 per cent relative to sterling and the yen. (The data in the three diagrams is extended back to January 1996 so as to determine the long-run trend in the euro exchange rate. Over this longer time frame, there is an even greater depreciation relative to the dollar and sterling.)

However, the fall in the euro came to an end late in 2000 and it regained some lost ground in 2002. But it was remarkable that the dollar remained strong in the aftermath of the terrorist attacks of September 11, 2001, the spate of financial scandals revealed during 2002, and the stock market decline. If these events have not shaken investors' confidence in the US economy, what will?

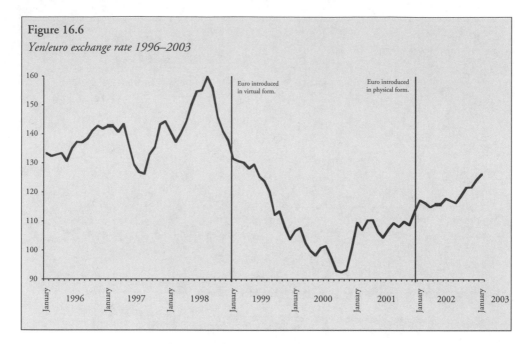

Figure 16.6
Yen/euro exchange rate 1996–2003

Why, contrary to expectations, has the euro been relatively weak? Since 1999, 'key indicators' such as the current account of the balance of payments and the inflation rate tend to favour the Eurozone over the US. The Eurozone has recorded a balance of payments surplus relative to a deficit in the US, and Eurozone inflation has also been relatively lower. Against this, the real growth rate has been faster in the US and interest rates are also relatively higher. This has resulted in a capital inflow into the US to take advantage of the higher returns both on Wall Street and in government bonds. This capital inflow is offsetting the balance of payments current account deficit leading to dollar appreciation. It has been estimated that in 2002, the US must import $2 billion of foreign capital every working day to cover the current account deficit, which was running at $500 billion a year.

While many commentators believe that this situation is unsustainable and a reversal of the euro's fortune is inevitable, others have argued that the world needs the liquidity that the US current account deficit pumps out. If the US reined in its deficit, the world economy would suffer a liquidity crunch. Only time will tell if the holders of all these extra dollar assets agree! (See Ronald McKinnon, 'The International Dollar Standard and Sustainability of the US Current Account Deficit', www.stanford.edu./mckinnon/papers/htm.)

16.6 Exchange Rate Policy in the Eurozone

The euro, dollar and yen are floating on the foreign exchange markets. There is no official — or as far as we know unofficial — target exchange rate between these currencies. When concerns were expressed about the weakness of the euro in 2000, Wim Duisenberg declared its level was far 'too low', but that it is not official policy either in Europe or in the US to intervene to keep the dollar/euro exchange rate at any particular level.

However, the ECB owns large reserves of non-euro currencies. In January 1999, €40 billion was transferred from the national central banks to the ECB. (Of this, 15 per cent was in gold (750 tonnes) and 85 per cent in dollar and yen holdings.) By March 2002, the ECB's external reserves had risen to €51 billion. An additional €358 billion is held by the NCBs and these reserves are managed in a decentralised manner. Table 16.2 outlines the external reserves position of the Eurosystem in March 2002. These funds could, in principle, be used to intervene in the market.

Table 16.2
Reserve assets of the Eurosystem, March 2002

	€ billions	%
Foreign exchange	237.4	58.0
Special drawing rights	5.5	1.3
Reserve position at the IMF	25.8	6.3
Gold	138.8	34.0
Other claims	1.5	0.4
Total	409.0	100.0

Source: European Central Bank, *Monthly Bulletin*, July, 2002.

In chapter 11 we explained how these reserves could be used to intervene under 'dirty floating' or a managed float. Intervention, however, is not consistent with pillar 1 of the ECB's monetary policy. As mentioned, when the ECB buys euro, this leads to a fall in the external reserves (R) on the asset side of the ECB's balance sheet (table 16.3) and a decrease in the commercial bank reserves (RE) on the liability side.

$$\downarrow R \Leftrightarrow \downarrow RE$$

The fall in R, however, affects high-powered money (the monetary base) and, via the money multiplier, the overall money supply. Conversely an increase in R will lead to a rise in H and the money supply. It is not possible to have a fixed exchange rate and simultaneously control the money supply.

STERILISATION

What is known as 'sterilisation' appears to allow a central bank some leeway by breaking the link between foreign exchange market intervention and changes in high-powered money. This is done by conducting an open market operation that offsets the foreign exchange market intervention (see section 11.4 in Chapter 11).

For example, if the ECB engages in an open market operation and buys government securities from the commercial banks, this will increase the Government securities entry on the asset side in table 16.3 and RE on the liability side. That is:

$$\uparrow \text{Government securities} \Leftrightarrow \uparrow RE$$

Table 16.3
European Central Bank balance sheet

Assets		Liabilities	
External reserves	−1	Currency	
Loans:		Commercial bank reserves	−1, +1
Banks			
Government		Government deposits	
Government securities	+1		
Other		Other	
High-powered money (H)		High-powered money (H)	

The open market operation offsets the fall in R with the result that H is unchanged. This strategy sterilises the effect of changes in external reserves on H. The only change has been in the portfolio composition of the balance sheet.

There is, however, a good deal of scepticism among economists about the effectiveness of sterilised intervention. It is argued that such a policy may work to smooth temporary fluctuations in the exchange rate. However, it is pointed out that central bank reserves are generally small, relative to international capital flows. Hence, sustained intervention will eventually lead to the depletion of the external reserves. That is, when the exchange rate is fundamentally weak, long-run sterilisation is not a viable policy option.

16.7 WHO DECIDES EXCHANGE RATE POLICY?

We noted that there is no formal target rate of the euro relative to other currencies. The Maastricht Treaty (Article 109) divides responsibility for exchange rate policy between the Council of Ministers (which is made up of ministers from all fifteen member states of the EU) and the ECB. The Council acting unanimously may conclude formal agreements linking the euro to non-Community currencies. It must consult with the ECB and try to achieve a consensus consistent with price stability, but once the Council has made an agreement the ECB will be bound by it. The Council may also promulgate less formal 'general orientations' for exchange rate policy.

Note:
This means that politicians from outside the Eurozone have a say on the euro exchange rate policy. The EU Council of Ministers includes finance ministers of countries, such as the UK, that are not EMU members and they could attempt to introduce an exchange rate policy that is in their own best interest.

At first sight these provisions would appear to compromise the ECB's independence. Some European firms are in fierce competition with their US rivals on world markets

(Airbus v. Boeing, for example). Politicians from the regions of Europe where these firms provide a lot of employment will lobby to have the euro at a 'competitive' (i.e. low) exchange rate relative to the dollar. This may not be consistent with the goal of price stability as a depreciation of the exchange rate would raise import prices.

Another issue is the problem of 'speaking with one voice'. In the US the Treasury secretary is the person responsible for exchange rate policy. But he has no counterpart in the Eurozone. If there is a currency crisis, who does he contact to resolve the problem? It is obviously very unsatisfactory if he has to deal with the entire Council of Ministers and the ECB. Exchange rate crises generally require quick and decisive action, but this may not be forthcoming if the Council of Ministers and the ECB have to arrive at a consensus decision.

WHY A FIXED EXCHANGE RATE SYSTEM MAY NOT BE DESIRABLE

There are a number of considerations that render concerns about a fixed exchange rate policy somewhat remote. Firstly, a 'formal agreement' of the type referred to in Article 109 implies a return to a global fixed exchange rate system similar to the post-war Bretton Woods agreement. There are now only three major, global currencies: the dollar, the euro and the yen (in that order of importance). If the European authorities wished to target a stronger euro, they could only succeed if the US authorities simultaneously wished to target a weaker dollar. There is little prospect of a formal agreement between the EU and the US to co-ordinate or peg exchange rate policy along these lines.

Secondly, a flexible exchange rate system does not necessarily mean a volatility exchange rate to the dollar and the yen. The monetary authorities in the US, the Eurozone and Japan are all committed to price stability and pursuing similar monetary policies, which is a recipe for relatively stable exchange rates. This would remove the need for a formal agreement to peg the currencies in the short- to medium-term.

A third reason for not worrying too much about the implications of EMU exchange rate policy for price stability is the fact that the Eurozone is a large and closed economy rather than a very open economy. In fact the Eurozone is a more closed economy than the US: only about 11 per cent of the Eurozone's output is exported outside the Eurozone. This makes it less open to trade than the US, where exports comprise about 16 per cent of GDP. As a consequence, the euro exchange rate is not a key determinant of price stability in Europe. An overvalued euro would impair the ability of firms in the Eurozone to compete with American or Asian firms on world markets. But because most of the output of the Eurozone firms is sold within the Eurozone, this issue will not be as vital as it was to individual countries in the pre-EMU period.

For Ireland, however, the value of the euro relative to the dollar and sterling will continue to be very important. With over €1.6 billion of Irish exports going to the US annually, a significant appreciation of the euro could have serious implications for trade, output and employment. Some of the excess inflation experienced in Ireland after 1999 was due to the relatively large impact of the weak euro on our economy, due to the continued importance of imports from the UK.

16.8 FISCAL POLICY IN EMU

In view of the constraints placed on national monetary policy by the Maastricht Treaty, it might seem that there would be greater reliance on fiscal policy as an instrument of national economic policy in EMU. However, a recurrent source of tension in the old European Monetary System (EMS) was the lack of co-ordination of national fiscal policies. This suggests that if EMU is to endure, the participants must pursue consistent and disciplined fiscal policies.

THE STABILITY PACT

In order to remove the possibility that individual countries would pursue divergent fiscal policies, tight constraints have been imposed on members of EMU. A Stability Pact (officially known as 'The Pact for Stability and Growth') was agreed in Dublin Castle on the 13-14 December 1996 and ratified in Amsterdam in June 1997. The objective of this Pact is to constrain fiscal policy in EMU.

The Stability Pact requires Eurozone governments to balance their budgets over the business cycle. It outlaws 'excessive fiscal deficits'. A fiscal deficit equal to or over 3 per cent of GDP was defined as excessive except in exceptional circumstances. A country that is approaching the 3 per cent ceiling must take corrective measures or face sanctions. The rationale for these constraints is that large deficits could over time undermine confidence in the euro, especially if they were financed by 'printing money'.

PENALTIES

The Pact specifies that penalties will be imposed on countries that violate its conditions.

Year one

If the fiscal deficit is equal to or exceeds 3 per cent of GDP, then a fixed deposit equal to 0.2 per cent of GDP must be paid. In addition, a variable deposit equal to 0.1 per cent of GDP must be paid for every point the deficit is above the 3 per cent threshold. The maximum deposit in year one has been constrained to 0.5 per cent (see figure 16.7).

Subsequent years

The fixed deposit is ignored and the government continues to pay 0.1 per cent of GDP for every point the deficit is above the 3 per cent threshold. The upper limit of 0.5 per cent remains and this means that the maximum penalty occurs when the fiscal deficit reaches 8 per cent of GDP (figure 16.7). Crucially, after two years, all the deposits become a fine if the deficit is not cleared.

Note:
Figures 16.7, 16.8 and 16.9 are taken from Peter J. Neary, 'The European Union Stability Pact and the Case for European Monetary Union', *Economic Outlook and Business Review*, December, 1997.

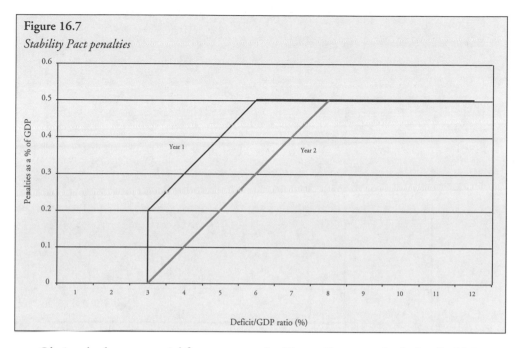

Figure 16.7
Stability Pact penalties

Obviously these potential fines are very significant. For example, Ireland's GDP was forecast at €104,325 million for 2002. A fine of 0.5 per cent in year one would come to €521 million. A similar fine in year two would more than cover the cost of building a new football stadium! Clearly, imposing these fines on countries that violate the deficit rule would cause a political crisis. How would Irish politicians react to being required to pay such a fine?

In 2002, there are a number of EMU countries, Germany in particular, with fiscal deficits close to the 3 per cent ceiling. A major shock, such as a rise in energy prices could easily push their deficits above the 3 per cent limit. If this should happen, the EMU would be severely tested by the requirement that the offending countries be fined. On the other hand, failure to impose fines would undermine the EMU's commitment to hard-nosed anti-inflation policies.

LET-OUTS

However, the Stability Pact may not be as strict as first appears. There are two let-out clauses. Firstly, a government may be excused the fines if the fiscal deficit is classified as 'exceptional' and/or 'temporary'. By exceptional means an 'unusual event outside the control of the state' or a 'severe economic downturn'. A severe economic downturn is deemed to be a fall of 2 per cent or more in GDP. Hence, if the real growth rate is minus 2 per cent or less, the penalties will not be imposed. By 'temporary' means a situation where the European Commission forecasts that the fiscal deficit will be short-lived and that the deficit will fall below the 3 per cent threshold in the very near future.

Note:

As discussed in the context of built-in stabilisers in chapter 4, during a recession government tax receipts fall and government expenditure automatically increases. The process goes into reverse

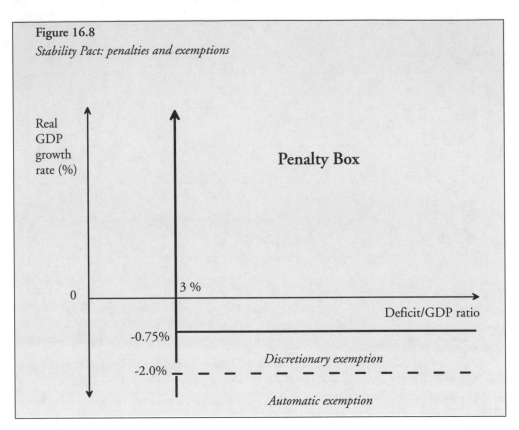

Figure 16.8
Stability Pact: penalties and exemptions

during an expansion. As a result, the budget deficit automatically increases during recessions and falls during booms. The Pact has the effect of choking off these automatic stabilisers.

The second let-out is that a government can put its case to the European Commission if the economy is in 'severe recession'. This is defined as a fall in the real growth rate of at least 0.75 per cent. This second let-out clause introduces a discretionary element into the Stability Pact.

Figure 16.8 summarises the let-out clauses. The real GDP growth rate is shown along the vertical axis. The fiscal deficit to GDP ratio is along the horizontal axis. Once the deficit reaches the 3 per cent *threshold* (horizontal axis) and as long as the real GDP growth rate remains above the upper discretionary limit of minus 0.75 per cent, the government is subjected to a fine. The co-ordinates of 3, -0.75 define the penalty box.

If the real growth rate falls to between −0.75 and −2, the fine is in the discretionary area. Finally, if the real growth rate falls below −2 per cent the government is exempt from the penalties.

There are, however, a number of other aspects to the Stability Pact that introduce ambiguity and which require a majority decision by politicians before the penalties can be imposed. For example, the text is sprinkled with terms like 'as a rule'. There is a fifteen-month lag before the initial 0.2 per cent deposit is actually paid. It will require a majority decision by all EU members to decide if a deficit is 'excessive' or not. In addition, it will require a majority of EMU members to decide if the sanctions should be imposed.

SUMMARY

The Pact, which was introduced in the 1990s to ensure that the Maastricht discipline did not evaporate as soon as the new currency was launched, has become an embarrassment to economies like France and Germany, which in 2002 came close to moving into the penalty area.

The irrelevance of the Pact is also illustrated by a consideration of the *dynamics of the public debt*. (We discuss this in detail in an appendix to this chapter.) Part of the rationale of the Pact is to ensure that excessive debt/GDP ratios do not undermine confidence in the euro. However, the debt/GDP in most European countries is at present very low and not rising rapidly. Much larger fiscal deficits would be needed to put national debt on an unsustainable trajectory or to threaten the euro as a currency.

Note:

Belgian economist Paul de Grauwe has argued that the Stability Pact's insistence on balancing budgets over the business cycle would eventually lead to the decline of government bond markets in Europe — a development that would cause its own problems.

By mid-2002 four Eurozone countries — Germany, France, Italy and Portugal — either already had breached the 3 per cent ceiling or were very close to doing so. The new governments in France and Germany, in particular, were framing budgets that seemed to ignore the limits imposed by the Pact. Faced with this situation the EU Commission seems likely to relax the requirement of achieving a balanced budget by the year 2004.

Most economists are not sorry to see the Pact unravel. They regarded it as a perverse and possibly harmful idea from the start. As pointed out above, it could choke off the operation of automatic stabilisers and make fiscal policy perversely pro-cyclical: aggravating rather than smoothing the business cycle.

Perhaps the main argument for continuing to try to enforce the Stability Pact is that, even though it was a bad idea to start with, to cave in now would be a clear sign of weakness and lack of discipline among the Eurozone governments.

THE IRISH ECONOMY AND THE STABILITY PACT

What would have been the Irish experience if the Stability Pact had been in operation since the early 1970s? Figure 16.9 summarises the outcome. Between 1975 and 1987, the Irish government incurred large budget deficits. However, at no time did the real GDP growth rate fall anywhere near the −0.75 per cent discretionary limit. The lowest real GDP growth rate recorded was -0.2 per cent in 1983. (However, GNP declined more frequently, illustrating the perils of choosing between GDP and GNP in the Irish context.) Hence, the government would have been obliged to pay the full penalty. The fines would have amounted to billions of pounds. Only in the 1990s when the real growth rate picked-up and the budget deficits fell did the economy move outside the penalty zone.

A similar situation applies for the other EMU countries. The Irish experience indicates that the exemptions rarely apply and that if a government incurs a budget deficit in excess of the 3 per cent limit, it can expect to incur significant costs.

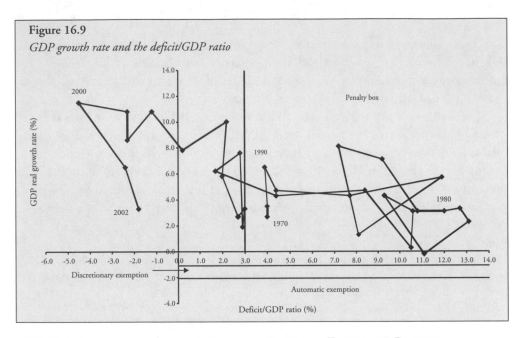

Figure 16.9

GDP growth rate and the deficit/GDP ratio

16.9 THE IMPLICATIONS OF THE STABILITY PACT FOR ECONOMIC POLICY

The drive to achieve the Maastricht criteria in 1997 imposed deflationary policies on Europe. Figure 16.10 shows the trend in unemployment and inflation in the Eurozone from 1979 to 2002. From 1983, an inverse relationship between the two series may be observed. As inflation fell in the 1990s, partly driven down by the desire to meet the Maastricht convergence criteria, unemployment rose.

With monetary and fiscal policy severely constrained, the policy framework of EMU leaves little scope for stabilisation policy. The countries that have joined EMU

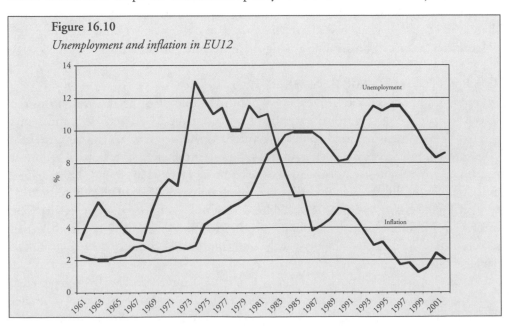

Figure 16.10

Unemployment and inflation in EU12

have signed up to a very 'classical' policy orientation, relying on wage and price flexibility to adjust to economic shocks. If prices and wages in the Eurozone countries continue to be as inflexible, and labour as immobile, as they have in the past, the result will be protracted recession and even higher unemployment than is presently recorded in Europe. This would add considerably to political tensions between the participating countries.

One possible solution would be for the EU itself to conduct an active counter-cyclical fiscal policy. But the EU has no fiscal instruments to stabilise the economy. Also because of the relatively small size of the EU budget (less than 2 per cent of EU GDP) there are no EU automatic stabilisers worth talking about. Unlike the situation in federal economic structures, such as the United States, there is no significant 'fiscal federalism'. That is, there is no mechanism for offsetting economic shocks by the taxes paid by the nations to Brussels or the transfers they receive from Brussels.

The current low inflation rate in the Eurozone has been achieved by tolerating a sharp rise in unemployment. The ECB consistently blames the poor performance of the European labour market on 'structural rigidities'; basically expressing the belief that Europe does not operate as flexibly as the US in matters or hiring and firing. (We discuss these issues in chapter 22.) If they are right about this, the fear is that when the economic growth rate in the core EMU economies rises, inflation is also likely to pick up again. The ECB will then be under pressure to prevent inflation rising above the level that prevailed at the launch of the euro. This could lead to the imposition of contractionary policies relatively early in the recovery phase of the cycle. Higher interest rates would cause severe budgetary problems in the highly indebted countries increasing the risk that they breach the Stability Pact. They could easily be forced to implement pro-cyclical corrective policies that would kill off the resurgence in economic growth.

The EMU project contains no proposals to address this issue. It is likely that the combination of the ECB's commitment to price stability and the constraints imposed by the Stability Pact could create a deflationary bias in EMU and contribute to the relative under-performance of the Eurozone compared with the US economy.

16.10 CONCLUSION

In this chapter we discussed in some detail monetary and fiscal policy in the Eurozone. Among the main points discussed were:

- Problems in controlling the money supply
- The ECB's interest rates and how they impact on inter-bank and commercial interest rates
- The main factors, other than the ECB, influencing interest rates
- Exchange rate policy in the EMU and the external value of the euro
- The concept of 'sterilisation'
- Who decides exchange rate policy in the Eurozone
- Fiscal policy in EMU under the Stability Pact
- The penalties and let-out clauses associated with the Stability Pact

- The conditions under which the fiscal deficit and the national debt can be stabilised
- The risk that the EMU will have a deflationary bias.

APPENDIX
THE DYNAMICS OF DEBT ACCUMULATION

In this appendix, we determine the conditions under which the government can stabilise the fiscal deficit and the overall national debt. The starting point is to note that the government spends money on its current and capital accounts, G, and to pay interest on its past borrowing. If we denote the stock of national (government) debt as ND and the interest rate payable on this debt as i, total government spending is:

$$G + i\text{ND}$$

The main source of government revenue is tax receipts, T. The *general government deficit* or fiscal deficit is defined as the shortfall of government spending over tax revenue:

$$[G + i\text{ND}] - T \tag{1}$$

A narrower definition of the deficit excludes interest on past debt. (The government has little control over interest rate payments.) This is called the *primary deficit*:

$$G - T \tag{2}$$

If we denote borrowing as ΔND (i.e. the change in national debt) the government's budget constraint is:

$$G + i\text{ND} - T = \Delta\text{ND} \tag{3}$$

The Stability Pact more or less constrains governments to borrowing from the non-bank public. Hence we can ignore the possibility of monetary financing.

BALANCED BUDGET

If the aim is to run a balanced budget (stabilise the absolute national debt), then ΔND = 0. The budget constraint now becomes:

$$T - G = i\text{ND} \tag{4}$$

In other words, to stabilise the level of the national debt the government must run a primary budget surplus equal to the interest on the national debt (iND). The government must pay the interest on past debt out of current tax receipts.

STABILISING THE FISCAL DEFICIT/GDP RATIO

To see how the fiscal deficit to GDP ratio (Stability Pact criteria) can be stabilised or kept below 3 per cent, divide the magnitudes in (3) by the level of GDP.

This gives us

$$G/\text{GDP} + i\text{ND}/\text{GDP} - T/\text{GDP} = \Delta\text{ND}/\text{GDP} \tag{5}$$

Writing ratios to GDP in lowercase letters (G/GDP = g, etc.) this becomes:

$$(g + ind) - t = \Delta ND/GDP < 3\% \tag{6}$$

The term, $\Delta ND/GDP$, is the fiscal deficit to GDP ratio. If this equals 3 per cent or more the government is subjected to the sanctions imposed by the Stability Pact. The equation states that taxes (as a proportion of GDP) must exceed spending (as a proportion of GDP) to pay the interest on the debt to GDP ratio. This suggests that the main variables influencing $\Delta ND/GDP$ are government spending, taxation, interest rates and GDP. A rise in government spending, higher interest rate, lower tax receipts and a slowdown in the growth rate could combine to move $\Delta ND/GDP$ into the penalty box zone.

STABILISING THE DEBT/GDP RATIO

A balanced budget (or stabilising the absolute level of the debt) implies that the debt to GDP ratio (ND/GDP) is falling. This is because GDP itself is increasing over time.

What are the conditions under which this ratio, ND/GDP, is stabilised? To obtain the necessary condition, we need to introduce the real growth rate into the analysis. This can be done as follows. By definition,

nd = ND/GDP.

Rearranging:

ND = nd × GDP

Total differentiation gives:

ΔND = nd ΔGDP + GDP Δnd

Dividing both sides by GDP yields:

ΔND/GDP = nd ΔGDP/GDP + Δnd

Letting y equal the rate of growth of GDP (that is ΔGDP/GDP)

ΔND/GDP = nd y + Δnd

Substituting into (6) above we obtain

$$g + ind - t = nd\, y + \Delta nd \tag{7}$$

Rearranging:

$$\Delta nd = g + ind - t - nd\, y \tag{8}$$

or

$$\Delta nd = g - t + (i - y)nd$$

The goal of stabilising the debt/GDP ratio implies setting nd = 0, which implies:

$$g - t + (i - y)nd = 0$$

or

$$t - g = (i - y)nd \tag{9}$$

Equation (9) states that a stable debt/GDP ratio will be achieved if the primary budget surplus as a percentage of GDP equals (or exceeds) the excess of the rate of interest over the rate of growth of GDP *times* the initial ratio of debt to GDP. (Note that both interest rates and GDP are in nominal terms.)

To stabilise the debt/GDP ratio, therefore, it is necessary to run a primary budget surplus whose size depends on:

- The level of interest rates relative to the rate of growth of GDP, and
- The initial size of the national debt.

In the present Irish situation, with GDP growing at or above the rate of interest on government debt, $y > i$, combined with a primary budget surplus, $t > g$, the debt/GDP ratio is falling, Δnd < 0. It is this combination of events, high growth, low interest rates and a primary budget surplus, that has led to a faster fall in the Irish debt/GDP during the 1990s and early 2000s than has been achieved in any other European country.

CHAPTER 17

The IS-LM Model

17.1 INTRODUCTION

In this chapter we outline a standard macroeconomic model that is often referred to as 'the IS-LM model'. This depicts the interaction between the goods and money markets. The 'I' in IS stands for investment and 'S' for savings. The 'L' in LM denotes liquidity preference (demand for money) and 'M' the money supply. The Nobel prize-winning English economist John Hicks (1904–89) developed the IS-LM framework very shortly after the publication of Keynes's *General Theory*. (J. R. Hicks, 'Mr Keynes and the Classics, A Suggested Interpretation', *Econometrica*, Vol. 6, April 1937.)

A key difference between this model and the 'open economy monetary model' developed in earlier chapters is that the *price level is fixed*. In its original form the IS-LM model does not shed light on the problem of inflation. Furthermore, the model is essentially a demand-side model that provides no insights into the workings of the supply-side of the economy. In the concluding sections of this chapter we use the IS-LM model to discuss the issues of 'crowding-out', the relative effectiveness of fiscal and monetary policy and the fiscal, monetary policy mix.

17.2 EQUILIBRIUM IN THE GOODS MARKET: THE IS CURVE

The IS curve describes the market for goods and services or, simply, the goods market. Equilibrium in this market requires that the value of what is being produced (GNP) equals total spending or aggregate demand (AD). Aggregate demand, in turn, is identically equal to the sum of consumer expenditure (C), investment (I), government current consumption (G) and net exports (exports minus imports). That is:

$$GNP = AD \equiv C + I + G + NX \tag{1}$$

The next step is to introduce the *consumption function*, which was first outlined in chapter 3. In its simplest form, the consumption function states that consumer expenditure is a function of income or GNP.

$$C = a + c\,GNP \tag{2}$$

The intercept term *a* represents autonomous consumer expenditure, that is, expenditure not influenced by changes in income or GNP. The coefficient c indicates what proportion of extra income is consumed and is referred to as the marginal propensity to consume (MPC).

We now introduce the relationship between the (real) interest rate (r) and aggregate demand. Note that as the price level is assumed constant we can use either nominal or

real interest rates. In chapter 8 we pointed out that changes in the real interest rate
affected consumer expenditure, investment and net exports. This type of expenditure is
called *interest-sensitive expenditure* (IE). To simplify the analysis we assume here that the
interest rate does not affect consumer expenditure or net exports. Hence, an increase in
the interest rate only leads to a fall in investment. Conversely, a fall in the interest rate
only increases investment. A curve depicting the relationship between the interest rate
and investment (I) is known as the *marginal efficiency of investment* (MEI) curve. The
relationship can be written:

$$I = d - b\, r \tag{3}$$

The intercept term *d* indicates autonomous investment, that is, investment not
influenced by changes in the interest rate. The coefficient *b* indicates how investment
reacts to changes in the interest rate (r). Substituting (2) and (3) into (1) we have:

$$GNP = a + c\, GNP + d - b\, r + G + NX \tag{4}$$

Rearranging:

$$GNP(1 - c) = (a + d + G + NX) - b\, r \tag{5}$$

Let total autonomous expenditure $(a + d + G + NX) = Z$ then:

$$GNP = [1/(1 - c)](Z - b\, r) \tag{6}$$

It can be seen from (6) that there is a negative relationship between GNP and r. Basically,
what happens is that an increase in the interest rate lowers the level of investment which
in turn reduces aggregate demand and ultimately GNP, and vice versa. In short:

$$\uparrow r \rightarrow \downarrow I \rightarrow \downarrow AD \rightarrow \downarrow GNP$$

Figure 17.1 outlines the effect of a decrease in the interest rate using the standard
aggregate supply (AS), aggregate demand (AD) diagram. Note that the AS curve is
assumed to be horizontal so as to ensure a constant price level. In the left-hand diagram
a reduction in the interest rate from r_1 to r_2 increases investment. The aggregate demand
curve shifts out to the right and the economy moves from the point A to the point B.
GNP increases along the horizontal axis from GNP_1 to GNP_2. In the right-hand
diagram the point C represents the initial combination of interest rate and GNP, which
is one point on the IS curve. The point B represents the second point on the IS curve
as it shows the r_2, GNP_2 combination. By changing the interest rate and thereby shifting
the AD curve to the left and to the right we can trace out each equilibrium interest rate,
GNP combination, and construct the complete IS curve. Each point on the IS curve
represents equilibrium in the goods market.

SLOPE OF IS CURVE
The slope of the IS curve indicates how a change in the interest rate affects GNP. It can
be seen from equation (6) that the interest rate affects GNP via the *b* coefficient and
the $1/(1-c)$ term. Hence the slope of the IS curve depends on the following factors:

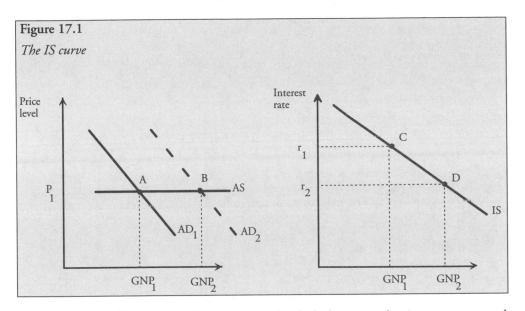

Figure 17.1

The IS curve

- The *b* coefficient, which represents the link between the interest rate and investment (the MEI curve).
- The $1/(1-c)$ term which reflects the link between investment and GNP (the multiplier).

It follows therefore that:

- The IS curve will be *flat* (elastic), if *b* is large (elastic MEI curve) and/or $1/(1-c)$, (the multiplier) is large.

Conversely,

- The IS curve will be *steep* (inelastic) if *b* is small and/or the multiplier $1/(1-c)$ is small.

Note:
To keep the analysis as simple as possible we ignore the marginal propensity to tax (MPT) and the marginal propensity to import (MPM) in deriving the multiplier. These two coefficients will also influence the slope of the IS curve.

LOCATION OF IS CURVE

Consider now the factors which determine the location of the IS curve. In the left-hand diagram in figure 17.2 the AD curve again shifts out to the right, but this time the movement is due to a change in autonomous expenditure. That is, an increase in the AD curve *not brought about by a change in the interest rate*. The economy moves from the point A to the point B and GNP increases along the horizontal axis.

In the right-hand diagram, the point C represents the initial r_1, GNP_1 combination. The increase in autonomous expenditure has increased output from GNP_1 to GNP_2. If the IS curve is shifted out to the right this enables us to examine the relationship between the initial interest rate r_1 and the new, higher level of output, GNP_2. The point

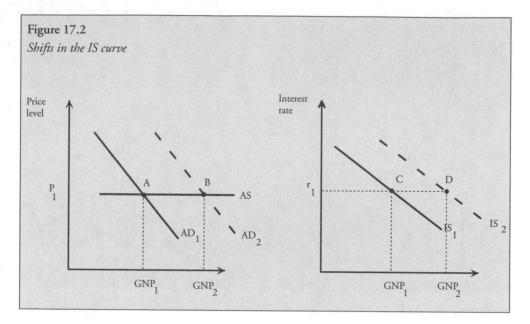

Figure 17.2
Shifts in the IS curve

D, for example, on the new IS curve represents the original interest rate, r_1, and the new higher level of output, GNP_2. It follows from this that a change in any of the components of autonomous expenditure, C, I, G or NX will affect the location of the IS curve. Thus an expansionary fiscal policy will shift the IS curve to the right and a deflationary fiscal policy will shift it to the left. Changes in the interest rate, on the other hand, will be reflected in movements *along* the IS curve.

17.3 EQUILIBRIUM IN THE MONEY MARKET: THE LM CURVE

Consider now the relationship between the interest rate and GNP as reflected in the money market. The level of nominal GNP and the interest rate determine the demand for money.

$$M^d = e\,GNP - f\,r \qquad (7)$$

There is a positive relationship between GNP and M^d due to the transaction and precautionary motives for holding money. The coefficient *e* indicates how a change in GNP influences the demand for money and is referred to as the *income elasticity of the demand for money*. The larger the coefficient *e*, the greater the effect GNP has on M^d.

The interest rate reflects the speculative demand for money. There is an inverse relationship between r and M^d. The coefficient *f* shows how changes in the interest rate affect the demand for money and is referred to as the *interest elasticity of the demand for money*.

Note:
In this chapter, the demand for money is a function of the real interest rate, r, whereas in chapter 8 we related it to the nominal interest rate, *i*. Given that the price level is assumed to be constant there is no inconsistency between these two treatments.

It is assumed that the central bank controls the money supply (M^s). Hence the equilibrium condition in the money market is:

$$M^s = M^d \tag{8}$$

Substitute equation (7) into (8) to obtain:

$$M^s = e\,GNP - f\,r \tag{9}$$

Solving equation (9) for the interest rate, we have:

$$r = [1/f]\,(e\,GNP - M^s) \tag{10}$$

Equation (10) shows that there is a positive relationship between GNP and the interest rate in the money market. The LM curve, which shows the r, GNP combinations consistent with equilibrium in the money market, is therefore upward sloping.

Figure 17.3 illustrates why this positive relationship exists. The left-hand diagram shows equilibrium in the money market. The supply and demand for money interact to determine the interest rate on the vertical axis. As demonstrated in chapter 8, an increase in GNP shifts the M^d curve upwards, and vice versa. Initially, we are at the point A in the money market. Suppose now GNP increases from GNP$_1$ to GNP$_2$. The M^d curve shifts upwards and the money market moves to the point B, with the interest rate increasing to r$_2$ along the vertical axis. Hence, in the money market there is a positive relationship between the level of GNP and the interest rate that is consistent with equilibrium in the money market. This is represented in the right-hand diagram as an upward-sloping curve labelled LM. In short:

$$\uparrow GNP \rightarrow \uparrow M^d \rightarrow \uparrow r$$

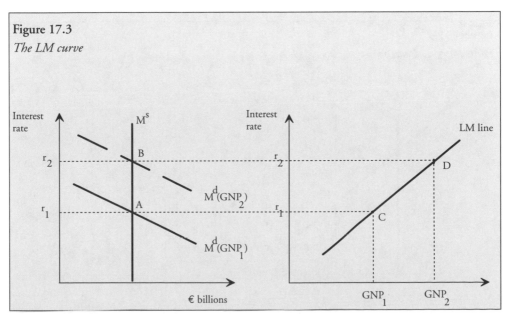

Figure 17.3
The LM curve

In the right-hand diagram the point C represents the initial r_1, GNP_1 combination. This is one point on the LM curve. The point D, in turn, indicates the new r_2, GNP_2 combination and is another point on the LM curve. By shifting the M^d curve in the money market we can trace out the various interest rate, GNP combinations consistent with equilibrium in the money market. These points lie on the LM curve.

SLOPE OF THE LM CURVE

Consider now the factors that determine the slope of the LM curve. A steep LM curve means that a given change in GNP has a large effect on the interest rate and vice versa. An examination of equation (10) indicates that the effect of changes in GNP on the interest rate depends on the coefficients e and f. Hence:

- The LM curve will be *steep* (inelastic) if e (income elasticity of the demand for money) is large and/or f (interest elasticity of the demand for money) is small.
- The LM curve will be *flat* (elastic) if e is small and/or the coefficient f is large.

LOCATION OF LM CURVE

The location of the LM curve depends on the level of the money supply. An increase in the money supply shifts the LM curve to the right and a decrease to the left. For example, in the left-hand diagram in figure 17.4 the money market is initially in equilibrium at the point A. This equilibrium point corresponds to r_1 and GNP_1. Holding GNP constant, an increase in the money supply shifts the M^s curve from M^s_1 to M^s_2 and the interest rate falls from r_1 to r_2. In the right-hand diagram the point C corresponds to the initial r_1, GNP_1 combination. By shifting the LM curve downwards, we can examine the relationship between GNP_1 and the new lower interest rate, r_2. For example, the point D corresponds to the new r_2, GNP_1 combination. Conversely, an increase in the money supply will shift the LM curve upwards.

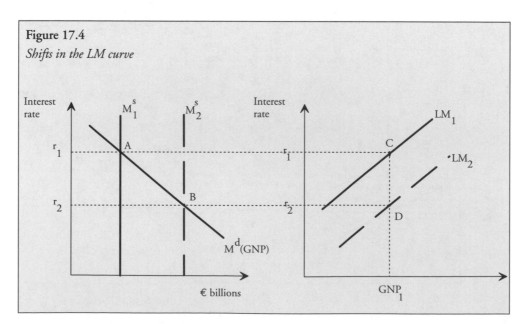

Figure 17.4
Shifts in the LM curve

17.4 EQUILIBRIUM IN THE GOODS AND MONEY MARKETS

Figure 17.5 amalgamates the IS and LM curves. Recall that points on the IS curve are consistent with equilibrium in the goods market, and points on the LM curve are consistent with equilibrium in the money market. Hence, at the point F, where the two curves intersect, there is equilibrium in both the goods market and the money market. At this point, and only here, aggregate demand equals planned production and the stock of money equals the desired holdings of cash balances by the public.

If a disequilibrium should arise, either because the interest rate or GNP is too high or too low, then it can be shown that the economy will adjust back to equilibrium. To

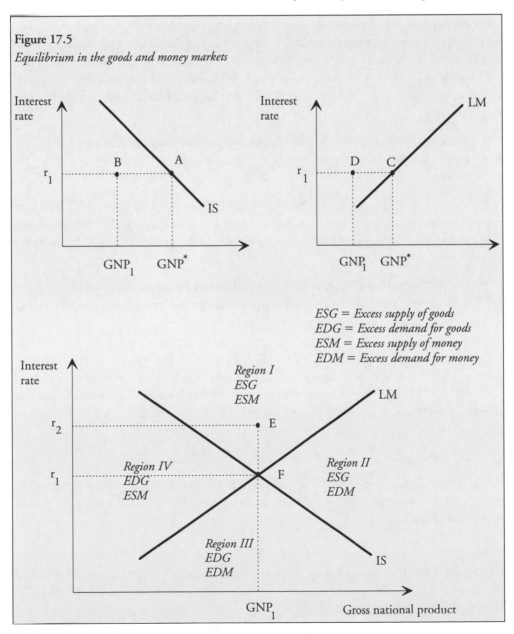

Figure 17.5
Equilibrium in the goods and money markets

establish this, consider the two diagrams at the top of figure 17.5. The diagram on the top left shows the IS curve. The point A corresponds to r_1 and GNP* and the goods market is in equilibrium. Suppose, however, that output is at GNP_1 so that the economy is at the point B, to the left of the IS curve. Since GNP is lower than what is necessary for equilibrium, there must be an excess demand for goods and services. Hence:

• All points to the left of the IS curve are associated with an *excess demand* for goods and services.

• All points to the right of the IS curve are associated with an *excess supply* of goods and services.

Consider now the LM curve in the top right-hand diagram. At the point C, r_1 and GNP* represent the interest rate and the level of output consistent with money market equilibrium. If, however, output is less than GNP*, say GNP_1, and the market is at a point such as D, then there is an excess supply of money. The reason is that GNP and therefore the demand for money is lower than that necessary for equilibrium. It follows, therefore, that:

• Points to the *left* of the LM curve represent an excess *supply* of money.

• Points to the *right* of the LM curve are associated with an excess *demand* for money.

We can divide the area in the diagram in the bottom panel of figure 17.5 into four regions, corresponding to combinations of excess supply and demand in the goods and money markets. The economy will adjust towards equilibrium (represented by the point F) because:

• Output rises whenever there is an excess demand for goods and vice versa.

• The interest rate rises when there is an excess demand for money and vice versa.

Region I

Points in region I correspond to an excess supply of goods and an excess supply of money. If the economy were at a point such as E in this region, the excess supplies in both the goods and money markets would interact in such a way as to drive the interest rate and GNP to an equilibrium point such as F. (As drawn, we show a fall in the interest rate only.)

Region II

Points in region II correspond to an excess supply of goods but an excess demand for money. In this situation, the interest rate will rise and GNP will fall until equilibrium is reached at the point F.

Region III

Points in region III correspond to an excess demand for goods and an excess demand for money. Both GNP and the interest rate will rise until equilibrium is reached at F.

Region IV

Finally, if the economy is in region IV, there is an excess demand for goods and an exccss supply of money. GNP will rise and the interest rate would fall until equilibrium is re-established.

Thus the combination r_1 and GNP_1 represents a stable equilibrium to which the economy will return if the economy is subjected to a shock.

PHILLIPS MACHINE

In the late 1940s a New Zealand economist A.W. Phillips (see chapter 21) built the first 'Phillips Machine' in a garage in Croydon. The photograph shows Phillips with his machine in the early 1950s. This machine is a hydraulic version of the IS-LM model. (One prototype is currently on display in the Science Museum, South Kensington, London. Approximately fourteen machines were built.) The machine could be used, among other issues, to quantify the effect on national income, the interest rate and the exchange rate of, say, an expansionary fiscal or monetary policy. It was, in effect, one of the first computers used in economics. It was, for a number of years, used for teaching

Bill Phillips and his economic computer (Source: London School of Economics)

James Meade lecturing at the LSE (Source: Barratt's Photo Press)

purposes at the London School of Economics (LSE). The second photograph shows Professor James Meade lecturing at the LSE using two Phillips machines (each representing a different country).

17.5 GOVERNMENT SPENDING AND PRIVATE INVESTMENT: CROWDING-OUT

In this section the IS-LM model is used to explore how an increase in government spending may affect private sector investment spending. Suppose that there are unemployed resources and the government embarks on an expansionary fiscal policy. This is shown in the left-hand diagram in figure 17.6 as the IS curve shifting outwards from IS_1 to IS_2. If, we ignored the effects of this on the monetary sector, the economy would move from the point A to the point B and GNP would increase to GNP_2. However, when we take account of the possible repercussions of the fiscal expansion on the money market, we see that the economy moves up along the LM curve and equilibrium is established at the point C. Output increases only to GNP_3, which is lower than the level GNP_2, which would have been reached if there had been no monetary repercussions.

The reason for the smaller increase in GNP is the *crowding-out effect*. Basically, what happens is that the rise in GNP leads to an increase in the demand for money. Given a constant supply of money, the increase in the demand for money pushes up the interest rate (along the vertical axis in figure 17.6) and this, in turn, reduces investment expenditure. Hence, increased government expenditure is partly offset by a reduction in investment and the impact of fiscal policy on GNP is reduced. The crowding-out effect reduces the effectiveness of fiscal policy.

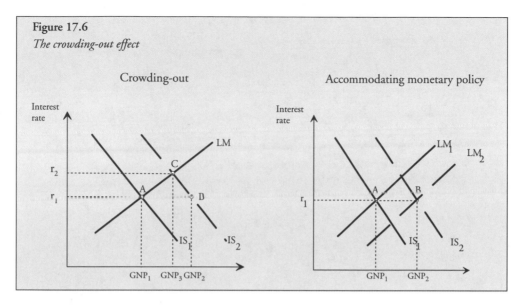

Figure 17.6
The crowding-out effect

ACCOMMODATING MONETARY POLICY

In practice, however, the crowding-out effect may be reduced if the government implements an accommodating monetary policy simultaneously with an expansionary fiscal policy. Instead of assuming that the money supply is held constant, let us suppose that the expansionary fiscal policy is accompanied by an increase in the money supply. In the right-hand diagram in figure 17.6 an increase in the money supply shifts the LM curve upwards from LM_1 to LM_2. The economy moves to the point B, GNP increases to GNP_2, and because there is no increase in the interest rate along the vertical axis investment expenditure is not crowded-out.

IMPLICATIONS FOR EMU COUNTRIES

The above analysis is relevant at the Eurozone level. If the large EMU countries were to embark on a co-ordinated fiscal expansion, it is likely that Eurozone interest rates would rise and private sector investment would be crowded-out. However, the analysis is not relevant at the level of a small EMU country operating in isolation. If, for example, the Irish government were to embark on an expansionary fiscal policy this would have no impact whatsoever on Eurozone interest rates. This is akin to the situation where the LM curve is perfectly horizontal. In this case, there would be no crowding-out and fiscal policy in the small country is, therefore, more effective. This illustrates that a small country participating in EMU is a 'free rider' with regard to interest rates. The government can embark on a particular fiscal policy knowing that it will not entail adverse effects emanating from the money market.

17.6 THE RELATIVE EFFECTIVENESS OF FISCAL AND MONETARY POLICY IN THE IS-LM MODEL

The IS-LM framework can be used to illustrate issues such as the relative effectiveness of fiscal and monetary policy. An expansionary fiscal policy shifts the IS curve to the right.

Figure 17.7

Fiscal policy and the slope of the LM curve

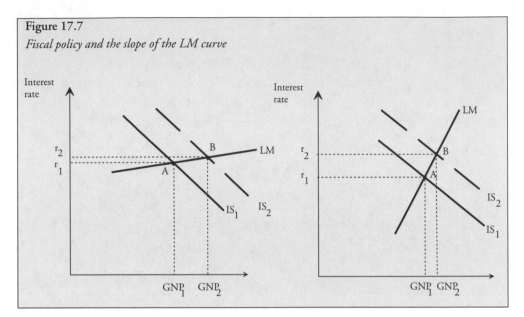

As the two diagrams in figure 17.7 illustrate, the resulting increase in GNP depends on the slope of the LM curve. In the left-hand panel, the LM curve is relatively flat and a shift of the IS curve to the right leads to a large increase in GNP. In the right-hand panel, the LM curve is steep and a similar shift of the IS curve has a small effect on GNP. The reason for the difference in the change in GNP is the crowding-out effect. When the LM curve is flat, there is a small increase in the interest rate on the vertical axis and the crowding-out effect is insignificant. On the other hand, if the LM curve is steep, there will be a large increase in the interest rate and the crowding-out effect will be significant.

Figure 17.8 examines the case of an expansionary monetary policy (shift of the LM curve to the right). In the left-hand panel, the IS curve is steep and an expansionary

Figure 17.8

Monetary policy and the slope of the IS curve

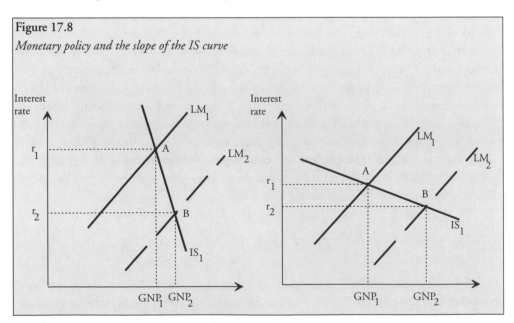

monetary policy has a small effect on GNP. The reason is that investment is not very sensitive to interest rate changes and, as a result, the decrease in the interest rate on the vertical axis has an unimportant effect on investment. As a result, monetary policy has only a small effect on the level of output and employment.

In the right-hand panel, the IS curve is relatively flat because investment is sensitive to changes in the interest rate, and a shift of the LM curve to the right has a large effect on GNP. As a consequence, a change in the money supply has a relatively large effect on GNP.

THE KEYNESIAN-CLASSICAL DEBATE

The debate between the Keynesian and classical views of macroeconomics can be summarised in terms of the IS-LM model. The Keynesian view requires:

- A *flat* LM curve and a *steep* IS curve (left-hand diagrams in figures 17.7 and 17.8).

Fiscal policy has a significant effect on GNP and monetary policy has little or no effect on GNP. An extreme Keynesian position is the concept of a *liquidity trap* when the LM curve is horizontal. Under this condition, there is no crowding-out of investment and fiscal policy is very effective.

The classical view is just the opposite, namely:

- A *steep* LM curve and a *flat* IS curve (right-hand diagrams in figures 17.7 and 17.8).

Now government spending crowds-out private sector investment and fiscal policy is ineffective. In contrast, changes in the money supply have an important effect on the level of nominal GNP. The extreme classical case is that the LM curve is vertical and an expansionary fiscal policy has no effect on output. With a vertical LM curve there is 100 per cent crowding-out.

It is possible to compromise and to suggest that the truth lies between the extremes represented by the Keynesian and classical views. When interest rates are low, for example, an increase in interest rates may not crowd-out investment and the Keynesian view that fiscal policy is effective may be valid. On the other hand, when interest rates are relatively high any further rise in interest rates may lead to significant crowding-out of investment. In this case, the classical view that fiscal policy is ineffective may be valid. However, it is clear that the interest elasticity of the demand for money is of crucial importance in assessing policy prescriptions. It is over seventy years since Keynes launched his *General Theory*, but the economics profession has still not reached a consensus on the controversies it provoked.

17.7 THE FISCAL-MONETARY POLICY MIX

If we assume that there are unemployed resources in the economy, the question naturally arises: which mix of fiscal and monetary policies should the government use to reduce unemployment? In figure 17.9, the economy is initially at the point A, which corresponds to an interest rate of r_1 and output of GNP_1. Suppose that the vertical curve

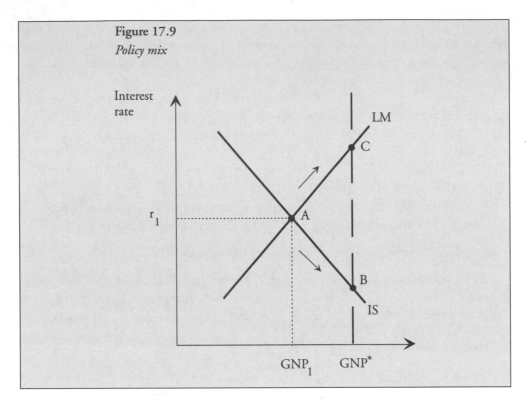

Figure 17.9
Policy mix

corresponding to GNP* indicates natural real GNP. If the government implements an expansionary fiscal policy the economy will move to the point C. Output increases, but the interest rate rises along the vertical axis. This implies some crowding-out of private sector spending.

If, alternatively, the government pursues an expansionary monetary policy, the economy moves to the point B. This time the increase in output is accompanied by a reduction in the interest rate, which would stimulate an increase in private sector investment. It might appear that this outcome is preferable. However, the IS-LM model does not consider the longer-run implications of the increase in the money supply and the reduction in interest rates for inflation (the quantity theory).

The choice between an expansionary fiscal or monetary policy is clearly in part a political one. Conservative politicians tend to prefer tax cuts to increases in public expenditure. They would also worry about the longer-run inflationary implications of an expansionary monetary policy. Left-wing politicians, who generally favour increases in public expenditure to tax cuts, tend not to be as worried about inflation as conservatives are.

17.8 CONCLUSION

In this chapter we introduced the IS-LM model and used it to analyse how the economy responds to fiscal and monetary policy. We reiterate again the point that the analysis presented in this chapter is only relevant in the context of the Eurozone as a whole. Only extreme versions of the analysis, for example a horizontal LM curve, is relevant for a small country like Ireland participating in EMU. Also the IS–LM model does not enable us to examine the problem of inflation. Nor does it provide any insight into the operation of the supply-side of the economy. The key points covered included:

- The IS curve shows the combinations of the interest rate and GNP that give an equilibrium in the market for goods and services
- The LM curve shows the combination of the interest rate and GNP that give equilibrium in the money market
- The intersection of the IS and LM curves represents a simultaneous equilibrium in both the goods and money markets
- The Keynesian case is represented by a flat (elastic) LM curve and a steep (inelastic) IS curve
- The classical case is represented by a steep (inelastic) LM curve and a flat (elastic) IS curve
- The crowding-out effect is important in the monetarist case but unimportant in the Keynesian model
- Expansionary fiscal and monetary policies have different implications for interest rates.

CHAPTER 18

The Mundell-Fleming Model

18.1 INTRODUCTION

In this chapter we extend the Keynes-Hicks IS-LM model so as to make it applicable to open economies. This extension was developed by John Fleming, an Oxford economist, and Robert Mundell, a Nobel prize-winning Canadian economist teaching at Columbia University. We then use the Mundell-Fleming model to explore the effects of fiscal, monetary and exchange rate policies on output and employment. This supplements our analysis in previous chapters, where similar issues were addressed using the 'open economy monetary model'.

18.2 INTERNAL AND EXTERNAL BALANCE

In an open economy a key issue is how the policy maker can achieve simultaneously both full employment (*internal balance*) and balance of payments' equilibrium (*external balance*). To start, we need to extend the IS-LM framework we introduced in the previous chapter to account for external balance. Recall that the IS line shows the combinations of GNP and the real interest rate consistent with equilibrium in the goods market. The LM line shows the combinations of GNP and the real interest rate consistent with equilibrium in the money market. At the point A in figure 18.1 the two lines intersect and there is, simultaneously, equilibrium in both the goods and money markets.

Note:
In figure 18.1 we show the nominal (i), and not real (r), interest rate on the vertical axis. The substitution of the nominal for the real interest rate does not affect the analysis because, with *prices fixed*, a change in the real interest rate will be completely reflected in a change in the nominal interest rate. The reason for making this substitution is to incorporate into the analysis, capital flows, through the balance of payments. These capital account flows are responsive to changes in nominal interest rates.

Any change in the components of aggregate demand consumption (C), investment (I), government expenditure (G) and net exports (NX) shifts the IS schedule. An expansionary fiscal policy, for example, would shift the IS curve to the right. Also an increase in NX will shift the IS curve out to the right, and vice versa. On the other hand, a change in the money supply (monetary policy) will shift the LM schedule.

EXTERNAL BALANCE

In chapter 9 we pointed out that under flexible exchange rates the balance of payments always balances in the sense that the current account surplus (deficit) is always offset by

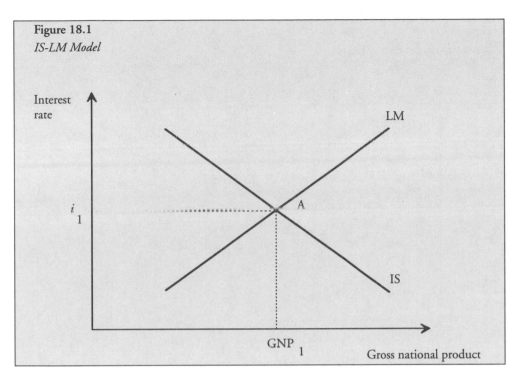

Figure 18.1
IS-LM Model

an equal deficit (surplus) on the capital account. If the exchange rate is fixed these surpluses (deficits) will be reflected in an increase (decrease) in the official reserves of foreign exchange held by the central bank. *External balance* can be said to exist when the central bank does not have to intervene in the foreign exchange market to stabilise the exchange rate. This implies that the sum of the current account and private capital flows is zero. This balance could happen even though there is a large current account deficit, provided it is financed by a private capital inflow. A good example of this is the US economy in 2002.

In figure 18.2 we draw a reference line BP = 0, which shows the combinations of GNP and the interest rate that result in the overall balance of payments being zero. The BP = 0 line slopes upwards because increases in the interest rate and in GNP have opposing effects on the balance of payments. Consider first the effect of an increase in the interest rate. If the exchange rate is fixed, an increase in the domestic interest rate relative to the world rate leads to a capital inflow as investors move funds to the country that offers the highest return.

- $\uparrow i$ (relative to the interest rate in the rest of the world) $\rightarrow$ $\uparrow$capital inflows $\rightarrow$ surplus on the capital account of the balance of payments.

On the other hand, an increase in GNP leads to an increase in imports (M) via the marginal propensity to import (MPM) and a fall in net exports, that is, a rise in the deficit on current account.

- $\uparrow$ GNP $\rightarrow$ $\uparrow$ M $\rightarrow$ rise in current account deficit

The BP = 0 line is drawn so that the positive effect of higher interest rates offsets the negative GNP effect and the overall balance of payments remains in equilibrium. In

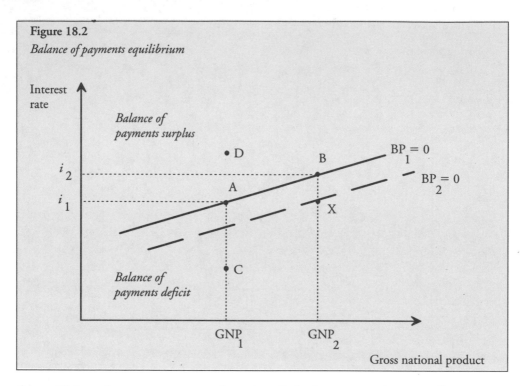

Figure 18.2
Balance of payments equilibrium

figure 18.2, as the economy moves from A to B the interest rate increases from i_1 to i_2 and this leads to a capital account surplus. On the other hand, the increase in GNP from GNP_1 to GNP_2 leads to a current account deficit.

If the economy is above the BP = 0 line, at a point such as D in the diagram, there is a balance of payments surplus. This is because the interest rate is higher than that necessary for equilibrium. If it is below the BP = 0 line, at C for example, there is a balance of payments deficit. The interest rate is lower than that required for equilibrium.

LOCATION OF THE BP LINE

The BP = 0 line is drawn for a given level of exports and imports, world interest rates, and exchange rate expectations. (Bear in mind from our discussion of interest rate parity that if the exchange rate is expected to depreciate, the interest rate will have to be higher than the world interest rate.) The position of the line changes if any of these variables change. An increase in exports or a fall in imports (not brought about by a change in GNP) will shift the BP = 0 line downwards to the right. To see why, suppose that the economy is initially at the point A and interest rates are kept constant at i_1. Suppose now that there is an increase in the demand for the country's exports. By shifting the BP = 0 line to the right we can again achieve BP equilibrium. The point X, for example, in figure 18.2 is on the lower BP = 0 line. At X the rise in GNP from GNP_1 to GNP_2 has increased imports sufficiently to offset the increase in exports and the balance of payments returns to equilibrium.

Similarly, an expected exchange rate depreciation would improve the trade balance and require a lower interest rate. The BP = 0 line would shift downwards. A fall in world interest rates would facilitate a fall in domestic interest rates. By shifting the BP line downwards, we can examine the relationship between the new lower interest rate and the initial level of GNP.

A fall in exports, a rise in imports (not due to changes in GNP), an increase in world interest rates or an expected exchange rate appreciation would shift the BP = 0 line upwards to the left.

SLOPE OF THE BP LINE

The slope of the BP = 0 line depends on (i) the degree of capital mobility, and (ii) the marginal propensity to import (MPM). If capital flows are very sensitive to interest differentials then the BP line will be relatively flat. Only a small change in the interest rate (relative to the world rate) is necessary to attract sufficient capital to compensate for the increased imports due to a given increase in GNP and maintain the balance of payments in equilibrium. If there is *perfect capital mobility*, the BP = 0 line will be *horizontal*. A small change in the domestic interest rate would lead to unlimited capital inflows or outflows. In this case, only the world interest rate, i^*, is consistent with balance of payments equilibrium whatever the level of GNP. Changes in exports, imports and the exchange rate will *not* shift the BP = 0 line because enough capital will always flow in to finance the current account deficit.

On the other hand, if capital flows are restricted by *exchange controls*, the BP = 0 line will be relatively steep. A large change in interest rates would be needed to attract the capital inflows to finance the current account deficit due to a given increase in GNP.

A large MPM means that a given increase in GNP will lead to a relatively large increase in imports and interest rates will have to increase accordingly to compensate; hence the BP = 0 line will be steep. In general:

- If there is a high degree of capital mobility and the MPM is small, then the BP line will be relatively flat.
- If there is a low degree of capital mobility and the MPM is large, then the BP line will be relatively steep.

In 2002 the Irish economy is best described by a horizontal BP = 0 line. This is because the degree of capital mobility between Ireland and our main trading partners is very high. Between Ireland and the other EMU countries it is not possible for domestic interest rates to deviate by any significant amount from the European Central Bank's (ECB) and the EMU inter-bank rates without provoking massive capital flows. Similarly, between the Eurozone, the US and UK there is a very high degree of capital mobility which results in a horizontal BP line.

While it is true that the Irish MPM is relatively large, any increase in imports as a result of increases in GNP is likely to be dominated by the effect of an incipient rise in interest rates on the capital account.

Note:
On a historical level the BP = 0 line was horizontal in Ireland up to 1979 when the Irish pound was pegged to sterling and capital flowed freely between Ireland and the UK. Between December 1978 and December 1988 exchange controls restricted capital movements between Ireland and

other countries. It is possible that during this period the BP = 0 line sloped upwards, allowing the Irish interest rate to deviate from that in the rest of the world. However, with the complete abolition of exchange controls in 1992 and the introduction of the euro in 1999, there is now near perfect capital mobility between Ireland and other countries.

18.3 INTRODUCTION TO THE MUNDELL-FLEMING MODEL

We can now extend our IS-LM analysis to include the effect of changes in the level of economic activity on interest rates and the balance of payments. The Mundell-Fleming model was developed for this purpose. (J. M. Fleming, 'Domestic Financial Policies under Fixed and Floating Exchange Rates', *IMF Staff Papers*, 9, 1962, and R. A. Mundell, 'The Appropriate Use of Monetary and Fiscal Policy Under Fixed Exchange Rates', *IMF Staff Papers*, 9, 1962.) The model is based on several assumptions.

- Firstly, and most importantly, it assumes that the *price levels in the domestic country and the rest of the world are constant*. This is obviously a strong assumption because as we have seen, even with the introduction of the euro, there is no single inflation rate between the Eurozone countries.
- Secondly, the model assumes that the economy is not supply constrained.
- Thirdly, crowding-out is less than complete and, as a result, fiscal policy is an effective policy instrument.

These three assumptions imply that the aggregate supply curve is perfectly horizontal and that changes in real output and employment are determined only by changes in aggregate demand.

- Fourthly, we assume that an expansionary fiscal policy is financed in a non-monetary way and does not result in an increase in the money supply.
- Finally, we assume perfect capital mobility so that the BP = 0 line is horizontal. The analysis below, however, does allow for imperfect capital mobility and shows how this alters the conclusions of the model.

Figure 18.3 incorporates these assumptions. A horizontal BP = 0 reference line is amalgamated with the IS-LM model. At the point A the IS and LM curves intersect with the BP = 0 line. At this point the goods and money markets and the balance of payments are all in equilibrium.

In the next section we use the Mundell-Fleming model to analyse the effects of fiscal and monetary policy on output and the balance of payments when the exchange rate is both *fixed* and *flexible*. In what follows, it is important to bear in mind that under fixed exchange rates the central bank intervenes in the foreign exchange market to stabilise the exchange rate. As a result, balance of payments' deficits or surpluses are reflected in changes in the external reserves, which in turn affect the domestic money supply and shift the LM curve. If the exchange rate were floating, then the central bank would not intervene in the foreign exchange market and balance of payments surpluses or deficits would result in an appreciation or depreciation of the currency. As we shall see, the effect of fiscal and monetary policy on output and employment is very different, depending on whether the exchange rate is fixed or floating.

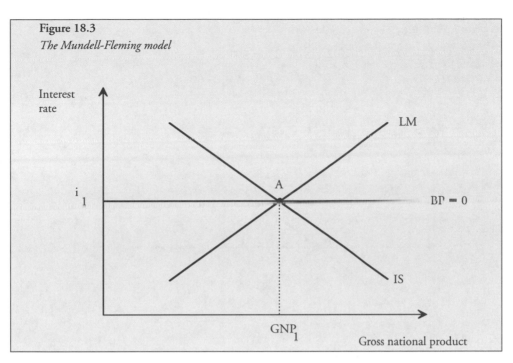

Figure 18.3
The Mundell-Fleming model

18.4 APPLYING THE MODEL UNDER FIXED EXCHANGE RATES

FISCAL POLICY

In figure 18.4 we show the effect of an increase in government expenditure on output when the exchange rate is fixed. This analysis is not applicable to the case of Ireland relative to the other EMU countries because, with the introduction of the euro, there is no longer any exchange rate between countries in the Eurozone. Hence, it is no longer necessary for the Central Bank of Ireland to intervene in the foreign exchange market. The analysis is relevant in, for example, some Eastern European countries such as the Czech Republic, which is pursuing a fixed exchange rate policy relative to the euro.

An increase in government expenditure shifts the IS curve outwards from IS_1 to IS_2 and the economy moves from A to B. At B, GNP has increased and there is a balance of payments surplus as the economy is above the BP = 0 reference line.

An expansionary fiscal policy results in a balance of payments surplus because:

- The increase in GNP leads to an increase in imports via the marginal propensity to import and this results in a *deficit* in the current account of the balance of payments.
- The increase in GNP increases the demand for money and therefore the domestic interest rate. This results in a capital inflow and a surplus on the capital account of the balance of payments.

$$\uparrow GNP \rightarrow \uparrow M^d \rightarrow \uparrow i \rightarrow \text{capital inflow}$$

Given perfect capital mobility, the second effect dominates the first, with the result that there is an overall balance of payments surplus: the deficit in the current account is more than offset by the surplus on the capital account.

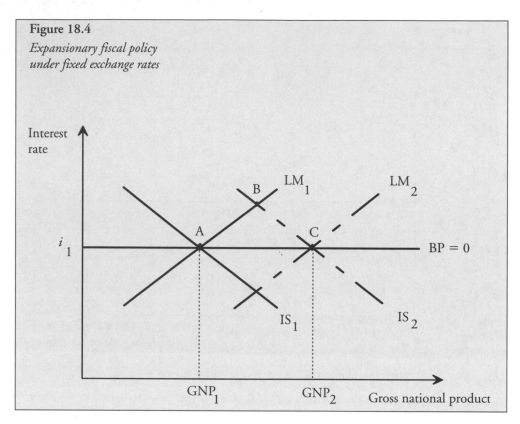

Figure 18.4

Expansionary fiscal policy under fixed exchange rates

Point B in figure 18.4 is not a final equilibrium. Because the exchange rate is fixed, the central bank must intervene in the foreign exchange market to stabilise it following the emergence of a balance of payments surplus. In the case of the Czech Republic, this intervention takes the form of selling crowns and accumulating euro, which are added to the external reserves. The rise in the external reserves, in turn, increases high-powered money and has a multiplier effect on the overall money supply. The LM curve now shifts outwards from LM_1 to LM_2. The economy moves from B to C.

Note:
When the exchange rate is fixed or pegged, a surplus (deficit) in the balance of payments will cause the external reserves to rise (fall) and shift the LM curve. Thus in an open economy, with a fixed exchange rate, the country's central bank loses control over the money supply. If, however, the central bank engages in *sterilisation*, it can try to offset this effect. We assume here that the central bank does not engage in sterilisation, which in any event tends to work only in the short run.

At C the domestic interest rate is again equal to the world rate and the overall balance of payments is zero. The current account is in deficit but this is offset by the capital account surplus. The level of GNP has risen as a result of the fiscal expansion. Fiscal policy is therefore *effective* when the exchange rate is fixed and capital is perfectly mobile. The magnitude of the impact of fiscal policy on output depends on the slopes of the IS-LM curves.

IMPERFECT CAPITAL MOBILITY

If there is imperfect capital mobility between the Czech Republic and the Eurozone, the BP = 0 line will slope upwards. If the degree of capital mobility is such that the BP = 0 line is steeper than the LM curve, the reader can verify that an expansionary fiscal policy will result in an overall balance of payments *deficit*. The LM curve will then shift back to the left, reflecting a fall in the central bank's external reserves. The increase in GNP will be smaller than when there was perfect capital mobility. This suggests that the greater the degree of capital mobility, the more effective is fiscal policy.

MONETARY POLICY

Figure 18.5 shows the effect of an expansionary monetary policy when the exchange rate is fixed. We reiterate the point that this analysis is relevant in the case of the Czech Republic, for example, and the Eurozone but not between countries participating in EMU.

The increase in the money supply shifts the LM curve from LM_1 to LM_2 and the economy moves from A to B. At B, GNP has increased, but the economy is below the BP = 0 line, indicating that there is a balance of payments deficit.

The balance of payments deficit arises for two reasons:

- The increase in the money supply leads to a fall in the domestic interest rate relative to the world interest rate, and this results in a capital outflow and a deficit on the capital account of the balance of payments.

$\uparrow M^s \rightarrow \downarrow i$ (relative to the world rate) $\rightarrow$ capital outflow

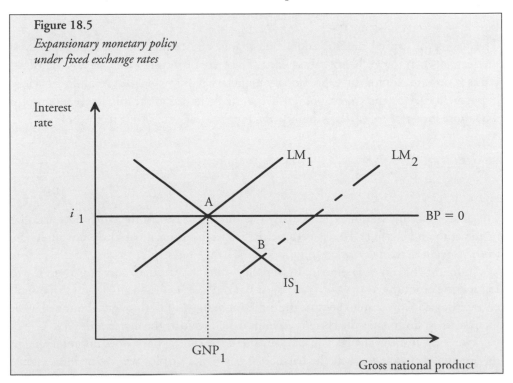

Figure 18.5

Expansionary monetary policy under fixed exchange rates

•   The increase in GNP leads to an increase in imports (via the marginal propensity to import) and a current account deficit.

$$\uparrow \text{GNP} \rightarrow \uparrow \text{M} \rightarrow \text{current account deficit}$$

An expansionary monetary policy therefore results in a deficit in *both* the current and capital accounts of the balance of payments, giving rise to an overall balance of payments deficit.

The economy will not remain at B. Because the exchange rate is fixed, the central bank must intervene in the foreign exchange market to offset the balance of payments deficit. It does this by buying Czech crowns with euro from the official external reserves. The fall in the reserves results in a contraction in the money supply. This is shown by the backward shift in the LM curve, which continues until the economy returns to its original position at A. At this point, the domestic interest rate is again equal to the world rate and GNP has returned to its initial level. From this sequence of events we see that:

•   When the exchange rate is fixed, the money supply is no longer controlled by the central bank.

Because capital is perfectly mobile, the fall in the interest rate leads to an immediate capital outflow and the money supply and the interest rate quickly return to their original levels. Given the speed with which capital flows out of the country, the interest rate does not remain below the world rate long enough to have any effect on the level of domestic economic activity. Monetary policy is therefore *ineffective* when the exchange rate is fixed and capital is perfectly mobile.

IMPERFECT CAPITAL MOBILITY

The degree of capital mobility does not change the result that monetary policy is ineffective when the exchange rate is fixed. The reader can verify that even if the BP = 0 line is upward sloping, an expansionary monetary policy will again result in a balance of payments deficit and the economy will eventually return to the initial level of output. The more imperfect is capital mobility, the longer it takes to revert to the point A.

18.5 THE MODEL UNDER FLOATING EXCHANGE RATES

FISCAL POLICY

The analysis in this section is particularly relevant in the case of the euro and the dollar or the euro and sterling. This is because the respective central banks do not intervene in the foreign exchange market to influence exchange rates.

In figure 18.6 an expansionary fiscal policy shifts the IS curve outwards from IS_1 to IS_2 and the economy moves from A to B. At B, GNP has increased and there is an overall balance of payments surplus because the capital account surplus (brought about by higher interest rates) dominates the current account deficit (due to the increase in GNP).

However, if the exchange rate is floating and the central bank does not intervene in the foreign exchange market, the balance of payments surplus will result in exchange

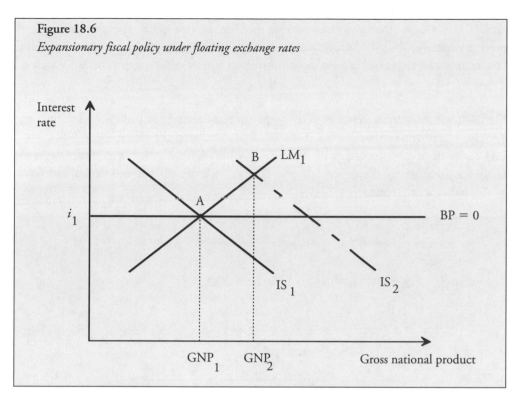

Figure 18.6
Expansionary fiscal policy under floating exchange rates

rate appreciation. The external reserves and the money supply remain unchanged. The LM curve is therefore not affected.

But the rise in the exchange rate reduces exports and increases imports, and the IS curve shifts backwards to the left. The *real* exchange rate (ϵ) is defined as:

$$\epsilon = (e \times P)/P_f$$

where P and P_f are domestic and foreign prices respectively and e is the nominal exchange rate. This real exchange rate is one determinant of net exports (NX), that is exports minus imports. It follows, therefore, that changes in the real exchange rate (brought about by nominal exchange rate appreciation) affect the position of the IS curve in an open economy.

This process will continue until the economy reverts to point A. The increase in GNP was therefore only temporary. In effect, under floating exchange rates, an expansionary fiscal policy crowds-out NX through exchange rate appreciation. Fiscal policy is therefore *ineffective* when the exchange rate is floating and there is perfect capital mobility.

IMPERFECT CAPITAL MOBILITY

If the BP = 0 line is steeper than the LM curve due to imperfect capital mobility, an expansionary fiscal policy will result in an increase in GNP and a balance of payments deficit. In this case, the exchange rate depreciates and this results in a further increase in GNP. The reader can verify that under these circumstances fiscal policy will have a greater effect on output and employment than in the case of fixed exchange rate and perfect capital mobility. Note, however, that we are assuming there are no supply-side constraints and that no domestic inflation follows from the exchange rate depreciation.

MONETARY POLICY

Figure 18.7 illustrates the case of an expansionary monetary policy under floating exchange rates with perfect capital mobility. The increase in the money supply shifts the LM curve from LM_1 to LM_2 and the economy moves from point A to point B. At B, GNP has increased and a deficit has emerged on both the current and capital accounts of the balance of payments.

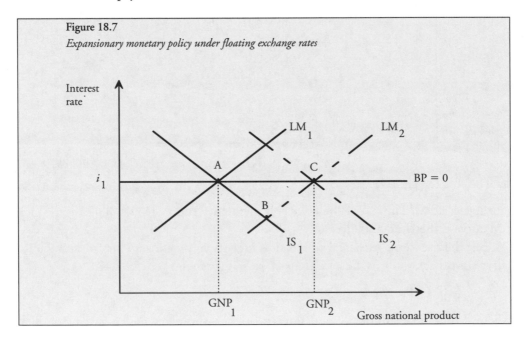

Figure 18.7
Expansionary monetary policy under floating exchange rates

The exchange rate now depreciates and this increases net exports. The IS curve shifts outwards from IS_1 to IS_2 and the economy moves from B to C. GNP again increases and equilibrium is restored to the balance of payments. This implies that monetary policy is very effective when exchange rates are floating, capital is perfectly mobile, and there are no supply-side constraints. This result is not changed if there is imperfect capital mobility and the BP = 0 line is upward sloping.

SUMMARY

Table 18.1 summarises our conclusions for fixed and floating exchange rate cases. Monetary policy is ineffective (in terms of achieving increases in output and employment) when the exchange rate is fixed but is very effective when the exchange rate is flexible. This is the case regardless of the degree of capital mobility.

Fiscal policy, on the other hand, is effective under fixed exchange rates and ineffective under floating exchange rates when there is perfect capital mobility. However, this finding tends to get reversed as capital becomes more immobile.

Table 18.1
The effect of fiscal and monetary policy on output

| | Exchange rate | |
	Fixed	Floating
Monetary policy	Ineffective (regardless of degree of capital mobility)	Effective
Fiscal policy	*Capital mobile* Effective	Ineffective
Fiscal policy	*Capital immobile* Relatively ineffective	Effective

Overall, the choice of exchange rate regime and the degree of capital mobility play an important role in determining the effectiveness of fiscal and monetary policy.

18.6 ECONOMIC POLICY, OUTPUT AND THE TRADE ACCOUNT

In the previous sections we focused on the overall balance of payments (current plus capital accounts). There we saw that as long as a current account deficit was offset by a capital account surplus the overall balance of payments was in equilibrium and external balance was achieved. In this section we focus on the current (trade) account only and examine how this account can influence the design of economic policy.

DEVALUATION AND THE TRADE BALANCE

An expansionary fiscal or monetary policy increases GNP, but in doing so creates a trade deficit (or reduces a trade surplus). This happens because the increase in GNP leads to an increase in imports via the marginal propensity to import (MPM). In certain circumstance, therefore, a *policy dilemma* can exist because an expansionary fiscal and monetary policy may increase employment (internal balance) and simultaneously create a trade deficit (external imbalance).

Devaluation, on the other hand, increases GNP through an improvement in the trade balance. Devaluation is therefore a particularly useful policy instrument if there is a trade deficit and high unemployment. The policy dilemma that can exist between achieving a trade balance and full employment can be resolved by devaluation. We emphasise once more that devaluation is not an option for any of the countries participating in EMU. It could be an option, however, for the Eurozone as a whole.

Note:
An improvement in the home trade balance resulting from exchange rate devaluation has to be matched by an increase in some other country's trade deficit. Hence the gain in output and employment at home must be at the expense of a reduction in output and employment in some other country. This gives rise to the accusation that devaluation is a 'beggar thy neighbour' policy in that the devaluing country is attempting to 'export its unemployment' to other countries.

TRADE ACCOUNT

In figure 18.8 we elaborate on this point by developing an NX = 0 reference line. The analysis is the same as it would be for the BP = 0 line, with zero capital mobility. Here we are concentrating on the current account or the *trade account* if the other sub-accounts are assumed to be independent of changes in GNP. One reason for focusing on the trade account is that the capital account does not enter into the calculation of aggregate demand.

With GNP on the horizontal axis and exports and imports on the vertical axis, the import schedule is shown as sloping upwards. This reflects the fact that imports increase as GNP rises. The slope of this line is determined by the MPM. The larger the MPM, the steeper the import schedule. The export schedule is shown as a horizontal line, indicating that changes in GNP do not affect the level of exports. Exports are determined by the exchange rate and by aggregate demand in our main trading partners. At GNP_1, exports equal imports and the trade account is balanced. We draw a vertical NX = 0 reference line to indicate this level of GNP. To the right of the NX = 0 line there is a trade deficit (imports exceed exports), and to the left there is a trade surplus.

A devaluation will shift the import schedule down to the right and the export schedule upwards. The NX = 0 line will now shift to the right and the equilibrium level of GNP (that level of GNP where exports equal imports) will move to the right along the horizontal axis.

Figure 18.9 shows an NX = 0 line that corresponds to a trade balance at GNP_1 and a natural real GNP reference line denoted by GNP*. To the right of natural real GNP, the economy is over-heating and there is 'over-employment'. That is unemployment is

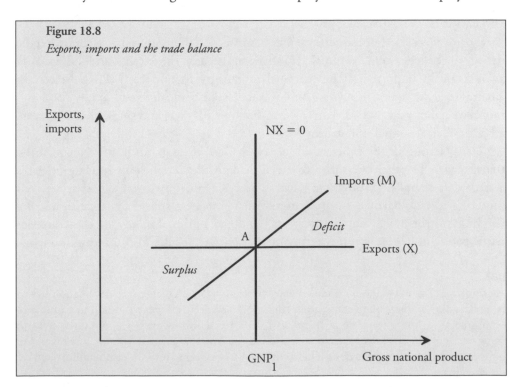

Figure 18.8
Exports, imports and the trade balance

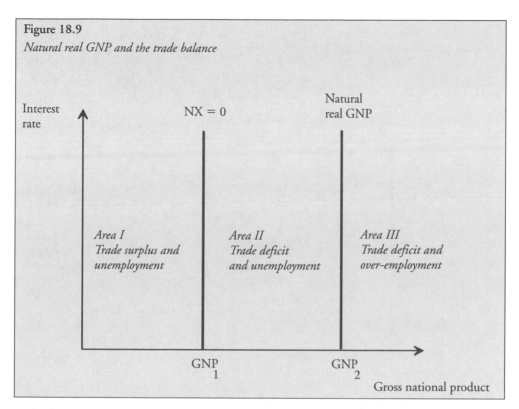

Figure 18.9
Natural real GNP and the trade balance

below its natural rate. To the left of natural real GNP, the economy is in recession and unemployment is above its natural rate. As drawn, the NX = 0 line is situated to the left of the GNP* (other combinations are possible). The economy can be in areas I, II or III. These areas are characterised as follows:

- Area I: trade surplus and unemployment
- Area II: trade deficit and unemployment
- Area III: trade deficit and over-employment.

To illustrate the various areas, in the early 1980s, the Irish economy was clearly in area II when the balance of trade deficit was about 15 per cent of GNP and unemployment was high and rising. In the early 1990s, with a trade surplus and a relatively high unemployment, the Irish economy was in area I.

If the economy is in area I or III there is no policy dilemma in using fiscal or monetary policy to achieve a trade balance and full employment. For example, if the economy is in area I, an expansionary fiscal or monetary policy can be used to reduce unemployment *and* reduce the trade surplus. Similarly, if the economy is in area III, a deflationary fiscal or monetary policy can be implemented to reduce over-employment *and* reduce the trade deficit.

A dilemma does however arise if the economy is in area II. An expansionary fiscal or monetary policy would reduce unemployment but aggravate the balance of trade deficit. In contrast, a contractionary fiscal or monetary policy would aggravate the problem of unemployment while improving the trade deficit.

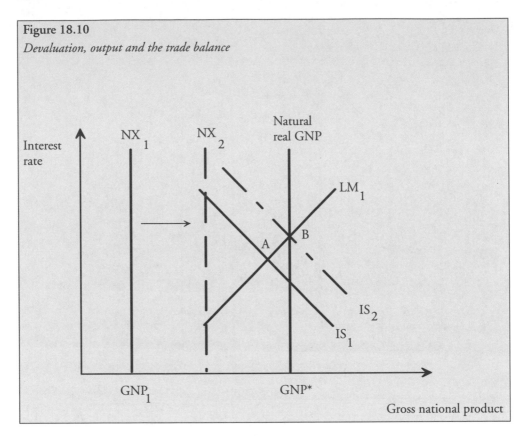

Figure 18.10
Devaluation, output and the trade balance

POLICY MIX

The dilemma between the internal and external policy objectives that exists when the economy is in area II can be resolved by resorting to devaluation. For example, as shown in figure 18.10, a devaluation would shift the NX = 0 line towards GNP* and move the IS curve from IS_1 to IS_2 (recall that a devaluation increases NX and therefore the IS curve). As a result, full employment could be restored while at the same time there should be an improvement in the trade account.

Suppose, however, the economy is at a point such as A in figure 18.11, which corresponds to natural real GNP and a trade deficit. A devaluation would move the NX = 0 line towards GNP*, but because of the shift to the right of the IS curve, the economy moves to the point B. At the point B, the trade account deficit has improved but the economy is now over-heating.

In this situation a deflationary fiscal or monetary policy is required to move either the IS or LM curves back to natural real GNP. Because of the fall in GNP this will further improve the trade deficit. This example shows that if the economy is close to natural real GNP, devaluation will have to be accompanied by an *expenditure reducing* policy if the objectives of internal and external balance are to be achieved simultaneously. Put another way, if the objective of devaluation is simply to improve the trade account without increasing output and employment, an expenditure reducing policy will have to accompany it. These applications illustrate how economists can analyse the appropriate policy mix for an open economy.

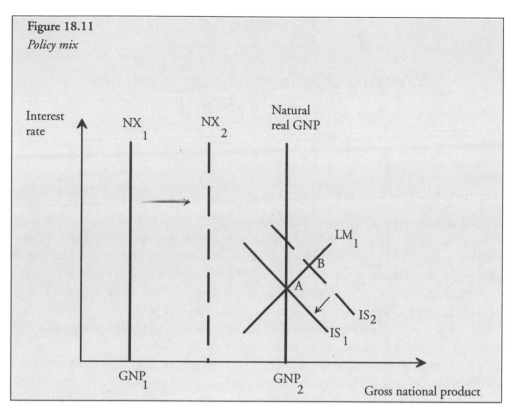

Figure 18.11
Policy mix

18.7 CONCLUSION

In this chapter we discussed how the open economy adjusts in the short run when prices are assumed to be constant and there are no supply-side constraints. Some of the main points developed in this chapter include:

* The concepts of internal and external balance
* The BP line
* The Mundell-Fleming model
* Fiscal policy is effective and monetary policy ineffective when the exchange rate is fixed and there is perfect capital mobility
* If the exchange rate is floating and capital perfectly mobile, fiscal policy is ineffective and monetary policy effective
* How a policy dilemma can exist when the objective is to achieve a trade balance and full employment
* Devaluation must be accompanied by a deflationary fiscal or monetary policy if the economy is close to natural real GNP and the objective is to remove a trade deficit.

CHAPTER 19

Hedging against Exchange Rate and Interest Rate Risk

19.1 INTRODUCTION

In this chapter we explore some technical aspects of international financial markets. Ireland is a small and open economy that is deeply integrated into the global economy. Buying and selling across international borders between countries that use different currencies involves *exchange rate risk*. This continues to be a problem for Irish exporters and importers even after the introduction of the euro in 1999. Trade between Ireland and the UK, the US, Japan, and other countries outside the EMU still involves exchange rates. Even if a firm's sales are entirely in euro, it may still be exposed to exchange rate risk if it imports some of its inputs from outside the Eurozone.

Because of its importance to a country like Ireland, in this chapter we provide a survey of some technical aspects of foreign exchange markets. We describe the various techniques that have been developed to hedge against exchange rate risk. Much of the discussion relates to the forward exchange rate, which is the most important external hedging technique. We examine the topic of forward market efficiency and the unbiased predictor hypothesis (UPH).

The concluding sections discuss *interest rate risk* and the various techniques that have been developed to hedge against this type of risk. Among the hedging techniques discussed are forward rate agreements, foreign currency swaps and futures contracts.

19.2 INTERNAL HEDGING TECHNIQUES

To see how significant exchange rate risk can be, it is relevant to consider the case of a firm exporting to the UK. As long as the UK remains outside the EMU, the pound sterling will fluctuate in terms of the euro. Consider, for example, an exporter who expects to receive £1 million in one month's time and anticipates that the exchange rate will be £0.64/€1. At this exchange rate, euro receipts will be €1,562,500 = (£1,000,000/0.64). Suppose, however, that the euro unexpectedly appreciates to £0.70796/€1. The exporter's receipts will translate into only €1,412,509. This is €149,990.8 less than was anticipated and could render the deal unprofitable. Traders naturally wish to hedge against this type of risk.

In this section we outline some of the more common *internal* hedging techniques. These techniques are less costly than *external* hedging techniques, but can achieve the same objective.

Use Eurozone suppliers

One way of eliminating exchange rate risk is to switch from a foreign to a domestic supplier. This was not very feasible prior to the introduction of the euro because many of the raw materials imported into Ireland had no domestic substitutes. However, with the introduction of the euro, the possibility of finding a supplier in the Eurozone has increased significantly. If it remains the case that no supplier can be found in the Eurozone, then a supplier operating out of a weak currency country is preferable to a strong currency country supplier. If the foreign currency depreciates, imports will cost less in euro.

Invoice in euro

If a company can invoice in euro, then exchange rate risk is eliminated. In effect, the exchange rate exposure is transferred to the other party in the transaction. Whether or not this is possible will probably depend on the relative strength of the parties to the deal. For example, a large buyer may be able to pressurise a small supplier into accepting the exchange rate risk. On occasions, both parties may agree to trade on the basis of a mutually acceptable hard currency such as the US dollar.

Match assets (liabilities) against liabilities (assets) in the same currency

Consider the case of an Irish firm with foreign assets, such as a subsidiary company in Britain. All of the assets and liabilities of the company in Britain will have to be translated from sterling to euro in order to prepare the balance sheet of the parent company in Ireland. If sterling depreciates on the foreign exchange market, then the euro value of the British subsidiary will fall and this will lower the value of the parent company. This type of exchange risk is referred to as *translation exposure*. One way to avoid or minimise it is to match overseas assets with liabilities in the same currency by, for example, borrowing in sterling. Then if the euro appreciates, the value of both the sterling assets and liabilities will fall. However, there is some debate as to the importance of translation costs and gains in determining a firm's stock price. Modern security analysis should disclose translation gains and losses in income statements and, as such, should not unduly influence prospective buyers of the firm's stock.

Foreign currency accounts

Another way of reducing exchange rate exposure is to match foreign currency receipts (from the sale of output) against foreign currency payments to suppliers. That way a loss on receipts will be matched by a reduction in payments. This technique will not, however, be possible unless the firm has a reasonable two-way flow in the same foreign currency.

To use this technique a firm will normally operate a *foreign currency account*. This is an account denominated in a currency other than euro. These accounts allow the trader to match inflows and outflows in the same currency. Another technique relates to a trader who has payments in one foreign currency (dollars) and receipts in another foreign currency (sterling). It is possible to convert from sterling to dollars using the cross exchange rate and thereby reduce conversion charges. Normally, the trader would convert his sterling receipts to euro and then use the euro to obtain dollars. However, the greater the number of conversions, the higher the charges and the lower the revenue to the trader.

BORROWING FOREIGN CURRENCY

Consider the case of an exporter who expects to receive a certain amount of sterling in one month's time. He or she could borrow the sterling now and convert it into euro at the current spot exchange rate. The foreign borrowing is subsequently repaid by the proceeds from the exports. By using this technique the exporter avoids exposure to exchange rate risk for the period he or she is waiting to be paid.

LEADING AND LAGGING OF PAYMENTS OR RECEIPTS

Importers and exporters can speculate on future exchange rate movements by leading and lagging. Importers and exporters can also minimise exchange rate losses through *leading* (importers paying before time) and *lagging* (exporters delaying receipts for as long as possible). If, for example, the euro were expected to depreciate, importers would pay their bills as soon as possible and exporters would delay converting their foreign currency receipts into euro. In the past, the very high exports/GNP and imports/GNP ratios in Ireland ensured that leading and lagging had a very significant impact on the level of Irish external reserves.

TRANSFER PRICING

Transfer pricing is concerned with setting intra-firm prices so as to minimise tax burdens. It is also possible to use transfer pricing to reduce exchange rate exposure. For example, suppose a company has two subsidiaries, one in a strong currency country and the other in a country whose currency is expected to depreciate. If the subsidiary in the weak currency country sells at cost to the other subsidiary, profits are maximised in the hard currency country and minimised in the weak currency country. The company will then gain if currencies move in the expected direction.

19.3 EXTERNAL HEDGING TECHNIQUES: THE FORWARD MARKET

In this section we describe one of the most widely used external hedging techniques, the use of the *forward exchange rate*.

FORWARD EXCHANGE CONTRACTS

A forward exchange contract consists of an agreement between a bank and a customer to:

- Buy or sell a specified amount of foreign currency for delivery some time in the future at an exchange rate agreed today.
- Payment and delivery are not required until the maturity date.

Consider the example of an Irish firm importing cars from the US. The cars will arrive in three months' time and the Irish importer will be required to pay, say,

$2,500,000 at that time. If the current (spot) exchange rate is $0.94/€1, the importer's bill will be €1,595,745 million. The importer, however, may be worried that over the next three months the euro could depreciate against the $ and not be prepared to take the exchange rate risk. (If the euro fell to $0.9/€1, the importer's bill would increase by €70,922.)

To remove this uncertainty the importer could enter into a contract that provides *forward cover* and removes the exposure to exchange rate risk. For example, he could arrange today to have $2,500,000 delivered in three months' time at an exchange rate (the three-month forward rate) agreed today. (Forward exchange rates are quoted for one, two, three, six and twelve months, and contracts can be arranged for longer periods. The rates are available from the banks and are published in the financial newspapers.)

Table 19.1
Spot and forward exchange rates, August 2002

	£/€		$/€	
	Bid	Offer	Bid	Offer
Spot	0.6570	0.6600	1.0035	1.0045
6 month forward	0.6625	0.6645	0.9677	0.9687

Source: AIB Bank.

Table 19.1 shows the spot and six-month forward exchange rates for the euro against sterling and the dollar in January 2002.

Recall from chapter 9 that:

- The *bid* rate is the rate at which banks buy euro (or sell foreign currency).
- The *offer* rate is the rate at which the banks sell euro (buy foreign currency).

The spot rates given in table 19.1 indicate that a bank dealer will buy euro at £0.6570 and sell euro at £0.6600. The difference between the bid and offer rates is referred to as the 'spread' and it provides the banks' profit from foreign exchange transactions.

The six-month forward rates in table 19.1 are the rates at which sterling and the dollar can be purchased or sold forward. Suppose, for example, an Irish importer wishes to obtain sterling six months from now. The bank will sell sterling forward to the importer (delivery is in six months' time) at an exchange rate of £0.6625/€1. Similarly, an exporter who is due to receive a certain amount of sterling in six months' time can eliminate exchange rate risk by selling sterling to the bank. The bank will buy sterling at a forward exchange rate of £0.6645/€1.

The forward exchange rate is normally at a *premium* or a *discount* relative to the spot exchange rate. Using indirect quotes (i.e. £/€), which is the convention in Ireland, if the forward exchange rate is lower than the spot rate, the euro is said to be at a discount relative to the foreign currency. Conversely, if the forward rate is higher than the spot rate, the euro is said to be at a premium relative to the foreign currency.

Comparing the spot and forward rates in table 19.1, we see that more sterling could be obtained for euro delivered in the future than today and hence the euro was at a premium relative to sterling. Fewer dollars could be obtained in the future for euro and hence the euro was at a discount relative to the dollar. If the spot and forward rates are exactly the same, the forward price is said to be *flat*.

Note:

There are two types of forward contracts. A *fixed* contract is where a specific date is chosen to fulfil the contract. This is used when the exact payment date is known. An *option* contract is where the customer can chose two specified dates to fulfil the contract. This type of contract will be used when the customer is unsure about the actual payment date. It is not an option to take or leave the contract.

HOW HEDGING CAN RESULT IN A LOSS OF REVENUE

It is important to note that while a hedging strategy minimises exchange rate losses, it also removes any possibility of making windfall profits from exchange rate movements.

As an example, suppose an exporter expects to receive £1 million in three months' time. He or she has a choice as to whether to sell sterling forward and avoid exchange rate risk, or sell sterling spot in three months' time and accept the exchange rate risk. Suppose, for example, that the forward rate (F_t) is £0.671/€1 and the spot rate three months from now (e_{t+1}) is £0.644/€1. The alternative outcomes are as follows:

- If he had sold £1 million three months earlier at a forward exchange rate of ($1/F_t$) = (1/.6710), his receipts would have been €1,490,313.
- If he accepted the exchange rate risk and sold £1 million on the spot market at ($1/e_{t+1}$) = (1/.644), his euro receipts would have been €1,552,795.

It is clear from this example that because F_t was not equal to e_{t+1}, the exporter's receipts differed significantly depending on which option he chose. If he had decided to hedge, his receipts would have been €62,482 lower than if he had accepted the exchange rate risk and sold sterling on the spot market.

In the above example the exporter would have forgone a profit by contracting forward. However, an importer would have gained by entering into a forward contract. The reason is that the importer is buying foreign currency when the exporter is selling. The two cases are mirror images of the same transaction.

This illustrates how hedging can entail forgoing a significant profit. In practice, treasury managers and others concerned with international cash flows do not always attempt to eliminate exchange rate risk because taking risks (or speculating) on foreign exchange movements can be profitable. For this reason, currency management is an integral part of treasury management in any large firm whose business involves extensive foreign exchange dealings.

FORWARD CURRENCY OPTIONS CONTRACT

A variation on the forward currency contract is the *forward currency options contract*. This gives the holder the right, but not the obligation, to buy or sell currency in the future. For this right, the holder will be charged a fee (or a premium) expressed as a percentage of the total amount of money involved. The right to sell a currency is referred to as a *put option* and the right to buy is known as a *call option*. The distinctive feature of option contracts is that while the holder can avoid exchange rate losses (downside risk), she can benefit from any favourable movements in the exchange rate (upside potential), or vice versa.

Take, for example, an Irish exporter who expects to receive $1 million in three months' time. To avoid exchange rate risk she enters into an options contract to convert dollars to euro at an exchange rate of, say, $1.060/€1. If the spot dollar exchange rate depreciates (euro appreciates) to $1.070/€1, the exporter should exercise her option contract in order to avoid incurring an exchange rate loss. If, however, the spot dollar exchange rate appreciates (euro depreciates) to, say, $1.050/€1, the exporter should allow the options contract to lapse and instead convert the dollar receipts to euro on the spot market. In this case she will gain from the exchange rate movement.

If the exporter had used a normal forward currency contract, she would have avoided any exchange rate loss but would also have forgone any gains. (A fee or commission is charged on these contracts, otherwise they would be preferable to using the forward market.)

Note:
There are two types of foreign currency option contracts. An *American option* is where the customer can exercise the option on any business day between the granting of the contract and the expiry date. A *European option* is where there is a single expiry date and a single settlement date. The customer must tell the bank if he or she intends exercising the contract on a particular date.

A variation of the forward option contract is a *participating forward contract*. This is where the trader has an options contract for part of her exposure and a fixed rate contract for the remainder. This allows the customer to benefit from exchange rate movements using only a part of their exposure. Another variation is known as a *zero-cost cylinder*. This involves buying a currency call option while simultaneously selling a currency put option. The details are rather technical, but the principle is essentially the same. The idea is to reduce exchange rate exposure while still being able to benefit from any windfall gains that might emerge due to currency movements. While the options contract allows for greater flexibility, in general, the simple forward currency contract is the most extensively used method of hedging against exchange rate risk.

19.4 Interest Rate Parity Theory

As explained earlier in chapter 10, the uncovered version of interest rate parity theory (UIP) relates the difference between domestic and foreign interest rates to the expected change in the exchange rate. In this section we outline the *covered* version of interest rate parity theory (CIP).

COVERED INTEREST PARITY

In chapter 10 the UIP formula was given as:

$$(e^e_{t+1} - e_t)/e_t = (i_{US} - i_{EUR})/(1 + i_{EUR}) \qquad (1)$$

This equation says that the expected change in the exchange rate, $(e^e_{t+1} - e_t)/e_t$, should equal the difference between foreign (US) and Eurozone (EUR) interest rates, $(i_{US} - i_{EUR})/(1 + i_{EUR})$. If the market expects the exchange rate to depreciate in the future, Eurozone interest rates will exceed foreign rates and vice versa.

The covered version of interest rate parity (CIP) is based on the same equation except that the forward exchange rate (F_t) replaces the expected exchange rate variable e^e_{t+1}. Hence:

$$(F_t - e_t)/e_t = (i_{US} - i_{EUR})/(1 + i_{EUR}) \qquad (2)$$

CIP states that the forward premium or discount (left-hand side) equals the interest differential (right-hand side). If the euro is at a premium ($F_t > e_t$), the foreign interest rate will exceed the Eurozone interest rate. Conversely, if the euro is at a discount ($F_t < e_t$), the Eurozone interest rate will exceed the foreign interest rate.

Note:
We have used the dollar in the above example to develop the basic CIP equation, but the theory can be generalised to include any currency and foreign interest rate. Hence in equation (2) the US can be replaced by the more general term 'interest rate in the rest of the world'.

Figure 19.1 gives a graphical representation of CIP. The interest differential (foreign minus domestic) is given on the vertical axis, and the premium (+) or discount (-) on the euro is given on the horizontal axis. The diagonal line represents the parity condition. At points on this line, such as A and B, CIP holds because the forward premium or discount is equal to the interest differential. If the interest differential exceeded the premium, as at point X, it is profitable to borrow in the Eurozone and invest in the US. This is true for all points above and to the left of the parity line. It is also true for points in the south-west quadrant of the diagram. At a point such as Y the premium on the euro exceeds the interest differential. If this were the situation, it would be profitable to borrow in the US and invest in the Eurozone.

Note:
It is possible that exchange controls might prevent arbitrage restoring the values on the left- and right-hand sides of the CIP equation. However, the leading and lagging by exporters and importers, respectively, cannot be prevented by exchange controls, and this would have the effect of re-establishing any divergence from interest rate parity.

The available evidence for the Eurozone and elsewhere suggests that CIP holds. In fact, banks tend to set forward exchange rates by looking at interest rate differentials, so in a sense it must hold! The interest rate differential determines the forward exchange rate. Does the forward exchange rate act as a good predictor of the future spot rate? This is the unbiased predictor hypothesis to which we now turn.

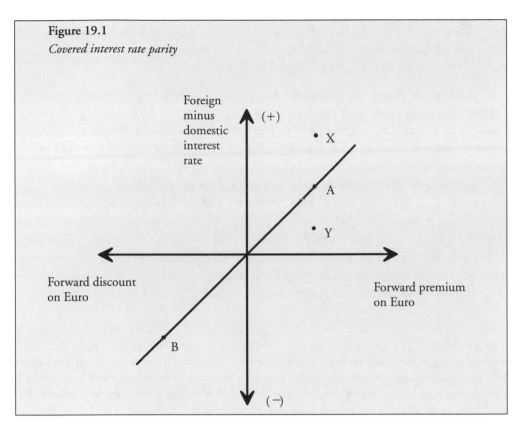

Figure 19.1
Covered interest rate parity

19.5 THE UNBIASED PREDICTOR HYPOTHESIS (UPH)

It is natural to ask whether the forward exchange rate is a good indicator of the future spot rate, that is, if the forward rate is a good predictor of exchange rate expectations? The forward exchange rate is said to be an unbiased predictor of the future spot rate if, over time, the forward rate is equal to the future spot rate *plus* or *minus* a random error. Mathematically, the *unbiased predictor hypothesis* (UPH) may be written:

$$e_{t+1} = \alpha + \beta\, F_t + u_t \qquad (3)$$

where e_{t+1} is the spot exchange rate in time t+1, F_t is the forward exchange rate in time t and u_t represents the forecast error. This error should be random with a mean of zero and a constant variance. If F_t is an unbiased predictor of e_{t+1}, the coefficients α and β will equal 0 and 1, respectively. F_t will equal e_{t+1} on average. If the UPH holds, today's forward rate is the best indicator of what the spot exchange rate will be in the future.

WHY F_t SHOULD REFLECT MOVEMENTS IN e_{t+1}

Suppose that the six-month sterling forward rate (F_t) is currently £0.64/€1 and that a speculator expects the spot exchange rate in six months' time (e_{t+1}^e) will be £0.6/€1. If the speculator's expectations prove correct, she could profit from the situation by:

- Contracting to buy, say, £1 million forward at £0.64/€1. The euro cost would be €1,562,500.

- Then in six months' time sell the £1 million on the spot market at £0.6/€1 and receive €1,666,667.
- Her profit on the transaction would be €104,166.7.

In general, if the speculator expects $e^e_{t+1} < F_t$, she should buy the foreign currency forward today and sell it on the spot market in the future. However, if a sufficient number of speculators believe this to be the case, their actions will have the effect of forcing F_t to converge to e^e_{t+1}. Buying sterling forward (selling euro forward) drives down F_t and selling sterling on the spot market (buying euro) drives up e^e_{t+1}.

Conversely, if the speculator expects $e^e_{t+1} > F_t$, she should sell the foreign currency forward and buy it on the spot market in the future. Again the effect will be to force F_t to converge to e^e_{t+1}. Selling sterling forward (buying euro forward) drives up F_t and buying sterling on the spot market (selling euro) drives down e^e_{t+1}. Hence, F_t should reflect what the market believes the future spot exchange rate will be. If this is not the case, the actions of speculators in the pursuit of profits will force a convergence of the forward and the future spot exchange rates as predicted by UPH.

Note:
The profit on such a deal cannot be expressed in percentage terms as no capital is actually invested when the speculator enters into the forward contract. The profit is simply the return from risk-taking. The amount that can be invested in this type of speculation will be limited by the amount of credit the speculator can draw down. There is, therefore, considerable scope for profitable speculation on the foreign exchange markets.

Historically, the Central Bank of Ireland attempted to constrain forward market speculation by introducing a number of controls. Up to January 1988 firms could only buy or sell currency forward if the transaction was *trade related*. Those dealing in services had to use some alternative hedging technique or accept the exchange rate risk. However, the exchange controls were relaxed in January 1988 to allow service industries access to forward cover, and in January 1992 to allow capital transactions and debt repayments cover. The Central Bank of Ireland cannot restrict trading on the euro forward market.

SOME HISTORICAL EVIDENCE ON UPH

Figure 19.2 uses the sterling, Irish pound exchange rate (from the start of the EMS in 1979 to the introduction of the euro in 1999) to compare the forward rate with the spot exchange rate three months from now. That is the spot rate three months from now (e_{t+1}) is 'taken back' and compared to today's forward rates (F_t). It is evident that these rates are not identical. In particular it is noticeable that the forward rate consistently *fails to predict turning points* in the future spot exchange rate. This is not the case, however, during the currency crisis of 1992–93. F_t correctly predicted the fall in e_{t+1} but over-stated the extent of the depreciation.

The unbiased predictor hypothesis (UPH) can be empirically evaluated by constructing a scatter diagram and then using regression analysis to estimate the 'line of

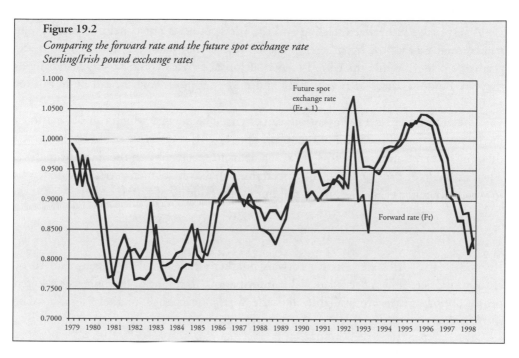

Figure 19.2

Comparing the forward rate and the future spot exchange rate
Sterling/Irish pound exchange rates

best fit'. This is done in figure 19.3. The slope of the trend line, the β coefficient in equation (3), is estimated to equal 0.7967, which is statistically different from the expected value of 1. Also the R^2 statistic suggests that F_t explains only 72 per cent of the variance of e_{t+1}. The forward rate does not appear to be a particularly good indicator of the future spot rate.

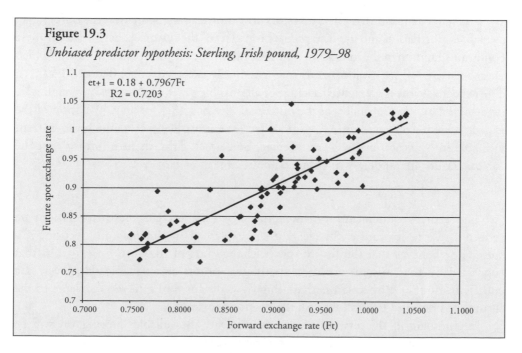

Figure 19.3

Unbiased predictor hypothesis: Sterling, Irish pound, 1979–98

A test of UPH between sterling and the Irish pound is not conclusive and it may still be the case that the hypothesis holds. UPH does not require F_t to be an 'accurate' predictor of e_{t+1}. While the period-to-period forecast errors could be large, so long as they are random, then UPH may hold and no better guide than F_t can be found for predicting e_{t+1}.

Therefore, there is a key question: can any rule be devised which can out-perform the forward rate as a predictor of the future spot rate? If such a rule could be developed then, in theory, unlimited profits are available from speculating in the forward market. The answer to this question is uncertain. The available empirical evidence is inconclusive and as such the jury is still out on the validity of UPH.

19.6 FORWARD MARKET EFFICIENCY

Related to the UPH are tests for forward market efficiency. A market is said to be efficient if prices fully reflect all available information. If this is not the case, unexploited profit opportunities are available and the foreign exchange market is said to be *inefficient*.

Note:
E. F. Fama, 'Efficient Capital Markets: A Review of Theory and Empirical Work', (*Journal of Finance*, 25, 1970, 383–417), distinguishes between three forms of market efficiency. *Weak form* efficiency is where current prices reflect only the information contained in historical prices. *Semi-strong* efficiency is where current prices reflect all public information. *Strong* efficiency is where current prices reflect all information, including insider information.

Efficiency requires that, first, investors are rational in the sense that they process all available information and use it to prepare forecasts of the future exchange rate. If these conditions hold, then the forecast of a currency in time $t+1$ formulated in time t (which we shall write as $_{t+1}e^e_t$) will equal its mathematically expected value, denoted $EV(e_{t+1})$. The expected value is a weighted average of all possible outcomes, where the weights are determined by the probability of the outcome. (See box 19.1 for an explanation of the expected value concept.) $EV(e_{t+1})$ is, in effect, the most likely outcome given current available information and will, on average, be correct. This, in turn, means that the forecast errors are randomly distributed about a mean of zero.

$$_{t+1}e^e_t = EV(e_{t+1}) \tag{4}$$

The second requirement for market efficiency is that exchange rate expectations are reflected in the forward exchange rate. As explained in the previous section, if a speculator believes that the future spot exchange rate of the euro differs from that suggested by the forward rate then speculative profits are available. However, if a sufficient number of speculators share this view, the forward rate will converge to the future spot rate and this will remove the profit opportunity.

In summary, if the forward market is efficient, all available information will be accurately processed by investors in calculating the expected value of the future spot rate.

Box 19.1
Expected value

As an example of how expected values are calculated, consider a lottery where half the tickets sold carry no prize money and the other half carry a prize of €10. This means that if someone were to purchase a ticket there is a 50 per cent change of winning €10 and a 50 per cent change of winning nothing. The following table shows the two possible outcomes and their associated probabilities (note that the sum of the probabilities add to one.) The third column shows the product of column 1 and column 2. The sum of the two products is the expected value. In this case the expected value is €5. What this means is that if someone were to buy 100 tickets, they would expect to win on average €5. The first few tickets may or may not carry any winnings, but on average over a hundred or so tickets the purchaser could expect average winnings of €5. The expected value is, in effect, the most likely average outcome from purchasing tickets. Note that no one ticket actually carries a prize of €5. In formulating a forecast of the exchange rate, the task of deciding on the probabilities associated with each possible outcome will, of course, be considerably more complex than in this example.

Outcome	Probability	Outcome × Probability
€0	0.5	0
€10	0.5	€5
Expected value		€5

Because of arbitrage, the forward rate will converge towards $_{t+1}e_t$, which will embody all the currently available information about the future spot exchange rate. If this happens, the forward market is said to be efficient. Thus simple market efficiency may be stated as:

$$F_t = EV(e_{t+1}) \tag{5}$$

Exchange rate expectations prove correct on average and the forward exchange rate equals the expected future spot rate.

UPH AND MARKET EFFICIENCY

If the simple market efficiency hypothesis is correct, then it follows from conditions (4) and (5) that:

$$_{t+1}e_t = F_t \tag{6}$$

Subtracting e_{t+1} from both sides:

$$_{t+1}e_t - e_{t+1} = F_t - e_{t+1} \tag{7}$$

or

$$v_t = F_t - e_{t+1} \tag{8}$$

where $v_t = {_{t+1}e_t} - e_{t+1}$ is the forecast error in time t. Rearranging (8):

$$e_{t+1} = F_t - v_t \tag{9}$$

When coefficients representing the intercept and slope are inserted into (9) we obtain the UPH equation given in (3) above. (v_t is an error term equivalent to μ_t. Because the mean of the error term is zero the sign change is of no consequence.) Hence, the unbiased predictor hypothesis is closely related to the forward market efficiency hypothesis. If UPH holds, then it is likely that the forward market is efficient.

RISK PREMIUM

Even if UPH does not hold, the foreign exchange market may none the less be efficient. The explanation could be that the market allows a *risk premium* on forward contracts. In the previous example speculators, in an attempt to make profits, drive F_t towards $_{t+1}e^e_t$. In practice, F_t need not exactly equal $_{t+1}e^e_t$ because at some point speculators may demand a risk premium in order to compensate them for the possibility of being wrong.

Market efficiency now requires that

$$F_t = {}_{t+1}e^e_t + RP_t \tag{10}$$

where RP_t is the risk premium demanded by investors. (The simple market efficiency hypothesis can be restored by assuming that investors are risk neutral, so that the risk premium does not enter into the analysis.) This is known as the *general efficiency hypothesis* and it requires that the forward rate embody all publicly available information on the future exchange rate (through $_{t+1}e^e_t$) as well as the market's attitude towards risk (given by RP_t). The important point to emerge from this discussion is that the relationship between F_t and e_{t+1} is no longer unambiguously defined. If a researcher estimates equation (3) and finds that F_t is a biased predictor of e_{t+1}, it does not necessarily follow that the forward market is inefficient. It can be argued that the general rather than the simple market efficiency hypothesis holds and that the researcher did not properly account for the risk premium. However, to avoid this rationalisation becoming a tautology, we need to have some measure of risk. If there is such a measure, say Z, the researcher can estimate an equation of the form:

$$e_{t+1} = \alpha + \beta F_t + \chi Z_t + \upsilon_t \tag{11}$$

Unfortunately, current research indicates that the risk premium can change signs over time and this makes it extremely difficult to measure.

Note:
There is a further complication in testing for market efficiency. Investors may not, in fact, be rational in formulating forecasts. In testing for market efficiency the researcher must therefore correctly measure *both* the manner in which expectations are formed and the risk. If the market efficiency hypothesis is rejected, it may be because expectations or risk or both were incorrectly modelled. This issue makes it extremely difficult to test the market efficiency hypothesis.

At the present time the evidence in the international literature is very mixed. The consensus would appear to be that UPH does not hold or, at least, there are important deviations from it. The implication is that a rule can be developed to out-perform the forward exchange rate in forecasting the future spot rate and profits could be made from forward market speculation. The results relating to market efficiency are less decisive and, because of the estimation difficulties involved, will probably never be satisfactorily resolved.

19.7 Interest Rate Risk

There are different types of interest rate risk. *Basis risk*, which mostly affects financial firms, results from a mismatching of interest rate base for assets (loans) and liabilities (deposits). A change in relative interest rate movements (the spread) results in a change in net interest income to the financial institution. For example, if the lending rate were to fall relative to the deposit rate due to market competition, the financial institution would experience a fall in net interest rate income.

Another form of risk is referred to as *gap risk*. This mostly relates to non-financial firms who typically have small amount of interest rate assets and large amount of interest rate debts. This mismatch means that the losses on the debts cannot be offset by the gains on the assets.

As an example of gap risk consider the case of a treasury manager who, in July 2002, anticipates a cash surplus of €1 million between mid-September and mid-December 2003. The treasury manager proposes to place this money in a bank deposit. The current interest rate is 10 per cent but the treasury manager expects interest rates to fall to 8 per cent sometime in September. If interest rates do fall, then the interest received on the deposit will be reduced. For example, if the interest rate equals 10 per cent the return on the deposit is:

$$\text{Deposit interest} = €1 \text{ m} \times 10/100 \times 90/360 = €25,000$$

that is, the deposit interest equals the sum deposited multiplied by the interest rate multiplied by the duration (ninety days). If the interest rate falls to 8 per cent:

$$\text{Deposit interest} = €1 \text{ m} \times 8/100 \times 90/360 = €20,000$$

Hence a reduction in interest rates from 10 per cent to 8 per cent leads to a loss of €5,000 on deposit interest. This loss will be partly offset by any gains from interest rate yielding assets.

If the treasury manager were borrowing money instead of depositing it, the opposite would be the case. This raises the question of, firstly, how can we tell which way interest rates will move in the future? And, secondly, how does a treasury manager or a borrower hedge against interest rate risk?

19.8 Anticipating Interest Rate Movements

In chapter 13 we pointed out that the interest rate yield curve can be used to derive the (implicit) forward interest rate. These forward interest rates are, in effect, the market's forecasts of future short-term interest rates. To illustrate this point consider the case of an investor who has a choice between:

1. A six-month investment.
2. A roll-over strategy which entails investing at the end of three months for a second three-month period. That is, invest for the first three months and then re-invest for a further three months.

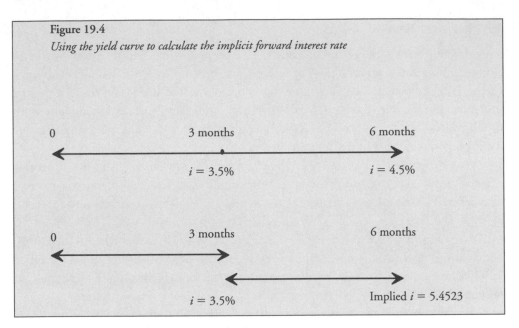

Figure 19.4

Using the yield curve to calculate the implicit forward interest rate

As outlined in figure 19.4 suppose the three-month interest rate (expressed in annual terms) is 3.5 per cent and the six-month rate is 4.5 per cent. What is the implied three-month interest rate starting three months from now (denoted $i_{3,6}$)?

Arbitrage should ensure that the two strategies give the same return. If this is the case:

$$(1 + (0.035 \times (90/360))) \times (1 + i_{3,6}) = (1 + (0.045 \times (180/360)))$$

That is the current three-month rate multiplied by the future three-month rate should equal the six-month rate. Solving this equation gives:

$$1.00875 \times (1 + i_{3,6}) = 1.0225$$

$$i_{3,6} = 0.01363.$$

That is 1.363 per cent for three months or 5.4523 per cent per annum (1.363×4).

In this case, the yield curve is positively sloped: the interest rate three months from now is higher than the current rate (see figure 15.5). This indicates that the market expects interest rates will rise in the future. Conversely, if the forward interest rate was lower than the current rate, this would indicate that the market expects rates to fall in the future. The yield curve, therefore, gives an indication of the future direction of interest rates. It should be noted, however, that market expectations may not always prove correct. Due to unanticipated developments, the future interest rate could differ significantly from current expectations.

19.9 HEDGING AGAINST INTEREST RATE RISK

As with exchange rates, a number of techniques have been developed to hedge against interest rate risk. In this and the next section we outline some of these techniques. The list is by no means comprehensive and is intended to act as an introduction to the various techniques that are available. In this section we discuss *forward rate agreements* and *foreign currency swaps*. The following section discusses *futures contracts*.

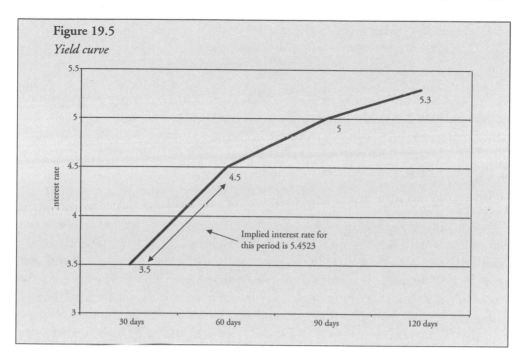

Figure 19.5
Yield curve

FORWARD RATE AGREEMENT (FRA)

This is an agreement that is used to lock-in or fix interest rates for a specific period of time. The agreement is generally between a borrower who is expecting interest rates to rise and a depositor who is expecting interest rates to fall. Hence, the two parties are taking *opposing views* on the direction of interest rates.

A forward rate agreement (FRA) is a contract where the seller (called the writer) pays the buyer (called the holder) if the actual interest rate is greater than the agreed rate. Conversely, the buyer pays the seller if the actual interest rate turns out to be less than the agreed rate.

Actual i > agreed i *seller pays buyer*
Actual i < agreed i *buyer pays seller*

Hence a firm would purchase a FRA if it intends to borrow and expects interest rates to rise. Conversely, a firm would sell a FRA if it intends to invest funds but anticipates a fall in interest rates.

As an example, suppose two firms enter into an agreed FRA for €1 million with an agreed interest rate of 7.5 per cent for ninety days starting in three months time. Suppose, however, the actual interest rate in three months time turns out to be 9 per cent. The buyer will receive from the seller the interest rate differential. This is calculated as follows:

$$€1m \times [(0.09 - 0.075) \times (90/360)] = €3,750$$

That is, the principal multiplied by the interest rate differential multiplied by the duration of the contract. The overall impact on the cost of borrowing to the firm is the 9 per cent interest payment minus the FRA inflow. That is:

Total interest payment (€1 m × 0.09) × (90/360) = €22,500
minus FRA inflow = €3,750
Total cost of borrowing (for 3 months) = €18,750

On an annual basis this is €75,000 (€18,750 × 4) which is 7.5 per cent of the €1 million borrowed. Hence the firm is able to use the FRA to fix its borrowing costs. The firm paying the FRA is not concerned because it earned extra income from its investments when interest rate rose unexpectedly. That second firm was content to lock-in the interest rate at 7.5 per cent.

FOREIGN CURRENCY SWAPS

A foreign currency forward swap is another technique for fixing interest rates but this time without actually taking out a loan. Suppose an Irish firm needs $1 million in three months for a three-month period. The firm has the equivalent in euro on deposit but is concerned about the interest rate on dollar borrowings. To fix the interest rate the firm could enter into two foreign currency forward swaps. Firstly, the firm will buy $1 million thirty days forward at a forward exchange rate of $0.94/€1. Secondly, the firm sells dollars forward sixty days from now at a forward rate of $0.96/€1. These two forward rates are quoted by the banks and other financial institutions. Hence:

Cost of obtaining dollars (30-days time) = $1 m ÷ 0.94 = €1,063,830
Receipts from selling dollars (60-days time) = $1 m ÷ 0.96 = €1,041,667

The *internal rate of interest* is derived as the percentage change between the sale and cost price, that is:

[(1,041,667 − 1,063,830)/1,063,830] = −0.208 or −2.08 per cent for three months.

This internal interest rate over a year is −8.32 per cent (2.08 × 4). This technique allows the firm to fix interest rates on a dollar exposure without actually having to take out a dollar loan.

19.10 FUTURES CONTRACTS

Futures markets have been around in one form or another for over 150 years. Initially, participants on the market agreed prices for the future delivery of commodities (oil, metal, wheat and sugar). Over the last thirty years *financial futures* have evolved which are designed to reduce risk relating to movements in exchange rates, interest rates and stock market prices. Hence, the function of a financial futures contract is to enable companies and individuals with positions in money, securities and foreign exchange markets to reduce their exposure to risk. Financial futures trading is conducted on the floor of an organised exchange. The main futures exchanges include (the year indicates the starting date):

- International Money Market (IMM) of Chicago 1972
- Singapore International Monetary Exchange (SIMEX) 1979
- New York Futures Exchange 1979
- London International Financial Futures Exchange (LIFFE) 1982

There are also other exchanges in Sweden, New Zealand, France and Canada and other parts of the world. In terms of trading volume, the IMM is by far the largest and most important exchange. These exchanges engage in a number of contracts including:

- Future on long-term government stock
- Future on short-term government stock
- Future on short- and long-run inter-bank interest rates
- Future on stock market index
- Future on commodity prices (gold, lead, zinc, etc.).

Each of these contracts has their own specifications. The contracts are for a standardised amount and are delivered on a standardised date in the future. In what follows we give an example of how the three-month Eurozone inter-bank interest rate (EIBOR) contract might be used in practice. This contract can be used to hedge against interest rate risk. The operation of this contract is very similar to other futures contracts on the various exchanges around the world.

Note:
In May 1989 the *Irish Futures/Options Exchange* (IFOX) commenced trading but was voluntarily closed down in August 1996. The reason IFOX closed down was due to a lack of demand for the product. Turnover fell from 27,000 contracts in 1990, to an unfeasible 7,000 in 1996. One of the main reasons for the lack of demand was that the Irish market was too small and this led to a lack of liquidity. If someone wanted to sell a particular contract it was often very hard to find a buyer and vice versa. As a result investors sought alternative hedging techniques. In addition only twenty-five shareholders were allowed to trade on the exchange and this further restricted the size of the market. Other traders and smaller institutions who were not members were directly excluded from participating on the exchange.

INTEREST RATE FUTURES CONTRACT
A typical specification on an EIBOR contract is as follows:

Contract size:	€100,000
Settlement date:	Third Wednesday of March, June, September, December
Quotation price:	100 *minus* the rate of interest
Tick size:	0.01 per cent
Tick value:	€2.50
Contract cash settlement.	

The EIBOR contract is a standardised size of €100,000. The standardised settlement dates are the third Wednesday of March, June, September and December. The quotation price is calculated as 100 minus the interest rate (the Eurozone inter-bank interest rate). Hence, if the interest rate is 10 per cent, the quotation price is $100 - 10 = 90$. If the interest rate is 8 per cent, the quotation price is $100 - 8 = 92$. This means that if interest rates decrease, the quotation price increases and (as explained below) the buyer of the futures contract gains. If, on the other hand, interest rates increase, the quotation price falls and the buyer incurs a loss.

The *tick size* is the minimum price movement and is set at 0.01 per cent. The tick value is calculated as the value of the contract multiplied by the tick size multiplied by the duration of the contract (three months or ninety days).

Tick value = €100,000 × 0.0001 × 90/360 = €2.50

This means that the price has to move by €2.50 before the price movement will be recorded.

HEDGING

To hedge against falling interest rates the treasury manager enters into a futures contract. The basic idea is to set up in the futures market an equal but *opposite* position to that in the deposit or cash market. If interest rates fall, the value of the futures contract will increase and the profits on the futures contracts will compensate for the loss of interest on the deposit.

In order to 'lock in' to an interest rate of 10 per cent on a deposit of €1 million, the treasury manager must purchase ten contracts of €100,000. (A borrower in the cash market would sell futures contracts.) Ten contracts at a price of 90.00 would cost €225,000.

10 contracts × 9,000 ticks × €2.50 = €225,000

Suppose that in September the treasury manager's expectations are realised and interest rates fall from 10 per cent to 8 per cent and the contract price rises from 90 to 92. Having bought the 10 contracts for €225,000, the treasury manager now sells the 10 futures contracts for €230,000.

10 contracts × 9200 ticks × €2.50 = €230,000

The profit on the futures contract of €5,000 exactly offsets the loss on the deposit interest. In effect, the treasury manager has achieved a 'perfect hedge'.

The profit (or loss) on the futures contract can also be calculated using the tick values. The difference between the sell price (92) and the purchase price (90) is equivalent to 200 ticks. The profit is equal to the number of ticks multiplied by the tick value multiplied by the number of contracts.

Profit on futures contract = 200 × €2.50 × 10 = €5,000

The treasury manager, by 'fixing' the interest on a floating rate deposit, also trades away any potential gains. If interest rates increased over the period, the gain made on deposit interest is offset by a loss on the futures contract. It should be borne in mind that it takes two parties to complete a transaction. If someone is purchasing a futures contract, someone else must be selling. This means that the two parties are taking opposing views on how interest rates will move in the future. If the buyer of the futures contract gains, the seller of the contract loses, and vice versa.

Note:
Because of arbitrage between the cash and futures markets, the interest rates on futures contracts are very closely related to the interest rates embodied in the yield curve. Hence, if the yield curve is upward sloping, indicating that interest rates will increase in the future, the interest rate on

futures contracts will be greater than current interest rates. This means that futures contracts only offer insurance against unexpected changes in interest rates, that is, changes in interest rates over and above changes reflected in the yield curve.

VARIATION MARGIN

The purchaser of a futures contract is required to deposit, as collateral, with the clearing exchange a sum of money known as the *initial margin*. This money is returned on completion of the contract. Each day the clearing exchange marks all accounts to the current market value and the purchaser is refunded or required to pay a maintenance margin, known as the *variation margin*, in cash each day. The variation margin is equivalent to the difference between yesterday and today's closing price. This feature of futures contracts is known as *marking-to-market*. As an example of how the variation margin works, consider the data in table 19.2.

Table 19.2
Variation margin

Day	Price	Initial margin €	Variation margin €
Monday	90	3,000	
Tuesday	89		(2,500)
Wednesday	87		(5,000)
Thursday	92		+ 12,500
Close			+ 5,000

On Monday the treasury manager buys ten contracts at a price of 90. Each contract requires an initial margin of €300. Hence the manager must deposit €3,000 with the futures exchange. Suppose the contract price falls on Tuesday to 89, a decrease equivalent to 100 ticks, reflecting an increase in interest rates. Because the price has fallen the manager must now pay the futures exchange €2,500 as a variation margin. This is calculated as:

10 contracts × €2.50 × 100 ticks = €2,500

Suppose that on Wednesday the contract price again falls, this time to 87. The treasurer must pay a further variation margin of €5,000.

10 contracts × €2.50 × 200 ticks = €5,000

Finally, suppose that on Thursday interest rates decrease and the contract price rises from 87 to 92. The treasury manager now receives €12,500 from the futures exchange.

10 contracts × €2.50 × 500 ticks = €12,500

Having incurred a loss of €7,500 on the first two days and a profit of €12,500 on the third day, the treasury manager has made an overall profit of €5,000. She may now close out her position by selling the ten contracts. As mentioned, the gain on the futures contract offsets losses in the cash market. The main point about the variation margin is that gains and losses are paid for on a daily basis. If the purchaser cannot pay the variation margin, the clearing exchange will close out his position and make good any losses from the initial margin. In this regard, the clearing exchange guarantees the performance of the futures contract.

19.11 COMPARING FORWARD AND FUTURES CONTRACTS

Foreign currency futures contracts can also be used to hedge against exchange rate risk. For this reason it is worthwhile to compare futures contracts to forward contracts. These two types of contracts differ in a number of important respects.

- Forward contracts are negotiated with a bank at any location. Futures trading is conducted by brokers on the floor of an organised exchange.
- Banks will enter into a forward contract for any amount. Futures contracts are for a standard size contract for delivery at a standard maturity date in the future.
- Forward contract prices are expressed by a bank in the form of bid and offer rates. Some futures prices are determined on the floor of the exchange by an 'open outcry' system.
- Futures contracts require the purchaser to put up an initial margin as a good-faith gesture. A variation margin is then required each day as the price of the contract is mark-to-market. Forward contracts require no margin prior to the settlement date. This is one of the most important differences between futures and forward contracts.
- Unlike the futures contract, there is no minimum price movement on forward contracts.

19.12 CONCLUSION

The main points discussed in this chapter were:

- Exchange rate risk and how it impacts on the operation of exporters and importers
- The various internal hedging techniques that can be used to reduce exposure to exchange rate risk
- The definition of a forward exchange transaction
- The concept of a premium or discount on forward exchange rates
- The link between the forward discount/premium and the differential between domestic and foreign interest rates. The theory underlying this relationship is known as 'covered interest parity theory'
- The hypothesis that the forward exchange rate is an unbiased predictor of the future spot exchange rate states that on average the forward exchange rate is a good predictor of the future spot rate and that the prediction error will be random
- The concept of forward market efficiency
- The role of risk premiums
- Interest rate risk
- How forward rate agreements and foreign currency forward swaps can be used to hedge against interest rate risk

- How financial futures contracts can be used to reduce interest rate and exchange rate risk
- A foreign currency futures contract is similar to a forward contract. One of the main differences is that in a futures contract the purchaser is required to put up an initial margin as collateral.

CHAPTER 20

The Labour Market

20.1 INTRODUCTION

In this chapter we expand the supply-side of the economy by introducing a production function and by explaining how the interaction of the supply and demand for labour determines the wage rate and employment. The labour market is then amalgamated with the aggregate supply (AS), aggregate demand (AD) model, the purchasing power parity (PPP) model, and the IS-LM framework developed in previous chapters to provide a detailed model of the economy. This expanded model is used to illustrate the differences between the Keynesian, monetarist and neoclassical schools of thought. As we shall see, different assumptions about price expectations and other factors lead to different conclusions about effectiveness of economic policy. An important issue in this regard is the nature of the short-run trade-off between inflation and unemployment. Can policy makers reduce unemployment at a cost of higher inflation?

20.2 THE AGGREGATE PRODUCTION FUNCTION

As discussed in chapter 2, land, labour and capital (which includes technology) are the three basic *factors of production*. These factors of production are combined to produce the output of the economy (GNP). This relationship between the factors of production and GNP is described by the *aggregate production function* and is written as:

$$\text{GNP} = f(\text{K}, \text{L}, \text{N}) \tag{1}$$

where N = labour input or hours worked, L = land, and K = the capital stock (plant, machinery and technology). Land is clearly not a variable input, at least in the short run. If we assume that the amount of capital available is fixed or constant in the short run, we can examine the relationship between output and employment. This is done in figure 20.1.

In the left-hand diagram, increasing employment along the horizontal axis leads to an increase in output (GNP) on the vertical axis. For example, employment of N_1 is associated with GNP_1. Note that the production function becomes flatter as the level of employment increases. This means that as more and more labour is hired, output continues to increase, but at a *diminishing rate*. For example, an increase in employment from N_1 to N_2 leads to a less than proportional increase in GNP. This reflects the assumption of diminishing returns to labour. As more and more labour is applied to fixed amounts of land and capital, the extra output produced by hiring one extra worker declines. This extra output of a particular worker is referred to as the *marginal product*

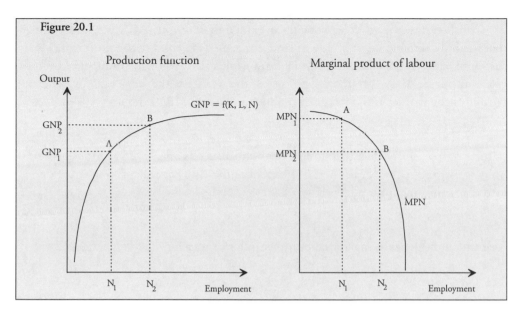

Figure 20.1

of labour (MPN). By marginal we mean 'extra' and by product 'output', so MPN stands for the extra output produced from hiring one more worker.

The right-hand diagram in figure 20.1 shows the marginal product of labour relative to the level of employment. The diagram has been drawn to reflect the assumption that, as employment increases along the horizontal axis, the MPN decreases along the vertical axis. The slope of the production function determines the MPN curve. As explained in the following section, this MPN curve underlies the *demand curve for labour*.

20.3 THE LABOUR MARKET

In this section we explain how the supply and demand for labour determine the wage rate (W) and the level of employment (N). We begin by deriving the demand for labour curve.

THE DEMAND FOR LABOUR

The basic rule for profit maximisation is that a firm will increase output up to the point where the *marginal cost* (MC) of producing an extra unit of output is equal to the *marginal revenue* (MR) from selling it:

$$MC = MR \qquad (2)$$

In a competitive market, each firm is so small in relation to the overall market that increases in its output will have no effect on the market price. That is, the demand curve for the firm's product is horizontal and not downward sloping as in the case of a monopoly. If the demand curve is horizontal it follows that marginal revenue will be equal to the output price (P). This is because the increase in sales does not lead to any fall in the price level. The profit-maximising rule becomes:

$$MC = P \qquad (3)$$

Consider now the cost of producing an extra unit of output, MC. We have assumed that the only variable input is labour: land and capital are fixed in the short run. MC is therefore equal to the cost of hiring one extra worker divided by the number of units of extra output he or she produces. The cost of the worker is the wage rate (W) and the output of the worker is the marginal product of labour (MPN). Hence:

$$MC = W/MPN \qquad\qquad (4)$$

If, for example, the wage rate is €500 a week and an additional worker produces twenty units of output in a week, the MC of a unit of output is €25. Substituting equation (4) into (3), a firm maximises its profits when:

$$W/MPN = P \qquad\qquad (5)$$

Rearranging, the profit maximisation rule can be written as:

$$W/P = MPN \qquad\qquad (6)$$

Equation (6) states that a firm's profits are maximised when the real wage rate (W/P) is equal to the marginal product of labour, MPN. Figure 20.2 shows the MPN curve with the real wage on the vertical axis and the level of employment on the horizontal axis. If the real wage is $(W/P)_1$ the profit-maximising level of employment is 200 workers. If the firm hired only 100 workers the MPN would exceed the real wage and profits could be increased by hiring additional labour. Similarly, if the firm hired 300 workers, then the MPN is less than the real wage and the firm is incurring a loss on the last 100 workers hired. The firm could increase profits by reducing its workforce to 200.

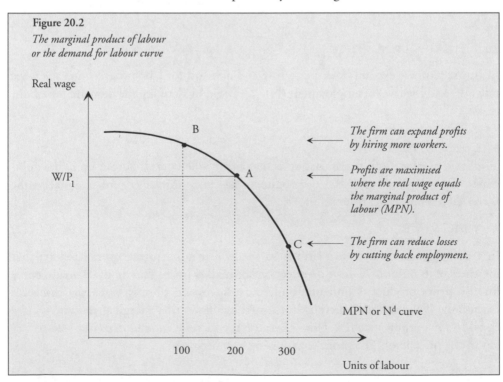

Figure 20.2
The marginal product of labour or the demand for labour curve

Real wage

B

The firm can expand profits by hiring more workers.

W/P_1

A

Profits are maximised where the real wage equals the marginal product of labour (MPN).

C

The firm can reduce losses by cutting back employment.

MPN or N^d curve

100   200   300

Units of labour

It follows that the point A in figure 20.2 is one point on the demand for labour curve. In fact, the demand for labour curve *coincides* with the MPN curve. For any level of W/P we can read off the profit-maximising level of employment by moving horizontally over to the MPN curve and then vertically down to the X-axis. Each point where W/P cuts the MPN curve corresponds to a point on the demand for labour curve. Because the MPN curve is downward sloping due to diminishing returns, the demand for labour curve is also downward sloping.

LOCATION OF THE DEMAND FOR LABOUR CURVE

The left-hand diagram in figure 20.3 shows the demand for labour curve with the real wage along the vertical axis and employment along the horizontal axis. The relationship between the real wage and employment is shown by movements *along* the demand for labour (N^d) curve. For example, a reduction in the real wage rate increases employment by moving firms down along the N^d curve.

The *location* of the N^d curve is determined by MPN. Productivity, in turn, depends on the level of capital, advances in technology, education and training. An increase in the capital stock, for example, increases MPN and more labour will be employed at a given wage rate. Hence, anything that makes workers more productive shifts the N^d curve outwards and increases the demand for labour at each wage rate. The demand for labour curve is labelled N^d(MPN) to indicate that the demand for labour is a function of the marginal productivity of labour.

ALTERNATIVE REPRESENTATION

The demand for labour can also be plotted as a function of the *nominal wage*. Rearranged, equation (6) can be written:

$$W = P \times MPN \tag{7}$$

Using this rule, firms hire workers up to the point where the nominal wage equals the value of the output produced by workers. The term $P \times MPN$ is the value of workers' output and is referred to as the *marginal revenue product* (MRP). In this representation, the relationship between the nominal wage (W) and employment (N) is shown by movements along the N^d curve. An increase in nominal wages reduces the demand for labour and vice versa.

The location or position of the N^d curve is now determined by the price level (P) and MPN. To reflect this the N^d curve is relabelled N^d(P, MPN). As illustrated in the right-hand diagram in figure 20.3, the N^d curve shifts out as the price level rises from P_1 to P_2. As we have drawn it, this leads to an increase in W along the vertical axis for a given level of employment, N. Conversely, a fall in the price level or MPN will shift the N^d curve down to the left.

EXPECTATIONS

An important qualification is necessary. An employer hires labour with a view to producing additional output and selling it profitably some time in the future. This is a *forward-looking* decision and involves expectations of the wage rates to be paid to

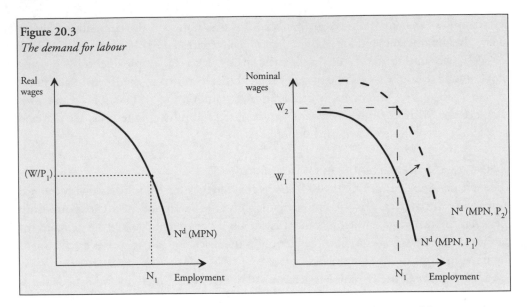

Figure 20.3
The demand for labour

workers in the future and the price at which output will be sold. We assume throughout this chapter that firms can predict future wages and prices accurately. If we write P^e for the expected price level, then we are assuming that for firms, $P^e = P$. This assumption allows us to use P, rather than P^e, throughout this chapter as the variable affecting the demand for labour. As we shall see, this assumption has an important bearing on the analysis.

THE SUPPLY OF LABOUR

We start from the basic assumption that the supply of labour depends on the real wage, W/P. This reflects the commonsense belief that people must be paid more if they are to work longer hours and that it takes a higher real wage rate to induce inactive people into the labour force. The supply of labour function is written:

$$N^s = f(W/P^e) \tag{8}$$

As in the case of firms, the willingness of a worker to commit themselves to an employer is a forward-looking decision. What matters is the real wage that prevails over the period for which the worker agrees to accept a job. This is not known because the future price level is uncertain. So whereas the worker knows what the nominal wage will be, he or she does not know with certainty what will happen to the price level. As a result the expected real wage is uncertain.

In the previous section we assumed firms correctly predicted future price movements. We do *not* invoke this assumption in the case of the workers. The relevant real wage is therefore (W/P^e). The question of how workers form price expectations is brought to the centre of the stage by this consideration.

LOCATION OF THE N^s CURVE

Figure 20.4 (left-hand diagram) shows the relationship between the (expected) real wage and the supply of labour (employment). The labour supply curve (N^s) is upward

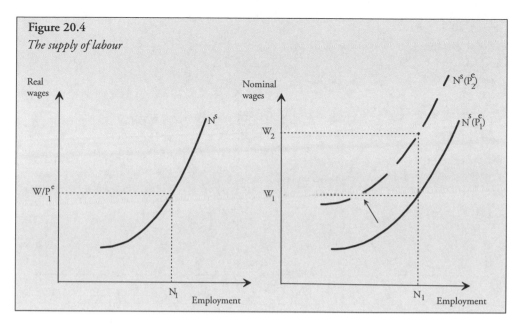

Figure 20.4
The supply of labour

sloping, indicating that firms must offer higher real wages in order to encourage workers to supply more labour or to induce entrants to the labour force.

An alternative representation (which we use throughout this chapter) is to put the nominal wage on the vertical axis and use price expectations (P^e) to determine the location of the N^s curve. In the right-hand diagram in figure 20.4, the relationship between the nominal wage (W) and the supply of labour is shown by movements *along* the N^s curve.

The N^s curve is now labelled $N^s(P^e)$ to indicate that changes in P^e shift the N^s curve. If P^e rises, the N^s curve shifts to the left. The increase in the price level reduces the real wage and workers will supply less work effort. Conversely, if P^e falls, the N^s curve shifts to the right. Workers will supply more work effort as the real wage has increased.

EQUILIBRIUM IN THE LABOUR MARKET

The labour market and the production function describe the supply-side of the macroeconomy. Figure 20.5 shows how they interact. In the left-hand diagram, the demand and supply of labour determine the nominal wage rate (vertical axis) and the level of employment (horizontal axis), at W_1 and N_1. It is important to bear in mind that MPN and P determines the location of the N^d curve. In contrast, P^e determines the location of the N^s curve. The important assumption here is that firms have perfect foresight with regard to future prices but workers do not have such foresight and can make forecast errors. The significance of this assumption will become apparent in due course.

In the right-hand diagram, the level of employment (N_1) determined in the labour market is used, via the production function, to produce output equal to GNP_1. If there is a change in employment, brought about by shifts in the N^d or N^s curves, this will lead to a change, via the production function, in output. A reduction in employment leads to lower output and vice versa.

Figure 20.5

Labour market and the production function

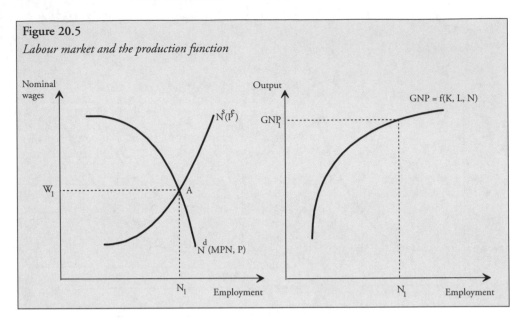

20.4 THE GENERAL MODEL

In this section we incorporate the labour market with some of the other models developed in previous chapters. Figure 20.6 gives an overview of the general model. The *IS-LM model*, developed in chapter 17, is shown in the lower right-hand diagram. The interaction of the IS and LM curves determines the interest rate and nominal GNP. In what follows it is important to bear in mind the variables that determine the location of the various curves in each of the markets. In the case of the IS-LM model, fiscal policy (government expenditure and tax rates) and the other components of aggregate demand (consumption, C, investment, I, and net exports, NX) determine the position of the IS curve. In contrast, the money supply (M^s) determines the position of the LM curve.

The diagram in the top right-hand corner shows equilibrium in the *goods and services market*. The short-run AS curve and the AD curve determines the equilibrium price level (P) and the level of real GNP. Also incorporated in this diagram in a line representing natural real GNP. To the left of this line the economy is in recession and to the right it is over-heating.

The location of the AD curve depends on the components of aggregate demand, C, I, G, NX and M^s. An increase in any of these variables shifts the AD curve to the right. This means that an expansionary fiscal or monetary policy shifts the AD curve outward and vice versa.

The location of the short-run AS curve depends on the cost of inputs (wages, raw materials, electricity, etc.) and productivity. An increase in costs or a fall in productivity shifts the short-run AS curve to the left and vice versa. The long-run AS curve (natural real GNP) is determined by the factors of production. It is possible that some changes in costs also impact on the long-run AS curve but we will not consider that possibility at this juncture.

The diagram in the top left-hand corner shows equilibrium in the *labour market*. The interaction of N^d and N^s determines the nominal wage (W) and employment (N).

Figure 20.6
The overall model

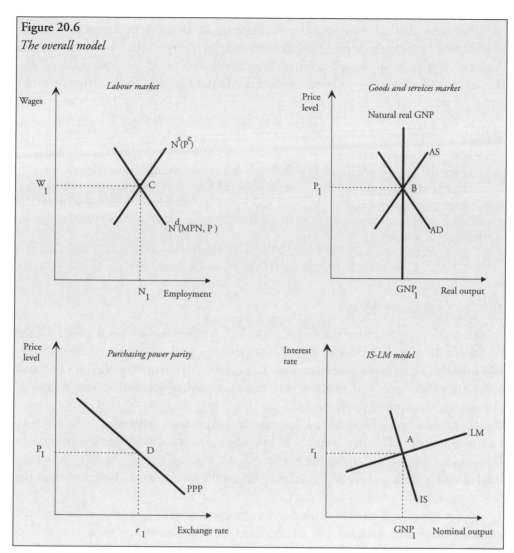

As explained in the previous section the variables in brackets determine the location of the N^d and N^s curves.

Finally, the diagram in the bottom left-hand corner shows the *purchasing power parity* (PPP) relationship developed in chapter 10. The price level is shown along the vertical axis and the exchange rate along the horizontal axis. At any point on the PPP line, domestic prices (adjusted for the exchange rate) are equated to foreign prices. Above the PPP line the home country suffers a loss of competitiveness and below the line the home country experiences a gain in competitiveness. The foreign price level determines the location of the PPP line.

We now use this general model to clarify some key issues in modern macroeconomics, particularly the relationship between the level of unemployment and the rate of inflation, as viewed by Keynesian, monetarist and neoclassical economists. (We exclude from the analysis the production function as this does not provide any useful insight into how economies adjust to economic shocks or disturbances.)

The terms classical, monetarism and Keynesian mean different things to different economists. In fact, the term 'classical economist' was first coined by Karl Marx to describe orthodox nineteenth-century British economics. A representation of the classical model was given by Keynes in chapter 2 of the *General Theory* so that he could replace it with his own 'Keynesian' model.

Note:

Mark Blaug has commented that

> perhaps the recent proliferation of definitely new but conflicting interpretations of the essential meaning of classical economics is simply an expression of the fact that modern economists are divided in their views and hence quite naturally seek comfort by finding (or pretending that they can find) these same views incorporated in the writings of the past.
>
> ('Classical economics' in *The New Palgrave: A Dictionary of Economics*, eds. John Eatwell, Murray Milgate and Peter Newman, London: Macmillan, 1987.)

20.5 THE KEYNESIAN MODEL

In this section we examine the implications of an expansionary fiscal policy in the context of the Keynesian model. Figure 20.7 (lower right-hand diagram) shows the IS-LM model. The IS curve is steep and the LM curve is flat, representing the Keynesian belief that fiscal policy is effective and monetary policy ineffective as a means of influencing output and employment.

An expansionary fiscal policy (increase in government expenditure or a cut in taxation) shifts the IS curve from IS_1 to IS_2. The economy moves from the point A to B. Nominal output rises along the horizontal axis and, because of the flat LM curve, there is only a small increase in the interest rate on the vertical axis. This means that the crowding-out effect will be very small.

In the goods and services market (top right-hand diagram), it is assumed that the economy is initially at natural real GNP. The increase in government expenditure shifts the AD curve from AD_1 to AD_2, and the economy moves from the point C to D. Because the short-run AS curve is positively sloped, both real output and the price level increase. At the point D, the economy is to the right of natural real GNP and is over-heating.

The important link from the goods and services market to the labour market is the price level. Recall that the price level determines the location of the N^d curve. Hence changes in the price level, brought about by shifts in the AS or AD curves, will impact on the labour market.

The increase in output prices from P_1 to P_2 in the goods market causes the demand for labour curve (top, left-hand diagram) to shift out to the right. That is, the N^d curve shifts from $N^d(MPN, P_1)$ to $N^d(MPN, P_2)$. The increase in output prices leads to an increase in firms' profits and this, in turn, encourages firms to expand output.

MONEY ILLUSION

But how do workers react to this development? In the Keynesian model it is argued that there will be no immediate change in workers' price expectations. In the Keynesian model,

Figure 20.7
The Keynesian model: expansionary fiscal policy

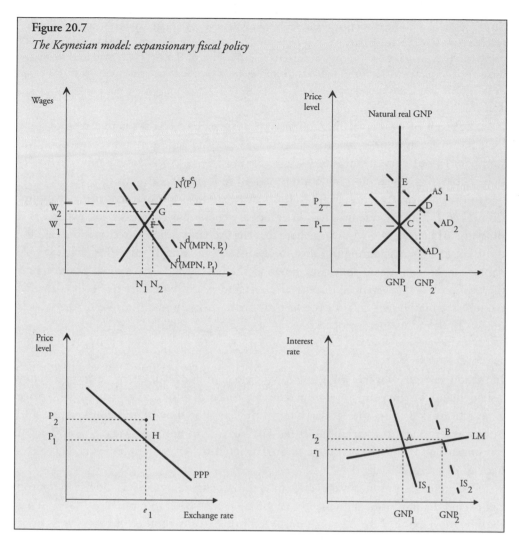

workers formulate price expectations by looking at the historical trend in prices. Price expectations are, in effect, backward looking and this gives rise to forecast errors. The effect of this is that the N^s curve does not shift. If this is the case, workers supply more labour in response to higher *nominal* wages whereas in real terms they are worse off.

This can be seen from a comparison of the change in the price level and the nominal wage in the left-hand diagram. It can be seen that the increase in W is *less* than the rise in P. This means that the real wage (W/P) has fallen. Because of errors in formulating price expectations, workers have supplied more labour in response to a higher nominal wage whereas, in fact, real earnings have declined. Workers are under the illusion that the wages they are offered are worth more than in reality is the case. In a sense they have been tricked. This is known as *money illusion*.

Note:

If money illusion exists, the steepness of the short-run AS curve depends on the slope of the labour supply (N^s) curve. The flatter (more elastic) the N^s curve, the flatter the short-run AS curve. To see this point, note that if the short-run AS curve is flat, an expansionary fiscal policy will lead to a large increase in real GNP. As before, the change in the price level will shift the N^d curve to the right. However, if the N^s curve is flat, the shift of the N^d curve will lead to a large increase in employment. It is this increase in employment that enables firms to increase real GNP in the goods and service market.

The result of workers failing to correctly anticipate price rises is that employment increases in response to a nominal wage increase as the economy moves up along the supply of labour curve from F to G. It is this increase in employment from N_1 to N_2 that enables firms (via the production function) to increase real output.

In the bottom left-hand diagram, the increase in the price level moves the economy from H to I. This represents a loss of competitiveness that depresses net exports and shifts the AD curve in. (We assume here that the exchange rate is fixed as is the case for those countries participating in European Monetary Union.) If this 'PPP effect' is very strong the AD curve will shift back down to the left towards its original position and the economy will revert to natural real GNP and prices will start to decline. In this section, we play-down this 'PPP effect' in order to highlight the role of the labour market in the adjustment process.

<h3>Long-run response</h3>

In the longer-term workers will recognise the effect of higher prices on real wages. They will demand an increase in nominal wages to compensate. The increase in price expectations (P^e) shifts the N^s curve up to the left (not shown) and employment and output revert back to their initial levels. The increase in nominal wages, W, will equal the increase in P and the real wage returns to its initial level. Employment, N, reverts back to its original level.

The increase in money wages also shifts the AS curve upwards to the left in the top right-hand diagram (not shown). The economy reverts back to natural real GNP. Note that the movement of the AS curve to the left brings forth another increase in the price level. It is assumed here that workers incorporate this additional price increase into their wage demands so that the real wage, consistent with natural real GNP, is restored.

The analysis suggests that the upward-sloping AS curve is only a short-run phenomenon. The AS curve slopes upwards only for as long as workers suffer from money illusion. As soon as workers demand higher wages to compensate for higher output prices, the short-run AS curve shifts to the left. In the Keynesian model, an expansionary fiscal or monetary policy can influence the level of output and employment in the short run, but as soon as workers adjust price expectations there is no effect in the long run. This means that there is a *trade-off* between inflation and real GNP (and indirectly unemployment) in the short run but not in the longer-term. That is, in the longer-term the policy maker cannot reduce unemployment at the cost of higher inflation.

Note:
The point E in figure 20.7 is not a long-run equilibrium position because the economy is above the PPP line in the bottom, left-hand diagram. At some stage this loss of competitiveness will impact on the AD curve and this will bring forth another round of adjustment.

20.6 DEFLATIONARY DEMAND-SIDE SHOCK

In this section we continue to use the Keynesian model to examine how the economy adjusts to a deflationary demand-side economic shock. In figure 20.8 (bottom, right-hand diagram), a fall in investment, I, shifts the IS curve to the left. The interest rate falls on the vertical axis but because the LM curve is relatively steep, this is not sufficient to 'crowd-in' some other component of aggregate demand.

In the top right-hand diagram, the decrease in investment shifts the AD curve from AD_1 to AD_2 and the economy moves from the point C to D. Both real output and the price level fall. The economy is now to the left of the natural real GNP line and is in recession.

In the labour market the decrease in the price level shifts the N^d curve to the left and the economy moves from the point F to G. The decrease in nominal wages is *smaller* than the fall in the price level and, as a result, real wages rise. Employment

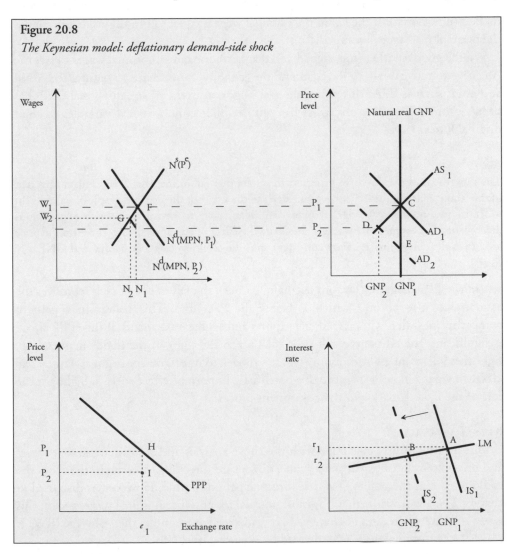

Figure 20.8
The Keynesian model: deflationary demand-side shock

decreases along the horizontal axis. The N^s curve does not immediately shift because the change in the price level is unexpected.

At the points D and G in figure 20.8, the economy is in recession and unemployment is rising in the background. The question now arises as to how long the economy will remain at the points D and G? If the economy remains in recession for a long time the costs in terms of lost output and unemployment will be high. We now discuss some of the factors that have a bearing on the adjustment process.

PROTRACTED RECESSION

Those who believe in a smooth-functioning, self-regulating economy claim that prices and wages will fall quickly in response to the rise in real wages and the emergence of unemployment and spare capacity. They argue that workers will realise that the price level has fallen and will accept a cut in the nominal wage so as to restore the real wage. This change in price expectations shifts the N^s curve down to the right in the labour market (not shown). If the fall in the nominal wage is equal to the fall in the price level, the original real wage is restored.

In the goods market (top, right-hand diagram), the fall in nominal wages causes the AS curve to move down to the right and the economy moves back to natural real GNP at a point such as E. At this point, the real wage consistent with natural real GNP has been restored. Thus, a *disinflation* has restored the economy's real variables to their original levels.

Note:
The movement of the AS curve brings forth yet another fall in the price level. This means that in the labour market, the N^d curve again shifts to the left (not shown) and employment falls. In order to restore the real wage, workers will again have to revise their price expectations downwards. We assume that workers anticipate the effect of a shift of the AS curve on the price level so as to achieve the real wage consistent with the economy being at natural real GNP.

In the PPP diagram (bottom left-hand corner), the fall in the price level moves the economy to the point I which is below the PPP line. This results in a gain in competitiveness that will increase net exports and aggregate demand. If this 'PPP effect' is significant, the AD curve will shift back up to the right in the goods market (top, right-hand diagram). The economy will revert back to its original position at natural real GNP. In what follows we ignore this potentially important effect so as to highlight the role of the labour market in the adjustment process.

KEYNESIAN ANALYSIS

Keynesian economists take issue with the above analysis and instead argue that wages and prices are inflexible, particularly in a downward direction. As a result, the economy could remain at the points D and G for some period of time. However, as discussed in chapter 2, while it is true that it is most unusual for absolute nominal wages to fall, this is not the case when rates of change are considered. For example, the real wage (RW) is equal to the nominal wage (W) divided by the price level (P):

$$RW = W/P \tag{9}$$

This implies approximately that:

$$\% \text{ change in real wage} = \% \text{ change in nominal wage} - \text{inflation} \tag{10}$$

That is, the percentage change in real wages is equal to the percentage change in nominal wages minus inflation. To bring about a cut in real wages all that is required is for inflation to exceed the change in nominal earnings. From this perspective, a fall in real earnings may not be so implausible. We now discuss two other considerations that have a bearing on the adjustment process.

THE KEYNES EFFECT

In the *General Theory*, Keynes identified an adjustment process that should help move the economy back to natural real GNP. The process is as follows: the increase in unemployment (due to the recession) reduces wages and therefore firms' costs. The reduction in costs, in turn, leads to a reduction in the price level. This leads to an increase in the real money supply and a reduction in interest rates. The fall in interest rates increases interest-sensitive expenditure (IE) such as consumer expenditure, investment and net exports. This, in turn, increases aggregate demand and real GNP. In short:

$$\text{Unemployment} \rightarrow \downarrow \text{Wages} \rightarrow \downarrow \text{Costs} \rightarrow \downarrow p \rightarrow \uparrow (M^s/P) \rightarrow \downarrow r \rightarrow \uparrow IE \rightarrow \uparrow AD \rightarrow \uparrow GNP$$

This adjustment process is known as the *Keynes effect*. However, it will be recalled that Keynesians believe that there is a weak link between the money supply and aggregate demand. Hence, having identified the effect, Keynes dismissed it as having little practical significance. Monetarist, who believe in a strong link between the money supply and GNP, would take the opposite view. They would see the Keynes effect as having an important contribution to the adjustment process. Note that a decrease in the Irish price level would have no impact whatsoever on Eurozone interest rates. Hence, the Keynes effect cannot be expected to move the Irish economy out of recession.

SLOPE OF THE AD CURVE

Anther important issue relates to the slope of the AD curve. Keynesians believe that the AD curve is steep (inelastic). This means that *large* changes in prices and wages are necessary before the economy reverts to natural real GNP. If the AD curve were relatively flat (elastic), only small changes in prices and wages would be necessary for the economy to revert back to natural real GNP. Clearly, the further prices and wages have to fall the more prolonged will be the recession.

Note:
Keynesians argue that the AD curve is steep because a given change in the price level has only a small impact on real GNP. In terms of the 'Keynes effect' discussed above, there is a weak link between interest rates and interest-sensitive expenditure and hence the AD curve is steep. In contrast, in the monetarist analysis, the AD curve is relatively flat because changes in interest rates have a significant impact on expenditure.

GOVERNMENT INTERVENTION

Faced with the above constraints on the adjustment process, Keynesian economists argue that the government should intervene in the economy and pursue a fiscal stabilisation policy. Hence, Keynesian economists advocate an *active* role for economic policy to offset the unemployment that results from deflationary shocks to the economy.

The speed with which economies adjust is crucially important in the context of membership of the European Monetary Union (EMU). As discussed in chapter 14 the burden of adjustment (following an adverse economic shock) falls on the labour market and on the 'PPP effect'. It is evident from the discussion in this section that if wages and prices are inflexible, particularly in a downward direction, the result could be a protracted recession.

20.7 DEFLATIONARY SUPPLY-SIDE SHOCK

Consider now the case of an adverse supply-side shock such as a temporary increase in the price of oil (a permanent increase in oil prices will affect natural real GNP but we do not consider this possibility here). A number of modifications are necessary in order for the general model to explain how the economy adjusts to a supply-side shock. Firstly, in figure 20.9, the IS-LM model is removed from the analysis. This is because this is a demand-side model, which provides no insight as to how the economy adjusts to a supply-side shock. In the goods market (top, right) the increase in firms costs (higher oil prices) shifts the short-run AS curve up to the left and the economy moves from the point A to B. This leads to an increase in the price level and a fall in real GNP. At the point B the economy is in recession and unemployment is rising.

In the labour market (top, left) the increase in the price level would normally shift the N^d curve out to the right. However, a second important modification must be made at this juncture. Recall from chapter 2 that a firm's profit is equal to total revenue minus total cost:

$$\text{Profit} = \text{total revenue} - \text{total cost} \tag{11}$$

where total revenue equals the price of output (P_q) multiplied by the volume of output (Q). Total cost equals the price of inputs (P_z) multiplied by the volume of inputs (Z), such as raw materials and labour. Substituting into equation (11):

$$\text{Profit} = (P_q \times Q) - (P_z \times Z) \tag{12}$$

Up until now the increase in the price level increased the firm's total revenue and therefore profits. Higher profits, in turn, created the incentive for firms to increase the demand for labour and produce more output (shift the N^d curve to the right). However, in this supply-side analysis, the rise in the price level is due to the rise in costs (higher oil prices). As such the firm's profits are at best unchanged. There is therefore no incentive for the firm to hire more workers or expand output. This means that the N^d curve does not shift to the right. (Note that it is possible for profits to fall in which case the N^d curve moves to the left. We ignore this possibility here.) In figure 20.9, we assume that the N^d curve is unchanged.

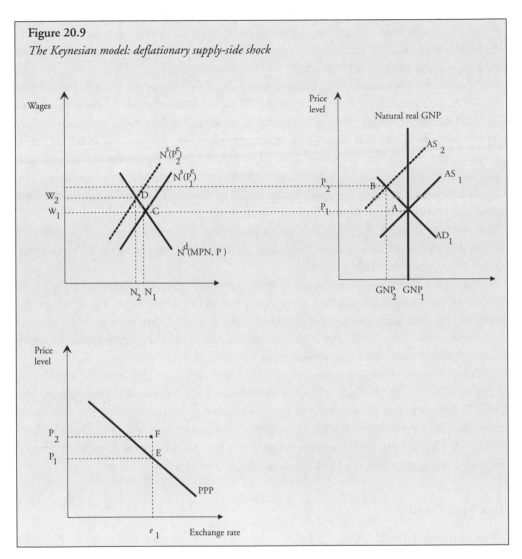

Figure 20.9

The Keynesian model: deflationary supply-side shock

The third modification relates to workers' expectations. Up until now we assumed that workers do not anticipate the effect on the price level of a demand-side shock. However, it is one thing to assume that workers do not correctly anticipate the consequences of a surprise fall in, say, investment on the price level. But it is quite another thing to assume workers are not aware of the consequences of a rise in oil prices (which will be loudly broadcast in the media). Hence, in the case of an oil price increase, workers gauge quickly and correctly the effects on the overall or general price level. That is, there is little or no money illusion when it comes to oil price changes. If this is the case, the N^s curve moves up to the left and the economy moves from the point C to D. The decrease in employment in the labour market is associated with a fall in real GNP in the goods market.

In the PPP model, the rise in the price level moves the economy from the point E to F. The economy is above the PPP line and suffers a loss of competitiveness relative to other countries (this assumes the rise in the price of oil had a disproportionate impact on the home country).

At the point D in the labour market, the real wage (W/P) has decreased. It can be seen from the diagram that the increase in the price level is greater than the rise in nominal wages. Hence, at the point D workers are worse off.

In order for the economy to return to natural real GNP, it is necessary for the short-run AS curve to shift back down to the right. This could come about if workers accepted a cut in nominal wages. The problem here, however, is that since workers already experienced a fall in real wages in the movement from the point C to D, such a development is likely to be resisted. If a fall in nominal earnings is not forthcoming, it is possible that the economy would remain at the points C and D for some time.

After a time, the rise in unemployment could be expected to put downward pressure on wages and shift the AS curve back down from AS_2 to AS_1. The economy will revert back to natural real GNP. This is the 'Keynes effect' discussed above. However, this whole process could take some considerable time and the costs in terms of lost output and employment are likely to be high.

Note that an expansionary fiscal or monetary policy cannot resolve the problem. Such a policy would shift the AD curve up to the right but, in doing so, increases the price level which leads to a further loss of competitiveness. This, in turn, will shift the AD curve back down to the left. This illustrates the point that a demand-side policy cannot be used to resolve a supply-side shock.

Furthermore, if the short-run AS curve is slow to adjust down to the right, it is possible that the 'PPP effect' will act to compound the adjustment problem. At the point F (bottom, left) the economy is experiencing a loss of competitiveness. This could shift the AD curve down to the left moving the economy even further away from natural real GNP. This is a potential source of instability which could intensify the recession and puts an even greater adjustment burden on nominal wages.

20.8 MONETARISM

Monetarism is a variant of the classical economics that incorporated some of Keynes's ideas but modified them significantly. The monetarist model is outlined in figure 20.10. The theoretical structure of the monetarist model is not very different from the Keynesian model. On the supply-side of the economy, the monetarists accept the Keynesian view that workers do not have perfect information on future price movements and that errors are made in forecasting. As a result, the short-run N^s curve is positively sloped and this, in turn, implies that the short-run AS curve is also upward sloping.

The difference between the monetarists and Keynesians lies in the slope of the IS and LM curves and also the AD curve. Figure 20.10 shows the monetarist view that the LM curve is steep and the IS curve is flat. This means that fiscal policy has a relatively small effect on output and employment. For example, an increase in government expenditure would shift the IS curve upwards to the right (not shown). The large increase in the interest rate along the vertical axis would crowd-out investment with the result that there is a small increase in real output on the horizontal axis.

Monetary policy, on the other hand, has a very significant effect on nominal output. In figure 20.10 (diagram, bottom right) an increase in the money supply shifts the LM

Figure 20.10

The Monetarist model: expansionary monetary policy

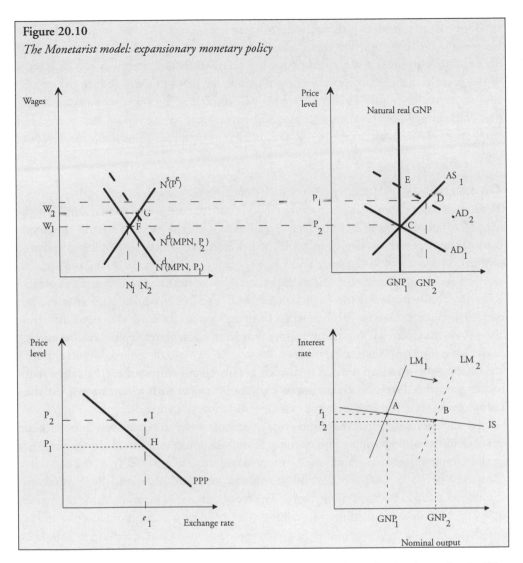

curve from LM_1 to LM_2 and nominal output increases along the horizontal axis. The small change in the interest rate along the horizontal axis does not crowd-out investment and as a result nominal GNP increases.

The increase in the money supply also shifts the AD curve from AD_1 to AD_2 (diagram top right) and both real output and the price level increases. In the short run real output increases along the horizontal axis.

As before, the increase in the price level shifts the N^d curve in the labour market (top, left) upwards to the right. Nominal wages and employment both increase. It is the increase in employment that enables firms (via the production function) to increase real GNP.

The N^s curve does not shift up to the left because workers unanticipated the increase in the price level. Workers are supplying more labour in response to a higher nominal wage even though in terms of real wages they are actually worse off. Hence, in the monetarist model, workers continue to suffer from money illusion.

One of the essential theoretical difference between the monetarists and the Keynesians is the proposition that changes in the money supply has a significant effect on nominal output, whereas fiscal policy has an insignificant effect. As before the rise in the price level erodes competitiveness (bottom, left) and this will reduce net exports and aggregate demand. This 'PPP effect' will offset the effects of the expansionary monetary policy and tend to shift the AD curve back to the left. Again we do not emphasise this particular effect in this section so as to highlight adjustment in the labour market.

THE NEUTRALITY OF MONEY

As discussed in previous chapters, monetarists argue that monetary policy should *not* be used to influence output or stabilise the business cycle. They reason that in the longer run increases in the money supply will, via the quantity theory of money, lead to a proportional increase in the price level. The process is as follows. In the labour market, workers eventually realise that real wages have fallen and demand an increase in nominal wages to compensate for the higher price level. The N^s curve shifts to the left and employment reverts to its original level. In the goods market, the short-run AS curve also moves up to the left and the economy returns to natural real GNP. This means that in the long run the AS and the N^s curves are *vertical*. An expansionary monetary policy has no long-run effect on real variables such as output and employment, but does result in a higher price level. That is, monetary policy is *neutral* with regard to real variables such as real GNP and employment.

Furthermore, monetarists argue that there are long and variable lags between changes in the money supply and changes in nominal output. They argue that changes in the money supply have been one of the major sources of instability in the economy. Monetary policy is likely to destabilise the economy and, as such, the government should not adopt an *active* policy stance. The monetarists therefore conclude that, given the role of money as a medium of exchange, the government should allow the money supply to increase in line with the predicted growth in real GNP. The targets should be announced beforehand and the government should adhere to this *monetary rule*.

POLICY IMPLICATIONS

A second important difference between the Keynesians and monetarists relates to the slope of the AD curve. In the Keynesian model the AD curve is very steep and the price level has to fall significantly in order to return the economy to natural real GNP. However, in the monetarist model the AD curve is relatively flat. This means that only a *small* fall in the price level is necessary to restore the economy to full-employment GNP. In this case, recessions will not persist and the costs in terms of lost output will be small. As such, monetarists do not advocate any form of government intervention instead relying on an automatic adjustment back to natural real GNP.

Note:
Monetarists realise that for the adjustment mechanism to work effectively, the labour market has to be flexible. Monetarists therefore argue that minimum wage legislation, trade union closed

shops, employment protection legislation and similar rigidities slow down wage adjustments and impede the movement back to natural real GNP. If wages can be made more responsive to shifts in the supply and demand for labour, the adjustment process will be faster. As we discuss in chapter 22, this view blames the high unemployment rate in continental Europe on what are called 'labour market rigidities'.

20.9 THE NEOCLASSICAL MODEL

The controversy surrounding the effectiveness of fiscal and monetary policy has developed largely around the way economic agents (firms and workers) form expectations about key variables such as the future price level or the rate of inflation. In this section we examine an alternative approach to forming expectations and assess the implications for economic policy.

Expectations formed on the basis of the current levels of economic variables are known as *static expectations*. The shortcoming with this approach is that it allows for no feedback from errors in previous forecasts.

The traditional view of how economic agents (workers and firms) form their expectations of the price level and the rate of inflation was that they looked back to the recent past and extrapolated from that to the future. If last year's inflation rate was 4.5 per cent, it is not unreasonable to expect this year's rate to be in the region of 4 per cent also. This method of formulating expectations is known as *adaptive expectations*. While the forecast is essentially backward looking, it has the merit of making an adjustment for previous forecast errors. However, this approach can also lead to systematic forecast errors. In a period of accelerating inflation, for example, the expected rate of inflation will always be less than the actual rate.

RATIONAL EXPECTATIONS

Adaptive expectations take account of past experience but not, for example, of changes in policy. In a period of rising inflation, the adaptive expectations approach would always tend to under-predict inflation. This kind of systematic error is a problem with backward-looking forecasts.

Rational expectations *avoid* systematic forecast errors. They are formed on the basis of all available information (including past inflation and changes in policy) and knowledge of how the economy works. This approach does not result in systematic errors. This does not imply that the forecasts will be always accurate — just that there will be no tendency to consistently over- or under-predict a variable such as the rate of inflation. In recent years, rational expectations have become a very influential way of thinking about the economy. This approach is associated with the name of Robert Lucas of the University of Chicago, who was awarded the Nobel prize in economics in 1996.

Note:
See Robert Lucas, 'Rules, Discretion and the Role of the Economic Advisor' in *Rational Expectations and Economic Policy*, ed. Stanley Fischer, University of Chicago Press, 1980. Rational expectations originated in a paper that attracted little attention when it was first published: John Muth, 'Rational Expectations and the Theory of Price Movements', *Econometrica*, 29 July 1961.

Other influential economists who developed the rational expectations approach include Thomas Sargent of the University of Chicago and Robert Barro of Harvard University.

A rational forecast of the price level or inflation is based on all available information and a valid model of what causes inflation. A belief in monetarism will lead the public to anticipate an increase in the rate of inflation when the rate of growth of the money supply increases. If the economy is close to full employment and the government pursues an expansionary monetary policy, firms and households will anticipate that the rate of inflation will increase.

Note:
Inflation expectations can influence actual inflation. If workers expect the rate of inflation to increase they will demand increases in nominal wages in compensation. If households anticipate a rise in inflation, they will rush to buy at today's prices. These reactions will of themselves tend to push up the rate of inflation. Feedback from expectations to outcomes is very important in economics. Things are very different in meteorology: unfortunately, a forecast of fine weather is not enough to ensure that the weather will be fine!

Figure 20.11 outlines the neoclassical model using the now familiar IS-LM diagram, the AS-AD model, the labour market and the PPP model. The neoclassical economists agree with monetarists on the slopes of the IS and LM curves and on the ineffectiveness of fiscal policy. They also agree on the slope of the AD curve.

Consider now the effect of an expansionary monetary policy. If the central bank increases the money supply the LM curve shifts to the right and output increases. The economy moves from the point A to B in the bottom right-hand diagram.

In the goods and services market, the aggregate demand curve also shifts to the right and both the price level and real output increase. In the labour market, the increase in the price level shifts the N^d curve to the right. So far the analysis is the same as in the monetarist model.

The neoclassical model assumes that workers realise that the increase in the money supply will raise prices and they demand an immediate increase in nominal wages in compensation. In contrast to the Keynesian and monetarist case, workers do not suffer from money illusion. Because expectations are formed rationally, workers anticipate that prices will rise following the increase in the money supply. That is, there is no delay or lagged effect as in the Keynesian model. The labour supply (N^s) curve therefore shifts to the left and the real wage is restored. That is, in the top, left-hand diagram the economy moves from the point E to F.

In the goods and services market, the short-run AS curve also shifts to the left and both employment and real output revert back to their original levels. The economy moves from the point C to D (top, right-hand diagram). Once the policy or the shock is anticipated, the N^s and the AS curves are vertical and there is *no trade-off* between inflation and unemployment other than in the very short run. The analysis of fiscal policy is similar except that fiscal policy is even less effective due to crowding-out of investment.

Figure 20.11

The neoclassical model: expansionary monetary policy

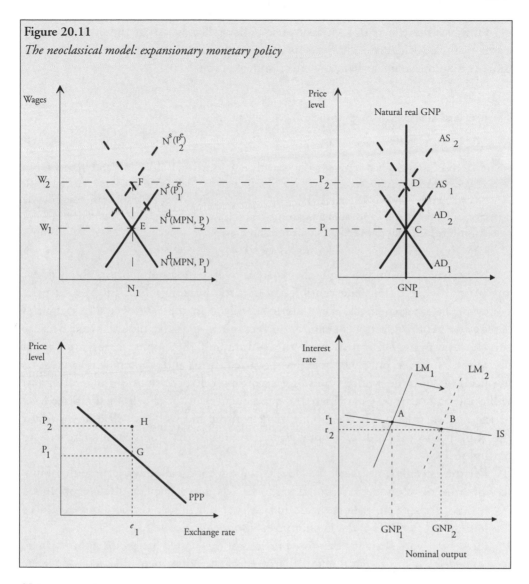

Note:

Both employers and employees forecast an increase in prices equal to the increase in the money supply. This forecast takes account of any secondary increases in the price level due to a shift of the AS curve.

UNANTICIPATED INFLATION

The above analysis suggests that if inflation is anticipated there will be no trade-off between inflation and GNP (or unemployment) even in the short run. The money illusion that we discussed earlier in this chapter can only come about through *surprise* or *unanticipated* inflation. Policy makers can only achieve this result by an *unannounced* change of policy that takes firms and households by surprise. Hence a surprise fiscal or monetary expansion could lead to an increase in real GNP in the short run by creating an unanticipated increase in the price level or the rate of inflation.

However the effects of such a surprise policy will not last: as the public quickly learns from the evidence and adjusts its expectations. This means that only in the very short run do these shocks have any effect on real output.

Note:
The neoclassical aggregate supply function can be written:

$$\Delta GNP = \Delta GNP^* + \alpha(\pi - \pi^e) \tag{13}$$

where ΔGNP^* and ΔGNP represent the growth rate in natural real GNP and actual GNP respectively. Note that $\Delta GNP - \Delta GNP^*$ is the output gap we defined in chapter 2. Actual GNP can exceed natural real GNP only if $\pi > \pi^e$. That is, the actual inflation rate exceeds the expected inflation rate. If expectations are formed rationally, such unanticipated inflation will not persist for long. Output gaps will be small and short-lived.

Neoclassical economists argue that there is no role for a stabilisation policy or for any form of government intervention to offset the instability brought by a surprise policy or an external shock. They argue that even in the case of a shock such as September 11, the government cannot do very much to resolve the situation. Because the shock was unanticipated, both the private and the public sector are caught unawares. However, once the shock has occurred, firms and workers will forecast its implications and adjust prices and wages accordingly. Expectations, formed rationally, will on average correctly anticipate the consequences of the shock for the price level or the rate of inflation. In the labour market, firms and workers will quickly adjust the supply and demand for labour curves to ensure that the economy reverts to natural real GNP.

For these reasons, neoclassical economists are sceptical about governments' ability to 'fine-tune' the economy in response to shocks. As Lucas comments about economists: 'As an advice-giving profession we are in way over our heads.' (Robert Lucas, 'Rules, Discretion and the Role of the Economic Advisor', *op. cit.*, 1980.)

However, people living in depressed regions of the United States, for example, may be excused for being sceptical about the speed of the adjustment that relies on wage flexibility. Areas that have suffered structural decline – the Detroit region has been badly hit by the decline in employment in the automobile industry – have adjusted mainly through migration. Those who have stayed behind have seen their wages and job opportunities decline. At the national level, the disinflationary process that began in the early 1980s in the US resulted in several years of above average unemployment rates. Clearly the experience of these people fits very uneasily with the neoclassical analysis and policies prescriptions expounded in this section.

20.10 CONCLUSION

In this chapter we expanded our understanding of the supply-side of the economy and discussed the policy differences between Keynesians, monetarists and neoclassical economists. Among the main topics discussed were:

- The aggregate production function
- How the supply and demand for labour determines the wage rate and the level of employment
- The role of price expectations particularly with regard to the supply of labour
- The concept of money illusion
- The Keynesian, monetarist and neoclassical models
- The effects of an expansionary fiscal and monetary policy
- The effects of a deflationary demand-side and supply-side shock.

CHAPTER 21

The Phillips Curve and the Inflation-Unemployment Trade-off

21.1 INTRODUCTION

In this chapter we examine the relationship between inflation and unemployment. The New Zealand economist A. W. H. Phillips (1914–75), working at the London School of Economics in the 1950s, presented evidence which showed an inverse relationship between the percentage change in wages and the rate of unemployment. A curve depicting this inverse relationship has come to be known as the *Phillips curve*. We begin this chapter by discussing the original version of the Phillips curve and its implications for economic policy. This is followed by a discussion of subsequent modifications and critiques of the Phillips curve. These developments gave rise to the *accelerationist theory of inflation*. We use this theory to discuss the costs associated with implementing a deflationary or anti-inflationary economic policy. We conclude the chapter by presenting econometric evidence on the Phillips curve for the Eurozone countries.

21.2 THE ORIGINAL PHILLIPS CURVE

Phillips noted that between 1861 and 1957 in Britain there was a tendency for periods of low unemployment to coincide with periods of rising wage rates. Conversely, during periods of high unemployment, the rate of increase in wages moderated. (See A. W. H. Phillips, 'The Relation Between Unemployment and the Rate of Change of Money Wages in the United Kingdom, 1861–1957' in *Economica*, Vol. 25, November 1958.) The Phillips curve simply shows the inverse relationship between the rate of unemployment and the rate of increase in nominal wages. Phillips drew a diagram depicting this inverse relationship. Variants of it have appeared in macroeconomic textbooks ever since.

   One modification is to replace the rate of increase in nominal wages by the increase in prices or the inflation rate. This adjustment, in effect, assumes that prices are set as a *mark-up* over wages. If wages rise, so too will the price of output, and vice versa. Expressed in terms of price inflation, the Phillips curve can be written as:

$$\pi = f(U) \qquad f_1 < 0 \tag{1}$$

where π is the rate of inflation and U the unemployment rate. Equation (1) states that the inflation rate is a function of the rate of unemployment. The $f_1 < 0$ indicates that we expect an increase in unemployment to lead to a fall in the rate of inflation and vice versa.

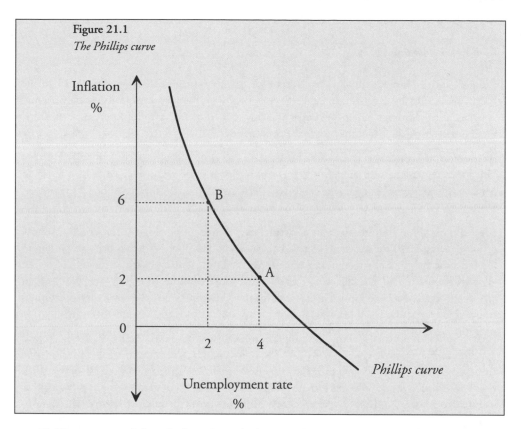

Figure 21.1
The Phillips curve

Phillips suggested that the best fit to the historical data was a non-linear one, as shown in figure 21.1. The Phillips curve shows the inverse relationship between unemployment (horizontal axis) and inflation (vertical axis). A low level of unemployment is associated with a high rate of inflation. Conversely, a high level of unemployment is associated with a low level of inflation. Note that at some stage, the Phillips curve cuts through the horizontal axis. This suggests that high levels of unemployment are associated with deflation.

Note:
In actual fact, Phillips obtained his curve using data over the sub-period 1861–1913 and *not* the entire period 1861–1957. He then applied the curve to the sub-periods 1913–48 and 1948–57 and discussed the appropriateness of the fit. What he found was that the data moved in loops around the curve. If he had estimated the curve for the entire period it is likely he would have obtained quite a different shape or slope. Other economists had examined the data over the entire period but thought the scatter diagram offered no discernible relationship between wages and unemployment. It is of interest to note that in obtaining the curve for the 1861–1913 period, Phillips did *not* appear to use any statistical technique but actually drew the curve freehand to obtain the best fit. A contemporary economist of Phillips comments: 'Early on, (Phillips) said that, since the curve had a logarithmic form and since there are no logs of negative numbers, he was forced to use unconventional methods of first averaging the data into a few points and then fitting a curve to those points by eye'. (Richard G. Lipsey, 'The Famous Phillips Curve Article' in *A. W. H. Phillips: Collected Works in Contemporary Perspective*, ed. Robert Leeson, Cambridge University Press, 2000.)

Box 21.1
Profile of Bill Phillips (1914–75)

Alban William Housego Phillips or 'Bill' to his friends was born in November 1914 in the North Island of New Zealand. In his early years he drifted between jobs in Australia working, at times, as a goldminer, cinema manager and crocodile hunter. During this period he qualified as an engineer through a correspondence course.

At the start of World War II, he joined the RAF as a Flying Officer and was initially based in Singapore. His plane was later shot down and he spent three-and-a-half years in a Japanese prisoner of war camp. For his war exploits, he was awarded an M.B.E. (Military Division) in 1946.

After the war, Phillips undertook an undergraduate degree in sociology at the London School of Economics (LSE) for which he received a pass grade. His poor grade has been attributed to his life-time habit of chain smoking unfiltered cigarettes. During exams, students were not allowed to smoke and this apparently affected his concentration. In actual fact, Phillips had already converted to economics and spent most of his time studying monetary economics rather than preparing for his exams.

Over the next ten years, Phillips rose rapidly through the academic ranks. In 1958, he was appointed Professor of Economics at LSE. Today, it would be a near impossibility for someone to progress from a pass degree to a full professorship at a leading university in such a short space of time. During this period he published a number of papers on topics such as stabilisation policy, optimal control theory, economic growth, and, of course, the famous 'Phillips curve' article in 1958.

In 1967, Phillips accepted a chair in economics at the Australian National University. Two years later he suffered a stroke and retired to Auckland, New Zealand. He died from a stroke on March 1975 at the age of sixty.

POLICY IMPLICATIONS

The thinking behind the Phillips curve was enormously influential in the 1960s. It led macroeconomic policy makers to believe, in a phrase used by Paul Samuelson and Robert Solow in 1960 (both Nobel prize laureates teaching at the Massachusetts Institute of Technology), that there exists a 'menu for policy choice'.

Note:
Soon after the publication of his paper in *Economica*, Phillips left for a sabbatical in Australia. When he returned he was amazed to find people referring to a 'Phillips curve'. In fact, the economists Paul Samuelson and Robert Solow coined the phrase 'the Phillips curve'. (P. A. Samuelson and R. M. Solow, 'Analytical aspects of anti-inflation policy' in *American Economic Review*, Papers and Proceedings, May 1960.)

This led to the belief that there was a trade-off between the two evils of inflation and unemployment. It is not possible to enjoy a low rate of inflation and a low rate of unemployment at the same time, but it is possible to have less of one if more of the other is tolerated. Countries have to decide how much extra inflation they are prepared to tolerate in order to achieve a reduction in unemployment. For example, suppose the economy is initially at the point A in figure 21.1, where an inflation rate of 2 per cent is combined with an unemployment rate of 4 per cent. If the government now uses a fiscal or monetary policy to move the economy to the point B, unemployment is reduced to 2 per cent but inflation rises to 6 per cent. The gain in terms of lower unemployment has been paid for in terms of a higher rate of inflation.

The choice between these two evils is essentially a political one. Conservatives might prefer low inflation and ignore the high unemployment that this entails, whereas Labour or left-wing parties might tend to opt for low unemployment and accept the consequences in terms of inflation.

Various attempts were suggested in the 1960s to improve the trade-off. For example, a prices and incomes policy could be used to constrain the rise in inflation. With inflation held constant along the vertical axis, fiscal or monetary policy could then be used to lower unemployment. The result would be to shift the Phillips curve down to the left and improve the trade-off. The British Prime Minister, Ted Heath, tried such a policy in the early 1970s with disastrous results. The prices and incomes policy lead to a pent-up demand for higher wages and caused major industrial strife.

THE PHILLIPS CURVE AND THE AD-AS MODEL

The economic rationale underlying the Phillips curve can be explained in terms of movements of the aggregate demand (AD) curve along the short-run aggregate supply (AS) curve. Shifts of the AD curve to the right, for example, lead to increases in both inflation and the real growth rate (not shown). The increase in real GNP is, in turn, reflected in a fall in unemployment. This is akin to a movement up the Phillips curve. Lower unemployment is associated with higher inflation. Conversely, a shift of the AD curve to the left (not shown) would reduce inflation and the real growth rate and increase unemployment. This is equivalent to a movement down the Phillips curve as lower inflation is associated with higher unemployment.

The slope of the Phillips curve is determined by the slope of the AS curve. At very low levels of unemployment, the short-run AS curve tends to become steep and the inflation rate increases more rapidly. Conversely, at high levels of unemployment, the short-run AS curve is relatively flat and there is a small increase in the inflation rate.

Note that prior to the publication of the Phillips article, economists tended to view the AS curve as been ⌐ shaped (inverted L). That is the AS curve is horizontal when unemployment is high and vertical when full employment is reached. This meant that as the AD curve shifts to the right, the economy went from a position of constant prices and variable unemployment to a position of constant unemployment and variable prices. The implication was that there is no *smooth* trade-off between inflation and unemployment.

BREAKDOWN OF THE PHILLIPS CURVE RELATIONSHIP

Attempts to exploit the trade-off between unemployment and inflation led to increasing disillusionment. The emphasis during the 1960s was on keeping the rate of unemployment low, and a fair degree of success was achieved in this regard. However, in many countries it became evident that the rate of inflation associated with what was considered full employment was rising. Even worse was the experience of the mid-1970s when the rate of inflation began to increase at a time of rising unemployment. This became known as *stagflation*. It appeared that the policies designed to move the economy up the Phillips curve were in fact causing the curve to shift upwards to the right. That is, a higher level of unemployment was associated with a higher level of inflation. The inflation/unemployment relationship, which apparently had been stable for over a hundred years, appeared to be breaking down.

There was much discussion of possible explanations for this: increased trade union militancy, a growing mismatch between the skills of the job seekers and the requirements of employers, a more generous social welfare system, and so on. Note that a shift of the short-run AS curve up to the left (due to an increase in raw material prices or a fall in productivity) would also explain stagflation. This would increase both unemployment and inflation, which is the equivalent of the Phillips curve shifting up to the right.

However, none of the above explanations seemed to go to the heart of the matter and explain what was happening. It seemed that a fundamental reformulation of the Phillips curve idea was required. In this regard, two economists, Milton Friedman, University of Chicago and Edmund Phelps, Columbia University, deserve credit for foreseeing in the 1960s the acceleration of inflation that would occur if the Phillips curve were used for policy purposes. These two economists provided a theoretical framework that significantly advanced our understanding of the relationship between inflation and unemployment. Before we turn to an explanation of the Friedman, Phelps analysis, we present some empirical evidence on the Phillips curve for the Eurozone countries.

EMPIRICAL EVIDENCE FOR THE EUROZONE COUNTRIES

As a preliminary exercise, we can study the relationship between inflation and unemployment across the countries of the Eurozone. This may shed some light on the validity of the simple original version of the Phillips Curve. Figure 21.2 shows a scatter diagram based on the inflation, unemployment combinations for Ireland over the period 1961 to 2002. That is, each point in the diagram shows the combination of inflation and unemployment for a particular year. For example, the years 1976, 1987 and 2001 are highlighted. A linear (as opposed to the logarithmic line used by Phillips) 'line of best fit' or trend line is then inserted into this scatter diagram. The distance from each observation to the trend line is called the 'error' associated with that observation. The trend line is placed in such a way that the 'errors' above the line cancel with the 'errors' below the line. In this sense, it is the 'line of best fit'.

The line slopes downwards, indicating that as unemployment increases along the horizontal axis, the inflation rate falls on the vertical axis and vice versa. The estimated equation is:

$$\text{Inflation} = 9.3 - 0.2 \, \text{Unemployment} \tag{2}$$

The slope of the line is estimated to be −0.2. (The 9.3 is the estimated intercept which may be ignored at this juncture.) The regression results suggest that for every 1 per cent

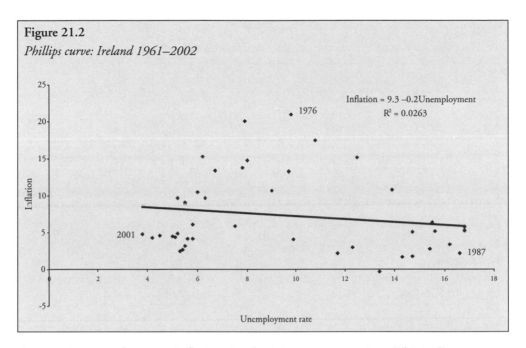

Figure 21.2

Phillips curve: Ireland 1961–2002

decrease in unemployment, inflation rises by 0.2 percentage points. This indicates a very favourable trade-off in the case of the Irish economy. It would appear the policy maker could reduce unemployment without have any major impact on inflation. The R^2 statistic indicates how much of the variance (fluctuation) in inflation is explained by the unemployment rate. The estimated R^2 for Ireland of 0.02 indicates that only 2 per cent of the variance of inflation is determined by unemployment. This is very low but is not particularly surprising as Ireland is a very open economy and external developments have a very important bearing on domestic inflation. We expect the R^2 coefficient to be higher in some of the larger, more closed, Eurozone countries.

Table 21.1 shows the estimated slope coefficient and the R^2 coefficient for the Eurozone countries. (Annual data over the period 1961 to 2001 was obtained from the European Commission, *European Economy*, No. 73, 2001.) All countries have the expected negative sign between inflation and unemployment with the exception of Portugal. It can be seen that the slope coefficient varies considerably from a high of –1.76 in Austria to a low of –0.2 in Spain and Ireland. Clearly there are some countries such as Austria, Finland, Greece and Italy where any attempt to reduce unemployment will have severe adverse implications for inflation. The opposite would seem to be the case in Belgium, Ireland and Spain. This points to a lack of homogeneity between the Eurozone countries. A deflationary monetary policy designed to reduce Eurozone inflation will, according to these results, have a very uneven impact on unemployment across the Eurozone countries.

The R^2 coefficient indicates that only in a small number of countries, Austria and Germany for example, does the original Phillips curve perform satisfactorily. From the basic empirical results presented in table 21.1, it would seem that the determinants of inflation are more complex than given by the original Phillips curve.

Table 21.1
Phillips curve estimates for the Eurozone countries: 1961–2002

	Slope coefficient	R^2
Austria	−1.76	0.59
Belgium	−0.19	0.06
Finland	−0.54	0.28
France	−0.41	0.18
Germany	−0.39	0.43
Greece	−0.69	0.06
Ireland	−0.20	0.02
Italy	−0.71	0.08
Luxembourg	−0.48	0.02
Netherlands	−0.41	0.20
Portugal	+2.30	0.45
Spain	−0.20	0.09

Source: Authors' estimates.

21.3 THE REVISED PHILLIPS CURVE

As mentioned, a fundamental critique of the Phillips curve analysis was advanced independently in the late 1960s by the monetarist economists Milton Friedman and Edmund Phelps. (See M. Friedman, 'The Role of Monetary Policy' in *American Economic Review*, March 1969; and E. Phelps, *Inflation Policy and Unemployment Theory*, Norton, 1973.) Basically, they argued that the original Phillips curve ignored the role of price expectations in wage negotiations. They incorporated *price expectations* into the Phillips curve and showed that in the long run there is no trade-off between inflation and unemployment. Put another way, they argued that the long-run Phillips curve is vertical. They argued that attempts to hold unemployment below the natural rate would result in *accelerating* inflation.

They argued that a vertical Phillips curve would intersect the horizontal axis at the natural rate of unemployment. This 'natural' rate is also known as the *non-accelerating inflation rate of unemployment* or NAIRU. The phrase NAIRU was introduced by James Tobin, of Yale University. It has the merit of avoiding the moralistic overtones of the 'natural' rate. We continue, however, to use the term 'natural rate' in the remainder of this chapter.

Note:
Economists mistakenly refer to a rising inflation rate as accelerating inflation! An inflation that goes from 2 to 4 to 6 per cent is rising. Only when the inflation rate is rising at an increasing pace — from 2 to 4 to 8 to 16 per cent — is it accelerating.

THE ROLE OF EXPECTATIONS

The starting point is to reformulate the Phillips curve in terms of how workers bargain for wage increases. Here it is essential to distinguish between the change in nominal wages (ΔW) and the change in real wages (ΔRW). The real wage is the nominal wage adjusted for inflation (π). That is:

$$\Delta RW = \Delta W - \pi \qquad (3)$$

The next point to note is that wage bargaining is forward looking and has to be based on an anticipated or ex ante rate of inflation. That is, because wage contracts last into the future, workers will try to anticipate the rate of inflation in order to protect their real wages for the duration of the contract. For example, if inflation is expected to be 20 per cent over the coming year, workers will demand a 20 per cent increase in nominal wages to compensate for anticipated inflation and maintain real wages at the present level. Hence the variable that matters in wage bargaining may be defined as:

$$\Delta RW = \Delta W - \pi^e \qquad (4)$$

where π^e is expected price inflation.

Given that prices are set as a mark-up over wages, it follows that an increase in inflationary expectations will increase wage demands which, in turn, will increase the inflation rate. In short:

$$\uparrow \pi^e \rightarrow \uparrow \Delta W \rightarrow \uparrow \pi$$

It follows from this that it is in the best interest of the policy maker to maintain a low inflation environment. If workers anticipate low inflation they will set their wage demands accordingly.

NATURAL RATE OF UNEMPLOYMENT

The second main strand in the Phelps-Friedman theory is to incorporate the natural rate of unemployment into the analysis. This is the level of unemployment that exists when the economy is growing at the natural real growth rate. It is a normal feature of any dynamic economy that some minimal frictional unemployment remains even when the economy is growing at its potential.

The natural rate of unemployment can vary from one period to another. That is the natural rate tends to rise during recessions and fall during boom periods. Economists use the concept of *hysteresis* when exploring this issue. (See Richard G. Layard, Stephen J. Nickell and Richard A. Jackman, *Unemployment: Macroeconomic Performance and the Labour Market*, Oxford: Oxford University Press, 1991.) Hysteresis refers to a situation where the natural rate of unemployment depends on the actual level of unemployment. This means that the natural rate of unemployment increases during recession (mid-1980s) and falls in boom periods (1990s).

Think of what would happen if every time you got the flu your body's normal temperature rose. Even after you had recovered, your temperature would remain above 37° Celsius. It would be exhibiting hysteresis. It sounds unpleasant!

The view that the natural rate of unemployment jumps around from decade to decade has led Robert Solow to question the usefulness of the concept: 'A natural rate that hops around from one triennium to another under the influences of unspecified forces, including past unemployment rates, is not natural at all.' (Robert Solow, 'Unemployment: Getting the Questions Right' in *Economica*, 1986, [Supplement] S54.)

Note:
The Irish experience tends to bear out the notion of a variable natural rate of unemployment. The National Industrial Economic Council in 1967 specified 2 per cent as the target (or natural) unemployment rate. The National Economic and Social Council (NESC) published a study in 1975 that defined it as 4 per cent. In 1977 the NESC used a rate of 5 per cent as equivalent to full employment. The use of numerical targets was then abandoned. Studies of unemployment by the Economic and Social Research Institute (ESRI) and official documents, including the *Programme for National Recovery* (1987), the *Programme for Economic and Social Progress* (1990), *Programme for Competitiveness and Work* (1994), and the national *Development Plan* 2000–06 have avoided specifying targets for full employment or the natural rate of unemployment. (Estimates of natural real GDP for the Eurozone countries are given in C. Denis, K. McMorrow and W. Roger, 'Production Function Approach to Calculating Potential Growth and Output Gaps: Estimates for the EU Member States and the US' in *European Economy*, European Commission, No. 176, September 2002.)

Clearly a variable natural rate of unemployment makes the policy makers task more difficult as they are, in effect, aiming at a moving target. In this chapter, in order to facilitate the analysis, we assume that the natural rate remains constant.

On this basis, Friedman and Phelps argue that inflation depends on the gap between the actual unemployment rate (U) and the natural rate (U_n). That is, inflation is influenced by $(U - U_n)$, rather than U. If U is greater than U_n, there is downward pressure on inflation. This is because in times of high unemployment, the trade unions bargaining position is weak and they settle for lower wage demands. Conversely, if U is less than U_n, there is upward pressure on inflation. This is because in boom times, there are bottlenecks and labour shortages and the unions are in a strong position and can demand higher wages. Unemployment does not affect inflation when U is equal to U_n.

EXPECTATIONS-AUGMENTED PHILLIPS CURVE

Taking the above two adjustments together, the *accelerationist* or *expectations-augmented* Phillips curve may be written:

$$\pi_t = \pi^e_t - \alpha(U - U_n) \tag{5}$$

Equation (5) states that the inflation rate in time t depends on the expected rate of inflation (π^e_t) plus an adjustment based on the difference between the actual rate of unemployment and the natural rate. The coefficient α indicates how the rate of inflation reacts to the difference between the unemployment rate and the natural rate of unemployment $(U - U_n)$. A high coefficient would indicate that inflation is very sensitive to the unemployment gap and a low coefficient indicates that inflation is not very responsive to the unemployment gap.

HOW ARE EXPECTATIONS FORMED?

In the Keynesian model, workers use *adaptive expectations* to forecast inflation. It is assumed that this year's inflation rate will recur next year; that is, $\pi^e_t = \pi_{t-1}$, where the subscript t indicates the year. This means that if inflation is 3 per cent in 2002, the same inflation rate is expected for 2003. This is a backward-looking approach to formulating expectations, and in periods of volatile inflation it is likely to lead to serious errors in the anticipated rate of inflation. Inserting this formulation of expectations into equation (5), we have:

$$\pi_t = \pi_{t-1} - \alpha(U - U_n) \tag{6}$$

Equation (6) states that the inflation rate in time t depends on inflation in the previous year plus an adjustment based on the unemployment gap.

Note:
Much more sophisticated techniques for formulating expectations can be employed. In chapter 20, for example, we discussed the neoclassical schools belief in 'rational expectations'. In this chapter we retain the adaptive expectations approach as it highlights the monetarists critique of the Phillips curve.

21.4 THE ACCELERATIONIST THEORY OF INFLATION

The expectations-augmented Phillips curve is illustrated in figure 21.3. The Phillips curve is again downward sloping, indicating an inverse relationship between inflation and unemployment. We have also inserted a vertical line labelled the long-run Phillips curve. As mentioned, the long-run Phillips curve is located at the natural rate of unemployment, which for illustrative purposes may be taken to equal 6 per cent unemployment.

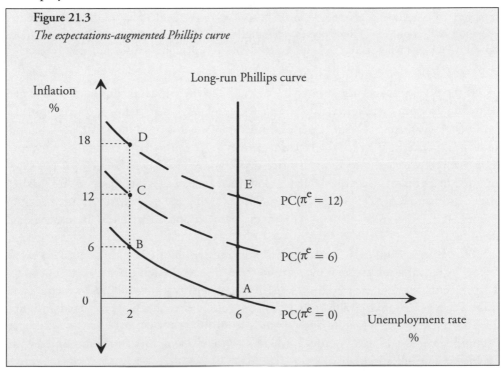

Figure 21.3
The expectations-augmented Phillips curve

Suppose now that the economy is at the point A in figure 21.3. At this point, expected inflation (π^e) equals zero and the actual unemployment rate equals the natural rate of 6 per cent. It can be seen from equation (6) that under these circumstance, the actual inflation rate will also be zero. Hence, at the point A, zero inflation is combined with a 6 per cent unemployment rate. Note that the Phillips curve is labelled PC(π^e = 0) to indicate that expected inflation is zero.

Let us suppose that the government decides that 6 per cent is an unacceptably high rate of unemployment. If the government uses monetary or fiscal policy to reduce unemployment the economy moves up along the Phillips curve to the point B. (Note that this is equivalent to shifting the AD curve to the right.) At the point B, inflation increases to 6 per cent and unemployment falls to 2 per cent.

The movement from A to B in figure 21.3 is a satisfactory outcome from the government's point of view. An expansionary macroeconomic policy has lowered unemployment to 2 per cent at the cost of a 6 per cent increase in inflation.

However, the point B is not a long-run equilibrium point. Inflation has increased from 0 per cent to 6 per cent, but workers were expecting it to be zero. In the next round of wage negotiations, workers will revise their inflation expectations upwards from zero to 6 per cent. This is reflected in the diagram as the Phillips curve shifts upwards from PC(π^e = 0) to PC(π^e = 6). In effect, price expectations determine the position or location of the Phillips curve. An increase in expectations shifts the curve upwards and vice versa. This means that the Phillips curves shown in figure 21.3 are only *short-run* Phillips curves.

Note:
When unemployment equals the natural rate, actual inflation is determined by expected inflation. In other words, the short-run Phillips curve intersects the long-run Phillips curve at the point corresponding to the expected rate of inflation. The long-run PC is the locus of points on short-run PCs where actual inflation equals expected inflation. Surprise inflation is zero.

If the policy makers persist in trying to maintain the rate of unemployment at 2 per cent, the economy will move, in the next round of wage negotiations, to the point C on PC(π^e = 6). At this point, 2 per cent unemployment is combined with an inflation rate of 12 per cent. Why has the inflation rate increased from 6 per cent to 12 per cent? The answer is that the revision in price expectations from 0 per cent to 6 per cent resulted in an increase in wage demands. This increase in wages (via the mark-up model) added a further 6 per cent to the inflation rate bringing the new rate to 12 per cent. At the point C, the trade-off between unemployment and inflation is becoming less favourable.

However, the point C is also not a long-run equilibrium point. Workers were expecting an inflation rate of 6 per cent whereas the actual inflation rate turns out to be 12 per cent. In the next round of wage negotiations, workers will again revise their inflation expectations upwards from 6 per cent to 12 per cent. This is reflected in figure 21.3 as the Phillips curve shifting upwards from PC(π^e = 6) to PC(π^e = 12). The economy now moves to the point D, where 2 per cent unemployment is combined with an 18 per cent inflation rate.

The crucial point that emerges from this analysis is that as long as policy is dedicated to maintaining the rate of unemployment below its natural rate, the economy will not remain in a steady equilibrium position. Inflation will go on accelerating as workers continually revise price expectations upwards.

The consequences of trying to maintain the rate of unemployment below its natural rate are now very unsatisfactory. The cost of the reduction in unemployment is a continuously rising rate of inflation. The expansionary macroeconomic policy has not just caused a once-off increase in inflation but has led to an *accelerating* rate of inflation.

Eventually, the policy maker will come to view the inflation problem as more serious than the unemployment problem, and policies will be introduced to stop inflation accelerating. This would entail introducing a deflationary fiscal or monetary policy that moves the economy down the Phillips curve from the point D to E. (Note that the models discussed in chapter 20 predict that the economy will automatically revert back to the natural rate of unemployment.) At the point E, unemployment is back to the natural rate and workers price expectations prove to be correct. (At the point E, the actual inflation rate equals 12 per cent.) Hence, the point E is a stable long-run equilibrium point.

By joining points such as A and E, we obtain the long-run Phillips curve. We can see that it is *vertical* because we started at the natural rate and ultimately we end up back at the natural rate. The inflation rate may differ, but the unemployment rate will, in the long run, be the same. Given that we started from the natural rate of unemployment and that we have now ended back at this rate, what has been gained by the expansionary macroeconomic policy? The answer is a temporary reduction in the rate of unemployment and a permanent increase in the rate of inflation.

This is obviously less attractive than the permanent reduction in unemployment that was promised by the original version of the Phillips curve. If the cost of maintaining unemployment below the natural rate was accelerating inflation, the attempt to do so would eventually have to be abandoned in order to prevent the breakdown of economic life. Accelerating inflation would lead to hyperinflation of the sort experienced in central Europe after World War II and in many Eastern European countries in recent years. Such inflation is so disruptive that it undermines normal economic processes and leads to a sharp decline in living standards.

On the basis of their critique of the earlier Phillips curve analysis, therefore, Phelps and Friedman rejected the notion that in the long run unemployment could be reduced by accepting a higher rate of inflation. The 'accelerationist' theory of inflation, as this theory has been called, left little or no room for expansionary macroeconomic policy as an instrument for lowering the rate of unemployment.

ALTERNATIVE EXPLANATION

The above analysis could also be conducted in terms of equation (6). Recall that:

$$\pi_t = \pi_{t-1} - \alpha(U - U_n)$$

The expansionary monetary policy reduced U below the natural rate of unemployment and this added 6 per cent to π_t in the first year. In the second year this increase in inflation feeds back into the π_{t-1} term and this pushes the actual inflation rate to 12 per cent. In the third year the increase in inflation again feeds back into the π_{t-1} term and inflation again rises, and so on. Eventually, the policy maker decides that the rise in inflation is no longer acceptable and introduces policies to move the economy back to the natural rate of unemployment.

21.5 DEFLATION, EXPECTATIONS AND CREDIBILITY

So far we have concentrated on accepting a higher inflation rate in order to lower unemployment. But what of the opposite case where a government is willing to accept higher unemployment in order to bring down inflation? This is essentially the type of 'monetarist' policy introduced by Mrs Thatcher in Britain in 1979 and by Paul Volcker, chairman of the Federal Reserve Board in America in the same year. This deflation policy is the reverse of the expansionary policy discussed in the previous section.

Consider figure 21.4, where the economy is initially at the natural rate of unemployment at A. Suppose also that inflation is 20 per cent and that this rate is unacceptable to the government. To reduce inflation the government introduces a deflationary fiscal or monetary policy. (This is akin to a shift to the left in the aggregate demand curve.) As a result, the economy moves from the point A to the point B along the Phillips curve labelled PC ($\pi^e = 20$). This Phillips curve is associated with inflation expectations of 20 per cent.

At the point B unemployment has risen from 6 to 10 per cent but actual inflation has fallen 16 per cent. (Note that the decrease in inflation depends on how far the economy moves down the Phillips curve.) At the point B the economy is said to be experiencing an inflationary recession.

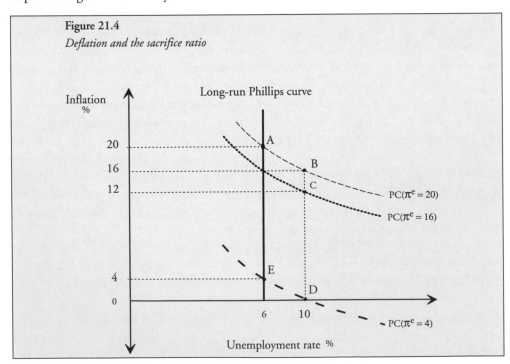

Figure 21.4
Deflation and the sacrifice ratio

In the next round of wage negotiations, workers realise that inflation is lower than expected and they revise inflation expectations from 20 to 16 per cent. This is reflected in a shift downwards in the Phillips curve. As workers inflation expectations fall, wage demands are moderated and the actual inflation rate falls to 12 per cent.

Over time, the Phillips curve will gradually drift down as price expectations are revised downwards. Eventually the economy will move to a point such as D. At this point, 0 per cent inflation is combined with a 10 per cent unemployment rate. The government may now decide to introduce an expansionary fiscal policy to move the economy up the Phillips curve from the point D to E. (Note that in line with the models discussed in chapter 20, the economy could also revert automatically back to the natural rate of unemployment.) The economy reverts back to the natural rate of unemployment and inflation increases to 4 per cent.

SACRIFICE RATIO

The cost of reducing inflation is the lost output and the rise in unemployment associated with the policy-induced recession. The sacrifice ratio is one measure of this cost. It indicates how much unemployment has to be increased in order to reduce inflation. To explain this sacrifice ratio, we first define a point-year of excess unemployment as being the difference between actual unemployment and the natural rate multiplied by the number of years. For example, suppose actual unemployment is 10 per cent and the natural rate is 6 per cent for two years. This is equivalent to 8 point-years of excess unemployment.

> Point-year of excess unemployment = 4 per cent excess unemployment $\times$ 2 years
> = 8 points

The sacrifice ratio is now defined as the point-year of excess unemployment divided by the decrease in inflation. That is:

> Sacrifice ratio = Point-year of excess unemployment/decrease in inflation

Hence if it takes 8 point-years of excess unemployment to reduce inflation by 2 per cent, the sacrifice ratio is 4 (8/2).

Equation (6) can be used to throw light on the potential size of the sacrifice ratio. By taking the π_{t-1} term to the left-hand side we have:

$$\pi_t - \pi_{t-1} = - \alpha(U - U_n) \tag{7}$$

or

$$\Delta\pi = - \alpha(U - U_n) \tag{8}$$

Suppose that the natural rate of unemployment is 6 per cent and that the α coefficient is estimated to be equal to 1. If the policy maker wishes to reduce inflation by 5 per cent, then equation (8) suggests that actual unemployment will have to be increased to 11 per cent for one year.

$$-5\% = - 1(11 - 6)$$

Inserting this information into the definition of the sacrifice ratio above we calculate that the sacrifice ratio is 1. (Five point-years of excess unemployment divided by a 5 per cent reduction in inflation.)

Alternatively, the policy maker could increase actual unemployment to 8.5 per cent for two years to achieve the same 5 per cent reduction in inflation. Again the sacrifice ratio is 1.

However, if the α coefficient is instead equal to, say, 0.5, the sacrifice ratio would be twice as high. For example, the policy maker would have to increase actual unemployment to 16 per cent to bring about a 5 per cent reduction in inflation in one year.

$$-5\% = -0.5(16 - 6)$$

Alternatively, the policy maker could opt for an actual unemployment rate of 11 per cent for two years to bring about a similar result. This analysis suggests that the sacrifice ratio depends, in part, on the α coefficient. The higher the α coefficient the lower the sacrifice ratio and vice versa. We present some empirical evidence on the α coefficient in section 21.6.

The sacrifice ratio also depends on how rapidly inflationary expectations are revised. If inflation expectations are quickly revised downwards, the adjustment costs will be relatively small. Conversely, if inflation expectations are slow to change, the adjustment costs will be relatively high. Equation (8) does not throw any light on this issue as we have assumed adaptive expectations. That is, we have assumed that this year's inflation rate is the best indicator of next year's inflation rate. This assumption is 'built-in' to the equation and hence cannot be empirical evaluated.

'Gradualist' or 'cold turkey'

As mentioned, the α coefficient, in part, determines the sacrifice ratio. However, there is some international evidence which shows that the sacrifice ratio tends to be lower, the quicker the disinflation. (See Laurence Ball, 'What Determines the Sacrifice Ratio?' in N. G. Mankiw ed., *Monetary Policy*, University of Chicago Press, 1994.) This raises the question of whether the policy maker should introduce a 'gradualist' or 'cold turkey' approach in deflating the economy. That is, should the policy maker slowly deflate the economy and move gently towards a low inflation rate? Alternatively should the policy maker introduce a once-off deflationary policy that hits the economy so hard that market participants cannot but recognise the government's intention and therefore revise their expectations? In this case, the movement to a low inflation rate should happen very quickly and unemployment would not remain above the natural rate for very long.

The problem with the 'cold turkey' approach is that it can lead to a severe recession that leads to civil unrest and political instability. Also it will impact disproportionately on vulnerable sectors of the labour market such as the unskilled and the young. In this context, one of the authors noticed the following headline in a Polish newspaper: '*Sachs obcial psu ogon przy szyi.*' Literally translated this means 'Sachs cuts dog's tail off at neck'! This is a reference to the American economist Jeffery Sachs who was responsible for introducing economic reforms in Poland during the late 1980s. Obviously, the media felt he had overdone the 'cold turkey' approach!

UK, US AND IRISH DISINFLATIONARY EXPERIENCES

Economists such as Robert Lucas of Chicago University, who believe in rational expectations, argue that the sacrifice ratio may be small under certain circumstances. Individuals take policy changes into account in formulating their expectations. If the central bank announces a reduction in the money supply, individuals would anticipate the reduction in inflation and quickly adjust their expectations. In this case, the unemployment costs involved in the disinflation would be small. An extreme form of rational expectation is the 'full information' assumption. According to this, price expectations prove correct not just on average but in all cases. If wages and prices are completely flexible and the public is well informed, then the adjustment to low inflation will be instantaneous and the costs of deflation will be negligible.

However, the evidence does not support this point of view. In the UK Mrs Thatcher's monetarist experiment resulted in a painful transition. Inflation fell from 18 per cent in 1980 to 4 per cent in 1983, but absolute GDP fell by 3 per cent between 1981–83 and unemployment increased from 1.1 million in 1979 to 3 million in 1984.

Similarly, in the US, the Fed under Paul Volcker pursued a deflationary monetary policy that reduced US inflation from 21.5 per cent in 1979 to 4 per cent in 1983. However, the real growth rate averaged only –0.3 per cent from 1980–82 and unemployment increased from 5.5 per cent in 1979 to 10 per cent in 1983. It took several years to return to the 5.5 per cent level.

In 1979, Ireland joined the European Monetary System (EMS) primarily to reduce inflation to the low German rate (see chapter 13). The 'sacrifice ratio' associated with this policy would seem to be relatively high. The number of point-years of excess unemployment between 1981–97 totalled 73, while inflation fell by 15 percentage points. This suggests a sacrifice ratio of 4.9, almost twice the ratio attributed to the Volcker disinflation in the US. High unemployment seems to be a very costly mechanism for reducing inflation in an Irish context.

POLICY CREDIBILITY

Another factor impacting on inflation expectations is the *credibility* of the policy maker in sticking to the measures needed to bring about the required adjustment. It is argued that if the policy is credible, then economic agents (firms and workers) will quickly adjust prices and wages to take account of the new policy. However, if the policy maker lacks credibility and is viewed as likely to waver under pressure, then adjustment will be prolonged and the costs will be high. Factors influencing the 'credibility' of the policy maker include:

* An ability to reduce, if not eliminate, excessive budget deficits.
* An ability to communicate the new policy effectively to the public.
* Reputation for hard-nosed indifference to temporary increases in unemployment.

This is likely to be highest when the policy makers are 'above politics'; that is, when they do not have to pander to the electorate. For that reason, if monetary policy is in the hands of an independent central bank, it is more likely that the public will believe their commitment to squeezing inflation out of the system. If, on the other hand, the central bank is ultimately controlled by politicians, the public will expect the politicians to instruct the bankers to ease up on disinflation as unemployment rises, especially if an election is in the offing.

An approach that has been widely used by small economies to gain credibility is to peg the currency to a 'hard' currency (the euro) and then implement appropriate fiscal, monetary and incomes policies to back up the peg. The ultimate logic of this approach is to abandon an independent monetary policy. Responsibility for domestic inflation is removed from the national central bank and transferred to the European Central Bank in Frankfurt. Ireland took this decision in 1998.

21.6 THE AUGMENTED PHILLIPS CURVE: EVIDENCE FROM THE EUROZONE

It would be informative if we could estimate equation (8) as this would give an indication of the sacrifice ratio for any particular country. However, estimating equation (8) is problematic because the natural rate of unemployment is unobservable. That is we do not know a priori the value for U_n and this makes it difficult to estimate the equation. An alternative to equation (8) is to estimate the following equation:

$$\Delta\pi_t = \beta - \alpha U \tag{9}$$

This equation examines the relationship between the change in the inflation rate and the unemployment rate. The β term is the intercept which may reflect how firms mark up prices over wages and other rigidities in the system such as national wage agreements and so on. The α term shows how the change in inflation reacts to the unemployment rate. This is the same coefficient as in equation (8) and can be used to estimate the sacrifice ratio. Box 21.2 demonstrates that equation (9) is consistent with equation (8). Equation (9) can easily be estimated without having to make any assumptions about the natural rate of unemployment.

Table 21.2 shows the results of estimating equation (9) for each of the Eurozone countries. Recall that the higher the α coefficient the lower the sacrifice ratio and vice versa. The results in table 21.2 indicate significant differences in the α coefficient across the Eurozone countries: from a low of −0.03 in Finland to a high of −0.99 in Austria. This suggests that if the Eurozone were subjected to a common deflationary monetary or fiscal policy, the transition back to the natural rate of unemployment would be very uneven across the Eurozone. That is, the sacrifice ratio would be relatively low for Austria, Greece, the Netherlands and Portugal. But it would be relatively high for countries like Finland, Germany, Ireland and Spain. This has important implications for the issue of convergence within the Eurozone.

NATURAL RATE OF UNEMPLOYMENT
The empirical results in table 21.2 can also be used to get an indication of the natural rate of unemployment. From equation (12) in box 21.2, we can write:

$$U_n = \beta/\alpha$$

Using the estimates of β and α, the natural rate of unemployment for each of the Eurozone countries is given in column 3 in table 21.2. Again there appears to be some

Box 21.2
Deriving the Phillips curve

Equation (9) in the main text states that:

$$\Delta\pi_t = \beta - \alpha U \tag{10}$$

We start with a definition. The natural rate of unemployment is the level of unemployment that prevails when actual inflation equals expected inflation. That is when $\Delta\pi_t = 0$. Setting equation (10) equal to zero and substituting the natural rate of unemployment for the actual rate we have:

$$0 = \beta - \alpha U_n \tag{11}$$

Rearranging:

$$\alpha U_n = \beta \tag{12}$$

Return now to equation (10) above. This equation can be rewritten as:

$$\pi_t = \pi_{t-1} = \beta - \alpha U \tag{13}$$

Substitute equation (12) into (13) to obtain:

$$\pi_t = \pi_{t-1} + \alpha Un - \alpha U \tag{14}$$

Rearranging:

$$\pi_t = \pi_{t-1} - \alpha(U - U_n) \tag{15}$$

which is equation (8) in the main text. Hence equations (8) and (9) are equivalent.

Table 21.2
Estimates of the augmented Phillips curve for the Eurozone countries: 1961–2002

	β	α	Natural rate of unemployment
Austria	4.88	−0.99	4.9
Belgium	0.84	−0.13	6.5
Finland	0.10	−0.03	3.3
France	0.72	−0.11	6.5
Germany	0.19	−0.06	3.2
Greece	2.45	−0.40	6.1
Ireland	1.39	−0.14	9.9
Italy	1.81	−0.23	7.9
Luxembourg	0.54	−0.25	2.2
Netherlands	1.93	−0.37	5.2
Portugal	1.93	−0.37	5.2
Spain	1.23	−0.10	12.3

Source: Authors estimates.

considerable variance in the natural rate: from a high of 12.3 in Spain to a low of 2.2 in Luxembourg. This would indicate the existence of 'different goal posts'. Countries like Spain, Ireland and Italy could be close to the natural rate of unemployment even when the actual rate of unemployment is relatively high. In contrast, countries like Luxembourg, Finland and Germany would have to achieve low levels of unemployment before the economy could be said to be at the natural rate.

THE IRISH, GERMAN AND SPANISH EXPERIENCE

Figures 21.5, 21.6 and 21.7 show the combination of price inflation and the unemployment rate in Ireland, Germany and Spain respectively from 1961 to 2002. We have inserted into each diagram a line indicating the natural rate of unemployment as given in table 21.2. Generally, the inflation, unemployment combinations for each country seem to oscillate around the natural rate of unemployment as predicted by the expectations-augmented Phillips curve analysis. That is, we may be observing a collection of short-run Phillips curves that shifted over time. The three countries seem to have experienced similar trends. The various decades can be described in the following ways.

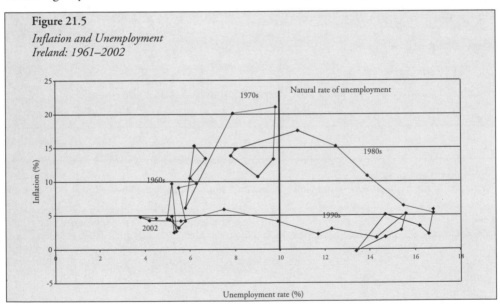

Figure 21.5

*Inflation and Unemployment
Ireland: 1961–2002*

In the 1960s low unemployment was combined with low inflation so the short-run Phillips curve in each of the three countries was down towards the left-hand corner.

In the 1970s each country experienced stagflation. That is, a rise in both unemployment and inflation. This suggests that the short-run Phillips curve representing this decade moved up towards the right.

In the 1980s high unemployment was associated with a high, but falling, inflation rate. The short-run Phillips curves seem to have moved downwards from right to left. In Ireland, this shift of the Phillips curve is a result of the painful deflationary policy associated with EMS membership.

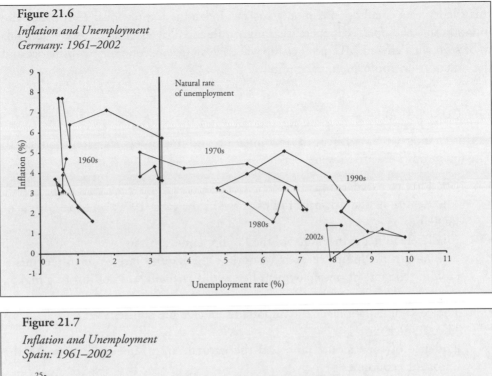

Figure 21.6

Inflation and Unemployment
Germany: 1961–2002

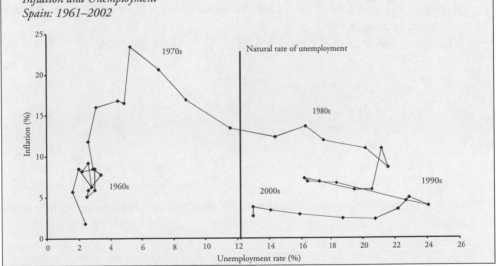

Figure 21.7

Inflation and Unemployment
Spain: 1961–2002

In the 1990s and early 2000s, however, the experience in the three countries is rather different. The Irish economy may have under-shot the natural rate of unemployment. Spain, on the other hand, appears to have made the perfect 'touch-down' arriving at the, albeit high, natural rate of unemployment. Germany is the odd country out as, following reunification in the early 1990s, it seems to be stuck in the mire of recession.

Generally, the Irish, German and Spanish experiences seem to conform to the predictions of the expectations-augment Phillips curve analysis. However, we reiterate the point that this theory was developed to explain inflation in large economies (the US and the Eurozone) which are relatively closed to international trade. The relevance of this theory to a small open economy such as Ireland is less obvious. This is because inflation in small open economies is strongly influenced by external factors. It remains to be seen what effect EMU membership will have on macroeconomic performance and the inflation-unemployment trade-off.

21.7 CONCLUSION

In this chapter we have discussed how inflation and unemployment are interrelated. The main topics discussed were:

- The Phillips curve
- The demise of the original Phillips curve in the early 1970s and the advent of stagflation
- The Phelps-Friedman critique of the Phillips curve analysis
- The long-run Phillips curve is vertical at the natural rate of unemployment. Holding the rate of unemployment below this rate will lead not just to a higher, but to accelerating inflation
- The costs of deflation and the importance of credible policies
- The sacrifice ratio
- Evidence of the sacrifice ratio and the natural rate of unemployment for the Eurozone economies
- The Irish experience and the expectations-augment Phillips curve.

CHAPTER 22

The Labour Market and Unemployment

22.1 INTRODUCTION

The gap between European and American unemployment rates widened markedly during the 1990s and early 2000s. In 2000, unemployment was 9.1 per cent in the Eurozone, compared with 5.5 per cent in the United States. The persistence of a high unemployment rate is the most intractable problem facing Europe today.

Following the economic boom of the 1990s, the Irish unemployment rate fell below 4 per cent in 2001. Even as the economy slowed, the Irish unemployment rate remained low and is no longer as serious problem as it was during the mid-1980s. However, long-term unemployment and non-participation in the labour force persist among many sectors of the population. In this chapter we focus on the macroeconomic and labour market aspects of unemployment, with special reference to the Irish and European situation.

The structure of the chapter is as follows. We start with a description of the Irish labour force and discuss the *labour force participation rate* and the *dependency ratio*. We then discuss the trend in employment and unemployment in Ireland since 1960. This is followed by an account of the dynamics of unemployment. That is, the links between economic growth and unemployment and the relationship between Irish and UK unemployment. We then look in more detail at the characteristics of unemployment. This is followed by a discussion of why the labour market may not 'clear' and the factors that affect the incentive to work. Finally, we discuss the policies that might reduce unemployment in Europe.

22.2 THE LABOUR FORCE

The labour force (or the economically active population aged between 16 and 65 years) is the sum of the employed and the unemployed:

$$\text{Labour force} = \text{employed} + \text{unemployed} \tag{1}$$

According to the International Labour Office (ILO), a person is classified as employed if he or she is working for pay or profit or in a family business for one hour or more during the week. The employed include employees, farmers, those working in family businesses, and the self-employed. It is surprising that working as little as an hour a week is sufficient to get a person classified as employed. Note that under this definition it is possible to be classified as 'employed' while being a student.

A person is classified as unemployed if he or she is (A) not working, and (B) actively seeking, and available for, work. People who are neither working nor looking for work are classified as economically inactive. They do not form part of the labour force. Calling unpaid workers in the home, such as housewives and farmers' wives, 'inactive' is clearly a misnomer. However, it is consistent with the convention of excluding unpaid home production from GNP.

The *unemployment rate* (UR) is the proportion of the labour force that is unemployed:

$$UR = (\text{unemployed/labour force}) \times 100 \tag{2}$$

The unemployment rate can be calculated separately for specific population groups (men, women, by age group, etc.).

Note:

In most countries the principal source of information on employment and unemployment is a household survey, such as the *Current Population Survey* in the United States or the *Labour Force Survey* (LFS) in Europe. The first Irish LFS was undertaken by the Central Statistics Office (CSO) in 1975. Annual surveys were conducted between 1983 and 1996 and a quarterly survey called the *Quarterly National Household Survey* (QNHS) was introduced in 1997. A sample of about 45,000 households is interviewed. The questionnaire has been refined over the years by the Irish CSO, the Statistical Office of the EU and the ILO.

Figure 22.1 shows the trend in employment, unemployment and the labour force in Ireland over the period 1971 to 2002. Over the period 1971–90 the labour force increased by 19 per cent. However, in the 1980s, much of this growth was reflected in rising unemployment. In contrast, between 1990 and 2002 the labour force grew by 38 per cent and employment by 51 per cent, an unprecedented growth in the numbers at

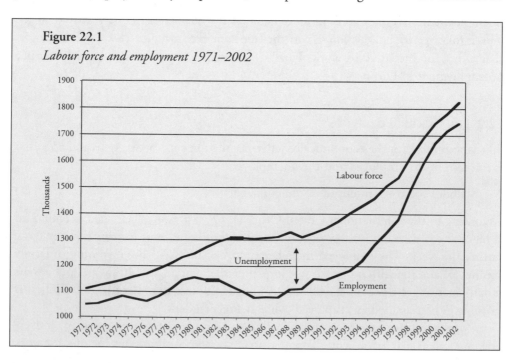

Figure 22.1

Labour force and employment 1971–2002

work. No other country in the OECD recorded a comparable rate of increase in employment over this period.

LABOUR FORCE PARTICIPATION RATE

The labour force participation rate (LFPR) is the proportion of the population that is in the labour force:

$$LFPR = (labour\ force/population) \times 100 \qquad (3)$$

In 2002 there were 1.825 million people in the labour force out of a population of 3.884 million, giving an LFPR rate of 47 per cent. This compares to a ratio of 36 per cent in 1976. Figure 22.2 shows the trend in the LFPR between 1961 and 2002.

The two influences on the LFPR are:

1.   The ratio of the working-age population (16 to 65 years) to the total population.

In the past this ratio was low in Ireland, due to the relatively high birth rate that results in a relatively high proportion of children in the population. However, since the late 1980s, the ratio has risen significantly. This is due to net immigration increasing the working-age population.

2.   The labour force participation rate of the working-age population. This depends on factors such as:

•   Educational participation rates. The higher the participation rate in second and third level education, the lower the labour force participation rate among young adults. Educational participation rates rose sharply in Ireland during the 1980s and 1990s, and this tended to depress the LFPR.

•   Age at retirement. In most western countries there has been a marked trend towards earlier retirement, especially among men. This has also tended to depress the LFPR.

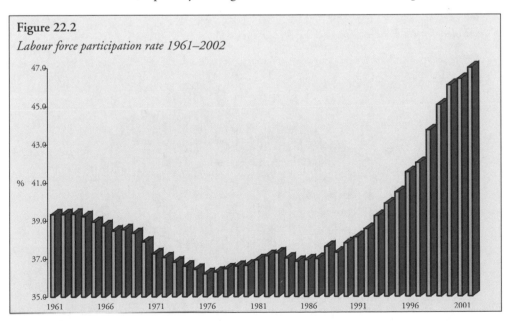

Figure 22.2

Labour force participation rate 1961–2002

- Women's labour force participation rates. In the past in Ireland the LFPR among adult women was very low due to the tendency for women with young children not to remain in paid employment. (Until the 1970s, women had to retire from employment in the civil service and the banks if they got married!) However, in recent years women are having fewer children. Also those with children are less likely to retire from the labour force. This has increased the LFPR significantly.

Note:
There has also been a contrasting trend in LFPRs among older men and younger women. There has been a dramatic increase in the LFPR among women aged 25–44. This is, in part, due to rising educational standards and a fall in the marriage rate. In contrast, there has been a significant fall in the LFPR for men aged 45–64. A fall in the demand for older, unqualified workers has led to many men dropping out of the labour force at a relatively early age.

THE DEPENDENCY RATIO

The employment dependency ratio is defined as the ratio of the non-employed to the employed.

$$\text{Dependency ratio} = (\text{Non-employed/employed}) \times 100 \qquad (4)$$

The non-employed is calculated as the population minus the labour force. The dependency ratio gives an indication of the burden that has to be borne by the employed (through taxation or transfers within households) to support those who are not employed.

Figure 22.3 shows the trend in the dependency ratio between 1961 and 2002. There was a steady rise in this ratio over the years 1961 to 1985 when the ratio peaked at 2.2. This meant that there were more than two dependants for every person at work. This

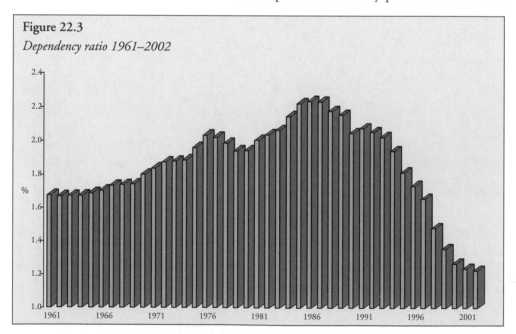

Figure 22.3

Dependency ratio 1961–2002

was due to the high birth rate, the high unemployment rate, and the low participation rate among women. This rising dependency ratio acted as a drag on the improvement in living standards.

However, since the mid-1980s the dependency ratio has fallen to 1.2. Even without any rise in the rate of economic growth, this would have allowed living standards to rise rapidly. The sharp drop in dependency since the mid-1980s reflects:

- The rising proportion of the population in the working-age groups.
- The falling unemployment rate.

Assuming no significant rise in the unemployment rate, the dependency ratio will remain low over the coming decades. This will considerably ease the burden on the working population of providing for the young and the elderly. Ireland is much better situated in this regard than are the continental European countries and Japan, where the burden of dependency is rising rapidly due to the ageing of the population.

22.3 EMPLOYMENT TRENDS

After a long period of stagnation, the rate of growth of private sector, non-agricultural employment since the late 1980s has been little short of astounding. Over the past twelve years the Irish economy has created proportionately more employment than any other OECD country. Not only did we outperform the relatively stagnant economies of Europe, our employment creation was at a much faster pace than in the dynamic US economy. Whereas in the 1980s there was widespread pessimism regarding our ability to absorb our rapidly growing population into employment, by the late 1990s labour shortages had become widespread and the high emigration rate of the late 1980s had been replaced by the highest immigration rate among the EU countries. Figure 22.4 shows the change in sectoral employment (services, industry and agriculture) over the period 1971 to 2002.

AGRICULTURE

Employment in agriculture fell by an average 2.6 per cent a year between 1971 and 2002. Productivity grew very rapidly. More output is being produced by a greatly reduced workforce. The share of agriculture in total employment is now down to 6.5 per cent, compared with 26 per cent in 1971. The decline in agricultural employment is likely to continue: in Britain and the US the share of agricultural employment in the total is below 2 per cent.

INDUSTRY

The rich countries of the world are often referred to as the 'industrialised countries', but this is a misnomer because the share of industry in total employment has fallen well below one-quarter in the world's advanced economies. In Ireland there was no net increase in employment in industry between 1971–91, although there was a radical change in its composition, with the older, protected industries declining and newer, mostly foreign-owned firms expanding. Between 1994 and 2002, industrial

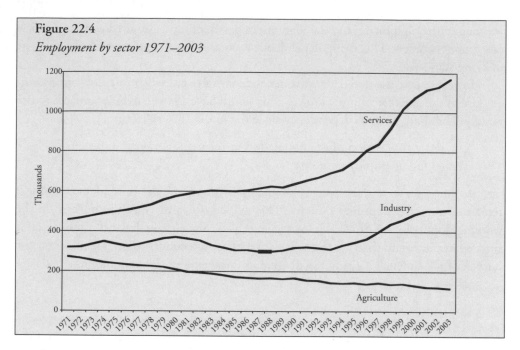

Figure 22.4

Employment by sector 1971–2003

employment increased an average 5 per cent per annum. Industries shared of total employment now amounts to 30 per cent.

Employment in a number of sectors has increased very rapidly: electronic engineering, 'high-tech' food, computer software and telemarketing. Most of this growth has been due to foreign direct investment (FDI) by multinational companies. (See chapter 24 for a discussion of why Ireland is an attractive location for FDI.) In 2002, many successful Irish manufacturing firms have reached maximum employment levels in Ireland and are now expanding abroad.

SERVICES

In the advanced countries of the world, employment is expanding rapidly in the services sectors. These include marketed and non-market services. Non-marketed services refer to those sectors that are provided directly by central and local government, by state-owned companies, and by tax-financed hospitals, schools, colleges and universities. Market services include a variety of sub-sectors such as banking, financial, professional and business services, tourism, hotels and restaurants, and retail and wholesale distribution.

As can be seen from figure 22.4, service sector employment increased on average, 3 per cent per annum between 1971 and 2002 (the growth rate was 5.4 per cent since 1994). Service sector employment now accounts for 65 per cent of total employment. Up from 43 per cent in 1971.

Note:

Believers in the importance of industry argue that service sector employment is 'unproductive'. This is as fallacious as was the eighteenth-century physiocratic view that only agricultural employment was genuinely 'productive'. Productive jobs are simply those that respond to consumers' needs. As people become wealthier they spend a rising proportion of income on services rather than on physical products. As a consequence, in rich countries the standard of living depends increasingly on the efficiency of the service sector rather than on industry and agriculture.

The services sector can act as an 'employer of last resort', providing jobs when no other employment opportunities are available. This is often the case in low-income countries where many young people are only able to find jobs like selling cigarettes or polishing shoes on street corners. In the United States much of the recent employment growth has been in relatively low-wage service jobs, giving rise to the label the 'working poor'. In the past young Irish people preferred emigration to the prospect of low-wage service employment at home. However, during the boom of the 1990s, the services sector has provided some of the best-paid and most sought-after employment opportunities.

22.4 THE DYNAMICS OF UNEMPLOYMENT

The behaviour of the unemployment rate is an important economic indicator. As we have stressed throughout this book, a low unemployment rate is one of the principal goals of macroeconomic policy. Figure 22.5 shows the unemployment rate in Ireland, EU15 and the US from 1961 to 2002. The Irish unemployment rate has been highly unstable relative to the EU15 and the US over the past four decades.

This is what one might expect for a region in a larger economy. During the recession in the mid-1980s, the Irish unemployment rate rose well above the rate in EU15 and the US. However, during the economic boom in the 1990s the Irish rate fell below the EU15 rate and even the US rate. In 2001, the Irish unemployment rate of 3.8 per cent represented 75,000 people out of work. The EU15 rate of 8.4 per cent represented

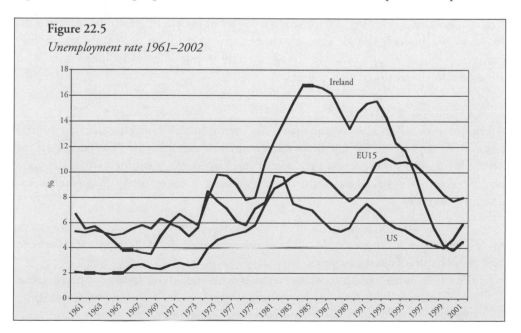

Figure 22.5

Unemployment rate 1961–2002

14,228,000 people unemployed (of this, 11,741,000 are in the Eurozone). The US unemployment rate of 5.5 per cent represents 6,742,000 people out of work. The smallness of the Irish labour market is evident from this comparison.

The unemployment rate refers to a stock of people measured at a point of time. Changes in stocks reflect the difference between inflows and outflows. The main flows into and out of the unemployment pool are illustrated in figure 22.6. This simple framework allows us to highlight some important points.

- Unemployment falls when the numbers leaving the pool of unemployment exceeds the inflow. The best way to increase the outflow from unemployment is to increase the rate at which job seekers find jobs. This depends above all else on the rate of economic growth.

- The rate at which unemployment falls also depends on the matching of vacancies with job seekers. This, in turn, depends on factors such as the skills of the unemployed and their willingness to accept the available jobs. An efficient labour market does a good job of pairing job seekers with vacancies. One of the problems with countries with persistently high unemployment rates is that job seekers seem unwilling or unable to fill the available vacancies.

- A less favourable way to increase the outflow from unemployment is to encourage people to withdraw from the labour force or to leave the country. Emigration has played a very important role in the adjustment of the Irish labour force in the past. One of the really great achievements of the 1990s was that we brought the unemployment rate down not by getting people out of the Irish labour force but by getting them into employment in Ireland.

In Ireland in the past we tended to blame our high unemployment on the rapid growth of the labour force. It is far from clear, however, that high unemployment is correlated with the growth of the labour force. Countries like Germany, France and Belgium have very low rates of population growth but persistently high unemployment. In the 1990s the Irish attitude abruptly changed from regarding 'our young and rapidly growing population' as a problem to — correctly in our view — looking on it as an attraction for investors coming to Ireland.

Duration of unemployment

A key question, of great social and economic importance is: how long does the typical entrant to the pool of unemployment remain unemployed? The duration of unemployment matters because the social costs of unemployment increase the longer a person is out of work. Long-term unemployment is more costly than short-term unemployment because:

- Savings may tide households over a short spell of unemployment.
- The long-term unemployed tend to lose motivation and self-esteem and come to be regarded as 'unemployable'.
- The long-term unemployed lose contact with the labour market. They exercise little influence on the wage-bargaining process. Short-term unemployment, on the other hand, moderates inflationary wage pressures.

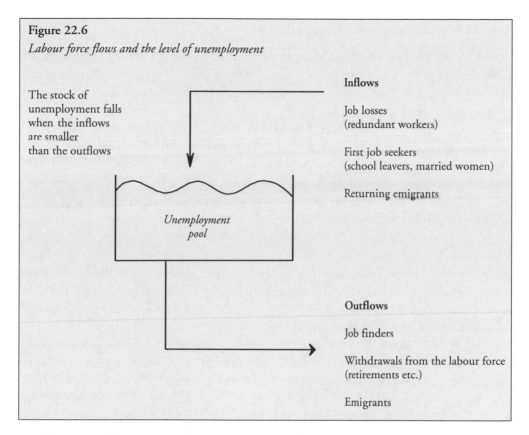

Figure 22.6
Labour force flows and the level of unemployment

The stock of unemployment falls when the inflows are smaller than the outflows

Inflows

Job losses
(redundant workers)

First job seekers
(school leavers, married women)

Returning emigrants

Unemployment pool

Outflows

Job finders

Withdrawals from the labour force
(retirements etc.)

Emigrants

The rate of long-term unemployment has fallen in Ireland from 10.4 per cent in 1988 to 1.3 per cent in 2002. The really surprising aspect of the Irish success story is that long-term unemployment — once regarded as the most intractable social problem — responded even more to the boom than the overall unemployment rate. Moreover, we did not rely on encouraging people to retire from the labour force as a way of disguising the long-term unemployment problem, unlike many European countries where early retirement was regarded as the only solution to the long-term unemployment problem. Participation rates among men aged 55–64 have actually risen slightly in Ireland in recent years.

Note:
There were some schemes to encourage the long-term unemployed to withdraw from the labour force, by taking early retirement or going on social employment schemes. There were about 20,000 people on 'pre-retirement allowance schemes' in 2002, just over 1 per cent of the labour force.

OKUN'S LAW
Figure 22.6 suggests that if people are finding jobs faster than they are losing them, unemployment will fall. This highlights the link between the rate of growth of the economy and changes in the unemployment rate. This relationship is summarised by Okun's law, which we introduced in chapter 2. This law states that changes in the unemployment rate can be related to the rate of growth of output:

$$\Delta U_t = \alpha(\Delta GDP - \text{natural growth rate}) \tag{5}$$

where ΔU = change in the unemployment rate, ΔGDP = the percentage change in real GDP, and α is the parameter to be estimated statistically. Using Irish data over the period 1960 to 2001 the α coefficient was estimated to be 0.25. This suggests that that for every 1 per cent increase in real growth, over the average (natural rate) of 4 per cent, unemployment falls by 0.25 percentage points

This equation is a systematic way of accounting for the behaviour of the unemployment rate in Ireland. For example, since 1994, the exceptionally rapid growth of the economy has progressively lowered the unemployment rate. Despite a significant increase in the labour force, the growth of employment has been so rapid that the rate of unemployment has fallen sharply.

IRISH AND UK UNEMPLOYMENT

After the rate of growth of output in Ireland, the most important influence on Irish unemployment is probably the economic situation in Britain. Some economists have argued that this influence is so strong that the Irish unemployment rate is determined primarily by UK labour market conditions.

Figure 22.7 shows the Irish and British unemployment rates between 1961 and 2002. There was a general tendency for unemployment in the two countries to move in tandem at least up until the Irish economic boom in the 1990s. In 1999, the Irish unemployment rate fell below the UK rate for the first time ever. (The current UK rate of 5.6 per cent is equivalent to 1,631,000 people out of work.)

The increase in the gap between the two unemployment rates during the 1980s raises the question of why people preferred to remain unemployed in Ireland rather than migrate to Britain at this time? Two possible explanations are:

- The Irish social welfare system became relatively generous and encouraged the unemployed to stay in Ireland rather than emigrate to Britain.
- Migration to Britain seems to depend not just on the gap between Irish and British unemployment but also on the unemployment rate in Britain. The unprecedented high level of British unemployment in the first half of the 1980s may account for the low-level of emigration from Ireland.

22.5 WHO ARE THE UNEMPLOYED?

We can gain a better understanding of the causes of unemployment, and its persistence, by studying the characteristics of the unemployed. The risk of being unemployed differs greatly between population groups. The following is a summary of the factors that have been found to affect the unemployment rate in Ireland.

EDUCATIONAL ATTAINMENT

There is a very striking association between educational attainment and the risk of unemployment. Those with low educational qualifications are much more likely to be unemployed than better-educated individuals. Furthermore, once they become

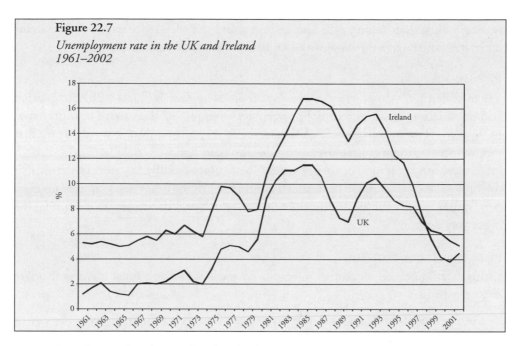

Figure 22.7

Unemployment rate in the UK and Ireland 1961–2002

unemployed, poorly-educated individuals are more likely to remain unemployed: their risk of long-term unemployment is high. Finally, they are more likely to drop out of the labour force by ceasing to look for employment. This holds for women as well as men.

AGE

The youth unemployment rate is higher than that among people of prime working age. Teenagers and those with little or no employment experience have the highest unemployment rate. In the European Monetary Union in 2002, the youth unemployment rate is 16.5 per cent compared to a total unemployment rate of 8.3 per cent.

MARITAL STATUS

Other things being equal, unmarried men are most likely to be unemployed. This could be because single people have become less committed to holding down a job or, alternatively, because those who cannot get a job are less eligible for marriage. It is difficult to decide the direction of causation between these two variables.

AREA OF RESIDENCE

Men living in large urban areas are more likely to be unemployed than their rural counterparts. Employment opportunities for men appear to be more plentiful in rural areas. There is some evidence of the reverse pattern for women.

THE PRESENCE OF YOUNG CHILDREN IN THE HOUSEHOLD

Both men and women are less likely to be employed when there are young children present in the household. Men, as well as women, may choose to devote time to child rearing rather than taking paid employment, and the social welfare and tax systems make it less attractive for those with families to accept offers of employment.

HOUSING TENURE

When all other factors are allowed for, those who live in local authority rented accommodation are significantly less likely to be employed than those in other types of housing. The negative effect of this factor is very strong, but it is not clear what mechanism is at work. Employers may discriminate against people with addresses in local authority estates or people may be influenced by a culture in which unemployment has come to be regarded as normal. On the other hand, an unemployed person may qualify for local authority house in which case the causation is running the other way around.

HOUSEHOLD COMPOSITION

Living in a household with other unemployed and/or inactive adults. It seems that like cluster with like.

While these findings do not help explain the reasons for fluctuations in the rate of unemployment, they should be taken into account in formulating policy towards the unemployed. The characteristics of the unemployed are discussed in Anthony Murphy and Brendan Walsh, 'The incidence of male non-employment in Ireland', *Economic and Social Review*, 1996, 467–490.

22.6 WHY DOESN'T THE LABOUR MARKET CLEAR?

Why should there be any significant unemployment over and above some minimal level of frictional unemployment? Why does the labour market not clear? The persistence of high unemployment in Europe has provoked an enormous amount of research on this topic in recent years. We now review the main explanations that have been suggested.

REAL WAGE RIGIDITY

In microeconomics students learn that excess supply in any market leads to a fall in the price until the market clears. Figure 22.8 shows the labour market analysis developed in chapter 20. The supply and demand for labour determines the real wage (vertical axis) and employment (horizontal axis). The equilibrium real wage is W_1 and the associated employment level is N_1. (If the price level is assumed to be constant, then W represents the real wage.) If, however, the actual real wage is W_2 firms will only hire N_2 workers, and unemployment emerges. By definition, a non-market-clearing real wage results in unemployment.

Note:
We can think of the equilibrium situation as one in which unemployment is at the natural rate. When the real wage is above the market-clearing level, unemployment rises above the natural rate.

But why does unemployment not lead to a fall in the real wage rate, encouraging employers to move down their demand for labour schedules and hire more workers until

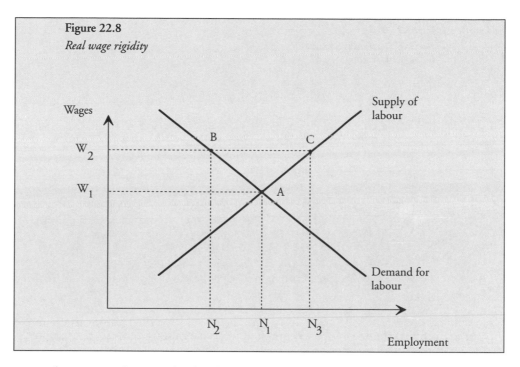

Figure 22.8
Real wage rigidity

unemployment is eliminated? If real wage cuts are resisted, unemployment will persist. This explanation of unemployment is called the real wage resistance hypothesis.

Figure 22.9 shows the annual percentage change in real wages per employee in Ireland and the unemployment rate from 1961 to 2002. There appears to be little correlation between the two variables. During the recession of the mid-1980s, real wages increased 2.2 per cent per annum. In contrast, during the boom of 1994–99, real wages rose only 0.2 per cent. Real wages actually fell by 1.3 per cent in 1998.

THE WAGE-BARGAINING PROCESS

To say that unemployment is high because the labour market does not clear due to 'real wage rigidity' only pushes the explanation back one stage. What accounts for this resistance to wage cuts in the face of high unemployment?

Many explanations have been offered. Most of them have to do with the wage-setting process and the role of trade unions. Trade unions exist in part to ensure that real wages do not fall. In inflationary periods unions look for indexation of wages, that is, automatic increases in nominal wages to compensate for rises in the cost of living. In Ireland during the 1970s and 1980s wage bargaining quickly focused on real, post tax pay. Trade unions sought to protect their members not only from inflation but also from the effects of higher taxation.

Different approaches have been tried to make the behaviour of real wages more responsive to the level of unemployment. Co-operation between the 'social partners' (unions, employers and government) or 'corporatism' is advocated. It has been argued that where a high degree of corporatism exists, as in Scandinavia and Austria, the growth of real wages has been moderated to prevent unemployment from rising. The Irish experience in the 1990s might be added to this list.

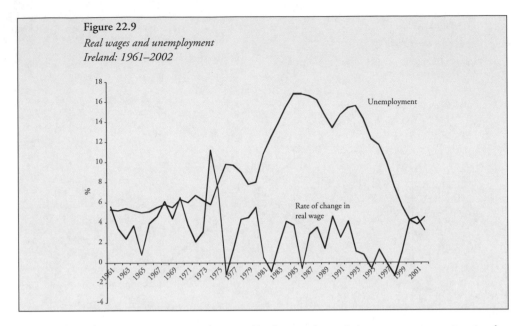

Figure 22.9
Real wages and unemployment
Ireland: 1961–2002

At the other extreme, a very decentralised wage-bargaining process, as exists in the US, may also impose a discipline on the labour market. The worst outcome is associated with situations where individual trade unions struggle to increase their members' pay but accept no responsibility for the effect of their actions on the national economy. This was the situation in Britain before the Thatcher government broke the power of the unions in the 1980s. In Ireland, five national wage programmes have been agreed since 1988. The programmes names and their duration are as follows:

- The *Programme for National Recovery* (January 1988 – December 1990)
- The *Programme for Economic and Social Progress* (January 1991 – December 1993)
- The *Programme for Competitiveness and Work* (January 1994 – December 1996)
- *Partnership 2000* (January 1997 – March 2000)
- The *Programme for Prosperity and Fairness* (April 2000 – December 2002)
- At the start of 2003, a new programme called *Sustainable Progress* was being negotiated.

The increase in nominal wages under each programme is summarised in table 22.1, column A. Columns B and C show the inflation rate and associated real wage increase for each sub-period. It can be seen that with the exception of *The Programme for Economic and Social Progress*, the increase in real earnings was very small. In fact, real earnings declined under the *Programme for National Recovery* (1988–91) and again at various stages in 1994 and 1999. This indicates that the trade unions and workers experience considerable difficulty in accurately forecasting inflation. Furthermore, given the upsurge in employment in the 1990s, workers have supplied more labour in response to a higher nominal wage whereas, in fact, real earnings have stagnated. This is an example of the *money illusion* discussed in chapter 20.

However, it should be emphasised that the wage awards in column A are only the basic, *minimum* awards. In addition to these minimum awards, employees could also

Table 22.1
National wage agreements

National wage agreements		Agreed change in nominal wages	Inflation	Change in real earnings
		%	%	%
		A	B	C
Programme for National Recovery	1988 (Jan–Dec)	2.5	2.6	−0.1
	1989 (Jan–Dec)	2.5	4.7	−2.2
	1990 (Jan–Dec)	2.5	2.7	−0.2
Programme for Economic and Social Progress	1991 (Jan–Dec)	4.0	3.6	0.4
	1992 (Jan–Dec)	3.0	2.4	0.6
	1993 (Jan–Dec)	3.5	1.4	2.1
Programme for Competitiveness and Work	1994 (Jan–Dec)	2.0	2.4	−0.4
	1995 (Jan–Dec)	2.5	2.4	0.1
	1996 (Jan–Jun)	2.5	0.8	1.7
	1996 (July–Dec)	1.0	1.0	0.0
Partnership 2000	1997 (Jan–Dec)	2.5	1.9	0.6
	1998 (Jan–Dec)	2.5	1.7	0.8
	1999 (Jan–Sept)	1.5	1.9	−0.4
	1999 Oct–2000 Mar	1.0	2.7	−1.7
Programme for Prosperity and Fairness	2000 April–Mar 2001	5.5	4.7	0.8
	2001 April–2002 April	5.5	4.8	0.7
	2002 April–2002 Dec	4.0	2.6	1.4

negotiate further increases at a local level, there was a special inflation compensation pay-out in 2001 and the government held out the prospect of tax reductions at budget time. As mentioned in chapter 4, it is estimated that the tax reductions alone added 1.8 per cent per annum to real, post-tax earnings over the period. Furthermore the national wage agreements only cover approximately 600,000 workers out of total employment of 1.75 million. Overall, the national wage agreements have been credited with helping to combine industrial peace with rapid growth in employment since the 1980s.

It does seem that the return to centralised wage bargaining in the 1980s coincided with — and perhaps should be credited for — the break in the tendency for Irish wage rates to rise at a faster pace than those of our main trading partners. When account is taken of the movements in exchange rates, Ireland began to gain competitiveness in the sense of falling relative wage costs towards the end of the 1980s and during the 1990s. This contrasts with the situation of losing competitiveness during the 1970s and early 1980s.

EFFICIENCY WAGES

Karl Marx (1818–83) believed that the capitalists of his day used the 'Reserve Army of the Unemployed' to force wages down to the bare subsistence minimum. Industrial relations are not so simple today. The unemployed do not knock at employers' doors offering to work for less than the going rate. If they did employers would probably be reluctant to hire them, suspecting that only a problem worker would offer to work for less than the going rate. Nor is it usual for employers to ask their employees to accept wage cuts or to threaten to replace them with new recruits at lower wages. In most firms there is an explicit or implicit contract between employers and workers which guarantees a certain stability of wages and employment.

The *efficiency wage hypothesis* says that employers use wages to recruit, retain and motivate their workers. By paying above the odds, firms retain a more productive labour force than they would get if they set wages in accordance with fluctuations in the supply and demand for labour. The employers have valid reasons for not allowing the existence of unemployment to drive wages down to the market clearing level.

LABOUR MARKET RIGIDITY

A number of special features of European labour markets have been blamed for the reluctance of employers to take on workers at the same rate that occurs in the United States. Among these are:

• Firing costs

In many European countries employers have to offer more or less permanent employment to their workers. It is difficult and costly to get rid of workers once they are hired. Understandably, this makes employers reluctant to take on workers in the first place. Paradoxically, the attempt to protect employment may result in less employment!

• Restrictive work practices

It is more costly for employers to do business if workers oppose flexible working arrangements, such as part-time and shift working. Demarcation rules could stipulate that employers hire two craftsmen where one would be sufficient. The result may be that no one is hired.

• Skills mismatch

A mismatch between the skills of the unemployed (particularly the long-term unemployed) and job vacancies can lead to shortages in key occupations even when the overall rate of unemployment is high. The evidence suggests increased mismatch in many economies since the 1980s.

• High reservation wages

A relatively generous social welfare system leads to high reservation wages, that is, the minimum wage that must be offered before a vacancy can be filled. The unemployed search longer for a 'suitable' job rather than taking the first job they are offered. A harsh social welfare system deprives the unemployed of this luxury. Perhaps, like Hamlet, the state has to be cruel (in the short run) to be kind (in the long run)!

• Labour mobility

Immobility of the unemployed to search for jobs reduces the efficiency of the labour market and increases the natural rate of unemployment. Factors such as the difficulty of obtaining housing in expanding regions or the desire to retain a subsidised council house affects labour mobility.

• Maximum working week

The Maastricht Treaty includes a 'Social Charter' that lays down numerous regulations concerning conditions of employment. One of them stipulates that employees may not work more than forty-eight hours a week — even if they want to! The UK has consistently opposed this approach to the labour market, citing its own better record at reducing unemployment than that of the continental economies. It obtained an 'opt out' from the Social Charter and advocates greater flexibility in the labour market as the way to reduce unemployment. New Labour has adopted the old Conservative view on this issue.

• The tax wedge

Taxes drive a wedge between what it costs the employer to hire a worker and what the employee actually takes home in pay. The difference between the two is known as the *tax wedge*. This arises due to the taxes levied on income and expenditure. The demand for labour depends on gross wages plus any levies the employer has to pay (such as employer's PRSI at 12 per cent in Ireland in 2002). The supply of labour depends on the after-tax purchasing power of the worker's income. This is reduced not only by income taxes (PAYE) and social security levies (PRSI) but also by indirect taxes (VAT and excise taxes) that are levied on expenditure. Taxes drive a large wedge between the cost of hiring a worker and the purchasing power of his or her wages.

For example, suppose the total cost of hiring a worker is €190 (€175 gross wages + 12% employer's PRSI). On a gross salary of €175, the worker will pay €28 in taxes giving a take-home pay of €149. VAT and excise taxes reduce the purchasing power of this by about 25 per cent or €34. Thus it costs the employer €196 to give the employee a net-of-tax purchasing power of €115. The wedge between the cost of hiring to the employer and the take-home pay of the employee was much higher in the 1980s than it is now. The tax wedge contributed to our poor employment record in the 1980s.

The effect of the tax wedge is to move the employer back up along the demand for labour schedule and the worker back up along the supply of labour schedule, leading to a reduction in employment. In figure 22.10 (where, with a constant price level, we depict the real wage as W), equilibrium in the absence of taxes would be at W and N. If the tax rate on employers is t_1 and that on employees is t_2, the cost of hiring a worker is $W(1 + t_1)$ and the after-tax income of the employee is $W(1 - t_2)$. The gap between these two magnitudes is the tax wedge. The new equilibrium level of employment is at N_1. That is, employment falls by $(N - N_1)$. The size of this fall in employment depends on the slopes of the demand and supply schedules. The more elastic (flat) the schedules, the greater the impact.

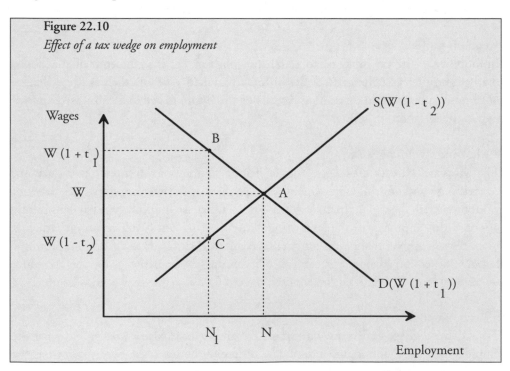

Figure 22.10

Effect of a tax wedge on employment

Note:

In Ireland both labour supply and labour demand are likely to be relatively elastic: the supply of labour, because of the possibility of emigrating or working in the 'black' economy rather than accepting low after-tax wages. The demand for labour, because much of our employment is in internationally-traded sectors, where Irish employers are not able to raise their prices in response to higher domestic costs.

Social charges like PRSI are relatively low in Ireland by European standards. One of the serious problems with the German economy is the enormous gap between take home wages and the total employment cost to an employer. This problem is likely to get worse as the population ages and the working population has to pay higher social charges to fund the ever-growing pensions bill.

22.7 FACTORS AFFECTING THE INCENTIVE TO WORK

There are a number of factors that affect the incentive to work and preclude a worker from accepting a job offer.

THE REPLACEMENT RATIO

High unemployment benefits combined with high rates of income tax can create an 'unemployment trap', which removes the incentive to accept a job. An unemployed person may find that going back to work may entail a *fall* in net income. If this is the case it is irrational for the person to accept a job offer.

One measure of this disincentive effect is the *replacement ratio*. This is defined as:

Replacement ratio = (net income while unemployed/net income while employed) × 100

For example, in 2001 a single person earning a gross wage of €244.24 a week (about €6.28 an hour) would have to pay €32.12 a week in PAYE and a further €4.6 a week in PRSI, leaving €207.69 a week in after-tax income. When unemployed he or she could be entitled to €98.64 a week in unemployment benefit. Hence:

Replacement ratio = €98.64/€207.69 = 47.4%

This may seem relatively low, and hardly enough to dissuade a person from accepting a job offer, but several other factors need to be taken into account. The *numerator* should include other benefits such as:

- Rent allowance
- Medical card
- Subsidised local authority housing
- Family income supplement (FIS)
- Non-cash benefits (fuel allowances, etc.)

The unemployed person may loose some of these entitlements if he or she accepts paid employment.

The *denominator* should reflect work-related expenses such as:

- Cost of commuting
- Child care costs
- Some unemployed persons are able to work occasionally in the grey economy while still registered as unemployed.

The upshot is that the interaction of the tax and social welfare systems can create situations in which an unemployed person does not find it very attractive to 'sign off' the Live Register and accept an offer of employment.

THE POVERTY TRAP

A related problem is the 'poverty trap'. This arises because employees face high marginal tax rates over certain income ranges. Table 22.2 is taken from a Department of Social Welfare report and relates to the year 1996. Hence we use £ rather than €. The table shows that a married man with two dependent children could be little better off earning £14,000 a year than he would be earning £7,000. He would actually be worse off earning £11,000 than £7,000! The reason is that as his income rises, the worker has to pay PAYE and PRSI at higher rates, becomes liable for income levies, and loses FIS (Family Income Supplement), the medical card and pays higher local authority rent. The worker may also lose 'secondary benefits' (fuel allowance, Christmas bonus, school clothing and footwear allowance and food vouchers). This sort of evidence prompted some of the tax changes that were influential in the late 1990s.

Table 22.2
Illustration of the 'Poverty Trap', 1995–96

Gross annual income £	Net weekly income[1] £
7,000	153
8,000	152
9,000	151
10,000	147
11,000	149
12,000	158
13,000	166
14,000	176

1.   Including estimated value of non-cash benefits

Source: Department of Social Welfare, *Report of the Expert Working Group on the Integration of the Tax and Social Welfare Systems*, June 1996, Table 2.1.

How important are these disincentive effects due to the replacement ratio (previous section) and the poverty trap? There is no agreement on this issue, but it is hard to believe that situations like those shown in table 22.2 do not reduce the willingness of people to work in the official, taxed labour economy.

There is evidence that countries where the unemployed are entitled to extended benefits have higher levels of long-term unemployment than countries where entitled is limited. In the US there is no federal unemployment insurance system, and most state and occupational systems do not provide benefits after six months' unemployment. In Ireland, on the other hand, entitlement to unemployment benefits (UB) can last up to fifteen months. If still unemployed after fifteen months, a person has to move to the means-tested unemployment assistance (UA), but entitlement to this can last indefinitely and the rate of benefit is much the same as for UB. It is argued that the availability of unemployment assistance affects the rate of long-term unemployment.

22.8 REDUCING UNEMPLOYMENT

There is a reasonable consensus among economists as to what has to be done to tackle Europe's problem of high unemployment. However, among politicians there is still a contrast between the flexible labour market approach favoured by the British and the more solidaristic approach favoured by the EU and the French in particular. The following, however, could be expected to reduce Europe's unemployment rate.

MAINTAIN A HIGH AND STABLE GROWTH RATE

A high and stable growth rate is the single most important factor in reducing unemployment and keeping it low. We have seen from the Irish experience in the 1990s that rapid economic growth will reduce unemployment to a low level. The challenge facing the German and French economies today is to maintain a steady growth rate in real GDP close to the natural rate. (Real GDP growth was 0.6 per cent in Germany and 2 per cent in France in 2001.) But there is a chicken and egg problem here. To some extent the slow growth of these economies is due to their rigid labour markets and high unemployment rates. They need some catalyst, such as Ireland experienced in the 1980s, to jolt them out of this low-level equilibrium.

REAL WAGE MODERATION

A favourable cost and wage structure helped Ireland to generate rapid employment growth in the 1990s. The cost of skilled workers in Ireland is low by international standards. This has come about:

- Because of an increase in the supply of educated young people eager to work in Ireland at rates of pay that are relatively low by European standards.
- Despite the tax wedge discussed above, non-wage costs (such as social security charges) are low in Ireland by comparison with continental Europe.
- Because of moderate increases in wage costs due to the national wage agreements and reductions in income tax which have boosted after-tax income.

REFORM OF THE TAX AND SOCIAL WELFARE SYSTEMS

The social welfare system should place a floor under those who are unable to support themselves by their own efforts, but it should not create a 'culture of dependency' by blunting the incentive to obtain employment. Many people blame the welfare state and the relatively generous support offered to the unemployed for the persistence of high unemployment in Europe. In the US, and more recently in Britain, the welfare system has been restructured to incorporate some form of 'workfare'. After a relatively short spell of unemployment, able-bodied people are required either to accept an offer of retraining or to enrol on a public works scheme. In the UK the Restart Programme, and the 'welfare-to-work' programme, introduced in 1997, has reduced unemployment by inviting the unemployed for an interview after six months.

Several reforms have been introduced in Ireland to reduce the disincentive effects of the tax and social welfare systems. These include:

- After 6 months of unemployment those claiming unemployment benefit are being called to interview.
- It is now permissible to work 'short-time' (up to three days a week) and retain some entitlement to unemployment benefits.
- A 'back to work allowance' has been introduced to allow a long-term unemployed person who returns to work to retain part of his/her unemployment assistance (on a sliding scale).
- Family Income Supplement will now be calculated on net rather than gross pay.
- Employers can claim a double tax allowance for hiring a long-term unemployed person.

While these changes were significant they hardly represented the radical overall or dismantling of the social welfare system that some economists call for in order to bring the European unemployment rate down. The Irish experience is fascinating, because it illustrates how important wage moderation and a favourable climate for investment triggered rapid growth, that in turn brought about a dramatic fall in unemployment (including long-term unemployment) without a radical social revolution. Economists in other countries are anxious to learn the secret of the Irish success on this front.

22.9 CONCLUSION

The main topics discussed in this chapter were:

- The influences on the growth of the labour force
- The labour force participation rate
- The dependency ratio
- The structure of employment and unemployment in Ireland today
- Short-term influences on unemployment: the rate of growth of output and the rate of unemployment in Britain
- The characteristics associated with the risk of becoming and remaining unemployed. The importance of education was emphasised
- The reasons why the labour market may not clear
- Factors affecting the incentive to accept a job
- Policies that will reduce the level of unemployment.

CHAPTER 23

Measuring the Economy's Performance: Introduction to National Income Accounting

23.1 INTRODUCTION

In this chapter we explore in some detail the relationship between national expenditure, output and income. The treatment is more specialised than that contained in most macroeconomics textbooks because of the complications that arise due to the structure of the Irish economy.

We begin by explaining the *circular flow of income* diagram. This diagram is used to illustrate how economic activity can be measured by three different methods: the *output*, *expenditure* and *income* approaches. This is followed by a discussion of the relationship between these measures. We then define *Gross National Disposable Income* (GNDI) and adjust this measure for both inflation and population growth to obtain what is probably the best indicator of living standards in an economy. The chapter concludes by explaining the relationship between saving, investment and the balance of payments.

23.2 THE CIRCULAR FLOW OF INCOME MODEL

Figure 23.1 presents a simplified version of the circular flow of income model. This model can be traced back to a court physician to Louis XV, François Quesnay (1694–1774). The modern version owes much to the work of the Cambridge economist John Maynard Keynes.

Initially, we assume that there is no government or foreign trade sector. We also assume that the *price level is fixed* or constant. These simplifying assumptions will be dropped later, and the model will be elaborated to correspond more closely to the real world.

There are only two kinds of economic agent in our simple economy, namely, households and firms. Consider the two loops on the left-hand side of the diagram. Households own the *factors of production*: land, labour and capital (which includes technology, entrepreneurship and natural resources). These factors of production are made available to firms in return for payments of rent, wages, interest and profit. Wages are paid for the use of labour, rent for the use of land, interest for the use of capital, and the owners of firms receive profits. The sum of rent, wages, interest and profit equals *national income*.

Note:

If we ignore rent, interest and profits, the two loops on the left-hand side simply represent people going to work and receiving a salary or wage for their labour, which produces output that is sold to consumers.

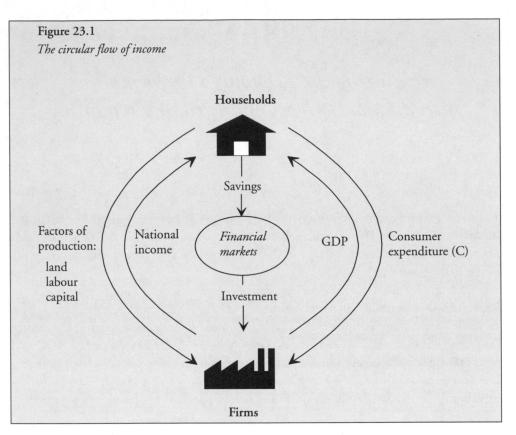

Figure 23.1
The circular flow of income

Consider now the two loops on the right-hand side. (Ignore for the moment the flows to and from financial markets.) Firms combine the factors of production to produce goods and services. We do not go into detail about the techniques of production. We shall just assume that inputs of land, labour and capital simply enter a 'black box' called the *production function*, and outputs of goods and services emerge on the other side. We use the term *Gross Domestic Product* (GDP) to describe the aggregate output of goods and services produced in a country over a period of time, usually a year. To close the loop, households, using the income they have earned (national income), purchase the goods and services produced by firms. We refer to this household expenditure as *private consumer expenditure* (C). Given that the two right-hand loops are equal, that is, expenditure equals output, it follows:

$$GDP \equiv C \tag{1}$$

where the symbol ≡ denotes an identity or something that is true by definition.

Going a stage further, since all of the money received by firms is passed on to households in the form of wages, rent, interest, and profit, it is also true that total expenditure equals national income (NI). Hence:

$$NI \equiv GDP \equiv C \tag{2}$$

The essential message of the simplified circular flow diagram given in figure 23.1 is that, in the aggregate, we consume what we produce, and we spend what we earn. People go to work and get paid, and spend their income purchasing the goods and services produced by the firms for whom they work.

SAVING AND INVESTMENT

Notice that in figure 23.1 there are two additional flows relating to saving (S) and investment (I), which we have not yet mentioned. The flow of savings reflects the fact that households do not spend all of their income. Some proportion of income is saved. This represents a *leakage* from the circular flow. Now given that people must either spend or save their income, it follows that the sum of consumer expenditure and saving equals NI. That is:

$$NI \equiv C + S \tag{3}$$

In the modern economy, household saving are channelled into the financial system (banks and building societies). Firms borrow from these institutions in order to finance *investment* (I). Investment refers to firms' expenditure on new machinery and buildings. Thus, households do not buy all of the goods and services produced by firms. Some firms purchase machines and materials from other firms. Total expenditure now equals consumer expenditure plus investment. Substituting into equation (2), we obtain:

$$NI \equiv GDP = \text{Total expenditure} \equiv C + I \tag{4}$$

This relationship states that NI equals GNP, which in turn equals total expenditure. Total expenditure, in turn, is divided into households' consumer expenditure and firms' investment expenditure.

Note:
In the *National Income and Expenditure* (NIE) accounts investment is referred to as 'gross domestic physical capital formation'. It includes both private and government investment. The word 'physical' tells us that the value of changes in stocks is included. A fall in the level of stocks is a negative contribution to investment; a rise is a positive contribution. Investment excluding changes in stocks is called *fixed* capital formation. The significance of 'gross' is that no allowance has been made for depreciation or 'capital consumption'. 'Domestic' investment takes place in the country. It excludes investment undertaken by Irish firms abroad.

GOVERNMENT

Figure 23.2 shows an expanded circular flow of income model that includes the government and the rest of the world. (We continue to assume that prices are constant.) The government affects the circular flow of income and expenditure because it levies taxes on households and makes *transfer payments* to them under various social welfare schemes. (Transfer payments are payments not in return for any goods or services supplied. They are sometimes called benefits or entitlements.) We shall denote the difference between taxes and transfer payments as *net taxes* (NT), the net flow from households to government. The government uses its net tax revenue to pay the people who work in the public sector and to purchase goods and services from private sector firms. These purchases are known as *government consumption expenditure*, G, and are shown on the right of figure 23.2. (To keep the diagram simple, we have omitted transactions between firms and government.)

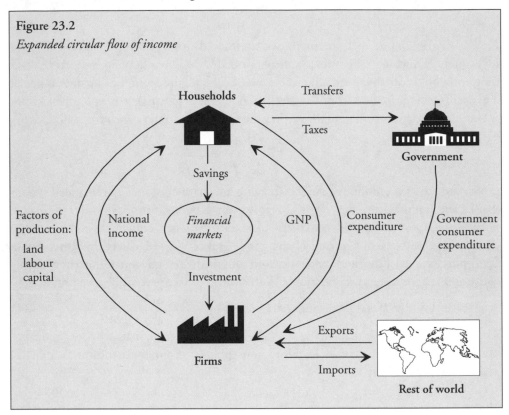

Figure 23.2
Expanded circular flow of income

Note:
In the NIE accounts, government expenditure, G, is called *net expenditure by public authorities on current goods and services*. It does not include current and capital transfer payments (e.g. social welfare payments, national debt interest paid to Irish residents, IDA grants, etc.) or government investment spending, which is included in I. G amounted to only 40 per cent of total government spending in the late 1990s.

FOREIGN SECTOR

Let us consider now the relationships between the foreign sector (the rest of the world) and the domestic economy. The output of Irish firms sold to non-residents is known as exports of goods and services (X). Purchases by Irish households and firms from abroad constitute imports of goods and services (M). The difference between the two is *net exports*, NX = X − M. The two arrows on the bottom right of figure 23.2 show these two flows.

This expanded circular flow diagram provides us with a framework for measuring the level of economic activity in a country.

23.3 Measuring the Nation's Output

The circular flow of income diagram highlights the concepts used by the national income accountants to measure the nation's output. Three different approaches are used to compile the statistics:

- The expenditure approach
- The value added or output approach, and
- The income approach.

The expenditure and the value added approach give similar measures of total output, but a number of important adjustments are necessary to go from the expenditure to the income approach.

The expenditure approach

In figure 23.2 four expenditure arrows point towards the firms. These refer to household consumption expenditure (C), government consumption expenditure (G), investment (I) and exports (X). There is one arrow pointing away from firms to the rest of the world, which represents imports (M). (To keep the diagram as simple as possible, imports by households are omitted.)

By adding up C, I, G and X and subtracting M we obtain one measure of the nation's output, which we call *Gross Domestic Product* (GDP), which measures the value of all the final goods and services produced in the country over a year:

$$GDP \equiv C + I + G + NX \qquad (5)$$

Table 23.1 shows the breakdown of expenditure on Irish GDP in 2001. The shares of private consumption (C), investment (I) and government consumption (G) in GDP are respectively 48 per cent, 24 per cent and 13 per cent of the total, which are all close

---

Table 23.1

Expenditure on Gross Domestic Product at current market prices, 2001

Symbol	Full description	€ million	As a % of GDP
C	Personal consumption of goods and services	55,144	48
+ I	Gross domestic capital formation	26,949	24
+ G	Net expenditure by public authorities on current goods and services	15,288	13
+ X	Exports of goods and services	112,368	98
− M	Imports of goods and services	−95,491	−83
	Statistical discrepancy	221	0
= GDP	Gross Domestic Product	114,479	100

Note: investment includes the value of changes in stocks.

Source: National Income and Expenditure, 2001, Central Statistics Office, Dublin, 2002, Table 5.

to the corresponding EU averages. However, exports (X) and imports (M) amount to 98 per cent and 83 per cent of GDP, respectively, which are among the highest in the world. Even net exports, (X − M), which amounts to 15 per cent of GDP, are also exceptionally large relative to GDP.

THE OUTPUT APPROACH

The output approach to measuring the value of national production concentrates on the value added at each stage of production. Value added is the difference between the value of a firm's output and the cost of the inputs it uses. Assume, for example, that only one good (e.g. a book) is produced in the economy. A sawmill produces the timber that it sells to a paper mill for €4. The value added at this stage is €4 (4 − 0). The paper mill uses the timber to produce €7 worth of paper, which is sold to the publisher. The value added at this stage is €3 (7 − 4). The authors produce a manuscript (using no inputs except their own labour) and sell it to the publisher for €10. The value added by the authors is €10 (10 − 0). Finally, the publisher combines the paper and the manuscript and produces a book that is sold in the bookshops for €30. The value added by the publisher and distributors is €13 (30 − [10 + 7]).

Table 23.2
Illustration of value added approach to measuring domestic production

	Cost of inputs	−	Value of output	=	Value added
Sawmill	0		4		4
Paper mill	4		7		3
Authors	0		10		10
Publisher	7+10 = 17		30		13
GDP					30

As shown in table 23.2, by summing the value added at each stage in the production process we obtain domestic output, which in this case equals €30 (= €4 + €3 + €10 + €13). Only one *final* product (a book) is produced and its value is €30. The same estimate of GDP is obtained using the value added and final output approaches.

The expenditure and value added approaches to estimating GDP in principle yield the same figure and could be used to cross-check the statistical accuracy of the estimates. In reality the information available does not allow both approaches to be completed independently.

THE INCOME APPROACH

National income is the sum of payments to the factors of production. Traditionally these are described as wages and salaries (payments to labour), rent (payments for the use of land and property), interest (payment for the use of capital), and profits, which can be thought of as a residual payment to entrepreneurs who take risks.

However, the data are not classified in exactly this manner in any table in the Irish *National Income and Expenditure* (NIE) accounts. Instead income is broken down into two broad categories, agricultural income and non-agricultural income. The latter is broken down into wages and salaries ('remuneration of employees'), profits and then into several sub-categories.

Table 23.3
National income by category 2001

	€ million	% of National income
Income from agriculture, forestry, fishing	3,310	5
Non-agricultural income	91,876	125
of which:		
Wages and salaries	43,651	60
Profits	38,642	53
Rent	5,268	7
Other	4,315	6
Adjustments	−4,257	−6
Net domestic product (at factor cost)	90,929	124
Net factor income from the rest of the world	−17,677	−24
Net national product (at factor cost) or national income	73,252	100

Source: *National Income and Expenditure*, 2001, Central Statistics Office, Dublin, 2002, Table 1.

Table 23.3 shows that the sum of agricultural and non-agricultural income equals *net domestic product at factor cost* (NDP_{fc}). (The 'adjustments' entry in the table relates to the financial services and a statistical discrepancy.) NDP_{fc} is, in turn, adjusted for *net factor income from the rest of the world* to arrive at *net domestic product at factor cost*. This is another name for *national income*. (In the next section we explain what is meant by 'factor cost' and 'net factor income from the rest of the world'.)

The table shows the distribution of national income between the various categories in 2001. Since most agricultural income is labour income, it follows that 65 per cent of national income accrues to labour. This is in line with international experience. In the US, for example, labour's share in national income has been approximately constant at 70 per cent over the post-war period.

23.4 RECONCILING THE INCOME AND EXPENDITURE APPROACHES

Three important adjustments have to be made to reconcile the expenditure and income approaches to measuring the level of national economic activity. These adjustments relate to:

*   Market prices and factor cost
*   Depreciation
*   Net factor income from the rest of the world.

In the next section we explain these adjustments.

MARKET PRICES AND FACTOR COST

Taxes levied on expenditure are called *indirect taxes* (T_i). In contrast, subsidies (S_u) are like negative taxes. Indirect taxes and subsidies drive another wedge between spending on output and the income of the factors of production. For example, a pint of beer may cost €4.00 in a pub, but indirect taxes (VAT and excises) account for about €2.00 of this. Only €2.00 goes to pay for the production and distribution of the beer and enters into national income. This requires us to distinguish between magnitudes measured at market prices and factor cost. The factor cost measure includes only payments made to the factors of production used to produce goods and services.

$$GDP_{fc} \equiv GDP_{mp} - T_i + S_u \tag{6}$$

where the fc, mp subscripts refer respectively to factor cost and market prices. In table 23.4, subsidies less indirect taxes are deducted from GDP at market prices to obtain GDP at factor cost.

Table 23.4
From GDP to national income, 2001

		€ million
GDP_{mp}	Gross domestic product at market prices	114,479
+	Subsidies (S_u) − indirect taxes (T_i)	−11,789
= GDP_{fc}	= Gross domestic product at factor cost	102,394
− D	− Provision for depreciation	−11,465
= NDP_{fc}	=Net domestic product at factor cost	90,929
+ F	+ Net factor income from rest of world	−17,677
= NNP_{fc} = NI	= Net national product at factor cost = national income	73,252

Source: *National Income and Expenditure, 2001*, Central Statistics Office, Dublin, 2002, Table 2.

DEPRECIATION

Another wedge between the value of output and income arises due to *depreciation*. The measure of investment (I) included in GDP is *gross domestic capital formation*, which is where the gross in GDP comes from. No allowance has been made for the using-up or depreciation of capital equipment in the production process. In reality, firms set aside allowances out of their revenue to provide for this depreciation and the eventual replacement of plant and equipment. This is another part of their receipts that is not passed on to households.

In table 23.4, *Net* Domestic Product (NDP) at factor cost is obtained by subtracting depreciation (D) from GDP at factor cost.

$$NDP_{fc} \equiv GDP_{fc} - D \tag{7}$$

In practice it is difficult to estimate depreciation and this is why GDP and GNP, rather than their net counterparts, are so often used to describe the economy's performance.

NET FACTOR PAYMENTS FROM THE REST OF THE WORLD

NDP is a measure of the total output of final goods and services *produced in the country*. Net *National* Product (NNP), on the other hand, is a measure of the value of the final output *accruing to the country's residents*. Thus the difference between NDP and NNP is *net factor payments to the rest of world* (F). ('Net' here refers to the difference between the gross inflows and outflows.)

$$NNP \equiv NDP + F \tag{8}$$

Although NDP (or GDP if depreciation is not subtracted from investment) is generally used in international comparisons of economic activity, NNP or GNP is a better guide to the trend in a country's living standards.

The distinction between NDP and NNP is of unusual importance in Ireland, where F is a large negative number (-€17,677 million in 2001) due to:

- The repatriation of profits by foreign-owned firms operating in Ireland.
- Interest on our national debt paid to non-residents.

These payments do not constitute part of the nation's income, but they have to be paid from the value of what is produced domestically.

In figure 23.3 we use the gross rather than the net data to highlight the increase in net factor income from abroad. By 2001, F equalled 15.4 per cent of GDP. This is a higher proportion than in any other OECD country. The magnitude of F has called into question the relevance of GDP for international comparisons involving Ireland. However, Irish

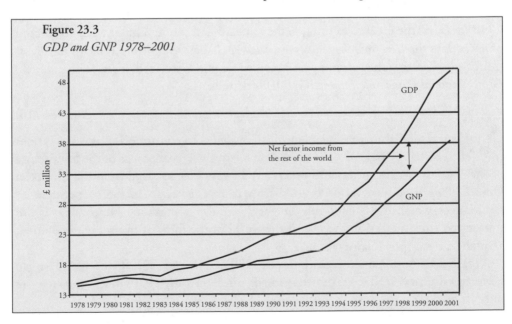

Figure 23.3
GDP and GNP 1978–2001

GNP may be meaningfully compared with the GDP figures for other countries because the main distortions arising from the operation of MNCs in Ireland have been taken out.

SUMMARY

We are now in a position to reconcile the income and expenditure approaches to measuring economic activity. Table 23.4 summarises the various stages involved using 2001 data. Firstly, an adjustment is made for indirect taxes and subsidies. The second adjustment is to allow for depreciation. Finally, when net factor income from the rest of the world (F) is added to NDPfc we obtain *net national product at factor cost* or *national income* (NI):

$$NI \equiv NDP_{fc} + F \tag{9}$$

It can be seen that NI accounts for only 64 per cent of GDP. This gap is unusually large in Ireland because of the outflow of income abroad, due to debt service and profit repatriation, as well as the other factors (depreciation, indirect taxes and retained earnings) that have to be deducted from GDP in all countries.

When estimating national income, the CSO starts by estimating agricultural income from data on crop production, etc. Non-agricultural income (wages and salaries, the income of the self-employed, profits, interest payments and rents) is estimated from data supplied by the Revenue Commissioners and other sources. These estimates of income form the basis of the GDP estimate. The expenditure figure is then reconciled with the income figure by treating personal consumer expenditure (C) as a residual. This may seem as somewhat unsatisfactory as C accounts for 48 per cent of GDP. Treating it as a residual risks accepting errors in the overall figures.

23.5 THE DISPOSABLE INCOME OF THE NATION

GNP measures the income accruing to the residents of a country, but it takes no account of *net current transfers from the rest of the world* (R). (These differ from F, factor payments from abroad, in that they are not paid in return for goods received or services rendered.) *Gross National Disposable Income* (GNDI) is defined as:

$$GNDI \equiv GNP + R \tag{10}$$

GNDI is the total amount available to Irish residents to consume and invest. Current transfers received by Ireland from abroad are relatively large, because of the importance of the support to farm prices and other current subsidies received from the European Union. They have however declined sharply in recent years. (In the past emigrants' remittances, which also fall into this category, were also important.) Some money is also transferred from Ireland to the rest of the world in the form of overseas development assistance, but this is relatively small.

Table 23.5 highlights the gap between GDP, GNP and GNDI in 2001. The gap between GDP and GNDI has grown markedly since the early 1970s due to the increases in both F and R.

Table 23.5
GDP and GNDI, 2001

		€ million	% of GDP
GDP	Gross domestic product	114,479	
+ F	net factor income from rest of world	−17,677	−15.4
= GNP	Gross national product	96,802	85.6
+ R	net transfers from rest of world	910	0.8
= GNDI	Gross national disposable income	97,712	85.4

ADJUSTING FOR INFLATION

In chapter 1 we discussed briefly the distinction between *real* GDP and *nominal* GDP (or GNP). Nominal GDP is also referred to as GDP at *market* prices or *current* prices. Real GDP is referred to as GDP at constant prices. Real GDP is equal to nominal GDP adjusted for inflation. The percentage change in real GDP is referred to as the *real growth rate* and measures the trend in living standards. Nominal GDP is a misleading indicator as increases in prices or inflation do not add to the standard of living.

Table 23.6 illustrates how the real growth rate is calculated. Column 1 shows the level of nominal GDP from 1995 to 2001. Column 2 shows the GDP *price deflator*. This price deflator is expressed in an index with the base year set equal to 100. To calculate real GDP we divide nominal GDP by the price deflator. That is, row 1 by row 2, and multiply by 100.

$$\text{Real GDP} = (\text{Nominal GDP/GDP deflator}) \times 100$$

The real GDP figures are given in row 3. The growth rates for nominal GDP, real GDP and the inflation rates are given in rows 4, 5 and 6. The real growth rates are calculated as follows:

$$\text{Real growth}_{2001} = [(\text{Real GDP}_{2001} - \text{Real GDP}_{2000})/\text{Real GDP}_{2000}] \times 100$$

It can be seen, for example, that the economy grew (in real terms) by 9.9 per cent and 5.4 per cent in 2000 and 2001, respectively. Note that the rate of growth in nominal GDP is approximately equal to the sum of the real growth rate and the rate of inflation.

In adjusting GDP for inflation, two approaches, the *expenditure* and *output* approaches are used. In the expenditure approach each component of expenditure on GDP is deflated using a different price index. C is deflated by the consumer price index, I by the price index for investment goods, G by an index based on rates of pay in the public sector, and X and M are deflated by export and import price indices respectively. The export price index is used to deflate F in years when the net flow is negative. (This is on the grounds that a net outflow can be used to purchase imports and ultimately has to be paid for with increased exports.) The import price index is used to deflate F in years when the net flow is positive.

In the output approach an attempt is made to measure value added in each sector at constant prices. Not surprisingly, the two approaches yield somewhat different

Table 23.6
Real and nominal GDP

	Nominal GDP € million 1	Price deflator Index 2	Real GDP € millions 3	Nominal GDP % change 4	Price deflator % change 5	Real GDP % change 6
1995	52,641	100.0	52,641			
1996	58,080	102.2	56,830	10.3	2.2	8.0
1997	67,098	106.4	63,068	15.5	4.1	11.0
1998	77,569	112.7	68,848	15.6	5.9	9.2
1999	89,770	117.4	76,466	15.7	4.2	11.1
2000	102,910	122.4	84,044	14.6	4.3	9.9
2001	114,479	129.2	88,618	11.2	5.5	5.4

Source: *National Income and Expenditure, 2001*, Central Statistics Office, Dublin, 2002.

figures. There is a persistent tendency for the expenditure approach to yield higher estimates of real growth than the output approach. To reconcile the two approaches it is usual to take the average of the two when quoting growth rates.

TERMS OF TRADE

One further aspect of taking account of inflation needs to be discussed. When discussing trade flows it is important to distinguish between price changes and quantity changes. We can write:

$$X = P_x \times Q_x$$

$$M = P_m \times Q_m$$

where X and M denote the value of exports and imports, respectively, P_x and P_m denote the price of exports and imports, and Q_x and Q_m indicate the quantity of exports and imports, respectively.

It follows that price changes have a direct effect on the balance of payments. Starting from an equilibrium position, an increase in P_x relative to P_m will result in a trade account surplus because the value of exports increases relative to the value of imports. (This is a short-run effect; over time, the quantities traded will respond to the change in relative prices.)

Another way of looking at it is: a country exports in order to earn foreign exchange to buy imports. If the price of its exports rises more slowly than import prices, it costs more in terms of exports to acquire a given quantity of imports.

The terms of trade are defined as P_x/P_m. An increase in this ratio is referred to as an *improvement* in the terms of trade. When such an improvement occurs, we need to

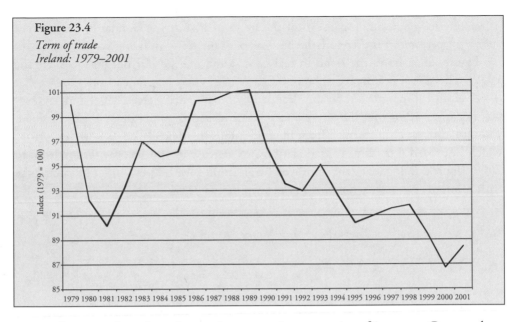

Figure 23.4

Term of trade
Ireland: 1979–2001

export fewer goods and services to import a given quantity of imports. Conversely, a decrease in the ratio is referred to as a *deterioration* in the terms of trade. We now need to export more Irish goods in order to import a given quantity of imports.

Figure 23.4 shows the terms of trade index (1979 = 100) for Ireland over the period 1975 to 2001. This index is strongly influenced by changes in the price of petroleum products on the import side, and of agricultural products on the export side. There was an adverse movement in the terms of trade between 1978 and 1982, but this was reversed between 1982 and 1986. In 1990 there was a significant deterioration in the terms of trade, due mainly to the fall in agricultural export prices. This decline has not, as yet, been reversed.

The terms of trade can have important implications for living standards in an economy as dependent on international trade as Ireland. This effect is not reflected in the constant price GDP figures. However, a terms of trade adjustment is published for GNDI at constant prices. The appendix explains how this is calculated. The inclusion of this adjustment is another reason for regarding constant price GNDI as the best index of the trend in the country's overall living standards.

ADJUSTING FOR POPULATION GROWTH

In most developed countries the rate of population growth is low and there is little need to worry about adjusting for it when analysing short-run economic performance. Ireland is unusual in this regard, however. During the 1950s the population declined by over 1 per cent a year. In the 1970s it grew by about 1.5 per cent a year, the highest growth rate in Europe. In the 1980s the population started to decline due to the resumption of large-scale emigration and the decline in the birth rate. During the 1990s the population again increased at about 1.5 per cent a year.

Our view of the country's recent economic performance would be distorted if we did not take these fluctuations in the rate of population growth into account, especially in making longer-run comparisons of the trend in Irish living standards. Income *per person* (or *per capita*) is therefore the best index of the trend in living standards.

Figure 23.5 shows the trend in real GNDI and real GNDI per person since the 1970s. The severity of the recession of the early 1980s may be gauged from the fact that the level of real income per person dropped by 8 per cent between 1979 and 1982. It was not until 1986 that the late-1970s level of real income per person was regained. The situation was transformed from the mid-1980s by the collapse of world oil prices, which improved our terms of trade and by an increase in real income. From 1987 to 2000, the real living standard improved by an impressive 87 per cent. The size of the Irish economy has nearly doubled in the last thirteen years.

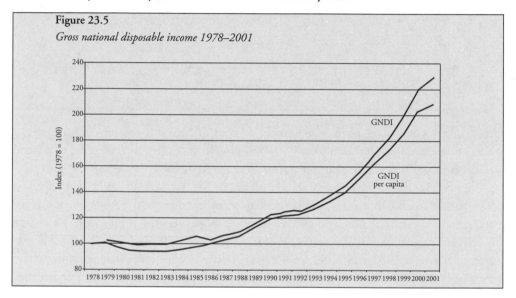

Figure 23.5
Gross national disposable income 1978–2001

Some people feel that livings standards did not improve as impressively as suggested by these figures. There has been a tendency for some people to focus on things that have got worse even as overall prosperity has improved: congestion, house price inflation, urban violent crime, even a supposed decline in friendliness and the sense of community. In fact, most people feel much better now than they did when unemployment and emigration were major problems and stagnation worried people more than congestion. However, over time the effects of the recent rise in prosperity will wear off, and people will end up feeling about as happy as they did when living standards were lower; except that a low unemployment rate will continue to represent a major improvement in human welfare. (For a discussion of some of these issues see P. Clinch, F. Convery and B. Walsh, *Beyond the Celtic Tiger*, Dublin: O'Brien Press, 2002.)

23.6 PUBLIC AND PRIVATE SAVING

National saving can be disaggregated into *public* and *private* sector saving. Public sector saving is the excess of current revenue (mainly from taxes) over current expenditure, on transfer payments and debt service as well as on current goods and services, (G).

Generally this balance has been negative, with the government spending more on day-to-day expenses than it takes in taxes. The government's current budget deficit is also called *public sector dissaving*.

Private sector saving can be broken down into household or *personal* saving and company or *corporate* saving. (The main component of the latter is the *retained earnings* of the larger corporations.) Figure 23.6 shows that corporate saving rose from a low level in the mid-1980s to a peak of 7.9 per cent of GNP in 1998. This reflects the increased profitability of Irish companies.

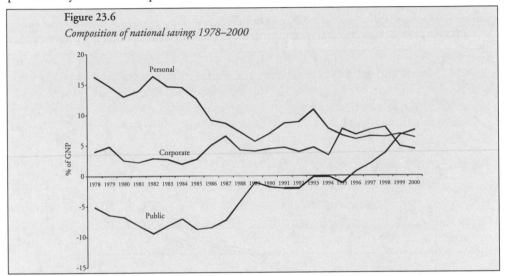

Figure 23.6
Composition of national savings 1978–2000

Personal saving reached over 16 per cent of GNP in 1982. This was an exceptionally high savings rate by international standards and one that could only fall in the longer run. Savings duly declined over the next few years reaching a low of 6 per cent in 1996.

However, the most dramatic change since the early 1980s has been the reduction in the level of public sector dissaving, from –9.5 per cent of GNP in 1983 to 7 per cent in 2000. Thus the rise in the national saving rate since the early 1980s has been largely due to the reduction in the public sector's current budget deficit.

It is significant that as public sector saving rose, the rate of personal saving declined, leaving the overall saving rate fairly stable. Some have interpreted this as evidence in favour of the Ricardian-Barro theorem, according to which a decrease in public sector deficits tends to be offset by a reduction in private sector saving.

23.7 SAVING, INVESTMENT AND THE BALANCE OF PAYMENTS

We now turn to the relationship between saving, investment and the balance of payments. National saving is one of the main determinants of the growth of living standards in the long run. This is because there is a close correlation between savings and investment. Investment, in turn, is a major source of economic growth. It can be shown (see box 23.1) that the following identity holds:

$$S - I \equiv CA \qquad (11)$$

Box 23.1
Saving, investment and the balance of payments

Recall from earlier sections in this chapter that:

$$GDP \equiv C + I + G + NX \tag{5}$$

$$GNP \equiv GDP + F \tag{8}$$

$$GNDI \equiv GNP + R \tag{10}$$

Note that in equation (8) we ignore depreciation and use gross rather than net. Substituting 5 into 8 and 8 into 10 we obtain:

$$GNDI \equiv C + I + G + NX + F + R \tag{12}$$

In this identity there are three variables that involve transactions with the rest of the world – NX, F and R. The NX variable represents the trade balance in goods and services, F is net income from the rest of the world and R represents international transfers. These three variables together comprise the *current account of the balance of payments*, which we shall label CA:

$$CA \equiv NX + F + R \tag{13}$$

We can rewrite the definition of GNDI as:

$$GNDI \equiv C + I + G + CA \tag{14}$$

Now just as a household either spends or saves its disposable income, the nation's disposable income must be either consumed or saved. Consumption consists of private consumption (C) and public sector consumption (G). Hence we can also define GNDI as:

$$GNDI \equiv (C + G) + S \tag{15}$$

where S equals gross national saving. (Gross national saving includes the allowance for depreciation; net national saving does not.)

Combining (14) and (15) yields

$$C + G + S \equiv C + I + G + CA \tag{16}$$

Cancelling C and G on each side and rearranging yields:

$$I \equiv S - CA \tag{17}$$

$$S - I \equiv CA \tag{18}$$

This is identity (11) in the main text. It states that the excess of saving over investment equals the current account surplus.

where S is saving, I is investment and CA is the current account of the balance of payments. This important identity shows that, whereas in a closed economy S must equal I, this is not true in an open economy. A country that trades with the rest of the world can finance some of its investment by running a current account balance of payments deficit and borrowing from abroad to finance this. Alternatively, it can use up some of its national saving by running a current account surplus, which is invested abroad.

Note:
We are dealing here with measured or *ex post* saving and investment and the relationships above are identities, that is, they hold by definition.

The typical experience of New World countries in the nineteenth century was for large investments in infrastructure to be funded by European investors. This was achieved by countries such as the US running sizeable current account deficits.

On the other hand, Japan in recent years has had a very high national saving rate (in excess of 30 per cent of GDP in the late 1990s) that has not been matched by an equally high rate of domestic investment. The result has been a large current account surplus, leading to a high level of overseas investment by the Japanese. Much of the outflow of money from Japan during the 1980s and 1990s was used to buy assets in the US, which financed the US balance of payments current account deficit. The American current account deficit, in turn, reflected a low saving rate relative to a heavy appetite for investment funds. These examples bring out the links between national saving, investment, and the balance of payments.

THE IRISH EXPERIENCE

The trend from 1978 to 2000 is illustrated in figure 23.7. (Saving include a small additional item, 'capital transfers', which are a further source of funding for investment. These are principally the non-current component of grants from the European Union.) In the late 1970s and early 1980s investment exceeded saving and this was reflected in an exceptionally large current account balance of payments deficit. In 1981, investment was 30 per cent of GNP (one of the highest levels in the OECD) compared to a saving rate of 15 per cent. The current account deficit was a massive 15 per cent.

Note:

As discussed in chapter 9, the current (CA) and capital (CP) accounts of the balance of payments must add to zero. Hence, a CA deficit is also reflected in a CP surplus. In Ireland in the early 1980s the CP surplus came about through foreign borrowing by the government and the private sector. It follows from this, that in the early 1980s, the Irish economy was engaged in heavy foreign borrowing in order to augment domestic saving and finance domestic investment.

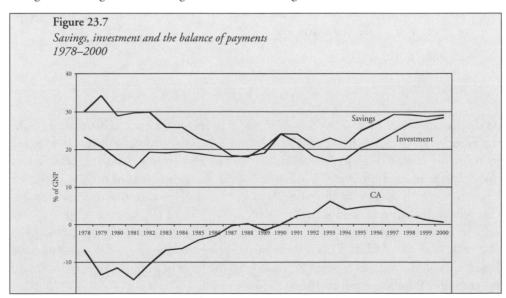

Figure 23.7

Savings, investment and the balance of payments 1978–2000

However, from 1991 onwards savings exceeded the investment rate, giving rise to a CA surplus. The CA surplus peaked in 1993 at 6 per cent. By the early twenty-first century the country was once again running a small balance of payments deficit. Of course the significance of the balance of payments had greatly diminished following entry into the Eurozone and the abolition of the national currency.

It is interesting to note that the Irish investment rate decreased at a time when exceptional real growth rates in GNP were achieved (late 1990s). Usually, an increase in investment is a pre-requisite for faster growth rates. However, the lower level of investment was offset by the much higher labour and capital productivity.

At the same time CA swung from deficit to surplus, the government's current account moved from deficit to surplus. It is often — but not always — the case that large balance of payments deficits reflect the inadequacy of national saving due to large public sector deficits.

23.8 CONCLUSION

In this chapter we examined the concepts of national income and product in some detail. We discussed the measures that are used in analysing the country's economic performance. Among the key concepts discussed were:

- The circular flow of income diagram
- The effect of government and the foreign sector on the circular flow of income
- Three methods of measuring economic activity: the expenditure, output and income approaches
- The relationship between these three approaches
- Gross national disposable income
- Nominal and real GDP and the GDP deflator
- The composition of national saving
- The relationship between national saving, national investment, and the current account of the balance of payments.

APPENDIX
ADJUSTING FOR CHANGES IN THE TERMS OF TRADE

As discussed in section 23.5. we export in order to import. Hence, what matters from the point of view of Irish living standards is how much our exports will allow us to buy in terms of imports. Think of Ireland as a country exporting dairy products and importing petroleum products. If the price of oil rises when that of milk is static, we have to export a larger quantity of milk to pay for a given quantity of imported oil. Conversely, if the price of milk rises relative to the price of oil, we have to give up less milk in order to import a given quantity of oil. In calculating real GNDI account has to be taken of these effects. This is done by adjusting for changes in the terms of trade index, that is, the price of exports, P_x, relative to the price of imports, P_m. (Both P_x and P_m are index numbers equal to 100 in the base year.)

If P_x/P_m increases, the terms of trade are said to have improved because we have to export less in order to obtain a given amount of imports. If the ratio falls the terms of trade are said to have deteriorated.

The terms of trade adjustment is the difference between the value of exports deflated by the price of imports and exports deflated by the price of exports, that is:

$$\text{Terms of trade adjustment} = (X/P_m - X/P_x) \text{ or } X(1/P_m - 1/P_x) \qquad (19)$$

In the base year both P_x and P_m are equal to 100 and hence the adjustment is zero. If in the following year $P_x > P_m$ then the adjustment is positive because the terms of trade have improved, allowing the country to buy more imports with the proceeds of a given volume of exports. If $P_x < P_m$ then the adjustment is negative because the terms of trade have deteriorated and the country has to export more in order to purchase a given volume of imports. The terms of trade adjustment given in (19) has to be added to GNDI in order to obtain GNDI adjusted for the terms of trade. The procedure has to start arbitrarily from a base year in which the adjustment is zero. The adjustment for any future year is relative to the base year.

The Irish statistician R. C. Geary (1896–1983) did some of the pioneering work on this topic. Dr Geary made important contributions to the theory of national income accounting and index numbers while Director of the Central Statistics Office in Dublin and of the United Nations Statistical Office in New York. He is also remembered for his contributions to economic theory, notably the 'Stone-Geary expenditure system'.

Table 23.7 shows how movements in the terms of trade have affected real GNDI between 1995 (the base year) and 2000. Because $P_x = P_m = 100$ in the base year, the effect is zero in that year. The adjustment has been significant and variable since then. We gained up until 1999 but suffered a significant reversal in 2000 due to higher oil prices and weaker agricultural export prices. Note that some of the gain was offset by smaller inflows through R (transfers from abroad) as farmers received less compensation for their beef exports outside the EU.

Table 23.7
Terms of trade adjustment

	GNP € millions	Terms of trade adjustment € millions	Current transfers from abroad € millions	GNDI € millions
1995	46,748	0	1,409	48,157
1996	50,227	105	1,729	52,062
1997	54,962	366	1,635	56,963
1998	59,303	648	1,286	61,237
1999	64,140	451	1,117	65,708
2000	70,816	−1,106	909	70,619

Source: National Income and Expenditure, 2000, Central Statistics Office, Dublin, 2001, Table 8.

CHAPTER 24

The Performance of the Irish Economy in the Long Run

> Little else is requisite to carry a state to the highest degree of opulence from the lowest barbarism, but peace, easy taxes, and tolerable administration of justice.
>
> Adam Smith

24.1 INTRODUCTION

Economists and historians generally gave Ireland's dismal economic performance between Independence in 1922 and 1960 low marks. In the 1960s and 1970s Ireland's growth rate rose but not sufficiently to close the gap in living standards with the richer European countries. In the early 1980s, the Irish economy went through a severe and protracted recession. Unemployment and emigration soared. However, these trends were dramatically reversed in the 1990s during the co-called Celtic Tiger period. The rapid growth of employment and output during these years led to a convergence of Irish living standards on those of the world's richest nations.

In this concluding chapter, we summarise the long-run trend in Ireland's population — always a key indicator of the country's fortunes. This is followed by an analysis of our economic performance during the following periods: 1922–60, 1961–94 and 1994–2002. Particular attention is given to the explanations that have been offered for the poor performance up to 1960 and the exceptional performance in the 1990s.

24.2 THE RECORD

The key indicators used to evaluate the economic performance of any economy are the real growth rate, the unemployment rate, inflation, the public finances and the balance of payments. In chapter 1 we presented the available data on each of these variables for the Irish economy. However, reliable data on the real growth rate only goes back to 1950 and the unemployment rate to 1960 and, as such, we have to resort to alternative indicators to gauge the long-run performance of the Irish economy.

One important additional indicator that is available since the 1840s is the level of *population*. Generally, when the economy is doing well and new jobs are made available, the population will tend to increase. Conversely, in times of recession, the population will decline. Note that the change in the population is the sum of the rate of *natural increase* (that is, the excess of the birth rate over the death rate) and *net migration* (immigration minus emigration). That is:

$$\Delta \text{Population} = \text{natural increase} - \text{net migration} \tag{1}$$

where

$$\text{Natural increase} = \text{birth rate} - \text{death rate} \tag{2}$$

and

$$\text{Net migration} = \text{inward migration} - \text{outward migration} \tag{3}$$

Net migration has been strongly influenced by the availability of jobs in Ireland. In periods of stagnant or falling employment and living standards, emigration increases and causes a decline in the population. Conversely, during boom periods, emigration gives way to immigration and the population increases.

IRELAND'S POPULATION HISTORY

Figure 24.1 shows the population of Ireland from 1841 to 2002. Due to the Famine and the depressed economic conditions that prevailed afterwards, the population of what is now the Republic of Ireland (26 counties) declined from 6,528,800 in 1841 to 2,972,000 in 1926. This 54 per cent decline in the population is a striking symbol of the long-run failure of the Irish economy during this period.

Between 1920 and 1945 the Irish economy suffered the effects of partition, civil war, the Great Depression, the Anglo-Irish Economic War, and World War II. In addition, the country turned its back on the world economy in the 1930s, embracing indiscriminate protectionism. Policy remained inward looking until the 1960s, when a gradual opening up to free trade occurred. As can be seen from figure 24.1, the population stabilised close to the three million mark until the late 1940s. The available indicators suggest that that the average standard of living was little higher in 1945 than it had been in 1914.

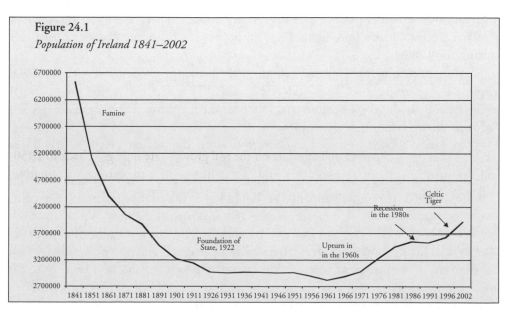

Figure 24.1

Population of Ireland 1841–2002

Note:
For an account of Ireland's economic history from Independence to the outbreak of World War II, see Cormac Ó Gráda, *Ireland: A New Economic History 1780–1939*, Oxford University Press, 1994. For the post-war period, see the same author's *A Rocky Road: The Irish Economy since the 1920s*, Manchester University Press, 1997.

The post-war experience was also disappointing. After a spurt of growth in the late 1940s, the 1950s were disastrous. Employment fell, emigration soared and the population dipped to a new low of 2,818,300 in 1961. (This proved to be the low point: 57 per cent below the peak of 1841.) With people streaming out of the country, serious concerns were voiced about the viability of an independent Irish economy.

Overall between Independence in 1922 and 1961 the population of Ireland had stagnated and living standards risen only marginally. Based largely on this experience, one influential study stated: 'It is difficult to avoid the impression that Irish economic performance has been the least impressive in Western Europe, perhaps in all Europe, in the twentieth century.' (J. J. Lee, *Ireland 1912–85: Politics and Society*, Cambridge: Cambridge University Press, 1989, 521.)

The country's economic fortunes changed markedly after 1960. Between 1960 and 1979 the annual average growth rate of GDP was 4 per cent compared to only 1 per cent in the 1950s. This rate of growth was above the average of the OECD countries. The decline of population was reversed and modest growth recorded, reaching 3,368,200 by 1979. The 1960s were a period of optimism when the phrase 'a rising tide lifts all boats' indicated that most sectors of society shared in the fruits of economic growth.

However, the era of sustained economic growth came to an end in the early 1980s. The oil crisis of 1979–80 and global recession caused the most severe recession in Ireland since the 1950s. Living standards declined, unemployment rose inexorably and emigration was held in check only by the severity of the recession in Britain and America. As can be seen from figure 24.1, the population of Ireland declined once more during the 1980s.

Lower unemployment in the UK and the US in the second half of the 1980s triggered a resumption of large-scale emigration. This was the period when illegal emigration by Irish people became established for the first time. The scale of emigration led to a renewed decline in population.

Population growth resumed in the 1990s with the advent of the Celtic Tiger economy. From 1994 to 2000, the average real growth rate was 9 per cent. By 2002 the population had reached 3,917,336, the highest level since the 1870s. Overall, between 1961 and 2001 the population of the Republic increased by nearly 40 per cent, proportionately the largest increase recorded in a European country over this period. However, this is still a long way short of the optimistic forecast of Padraic Pearse made during the Rising in 1916. '[In a] free Ireland, gracious and useful industries will supplement an improved agriculture, the population will expand in a century to 20 million and it may even in time go up to 30 million.' (Cited in J. F. Meenan, *The Irish Economy since 1922*, Liverpool University Press, 1970.)

NATURAL INCREASE AND NET MIGRATION

Figure 24.2 shows the rate of natural increase and net migration (per 1,000 of average population) from 1871 to 2002 (data is not available prior to this date). The rate of natural increase rose steadily up to 1971 and has declined sharply since then. By the early twenty-first century the population was growing at an annual rate of about 1.5 per cent, comprised almost equally of 0.75 per cent natural increase and 0.75 per cent net immigration.

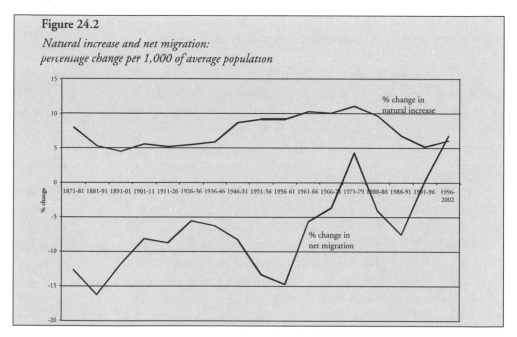

Figure 24.2

Natural increase and net migration:
percentage change per 1,000 of average population

It can be seen from figure 24.2 that net migration is considerably more volatile than the natural increase and has been the dominant influence on population change.

From the beginning of the nineteenth century, emigration from Ireland was encouraged by easy access to Britain and America. The outflow became a torrent after the Famine of the 1840s. As can be seen from figure 24.2, over most of the period between 1871 and 1961, and again in the 1980s, there was a high emigration rate. Net migration rate reached 15 per cent (per 1,000 population) between 1950 and 1956: a dismal record surpassed only by Communist East Germany. This offset a positive natural increase and, as a consequence, the population fell.

Only during the 1990s (and a brief period in the late 1970s) has there been a net inflow of people into Ireland resulting in positive net migration. However by the end of the 1990s Ireland was attracting immigrants not just from the Irish-born population living abroad but from people with no previous connection with the country, from both inside and outside the EU. For the first time in our modern history, immigration had become an important phenomenon, giving rise to a heated debate about policy towards asylum seekers, economic refuges, and so on. The question of the social welfare and housing entitlement of these newcomers, as well as whether they should be freely permitted to take up employment here, are now hotly debated.

24.3 REAL CONVERGENCE

In recent years economists have devoted a great deal of attention to the idea of *real convergence*. That is the process by which countries with initially low standards of living tend to grow more rapidly than richer countries. This leads to catching up and a narrowing of the gap between rich and poor. Formerly poor countries like Hong Kong, Singapore and South Korea achieved spectacular growth in the 1950s and 1960s. Since the economic reforms of the 1980s real GDP in China has been growing at almost 10 per cent a year, compared with much lower growth rates in the already rich countries. These differentials, if maintained, would quickly move these countries up the international league tables.

The evidence suggests that economic convergence is most likely to occur across regions and countries with similar levels of human and physical investment and similar institutional structures. That is to say, real convergence is conditional on several preconditions being in place. Many of the world's poorest countries (especially in Africa) have fallen behind the richer countries since the 1970s.

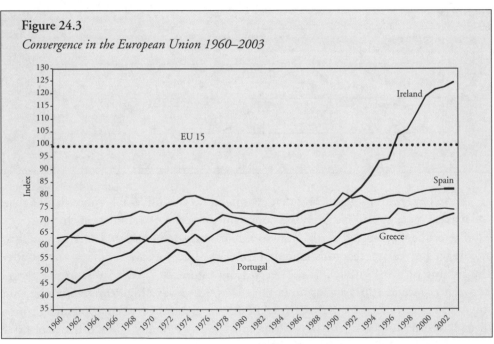

Figure 24.3

Convergence in the European Union 1960–2003

Ireland provides a clear-cut example of an economy that has made substantial progress towards closing the gap with the world's richest countries. Figure 24.3, for example, shows the experience of the four poorest countries in the EU between 1960 and 2003. The average standard of living in the EU is measured as an index and set equal to 100.

Note:

The standard of living is measured as Gross Domestic Product (GDP) at market prices per head of population adjusted for a purchasing power standard. (Source: European Commission, *European Economy*, Table 9, No. 73, 2001.) As emphasised in chapter 23, a note of caution must be sounded about comparisons based on GDP. GDP overstates the living standards in countries, such as Ireland, where foreign firms are a significant proportion of the industrial base. It is more valid to compare the level of Irish GNP with GDP in other countries. Even on this basis, however, Ireland closed the gap during the 1990s.

Back in the 1960s, the standard of living in Ireland was around 63 per cent of the EU average and similar to that in Spain, Portugal and Greece. However, as a result of accelerated growth in the 1990s, Irish living standards by 2002 were 25 percentage points above the EU average. Spain, Portugal and Greece, on the other hand, have only marginally narrowed the gap with the other EU countries.

Table 24.1
Comparing the standard of living in Ireland and the UK
Irish GDP per person as a % of UK level

	%
1913	51.6
1938	48.5
1947	46.6
1961	47.9
1971	62.9
1981	60.9
1991	77.3
2001	113.7

Source: Derived from European Commission, *European Economy*, No. 73, 2001 and OECD publications.

The long-run position relative to the UK is also informative. Table 24.1 shows Irish GDP per person as a percentage of the UK level from 1913 to 2001. It can be seen that between 1913 and 1961 Irish living standards declined somewhat relative to the UK. This poor performance reinforces the view that the policies pursued during the first four decades of Independence hindered any tendency that might have existed for Ireland to catch up with its nearest neighbour and closest trading partner. Between 1961 and 1991, the trend was reversed and Ireland's standard of living grew slowly relative to the UK. However, by 2001, after the boom years in the 1990s, the standard of living in Ireland climbed to 14 percentage points *above* that in the UK. Adjusting for the GDP, GNP gap implies that by the turn of the century, Irish and British living standards had drawn level.

Perhaps the real puzzle about Ireland's long-run performance is why it took so long for this convergence process to materialise. Even though Ireland had gained some ground in the 1960s, it slipped behind again in the 1980s, and had a lot of ground to make up at the beginning of the 1990s. With a modern educational system and a favourable business environment in place, the country would have been expected to grow very rapidly once it had sorted out the fiscal mess of the 1980s. And indeed this proved to be the case.

Note that 'catching up' is a transitional phenomenon. Once a country is on the frontier its growth rate may be expected to fall back to that of the leaders. As a rule of thumb the natural real growth rate of the US economy is generally seen to be in the region of 3 per cent. It is unrealistic to expect growth in Ireland to be much higher than this over the long run.

24.4 INTERPRETING THE RECORD: 1922–61

In this section we discuss some of the factors that explain Ireland's poor economic performance in the first half of the twentieth century. An important lesson to learn from Irish economic history is that policies matter. We do not attribute Ireland's backwardness and poor economic performance to the laziness of the population, the isolation of the economy or a lack of natural resources, but mainly to bad economic policies.

POST-INDEPENDENCE CAUTION

During the first decade of Independence, Ireland pursued basically conservative economic policies. In the monetary and financial areas, continuity with the past was maintained and no radical initiatives were launched. The government pursued a balanced budget approach to fiscal policy and the public finances were carefully managed. Although a major state monopoly, the Electricity Supply Board, and a state bank, the Agriculture Credit Corporation, were created in 1927, the role of the state in the economy remained limited. Agriculture, in which half the labour force was still engaged, was viewed as the engine of economic growth.

PROLONGED INWARD ORIENTATION

It was not until the Great Depression and the collapse of the global free trade system in the early 1930s that more radical and, in the long run, damaging policies were adopted. The Fianna Fáil government that took office in 1932 responded by introducing a wide-ranging set of inward-looking policies. Foreign investment was virtually excluded through the *Control of Manufactures Acts* (1932–34). High tariffs were imposed on imports to protect anyone willing to manufacture products in Ireland. In addition, measures were introduced to encourage the growth of native Irish industry, as well as a more labour-intensive pattern of farming. The level of protection of Irish industry remained extremely high for the next forty years. Even as late as 1966 the average rate of 'effective protection' of Irish manufacturing industry was almost 80 per cent, one of the highest in the Western world.

Note:
'Effective protection' measures the extent to which a tariff allows an industry to be inefficient relative to international competitive standards and still survive.

The firms that set up behind these high tariffs were Irish owned, although in many cases all that happened was that British firms went into joint ventures with Irish residents and formed subsidiaries to cater for their existing Irish markets. Due to the small scale of this market, separate production facilities proved very inefficient. An extreme example was the car industry, where British manufacturers had to dismantle new cars, put them in special kits and ship them to Ireland for reassembly. A limited number of semi-skilled jobs was created in this manner, but at the cost of much higher car prices in Ireland. Within ten years of the ending of protectionism hardly any of these jobs survived.

The fact that between 1932 and 1966 the Irish economy was one of the most heavily protected in the world is probably the single most important reason for the country's relatively poor economic performance over these years. Prolonged reliance on generalised protectionism has not proved to be an effective way of promoting economic development anywhere in the world. Whatever the merits of imposing tariffs on selected 'infant industries' at the early stages of industrialisation, there is no example of a country that has successfully used indiscriminate protection extending for over a generation to create a viable industrial sector.

A start was not made on dismantling tariffs until the 1960s. The *Anglo-Irish Free Trade Area Agreement* (1965) led to the elimination of tariffs between Ireland and Britain. The phased elimination of tariffs with European countries was negotiated as part of the terms of our accession to the EEC in 1973. It is hardly a coincidence that the country's relative economic performance improved dramatically as more outward-looking policies were adopted.

EXCESSIVE STATE INVOLVEMENT IN THE ECONOMY

After 1932 numerous state-sponsored bodies (or 'semi-state companies') were created to fill what were regarded as gaps left by enterprise. The areas in which they operated included radio and TV broadcasting, turf development, air, sea, road and rail transport, hotels, and food processing, manufacturing steel and chemical fertilisers — the list is long! Most of the state-owned companies enjoyed significant monopoly power and with the passage of time became overmanned and inefficient. They were also asked to achieve a variety of political and social objectives, which burdened them with high-cost operations.

Note:
A sensitive example of this is the requirement that all transatlantic flights had to stopover in Shannon Airport. This was imposed on Aer Lingus and other carriers with a view to developing the Mid-West region, even though it conflicted with the airlines' commercial objectives.

By the 1970s the role of the state in the Irish economy was probably more extensive than in any other country that had not formally adopted socialism. The result was a high tax burden on the economy, which acted as a deterrent to private enterprise. By the 1980s it was clear that the expansion of the role of the state in the economy since the 1930s had not succeeded in its aim of promoting the long-run development of the economy.

This recognition — prompted by changes in attitude towards the economic role of the state in Britain and America — led to the gradual introduction of deregulation and privatisation. Some state companies (Nítrigin Éireann, the Irish Life Assurance Company, Irish Steel, the Industrial Credit Corporation, the Agricultural Credit Corporation, the Irish Sugar Company, Telecom Éireann and parts of the Irish Airlines group) have been, or are due to be, privatised. The monopoly privileges of those in areas such as access transport, inter-city bus transport, health insurance, TV and radio broadcasting, and electricity generation have been reduced.

However, despite these changes the state still plays a major role in the productive sectors of the Irish economy. The level of state ownership and regulation of the economy is probably still higher than in many of the former socialist economies of Central and Eastern Europe. We have consistently delayed implementation of EU regulations for liberalisation of civil aviation, insurance and banking. In many areas we have liberalised reluctantly, under pressure from the EU.

THE LEVEL AND STRUCTURE OF INVESTMENT

Modern growth theory attributes great importance to the level and structure of investment as a determinant of growth. In the 1950s Ireland had a relatively low savings rate. A high proportion of the funds available for investment was used by government for social overhead projects such as housing and hospital building. The result was a low rate of investment in productive assets. In the 1970s the rate of investment rose but the government directly or indirectly controlled an inordinate proportion of it and its productivity was low.

THE BRITISH CONNECTION

Political independence did little to reduce Ireland's heavy economic dependence on Britain. As late as the 1950s, almost 90 per cent of Irish exports went to the UK and almost three-quarters of them consisted of live animals and foodstuffs. Our banking system and financial markets remained integrated with their British counterparts. With such close links to Britain it is hardly surprising that the growth rate of the Irish economy was closer to that of Britain than of the continental European countries. The relatively slow growth of the UK economy acted as a constraint on Irish economic development.

EMIGRATION

The persistence of high emigration from 1840 to 1961 is often cited not just as a symptom of under-achievement but also as a *cause* of poor economic performance. This is because emigration and a declining population can have a number of adverse effects on economic development.

- A contracting domestic market acts as a deterrent to new investment.
- Emigration distorts the age structure of the population, leading to a relatively high proportion of both young and old dependants, and a relatively small proportion of young adults.

- The psychological and social effects of emigration are negative. It is dispiriting if almost half of the school-leaving cohort leaves the country, as was the case during the 1950s, especially if those who go are the more energetic and enterprising. The remaining population will tend to be conservative and reluctant to take risks.

- Until the 1980s the highest rates of emigration from Ireland were recorded among farm labourers, the sons and daughters of small farmers, and unskilled manual workers, but in the 1980s higher rates of emigration occurred among those with third level and professional qualifications. This outflow of highly-educated young people represented a major loss of human capital and the state enjoyed no return on the public money spent on their education.

The adverse effects of emigration can, however, be exaggerated. In actual fact it is surprisingly difficult to find evidence that high rates of emigration have an adverse effect on the rate of economic growth. In assessing the costs of emigration account should be taken of the compensating benefits.

- In the absence of emigration the living standards of those who left and of those who stayed would have been even lower. Emigration afforded many young Irish people the opportunity of raising their living standards and relieved pressure on the welfare services in Ireland.

- When the rate of growth of the Irish economy picked up in the 1990s, return migration proved to be a valuable source of skilled personnel.

24.5 Interpreting the Record: after the 1950s

The reasons for the improvement in Ireland's economic performance after 1960 are largely the reverse of the negative factors that we listed in the previous section.

Outward orientation

Economists agree that the most important contribution to turning the Irish economy round was the dismantling of protectionism and the return to free trade in the 1960s. By the end of the 1950s it had come to be recognised that inward-looking economic policies offered little hope of raising Irish living standards. The growing momentum towards free trade in Europe and the prospect of eventual entry to the EEC forced Irish policy makers to think about opening up the economy. After 1960, successive governments were consistent in their commitment to export-led growth.

Note:
While most economists argue that free trade promotes growth, the international evidence is not conclusive. See Francisco Rodriguez and Dani Rodrik, 'Trade Policy and Economic Growth: A Skeptic's Guide to Cross-National Evidence' in *NBER working paper*, No. 7081, April 1999.

Industrial policy

As tariffs were dismantled in the 1960s an elaborate system of industrial grants and tax incentives was introduced. Instead of giving priority to Irish-owned firms willing to substitute for imported goods, the emphasis of policy was switched to attracting export-oriented *foreign direct investment* (FDI). The Industrial Development Authority (IDA) and An Foras Tionscal (which had been established in 1949 and 1952, respectively) were given this remit.

The success of the IDA in attracting high-tech foreign multinationals companies (MNC) to Ireland contributed to the improved economic performance after 1960. In 2001, for example, the IDA supported 1,237 companies which employed 138,009 people. This level of employment accounts for 27 per cent of total industrial employment. Sales amounted to €52.6 billion of which 90 per cent or €47 billion was exported. Irish economy expenditure by multinational firms amounted to 27 per cent of total sales, indicating considerable spin-off effects for the domestic economy.

The IDA paid out grants of €109 million in 2001. This expenditure is funded by the Irish government and by transfers from the EU budget. This resulted in a cost per job sustained of €13,375, down from €20,743 in 1986. Ireland now spends less than the EU average on state aid to industry.

However, the contribution of the MNCs to the Irish economy can easily be exaggerated by failing to take account of their high level of imports (including payments for patents, royalties, and other intangible inputs) and the very high level of repatriated profits.

Table 24.2
Contribution of the top 34 enterprises to the Irish economy, 1998

	€ billion
Exports	31.60
Capital expenditure	1.60
− Imports	19.68
= contribution to GDP	13.52
− repatriated profits	8.76
= contribution to GNP	4.76

Source: W. Keating, 'Measuring the Economy – Problems and Prospects', *Statistical and Social Inquiry Society of Ireland*, October, 2000.

Table 24.2 summarises the contribution of the top thirty-four enterprises (almost all of them MNCs that have been aided by the IDA) to the economy on a national accounts basis in 1998. Exports amounted to €31.6 billion and capital expenditure to €1.65 billion. However, when imports of €19.68 billion and profit repatriation of €8.76 billion are deducted, the direct contribution to GNP is only €4.76 billion. This is a significantly lower contribution to GNP than that suggested by the export figure.

Another issue is why any subsidies should be given to increase employment in a country that is close to full employment (Ireland in 2001)? Some valid reasons may be advanced: to upgrade and secure existing employment, to 'move up the value added chain' by obtaining better (higher paying) jobs, and to rebalance employment across the regions. But again these considerations can be exaggerated.

WHY IS IRELAND AN ATTRACTIVE LOCATION FOR MULTINATIONAL COMPANIES?

A number of inter-related factors may be suggested to explain why multinational companies choose to locate in Ireland.

* Corporation tax rate of 12.5 per cent.

Initially, the incentives used to attract foreign investment included fixed asset grants, generous capital allowances, and export sales tax relief. These were given to overcome the disadvantages of locating in a 'peripheral' location like Ireland. Most of these grants and taxes have now been phased out. In the 1960s a zero rate of tax was applied to profits arising from exports. This was deemed discriminatory by the EU and in its place a 10 per cent tax rate was applied to all manufacturing profits. This was replaced by a 12.5 per cent corporation tax rate on all profits from 2003. This compares very favourably with the much higher rates (nearly 40 per cent) prevailing in some European countries (see table 24.3).

Undoubtedly the low tax rate is the major attraction of Ireland for FDI. Although the tax rate is now higher than in the past, there is evidence that 'footloose' capital has become more sensitive to tax differentials and more willing to seek out locations that offer higher profitability. This would help explain why the low tax rate acted as a more powerful magnet in the 1990s than in earlier decades. So successful has Ireland's policy been that it has given rise to complaints of 'unfair tax competition' and pressure on Ireland to raise the tax rate to the average European rate.

Note:
One of the consequences of the low Irish corporation tax rate is an incentive for MNCs to attribute to Ireland as much as possible of their worldwide profits. As a result the profitability of some sectors of the Irish manufacturing are incredible. Industries like pharmaceuticals, cola concentrates, and software reproduction report value added per employee of well over €1,000,000. Much of the resultant profit flows back out of the country in form of 'repatriated profits' and swells the GDP, GNP gap discussed in chapter 23. One advantage of this is that 12.5 per cent of these exaggerated profits are paid as taxes to the Irish exchequer.

* The increased outflow from the Irish educational system of well-educated English speaking, young workers, who are prepared to work for relatively modest salaries. (Ireland is the only English-speaking country in the European Monetary Union).
* Flexible working practices. Most of the new foreign-owned firms that have located in Ireland are not unionised.
* Efficient institutional structures. For example, enforcement of the law, the efficiency of public administration and the financial sector in Ireland. Also the Irish and American 'cultures' are similar in a number of important respects.
* Ireland acts as a gateway to European markets particularly for US firms. The country also offers easy access to the US.

Table 24.3
Corporate tax rates in Europe

State	Corporation tax rate %
Ireland	12.5
Austria	34
Belgium	40.17
Denmark	30
Finland	29
France	34.33
Germany	38.36
Greece	35
Italy	40.25
Luxembourg	30.38
Netherlands	34.5
Portugal	33
Spain	35
Sweden	28
United Kingdom	30
Czech Republic	31
Cyprus	28*
Estonia	0**
Hungary	18
Latvia	25
Lithuania	24
Malta	35
Poland	28
Slovak Republic	25
Slovenia	25

* Cyprus is planning to introduce a 10% rate.
** Estonia has a 0% rate of tax on retained profits. Otherwise a rate of 35% aplies.

Source: KPMG Financial Services

• Success breeds success. Ireland has established a reputation as a suitable location for new foreign investment. In the microelectronic area, for example, numerous computer companies (Intel, IMB, Digital, Hewlett Packard, Gateway 2000, Dell) have set up and expanded here, this gives a clear signal to other computer companies looking for a suitable location within the EU. There is now a critical mass of workers with experience in computer-related occupations and the necessary sub-suppliers are in place. The same applies to some extent to sectors such as pharmaceuticals, high-tech food industries, medical equipment, financial services and telemarketing.

An important feature of Irish industrial policy is that it does not involve the state either in direct participation in industry or in explicitly picking winning sectors or firms.

Although sectors such as electronics, pharmaceuticals and medical instrumentation are undoubtedly targeted, the IDA is willing to provide similar assistance to all firms that regard Ireland as a suitable location. This contrasts with, for example, the approach taken in South Korea or Singapore, where the state has been directly involved in directing the pattern of investment.

Note:

While it is true that FDI accounts for most of the growth of industrial employment, output and exports, the importance of 'indigenous' Irish industry should not be overlooked. Since the 1960s a core of strong Irish firms has expanded and have become multinationals in their own right. Companies such as Smurfit, CRH, Ryanair, Bank of Ireland, Allied Irish Banks, Kerry, Elan, Glen Dimplex, Independent Newspapers, Waterford-Wedgwood, Greencore Waterford-Avonmore, IAWS, among others, derive large and increasing proportions of their profits from their international activities. However, non-Irish investors own significant proportions of their equity and it is becoming increasingly difficult, and less relevant, to distinguish between 'Irish' and 'foreign' industries. Some of the most famous 'Irish' branded products, such as Guinness stout, the main Irish whiskies, and Bailey's Irish Cream, are owned by multinational companies.

EXTERNAL ASSISTANCE

In 1922 the new Irish Free State was cut off from the financial support that it would eventually have enjoyed as a poorer region of the UK. This loss of support became quite significant as the welfare state was established and various regional policies implemented in the UK after World War II. Ireland did, however, benefit from the *European Recovery Programme* (Marshall Aid) launched by the United States in 1949. Under this programme Ireland received low interest loans amounting to over 3 per cent of GNP for three years. These funds were used to finance the development of agriculture and forestry and local authority housing and hospitals.

With the ending of Marshall Aid, however, Ireland had to rely exclusively on its own resources until it entered the EEC in 1973. Since then the country has benefited from high prices for farm products paid for through the Common Agricultural Policy and grants from the Regional and Social Funds. During the 1980s the level of aid under the Social and Regional Funds increased significantly and in the 1990s a new Cohesion Fund was established to narrow the gap between rich and poor countries.

Table 24.4 shows Irish payments to and receipts from the EU. Net receipts reached a peak of 6.6 per cent of GNP in 1991. Total net receipts over the period 1973 to 2001 amounted to €33,853.5 million, an annual average of €1,167.4 million or 3.9 per cent of GNP.

Table 24.5 shows the breakdown of total receipts since 1973. By far the most important source of funding is from the FEOGA guarantee section, which is the main channel of funding to the agricultural sector. Total receipts over the period 1973 to 2001 amounted to €45,379.7 million or an annual average of €1,564.8 million.

Note:

In table 24.5 FEOGA stands for *Fund European Orientation Guidance Agriculture*. It is also known as EAGGF, an abbreviation of *European Agriculture Guidance and Guarantee Fund*. The

Table 24.4
Ireland's net receipts from the EU

	Receipts €m	Payments to EU €m	Net receipts €m	Net receipts as a % of GNP
1973	47.1	5.7	41.4	1.2
1974	85.6	7.0	78.6	2.0
1975	138.8	12.4	126.3	2.6
1976	153.5	17.0	136.5	2.3
1977	349.9	28.1	321.9	4.4
1978	525.5	58.5	467.0	5.4
1979	678.3	76.9	601.3	5.9
1980	714.6	112.9	601.7	5.0
1981	651.2	133.8	517.4	3.5
1982	773.8	173.6	600.2	3.5
1983	940.4	234.5	705.8	3.6
1984	1,129.7	257.1	872.6	4.0
1985	1,452.8	270.8	1,182.0	4.9
1986	1,468.2	305.1	1,163.1	4.6
1987	1,408.4	324.0	1,084.4	4.0
1988	1,474.9	314.6	1,160.3	4.0
1989	1,644.7	362.6	1,282.1	4.0
1990	2,210.6	359.2	1,851.4	5.4
1991	2,794.9	442.1	2,352.8	6.6
1992	2,531.9	448.7	2,083.1	5.4
1993	2,850.9	575.8	2,275.1	5.5
1994	2,338.1	641.9	1,696.2	3.8
1995	2,568.7	689.2	1,879.5	4.0
1996	2,818.2	687.1	2,131.1	4.1
1997	3,179.9	652.0	2,527.9	4.3
1998	3,015.9	989.4	2,026.5	3.0
1999	2,678.9	1,051.0	1,627.9	2.1
2000	2,602.1	1,075.0	1,527.1	1.8
2001	2,152.1	1,220.0	932.2	1.0
Total	45,379.7	11,526.2	33,853.5	

Misc. section includes receipts under the EMS interest rate subsidies and from FIFG (*Financial Instrument for Fisheries Guidance*).

EU assistance is often cited as a reason for Ireland's improved economic performance since the early 1970s and, in particular, in the 1990s. The money was spent on roads and railways, telecommunications, and aid to industry, agriculture and tourism. The strategy was to strengthen the country's productive capacity by upgrading infrastructure, developing the skills of the population and encouraging local initiatives. It is now generally accepted that EU funding did raise Ireland's growth rate and lead

Table 24.5

Ireland's receipts (grants and subsidies)

	FEOGA Guarantee Section €m	FEOGA Guidance Section €m	European Social Fund €m	Regional Development Fund €m	Cohesion Fund €m	Misc. €m	Total €m
1973	47.1	47.1					
1974	81.0	4.6	85.6				
1975	129.8	0.8	5.1	2.3		0.9	138.8
1976	129.5	3.3	5.8	10.8		4.1	153.5
1977	311.2	9.4	10.4	10.8		8.1	349.9
1978	464.2	12.3	24.5	14.1		10.4	525.5
1979	503.5	23.5	36.6	32.4		82.4	678.3
1980	483.9	40.4	59.3	58.9		72.1	714.6
1981	386.8	53.2	57.5	69.3		84.4	651.2
1982	437.2	75.7	92.9	83.9		84.1	773.8
1983	560.8	80.9	117.7	73.9		107.0	940.4
1984	818.5	62.6	107.0	82.8		58.8	1,129.7
1985	1,062.3	70.9	179.4	96.5		43.8	1,452.8
1986	1,122.4	59.2	161.8	97.9		26.9	1,468.2
1987	939.1	86.2	245.7	111.0		26.4	1,408.4
1988	1,064.7	81.8	161.0	164.6		2.9	1,474.9
1989	1,223.3	97.4	176.0	143.4		4.7	1,644.7
1990	1,633.8	119.2	163.2	285.8		8.6	2,210.6
1991	1,694.3	182.0	470.7	434.1		13.8	2,794.9
1992	1,414.0	187.2	352.1	564.5		14.1	2,531.9
1993	1,627.6	159.9	395.7	589.7	52.8	25.4	2,850.9
1994	1,490.3	166.2	351.8	223.0	86.7	20.1	2,338.1
1995	1,460.5	181.4	325.3	454.7	129.5	17.3	2,568.7
1996	1,732.6	191.2	321.1	377.2	174.1	22.0	2,818.2
1997	1,929.7	210.6	344.1	452.3	206.6	36.6	3,179.9
1998	1,618.7	235.7	397.6	596.8	143.4	23.9	3,015.9
1999	1,723.0	106.3	265.5	265.0	290.0	29.1	2,678.9
2000	1,681.4	34.7	220.6	513.2	152.2		2,602.1
2001	1,247.7	20.7	135.0	359.5	297.0	92.3	2,152.1
Total	29,018.6	2,552.4	5,187.9	6,168.3	1,532.3	920.2	45,379.7

to convergence in living standards with the richer EU countries. However, it does not account for the massive growth spurt that was recorded between 1994 and 2000.

INVESTMENT IN EDUCATION AND THE SUPPLY OF SKILLED LABOUR

At various stages in this book we have stressed the importance of investment in human capital in the growth process. It holds the key to raising the productivity of the labour force and attracting high quality FDI. In 2000, the Irish government spent €1,356 million on primary, €1,578 on secondary and €1,064 million on third level education.

As a consequence of this expenditure, young people with relatively high quali-fications increasingly dominated the outflow from the educational system. As already mentioned, the availability of a well-educated labour force has acted as a magnet attracting foreign firms in high-technology fields to Ireland.

SUMMARY

While factors such as industrial policy, external assistance, and investment in education may have allowed Ireland to shake off the stagnation of the 1950s, they did not insulate it from the global recessions of 1973–74 and 1980–83. However, these factors partly explain the country's exceptional economic record in the 1990s; an issue to which we now turn.

24.6 THE 'CELTIC TIGER' PERIOD: 1994–2000

Recall that between 1980–87, the Irish economy experienced negative real growth, rising unemployment, and inflation (stagflation), a crisis in the public finances, a balance of payments deficit and a depreciating exchange rate. This led to mass emigration and rising poverty levels.

In contrast, after 1987 the economy outperformed its European partners and from 1994 to 2000 achieved seven years of spectacular growth, full employment, low inflation and surpluses on both the public finances and the balance of payments. There is little doubt that the performance of the Irish economy over this period was exceptional. As one economist commented: 'The performance of Irish productivity and Irish employment since the mid-1980s is very impressive. I do not know the rules by which miracles are officially defined, but this seems to come close.' (O. Blanchard, discussion of Patrick Honohan and Brendan Walsh, 'Catching-up with the Leaders: The Irish Hare', *Brookings Papers on Economic Activity*, 2002, 61.)

Note:
There is some debate as to when the Celtic Tiger economy first emerged. Economic growth did pick up in 1987 and rose to an impressive 8.3 per cent in 1990 (see figure 24.5). However, this was followed by three years where the growth rate averaged 2 per cent. This was an average performance and not the stuff of a booming economy. From 1994 to 2000 the average growth rate was 9 per cent. The growth rate then declined in 2001 and 2002 and unemployment again edged upwards. On the basis of the growth data, the Celtic Tiger period would seem to be between 1994 and 2000. Also, during this period, inflation remained relatively subdued.

The image of Ireland abroad changed radically as our economic performance improved. The phase 'Celtic Tiger' was coined in 1996 to compare Ireland's growth with that of the successful economies of East Asia such as Singapore, Malaysia and Thailand, where tigers do exist outside the zoos! It has been suggested that a more appropriate label for the Irish record would be the 'Irish hare'. Apart from the fact that there is such a creature, the idea of a hare suddenly coming to life and running very rapidly for a while is an accurate summary of what actually happened in Ireland during the 1990s. (For a detailed account of this period see Patrick Honohan and Brendan M. Walsh, *op. cit.*)

The Celtic Tiger idea was publicised by *The Wall Street Journal* (5/12/1996) and *Newsweek* (23/12/1996). In January 1988 *The Economist* carried a survey of Ireland called 'Poorest of the Rich', the cover showing a woman begging on O'Connell Street, Dublin. The basket in the woman's hand perhaps metaphorically implying that the Irish economy was a 'basket case'. In May 1997 the same magazine published another survey of Ireland entitled 'Europe's Shining Light'. This time the cover showed a map of Europe with the Republic of Ireland surrounded by a halo.

ACCOUNTING FOR THE TIGER ECONOMY

What changed and transformed the economy after 1990? There is a reasonable level of agreement among economists that several factors contributed to the sudden growth spurt of the 1990s. Some of these we have already discussed including the increase in EU assistance in the 1990s and the increased inflow of FDI. Additional factors include:

1.   The fiscal correction and halting of the upward spiral of debt and taxation in the 1990s.
2.   Wage moderation following the return to centralised wage bargaining.
3.   Favourable external conditions including the boom in the US economy.
4.   Consequences of qualifying for European Monetary Union (EMU).
5.   Exchange rate policy.
6.   Small is beautiful.

We now discuss each of these factors.

THE FISCAL CORRECTION AND TAXATION

The macroeconomic situation in Ireland at the start of the 1980s was unsustainable. The country was facing insolvency due to the rising debt/GDP ratio and the exceptional current account balance of payments deficit. The result was a flight of capital from the country and a reluctance of foreign firms to locate here.

Restoring order to the public finances was a precondition for a resumption of economic growth. The sharp cuts in public sector spending in 1987 restored private investors' confidence in the economy and laid the foundations for the subsequent expansion of the economy.

Also the rising tax burden encouraged widespread evasion and avoidance. Part of the approach to centralised pay bargaining adopted in 1988 was a commitment to reducing the burden of taxation on employees. In 1988 the standard rate of income tax was 35 per cent and the higher rate 58 per cent; by 2002 these rates had been lowered to 20 per cent and 42 per cent, respectively, and the thresholds at which they are applied have been raised in real terms. The rates of social insurance tax on lower paid workers have also been reduced slightly.

Ireland is one of the few EU countries where the share of taxes in GDP is significantly lower now than ten years ago. Because high rates of taxation act as a

Conflicting views of the Irish economy

disincentive to economic development, especially in a small open economy, the reversal of the upward trend in taxation since the mid-1980s is another factor that contributed to Ireland's improved performance.

Note:

We must acknowledge that the rapid growth of the economy has facilitated tax reductions and it is difficult to disentangle cause and effect. What matters is that since the early 1990s Ireland has enjoyed a virtuous circle with faster growth leading to lower tax and public debt burdens. This, in turn, has reinforced the economy's performance.

It should also be noted that government spending under the 1994 and 2000 National Development Plans amounted to 28 billion and 51 billion respectively. Most of this money was earmarked to improve infrastructure, alleviate road congestion, reduce environmental pollution, expand education and training and increase the supply of social housing.

CENTRALISED WAGE BARGAINING

A factor frequently invoked to explain Ireland's good economic record is the return to centralised wage bargaining or National Wage Agreements (NWAs) in the second half of the 1980s. These wage agreements are often referred to in Ireland and Europe as 'social partnership'. The phrase 'social corporatism' is also used.

There were several NWAs in the 1970s, but this approach broke down under the strain of rising inflation and unemployment in the 1980s. The high and rising level of unemployment exercised a harsh discipline on wage claims: real take-home pay fell by about 20 per cent between 1981 and 1986. In order to preserve moderation in wage inflation as the recovery gathered momentum, a new series of NWAs was launched from 1988. There have been five programmes up until the end of 2002. We summarised the experience with these agreements in chapter 22. A feature of these agreements has been that in return for low nominal wage demands the government held out the prospect of a reduction in income taxation, improvements in social benefits and a wide variety of other measures.

Centralised wage bargaining contributed to pay moderation and enhanced Ireland's competitive advantage after 1987. The wage agreements also resulted in a virtual absence of industrial strife. However, it should be noted that other countries, including Britain and the United States, have achieved pay moderation and low unemployment under decentralised pay bargaining. In 2002, the Irish system of social partnership is being severely tested by low unemployment and rising wage demands. In order to pacify wage demands, the *Public Sector Benchmarking Body*, which reported in June 2002, recommended significant pay awards for workers in the civil service, local authorities, health, defence, Garda, prison and education sectors. It remains to be seen whether or not these pay awards are consistent with maintaining competitiveness and constraining public sector expenditure.

WORLD ECONOMY

Ireland is very open to international trade. In 2001, for example, non-EMU countries accounted for 80.4 per cent of Irish trade. Ireland is particularly dependent on the US economy. In 2001, Irish exports to the US amounted to €1.6 billion. This means that Ireland is heavily dependent on US-owned firms in a few key sectors and this has increased our exposure to the world business cycle and to conditions in these sectors. The high growth rate in the US economy, particularly during the Clinton era, has a very beneficial effect on the Irish economy.

The slowdown in 2001 and 2002 is due in large part to the cooling of the US economy due to the terrorist attack on September 11. A serious downturn in the world microelectronics market, for example, would have grave repercussions for employment in various parts of Ireland.

Another factor is the increase in tourism revenues. Due, in part, to airline deregulation, a vigorous promotional strategy and price competitiveness, tourism receipts increased by 8 per cent per annum throughout the 1990s.

EMU ENTRY CRITERIA

To join EMU, Irish inflation had to drop to 2.7 per cent or lower in 1997. Hence, the commitment to participate in EMU forced the government to adopt an anti-inflation policy stance. This undoubtedly contributed to maintaining competitiveness particularly relative to non-EMU countries.

In addition, EMU membership entailed a fall in Irish interest rates down to the low German rates. This fall in interest rates stimulated the demand-side of the economy by increasing interest-sensitive expenditure. (See figures 14.1 and 14.2 in chapter 14.)

EXCHANGE RATE POLICY

An overvalued exchange rate combined with high interest rates can seriously curtail economic growth. The devaluations in August 1986 by 8 per cent and January 1993 by 10 per cent prevented the Irish currency from becoming seriously overvalued.

In the summer of 1993 the EMS bands were extended from ±2.25 per cent to ±15 per cent. This meant that the EMS has ceased to exist in all but name. It is remarkable how well the Irish economy performed during this period of free floating. The Central Bank of Ireland appears to have pursued a successful policy of stabilising the *effective* exchange rate. This involved playing off the strength of sterling against the weakness of the Deutsche mark (see chapter 13). From August 1997, the Irish pound was allowed to drift down against the Deutsche mark to the EMU entry rate of DM2.4838. At this exchange rate, the Irish economy was also competitive relative to both Britain and the US. This gain in competitiveness contributed to the exceptional boom of the years 1999 and 2000.

SMALL IS BEAUTIFUL

It is easier to turn around a small country like Ireland than a very large country like Germany, France or Spain. The level of foreign direct investment that came into Ireland during the 1990s would have had much less of an impact on a larger country. Similarly, immigration has had a much greater relative impact on Ireland than on larger countries. In this regard the Irish economy resembles a region of a larger economy (the Eurozone) more than a large, national economy.

SUMMARY

The list of factors that can be invoked to account for the dramatic improvement in Ireland's economic fortunes since the early 1990s is long. The financial stabilisation of the 1980s, the reversal of the rising tax burden, the refinement of our industrial policy, the coming on to the labour market of a large cohort of well-educated young people, the increased inflow of EU aid, the reintroduction of centralised pay bargaining, and favourable exchange rate developments — all played their role. Furthermore, there was an element of luck in that most of the above mentioned factors complemented each other in moving in the right direction at the same time.

It is not possible to measure the relative importance of the various factors. But it is clear that the period since 1994 has been unique in Irish history, because never before have so many favourable factors combined to transform the country's economic base and propel exports, employment and productivity to heights that were undreamed of in earlier decades.

24.7 GRAPHICAL REPRESENTATION

In this section we examine how the factors discussed in the previous section impact on the aggregate supply (AS) curve (supply-side of the economy) and the aggregate demand (AD) curve (demand-side of the economy). This analysis is imprecise because, firstly, we cannot *quantify* the effect of each factor; secondly, some factors impact on *both* the supply-side and the demand-side, and thirdly, the various factors *inter-act* with each other and ideally should not be examined in isolation.

SUPPLY-SIDE OF THE ECONOMY

As a starting point recall from earlier chapters, that natural real GNP (or the long-run AS curve) is determined by:

1. *Quantity of labour.* This, in turn, is affected by the labour force participation rate, hours worked per person and by net migration.
2. *Physical and human capital.* Labour quality is determined by education, knowledge, skills, job training, learning by doing and work experience.
3. *Technology.* This is primarily determined outside the country. During a 'catch-up phase' a country's rate of technological advance can be very high.

Of the factors discussed in the previous section, the following could be expected to affect the natural real GNP or the supply-side of the economy:

*   Investment in education can be expected to improve human capital and also research and development. As such it increases 2 and 3 above.
*   FDI (or industrial policy) can also be expected to increase 2 and 3. FDI clearly increases physical capital and introduces state-of-the-art technology into the domestic economy.
*   External assistance increases physical and human capital and therefore affects 2.
*   Fiscal policy (tax policy and the National Development Plans) and centralised wage bargaining could be expected to affect 1, 2 and 3. A reduction in the tax rate

for example, increases the labour force participation rate, government expenditure increases physical and human capital and also contributes towards research and development.

- The NWAs in so far as they constrained wage inflation can be expected to reduce firms' costs and thereby shift the AS curve to the right.

Taking these factors together, the result is a shift of both the long-run (LAS) and the short-run AS (SAS) curves to the right (figure 24.4).

DEMAND-SIDE OF THE ECONOMY

Turning now to the demand-side of the economy. Factors affecting the AD curve include:

- FDI increases net exports and shifts the AD curve to the right.
- World economy. An upturn in the world economy can be expected to increase net exports and also investment.
- EMU entry criteria. Low inflation and interest rates can be expected to increase consumer and investment expenditure and improve competitiveness.
- Exchange rate policy. A competitive exchange rate policy could be expected to increase net exports.
- Fiscal policy (tax cuts and government spending under the National Development Plans). This will increase consumer expenditure, investment and government expenditure.

The combined effect is to shift the AD curve to the right.

Figure 24.4 summarises the outcome. With both the AD and the short- and long-run AS curves shifting to the right the economy moves from the point A to B. The rate of economic growth increases along the horizontal axis. As we have drawn it the shift of the AS curves is exactly equal to the shift of the AD curve and as a consequence there is no increase in inflation along the vertical axis. This was certainly the case in Ireland up to mid-2000.

This suggests that the Celtic Tiger period was the result of a combination of demand-side and supply-side factors. That is, the supply-side of the economy expanded as much as the demand-side and this facilitated non-inflationary growth. Note that if the shift of the AD curve had been greater than the movement of the AS curve the inflation rate would have increased. Alternatively, if the AD curve movement had been less that the AS curve, the result would have been deflation.

NATURAL REAL GROWTH RATE

Between 1994 and 2000, the average actual real growth rate was 9 per cent. It is estimated that during this period the natural real growth rate was approximately 8 per cent. (See J. Fitzgerald, 'Fiscal Policy in a Monetary Union: The Case of Ireland' in *Quarterly Economic Commentary*, 2001.) Hence, the economy was growing slightly faster than its sustainable rate. Why was the natural real growth rate so high during this period?

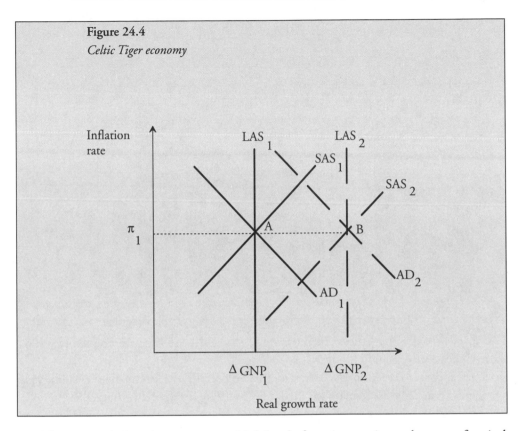

Figure 24.4
Celtic Tiger economy

The answer is that there was a very high level of excess capacity at the start of period and this enabled the economy to grow at a rapid rate. The growth in natural real GNP can be decomposed into two elements:

- The growth in employment.
- The growth of output per worker or productivity.

Consider first the growth in employment. Between 1994 and 2000 the unemployment rate fell from 14.5 per cent to 3.6 per cent, labour force participation rate (LFPR) rose from 38 to 47 per cent and net emigration turned into net immigration. Employment increased from 1,118,300 in 1993 to 1,745,000 in 2002. This resulted in a rise in the employment/population ratio from 33 per cent in 1993 to 45 per cent in 2002. This increase in employment accounts for about half the rise in GDP per person recorded in the 1990s.

The other half comes from productivity growth, that is, the growth of GDP per worker. It is estimated that productivity growth averaged about 2.5 per cent per annum over the period. This is a respectable rate of productivity growth, but not 'miraculous'. The sober fact is that during the Celtic Tiger period there was no productivity revolution. The real 'miracle' was the extraordinary increase in the numbers at work.

The increase in employment was a transitional phenomenon that could not be sustained indefinitely. It is estimated that by 2000 the natural real growth rate had fallen to 5 per cent. This was primarily due to a decline in the growth of the labour supply.

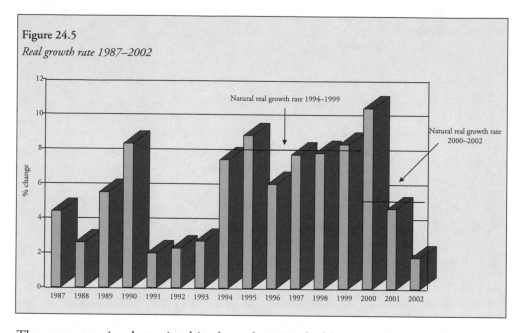

Figure 24.5
Real growth rate 1987–2002

The spare capacity that existed in the early 1990s had been used up and shortages of skilled labour increasingly hindered expansion.

Furthermore, the country's infrastructure, especially the urban road system, had become increasingly inadequate for the level of activity it now had to bear.

The level of house price inflation in the main urban centres was also of concern, not only from a social perspective, but also because it affects the cost of recruiting employees and the willingness of people to work and live in Ireland.

THE INFLATION PROBLEM

Figure 24.5 shows the real growth rate in Ireland from 1987 to 2002. A straight line is inserted at the 8 per cent mark to indicate the natural real growth rate between 1994 and 2000.

A second horizontal line is inserted to reflect the new natural real growth rate over the period 2000 to 2002. It is apparent that a large inflation gap emerged in 2000. As a consequence, inflation rose in 2000 from 1.6 per cent to 7 per cent, considerably above the EMU average (figure 24.6). Despite the slowdown in economic growth, the level of inflation has remained stubbornly high since 2000.

In 2001, the Irish economy was hit by a series of adverse economic shocks. These included the foot and mouth crisis in agriculture, downturn in the US economy, September 11 terrorist attack and a fall in tourism. The result was a fall in the real growth rate to 4.6 per cent in 2001 and (Department of Finance forecast) of 1.8 per cent in 2002. Since the 2002 growth rate is below the estimated natural growth rate, and given the upsurge in inflation, the era of the Celtic Tiger would seem to have ended in 2000.

Note:
Up to 2000, the Irish economy represented a clear-cut example of an over-heating economy within EMU. After nearly nine years of rapid economic expansion and a shift to full employment

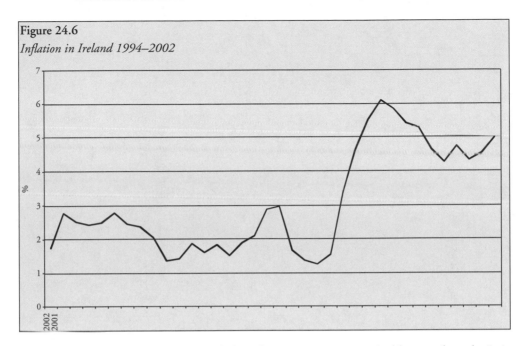

Figure 24.6

Inflation in Ireland 1994–2002

it was inevitable the economy would slow down to a more sustainable growth path. It is somewhat unfortunate that just as the evidence on the effectiveness of the key internal adjustment mechanisms (the 'wage effect' and 'PPP effect' discussed in chapters 14 and 20) was becoming increasingly apparent, adverse external shocks should emerge to partly bring about the transformation. These adverse shocks (September 11, foot and mouth disease etc.) are exogenous and not part of the internal adjustment process.

24.8 CONCLUSION

The main topics covered in this chapter included:

- The long-run economic performance of the economy as indicated by the trends in population and emigration
- Real convergence
- Factors that constrained the development of the economy prior to 1960, such as protectionism, state involvement in industry, reliance on the UK economy, and emigration as an escape hatch
- Factors that contributed to the improved economic performance after 1960, such as the increased openness of the economy, higher investment in education, and fiscal prudence
- Factors behind the boom years of the late 1980s and 1990s.

INDEX

accelerationist theory of inflation, 409–12
adaptive expectations, 395, 408–9
Aer Lingus, 469
aggregate demand (AD), 21–5, 28–30, 41, 142, 389
  Celtic Tiger and, 484
  interest rates and, 152–3
  natural real GNP and, 36–7
  Phillips curve and, 403
  stabilisation policy and, 69–70, 83–4, 390
  see also consumption function
aggregate price level, 8–9, 56
aggregate production function, 376–7
aggregate supply (AS), 21, 22, 25–9, 41, 142
  Celtic Tiger and, 483–4
  long-run aggregate supply (LAS), 36
  multiplier model and, 55–6
  natural real GNP and, 34–6
  Phillips curve and, 403
  stabilisation policy and, 69–70, 83–4
Agricultural Credit Bank, 140
Agriculture Credit Corporation, 468, 470
Ahern, Bertie, 92, 93, 239, 240, 251
Akerlof, George A., 47
Allais, Maurice, 46
Allied Irish Banks, 116, 138, 139, 475
Ando, Albert, 62
Anglo-Irish Free Trade Area Agreement (1965), 469
anti-inflationary credibility, 208
Antweiler, Werner, 309
arbitrage, 146, 147, 184, 201–2, 265, 372
Arrow, Kenneth, 45
automatic stabilisers, 74, 315–16

balance of payments, 15–17, 163–8
  capital and financial accounts, 166, 167, 459
  current account, 163–5, 458, 459–60
  errors and omissions, 166–7
  Eurozone, 163–8, 305–6
  external balance, 338–42
  in Ireland, 16–17, 163, 164–5, 459–60
  MAB theory, 215, 225–6
  multinationals and, 165–6
  real growth rate and, 179
  saving and investment, 457–60
    in Ireland, 459–60
  significance of, 167–8
  terms of trade, 454–5
  see also Mundell-Fleming model

Balassa, Bela, 196
Balassa-Samuelson effect, 185, 196–7
Bank of Credit and Commerce International (BCCI), 116
Bank of England, 119–20, 217, 236, 237
Bank of Ireland, 139, 475
  central bank development and, 133, 135, 136, 137, 138
bank rate, 119
banking, 108–12
  central bank role, 114–16, 118–20, 142
    exchange rates, 174–5
    independence and inflation, 287–9
    see also European Central Bank
  high-powered money, 117–18, 119, 212–13
  Ireland, 133–9
    central bank, 114, 120, 134, 135–9
    Currency Commission, 134, 135, 136–7
    financial sector, 139–41
    growth of banks, 138
    private banks, 135–6
    profits, 111, 112
  monetary base, 117–18, 119
  monetary policy, 118–20
    credit guidelines, 120
    discount rate, 119–20
    open markets, 119, 120
  money creation, 112–14
  money multiplier, 114, 117–18
  money supply, 108–10
  profits and bad debts, 111–12
  reserves, 111, 120, 166, 210–11
    fractional, 110–11, 113
  solvency and collapses, 116
  types of accounts, 108
Banking Commissions, 136–7, 245
Banque de France, 236–7
Barrington, Tom, 96
Barro, Robert, 43, 80, 396
Barro-Ricardo equivalence theorem, 80–1, 457
barter system, 104, 105
basis risk, 367
Becker, Gary, 46
bill discounting rate, 120
black economy, 3, 83, 438
Blair, Tony, 237
Blanchard, O., 478
Blaug, Mark, 384
Blythe, Ernest, 93
bonds, 70, 80, 115, 119, 145–7, 302–3
BP line, 339–42
Brandt, Willy, 278

Brennan, Joseph, 134, 136, 137, 138
Bretton Woods system, 215, 220–2, 278
Brumberg, Richard, 62
Bruton, John, 93, 98, 99
Bryan, William Jennings, 108
Buchanan, James, 46
budgets, 70–7
  balanced budget multiplier, 59
  expenditure, 70, 71–2
  full-employment budgets, 75, 76–7
  revenue, 70, 72–4
  surplus/deficit, 74–7
Building on Reality (1984), 90
building societies, 141
Bundesbank, 120, 211, 230, 234, 286, 287, 289, 292
Bush, George W., 24
business cycle, 5–6, 36, 37

call option, 359
Calmfors, Lars and Driffill, John, 91
Cantillon, Richard, 122
capital budget deficit, 70
capital flight, 83, 248, 479
capital formation
  fixed, 445
  gross domestic, 450–1
capital gains, 146
capital mobility, 341, 345, 346, 347–8
capital stock, 34, 63
Cassel, Gustav, 186–7
CBD (current budget deficit), 70
Celtic Tiger, 5, 464, 467, 478–87
  accounting for, 479–83
  AS-AD curves, 483–4
  inflation, 486–7
  natural real growth rate, 484–6
Central Bank of Ireland (CBI), 120, 169, 192, 211, 216
  background and history, 134, 135–9
  during currency crisis, 251, 252, 255
  ECB and, 114, 264
  EMS and, 243–4, 250, 258, 482
  forward market speculation and, 362
  governors, 138
Churchill, Winston, 218, 219
CIP (covered interest rate parity), 203, 359–61
  see also UIP
circular flow of income model, 443–6
classical dichotomy, 124
classical economics, 20, 21, 41–3, 156–9, 335, 384
  see also neoclassical model
Coarse, Ronald, 46

Cohesion Fund, 475, 477
Coinage Act (1926), 134
Colley, George, 93, 95
commercial banks, 140
Committee on Costs and
    Competitiveness, 89, 90
Common Agricultural Policy (CAP),
    222, 278, 475
competitiveness
    exchange rates and, 177, 189, 191,
        192–4
    national competitiveness indicators
        (NCI), 192–3
    real unit labour costs (RULC),
        193–4
compounding, 160
Consumer Price Index (CPI), 9, 10,
    11, 284
Consumers Association of Ireland, 269
consumption function, 48–53
    average propensity to consume and
        save, 59–61
    consumer behaviour theories, 61–5
        life-cycle theory, 61–4
        permanent-income hypothesis,
            64–5
    consumer expenditure
        income determination theory,
            22, 23, 24, 28
        interest rates and, 25, 152
        private, 444
    consumption smoothening, 62
    in Ireland, 48, 49, 52–3, 61
    IS-LM model and, 323–6
    saving and, 50, 51–2, 59–61
Continental Illinois Bank of Chicago,
    116
contraction in output, 5
Control of Manufactures Acts, 468
convergence, 196, 466–8
    in EMS, 230–3, 245–6
corporate profits tax, 74
corporation tax, 473, 474
corporatism, 91
counterfeiting, 106–7
covered interest parity (CIP), 359–61
CPI (Consumer Price Index), 9, 10,
    11, 284
credit guidelines, 120, 226
credit rationing, 226
credit unions, 141
crowding-out, 80, 158–60
    IS-LM model, 332–3
Currency Act (1927), 134
Currency Commission, 134, 135,
    136–7
currency crisis (1992), 180, 216–17,
    233–8
    causes, 233–6
    Irish pound and, 171, 204–5,
        251–7
currency holdings (CU), 306
currency peg, 208

current budget deficit (CBD), 70
Czech Republic, 343–6

Debreu, Gerard, 46
debt, national, 15, 167
    dynamics of debt accumulation,
        317, 320–2
    Irish, 71, 97
debt monetisation, 127
deferred payment, standard of, 105
deflation, 10, 412–16
    'gradualist/cold turkey', 414
    policy credibility, 415–16
    sacrifice ratio, 413–14, 415
    UK/US/Irish experiences, 415
deflationary demand-side shock,
    387–90
deflationary supply-side shock, 390–2
Delors, Jacques, 260, 279
Delors Report, 260, 262, 263, 279
demand for money, 144–9
demand-side policy, 29–30, 31, 81,
    392
    Celtic Tiger and, 484
demand-side shock, 29–30, 38–9, 41,
    274–5
    deflationary, 387–90
Denmark, Maastricht Treaty
    referendum, 235
deposit facility, 301
depreciation, 450
depression, 5, 41, 398
    Great Depression (1920s–30s),
        20–1, 41, 77, 219
deregulation, 42
devaluation and trade balance, 349,
    352
Development Plan (2000–06), 408
discount rate, 119–20
discounting, 160–1
disinflation, 388, 398, 412–16
disposable income, 48–53
    consumption and saving, 50,
        51–2, 59–65
    in Ireland, 52, 61
    national, 452–6
dissaving, 62, 457
dollar, 308, 313
    euro exchange rate, 171, 308–10
    exchange standard, 220, 221–2
dollarisation, 13, 126, 308
Domingo Solans, Eugenio, 284
Dornbusch, Rudiger, 250–1, 294
Doyle, Maurice, 138, 251, 260
drachma, 269
Duisenberg, Wim, 283, 284, 289, 310
Dukes, Alan, 93, 99

EBR (exchequer borrowing
    requirement), 70
    Irish figures, 96, 99, 101
ECB see European Central Bank
econometric theory, 19–20

Economic and Social Research
    Institute (ESRI), 408
economic performance see measuring
    economic performance
Economic Planning and Development,
    Dept of, 89
economic plans, 86–92
economic shocks see shocks, economic
economies of scale, 266
Economist, The, 479, 480
ECU (European Currency Unit),
    227–30
effective exchange rate index, 181–3
efficiency wage hypothesis, 436
EIBOR (Eurozone inter-bank interest
    rate) contract, 371
elections, political, 79
Electricity Supply Board, 468
EMCF (European Monetary Co-
    operation Fund), 230, 239
EMI (European Monetary Institute),
    263, 279, 282
emigration, 31, 37, 87, 272, 425, 427,
    428, 430
    net migration, 462–3, 465
    population and Irish economy,
        462–5, 470–1
employment
    definition, 421
    dependency ratio, 424–5
    trends, 425–7
    see also labour market;
        unemployment
EMS see European Monetary System
EONIA (Euro overnight index average),
    298–9, 301, 302–3, 304–5
equation of exchange, 123
ERM (exchange rate mechanism), 170,
    210, 211, 227, 230, 236–8, 258
    Ireland and, 245–50, 258
ERSI (Economic and Social Research
    Institute), 408
ESCB (European System of Central
    Banks), 282, 283, 285
EU see European Union
EURIBOR (Euro inter-bank offer
    rates), 298–9, 303, 305
euro, 139, 170–4, 262, 263
    ECU as forerunner of, 230
    as a global currency, 308–10
    see European Monetary Union
European Central Bank (ECB),
    282–96
    balance sheet, 300, 304, 312
    design of, 282–4
        Executive Board, 283–4
        Governing Council, 139, 264
        parallels with Federal Reserve
            System, 285, 286
    independence of, 286–90
        related to inflation, 287–9
    reserves, 110, 111, 115, 166, 211,
        301–2, 304, 305–6, 311

role of, 80, 114–15, 208, 262
  responsibilities, 284
  speculation and disclosure, 291–2
European Monetary Co-operation
  Fund (EMCF), 230, 239
European Monetary Institute (EMI),
  263, 279, 282
European Monetary System (EMS),
  227–40
  adjustment to, 231–2, 233, 244–5
  credibility, 232–3, 244–5, 248
  currency crisis (1992), 180,
    216–17, 233–8
    causes, 233–6
    Irish pound and, 171, 204–5,
      251–7
  ECU, 227–30
  EMCF, 230, 239
  ERM, 170, 210, 211, 227, 230,
    236–8, 258
    Ireland and, 245–50, 258
  flexibility in, 230
  history of, 227, 233–8, 239–40
  inflation convergence, 230–3,
    245–6
  Ireland see European Monetary
    System and Ireland
  speculation and, 180, 216–17
  unco-ordinated policies, 216
European Monetary System and
  Ireland, 243–59
  adjustment and credibility, 244–5,
    250
  background, 170, 241–3
  currency crisis, 171, 204–5, 251–7
    devaluation, 252–6
    policy following, 258–9
    PPP theory and, 257
  expectations and outcomes, 206,
    248–51
    fiscal and monetary policy,
      248–50, 482
  Irish experience, 245–8
    capital flight, 248
    inflation, 245–6
    interest rates, 204, 246, 247
    yield curve, 246–8
  rationale for joining, 206, 243–4
  wage adjustments, 244–5, 250,
    256–7
European Monetary Union (EMU),
  260–81
  background to, 230, 238, 260–3
  balance of payments, 163–8,
    305–6
  central bank role see European
    Central Bank
  chronology, 278–80
  cohesion fund, 261
  concept of, 261–2
  constraints on adjustment, 270–3
    asymmetric shocks, 270
    exchange rate option, 270–1

fiscal federalism, 272
labour mobility, 272–3
monetary and fiscal policy,
  271
countries comprising, 2, 170–1
criteria for joining, 263, 267,
  280–1, 482
euro, 139, 170–4, 262, 263
  ECU as forerunner of, 230
  as a global currency, 308–10
  exchange rate, 171–4, 265–6,
    270–1, 308–13
    fixed system concerns, 313
    sterilisation, 311–12
GDP statistics, 2, 15–16
inflation, 17, 130, 234, 266–8,
  284–6, 296
  central bank independence,
    287–90
  inflation targeting, 292–5
  Phillips curve, 404–6, 416–20
  quantity theory, 290–2, 294–5
  unemployment and, 318, 319
interest rates, 268–9, 298–308
  bonds and securities, 302–3
  compulsory deposits, 301–2
  determination, 304
  government borrowing, 307–8
  MRO interest rate, 120
  open-market operations,
    300–1
Ireland and, 17, 80, 101, 139,
  152, 482, 484
  benefits, 264–9
  costs, 269–73
monetary policy, 271, 290–6
  inflation targeting, 292–5
  quantity theory, 290–2, 294–5
money multiplier, 118, 298
money supply, 108–10, 118–19,
  124, 290–2, 295–6, 297–8
Okun's law coefficients, 33–4
Phillips curve evidence, 404–6,
  416–20
PPP theory and, 270, 274–5
price inequalities, 186, 187, 188
prospects for, 264
scale economies, 266
shocks, adjusting to, 270, 273–7
  Keynes effect, 276–7
Stability Pact, 77, 80, 160, 238,
  272, 314–19
  Ireland and, 317–18
  penalties and let-outs, 314–16
  policy implications, 318–19
TWERI, 181–3
unemployment, 7, 37, 318, 319,
  416–20
European Recovery Programme, 475
European snake, 222–3, 279
European Social Fund, 475, 477
European System of Central Banks
  (ESCB), 282, 283, 285

European Union (EU)
  chronology, 278–80
  convergence, 466–7
  Council of Ministers, 312–13
  grants, 459, 475–7
Eurozone see European Monetary
  Union
excess returns, 246
exchange rate mechanism (ERM), 170,
  210, 211, 227, 230, 236–8, 258
  Ireland and, 245–50, 258
exchange rates, 163–83
  balance of payments and, 163–8,
    179
  bid and offer rates, 169, 374
  currency appreciation/depreciation,
    168–9, 175
  determination, 173–5, 304
  EMU, 171–4, 265–6, 270–1,
    308–13
    fixed system concerns, 313
    sterilisation, 311–12
  ERM see Exchange Rate
    Mechanism
  euro, 171–4, 308–10
  factors influencing, 177–9
  fixed see fixed exchange rate
    systems
  floating, 174–5, 177, 180, 210,
    265
    advantages/disadvantages,
      223–5
    Mundell-Fleming model, 342,
      346–9
  foreign exchange market, 168–71
    equilibrium, 173, 174, 175–7
  forward exchange rates, 356–9,
    363
  importance of, 172–3
  inflation and, 126, 177, 179
  Ireland, 169–72, 185, 189–92,
    482
    ECU exchange rate, 229
    sterling link, 132, 170, 171,
      190, 203, 241–2, 243,
      245
    UIP, 203–6
    see also European Monetary
      System and Ireland
  J curve, 175–7
  net exports and, 153
  PPP see purchasing power parity
  real exchange rate, 189–92
  speculation, 179–81, 202, 216–17
    see also hedging
  supply and demand shifts, 177,
    178
  trade-weighted exchange rate index
    (TWERI), 181–3, 192
  UIP, 200–6
exchequer borrowing requirement
  (EBR), 70
  Irish figures, 96, 99, 101

excise duties, 72, 74, 185
expansion in output, 5
expansionary fiscal contraction (EFC),
    100
expenditure approach, 447–8, 449–52,
    453
exports
    as GDP percentage
        Eurozone statistics, 15–16
    Irish, 165, 470, 482
    net exports, 23, 28, 53, 153, 446
    terms of trade, 454–5, 460–1
    see also balance of payment

factor cost, 449, 450, 452
factors of production, 31, 443
Fama, E.F., 364
FDI (foreign direct investment), 426,
    472–5, 482, 483, 484
Federal Reserve Board (Fed), 119, 120,
    285, 412, 415
Federal Reserve System, 219, 234,
    285, 286
federalism, fiscal, 272
FEOGA (Fund European Orientation
    Guidance Agriculture), 475, 477
fiat money, 106
financial sector in Ireland, 139–41
First Programme for Economic
    Expansion, 87–8, 89, 90
fiscal deficit, 15
fiscal federalism, 272
fiscal policy, 68–85
    assessing the stance of, 74–7
    Barro-Ricardo equivalence
        theorem, 80–1, 457
    budgets, 70–7
        balanced budget multiplier, 59
        expenditure, 70, 71–2
        full-employment budgets, 75,
            76–7
        revenue, 70, 72–4
        surplus/deficit, 74–7
    contractionary, 24
    crowding-out, 80, 158–60
        IS-LM model, 332–3
    deflationary, 30, 128, 156, 412–16
    discretionary, 24, 70, 76, 125
    expansionary, 24, 30, 39–40, 78,
        84, 158, 159, 344, 347
        Keynesian model, 384–6
    interventionist, 41
    IS-LM model, 332–6
    Keynesian/classical debate, 156–9
    lags, 78, 128, 156
    laissez-faire, 42
    monetary financing, 159–60
    Mundell-Fleming model, 349–53
    policy dilemma, 30, 349
    politics and, 79–80, 289, 403
    stabilisation policy, 68–70, 390,
        398
        automatic stabilisers, 74

problems in implementing,
    77–82
supply-side shocks, 81
taxation and supply-side, 82–4
    work incentives, 83
see also Ireland, economy and fiscal
    policy
Fisher, Irving, 150, 157
Fisher equation, 150–1, 154, 179,
    207, 208, 290, 292
Fitzgerald, J., 484
fixed capital formation, 445
fixed exchange rate systems, 175,
    210–26
    Bretton Woods system, 215,
        220–2
    compared to floating, 223–5
    co-ordination, 215–16, 223
    EMU and, 313
    European snake, 222–3
    gold standard, 187, 188, 217–19,
        220
    how it works, 210–12
    MAB theory, 215, 225–6
    monetary exchange mechanism,
        212–14
    Mundell-Fleming model, 342,
        343–6, 348–9
    PPP and, 198–200
    problems facing, 215–17
    speculation, 216–17
    sterilisation, 214–15, 311–12, 344
Fleming, John, 338
Fogel, Robert, 46
Foras Tionscal, An, 472
foreign currency accounts, 355–6
foreign currency swaps, 370
foreign direct investment (FDI), 426,
    472–5, 482, 483, 484
foreign exchange market, 168–71
    equilibrium, 173, 174, 175–7
    forward market, 180, 364–6
    see also exchange rates
forward currency options contract,
    358–9
forward exchange contracts, 356–9,
    374
forward exchange rates, 356–9, 363
forward market efficiency, 180, 364–6
    risk premium, 366
forward rate agreement (FRA),
    369–70, 374
fractional reserve banking, 110–11,
    113
frictional unemployment, 8, 432
Friedman, Milton, 43, 45, 64–5, 125,
    128, 156, 157, 284
    Phillips curve critique, 404,
        406–9, 411
Frisch, Ragnar, 45
full-employment budgets, 75, 76–7
Fullerton, M., 260
futures contracts, 370–4

G7, 223
gap risk, 367
GDP (Gross Domestic Product), 1–4
    debt accumulation dynamics,
        320–2
    differentiated from GNP, 3–4
    in Eurozone, 2
    exports as GDP percentage,
        15–16, 164
    GNDI and, 452–3, 456, 458
    gross domestic capital formation,
        450–1
    in Ireland, 1, 2, 315, 451–4, 485
        expenditure breakdown, 447–8
        percentage of UK level, 467
        measuring output, 444, 447–8,
            450
    net domestic product (NDP), 449,
        450–1
    price deflator, 10
    problems in estimating, 3
Geary, R.C., 461
general efficiency hypothesis, 366
general government surplus, 70
Germany
    inflation and unemployment,
        418–20
    unification, 233–5, 236
Giavazzi, F. and Pagano, M., 100
Giscard D'Estaing, Valéry, 227, 239
GMF (government monetary
    financing), 159
GNDI (Gross National Disposable
    Income), 452–3, 456, 458
GNP (Gross National Product), 3–6
    aggregate supply and demand, 22,
        23–5, 28, 29
    balance of payments and, 17, 459
    budgets and, 75–7
    differentiated from GDP, 3–4
    economic shocks and, 38–41
    imports and, 58
    interest rates and, 142–3
    Ireland, 5–6, 14, 451–2, 459, 485
    multiplier model and, 53–9
    natural real GNP, 34, 485
        and aggregate demand, 36–7
        and aggregate supply, 34–6
        growth rate, 68, 69
        unemployment and, 36–7
    nominal GNP, 4
        price level and, 123–4, 128
    potential/full-employment GNP,
        34
    production function, 376–7
    real GNP, 4
        unemployment and, 31–4
gold standard, 187, 188, 217–19, 220
Goodhart's law, 118
government consumption expenditure,
    445–6
Grauwe, Paul de, 317
Greenspan, Alan, 285

Gresham's law, 107–8, 134
gross domestic capital formation, 450–1
Gross Domestic Product *see* GDP
Gross National Disposable Income (GNDI), 452–3, 456, 458
Gross National Product *see* GNP
growth, real, 4, 68–9, 453–4
    balance of payments and, 179
    inflation and, 4–5
    in Ireland, 5–6, 454, 484–6
Gulf War (1991), 180–1

Haavelmo, Trygve, 46
Hamalainen, Sirkka, 284
Harmonised Index of Consumer Prices (HICP), 9
Harsanyi, John, 47
Heath, Ted, 403
Heckman, James J., 47
hedging, 172, 265, 354–75
    external techniques, 356–9
    foreign currency swaps, 370
    forward currency options contract, 358–9
    forward exchange contracts, 356–9, 374
    forward market efficiency, 364–6
        expected value, 365
        risk premium, 366
    forward rate agreement (FRA), 369–70, 374
    futures contracts, 370–4
        variation margin, 373–4
    interest rate anticipation, 367–8
    interest rate parity theory, 359–61
    interest rate risk, 367–75
    internal techniques, 354–6
    revenue loss from, 358
    unbiased predictor hypothesis (UPH), 361–4
        market efficiency and, 365–6
Hibernian Bank, 138
Hicks, John, 23, 45, 323
HICP (Harmonised Index of Consumer Prices), 284
high-powered money, 117–18, 119, 212–13, 297–8, 307
hire-purchase finance companies, 141
Honohan, Patrick, 106, 255, 478
Household Budget Survey, 9
Hume, David, 41, 122
hyperinflation, 13, 125–8, 198, 411
    causes of, 126–8
hysteresis, 407

IDA (Industrial Development Authority), 472, 475
IE (interest-sensitive expenditure), 142, 153, 154, 156, 157, 158–9, 324
IFOX (Irish Futures/Options Exchange), 371

IMF (International Monetary Fund), 127, 193
    function of, 220
    SDRs (special drawing rights), 105, 210–11
IMM (International Money Market), 370–1
immigration, 31, 423, 425, 465, 482, 485
imports
    GNP and, 58
    in Ireland, 165
    multiplier model and, 55, 58, 66–7
    terms of trade, 454–5, 460–1
    see also balance of payment
income
    approach, 448–52
    circular flow of income model, 443–6
    see also disposable income; measuring economic performance
income determination theory, 19–41
    aggregate demand (AD), 21–5, 28–30, 36–7, 41
    aggregate supply (AS), 21, 22, 25–9, 34–6, 41
    economic shocks, 24, 25, 37–41, 42
        adjusting to, 38–41
        demand-side, 29–30, 38–9, 41
        supply-side, 27, 31, 40–1
    equilibrium in goods and services, 21–2, 28–9, 42
        stock changes, 22, 44
    general theory, 20–1
    macroeconomic models, 19–20
    natural real GNP
        and aggregate demand, 36–7
        and aggregate supply, 34–6
    real GNP and unemployment, 31–4
        Eurozone coefficients, 33–4
        Okun's law, 32–4
indexation, 105
individualisation policy, 101, 102
industrial banks, 140
Industrial Credit Corporation, 140, 470
Industrial Development Authority (IDA), 472, 475
inflation, 8–14
    accelerating, 406
    accelerationist theory, 409–12
    band, 285
    bias and time inconsistency, 288–9
    convergence in EMS, 230–3
    effects of, 10–14, 126, 177, 179
        income distribution, 14
        international competitiveness, 13
        menu and shoe leather costs, 13–14

transparency/confusion, 13
    value of money, 10–12, 14, 105, 116
    wages, 12
    in Eurozone, 17, 130, 234, 266–8, 284–6, 296
        central bank independence, 287–90
        inflation targeting, 292–5
        Phillips curve, 404–6, 416–20
        quantity theory, 290–2, 294–5
    exchange rates and, 126, 177, 179
    gap, 36, 68
    hyperinflation, 13, 125–8, 198, 411
        causes of, 126–8
    interest rates and, 12, 13, 14
    in Ireland, 11, 129–31, 243, 245–6, 482
        Celtic Tiger period, 486–7
        Phillips curve, 404–5, 415, 418–20
    monetary policy and, 118–19, 124–5
    price indexes, 9–10, 11, 284–5
    quantity theory, 122–5, 128, 129, 156, 213–14
        in Eurozone, 290–2, 294–5
    rate of, 10
    real growth and, 4–5
    real wages and, 42
    recession, inflationary, 412–13
    tax, 115, 116
    unemployment and, 318, 319 *see also* Phillips curve
    see also purchasing power parity
initial margin, 373–4
Insurance Corporation of Ireland (ICI), 116
interest rates
    aggregate demand and, 152–3
    consumer expenditure, 25, 152
    demand for money and, 144–50
        interest elasticity, 157, 159
    in Eurozone, 268–9, 298–308
        bonds and securities, 302–3
        compulsory deposits, 301–2
        determination, 304
        government borrowing, 307–8
        MRO interest rate, 120
        open-market operations, 300–1
    exchange rate and, 177–9
    inflation and, 12, 13, 14
    interest rate parity theory, 359–61
    interest-sensitive expenditure, 142, 153, 154, 156, 157, 158–9, 324
    investment and, 152–3, 156, 160–2
    in Ireland, 111, 112, 246, 247, 482
        industrial banks, 140

interest rates (*cont.*)
  UIP, 203–6
  Keynesian/classical debate, 156–9
  Keynes's 'normal' rate, 147–8
  monetary policy, 118–20, 142–4
    in closed economy, 153–6
    deflationary, 156
  MRO rate, 120
  net exports, 153
  nominal and real, 142, 150–1,
    154–5, 156
  UIP (uncovered interest rate
    parity), 200–6
  see also hedging; purchasing power
    parity
International Financial Services Centre
  (IFSC), 138
International Labour Office (ILO),
  421, 422
International Monetary Fund (IMF),
  127, 193
  function of, 220
  SDRs (special drawing rights),
    105, 210–11
International Money Market (IMM),
  370–1
international substitution effect, 25
internet shopping, 265
inter-temporal substitution, 25
investment, 152–3, 156
  circular flow of income model, 445
  net present value (NPV), 160–2
  saving and balance of payments,
    457–60
    in Ireland, 459–60
  UIP and, 200–6
Ireland, economy and fiscal policy,
  86–103, 462–87
  (1922–60), 86–8, 93, 203, 463–4,
    467, 468–71
  (1961–94), 88–91, 93–100, 464,
    467, 471–8
  (1994–2002), 91–2, 100–2,
    204–5, 258, 464, 467,
    478–87
    accounting for Celtic Tiger,
      479–83
    AS-AD curves, 483–4
    inflation, 486–7
    natural real growth rate, 484–6
  assistance and EU grants, 475–7,
    483
  budgets, 70–4, 95
  central bank role, 80, 114
  currency crisis, 171, 204–5, 251–7
  European Monetary Union, 17,
    80, 101, 139, 152, 482, 484
    benefits, 264–9
    costs, 269–73
  exchequer borrowing requirement,
    96, 99, 101
  finance ministers, 93
  free trade, 469, 471

industrial policy, 471–5, 483
investment, 470
  in education, 477–8, 483, 484
  foreign (FDI), 472–5, 482,
    483
monetary financing, 160
multinationals, 472–5
national debt, 97
population and emigration, 462–5,
  470–1
protectionism, 88, 463, 468–9
real convergence, 466–8
stabilisation policy experience, 78,
  92–102
standard of living, 467
state companies, 468, 469–70
supply-side policy, 30–1, 102
targets and outcomes, 86, 87
taxation, 72–4, 83, 100, 101,
  479–81, 483–4
wage agreements, 90–1, 101, 481,
  483
world economy and, 481–2, 484
see also European Monetary System
  and Ireland
Irish Banks' Standing Committee
  (IBSC), 112
Irish Congress of Trade Unions, 254
Irish Currency Report (1804), 133–4
Irish Futures/Options Exchange
  (IFOX), 371
Irish Life Assurance Company, 470
Irish Steel, 470
Irish Sugar Company, 470
Irish Trust Bank, 116
IS-LM model, 323–37
  crowding-out, 332–3
    implications for EMU, 333
  debate on, 335
  external balance and, 338–42
  fiscal/monetary policy, 333–6
  goods market and IS curve, 323–6,
    329–32
  labour market and, 382–3, 384,
    392–3, 396
  money market and LM curve,
    326–32
  Phillips machine, 331–2
Issing, Otmar, 284

J curve, 175–7
Jabobsson, Per, 136
Japan, saving and investment, 459
Jenkins, Roy, 227

Kahneman, Daniel, 47
Kaldor, N., 128
Kantorovich, Leonid, 45
Kearns, Adrian, 251
Kemmy, Jim, 98
Keynes, John Maynard, 20, 21, 23, 42,
  443
  Bretton Woods system, 220

Currency Commission and, 136–7
  General Theory, 20, 21, 49, 60,
    144, 323, 335, 384, 389
  on German hyperinflation, 126
  on gold standard, 219
  on Lenin debauching currency,
    107
Keynesian economics, 41
  consumption function, 49, 60,
    63–4
  debate with classical school, 41–3,
    156–9, 335
  Keynes effect, 276–7, 389, 392
  Keynesian model and labour
    market, 384–92
  liquidity preference theory, 144–9
  'normal' rate of interest, 147–8
  see also income determination
    theory; multiplier model;
    quantity theory of money
Klein, Lawrence, 20, 46
Kohl, Helmut, 264
Koopmans, Tjalling, 45
Kuznets, Simon, 45, 61, 63–4, 65

Labour Force Survey (LFS), 422
labour market, 376–99
  aggregate production function,
    376–7
  deflationary demand-side shock,
    387–90
    protracted recession, 388
  deflationary supply-side shock,
    390–2
  demand for labour, 377–80
  equilibrium in, 381–2
  general model, 382–4
  Keynesian model, 384–92
    long-run response, 386
    money illusion, 384–6, 396,
      434
  labour force, 6, 31, 421–5
    dependency ratio, 424–5
    employment trends, 425–7
    in Ireland, 34, 37, 272, 422–4
    participation rate (LFPR),
      423–4, 485
  mobility, 272–3, 437
  monetarist model, 392–5
    neutrality of money, 394
    policy implications, 394–5
  neoclassical model, 395–8
    rational expectations, 395–7,
      409
    unanticipated inflation, 397–8
  rigidity, 395, 436–9
  supply of labour, 380–1
  see also unemployment
labour productivity, 27, 193
Laffer, Arthur, 82
Laffer curve, 82–3, 84
Lafontaine, Oskar, 289
lags, and fiscal policy, 78, 128, 156

Lamont, Norman, 236
law of one price, 184–6
Lawson, Nigel, 235
leading and lagging, 181, 356
Lee, J.J., 464
legal tender, 106
Lenin, 107
Leontief, Wassily, 45
Lewis, Arthur, 45
LFPR (labour force participation rate), 423–4, 485
life-cycle theory of consumption, 61–4
liquid assets, 144
liquidity preference, theory of, 144–9
liquidity shortage, 303
liquidity trap, 150, 157, 335
Live Register, 6
living standards, 1–6, 10, 453, 456, 467
Lombard rate, 120
London International Financial Futures Exchange (LIFFE), 370
Lucas, Robert, 43, 47, 395, 398, 415

Maastricht Treaty (1992), 235, 238, 263, 266, 279, 280, 282, 284, 286, 307, 308, 312
MAB theory, 215, 225–6
MacBride, Seán, 86
McCreevy, Charlie, 78, 93, 101, 102
McFadden, Daniel L., 47
McKinnon, Ronald, 310
McNeely, Dr, 137
macroeconomics
    business cycle, 5–6
    constraints, 14–17
        balance of payments, 15–17
        fiscal deficit, 15
    goals and policy, 1, 14, 17
    Keynesian/classical debate, 41–3
    models, 19–20
MacSharry, Ray, 93, 99
main refinancing interest rate (MRIR), 300, 302–3
Major, John, 236
Malthus, Thomas, 41
marginal efficiency of investment (MEI), 324
marginal lending facility, 301
marginal product of labour (MPN), 376–7, 378–9
marginal propensity to import (MPM), 341, 349, 350
marginal revenue product (MRP), 379
market efficiency, 364–6
    risk premium, 366
market prices and factor cost, 450
marking-to-market, 373–4
Markowitz, Harry, 46
Marshall Plan, 86, 475
Marx, Karl, 384, 436
Meade, James, 45, 332
mean reversion, 190

measuring economic performance, 443–61
    circular flow of income model, 443–6
    depreciation, 450
    disposable national income, 452–6
    expenditure approach, 447–8, 449–52, 453–4
    income approach, 448–52
    inflation adjustment, 453–4
    market prices and factor cost, 450
    national income by category, 449
    national output, 447–9
    net factor income from the rest of the world, 449, 451–2
    output approach, 448, 453–4
    population growth adjustment, 455–6
    saving, investment and balance of payments, 457–60
        in Ireland, 459–60
    saving, public and private, 456–7
    terms of trade, 454–5, 460–1
Meenan, James, 137
Merchant Banking, 116
merchant banks, 140
Merton, Robert, 47
microeconomics, 8
migration, net, 462–3, 465
Mill, John Stuart, 41
Miller, Merton, 46
minimum lending rate, 119
Mirrlees, James, 47
Mitterrand, François, 233, 264
Modigliani, Franco, 46, 61–2
monetarism, 43, 156–9, 389, 392–5
    model, 392–4
        neutrality of money, 394
        policy implications, 394–5
    quantity theory and, 123, 125, 128
monetary base, 117–18, 119, 297
monetary exchange mechanism, 212–14
monetary neutrality, 124
monetary policy, 142–4
    closed economy, 153–6
    deflationary, 156
    in EMU, 271, 290–6
        inflation targeting, 292–5
        quantity theory, 290–2, 294–5
    expansionary, 345, 348, 397
    financing, 159–60
    IS-LM model, 333–6
    Keynesian/classical debate, 156–9
    see also quantity theory of money
money, 104–8
    circularity in its acceptance, 106–7
    counterfeiting, 106–7
    functions of, 104–5
    Gresham's law, 107–8, 134
    Irish currency, history of, 131–5
    types of, 105–8

commodity money, 106
token money, 106
value during inflation, 10–12, 14, 105
see also banking; quantity theory of money
money illusion, 384–6, 396, 434
money market and interest rates, 142–62
    aggregate demand and, 152–3
    consumer expenditure, 152
    crowding-out, 80, 158–60
        IS-LM model, 332–3
    demand for money, 144–50
        bond market, 145–7
        Keynes's 'normal' rate of interest, 147–8
        interest elasticity, 157, 159
        speculative, 145–7, 148–9
        transaction and precautionary motives, 145, 148–9
    equilibrium, 149–50
    investment, 152–3, 156, 160–2
    IS-LM model, 326–33
    liquidity preference theory, 144–9
    monetary policy, 142–4
        closed economy, 153–6
        deflationary, 156
        financing, 159–60
        Keynesian/classical debate, 156–9
    net exports, 153
    nominal and real interest rates, 142, 150–1, 154–5, 156
Money Market Committee, 169
money multiplier, 114, 117–18, 213, 298
money supply, 108–10, 288
    in EMU, 108–10, 118–19, 124, 290–2, 295–6, 297–8
    and Irish inflation, 129–31
    quantity theory, 119, 122–5, 128, 129, 156, 213–14
moral hazards, 112
MPM (marginal propensity to import), 341, 349, 350
MPN (marginal product of labour), 376–7, 378–9
MRIR (main refinancing interest rate), 300, 302–3
MRO interest rate, 120
MRP (marginal revenue product), 379
multinationals (MNCs), 3, 165–6, 472–5
multiplier model, 53–9
    AS curve and, 55–6
    balanced budget multiplier, 59
    calculating formula, 56–7
    generalising, 57–8
    imports and, 55, 58, 66–7
    in Ireland, 59
    savings and, 55, 66–7
    taxes and, 55, 58, 66–7

Mundell, Robert, 47, 102, 262, 338
Mundell-Fleming model, 338–53
    capital mobility, 341, 345, 346,
        347–8
    economic policy, output and trade
        account, 349–53
        devaluation and trade balance,
          349
        trade account, 350–1
    fixed exchange rates, 342, 343–6,
        348–9
        monetary policy, 345–6
    floating exchange rates, 346–9
        monetary policy, 348
    internal and external balance,
        338–42
Munster and Leinster Bank, 138
Murphy, Anthony, 432
Murray, Charles, 138, 170, 243
Myers, Kevin, 96
Myrdal, Gunnar, 45

NAIRU (non-accelerating inflation
    rate of unemployment), 406
Nash, John, 47
National Bank, 138
national competitiveness indicators
    (NCI), 192–3
National Development (1977–80), 89
National Development Plan (1994–99),
    91
National Development Plan (2000–06),
    72, 91–2
National Economic and Social Council
    (NESC), 408
national income *see* measuring
    economic performance
National Income and Expenditure
    (NIE) accounts, 445, 446, 449
National Industrial Economic Council,
    408
National Irish Bank, 139
National Planning Board, 90
National Wage Agreements (NWAs),
    481, 484
NCI (national competitiveness
    indicators), 192–3
NDP (net domestic product), 449,
    450–1
Neary, Peter J., 314
neoclassical model, 395–8
    neoclassical synthesis, 43
    rational expectations, 395–7, 409
    unanticipated inflation, 397–8
NESC (National Economic and Social
    Council), 408
net domestic product (NDP), 449,
    450–1
net factor income, 3
    from the rest of the world, 449,
        451–2
net factor payments to the rest of the
    world, 451

net migration, 462–3, 465
net national product (NNP), 451, 452
net present value (NPV), 160–2
New York Futures Exchange, 370
Nítrigin Éireann, 470
Nixon, Richard, 222
NNP (net national product), 451, 452
Nobel Prize winners, 45–7
North, Douglass, 46
Noyer, Christian, 284
NPV (net present value), 160–2

O'Brien, George, 136
O'Brien, Ken, 170
O'Connell, Maurice, 251
OECD (Organisation for Economic
    Co-Operation and
    Development), 18
Ó Gráda, Cormac, 135, 137, 464
Ohlin, Bertil, 45
oil price increases, 40–1, 89, 94, 95,
    96, 222, 390–1
Okun, Arthur, 32
Okun's law, 32–4, 429–30
    Eurozone coefficients, 33–4
OPEC (Organisation of Petroleum
    Exporting Countries), 40–1, 94,
    95, 222
open economies, 15–16, 119, 120,
    129
    open economy monetary model,
        206–8, 273
        currency peg, 208
    see also purchasing power parity
open-market operations, 300–1
opportunity cost, 148, 153
Optimum Currency Area (OCA)
    theory, 262–3
output
    approach, 448, 453
    contraction/expansion in, 5
    gap, 36, 41, 69, 94
    measuring, 447–9
overnight deposits, 109

Padoa-Schioppa, Tommaso, 284
Papademos, G., 283
Parker-Willis Commission, 134
participating forward contract, 359
Partnership 2000, 91, 434, 435
Pearse, Padraic, 464
performance *see* measuring economic
    performance
permanent-income hypothesis, 64–5
perpetuity, 146
peso problem, 205–6, 224–5
Phelps, Edmund, 404, 406–9
Phillips, A.W.H., 331, 400, 402, 411
Phillips curve, 400–20
    accelerationist theory of inflation,
        409–12
    augmented, 408–9
        Eurozone evidence, 416–20

deflation, 412–16
    'gradualist/cold turkey', 414
    policy credibility, 415–16
    sacrifice ratio, 413–14, 415
    UK/US/Irish experiences, 415
original, 400–6
    AD-AS model and, 403
    breakdown of, 403–4
    Eurozone evidence, 404–6
    policy implications, 402–3
revised, 406–9
    expectations-augmented
        Phillips curve, 408–9
    natural rate of unemployment,
        406, 407–8
    role of expectations, 406–7
Phillips machine, 331–2
Physiocrat movement, 41–2
Pigou, Arthur, 25
Pigou effect, 25
Ponzi, Charles, 168
population
    growth, 455–6
    Irish economy and, 462–5, 470–1
post office savings bank, 140
poverty trap, 440
PPP *see* purchasing power parity
price indexes, 9–10, 11, 192, 284–5
price level
    aggregate, 8–9, 56
    aggregate demand and supply,
        23–9
    quantity theory of money, 122–5,
        156, 213–14, 290–2, 294–5
price stability in Eurozone, 284–6
private consumer expenditure, 444
Private Motorists Protection Assn, 116
production, factors of, 31, 443–4
production function, 376–7, 382, 444
productivity, 27, 193
profit, 26
profit-maximising rule, 377–8
*Programme for Competitiveness and
    Work*, 91, 408, 434, 435
*Programme for Economic and Social
    Progress (PESP)*, 91, 257, 408,
    434, 435
Programme for National Recovery, 90–1,
    408, 434, 435
Programme for Prosperity and Fairness,
    30–1, 91, 101, 434, 435
Proposals for Plan 1984–87, 90
protectionism, 88, 463, 468–9
Provincial Bank, 138
public capital programmes, 86, 91, 92,
    93
Public Sector Benchmarking Body,
    481
purchasing power parity (PPP),
    184–200, 231
    Balassa-Samuelson effect, 185,
        196–7
    convergence effect, 196

currency crisis and, 257
Eurozone, 186, 187, 188, 198,
    270, 274–5
factors impeding
    absolute PPP, 185–6
    relative PPP, 196–7
fixed exchange rates and, 198–200
flexible exchange rates and, 198
graphical representation, 194–5
Ireland, 189–90, 196–7
labour market and, 383, 386, 388,
    392, 394, 396
law of one price, 184–6
open economy monetary model,
    206–8
    currency peg, 208
    PPP exchange rate, 186–9
    real exchange rate, 189–92
    relative PPP, 195–7
sterling link and, 241–2, 243
traded and non-traded goods, 186,
    196
put option, 359

quantity theory of money, 119, 122–5,
    129, 144, 156, 213–14
    EMU policy, 290–2, 294–5
    Keynesian perspective, 128, 131
*Quarterly National Household Survey
    (QNHS)*, 6, 422
Quesnay, François, 41, 443
quotas, 185

rates, abolition of, 74, 95
rational expectations, 43, 395–7, 409
raw materials, 35
Reagan, Ronald, 31
real balance effect, 25
real unit labour costs (RULC), 193–4
recession, 5, 6, 36, 41, 74, 77, 78,
    456, 464
    inflationary, 412–13
    protracted, 388
Regional Development Fund, 475,
    477
replacement ratio, 439
repurchase agreement (REPO), 300
residential property tax, 74
Ricardo, David, 41, 80
risk premium, 366
Rose, Andrew, 266
Royal Bank of Ireland, 138
RTGS (real-time gross settlement),
    299
RULC (real unit labour costs), 193–4
Ryan, Richie, 89, 93, 95
Ryan, W.J.L., 169

Sachs, Jeffery, 414
sacrifice ratio, 413–14, 415
Samuelson, Paul, 43, 45, 196, 402
Sargent, Thomas, 43, 396
saving

average propensity to save (APS),
    59–61
circular flow of income model, 445
disposable income, consumption
    and, 50, 51–2
    function, 51–2
    inflation and, 14
    investment and balance of
        payments, 457–60
    in Ireland, 459–60
    multiplier model and, 55, 66–7
    national savings in Ireland, 457
    public and private, 456–7
    Special Saving Incentive Scheme,
        78
    store of value, 105
scale economies, 266
Schmidt, Helmut, 227, 239
Scholes, Myron, 47
Schultz, Theodore, 45
Schwartz, Anna, 125
SDRs (special drawing rights), 105,
    210–11
Second Programme (1964–70), 88–9
seigniorage, 115, 116, 134–5
Selten, Reinhard, 47
Sen, Amartya, 47
September 11 terrorist attacks, 24, 25,
    177, 270, 298, 309, 398, 482,
    486
Shanahan's Stamp Auctions, 168
Sharpe, William, 46
shocks, economic, 24, 25, 37–41, 42
    adjusting to, 38–41, 78, 79
    asymmetric, 270
    demand-side, 29–30, 38–9, 41,
        274–5
    deflationary, 387–90
    in Eurozone, 270, 273–7
    Irish economy and, 486–7
    Keynes effect, 276–7
    oil crises, 94, 95, 96
    supply-side, 27, 31, 40–1, 81,
        275–6
    deflationary, 390–2
Simon, Herbert, 45
Singapore International Monetary
    Exchange (SIMEX), 370
Smith, Adam, 41, 82, 104, 462
Smith, Vernon L., 47
Smithsonian Agreement (1971), 222
Social Charter, 437
social employment schemes, 429,
    441–2
social insurance contributions, 72
social partnership, 481
social welfare system, 430, 437,
    439–40, 441–2, 445
Solow, Robert, 46, 402, 407–8
Somers, Michael, 251
Soros, George, 180, 217, 236
Spain, inflation and unemployment,
    418–20

Special Saving Incentive Scheme, 78
speculation, 145–7, 179–81
    disclosure and, 291–2
    fixed exchange rates, 216–17
    leading and lagging, 181, 356
    selling short, 180–1
    Tobin tax, 181
    UIP and, 202
    see also hedging
Spense, Michael, 47
spillover effects, 3
stabilisation policy, 68–70, 390, 398
    automatic stabilisers, 74, 315–16
    Irish experience, 92–102
    problems in implementing, 77–82
Stability and Growth Pact, 77, 80,
    160, 238, 272, 314–19
    Ireland and, 317–18
    penalties and let-outs, 314–16
    policy implications, 318–19
stagflation, 31, 43, 94, 404
standard of deferred payment, 105
standard of living, 1–6, 10, 453, 456,
    467
state-owned companies, 468, 469–70
static expectations, 395
sterilisation, 214–15, 311–12, 344
sterling, 105–6, 190, 245–6
    sterling link, 170, 171, 203,
        241–2, 243, 245
    see also currency crisis
STFC interest rate, 120
Stigler, George, 46
Stiglitz, Joseph E., 47
stock market crash (1987), 63
stocks
    capital stock, 34, 63
    equilibrium and changes, 22, 44
    variables, 63
Stone, Richard, 46
Stone-Geary expenditure system, 461
store of value, 105
structural adjustment programme, 90
subsidies, 450
supply-side policy, 30–1, 102
    Celtic Tiger and, 483–4
    taxation, 82–4
supply-side shocks, 27, 31, 40–1, 81,
    275–6
    deflationary, 390–2
Sustainable Progress, 434
Swift, Jonathan, 133
symbols, use of, 23

Tallaght Strategy, 99
TARGET, 299
tariffs, 185, 468, 469, 471
tax havens, 83
Tax Incentive Scheme, 100
tax incentives, 100, 471, 473, 474
taxes
    corporate profits tax, 74
    corporation tax, 473, 474

taxes (*cont.*)
  government revenue, 72–4, 445
    inflation tax, 115, 116
    unemployment and, 7–8
  indirect, 185, 450
  in Ireland, 72–4, 83, 101, 185
    Celtic Tiger period, 479–81,
      483–4
  multiplier model and, 55, 58,
    66–7
  net taxes, 445
  recent trends, 72–4
  residential property tax, 74
  supply-side and, 82–4
  tax wedge, 437–9
  wealth tax, 95
Taylor, John, 292
Taylor rule, 292, 294
Telecom Éireann, 470
terms of trade, 454–5, 460–1
Thatcher, Margaret, 31, 235, 245,
  412, 415, 434
theory of income determination *see*
  income determination theory
*Third Programme, Economic and Social
  Development (1969–72),* 88–9
tick value, 372
Tinbergen, Jan, 45
Tobin, James, 46, 181, 406
Tobin tax, 181
'Too Big To Fail' syndrome, 112
total expenditure, 21, 22–3, 28
trade account, 350–1
trade in goods and services, 164–5
trade unions, 90–1, 224, 254, 257,
  433, 434
trade-weighted exchange rate index
  (TWERI), 181–3, 192
transfer payments, 445
transfer pricing, 165–6, 356
transitory income, 65
translation exposure, 355
Trichet, Jean Claude, 283
troughs, 5
Troy ounce, 217
Truman, Harry S., 5
trustee savings banks, 140
TWERI *see* trade-weighted exchange
  rate index

UIP (uncovered interest rate parity),
  200–6, 207, 208, 359
  Celtic Tiger and, 482
  euro and, 205, 268
  excess returns and peso problem,
    205–6

Irish experience, 203–6
  see also CIP
Ulster Bank, 139
unemployment, 6–8, 421–42
  characteristics of unemployed,
    430–2
  costs of, 7–8
  definition of unemployed, 6,
    421–2
  disincentives to work, 439–40
    poverty trap, 440
    replacement ratio, 439
  duration of, 428–9
  dynamics of, 427–30
  Eurozone, 7, 37, 272, 404–6
    and inflation, 318, 319,
      416–20
  gap, 69
  GNP and, 30, 31–4, 36–7
    Eurozone coefficients, 33–4
  Great Depression and, 20–1
  and inflation *see* Phillips curve
  in Ireland, 6–7, 14, 404–5, 421,
    422–3, 427–8, 429, 485
    natural rate, 408
    Phillips curve, 418–20
    real wages and, 434
    UK influence, 430, 431
  labour force, 6, 31, 421–5
    dependency ratio, 424–5
    employment trends, 425–7
    in Ireland, 34, 37, 272, 422–4
    participation rate (LFPR),
      423–4, 485
  labour market not clearing, 432–9
    efficiency wages, 436
    labour market rigidity, 436–9
    real wage rigidity, 432–3, 434
    wage-bargaining process,
      433–6
  measurement of, 6, 422, 428
  natural rate, 34, 35, 406, 407–8,
    417
  Okun's law, 32–4, 429–30
  policies reducing, 441–2
  rate, 6, 422, 428
  tax wedge, 437–9
  trade account and, 350–2
  types of, 8
  see also labour market
United Kingdom exchange rate policy,
  235 *see also* sterling
UPH (unbiased predictor hypothesis),
  361–4
  market efficiency and, 365–6
  risk premium, 366

value added approach, 448
variation margin, 373–4
VAT (value added tax), 72, 74, 95, 98
velocity of circulation of money,
  122–3, 128, 213
  in Ireland, 131
Vickrey, William, 47
Volcker, Paul, 412, 415
Von Hayek, Friedrich August, 45
VSTFF (Very Short-Term Financing
  Facility), 230

wages
  efficiency wages, 436
  EMS and, 244–5, 250, 256–7
  inflation and, 12, 156 *see also*
    Phillips curve
  nominal, 38–9, 41, 42, 124, 156,
    275, 379
  real, 38–40, 41, 42, 156
    and unemployment in Ireland,
      434
  real wage moderation, 441
  real wage resistance hypothesis,
    433
  real wage rigidity, 432–3, 434
  wage agreements, 90–1, 101,
    433–6
  wage bargaining, 406–7, 410–11,
    413
    centralised, 481, 483
    process, 433–6
  see also labour market
Walsh, Brendan, 90, 432, 478
Walters, Alan, 235
Way Forward, The (1982), 89
wealth, 63–4, 144
wealth tax, 95
Werner Report (1970), 238, 278
Whitaker, T.K., 86–7, 138
White, Harry Dexter, 220
Williams, D. and Reid, R., 287
work incentives, 83
World Bank, 220

yield curve, 246–8, 367–8, 369,
  372–3

zero-cost cylinder, 359